Rethinking Corporate Governance

The Forming of Operative and Financial Strategies in Global Corporations

Sven-Erik Sjöstrand

Professor Emeritus, Stockholm School of Economics, Sweden

Edward Elgar
PUBLISHING

Cheltenham, UK • Northampton, MA, USA

Published by
Edward Elgar Publishing Limited
The Lypiatts
15 Lansdown Road
Cheltenham
Glos GL50 2JA
UK

Edward Elgar Publishing, Inc.
William Pratt House
9 Dewey Court
Northampton
Massachusetts 01060
USA

A catalogue record for this book
is available from the British Library

Library of Congress Control Number: 2015959652

This book is available electronically in the **Elgar**online
Business subject collection
DOI 10.4337/9781781951439

MIX
Paper from
responsible sources
FSC
www.fsc.org
FSC® C013056

ISBN 978 1 78195 142 2 (cased)
ISBN 978 1 78195 143 9 (eBook)

Typeset by Servis Filmsetting Ltd, Stockport, Cheshire
Printed and bound in Great Britain by TJ International Ltd, Padstow

Contents

PART II THE EMPIRICAL STUDY

Figures

About the author

Sven-Erik Sjöstrand (b. 1945) has been Professor of Business Administration at the Stockholm School of Economics since 1977 (Swedish Employers Association's Chair in Management), and from 1993 he became the first holder of the Matts Carlgren's Chair in Management. He has also been the head of the Stockholm School of Economics' Center for Governance and Management Studies since 1975, received some SEK 200 million in research grants, supervised close to 50 doctoral students, and served both as the Stockholm School of Economics' Deputy President and on its board.

Sjöstrand has also been a board member both in listed companies and in large state-controlled organizations, and he has been senior adviser to many of the 'captains of Swedish business' (i.e. to controlling shareholders, chairs and CEOs of large Nordic corporations).

Sjöstrand's current research addresses corporate governance, corporate control and general management issues. His list of publications in English (several of the volumes below are co-authorships) includes: *Organizational Myths* (Harper & Row, 1979); *Institutional Change: Theory and Empirical Findings* (M.E. Sharpe, 1993); *On Economic Institutions: Theory and Applications* (Edward Elgar Publishing, 1995); *The Two Faces of Management: The Janus Factor* (Thomson, 1997); *Invisible Management* (Thomson, 2001); *Aesthetic Leadership* (Palgrave, 2007); and *Corporate Governance in Modern Financial Capitalism* (Edward Elgar Publishing, 2010). Sjöstrand has also published books in Chinese, Finnish, German and Swedish (together, approximately 25 titles).

Preface

This book is the result of extensive fieldwork that could not have been completed without the most generous support of a great number of individuals, all of whom have devoted considerable time to share their insights and knowledge with the author. Many of them have also spent time checking the accuracy of (parts of) the voluminous and complex empirical materials that form the heart of the book. For all these dedicated, unreserved and thorough contributions, I express my deepest gratitude.

This study has been carried out as part of an on-going research programme called Corporate Governance in Financial Capitalism that has been conducted at the Centre for Studies in Corporate Governance and Management at the Stockholm School of Economics' Institute for Economic Research (SIR) since 1977.

Most of the material in this book has been discussed at seminars together with researchers active in the field, and I am most grateful for their feedback and suggestions for improvement. Particular thanks go to Associate Professor Markus Kallifatides and Assistant Professor Sophie Nachemson-Ekwall for their constructive comments.

I would also like to thank 'Handelsbanken's Research Foundations and Matts Carlgren's Foundation for Management Research for generously providing funding for this extensive research project. Many thanks also to Ingrid Kollberg for her assistance in the production of the manuscript, and Regina List for her professional language editing and general advice.

The responsibility for all the contents of this book, of course, remains with the author.

Sven-Erik Sjöstrand
Stockholm, September 2015

PART I

A theoretical platform

1. Points of departure

1.1 RESEARCH FIELD AND PURPOSE

This volume addresses a set of fundamental questions that too seldom has been raised in the socio-economic sciences: what are the main forces that decide the long-term (development) paths for large global corporations,[1] and how and under what circumstances do those forces operate? Theoretically, this set of research questions will be approached by integrating corporate governance theory with certain other key academic subfields, thereby building one coherent socio-economic frame of reference. These other key fields include theories about human rationality, institutional theories, theories of the firm/corporation and theories about corporate paths.

Basically, corporate governance theory focuses on drivers of co-ordinated action, addressing both the forces directly conducted by individual actors and the collectively (re)produced[2] indirect ones (i.e. culture and institutions). For some decades (the late 20th century) scholars in Economics and Finance dominated the theoretical development in the corporate governance field. Thus, much of the research was based on rather idealistic assumptions regarding actors, corporations and settings, and it almost exclusively addressed listed corporations. In recent decades, however, that classic theoretical body has been both questioned and widened. Socio-economists and legal scholars have added realism and complexity to the theory building, thereby improving its empirical relevance and practical value for corporate actors. These researchers[3] have also extended governance theory, so that it also embraces other kinds of organizations than just corporations.

Governance activities involve the whole repertoire of cultural and institutional structures and processes that single actors and actor collectives directly or indirectly (re)produce when they influence corporate development over time. Thus, both emerging and historical norms are involved in the governing processes (cf. laws, regulations, codes and customs).[4] The word repertoire is chosen to stress that many of these norms are uncoordinated, that is to say, that they lack systemic qualities. The actor construct should then be understood in a broad sense – that is to say, as referring to all kinds of corporate stakeholders, not merely to shareholders. Stakeholder then refers to those actor categories whose presence and activities are necessary for the very existence of corporations.[5]

The theoretical model used here to describe and explain the forces deciding corporate development is based on three core concepts, namely driving forces, governance arenas and corporate paths (cf. Figure 1.1). The left box containing the forces driving corporate development will be discussed in detail in this chapter, while the arenas (i.e. the corporation and its setting) will be elaborated in Chapter 2 (cf. the middle box). The theoretical part of this volume ends with a discussion of corporate paths (cf. the right box, and Chapter 3).

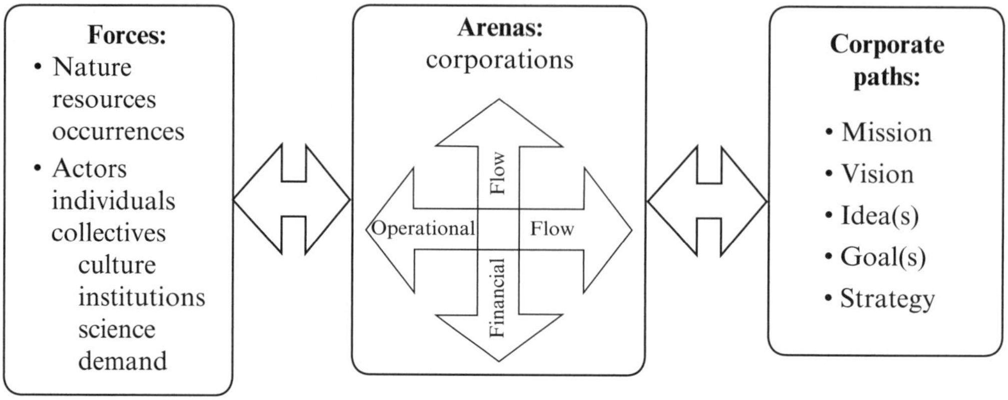

Figure 1.1 Corporate governance: its deciding forces, arenas and manifestations

Although a governance process runs both inside and outside a corporation, that arena will here be used as the basis from which the other governance processes are derived. Among the basic actor agencies identified inside corporations – shareholders, boards and top management – shareholders will be used as the main hub and taken as the basis in many of the analyses. To many actors the general research question initially formulated is accompanied by a second much more specific one addressing various aspects of shareholding, namely to what extent does its kind, legal form, structure, autonomy, organization and enactment influence corporate paths?

1.2 A BASIC THEORETICAL PLATFORM

What here is denoted as (driving) 'forces' influencing corporate development basically emerges from two sources: nature and actors. The latter category is here seen as the more important one of the two, and will therefore be discussed at some length below. The former category includes both occurrences that lie outside human control, and natural resources as such. Nonetheless, it is always human actors that are exposed to, discover, interpret and handle natural occurrences. Some of them hit specific companies (e.g. a fire in a paper mill), others whole industries (e.g. a tree-felling storm), and still others a large part of the business world (e.g. climate change). Some natural occurrences might actually be regarded as favourable by concerned actors/corporations (e.g. damages that hit competitors only), while others will be treated as deleterious and force shareholders and executives to reconsider corporate strategies (e.g. location of forestry investments). In both cases some actors react and deal with the upcoming opportunities or problems. So, although natural occurrences are not triggered by human action, they certainly evoke actor activity. Regarding the other aspect of nature – its resources – it is claimed that what qualifies for that category very much is decided by the context and the current (constellations of) actors.

The second basic force influencing corporate paths embraces all drivers that emerge from initiatives taken by actors. Such activities could be of many different kinds and also more or less collective and historical in character. In this study, four kinds of forces based on collective actorhood[6] have been identified as particularly important for corporate development: culture, institutions, science and demand.[7] Two of them – culture and institutions – basically refer to historical processes and represent the outcomes of past actor interactions and performances.

Culture is probably the most elusive of the actor-based forces, and the academic literature has attached several meanings to that construct. Here, culture denotes the overall world view and ethos prevalent in a society or in some other kind of unit that manifests in common values, attitudes, postures, emotional patterns and practical habits.[8] Thus, culture embodies the expectations, norms and episodic individual actions that appear in an entity regardless of whether its actors are interrelated or not. Culture is not something that could be exclusively linked to a specific individual. It is a truly collective phenomenon that rather refers to actions linked to human constructs and artefacts than to activities evoked by nature.[9] Many entities, for example, nations, corporations and professional associations, (re)produce and house powerful cultures that more or less strongly influence corporate paths.

The second of the collective drivers of corporate development – institutions – permeates the more general phenomenon of culture. Institutions comprise various systems of embedded and enforced social norms of at least some durability. A single norm is then understood as a socially communicated, value-based expectation or obligation – that is to say, it is a normative force that compels someone in a certain context or position to act in a specific way. Societies are then infused by – and infuse – numerous institutions that might be complementary, competing and decoupled as well as unrelated. Individuals could activate a collection of these institutions and their enforcement mechanisms forming what could be denoted as an institutional 'bricolage'.[10] The bricolage concept not merely underscores the fact that institutionalized norms applicable to a certain situation might be plentiful, but also indicates that even in well-defined specific situations such norms might be conflicting or even contradictory.

Institutions appear in several forms like, for example, laws, regulations, customs, professional traditions, codes of conduct, and so on. Each such institution and its normative power are then underpinned by some kind of mixture of rewards and sanctions that could be physical, economic or social in character. Human actors continuously build, reproduce, change, exceed, abandon and destroy institutions at the same time as these same institutions influence, enable and constrain human activity. Thus, institutions have the power to mould the dispositions of human beings; they even have the capacity to change people's ideals, attitudes and aspirations. An institution can therefore function as a kind of collective or 'macro actor' in society. In that role, institutions function as arbitrators between individuals and influence their opinions and relative power. In that way they also work as tools for the mobilization of human effort.[11]

As institutions emerge, develop and change over time they represent historical forces that materialize in physical artefacts (e.g. buildings) as well as in explicit discourses (e.g. economic theory) and invisible dispositions (e.g. tacit knowledge). Sometimes they also constitute the foundations for organizations that are built to (re)produce cherished norm systems. Thus, institutions do not exclusively represent 'mental' structures although they depend on individuals for their existence.[12] In all these ways (i.e. through artefacts, discourses, human dispositions and organizations), history provides the material – that is to say, the mental and habitual resources – for the thinking and acting of individuals.[13] Then it becomes apparent that past actor struggles also are a primary source for current sets of institutions. In modern societies old elites have left their strongest traces in the specific institutions they have (re)produced. Once old elites have left the governing arenas, they bequeath their influence in an institutionalized form (thus, some doctrines outlive their creators).

The impact of institutions on corporations is well documented. That insight was confirmed during the second half of the 20th century, when primarily organization researchers re-introduced the institutional phenomenon on the socio-economic scene through empirical investigations of various kinds of associations. Some economists had argued all along for the importance of institutions for economic processes and structures, but for decades they had been rather marginalized and obliged to establish their own journals[14] and associations.[15] However, it was not until the 1970s that a more general interest in linking the institutional perspective to the corporate phenomenon really took off. That scientific turn involved a revival of Knight's, Berle and Means', Coase's and other neglected or forgotten interwar theorists' writings on the theory of the firm.

The second half of the 20th century represented an explosion of perspectives and writings addressing the theory of the firm/corporation. It was not only the behavioural sciences that added knowledge about the functioning of corporate processes.[16] Both economists (e.g. agency theorists) and law scholars (e.g. regulation providers) elaborated the defining characteristic of a corporation – the hierarchy.[17] Institutionally oriented economic historians also contributed to the renewed interest in the corporation by investigating the forces behind – and the consequences of – increasing organizational sizes.[18] The most important outcome of all those efforts was probably the theories that addressed the financial flows that ran inside and outside the corporations.[19] Eventually these research efforts institutionalized a legal regime that all over the world enforced a rather similar hierarchical arrangement (containing three main agencies: shareholders' general meetings [GMs], boards and the Chief Executive Officer [CEO] position). The impact of institutionally oriented approaches to corporate governance processes became decisive, so some of that development is further addressed later in this volume.

Science represents the third of the collective driving forces that influence corporate paths. However, its collective charter could sometimes be questioned since it is possible both to attach scientific progress to actions taken by single individuals, and to regard such steps forward as basically outcomes of collective (interactive) processes. The term 'scientific development' is here used to represent the outcome of progress, taken in a broad sense, covering outcomes from all kinds of research efforts (i.e. from the humanities as well as from natural science and the socio-economic field). That progress usually enters corporations as inputs in their operative flows – as breakthroughs that improve their internal processes and/or market outputs (cf. innovations). Thus, many corporations house powerful research and development (R&D) activities that through innovations influence strategic options and paths, for example, by introducing new materials and more advanced technologies, and by pioneering distribution methods. Research findings might also address and influence the financial flows in corporations (e.g. by providing more efficient financial instruments). Thus, science tends to have a 'push effect' in both of the basic corporate flows.

The fourth and final collective actor force influencing corporate development – demand – is basically formed by two different actor collectives, namely customers and competitors. Competitors contribute to the sizes and compositions of the various markets, while customers constitute the actual demand on each of them. Customers tend to have a 'pull effect' in the operative flows, and in that role they influence most corporate paths (cf. Chapter 3). Their impact could take several different forms (e.g. buying and opinion building) and trigger substantial changes (e.g. stimulate product differentiation and innovation).

Thus, human actors are involved in almost all kinds of forces influencing corporate futures with the possible exception of the ones based on natural occurrences. In that function they often act as (parts of) collectives that (re)produce culture and institutions over longer periods of time. They also form constellations that enable scientific progress and arouse demand. Still, however, the individual actor is regarded as an important impact source in its own right. Thus, individual actorhood is important both as a force of its own, and also – in some way or another – as a component in all the other forces. It will therefore be elaborated in more detail in the following section.

1.3 ACTORS AND ACTOR CONSTELLATIONS

1.3.1 Bounded Rationality

When focusing on the last of the forces influencing corporate paths, the individual human actor, things become more complicated and require a lengthier discussion. The conviction that there exists a substantial amount of human discretion in most contexts indicates that individual action is seen neither as fully determined by outside forces, nor as mainly executed in non-reflective or 'non-conscious' habitual ways. Instead, actors, culture and institutions determine each other in 'eternal' on-going interaction processes.[20]

As actorhood is regarded to be one of the crucial forces in corporate governance, it becomes important to describe the notion of the individual that is applied throughout this volume. The conception of the partly autonomous human actor that is used here originates from the classical one that for long has dominated the economic sciences and usually has been labelled 'economic man'[21] or homo oeconomicus. However, that ideal type[22] construct of the human being is radically revised below. The homo oeconomicus construct was built upon the idea that individuals are perfectly informed and possess unlimited calculative capabilities, so that they are able to maximize their known utilities. Many problems are associated with that ideal type construct, particularly when empirical studies are to be carried out. Today, there is an overwhelming amount of both experimental studies and fieldwork that shows that human beings act in much more diversified and complex ways than the homo oeconomicus construct indicates. Nevertheless, the applicability of that rationale is still taken for granted in many studies.[23]

To many actors, calculations (i.e. mathematical methods, statistics and other quantitative approaches) represent the valid way of approaching the various decisions that have to be taken in corporations; thus, to them the citing of figures often represents 'the undisputed decision method'. When choices have to be made such calculations build certitude – they inform what stance it would be best to take. However, such confidence might be illusive when confronted with reality, as it is difficult to successfully apply such a purely calculative rationale except in fully transparent and cognitively uncomplicated situations. So, in most practical situations, human judgement has to be added, and such evaluations are to a large extent also based upon non-cognitive processes.[24]

Bounded rationality[25] is an expression that often is used to describe the calculative shortcomings that people in general exhibit. One consequence of those shortcomings is that actors usually have to tackle complexities (also) with the help of non-calculable simplifications such as, for example, various heuristics.[26] They become necessary because many decisions involve dimensions that are difficult or even impossible to measure. The use of heuristics also makes it possible for individuals to avoid cognitive stress (time is not unlimited). Heuristics also economize on actors' calculative capacity, as they provide well-established rationales and guidelines for most decision situations. Many of these heuristics also have cultural and institutional roots that link to specific (historical) values and settings.[27]

In reality, actors tend to confine themselves to solutions that are perceived as satisfactory and do not even try to maximize them. That behaviour implies that actor expectations and aspiration levels play a significant role in human decision processes.[28] Maximization is a most problematic criteria for action, as individuals often do not even know what to maximize, that is to say, they do not recognize their (instable) preferences, and it is sometimes actually the action (outcome) as such that helps an actor to decide what to seek. Moreover, actors often do not know what utilities are (potentially) available.

Another basic problem with the use of homo oeconomicus as the theoretical platform for empirical investigations is its purely cognitive basis. As mentioned earlier, that ideal type construct disregards the fact that individuals also have emotions, intuition and aesthetical preferences, and that they also make use of those qualities when deciding and acting. That idea is elaborated further below, where the notion of the multi-rational human being is introduced.

1.3.2 The Multi-rational Actor

If one combines the discussion above regarding actors' bounded rationality with the four dominating intrapersonal bases for human action (cognition, emotions, intuition and aesthetics), a more empirically valid construct of the human being emerges: that of homo complexicus or the multi-rational actor.[29] That construct indicates that individuals do not base their action on cognition only. They also rely on emotions, intuition and aesthetics.[30] Thus, most human activities have an emotional component. Its strength and relative importance for specific actions vary, but it is always present.[31] That means that human actors can develop strong emotional ties over time not only to certain ideas, values or interests but also to particular individuals. It also indicates that such attractions will guide many of their decisions and actions. Individuals also use intuition when they decide and act. Intuition then refers to those experiences that are hard to explain to others in an unambiguous way. The actor might actually even have difficulties in articulating that action rationale inwards. The same reasoning applies to aesthetics, which underpins a rationale that puts something that looks or sounds good in the driver's seat.[32]

The multi-rational individual is also seen as an interactive social being, which means that actors try to respond to one another by way of collectively constructed meanings. Thus, human action is oriented towards – and inspired by – inter-subjective representations.[33] Moreover, much of what a single individual perceives is also perceived by others, and in a seemingly similar way. By their actions, individuals continuously indicate what is expected of the others, and vice versa, and each individual, in a never-ending process, interprets the indications given by the others.[34] These processes usually imply a series of mutual adjustments; to put it another way, empathy and inter-subjectivity come into play. Labelling also occurs, as actors in the course of their interactions attribute roles and stereotypes to each other.

This view of the basis for human action opens up for the aforementioned interpersonal path for handling uncertainties. It means that individuals – when acting – take into consideration the expectations and activities of others, whether they be present or absent. Therefore, the word 'action' should be read and understood as representing a mutuality or interaction. However, an individual's capacity to relate to and interact with others has its limits. Previous (inter)actions, too, restrict individual activity, as they influence (and simultaneously are influenced by) an actor's cognitive map, intuitive capacity, emotional memory and aesthetic preferences. These 'action sediments' often build up over a long period of time, and as the present acting constitutes no more than a 'split second', the traces of earlier actions become particularly important (cf. path dependence, routines, habits, and the like). Also expectations about the future (i.e. goals, visions, dreams, etc.) influence the current behaviour of individuals.

1.3.3 Actors, Uncertainty and Risk

Actors linked to corporations have the capacity to influence their long-term development by providing perspectives, judgements and actions that create, reproduce, modify, alter or destruct existing conditions.[35] In those situations it is believed that various combinations of more or less related ideas, values and interests drive the individuals' actions. Thus, it is assumed that individuals at least sometimes have (conscious) intentions linked to their actions, although it is not always possible for others to detect them. When individuals put some of their ideas, values and interests into practice, they face uncertainties of various kinds. Such sources of ambiguity follow from the simple fact that nobody perfectly remembers 'the past', fully knows 'the present' and is able to safely predict 'the future'. To deal with the last, actors can sometimes gain some substance in their predictions by transforming them to risk (if both outcomes and their probabilities could be meaningfully estimated). Such risk-taking could be both rewarding (build fortunes) and disappointing (produce bankruptcy). Its presence is certainly crucial for the emergence of firms and corporations – those units could in fact be seen as tools for risk-taking.

However, actors' attitudes towards risk tend to differ a lot. Some individuals are simply more inclined to take risks (cf. risk-seekers) than others (cf. risk-avoiders). A risk-averse actor is one that, when faced with two investments with the same expected return but differing probability distributions, prefers the alternative with the lower variance. A risk- seeker is one that either absorbs lots of uncertainty or – at least – prefers alternatives with strong possible advantages even when accompanied with analogously strong disadvantages. Sometimes marked risk-seekers even prefer paths that have negative expected values but contain high (but rather improbable) possible benefits. Despite these interpersonal variations, individual risk attitudes tend to be relatively constant over time (i.e. linked to personality and/or culture), but it has also been shown that risk attitudes sometimes could change due to situational and/or contextual factors. For example, current mood[36] and feelings,[37] as well as the ways problems or situations temporary are framed,[38] might influence human risk-taking.

Individuals also face a kind of uncertainty that could not be transformed to risk: genuine uncertainty. Basically, that kind of 'remaining' uncertainty could be dealt with in three ways: through disconnection, intrapersonal processes and interpersonal processes. Disconnection processes simply represent the ones where various kinds of barriers are established between actors (e.g. physical ones like prisons). The other two processes are much more complicated and also more relevant in a discussion of corporate governance. The first of these two processes, the intrapersonal one, refers to situations where individuals use cognition, emotions, intuition and aesthetics in their thinking and acting. That intrapersonal path was thoroughly described above. In the second process, the interpersonal one, actors try to gain different degrees of certainty by building relationships to more or less known others. Such relations could be built on shared values and ideals, as well as on family ties or friendships, and that variety indicates that the accompanying actions will be more or less predictable/certain.[39]

Basically, actors reduce interpersonal uncertainty by more or less voluntarily engaging in relationships characterized by coercive, calculative, ideal-based or genuine qualities. Coercion is seldom discussed in management contexts, as it is not supposed to exist in such arenas, with the obvious exception of organizations explicitly concerned with that aspect of life (e.g. the police). Nonetheless, this way of coping with uncertainty is to a greater or lesser extent also present in many corporations. Although it is more unusual in its more brutal forms, such things as sexual abuse, kidnapping and wilful damage do sometimes occur. Moreover, in its more 'modest' and/or hidden forms coercive relationships might be fairly frequent in many organizations, for instance, as threats, blackmailing, bullying, and so on.[40]

The high dependency on innumerable unknown others that characterizes conditions for members of a modern society, as well as the accompanying physical and mental distances between dependent individuals, have made interaction based on a calculative rationale a necessity. That situation is also a direct consequence of a capacity barrier – actors have to manage the number and depths of their contacts. Indeed, most dependent individuals are (cognitively) incapable of identifying and building personal relationships to all linked actors. So, they base some of their uncertainty reduction on a calculative approach reducing the others to titles, positions, occupations, and the like.

However, dependent individuals are obviously not always anonymous to each other. Many interactions and exchanges take place between individuals who have at least some knowledge about the others involved, and actors tend to put particular faith in judgements made by such partially known others. Then the set of values and ideals that individuals hold and (sometimes) express in their interactions with others becomes particularly important. If these values and ideals become known and even shared, that knowledge tends to reduce uncertainty and builds interpersonal reliance. Thus, both shared values and ideals bridge many gaps and distances between actors – psychological, physical, geographical, temporal and organizational ones.[41] Indeed, they promote co-operation and exchange and hamper both opportunistic[42] behaviour and moral hazard.[43] A judgement made on the basis of a value-based rationale could be so important in a certain situation that it even overthrows a position built upon the classic calculative rationale. However,

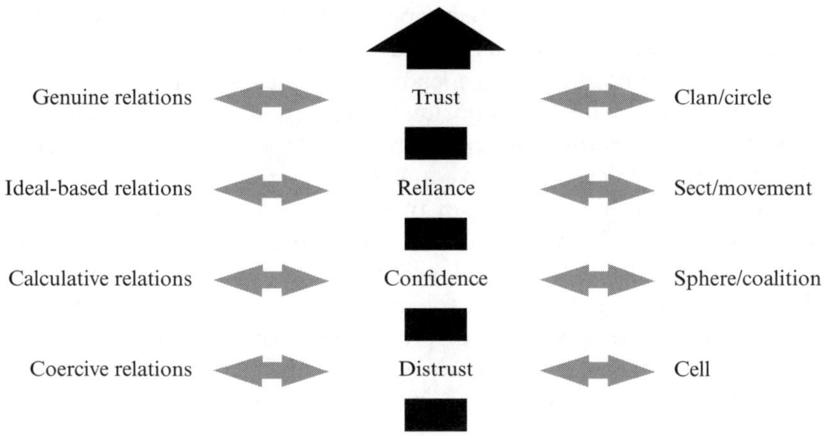

Figure 1.2 Faith in others and their sources

basically, this ideal-based rationale works as a complement to the calculative one providing actors with some extra capacity to deal with ambiguous situations.[44]

Sometimes dependent individuals are well known to each other. In those cases people know much more than the names, titles and positions of the others. They are also familiar with their personalities, networks, education, experiences, attitudes, interests, and so on. It usually takes a long time before such strong ties – 'genuine' relations – emerge between individuals. First and foremost they tend to appear among mates, friends, life partners, cohabitants, family members, and the like. Such genuine relations then create situations and circumstances where the strongest form of interpersonal faith – trust – might emerge. Figure 1.2 illustrates the whole range of 'faith in others' (distrust, confidence, reliance and trust), as well as their different sources (coercive, calculative, ideal-based and genuine relations).[45]

1.3.4 Actor Constellations

As mentioned above, a third way to cope with (genuine) uncertainty is through the interpersonal path. It builds on – and tends to simultaneously form – four structured kinds of actor constellations. They are denoted cell, sphere/coalition, sect/movement and clan/circle. Starting at the 'distrust' end of the scale (cf. Figure 1.2), coercive relationships could form groupings that have two different but connected kinds of bases: those built on physical force (cf. violence) and those that (in other ways) threaten the survival of individuals (cf. material and economic circumstances). These constellations based on coercion are denoted cells. It is also possible to identify actor constellations that are based on calculative relationships. That kind of constellation is here denoted sphere or coalition depending on whether it is hierarchically constructed or not. Because of its constituting mechanism – the calculative rationale – it is seen as a relatively fragile and short-lived grouping and represents a constellation where actors unknown to each other have agreed to co-operate – at least temporarily – for some common purpose.

When the defining characteristic of a constellation is based on (shared) values and/or ideals, a movement or sect appears. A sect represents the hierarchical form of the constellation and refers to a set of individuals that are linked through shared values (i.e. some kind of ideology) and subordinated to a leader.[46] The ideal type movement has the same characteristics as the sect with one important exception: it is non-hierarchic. The fourth and final constellation of actors has genuine relationships as its basis, and like the others it contains both a hierarchical – the clan – and a non-hierarchical – the circle – form. The basis for genuine relationships could be of two kinds. The theoretical concept clan refers to individuals who are tied together by various kinds of kinship, while circles instead are constituted by friendship relationships. Some researchers claim that still in the 21st century the family tie linkage represents the most important kind of human relationship, and that it actually functions as a kind of prototype for most of the other ones.

A clan is based on either (foremost) biologically defined relationships or built on love or different kinds of contracts between biologically distant individuals. That means that the former kind is built on those relationships that prevail in dynasties and families (blood-based ones), and such links cannot be broken, while the latter refers to relations between biologically (at least relatively) unrelated individuals, and such connections could be broken and terminated. In both cases, status and positional conditions are the defining characteristics.

A clannish inclusion is not always voluntary. For the kinship kind of clan the tie might actually be compulsory – the individual is born into the constellation. Accordingly, clan memberships are relatively stable, as position or status can only be established, changed or terminated via (biological) reproduction, marriage or death (or the like). Clan ties are particular, in that they involve people as unique individuals (linked to their status/positions), and they are universal, as they permeate most types of situations and actions as far as the individual is concerned. Such collectively flavoured interactions among relatives give rise to ideas about moral obligations, solidarity, feelings, concern for others, and an interest in relatives and kinship. In its ideal type form clans create emotional ties and produce opportunities for never-ending co-operation. Thus, clans represent genuine relationships that underpin the (re)production of trust between actors.[47]

As mentioned previously, trust may also emanate from friendship – a kind of lasting genuine relation between individuals that in certain respects differs from the kinship-based kind. Friendships emerge and grow over time from experiences that reveal matching personalities, mutual or complementary values, shared interests, and the like. In circles, that is to say, close and lasting non-clannish relationships, individuals' exchanges of information, thoughts and feelings become important as (re)producers of identities. Those processes presuppose that there are no pretences in the relationships – friends are expected to be spontaneous, open and 'natural' in their interactions, continuously expressing their 'true selves'. As a consequence, the individuals in a friendship relation are almost indispensable to each other – it is most difficult for other actors to replace them. Thus, friendship relationships concern the most private sphere; they involve the genuine unfeigned individuals (their core personalities). Such relations are not based on organizational roles or positions (or on other more formal and official aspects of life). As a result, friends and friendships are not described and evaluated in public – they are exclusive relationships that flourish in the private sphere. Moreover, like other genuine relationships, they involve strong emotions, care and compassion.[48]

Unlike for the clan, the circle is characterized by horizontal relationships built on voluntariness; that is to say, there is no biologically determined (or otherwise imperative) hierarchy around. Thus, an individual is not born into a circle, but when an individual has won such a status or membership, it tends to last for a long time. Like a clan, a circle is founded on ties that are particular; thus, they involve individuals that are regarded to be unique and irreplaceable by the others. Another similarity with the clan constellation is that membership in a friendship-based circle has a universal character, as it tends to permeate all kinds of situations and actions (with the [possible] exception of those linked to human sexuality).[49]

Thus, the circle denotes a 'complete' or all-embracing relationship, which implies that the involved individuals participate with a high proportion of their overall personalities, and so for longer periods of time. Like a clan, a circle also (re)produces moral obligations, solidarity and concern for others among its companions. As the circle is composed of close individuals, it offers each of them a possibility to expand their own capacity to reduce uncertainty, and handle it through collectively utilizing – trusting – the judgements of the well-known others.[50] As they know each other well – heritage, experiences, personalities, networks, and so on – they can evaluate the underlying bases for the suggestions and advice provided. They can also be almost sure that these close individuals do their very best, and that no one tries to deceive or betray the others. Circles also make it less risky for actors to share and exchange private and confidential information regarding delicate topics, and usually that possibility tends to improve decision quality.[51] However, even if most (interpersonally generated) uncertainties might be reduced substantially through disconnection, intrapersonal processes and interpersonal processes, as described above some genuine uncertainty will still remain, because individuals never fully can ascertain other people's intentions and actions rationales.

1.4 THE STRUCTURE OF THE BOOK

In this first chapter of the three that make up the first part of this volume ('A Theoretical Platform'), four core ingredients have been presented: the topic being focused upon, the purpose, the two research questions and the theoretical platform. In Chapter 2, a theory of the corporation will be presented to make the governance arena more elaborated and realistic. In that chapter two governance flows are highlighted – the operative and the financial.[52] There is also a focus on the variety of individual actors and actor collectives (cf. culture, institutions, science and demand) that are involved in the two flows, and on their differing roles and rationales. Chapter 3, finally, explains the more important theoretical concepts that are used to characterize corporate paths. It includes discussions about various kinds of missions, visions and goals, as well as operative and financial strategies. The forces presented in this chapter are also examined in relation to different corporate settings, allowing for the presentation of some of the more powerful tools that human actors use when trying to influence corporate paths.

The extensive empirical material is presented in the second part of this volume ('The Empirical Study'). Its first two chapters provide a presentation of how the four corporations in focus developed before World War II (WWII), with Chapter 4 unfolding the paths that materialized before World War I (WWI), and Chapter 5 unfolding the developments that took place during the interwar period. This second part of this volume continues with a presentation of four extensive 'master cases' focusing on corporate paths and on the main governing forces that have (re)produced them. The four master cases embrace differing time periods, as the four included corporations have very different dates of founding (ranging from the 14th century to the 19th century). The cases also end at slightly different points in time (1998, 2002, 2004 and 2004).

All the focused upon corporations are major global enterprises belonging to the same industry, the forest-based one, and they have sometimes – but not always – competed. The four master cases' corporations are: (1) Sveaskog (Chapters 6 and 7), which also, for example, contains companies like Domänverket, AssiDomän, Segheza, Kappa (Holding) and Ncb; (2) Holmen (Chapters 8, 9 and 10), which also, for example, involves companies like MoDo, Alicel/Alipap, Iggesund, Modo Paper, Metsä-Serla and Holmens Bruk; (3) Stora (Chapters 11 and 12), which also, for example, contains companies like Swedish Match, Papyrus, Billerud, Feldmühle (Nobel), UPM-Kymmene and Enso-Gutzeit; and (4) SCA (Chapters 13 and 14), which also, for example, involves companies like Mölnlycke, Laakirchen, Peaudouce, Italcarta, Reedpack, Procter & Gamble and Papierwerke Waldhof-Aschaffenburg (PWA).

In the concluding third part ('Analyses and Conclusions'), consisting of three chapters, the empirical material is analysed using the approach and theoretical platform presented in the first part of this volume. Thus, the final third part contains the most important conclusions that could be drawn from the encounter between the theoretical platform and the extensive longitudinal empirical material. Basically, then, Chapter 15 contains analyses and preliminary conclusions based on the empirical material that refers to the period before WWII (cf. Chapters 4 and 5), while Chapters 16 and 17 include conclusions and tentative hypothesis based on the empirical material that refers to the years after WWII (cf. Chapters 6–14). The appendix focuses on methodology issues and discusses the general design of the investigation including its extension in time, as well as the data sources that constitute the basis for the empirical chapters. It also contains a description of how the industry, the four master cases and the actors were selected. The appendix ends with a listing of all the interviewees, as their contributions represent the main basis for the empirical narratives.

NOTES

1. The two concepts corporation and company are used without distinction. In certain contexts, however, one or the other is preferred (e.g. 'company law' but 'corporate governance'). A corporation is seen as an association of individuals created under the authority of law that houses powers and liabilities and exhibits continuous presence independent of its actors. Corporations (companies) come in many different types but are usually divided by the law of the jurisdiction where they are chartered into two kinds: by whether or not they can issue stock, or by whether or not they are for profit (cf. Dictionary.com).
2. The use of (re)production in this volume is used to emphasize a presence of both historical and emerging elements.
3. Osborne (2009) and Steen-Johnsen et al. (2011).
4. The Organisation for Economic Co-operation and Development (OECD) defines corporate governance as 'the procedures and processes according to which an organization is directed and controlled'. There are other definitions, too. For example, one that is rather frequently used by financially oriented researchers: 'the ways in which suppliers of finance to corporations assure themselves of getting return on their investments' (Shleifer and Vishny [1997, p. 738]).
5. Freeman and Reed (1983).

6. That concept stresses that the actor activity is embedded in a specific and known setting.
7. 'Demand' refers to the aggregate (i.e. total) actor demand that exists on a particular market.
8. Geertz (1973) and Jackall (1988).
9. Hodgson (2007, pp. 98–9) and Kallifatides et al. (2010, Ch. 1).
10. Kallifatides et al. (2010).
11. Sjöstrand (1995).
12. Bhaskar (1989), Archer (1995) and Hodgson (2007, p. 104).
13. Sjöstrand (1995).
14. E.g. *Journal of Economic Issues* and *Journal of Socio-Economics*.
15. E.g. The Society for the Advancement of Socio-Economics and the European Association for Evolutionary Political Economy.
16. Cyert and March (1963) wrote a classic volume on that topic.
17. To name just one from each discipline: Williamson (e.g. 1975 and 1985) was probably the most influential researcher that addressed 'the economics of organization' in those days, and Masten (1988) was a recognized scholar that made a significant contribution to the theory of the corporation based on a legal perspective.
18. Chandler (1977) was perhaps the most influential researcher among those coming from Economic History.
19. Jensen and Meckling (1976) and Fama (1980) early addressed the agency issue.
20. Sjöstrand (1985 and 1995).
21. The expression 'economic man' is at least known from the 19th century. Marshall introduced it in 1885 when he raised objections regarding that construct. Later many economists have recognized that construct as a useful theoretical abstraction (ideal-type construct). Cf. Andrén (1995).
22. Ideal type (cf. the German *Gedankenbild*) has nothing to do with the usual definition of ideal as meaning 'to be preferred above all else'. Instead, an ideal type refers to an established construction with a distinct and commonly accepted scientific meaning. An ideal type is formed by an accentuation of certain selected characteristics that are ascribed to an empirical phenomenon (some scholars even suggest that ideal types represent constructions of theoretical extremes; cf. McNeil [1981]). Hence, an ideal type expresses conceptual purity and is, thus, similar to an elaborate construct with no obvious empirical counterpart. In other words, ideal types do not simply reflect empirical phenomena, nor do they correspond to anything wholly separated from empirical knowledge.

    Ideal types are usually based upon scientific explorations that explicitly or implicitly involve empirical elements. Therefore, they are often based upon ingredients drawn from the best existing scholarly knowledge. However, the value of a construct of this kind is not only determined by testing single ideal types against single empirical organizations; rather, its prime value is often revealed when the whole theoretical repertoire (the system of theoretical ideal types) is confronted with an empirical material. In brief, the relationship between ideal types and empirical phenomena is, thus, an analytical one – ideal types represent tools of an 'as if' kind for use in theorizing (cf. Collin, 1990, p. 73). Human organizing, it is assumed, occurs as if it were governed by rationales associated with a mixture of ideal types. The ingredients that compose the 'as ifs' for each ideal type then play a crucial role in theory construction (Sjöstrand [1997, p. 200]).
23. Sjöstrand (1997).
24. Kahneman (2003), Kahneman and Tversky (1993) and Guve (2003).
25. Simon (1957).
26. Sjöstrand (1997) and – first and foremost – the many writings of Kahneman and Tversky (e.g. 1972, 1973 and 1982) and Tversky and Kahneman (e.g. 1974 and 1981).
27. Westerlund and Sjöstrand (1979, Ch. 8).
28. See the writings of Simon. The Carnegie Mellon University has a complete corpus of his work.
29. The notion of the 'multi-rational' human being was introduced in Sjöstrand (1997).
30. Sjöstrand (1997).
31. Izzard (1977).
32. Sjöstrand (1997).
33. E.g. the classical writings of Durkheim (1984/1893) and Weber (1978/1920).
34. Blumer (1969, p. 20).
35. Sjöstrand (1995), Aoki (2001) and Hodgson (2007).
36. Hastorf and Isen (1982).
37. Johnson and Tversky (1983).
38. Early shown by Kahneman and Tversky (1979) and Tversky and Kahneman (1981). Cf. Zhapira (1995) for further references.
39. Sjöstrand (1997).
40. Ibid.
41. Ibid.

42. If there was no opportunism there would not be any moral hazard, adverse selection, shirking, filtering, disguised goal seeking or other strategic deceits (Williamson [2000, p. 39]).
43. Moral hazard is a situation where a party will have a tendency to take risks, because the party taking the risks would not incur the costs that could arise.
44. Zucker (1986) and Sjöstrand (1997).
45. Sjöstrand (1985 and 1997).
46. 'Sect' is a term that could be traced back to the Latin word 'secta' meaning principle, ideology, philosophical school, manifesto, etc.
47. Sjöstrand (1997).
48. Ibid.
49. Ibid.
50. Ibid.
51. Ibid.
52. Sjöstrand (1993 and 2005), Östman (1993 and 2009) and Kallifatides et al. (2010).

2. Towards a theory of corporate governance

2.1 TWO BASIC GOVERNANCE FLOWS

Many economists addressing governance issues have used a combination of the classic theory of the firm and agency-like theories as their conceptual platform; therefore, in their writings, they have foremost adopted a financial perspective that ultimately is rooted in ideas about an 'effective' capital market. Those researchers have often concentrated their efforts on the functioning of that market, expressing less interest in its connections to (individual) corporations. In the theoretical effort that is at the core of this book, that one-dimensional theory is expanded to a two-dimensional one through the addition of an operational perspective.

A corporation (company) is defined as an association of actors created under the authority of law that houses powers and liabilities and exhibits a continuous presence independent of its actors (cf. note 1, Chapter 1). It is then essentially composed of two flows (cf. Figure 2.1) – an operational one and a financial one. A double vertical arrow is used to illustrate the financial flow, and a double horizontal arrow is in a similar way used for the operational flow. That view means that two different constructs together determine the practical demarcation of a corporation: one determines what counts as a financial unit and one defines what makes up an operational unit. Thus, the financial rationale and the operational rationale are treated as two simultaneous and equally important elements both for the defining of the corporation and in its governance process. The financial flow has its origins both in the capital market (allocated capital) and in the capital derived from operations (generated capital), in the former case both in the public ('open') market for corporate control and in the more informal and hidden one (cf. below). The financial flow is also (although somewhat improperly[1]) often referred to as 'the allocation chain'. The operational flow has also two formative sources, namely the 'R&D push' and the 'demand pull'. The operational flow is usually (properly) labelled 'the value chain' (cf. Figure 2.2).

Corporate governance is a rather broad construct that embraces several of the forces that will be specified and explored in this chapter. It refers to the whole repertoire of cultural and institutional structures and processes that directly or indirectly through various actors and actor constellations influence how corporations (are allowed to) develop over time.[2] Thus, corporate governance involves most normative sediments that exist in a society that in some way or another regulate corporate activities, for example, laws, prescriptions, rules, codes, custom and (normative) expectations. The word repertoire is used to emphasize that many of those governing norms and activities are unco-ordinated, that is to say, they lack systemic qualities. Thus, corporate governance is something broader than 'shareholder governance', as it involves a much wider population of actors, including both stakeholders[3] and social interest groups.[4] Stakeholders' inputs in governance

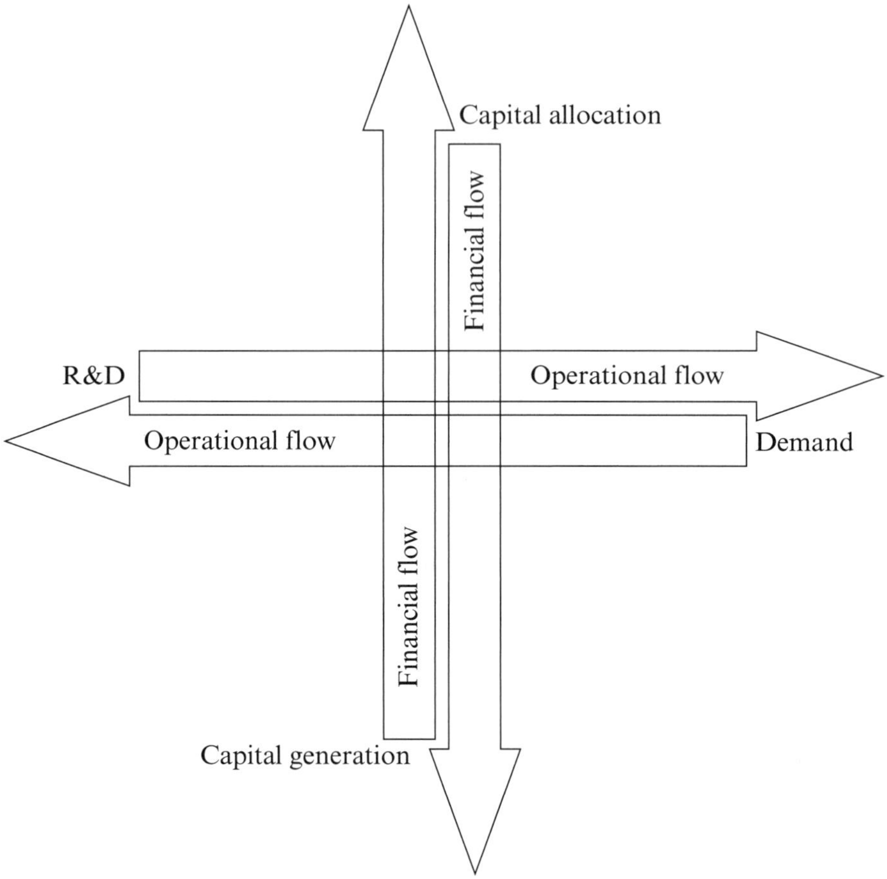

Figure 2.1 Two basic governance flows

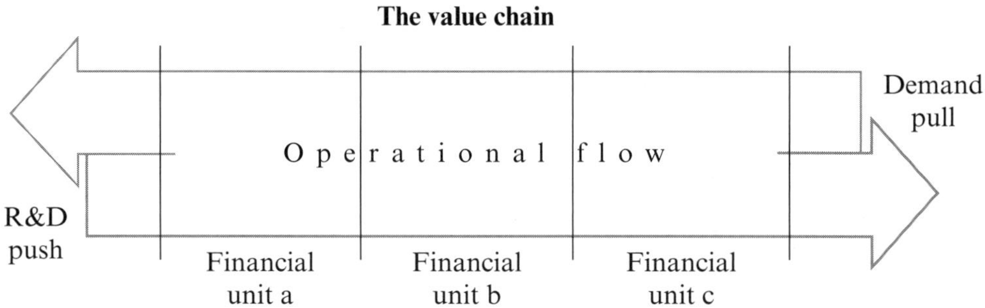

Figure 2.2 The value chain

processes tend to focus on two different targets: institutions (which could be [re]produced, changed or dissolved) and corporations (whose links to other companies, groups, actors, etc. could be built, developed or broken). Social interest groups have instead much wider agendas and more varied targets, so even if their activities sometimes affect certain corporate governance processes, they are usually not specifically addressing them.

Three different markets play important roles in corporate governance processes: the market for output, the market for corporate control and the market for executive capacity. The first one, competition on output markets, affects in particular the operational flows and disciplines executive action foremost through the emerging revenue streams. However, the second one, the market for corporate control, is a more complex construct. Basically, it is an arena for shareholder competition, and in that function, it especially influences the financial flows. More specifically, the market for corporate control refers to the many public (or 'open') marketplaces for corporate shares – that is to say, stock exchanges – that any investor can use to (directly or indirectly) acquire holdings in an almost innumerable amount of companies around the world. Those global marketplaces allow both for small-scale shareholding (investments without ambitions to participate in the corporations' governance processes) and for major control battles (attempts to buy large holdings and exert influence). Thus, current as well as potential shareholders with varying rationales, time perspectives and competences compete in that arena to obtain different degrees of control over corporations.[5]

There is also a more 'hidden' part of the market for corporate control that is populated by all those companies that are unlisted (and in a global perspective more difficult to find). Thus, quite a lot of the potentially available share capital is not present on the public control market because those actors that know (about) each other (e.g. through family, professional or friendship links) often also utilize interpersonal networks and ties to conduct share transactions, a practice that sometimes hampers significant changes of control structures. Thus, some of the discussions between (potential) owners take place as informal talks in rather closed circles, which have been built up and reinforced over many generations. That means that changes of control occur in that 'invisible' population, too, but in somewhat different ways than those on the public marketplaces. The third market, finally, the one for executive capacity, refers to arenas where shareholders look for particularly capable directors, CEOs and Chief Finance Officers (CFOs), and the outcomes of those search efforts influence both the operational and the financial flows.

2.2 A FEW GLOBAL DIFFERENCES

Corporate governance models and practices vary considerably around the world, mainly because they all are embedded in country-specific or regional institutional settings.[6] That diversity originates from the relative uniqueness of almost all nations' business histories. The varying institutional arrangements have emerged over long periods of time, basically from differences in constitutions, population structures, education levels, natural resources, cultural norms, (religious) belief systems, and the like. So, regulations relating to operational and financial flows tend to differ a lot, although some nations and regions exhibit similarities.[7]

Large parts of the governance repertoire found around the world have been portrayed in detail with both comparative[8] and descriptive[9] ambitions. Several Western European countries have been examined (e.g. France, Holland, Italy, Spain and the UK), as have some Eastern European nations (e.g. Poland and Russia), and a few non-European ones like Australia, China, Japan, Singapore and the US.[10] Generally speaking these descriptions indicate both that most national regulations are systemic only to a limited extent (they seem to emerge incrementally and lack holistic co-ordination), and that the inter-regional differences are large.

The first decade of the 21st century saw intense discussions about whether the ongoing globalization of the financial markets would produce convergence in relation to corporate governance regulations.[11] Some authors claimed that the Anglo-American model already had taken the lead in such a process, and that several of the model's fundamental elements had invaded many of the other regulatory systems.[12] However, rather quickly that tendency to adopt (parts of) the US and the UK regulations waned in several countries.[13] It became quite clear that in most national settings the existing constructs were much more complicated and slow to change than had been assumed – their different parts were linked by strong and complex ties that made it hard to successfully replace single elements. But it was not merely the national institutions as such that differed and obstructed changes. Equally important were the varying actor rationales that had evolved over centuries and (also) left their marks in the governance processes.[14]

Thus, the operational and the financial flows are both embedded in cultural and institutional settings that differ across countries and regions. Speaking specifically of the financial flows, the differences primarily are found in the shareholding situations and the status of the respective market(s) for corporate control. Particularly in the US, but to some extent also in the UK and other countries, shareholdings in large corporations tend to be dispersed and therefore closely linked to the activities on the capital market. Furthermore, the shareholdings are largely handled by various kinds of intermediaries. All that taken together indicates that in those countries changes in corporate shareholdings are driven foremost by the capital market, although corporate executives (i.e. directors and CEOs) sometimes could be so strong that they influence the outcomes of such transactions.

In a large part of the world – for example, continental Europe, the Nordic countries and Japan – the governance order differs significantly from the one(s) practised in the Anglo-American settings. Firstly, because corporate shareholdings in the non-Anglo-American countries are much more stable (usually based on controlling blocks), the role of their public control markets is more limited than the role of those in the US/UK. Secondly, because in most countries around the world, the national regulations (still) contain various 'frictions' or barriers that significantly complicate (or even obstruct) changes of the shareholding structures (cf. 'golden shares', state shareholding, shares with different voting rights, shareholding foundations, etc.[15]). In some countries (e.g. Japan[16]) regulations explicitly promote specific stakeholder interests, which also contributes to a somewhat more limited role for the public control market. However, having said that, one has to keep in mind that the variations are substantial also within the two basic systems, that is to say, between the UK and US governance regulations, and between, for example, the systems enforced in Sweden and Germany.

2.3 CORPORATE GOVERNANCE: ACTING IN THE FINANCIAL FLOW

The capital market represents the beginning of many vertical corporate governance processes. It is made up of traded contracts that directly or indirectly refer to underlying assets. A characteristic of the capital market is that it is intangible, and it is sometimes argued that its abstract quality feeds much of the 'casino' character of the current financial system.[17] The word casino is then supposed to capture the idea that more or less sophisticated financial actors speculate in more or less co-ordinated forms both about various economic futures and about possible (re)actions from other more or less sophisticated financial actors. It also refers to the well-documented herd mentality on financial markets, which contributes to sizeable volatility in terms of prices and volumes. Those fluctuations sometimes even develop into 'bubbles', where the value of the traded contracts has lost all intelligible connections to the underlying assets (be it in markets for tulips, real estate or stock derivatives).[18] For those reasons, the capital market has been subject to many regulatory efforts within and across states, basically with the ambition to prevent its instabilities from spilling over to the real economy.

The vertical financial flow is a manifestation of the forces active on the capital market, particularly on its 'submarket' for corporate control, but also in the more 'hidden' network-like talks described above. Those forces are then foremost described in terms of principal–agent relationships, which (too) often are assumed to (almost exclusively) characterize corporate governance processes; in other words, as flows in which the shareholders are seen as the ultimate decision-makers (i.e. as peak co-ordinators). Thus, the agency theory tradition puts the corporate shareholders alone in the driver's seat. It also defines corporations as 'a bundle of assets' that it is possible to capitalize either one by one or in full. The basic idea is then that corporations are units used by shareholders to maximize their returns on the invested capital. A strict application of that idea reduces corporations to being market-like financial arenas where shareholders only deal with corporate improvements through (re)allocations of capital. Unfortunately, academic studies of such capital-based governance processes too seldom fully incorporate the core elements of the operations being examined. Thus, the operational flow and the value chain are often almost absent phenomena in those analyses. That is rather surprising both because many of the financial resources in a corporation have their origin in the operational flow (payments for output sold), and because operationally generated capital streams usually become inputs in the allocation processes.

Moreover, research examining shareholding and its impact on corporate development has too seldom been based on longitudinal 'unfiltered primary data' (e.g. recurrent interviews and lengthy participant observations).[19] Therefore, it comes as no surprise that its results often have been rather difficult to 'translate' and utilize for practical action.[20] To a certain extent that scarcity of 'primary' data could be traced back to educational shortcomings, self-absorbed academic institutions and general access difficulties (weak links between researchers and practitioners).[21] So, as such, shareholder governance is still a rather unexplored field, particularly when it comes to those concrete actor activities that affect the operational and financial flows.

Shareholder governance could take place both through exchanges of shares (entry/exit) and through direct interventions in corporate flows (voice).[22] The shareholding distribution in each individual corporation (evenly distributed among all shareholders or concentrated in one single actor [constellation]) essentially influences what governance mode will be put into practice. When shareholding is distributed, shareholder control becomes difficult to exert, and shareholders might need to organize to defend their interests against those of other stakeholders (including the executive actors). Legislators around the world have therefore established a special arena that makes it easier for shareholders to mobilize influence – the GM. However, the regulations surrounding that agency vary considerably from country to country. Thus, it is not always such a powerful body as it is in the Nordic countries.

Ultimately, the crucial decision for controlling shareholders concerns which part of the vertical financial flow they should try to populate. Some of them act exclusively on the open market for corporate control and take distant financial positions, basically ignoring the operational flows. Others also engage in the 'corporate parts' of the financial flows, and then some of them become involved as executives (usually as chairs/directors). In all cases, it becomes important for them to decide at what hierarchical level the crucial allocation decisions ought to be taken (and, consequently, by what actor category). Another key decision concerns at what level the financial flow should connect with the operational one. How well that link works is critical for most corporations, because it is at this point that the fundamental trade-offs between the two flow rationales present themselves and decisions have to be taken about their relative impact on the governance processes and the structuring of the strategic paths.

2.4 ON INSTITUTIONAL BASES FOR FINANCIAL FLOWS

There is no shortage of academic literature addressing the many different institutions influencing corporate governance.[23] These institutions develop as part of national/regional politics and involve governments, political parties, employer associations, labour unions, social movements, 'big business', lobbyists, 'think-tanks', professional associations, academic organizations, and so on. Most of those actor constellations contribute in one way or the other to national/regional governance regimes, and all of them are embedded in relatively unique historical and environmental contexts that strongly affect the emerging institutional structures.[24] As a consequence, corporate governance regimes usually form inflexible (and even 'petrified') regulations, thereby making changes of individual institutions/norms rather difficult. However, when partial modifications are proposed,[25] the regimes often trigger counter actions from those reputable and powerful actors that support (certain parts of) the prevailing governance regulations. They defend those institutions and cultural bases that they think have worked well and favoured their particular interests.[26] As a result, corporate governance regimes (and their elements) can be expected to be rather stable.[27]

Figure 2.3 shows some of the institutions that influence financial flows. They represent legislative forces (e.g. company laws), public regulations (e.g. stock exchange stipulations) and self-regulating codes (e.g. corporate governance codes). Four main actor categories could also be identified in that flow: the shareholder, the lender, the financial adviser and the financial authority (controller). The action rationales of these various financial actors do not deviate from those of other actors, although their specific

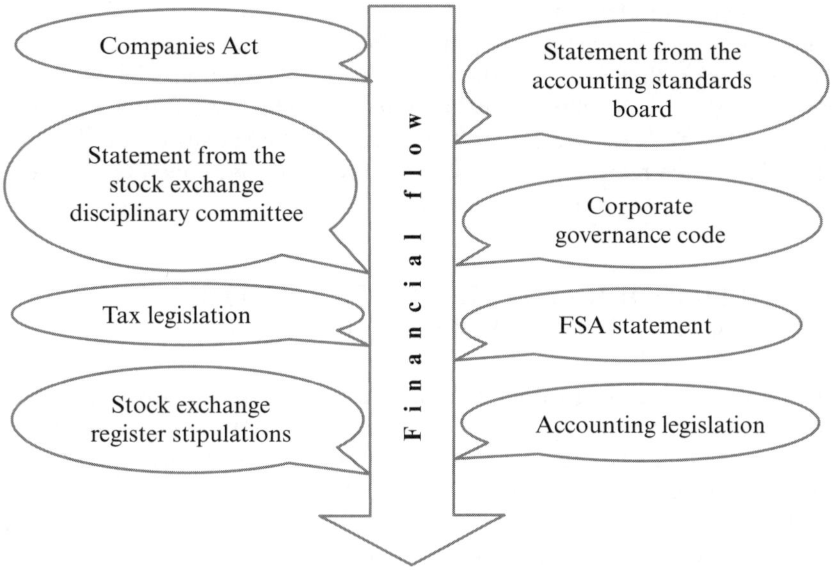

Figure 2.3 Examples of institutions that influence financial flows

functions in the governance process might to some extent influence what rationales they will prioritize.

All institutions forming the financial flow that is illustrated in Figure 2.3 have external origins, although the associated norms are (re)produced by both internal and external actors/agencies. The internal actors usually control the 'corporate part' of a flow with the intent to ensure that all processes work well and are reliable. For the external actors the basic function is to do something similar on behalf of the stakeholders (especially for the shareholders), although it has become rather common that they also give advice to the executive bodies regarding, for example, accounting matters, environmental issues and ethical codes. Some of those external agencies are particularly powerful, as they represent the public authorities.

However, many professional actors work independent of both corporations and authorities, expressing more or less qualified opinions on vital corporate matters. Media actors (e.g. economic journalists), analysts and rating agencies are prominent examples of a kind of external evaluator that foremost bases its conclusions on information linked to the financial flows. Media make large quantities of corporate material and data from open sources available and accessible to broader audiences including all kinds of (potential) shareholders, and they also publish narratives to inform their readers about less visible/accessible actor performances. In doing so, they try to 'get behind the figures' and add qualitative information in order to level out the information asymmetries that exist on the public market for corporate control. Analysts do something similar but only for a more limited group of actors.

What is noticeable is that since the 1980s media have increased their use of the financial perspective as the main platform for their narratives and analyses, and that has occurred at the expense of the perspective of the employee. Thus, many media actors have begun to act as 'vicarious shareholders'. That 'bias' could to some extent be explained by a change of audience – they rather write for (potential) investors[28] than for those employed in the companies. However, that focus on the financial flows could also be explained by the distant positions that media actors usually hold, from which it is difficult to become well informed about the more concrete operative issues. That disposition could also be due to the way they have been recruited – they seldom have extensive concrete experiences from relevant industries and top corporate positions.[29]

2.5 SHAREHOLDER GOVERNANCE: VISIONS, PERSONALITIES AND COMPETENCES

Shareholders are treated in a rather one-dimensional way in many corporate governance studies. They are portrayed as simple maximizers of the value of their shares over a certain often unspecified time period, and nothing else. However, many empirical studies and actor biographies have revealed that shareholders often also want to accomplish something beyond profit with their investments. Such broader ambitions are often present and both legal and possible, and usually other stakeholders tend to appreciate them.

There are (at least) two reasons why such more complex corporate purposes have materialized during the 20th century: national laws usually do not require that corporations maximize profit – to seek (any level of) profit is sufficient (cf. e.g. the Swedish legislation[30]) – and stakeholder activity has increased and become more visible and powerful due to the new media landscape, and that has forced corporations to consider a wider spectrum of perspectives and take new stances. It is also almost impossible to determine whether observed shareholder actions are triggered by profit maximization ambitions only, or if other motives are involved, too. Thus, shareholders might also exercise influence over corporations based on more personal values, and in such a way that they modify the traditional profit ambitions. That freedom of action makes it possible for shareholders to use the whole repertoire of actor rationales in their governance processes. So, as for actors in general, shareholders' governance efforts are both boundedly rational and multi-rational, although somewhat 'special', as the calculative rationale tends to dominate.

A controlling shareholder usually voices ideas regarding three fundamental issues: why the corporation exists at all, why its current operations are preferable and how the corporation is expected to develop over the long term (a vision). Shareholders' answers to the first question sometimes deviate from the classic 'to increase shareholder value', although that is far from always the case. Many corporate actors are fully convinced that a corporation's exclusive raison d'être should be to enrich its current (and future) shareholders, thereby simultaneously contributing to the general welfare in society, while others instead argue that additional purposes almost always play important roles, too. Those other purposes might then be linked to a specific geographical territory (e.g. benefit a certain nation), a population (e.g. favour a certain family/dynasty), a certain business (e.g. promote people's health), and the like.

The time perspective used by a controlling shareholder is usually linked to the corporate idea. Some controlling shareholders even express corporate ideas that breathe eternity – 'their' corporations are supposed to live on forever – while other shareholders act solely in the moment and avoid all commitments that involve the future. So, the choice of time horizon influences what mix of governance rationales a shareholder ultimately decides to bring into play.

The more concentrated the shareholding, the more likely it is that the traditional economic rationale is supplemented – and in exceptional cases even outdone – by the non-calculative ones. However, controlling shareholders do not always describe and communicate such more personal reasons behind their investments. Often the presence of such rationales is hidden or – if apparent – denied, as several of them tend to be in conflict with the dominating ideals that generally are associated with corporate governance. To apply them is also sometimes assumed to negatively affect the valuations of the corporations (i.e. lower the share prices).

Another way to describe shareholders' governance capacity addresses their personalities. As providers of capital, shareholders handle risks and absorb uncertainties, and those efforts are expected to (re)produce wealth both for them and for society as a whole. It is through investments in specific businesses that shareholders take operational and financial risks and internalize genuine uncertainty. They do that by allocating (cf. 'locking-in') capital to those corporations they believe will be the best at creating value.[31] However, individual shareholders' inclination to take risks and absorb uncertainties varies a lot – their differing personalities make some of them risk-seekers and others risk averse, and those attitudes have substantial impact on how corporations develop over time.

Other personality traits are supposed to have bearing on shareholder governance as well. The most commonly mentioned ones are (degree of) optimism–pessimism, cognitive–emotional balance and position on introversion–extroversion scales. The first trait is supposed to influence shareholders' expectations, and that, in turn, determines both the amount of capital they invest and how it is distributed over time. The second characteristic distinguishes between those actors that almost exclusively rely on calculations and figures in their capital allocations, and those that also put faith in intuition, gut feeling (cf. emotions) and aesthetic judgements. The third trait, finally, is said to influence how much personal leadership a shareholder will express when a corporate path is to be carved out, decided and implemented.

However, the most important shareholder trait might be inclination to act. That disposition could to some extent be personality driven (cf. above), but it is basically also a consequence of the size of the shareholding. Most shareholders – especially the minor ones – are almost obliged to take a passive role and avoid all kinds of involvement in 'their' corporations, while some others – foremost the major ones – tend to be active and even seek executive positions (usually as chairs/directors). The minor shareholders basically exert their almost negligible influence indirectly through entries/exits, while the major (or controlling) shareholders exert their influence directly through advice and commands ('voice'). The latter also have to decide at what corporate level the financial governance efforts should take place. Several levels in the vertical financial flow are available, and each of them will involve meetings and discussions with different categories of executives.

Shareholders' most decisive contribution to a corporation is to provide risk capital – a step that is necessary for its formation. That capital also to a large extent determines (at least theoretically and legally) what competences and actions will matter the most for how a corporation is governed. However, capital input is not always enough – a controlling shareholder usually also needs to make contributions beyond providing equity to be able to successfully govern a corporation. Then certain competencies stand out as the most important ones, in particular the capability to exert economic control and evaluate strategic proposals. In general, to carry out the monitoring function, major shareholders need to be educated and/or experienced in the fundamentals of accounting and control (economic and financial competence). Furthermore, to be able to challenge the executives' strategic proposals, they should have substantial experience of complicated operational and financial assessments (general business competence). A capacity to distinguish between disturbances (passing incidents that could be handled without a major change of course), tendencies (recurring incidents that require certain changes) and paradigm shifts (dramatic incidents that require substantial transformations) is also necessary. However, the most important non-financial competence governing shareholders should possess is probably the capacity to identify those activities that contribute the most to a corporation's value creation processes, and that, in turn, implies a high level of familiarity with the current operations.

At the top, that is to say, for those acting on the open market for corporate control, the span of investment opportunities will be the greatest, at least in principle, since the possibilities to specialize in mapping, scrutinizing and comparing corporations will be the best from such a 'universal' position. In comparison with all other loci, it will also treat all investment options equally (without 'biases' and restrictions), because that universal position tends to lack both psychological and historical ties to specific investment targets (corporations). However, for executive actors and employees at lower echelons the situation is reversed. They usually possess the best knowledge about specific corporations and their operations. By contrast, their opportunities to scan, evaluate and compare the possible investment alternatives outside the corporation are usually much more circumscribed. That means that the span of the allocation options tends to narrow along the financial flow. Obviously, universal investors could also take many in-between positions along the allocation chain (cf. Figure 2.4) and, for example, concentrate on some segment of the market (fewer alternatives). That is also common practice.

2.6 SHAREHOLDER GOVERNANCE: ACTOR DIFFERENCES

First of all, it is important to recall that direct shareholding varies significantly in scale from a situation in which an investor owns a controlling block of shares in a corporation to a context where the investors only hold minor or insignificant holdings. In the latter case, the ultimate shareholders' values and preferences could be both numerous and divergent, and therefore rather difficult to activate and organize in joint efforts. The relative sizes of those two shareholder categories vary around the world. In most countries it is the controlling shareholders that dominate the corporate governance processes, while in others it is instead the public market for corporate control or the executive bodies that carry out much of that function. However, common to all public markets for corporate control is that many new (kinds of) intermediaries have arrived on the scene, offering to act in the interests of their ultimate investors.

The most common corporate shareholder situation around the world is probably the one where one single actor (constellation) controls a corporation. That actor could be an

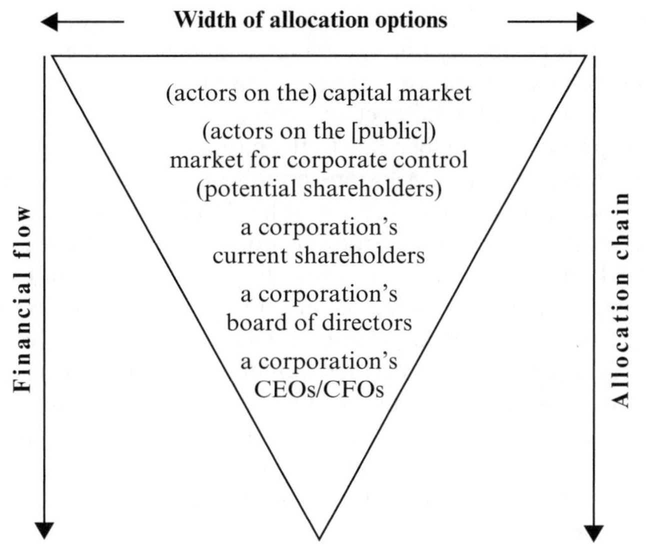

Figure 2.4 Width of allocation options along the financial flow

individual acting as such, or a representative for some kind of sphere, whether composed of a family/dynasty, a state, a member collective, a circle, a group of executives, or the like. For obvious reasons, such controlling shareholders tend to engage deeply in the financial flows, but they also often take active roles in the operational ones. Moreover, if they are the founders of the corporations, they might even hold symbolic roles and (re)produce family values and traditions through their corporate actions. Corporations that for decades or centuries have evolved in that way tend to have strong links to the surrounding community, which in turn might strengthen stakeholder interests and affect governance processes. Such long shareholdings also usually enable successful integrations of financial and operational flows, thereby fostering the emergence of robust corporate paths.

Corporations with controlling shareholders also provide opportunities for its leading actors to promote qualities that lie outside the classic profit maximization norm. In such small-number situations, the importance of actor personalities might grow particularly strong, although personalities always matter to some extent, even for corporations where shareholding is dispersed and/or handled by intermediaries. As such, corporations constitute arenas where differing, conflicting and even incompatible shareholder ideas and values meet and sometimes clash. However, much of the total shareholding lies in the hands of actors that never even have considered participating in corporate governance processes.[32] For various reasons many of them do not even care about in which corporations their capital is invested (but they do care about economic returns). Instead, numerous intermediaries (e.g. funds) have been set up to link those 'countless' investors (usually small savers) with the public market for corporate control. The intermediaries have been given the right to allocate those passive investors' capital (buy and sell shares) and handle the accompanying governance opportunities.

Thus, many intermediaries exert agency functions with fiduciary responsibility to generate 'optimum' returns to their beneficiaries. However, that goal is not always easy to define, since that investor category both is numerous and constitutes a rather heterogeneous population with elusive/unknown preferences and mostly varying commitments. The establishment of those units for indirect shareholding rests upon the expectation that such arrangements provide several benefits to the ultimate investors: the contracted intermediaries can base their allocation decisions on advantages of scale, early and exclusive information and advantages of specialization. That kind of indirect shareholding that is entrusted to place people's capital in corporate stock (as units in funds) has grown substantially in recent decades.[33] Because it is almost impossible to identify common denominators among all those pooled investors, the intermediaries themselves often decide both the allocation rules and the target corporations. That means that the focus will be almost solely on economic returns (for time periods ranging from short term to long term).

An important feature of most institutional investors is that they, as intermediaries, take on a perspective that resembles that of the 'universal shareholder' and invest in a wide range of corporations. That behaviour makes their allocation rationale differ significantly from that of investors with concentrated shareholdings, regardless of time horizons and risk attitudes.[34] In the new era of financial capitalism that evolved around the 1990s, many capital-market-based actors (i.e. various kinds of funds/intermediaries) became more influential, partly because their numbers and sizes increased, partly because the global financial market was deregulated. The deregulation trend also opened up opportunities in Europe for the emergence of 'new' forms of shareholding units – primarily ones with rationales that were imported (or copied) from the US. However, most of these 'new' constellations had no impact on the processes described in this book, partly because most of the empirical material focuses on European corporations, partly because it covers a time period that also embraces trade capitalism (≈ 19th century) and industrial capitalism (≈ 20th century). Thus, most of the corporate governance efforts were carried out in the long-established (European) business networks, that is to say, in the more 'invisible' market for corporate control.

Among the intermediaries/funds that became more important on the global financial scene in the late 20th century was the pension fund (cf. Figure 2.5). Its various configurations represent assets pools that are designed to generate stable growth over long periods of time. They may be national (and run by the state) or private (linked to corporations or other kinds of associations), and they often control considerable amounts of capital. Sometimes pension funds use their 'voices' in corporations but more often they act through 'entries/exits' on the market. Another fund that has become increasingly important in the era of financial capitalism is the mutual fund, which essentially represents a collection of stocks and/or bonds and other securities, for which economic returns are sought. That category primarily includes retail funds that are sold to individual investors through dealers on competitive markets. Such mutual funds have a fiduciary obligation to act in the sole interest of their investors, who also can reclaim their capital on short notice. Quarterly, monthly and even daily performances are tracked, and the competitive pressure ensures that the funds continuously try to get the best return on their investments. Usually, that type of institutional investor has an inherent focus on short-term earnings, which influences the way its actors participate in corporate governance processes.[35]

A third category is the hedge fund. The amount of global hedge fund capital has

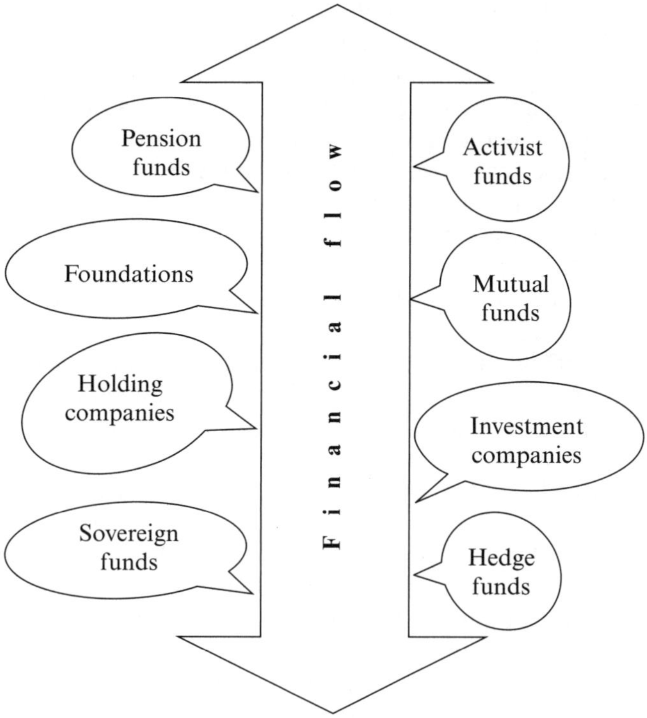

Figure 2.5 Important actors in the financial flows (examples)

grown remarkably during the relatively short era of financial capitalism.[36] The impact of those funds, however, exceeds the capital deposited by their owners. Some funds have therefore become significant actors on the stock market and have participated in many corporate control struggles (e.g. as early catalysts or as late trading arbitrageurs).[37] The activist[38] fund is yet another kind of intermediary that is associated with financial capitalism. Those units work in a mid-term perspective and position themselves so that they can encourage (or 'force') the board of a supposedly underperforming corporation to take measures in order to increase shareholder value. Activists often agitate publicly for specific operational and/or financial changes in target corporations, because their minor holdings usually require the active support of other investors.

The increased presence in the 21st century of actors such as pension funds, mutual funds, hedge funds, activist funds, sovereign funds and private equity constellations does not mean that all other kinds of investors have been pushed out – it rather means that their significance has declined, and that the classic kind of owners have to take the 'new' constellations into account when they act. It is then important to note that in the 21st century quite a lot of the buying/selling of companies still takes place within the (hidden/'invisible') business networks. Moreover, for this extensive study that covers a time period that goes far beyond that of the last two decades, those (hidden/'invisible') processes involving individuals, families/dynasties, spheres and states have been the most influential arenas for the buying/selling of companies.

The classic – and still potent – kinds of corporate ownership include the private company, the family-owned company, the co-operative, the foundation, the investment company, the insurance company and the state-owned company. In the Nordic countries (and many others) companies controlled by individuals or families/dynasties dominate the scene. While the co-operative is less used for running businesses, that form[39] of dispersed (i.e. democratic) ownership is still attracting individuals in several European countries. The foundation represents an asset or amount of capital that has been locked in for a specific, practically unalterable purpose for a long period of time (in principle, in perpetuity). It contains allocation and governance policies that embrace everything from securing control for a certain shareholder sphere to using the dividends for some stipulated purpose.

The (Nordic kind of) investment company is a constellation that usually takes specific risks by investing in relatively few corporations and that typically participates in the governance of those units. Spheres often use investment companies to control 'their' corporations. Insurance companies may appear in several forms, but many of them could be described as 'dual' businesses, that is to say, they function both as large investors in stock and as providers of financial or other services. Finally, states, too, including sovereign wealth funds, continue to invest in the 21st century, sometimes as shareholders in a smaller number of more or less related corporations, where they tend to favour certain investment and governance practices, sometimes as more passive universal investors.

The discussion above about classic as well as 'new' forms for organizing ownership of corporations indicates that the inclination to put pressure on executives might vary between different shareholder categories, and that it is not only among the controlling shareholders that intentions to govern can be found – several minor/mid-sized shareholders also express similar ambitions. Of course, the activist fund is the most obvious example of that conduct, but a similar reasoning is also applicable, for example, among foundations, mutual funds and hedge funds. It is then not merely the intensity of the pressure that matters – its content could also vary considerably (operational vs financial), as could its form (open vs hidden) and time horizon (short vs long).

Sometimes a corporation is the sole or dominating shareholder in another corporation. Then the latter is not always evaluated on its own merits; often its stand-alone performance is not the primary concern of the shareholders of the controlling entity. Instead, the governance process has its origin outside the corporation/subsidiary, making a holding company or a sphere constellation the ultimate decision-making body. On occasion, also more loosely connected shareholders join forces and establish what usually are referred to as consortia or 'actors in concert'. In such constellations the members themselves regulate the internal control processes, that is to say, establish procedures for how shareholder power should be exerted, and decide how changes in shareholdings should be conducted. It is also rather common that members of consortia build strong personal links that, for example, materialize as overlapping/cross-board memberships. Generally, spheres, consortia and similar constructs tend to put relatively more weight on the vertical governance processes, particularly if the operational connections between the controlled corporations are weak.

2.7 CORPORATE GOVERNANCE: ACTING IN THE OPERATIONAL FLOW

Basically, operational flows capture the ways financial capital is transformed to actor utilities, that is to say, to use(r) values. Capital cannot exclusively – and all the time – be kept in liquid form because (re)allocations alone – perpetual capital movements – cannot in the long run generate wealth. Thus, in its most general form, capital is tied up in specific investments, that is to say, as (part of the) operating capital,[40] to make processing – concrete value creation – possible. Such operating capital is largely used in the (re)production of those commodities that people consume – especially those goods and services that are most indispensable for their survival. The kind of commodities people really need are then evaluated on the basis of their 'use(r) values' (cf. utilities) rather than on their 'exchange values' (cf. prices).[41] Introduction of the time dimension produces a similar distinction: the commodities that people need instantly tend to be evaluated on a use(r) basis, while the goods and services whose consumption can wait for even long periods of time tend to be evaluated in price terms.

A corporation's operational process begins with its input (i.e. the resources needed for the processing), and ends with its output (i.e. the goods or services offered to the users). However, that does not mean that all processing activities have to be carried out inside a single corporation. The value chain segment that it is technologically feasible to carve out and hold together usually delineates the corporation's operations, and that border is then set, for example, on the basis of exchange frequencies, asset specificities and physical considerations.[42] Parts of the operations could also be outsourced to other corporations, or be dealt with through various kinds of networks, but the important thing is to decide what segment of a value chain an individual corporation should try to enter, dominate or control. The opposite situation, in which technological phases are difficult to discern, could instead give rise to a kind of 'super-hierarchical' solution (i.e. a 'giant corporation'), particularly if the operational dependencies require innumerable adaptations that are difficult to foresee and plan.

Essentially, a corporation's operational flow embraces a selected segment of a value chain, and it is the executive actors rather than the shareholders that govern that process (at least between the GMs). As mentioned above, operational flows represent the processing of resources 'locked up' in corporations (i.e. in financial units) for a certain period of time. In that flow, actors attract, recombine and develop the utilized resources, and deliver the resulting revenues to the actors who are engaged in the financial flow (cf. the allocation chain). Like the capital-based governance flows, operational flows move both ways (as described already in Figure 2.1 above).

Financially autonomous and semi-autonomous units penetrate all value chains (Figure 2.2 above). The accompanying borders indicate that separate and differing financial demands could be put on the various parts of a value chain. Within these borders, each corporation or corporation-like financial unit tends to function semi-autonomously, governing its particular segment of the chain. Thus, a financial unit takes all the risks associated with its specific activities. As such, it does not belong to any superior unit – its system for ranking alternatives and allocating resources is therefore a truly internal one.[43] In this way, value chains are imbued with corporations, all acting on their own merits.

Operational flows include not only the activities of management and other employees,

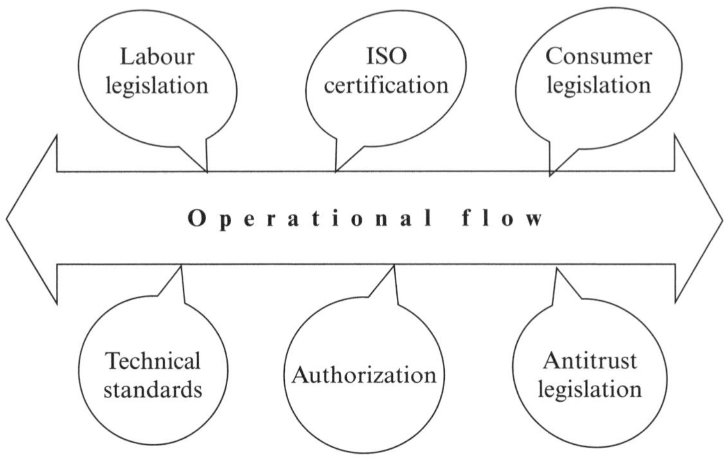

Figure 2.6 Institutionalized norms affecting operational flows (examples)

but also the efforts of various kinds of consultants, union representatives, customers, resource suppliers, head-hunters, local politicians, authorities, advisers, and so on. Several of those (inter)actions occur directly (i.e. face-to-face), but a growing number of them are nowadays mediated (i.e. take place through mass media and other intermediaries). Thus, many of the norms emerging from various kinds of external actors (stakeholders) penetrate operational flows (cf. Figure 2.6). First and foremost, legislation influences operations, making government agencies important actors (as they interpret the regulations). Those rules are often constructed to protect or favour certain stakeholder interests. Employees, for example, tend to benefit from several of those efforts: some deal with working conditions in a broad sense, while others address in what situations employees could exert (some) power.[44] Certain categories of employees also get support from other agencies, such as professional associations and social movements.

However, the government is not alone on the regulating scene. Quite a few authorization agencies and legitimizing bodies also have the potential to affect corporations, as do many standardization units. Most of them regulate the production processes as well as their inputs and outputs. Many other organizations raise their voices about how operations ought to be run, addressing both external effects (cf. e.g. emissions) and what resources a corporation should be allowed to use (cf. e.g. child labour). The operational flow is also populated by many consultants that provide advice regarding almost all possible production aspects ranging from input (e.g. how to recruit competent staff) to output (e.g. how to market commodities).

Many external actors take or represent specific positions on selected topics and act upon them when they engage in the operational flow. Consultants, for example, often side with the actors who contracted them, political organizations usually speak for parts of a population, voluntary associations leverage the power of their members, and so on. Corporations may also need to deal with various kinds of benefactors and sponsors, that is to say, actors and organizations that support their operations (even anonymously).

Some of the regulations focus especially on corporate outputs, giving priority to certain interests linked to customers. For example, in an effort to keep markets effective, governments try to get rid of monopolies, cartels and similar kinds of unwelcome co-operation between companies that might disadvantage other market players. Laws also often define what information a consumer ought to receive from producers regarding their commodities, so that the consumer can make informed choices. Regulations could also forbid, for example, certain ingredients, consumer uses and seller behaviour. In addition to state legislators and government regulators, quite a few other associations – idealistic as well as interest driven – make their voices heard regarding different kinds of corporate outputs (e.g. Greenpeace, Association of European Consumers and Consumers Union [US]).

In sum, corporate governance involves many different internal as well as external actors, including many kinds of institutions. That is valid both for operational and financial flows. The crucial question is then how to integrate them so that long-term stakeholder value can be built successfully. It is in those governance processes that financial capital is transformed into operational investments, and operational results become financial assets. Such 'meetings' between financial and operational flows require an arena; the key question then becomes on what hierarchical level those encounters ought to take place. That choice simultaneously determines the degree of shareholder/executive involvement in the strategic work. If the 'flow intersection' is set at the investor level, shareholders will have significant influence on the allocation processes, thus making financial considerations decisive for which segments of a value chain single corporations will try to control. That arrangement simultaneously allows the executive levels substantial influence over how the (financially) determined operational processes ought to be run. If, by contrast, the intersection of the two flows occurs at the executive levels, the shareholders can have greater bearing on a corporation's current operations, and the executives can have some impact on allocation decisions.

Finally, it is important to add that the two corporate flows vary in their degree of transparency. At one end, the financial flow gains very much from clarity and veracity, two qualities that are especially sought by those actors that are involved in that part of the overall governance process. At the other end, the operational flow rather often benefits from some level of 'opaqueness', since such fuzziness might help defend and utilize technological innovations and core competencies. Competitive strengths are usually built upon some measure of confidentiality or secrecy regarding the key operational processes.

2.8 SHAREHOLDING INERTIA

Shareholders' capacity to initiate changes in industry structures varies significantly. Some explanations are 'external', that is to say, refer to industry characteristics, while others are to be found 'inside' single corporations. For industries, the barriers to entry, the existence of shareholding spheres, the intensity of competition, the (expected) profitability level, the rate of innovation, and so on, all contribute to the development of its boundaries and structure. For single corporations the potential to accomplish industry changes depends on the concentration of the shareholdings, the ambitions and capacities of the actors involved, the available financial resources, the uniqueness of the market offerings, and so on. Thus, there are many factors that make it difficult even for controlling shareholders to make 'their' corporations promote and work for major restructurings. Instead, it is often newcomers (entrepreneurs) that trigger the radical structural transformations, for example, by introducing new path-breaking products, services or processes that have the potential to reshape both markets and competitive conditions.[45]

Obviously qualities such as corporate indebtedness, risk level, profitability and dividend policy influence (potential) shareholders' inclination to enter/exit, that is to say, to increase/reduce holdings over time. A long-term shareholding could also in itself (re)produce a strong motivation to stay in charge. The presence of spheres among shareholders could therefore create problems when industrial (re)structurings are on the agenda. The reluctance of sphere actors to take initiatives that also involve actors from other constellations tends to (re)produce a kind of 'shareholding inertia' that perpetuates the status quo. Basically, such rigidity is a consequence of how spheres emerge – usually they have their origins in various kinds of clan or circle relationships, which have been reinforced over long periods of time, and become both cherished and petrified. So, at least sometimes, the presence of spheres could be seen as a form of 'market imperfection', as they effectively 'lock in' corporations in different (sub)markets for control. Such solidified settings then sometimes obstruct (re)allocations of capital by restricting the investment options. This 'shareholding inertia' is of course also affected by the robustness of the spheres' shareholdings, that is to say, how probable it is that the current bases for control might disintegrate with time.

When sphere borders block transformations of industrial business structures, other kinds of changes tend to take place, especially those that could be carried out inside a sphere (or among units lacking controlling shareholders). Obviously, for clan-based spheres the important task is to ensure that the dynasties are reproduced and that they provide capable successors. Circle-based constellations face rather similar reproduction problems, although there the career paths of the up-and-coming young actors are based on merit (cf. meritocracy) rather than on kinship (cf. nepotism). Thus, it is sometimes what is best for a sphere or a consortium that shapes the future of a corporation, rather than its executives' ambitions or the global market for corporate control. As long as the controlling shareholders lack ambitions, incentives and competences to cross sphere borders and create new industry structures, their corporations face the risk of being left in the backwater.[46]

2.9 THE THEORY OF CORPORATE GOVERNANCE SUMMARIZED

The theoretical model of the corporation identifies two fundamental governance flows (cf. Figure 2.1) – the operational one and the financial one. A corporation is seen as an association of actors created under the authority of law that houses powers and liabilities and exhibits a continuous presence independent of its actors. Corporate governance is a rather broad construct that embraces most of the forces that were presented in Chapter 1 (Figure 1.1). Thus, corporate governance involves most normative sediments that exist in a society that in some way or another regulate corporate activities. Moreover, corporate governance is something much broader than 'shareholder governance', as it involves a much wider population of actors, including both stakeholders and now and then certain social interest groups.

The market for corporate control has been through several major changes over the last decades; it has become a global arena, its capital base has grown dramatically, and the number and kind of players have increased considerably.

As noted above, however, there is also a large part of the 'market' for corporate control that works more like a 'network', namely the 'hidden' part that houses most non-listed companies around the world. There, transactions often occur between actors who know (about) each other, which makes many control changes a result of bilateral negotiations rather than of auctions or bidding contests. Regardless of which part of the 'market/network' for transfers of corporate control that is examined (the visible or invisible one), it has become obvious that the allocated capital represents a variety of applied actor rationalities (i.e. emerges from actors with different competencies, experiences and judgement capacities).

The operational flow, illustrated with a horizontal arrow, starts either from technology-push or from demand-pull, and includes all the operational forces that influence corporate paths. In the theory, both flows are integrated, forming a two-dimensional conception of corporate governance. Thus, the capital-based rationale and the operational rationale are treated as two simultaneous and (usually) equally important elements in the overall corporate governance process. Sometimes, however, a corporation makes the financial needs of the operations the key issue (a corporate finance approach); sometimes it is the expected returns from the operations that are put in the foreground (a capital market approach). Thus, a crucial governance task will be to simultaneously handle the horizontal co-ordination of the vertical process and the vertical control of the horizontal process, so that successful corporate paths can be established.[47] The latter, that is to say, the 'corporate path theme', will be treated at length in the next chapter (cf. Figure 1.1 in Chapter 1).

NOTES

1. That description disregards its generative function.
2. Sevenius (2007), Kallifatides et al. (2010) and Sjöstrand and Hammarkvist (2014).
3. Any actor (constellation) that has a significant economic or other interest in a corporation's existence and success.
4. Freeman and Reed (1983).
5. 'Control' refers to voting power. A controlling shareholder (constellation) is present if more than 50% of the votes are owned (or are under control in some other way). However, since corporate control usually does not require that many votes in practice, the required percentage is often lower than 50%. Thus, it is usually the shareholding structure that defines what percentage establishes 'practical control' of a corporation. Nevertheless, control problems could turn up, for example, when corporate shares entail different voting rights, as that sometimes makes it possible to control a corporation despite a rather small capital investment. Such situations might create legitimacy problems, hamper expansion and/or activate new (kinds of) players.
6. Monks and Minow (2004).
7. Cf. e.g. Roe (2003).
8. Mallin (2004) and Monks and Minow (2004).
9. E.g. Arun and Turner (2009).
10. Mallin (2006a) and Mallin (2006b). Also notice the special legislation linked to the US state of Delaware. Cf. also Cicon et al. (2012).
11. Becht et al. (2002) and Hansmann and Kraakman (2011).
12. Ohmae (1995), Brodin et al. (2000), Henrekson and Jakobsson (2001 and 2011) and Mallin (2004).
13. Bratton (2001).

14. Grandori (2004), Mueller (2009), Kallifatides et al. (2010) and Henrekson and Jakobsson (2012).
15. Actually such qualities could also be found in the US and the UK but to a much lesser extent. Cf. Sjöstrand and Hammarkvist (2014) regarding state shareholding in Sweden.
16. Allen and Zhao (2007).
17. Sjödin (2006) provides an elaborate philosophical grounding of this fundamental conception of financial markets.
18. Brenner (2002).
19. That theme is elaborated in Kallifatides et al. (2010). Cf. also Aguilera et al. (2008) and García-Castro et al. (2013).
20. Pettigrew (1985/2011). Cf. also the special issue of 'Corporate Governance: An International Review' (2011, Vol. 19, No. 1) that addressed that issue.
21. Brown et al. (1976).
22. Hirschman (1970). However, he never discussed the 'entry' alternative.
23. E.g. Sjöstrand (1993), Aoki (2001), Hall and Soskice (2001), Fligstein (2001), Mantzavinos (2001), McCahery et al. (2002) and Campbell (2004).
24. Gao (1998).
25. The limited 'systemic character' of the regulations makes such partial efforts easier.
26. Following Teubner (2001), specifically discussing the 'legal irritant' of 'good faith' as a legal principle injected from continental European legal systems to the British one as part of European efforts at 'harmonization'.
27. Hall and Soskice (2001).
28. The percentage of the Swedish population that indirectly owns shares has increased in recent decades, as has the general interest for business issues.
29. Porac and Thomas (2002).
30. Johansson and Nial (2007).
31. Kallifatides et al. (2010).
32. Bengtsson (2005) discusses the problem with poor 'rational' incentives to engage in activism.
33. Blyth (2002). Swedish citizens, as long as they are employed, cannot avoid being major indirect shareholders through collective pension schemes.
34. Hawley and Williams (2000).
35. Windolf (2005).
36. Nobody really knows the total size of these funds, since they rather often are set up in tax havens or countries that do not furnish the necessary information.
37. Sassen (2001), Brenner (2002), Dodd (2005), Parenteau (2005) and Krugman (2008).
38. However, the word 'activist' could also be used to characterize other kinds of intermediaries and actor constellations. Cf. e.g. Gilson and Gordon (2013).
39. An economic association.
40. It should be noted that operational processes for some corporations have a pure financial content (cf. banks).
41. Östman (2009).
42. Williamson (1985).
43. Östman (2009).
44. In Scandinavia many of these norms are outcomes of negotiations between employer associations and employee unions, and they are also often controlled and executed by these organizations (although the basic framework is legally defined).
45. Other forces that also might trigger the (re)structuring of industries are governmental interventions and economic crises.
46. Sjöstrand (1997).
47. Östman (2006).

3. The (re)production of corporate paths

3.1 UNCERTAINTY, AMBIGUITY AND RISK

In this third and final theoretical chapter some of the basics regarding corporate missions, visions, ideas, goals, strategies and (development) paths will be described and linked to the theory of corporate governance presented in Chapter 2. Rather than providing an overview of the state of the art in the strategic management field, this chapter offers a brief description of the basic strategic options that corporations generally face and a review of the forces that shape those options.

When discussing corporate paths, uncertainty and risk qualify as key phenomena. As described in Chapter 1, an actor's ability to act in uncertain conditions is a consequence of resources and experiences, and it is in essence a subjectively formed capability. Uncertainty generally emerges from perceived differences between information needed and information at hand. Thus, it is related to the degree of confidence that actors feel when they intend to act.[1] Uncertainty could also emerge from information overload, that is to say, from an actor's inability to organize and evaluate abundant and unstructured information. That situation will here be referred to as one of ambiguity.[2]

Both uncertainty and ambiguity can be reduced at least to some extent. Thus, corporate actors are regarded as capable of acquiring more and more reliable information, which make them increasingly motivated to act, although never with full security. It is also assumed that actors possess considerable calculative competences (e.g. skill in transforming [some] uncertainty to risk). Such capabilities allow the actors to make educated guesses about probabilities (expectations that something will happen) and about stakes (expected outcomes). In that context mathematical and statistical reasoning sometimes makes a significant contribution. Regardless of the availability of such techniques that create more certainty, there will always remain a substantial amount of genuine uncertainty and ambiguity in almost every situation. Thus, irrespective of the information situation and the computation techniques used, uncertainty/ambiguity is only reducible up to a point and will always be an important feature in the thinking, conversations and actions relating to corporate development.

As it is impossible for corporate actors to move into the future without uncertainty, there will be plenty of room for human values, preferences and judgements in the path-formation processes.[3] The uncertainty and ambiguity surrounding those processes leave room for many differing demands and rationales. Thus, there is room for both subjectivity and multi-rationality when a corporation's best way ahead is decided.

The theoretical platform presented in Chapters 1 and 2 above was based on the idea that two main forces drive most corporate development, namely nature (resources and occurrences) and (individual and collective) actors. Individual actors often try to run such development processes through the use of five conceptual tools, namely mission, vision, (corporate) idea,[4] goal and strategy. However, the possibility for individuals to act is severely restricted by their embeddedness in the current settings (cf. culture and institutions), and by the simultaneous actions of competitors, customers, advisers, regulators, and so on.

3.2 CORPORATE MISSION, VISION, IDEAS AND GOALS

A mission represents a statement of why a certain corporation exists. Basically, the mission (or main purpose) of a corporation is to (re)produce sustainable structures and processes that over time create value for its stakeholders (with a privileged position for the shareholders) and society in general.[5] Obviously, the inclination to fulfil that universal ambition varies a lot among corporations. Some actors stress that the only adequate mission for a corporation is to maximize value creation for its current shareholders; they claim that all (inter)actions and exchanges with potential/future shareholders, as well as with other kinds of stakeholders, only represent means to achieve that purpose. Other actors instead describe corporate missions in terms of value creation for shareholders over time. Still others have formulated corporate missions that (also) stress non-profit dimensions. However, regardless of kind, a stated mission will only have impact if it is put into practice, and that is usually done through the application of the other four path-generating tools (i.e. corporate visions, ideas, goals and strategies).

Usually the dominating shareholder (more or less influenced by other stakeholders) formulates the corporate mission, and that statement functions as long-term guidance for the corporate actors involved. It is then rather common that it is the founder of the firm that states its raison d'être, although, now and then, subsequent controlling shareholders could add to – and even change – such an initial statement. Thus, deciding about a corporate mission is usually not an issue for the executive bodies, even if they sometimes might exert some influence on its content.

An operative or business vision is a description of what an organization seeks to become in a mid- or long-term perspective. It tends to represent a target that changes step by step at irregular intervals. Visions add emotional features to ideas about corporate futures, thereby inspiring actors by arousing expectations, hopes and dreams. However, one has to keep in mind that such appeals to emotions sometimes cloud judgement by encouraging actors to play down facts and figures. It is not always obvious if it is shareholders, stakeholders or executives that should develop the vision. Sometimes the major shareholder formulates both the mission and the vision; sometimes the vision is provided by the corporate board (or even by the CEO).

A corporate idea contains both operational and financial perspectives. The operational dimension includes descriptions of the services/goods to be offered and the anticipated customers (i.e. a product-market statement). Operative ideas could be more or less replicable, although the ambition is often to find a market 'niche', that is to say, a rather unique product or service offered to a certain set of customers. The financial dimension includes descriptions of what amounts and kinds of capital are needed for a pursued business mix. Corporate goals, finally, tend to focus on figures, that is to say, on various measureable targets for the efforts of most actors. Thus, goals are concrete constructs that relate to cognition rather than to emotion. Goals could link to almost everything ranging from sales to solidity, that is to say, they usually address both operative and financial matters, and can be broken down to influence actions also at the lowest hierarchical levels.

3.3 ON STRATEGIZING

In the economic sciences, strategy emerged as a key concept during the second half of the 20th century. An impressive number of researchers have published in the strategy field, and some of them have also contributed with extensive overviews.[6] Here, the more dynamic term 'strategizing' will be used. It refers to the process where it is decided how a corporation should move from its current position to a preferred one. That process is a core ingredient in the two governance flows described in Chapter 2, that is to say, the financial and the operational ones. Most of the talking, decision-making and acting that ultimately determine the long-term development of corporations will have taken place in those flows. Thus, they constitute the 'battleground' for corporations' strategic processes, regardless of whether the actors act from internal or external positions. Basically, the content of the strategy decided upon reflects the trade-off between, on the one hand, keeping assets liquid as financial capital, which makes re-allocations easy, and, on the other hand, putting capital to specific operative uses, which means investing in various kinds of assets[7] to obtain the benefits of value-adding processes. Two categories of actors are particularly important when that trade-off is being decided, namely shareholders and executives.

Shareholders tend to apply financial strategies that are based on their opportunities to evaluate all the investment options offered on the global capital market (i.e. the ones for corporate control[8]). Those that refrain from major holdings usually apply such a pure financial approach, focusing on their own risk position and flexibility. In doing so they tend to challenge how corporations are composed, that is to say, focus on the possibilities of buying/selling units. As they act from a distance and lack historical commitments and 'moral obligations' to invest in specific corporations, they apply an outside-in logic. As such, these shareholders tend to put relatively less emphasis on the particular financial needs of the corporations in which they invest. Instead, capital market considerations are given priority over operative requirements. The presence of that actor rationale indicates that the strength of the linkage between the two governance flows could vary among corporations.

By contrast, controlling and major shareholders tend to act in both flows, but it is primarily their experiences of the operative flows that determine how they act financially. Thus, basically, they make use of an inside-out logic. It is through staying power and/or affiliation that such shareholders develop solid knowledge bases – and perhaps even emotional ties – that are of benefit to the operations of the corporations in which they invest. Not surprisingly, those shareholders are eager to participate in the discussions about the corporations' future resource structures. It is their informed judgements regarding the expected success of the corporate path embarked upon that decide whether – and to what extent – they keep their capital in flexible form (focusing on entry/exit) or convert it to asset-specific uses (focusing on voice/loyalty).

Obviously, strategic decisions are not a matter for shareholders only. The executive levels are involved, too, particularly in large corporations. The location of the strategic decisions – at the shareholder or executive level – has significant consequences for the strategizing process, as the shareholders tend to act in the financial flow and stress the financial aspects of the strategy and the buying/selling of units, while the executives instead act in the operative flow and focus on the business aspects of the strategy and organic development. Thus, top management tends to consider the operative flow to be the main arena for governance efforts and investment considerations, although they also have to co-operate with those actors that dominate the financial flow in order to acquire the necessary resources. The financial flow also provides most of the evaluations and measurements of performance, making the connection between the two flows concrete.

CEOs are usually the ones who have to explain the operative requirements (including financial needs) to the shareholders, while shareholder preferences have to be explained to the operative actors. In some cases, however, CEOs function more like capital allocators – as performers of an 'internal shareholder' function working at a certain distance from operations (cf. holding companies). There exist also corporations where the board has become the unit that balances the financial and the operative needs. Such situations make the CEO's role more operational (and resembles that of a Chief Operating Officer [COO]).

Usually, lots of both formal and informal discussions take place between insiders (shareholders, directors, top management, etc.) and outsiders (analysts, economic journalists, consultants, investment banks, etc.) before a strategy is decided and implemented (i.e. translated into operative and financial investments). In general, such strategizing processes involve small-talk activities carried out by several kinds of actors – not just by shareholders and executives. However, at some stage, the truly important strategic ideas tend to cross at least one of the primary (legal) corporate bodies (i.e. a shareholding constellation, a board or a top management team).

Actor judgement is the crucial 'commodity' that is continuously expressed and exchanged in strategic discussions (it works almost like a currency). Human judgements become particularly important in situations characterized by genuine uncertainty and/or ambiguity, as all forms of uncertainty make the calculative rationale either insufficient or inappropriate.[9] Even various kinds of norm-based rationales like heuristics become invalid in those cases. Strategizing is a clear-cut example of those processes in which individuals must use their judgement capacities to be able to act in a non-gratuitous way. Thus, expressing judgements becomes a kind of last resort for non-random decision-making.

3.4 ON ACTOR JUDGEMENT

When providing judgement an actor usually relates to some kind of 'audience'. There are different kinds of talk and many sorts of audiences that, when combined, occupy a significant part of corporate life. Several philosophers[10] have written about how actors through small talk (cf. chat, gossip, natter, etc.) learn about and influence how other people think, decide and act.[11] The main source of most of that small talk – conscious and planned as well as spontaneous and haphazard – is experience.

Through small talk, actors (re)produce both the basis for their moral understandings and their notions about 'reality'. Often such non-instrumental, unstructured verbal communication is as important for human action as are well-thought-out stories, tales[12] and narratives[13] that also are part of the same general process. Small talk also sometimes serves as means for people to create a nice atmosphere, rather than as a method for systematic exchange of information about a particular topic. Moreover, small talk often also represents the on-going act of relating to others, that is to say, talk for the sake of talking.[14] So, verbal communication is a cornerstone in all forms of actor (inter)actions and decision-making, including those involving strategy formations. Indeed, small talk significantly contributes to the (re)production of the values and criteria that influence what in the end will be seen as the best path for a corporation.

All that talking and listening means that people communicate their experiences and values to one another, thereby (re)producing shared knowledge. In these processes some ideas or topics are neglected while others are stressed, and judgements represent both the outcomes of and premises for such filtering. As such, judgement is one form of speech act, that is to say, a human performance, unlike 'constatives',[15] which can often be identified as true or false, while 'performatives', which some researchers[16] claim are the only kind of utterances that qualify as judgements, have to be evaluated in other ways than through a true/false paradigm. Instead, it is the relevant audiences – that is to say, the individuals involved – that ultimately decide which judgement should be trusted.

Judgements then should be considered in relation to human constellations, such as a sphere, clan, circle or other kind of fellowship. That means that most judgements are formed in the context of a collective body of some kind. Thus, they are offered to earn support from others one knows (rather) well (cf. e.g. confirmatory and integrating statements). Such collective backing rests on the qualities other individuals attribute to the actors providing the judgement (cf. e.g. their track records[17]) and the content/form[18] of the statements (the quality of the judgements). In this way, such constellations simultaneously confirm/reaffirm the criteria for what constitutes a reliable and trustworthy actor.

In most situations more than one judgement exists, and the competition between them could be tough. Usually corporate actors try to establish their own position as the 'true' or most 'useful' one, in that way promoting what should look like a 'natural', logical or inevitable next step in a strategizing process. In other words, they state which – and whose – judgements it is wise to follow. For a judgement to be powerful, the actor making it must be confident that most of the others could be convinced about the same thing. So, there is a struggle to win over the others involved.

To be convinced means that most of the doubts surrounding a stance have been cleared. Such confidence is usually built on personal devotion – its emergence requires an emotional element.[19] Basically, such an emotional, intuitive and/or aesthetic commitment makes an individual think further and act, despite the absence of a satisfying calculative basis. It makes forward 'leaps' possible, particularly in situations of genuine uncertainty and ambiguity. Such leaps materialize as a consequence of actors' strong conviction that certain paths ought to be followed. In a sense, therefore, leaps represent acts without solid bases.[20] Thus, to furnish a judgement is to act with personal conviction, but without the necessary tools to 'prove' to others the correctness of the statement.

Judgement differs from calculative reasoning in that it does not follow any stable rules, heuristics or logical principles – instead both experiences and imagination could be its bases. A strong personal responsibility emerges for the positions taken, as it is not possible to refer to an established (and shared) logic, rationale or rule of some kind.

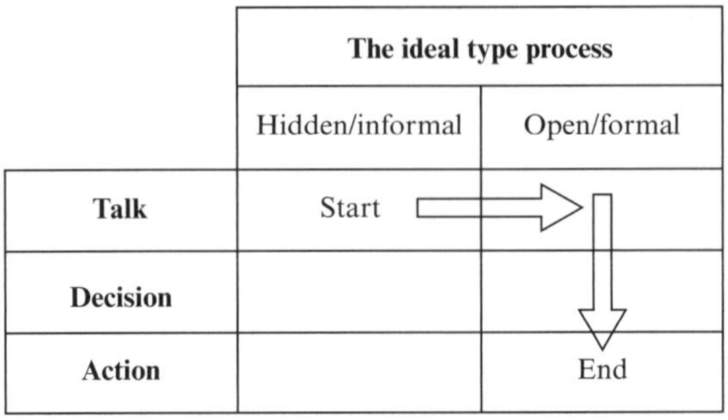

Figure 3.1 From idea to action: an ideal type construct

The suggested path becomes attached to or identified with the actor advocating it. The presence of such strong commitment in executive decision-making has been verified in several empirical studies.[21] Some scholars have even addressed the impact of, for example, mythomania, narcissism and bipolar illness on executive judgement.[22] One could add that arguments sometimes appear after a judgement has been formed. However, that does not imply that such arguments simply express hindsight wisdom – they could also represent restorations.

The process that takes individuals from exchanging and evaluating judgements to concrete acting varies significantly. The ideal type one is shown in Figure 3.1, where the arrows show a path starting from a few individuals' informal small talk, passing through some individuals' formal decisions and ending in open collective action. However, that ideal type procedure does not dominate corporate practice – most of the other conceivable paths are also followed.

3.5 STRATEGY AND RISK

Corporate strategic development is very closely linked to shareholders' and executives' operational and financial risk-taking. The basics regarding risk, ambiguity and uncertainty were presented in the previous chapters, where risk-taking also was linked to various kinds of shareholding. In this section, risk will instead be linked to the different kinds of strategies that are available to a corporation.

The most radical operative approach is to enter new markets with new products/services – that is to say, to simultaneously diversify the output and expand the operations into untested areas. For a corporation, that strategic choice represents high operative risk. However, for (some of) the shareholders the risk situation is different, as they might have other holdings that put individual diversification efforts in quite different contexts (e.g. in a sphere perspective). Operative risks are generally associated with (geographical) markets, R&D, production, distribution, mergers and acquisitions (M&As) and divestment. All these risks are also influenced by the actions taken by significant external actors (authorities, competitors, suppliers, social movements, customers, etc.).

Shareholders and executives differ in their views on corporate risk-taking primarily because of their divergent positions and interests. For example, it is usually assumed that shareholders value profitability more highly than they do growth, while executives instead are supposed to put growth before profitability. The reason is that expansion (and large size) usually strengthens the status of the executives involved (and increases their remunerations). Differing preferences could also be expected regarding dividend policies, since the retention of profits inside a company furnishes management with larger capital resources and a stronger voice in allocation decisions. Executives might also try to defend their corporations from (hostile) takeovers to lessen 'management risk', although such attacks sometimes might be advantageous in the eyes of the shareholders. Executives could also be expected to make efforts to become indispensable by increasing the value of their personal capital. That could be done, for example, by making the operations more and more in tune with their distinctive competences. Thus, there are many ways for executives to increase their power and lower their personal risk.[23]

Executives' inclination to promote operative risk-taking tends to be quite insensitive to (estimates of) probabilities of possible outcomes simply because they[24] are more comfortable with descriptions of concrete events than they are with summary statistics. Moreover, when they deal with risk, the magnitude of the outcome value is more crucial than some kind of weighting of that value by its likelihood to occur. Furthermore, as executives usually only consider a few aspects at a time (the 'key' factors), they often conclude that operative risks are 'controllable'. That conviction also follows from the fact that they have become more and more comfortable over time with their corporations' current business processes and settings. That comfort has made it possible for them to add judgements based on intuition to the more traditional, cognitively built convictions. Executives also tend to treat each decision involving risk as a unique one – only too seldom do they use compilations of total operative risks.[25]

When actors decide about corporate paths, they also affect financial risks that are not an issue just for the shareholders, but also for the corporation as such and all its stakeholders. Financial risks are primarily associated with developments on the financial markets, interest rate fluctuations, currency movements, default conditions, credit losses, borrowing terms and asset evaluation principles. Such risks also appear in figures for liquidity and solidity, and how those measurements stand in relation to industry standards and stakeholder requirements. Thus, financial risks are closely related to the size and composition of balance sheets, where composition refers to the relationship between, on the one hand, (various forms of) equity or assets and, on the other hand, liabilities. Financial risk is also linked to the qualities of these items, and how they are estimated. Usually, liabilities are concrete and easy to characterize in terms of size, 'stability' and type, while assets have more highly fluctuating values that depend on the continuously changing market evaluations.[26] Like for operative risks, a shareholder has two different contexts to consider – the corporate one (cf. the specific investment) and a broader one (cf. the total investment).

3.6 BASIC STRATEGIC ALTERNATIVES

When discussing the different forces that are particularly relevant for the emergence of corporate paths, most research tends to neglect or downplay some of those described back in Chapter 1, that is to say, (natural) occurrences, cultural influences, regulating institutions, scientific progress and (customer) demand. Instead, some groupings of scholars place emphasis on the individual actors (cf. e.g. the entrepreneurial and the cognitive schools), while others rather stress the group/team level (cf. e.g. the learning school). Still others address the corporation (cf. the design and planning schools) and some the industry level (cf. the positioning school).[27]

The crucial question in this study is whether a corporate path is primarily an outflow of human activities (i.e. talk, decisions and actions), or is basically formed by (some of) the other forces mentioned above. That rather controversial – and difficult – issue is addressed more extensively later in this chapter when the focus turns to actorhood. There, the discussion examines whether strategies are more often based on planning and ex ante decisions (cf. intended strategy), or rather tend to emerge in the minds of corporate actors as a consequence of on-going activities and occurrences (cf. emergent strategies).[28] Of course, a mix of these two kinds of processes is also possible; some parts of a strategy could be traced to documents or decisions of an ex ante kind, while others are ex post outflows of continuous adaptations (or of sheer twist of fate).

The use of the word 'path' signals that history matters when corporate strategies are developed and implemented. The use of that concept also indicates that corporate inertia could be substantial, and that some kind of crisis often is needed to push a corporation out of a well-established course. One could then talk about a basic clash between the past and the future – between what has been (re)produced over a long period of time and what might be attained. Thus, continuous struggles go on between those forces that try to keep, consolidate and defend a current path, and those that are open to and advocate a new course.

Strategizing is all about promoting the existence and development of a corporation by improving its capability to make use of its resources in an ever-changing context. Very often such corporate resources are classified under headings such as 'land', 'labour' (including human energy, knowledge and capability in general) and capital (real as well as financial capital; tangible as well as intangible capital). Strategy is also often contrasted with tactics, stressing that strategic decisions and actions are characterized by a certain degree of 'grandiosity' (i.e. they involve both big values and long time perspectives). That distinction, however, does not imply that the everyday activities in the lower echelons of corporations are of less importance for the way a 'grand' strategy is constructed and/or carried out. Many truly important strategic candidates or inputs tend to come from fairly remote organizational corners.[29]

Basically, strategic decisions and actions refer to substantial, durable investments/divestments of various kinds, that is to say, activities that significantly influence the general resource structure of a corporation. That structure includes both assets that the corporation owns – for example, factories, machines, tools, patents and brands – and assets that are controlled in other ways (through employment and/or other kinds of contracts) – for example, human competences, capabilities and skills. Such resource structures constitute the key platforms for corporate actors when they construct and head out along corporate paths.

Applying a long-term perspective and building sustainable competitive advantage might be a risky strategy because it represents a lengthy lock-in of resources for specific purposes, a situation that makes a corporation vulnerable to changes. So, when circumstances shift, such a long-term investor might be beaten by a corporation that instead has built capability to react quickly by keeping most of its capital available (liquid) for short-term activities. Thus, each corporation must find where on that 'short-termism'–'long-termism' scale it ought to be located, so that it can develop its operations successfully over time.

Corporate strategies emerge and materialize through activities in the two basic organizational flows described previously, namely the operational and the financial ones. An overall strategy is the product of both of these connected flows, implying the presence of separable underlying operational and financial strategies. Depending on the situation, one or the other of the two flows eventually becomes the dominating one, and its main actors capture the driver's seat. That outcome and its associated action rationale then determine to a large extent what path a corporation will follow. Usually, however, corporate strategies tend to be described in terms of the applied product–market combinations.

If one takes the corporation as the focal unit and applies the financial perspective, one finds that, in principle, a strategy could materialize in six different ways. The available financial resources could be used to pay off debts, invest in the current business, integrate 'horizontally' through M&As (to take control over competitors), integrate 'vertically' (i.e. backward or forward) through M&As to gain control over suppliers and/or customers, diversify and redeem shares. Four of these paths are in some way linked to operative considerations (investments), basically determining what to include in a certain financial unit, and what to handle through the market governance mode.

M&As differ somewhat from traditional 'in-house' investments (organic growth). They tend to occur more irregularly and are often initiated by outside actors or unforeseen occurrences. The information situation is also different, as knowledge about the 'other' is rather limited. The time dimension also differs, as M&A activities usually tend to happen fast (i.e. there is not time to collect all the 'necessary' information). Finally, M&As also bring a whole package of 'unwanted' businesses into a deal. Taken together, ceteris paribus, genuine uncertainty and risk tend to be greater in conjunction with M&A activities.

Staying with the corporation as the analytical unit but applying an operational perspective, strategies materialize both in the activities performed (ultimately in products/services), and in the markets that are exploited. An operative strategy then defines the span of the businesses along one or several value chains. As most value chains are composed of semi-separable or partially autonomous processes, it becomes possible for corporate actors to select and put into practice varying operational spans. However, as few corporations are capable of controlling all of a value chain, that is to say, engage in everything ranging from basic research to end-consumer sales, corporate actors must identify the most attractive operative range.

Extension along the operational process is usually called 'vertical' integration – a term that obviously does not particularly well suit its horizontal visualization in the revised theory of the corporation described in Chapter 2. Therefore, another pair of concepts referring to 'vertical' integration will be used here – a set that discriminates between the two directions embedded in the value chain: integrating towards the R&D push, hereafter referred to as 'backward' integration, and integrating towards the customer pull, hereafter denoted 'forward' integration. Attempts to integrate backward and forward are more likely to be made when the specific resources (assets) that are essential for the effective operation of a part of a value chain are controlled by more than one peak co-ordinator (i.e. several financial units are involved). Achieving unitary hierarchical control of such a segment – integrating market-based units into a single corporation – is presumed to circumvent the risks associated with dependencies of indispensable resources.

What in most strategic management research is named 'horizontal' integration is here instead labelled 'scale-based' integration, indicating a situation where a corporation benefits from all kinds of size economies connected to a certain span of a value chain.[30] In such scale-based integration efforts there are no positional moves either backwards or forwards – the range of the operations stays the same. Here the concept of scale refers not only to technology understood in a broad sense – there is also a spatial (geographical) aspect to it.[31]

A corporation might benefit from several kinds of scale-based economies. First of all there is the opportunity to lower the average ('unit') costs in the operative flow (up to a point). However, this kind of cost reduction could be done in more than one way depending mainly on the time perspective applied. Economies of scale could stem from increased capacity utilization both by using a given production technology and by applying a new/modified technology that generates a more profitable mix of fixed and variable operational costs. Thus, reductions in average costs due to increases in capacity utilization are based either on short-run economies of scale (they occur within a plant of given size and kind), or on long-run economies of scale (following the adoption of a new or improved technology).[32]

However, scale could also bring other advantages to a corporation beyond just lower average unit costs. Size is also associated with 'network externalities', that is to say, the benefits that a buyer of a commodity gains from an increase in the total number of buyers of the same article. On such markets, the existing customer base is the critical object of strategic rivalry. It creates an opportunity for a corporation to benefit from a dominating and lasting standard of some kind. Moreover, a large size also makes a privileged market position possible by allowing for a more extensive use of product/service differentiation. Thus, in many industries, a corporation might choose to provide a variety of products/services that differ according to brand (cf. name), characteristics (cf. content), location (cf. place), and so on, and use such market crowding to compete against the other corporations. Several authors[33] have argued that large corporations actually can cram a product space in order to gain and secure market dominance.

A large size also makes it possible for a corporation to invest in competence depth, that is to say, put into practice the advantages of specialization. Thus, large-scale investments in people, factories, patents and brands, and so on, make competence-based 'excess' returns possible. Scale economies could also utilize the possibility of more efficiently storing input resources and/or output (cf. inventories). Size could also build a power position that, for example, could be used in various kinds of bargaining situations and in other efforts to dominate an industry or a market.[34]

Scale is related as well to indivisibles, that is to say, to situations in which a certain resource cannot be acquired or withheld in (infinitely) small quantities. When fixed capital costs are a significant percentage of total costs (i.e. in capital intensive operations) and appear, for example, in the form of factories, assembly lines and specialized tools/instruments, indivisibles might be present that create opportunities for capturing advantages of scale. However, when most operative expenses are linked to materials and/or labour, the reverse is usually the case.[35]

In addition, a corporation has the possibility to control parts of more than one value chain, that is to say, several 'unrelated' operational flows. Such extensions of the operative range are traditionally discussed under the label 'diversification', but it is here also called 'scope integration' corresponding to operational scope economics. It exists if a corporation achieves economic benefits and advantages when it increases the variety of the commodities it offers. Economies of scope[36] could arise if the relative total cost of producing a variety of goods and services in one hierarchically controlled unit is lower than doing it separately in several autonomous units. Such 'synergy effects' refer to the supposed advantages that emerge from exploiting connections between 'unrelated' but yet in some ways linked activities in a coherent hierarchical unit. Such resource 'relatedness' has drawn attention to the question of how resources and capabilities can be effectively shared across differing operative and financial flows. Some researchers find merit in such corporate constructs (conglomerates), while others instead express doubts.[37]

Relatedness could be a rather ambiguous concept when applied to corporate businesses. Traditionally, it has been measured in two ways, either through the use of an index like the entropy index or Standard Industrial Classification Code (SIC Code) or through a more subjective measure by which businesses are considered to be 'related' when a common skill, resource, market or purpose applies to each of them.[38] The first type of measurement assumes that if two businesses share the same SIC, they must have common input requirements and similar technology functions. In terms of the more subjective type of measurement, several researchers have stressed that both technological and market links have to be considered when the (degrees of) relatedness between the various businesses of a corporation is judged. When such links are missing, a conglomerate exists representing a collection of 'unrelated' horizontal flows monitored by a peak co-ordinator that form a single financial unit.

Since conglomerates have survived for a long time, they must be associated with some particular advantage or strength that has contributed to their existence and growth (otherwise the market mechanism must be inefficient). Several reasons for their presence have been suggested. One explanation stresses that the typical conglomerate was established over a long time period by a family/dynasty or a state, and that the controlling shareholders in such cases had been satisfied with the privileges and opportunities in society that ownership of a large organization offered. So, sometimes they have kept control at the cost of traditional economic benefits.[39] Others have traced the origin of the conglomerates to speculation-driven US banks and consultancy firms and their view of corporations as portfolios of investment opportunities.[40]

However, several other reasons for the rise and development of conglomerates have also been offered. Several decades ago, it was proposed that excess capacity in core resources sets diversification in motion.[41] That tendency to try to utilize economies of scope is particularly evident when high transaction costs and/or other barriers prevent market trading. The scope discussion stressed the role of technology and the possibility for a corporation to use it for differing applications and/or on different markets.[42] 'Brand capital' and 'corporate reputation' were also mentioned as (potential) drivers of diversification, as such qualities provide opportunities to benefit from scale. Other suggested drivers were distribution networks, communication infrastructures, 'executive rationales'[43] and sales forces. Economies of diversification could also be obtained from centralized provision of support (i.e. scale advantages associated with, e.g., accounting, finance, legal expertise and IT services). When executives have better and earlier access to crucial information from within the corporation, other advantages might also be created. The common characteristic of all these (and other) potential conglomerate drivers is that they can be successfully applied (also) across unrelated operative flows. Thus, economies of scope could materialize as a result of cost savings from sharing resources and transferring capabilities between financial units. In the end the extent of these activities – and the possible growth of conglomerates – depends upon the cost of such transactions administered within a corporation compared to that of similar transactions carried out on markets.

Another suggested advantage linked to unrelated diversification is its potential to reduce operative risk at the corporate level.[44] That formula, however, is relevant primarily to executives, since shareholders could reduce that risk by making capital allocations on the market for securities. That observation brings up the issue of where in the vertical flow risk-taking ought to be carried out in order to be most productive (from a societal perspective) – at the corporate level, on the capital market or in both these arenas. Thus, the crucial question becomes whether executives can create additional corporate value by diversifying the corporation's operations 'on behalf of' the shareholders, in spite of the fact that the shareholders could manage such risks themselves by holding portfolios of securities.

In short, the main argument for the presence of conglomerates (diversification) can be summarized as follows: a common peak co-ordinator – a holding company or a head office – can add value (even) to unrelated businesses through obtaining scale economies, utilization of selected standardized managerial tools across businesses, obtaining scale economies or synergy by creating cross-fertilization between various businesses (e.g. the transfer or sharing of technologies, brands, core competences and capabilities), making use of the informational advantages associated with internal processes in hierarchical organizations, and utilizing the general power advantages that usually follow from a larger size.

Much of what is described above regarding what drives the development of conglomerates has primarily addressed value chains and operational flows. The sharing of activities across such chains or flows may in some cases require hierarchical integration (rather than market solutions), but that does not necessarily mean that it works efficiently. Sharing and integration of activities typically impose substantial co-ordination costs. Such diseconomies have been analysed by many researchers, who, for example, have looked at diversification costs in relation to information processing in complex organizations. The loss of information and the inefficiencies that are created as a result of such complex communication processes constitute significant diversification costs that establish upper limits for corporate sizes. Other sources of such costs include loss of control and effort wasted as a result of increased (opportunities for) shirking. Furthermore, executives who continue to apply their existing 'dominant rationales' on newly acquired, strategically dissimilar businesses also tend to cause diversity-based losses, as do corporate staffs who make inappropriate, incompetent and untimely interventions in acquired operations.[45]

3.7 INDUSTRIAL SETTINGS AND CORPORATE PATHS

As was described already in Chapter 1, the forces that influence the content of corporate paths have several different origins: natural occurrences and resources, collective actors (cf. culture, institutions, science and demand) and individual actors. However, natural occurrences with substantial impact on corporate actions are relatively rare, although they can be really devastating when they strike. And when they do occur, such catastrophes can trigger drastic revisions of both industry recipes and corporate strategies. The same reasoning applies to scientific breakthroughs and pioneering innovations. The demand situation could also change dramatically in both cases, which usually also precipitates reconsideration and adjustments of corporate strategies.

Industrial settings and institutions frequently and markedly influence corporate paths, as they tend to mirror the characteristics of the societies in which they are embedded. Thus, like most other human activities, corporate path building is interwoven in a web of cultural relationships that link to local communities, counties, nations, regions, and the like.[46]

'Industry' is a somewhat ambiguous construct populated by a network of more or less organized individual and corporate actors, which are bound together through innumerable 'invisible' mutual understandings and 'visible' (i.e. manifested) interactions that influence – and are influenced by – the embedded institutions and the surrounding culture. So, it is difficult to unambiguously define an industry. It is almost always possible to question the criteria used in such demarcation efforts. However, one way of partly getting around that definition problem is to base the delimitation on how the involved business actors themselves understand the boundaries.[47] Such notions are important, as they limit – lock in – inter-firm comparisons, which in turn contribute to manageable competitive settings. Thus, industries could be demarcated by identifying those corporations whose actors tend to view each other as rivals. In reality, actors rarely record more than a handful of competitors, and those that are listed are almost always those that offer 'similar' (i.e. substitutable) commodities on the same markets. These listings form stable cognitive orderings that to a large extent structure an industry's competitive activities, as well as its long-term development.

Nevertheless, it is a bit problematic to relate the industry construct to the market construct. There certainly exists an overlap, as industries tend to be linked to particular output markets. However, an industry could also be described as composed of many different 'submarkets' or complementary markets – each of them showing substantial differences regarding, for example, technology, regulations and customer populations. So, the relationship between industries and markets is complicated and very much open to subjective considerations. The impact of markets on corporate paths will therefore be discussed in a separate section below.

The strong impact of industry perspectives on corporate paths is indicated by the fact that the actors involved share many assumptions and express common frames of reference. These 'collective thoughts' are usually manifested as industry belief systems or as industry recipes,[48] where both contribute to a co-ordination of corporate strategies (in more or less collaborative ways). Such shared beliefs usually include descriptions of the anticipated positions and roles of most of the actors and corporations that are engaged in an industry.[49] Thus, choosing strategies is not an unfettered act – it is constrained by industrial prescriptions.

Industry belief systems are foremost disseminated through small talk and narratives, that is to say, through conversations among all kinds of industry actors (including journalists, analysts, consultants, etc.). That talk and its corresponding stories externalize internal representations, and put them into play as public interpretations of industry events, conditions and practices. Much of that collective 'regimentation' emerges from role imitations, coercive influence of authorities and expert advice (codified and diffused by professionals). A problem with that consensus is that actors might underestimate the impact of intra-organizational forces, and thereby exaggerate the degree of coherence in corporate strategic acting.[50] However, once perceptions and interpretations have become widely shared in an industry, that uniformity as such might stimulate revisions of corporate strategies and efforts to modify industry recipes.[51]

Researchers[52] examining 'industrial organization' have listed several industry characteristics that influence the development of corporate paths: entry barriers, rivalry between industry field incumbents, the presence (or not) of substitute products/services (or of a superior commodity), the relative bargaining power of suppliers, the relative bargaining power of buyers, production factor conditions and the demand situation. The presence of entry barriers indicates that markets function far from the way their idealized theoretical construct predicts. As most real markets are 'imperfect' ones, parts of the strategic analyses have focused on finding ways by which a corporation could utilize these 'imperfections' to reap monopoly-like profits. Barriers to entry often emerge when certain companies' early investments in physical assets and associated non-divisible resources have exploited scale economies. Such corporate initiatives often make it difficult for 'latecomers' to compete effectively, and the large investments also signal a capacity to endure protracted (price) competition. Property rights to scarce resources, copyrights and patents represent other arrangements that build entry barriers.

One consequence of barriers to entry is that rather few corporations dominate on many markets making up what usually is referred to as oligopolistic competition. The low number of weighty corporations on such a market makes all of them well known to each other, so that most actors know each other's strategic moves (sometimes even in advance). Moreover, oligopolies typically also contain stable populations of corporations. Such stability over longer periods provides time for the emergence of more or less visible (and legal) forums for negotiations that promote co-ordination and co-operation, that is to say, for arrangements that regulate or even eliminate competition.

If 'competing' corporations in an industry offer rather similar products/services, cartels tend to develop for the purposes of reducing corporate risk-taking and securing profitability for each organization. Cartels are more common in capital-intense industries, where the risks are particularly high (lots of financial capital has been transformed for specific operative uses). Such an informal and preferably invisible way of organizing usually divides up geographical markets (i.e. outputs and prices become fixed). Corporations that break such informal (and sometimes illegal) agreements are usually punished by the others according to some system of sanctions. So, most corporations in oligopolistic industries tend to stick to the institutionalized 'industry rules', which means that their strategies are determined to a large extent by a shared understanding of – and support for – a specific and rather stable industry structure.

However, if an industry's commodities gradually become more diverse, corporations instead get an opportunity to avoid competition by going for specialization, that is to say, they look for 'niches' that constitute less competitive submarkets. Such activities loosen up corporate links (including cartels), although usually only to a limited degree. Some actions might also be taken to prevent rivals from becoming stronger (and a tougher competitor in the future), even if the steps taken do not build value or create synergies for the acting corporation itself. In the end, acquisitions are sometimes made not by the corporation that has the best 'operative fit' or most potential to benefit, but rather by the corporation that seeks to eliminate promising opportunities for its competitors.

Many industry-focusing researchers stress the need for any corporation to seriously recognize the possible moves of its competitors to avoid 'strategic myopia'. Such near-sightedness could have several sources; it could emerge from lack of longer time perspectives, underestimation of competitors, disregard of related industries, whitewashing of the corporation's own failures and overestimation of own successes. The undervaluing of the importance of other industries sometimes makes corporations overlook many productive cross-industrial activities – that is to say, they fail to consider those relatively rare but ground-breaking external challenges of a dominating industry recipe that sometimes take place.[53]

3.8 MARKET DETERMINISM?

Researchers that stress the impact of natural occurrences, culture and institutions on the development of corporate paths simultaneously tend to express a rather sceptical view regarding the presence of actor-influenced corporate strategies. Certain researchers (sometimes denoted 'evolutionists') claim that such ex ante kinds of corporate strategizing do not work because of the unpredictability of market contexts. Some of them even claim that most markets are 'too effective' to allow any corporation to develop sustainable advantages. In such a (close to) perfectly competitive environment, even well-thought-out strategies only work for a (too) short period of time – the other companies in the industry will soon imitate any new success recipe. Thus, it is competition as such that mercilessly determines which corporations will last on a market – that is to say, it is only those organizations that immediately adapt to changing circumstances that survive.

Thus, in evolutionary-flavoured economic theory, it is markets rather than executives that shape the crucial corporate paths – what is left for executives is to try to run the corporation in such a way that the correspondence to changing circumstances will be as high as possible. Some researchers even contend that successful adaptation to changing settings is mainly the outcome of luck and coincidence – not a consequence of conscious context-matching efforts.[54] As a response to the massive critique of such market-based determinism, several researchers have stressed the importance of other kinds of markets for the emergence of viable corporate paths. They have broadened the general picture and discussed corporate survival in terms of the functioning of the factor markets (e.g. markets for corporate control, executives and financial capital).[55] Many of the critical voices have also pointed at the abundance of industries that feature monopoly, monopsony, monopolistic competition (cf. niche dominance) and oligopoly (cf. market leadership) – all structures that indicate substantial actor impact on how industries develop.

The incapacity of corporations to act in 'optimal' ways is still another explanation for the relative inefficiency of market forces when it comes to determining corporate populations and paths. A kind of 'slack'[56] is often present in organizations, and it constitutes a bumper against market changes. However, the competitive pressure has increased in the era of financial capitalism (i.e. in the early 21st century) making truly competitive markets more common, and the exclusion mechanisms more effective.[57]

3.9 PATH DEPENDENCE?

Another point of departure when discussing corporate paths is the organizational unit as such. Already in the middle of the 20th century several researchers[58] claimed that corporate resources were the crucial driving forces. They argued that unused resources together with the preferences, knowledge and experiences of its executives decide a corporation's future path. Thus, corporations strive to add operations that are related to its 'latent' resources, which then tend to strengthen their already well-established core activities (cf. path dependence). When a critical mass of investments has been made in a corporation's operational flow and a certain strategic path has been established, reorientation becomes difficult. Path dependence tends to materialize over time when pre-existing specialized and fixed investments favour the use of hierarchy (e.g. in the form of corporations) rather than the market as co-ordinating device. Such a corporate path reflects transfers of idiosyncratic capital between related operational activities, and such inimitable processes make it difficult for other corporations to compete. However, it should also be added that corporate path dependency often also is a consequence of the most general of all forces building organizational inertia – the difficulties that actors often have when required to adapt to changing circumstances.

Many of the researchers that stressed the historical and structural features of corporations have applied a 'resource perspective' in their studies of strategies and paths, thereby moving the focus from industry structure and market dynamics to organizational resources.[59] Those resources include both owned and 'semi-permanently tied' assets,[60] that is to say, all financial and operative capabilities in a corporation. The advocates of resource-based theories also saw corporations as compilations of tangible (plants, machinery, tools, financial capital, etc.) as well as intangible (reputation, routines, networks, tacit knowledge, etc.) resources. Competitive advantages then emerge from those resources that are seen as indispensable for the operating processes, and unique (or at least not easily accessible to competitors), imperfectly substitutable, imperfectly imitable, imperfectly mobile and non-tradable.

Imperfectly mobile resources, for instance, refer to those resources that are tradable but more valuable within the corporation that currently employs them than in any other organizational context. Imperfect mobility may result from synchronized or matched investments building idiosyncrasies in a corporation's resource structure, or from co-specializations of assets.[61] The concept 'non-tradable' refers to resources that cannot be acquired on traditional factor markets (corporate culture, brand value, reputation, customer loyalty, etc.). Instead, such resources tend to emerge inside corporations in complex and time-consuming processes. They also often have an intangible character, and the links between them and corporate performance are often ambiguous. Moreover, since these resources are built up over long periods of time, it is less likely that their full value will be incorporated in the costs of acquiring them. That could create evaluation problems in many acquisition processes.

A basic uncertainty exists regarding the connection between intangible resources and corporate performance, as most of the intangible resources resist more precise identification and definition. As a consequence, competitors often have difficulties understanding the true sources of each other's strengths. Such ambiguities could effectively protect competitive advantages and lock market situations. Three qualities of intangible resources work that way: tacitness, complexity and specificity. Tacitness refers to the implicit and non-codable accumulation of human capabilities that primarily results from learning by doing, while complexity describes the simultaneous presence of a large number of interdependent assets and competences. Finally, specificity refers to the degree of uniqueness of the intangible resources in question. Taken individually or in some combination, these characteristics may obscure the links between corporate resource endowments and output, thus creating barriers to imitation.

Another barrier to imitation is related to the time dimension. Latecomers to an industry or to a market usually need to shorten the time required to build certain strategic resources – otherwise they will not be competitive. However, doing strategic things fast has a cost – latecomers have to accept the diseconomies associated with time compression. Other 'isolating mechanisms' that have the effect of protecting a corporation's core capabilities by preventing imitation include, for example, legal restrictions linked to patents, copyrights and trademarks. They might also take the form of (long-term) exclusive contracts with units controlling indispensable, scarce resources necessary for competitive supremacy. Such core capabilities are embedded in the general resource structures of corporations, and are often hard to distinguish (at least by outsiders), as they usually refer to complex processes of co-ordinated activities, that is to say, ultimately to the ability to make use of a unique set of resources. Thus, it is the capability to make use of core competencies that might produce superior performance – not the competences as such.

Once based on discussions about portfolios of businesses, strategic management theory has become a field that primarily addresses portfolios of internal capabilities.[62] Thus, the focus of strategy is no longer on industry imperfections and how those could be utilized through various kinds of positioning, but rather on the development and leverage of organizational capabilities. In that spirit, several researchers claim that corporate strategic action is mainly a matter of building a portfolio of relationships. From there, a kind of 'knowledge transaction economics' emerges, where reputation represents an important type of capital that facilitates interactions and exchanges. So, to survive and prosper, a corporation needs to link to a wider range of capabilities than it could (re)produce and control 'internally' – capabilities that only can be captured outside the organization.[63]

The utilizing of 'economies of expertise' across industries requires different sets of strengths, both in terms of understanding where the potential sources of knowledge reside and regarding the ability to absorb and deploy external knowledge in internal operations. Then, the strategic focus shifts from strengthening internal processes and routines to building mechanisms that enable the identification, sharing and absorption of knowledge located in a broader network of organizations.[64] However, such processes also destabilize path dependences, as they expose corporations to external impressions and ideas. Furthermore, for those companies that enter into cross-licensing, co-sourcing and joint venturing in order to leverage their knowledge and information resources, boundaries could be blurred.

3.10 STRATEGIC ACTORHOOD?

In Chapter 1 it was proposed that actors, both as individuals and as collectives, have substantial impact on corporations' strategic development. In this section, the focus will be on the former force – the individual acting – here referred to as 'actorhood'. In essence, such individual actors attempt to align corporate strengths with some of the opportunities and obstacles presented by the existing cultural and institutional settings. In this sense, strategic management refers to those activities that more or less successfully co-ordinate corporate activities over time, simultaneously (re)producing what at least looks like a well-thought-out, coherent path.[65] Strategic management is also very much about making it possible for organizational actors to deal with ambiguous circumstances in a consistent and foreseeable way. However, it is also about executives' attempts to catch the attention of the members of the organization and increase their understanding of the intended strategies.

Many researchers look upon corporate strategy as something that executives could (and should) construct 'in advance', and then put into practice (a classic 'rational' approach[66]). Researchers working in that tradition also often look upon corporate settings as something comprehensible and relatively stable, as something that it is possible for leading actors to handle successfully through a combination of initiatives and adaptations. However, other scholars have raised doubts about the merits of such ex ante strategies. As they see it, actors are not capable of such advanced planning, as circumstances are both too complicated and continuously changing. Even if actors were able to tackle that demanding task, critical researchers claim that the required degree of actor co-ordination is unattainable because actors have limited capabilities. Indeed, most (if not all) actors have incomplete knowledge of what is going on both inside and outside a corporation. As a result, official strategies – that is to say, those that executive actors have proclaimed for their corporations – tend to be interpreted in many different ways (sometimes even along thoughtless, incompetent or haphazard lines). Moreover, the idea that corporate actors could act in concert based on a shared strategic understanding also fails to appreciate the substantial differences that exist among actors in terms of their resources, interests, preferences, ambitions, attitudes, and so on.

Official strategies could be seen as a way for corporate executives to simplify a complex and chaotic world and to communicate a sanctioned path to the involved actors. The illusory accuracy of the accompanying texts and figures is then supposed to create confidence and security among the actors – a sense that there exists an idea regarding the corporation's future that actually might work.[67] By contrast, most researchers that play down the real possibilities for corporations to decide their futures stress the presence of adaptive processes. Adaptation has to take place, as no one knows beforehand which of all the possible strategies might turn out to be the best one. Moreover, although no corporation is capable of sticking to a path 'forever', institutionalized strategies will only be modified when the powerful actors find such adaptation necessary to retain the respect, support and compliance of their subordinates. In order to still allow for gradual or minor changes, corporate strategies tend to materialize as rather loosely coupled and partly incompatible actor practices.

The presence of informal constellations of internal actors – power blocs – also complicates the formation of coherent and sound corporate strategies.[68] Such spheres or coalitions often constitute a breeding ground for micro-politics that initiate and influence various 'strategic candidates'.[69] Although the presence of organizational politics might indicate that many corporate members are involved in the strategic planning efforts, such activities still tend to be dominated by rather few actors – those that hold top positions and those that for formal or other reasons have access to the crucial arenas for such discussions.[70]

Actor distance also reduces the likely effectiveness of ex ante strategizing, particularly in relation to operational flows. Some researchers doubt whether it is possible at all to establish practicable strategies from a distance, for example, from the top executive levels, and claim, instead, that such planning has to be carried out close to operations – otherwise it is seldom possible to really understand what paths corporations ought to take. To these researchers, long-term strategic planning carried out 'from the stands' resembles hubris.

Indeed, many researchers consider strategy to be something that actors construct ex post, that is to say, when they reflect on what path a corporation actually has taken. Thus, strategy is not a planned activity but rather a set of emerging convictions about experienced practices; in other words, strategies unfold over time. Such a view blurs the distinction between 'formulating' and 'implementing' a strategy. Instead, the two processes mutually reinforce each other.[71] Still, that rather 'irrational' view could be taken one step further. Many researchers even regard managerial strategies merely as outcomes of coincidences, step-by-step adaptations, guesstimates, 'muddling-through',[72] 'logical incrementalism',[73] trial and error, luck and conciliation.

Basically, then, modifications of strategies are first and foremost based on gradual changes of the activities in a corporation *pari passu* with the growing and inescapable impact of a dynamic and uncontrollable environment. Such slow and rather haphazard adaptations entail continuous comparisons of different pieces of information, as well as serious efforts to obtain consensus in the leading executive constellations. Strategies might still foster a long-term perspective, but they also, at the same time, stimulate short-term views in iterative, trial-and-error-like processes. In essence, strategizing represents continuous adjustments of impressions, ideas, proposals, decisions and actions.

Strategic decisions are often associated with verbal commitments, but it is important to understand that such obligations could be difficult to translate into concrete actions. As described earlier in this chapter, the link between talk, decision and action is a complicated one (cf. Figure 3.1). As such, a strategy might be (re)produced in several ways. The ideal type process starts in informal (hidden) small talk that only involves a few actors who together try out more or less controversial or innovative ideas. Such an initial state is characterized by low risk for the actors involved, as the talking proceeds among those that trust each other. Some of these talks result in informal agreements to pass on the conclusions to those arenas where the strategies are formally decided. Many (but not all) of these decisions are later also put into practice and, consequently, manifested as a corporate path.

However, such an ideal type strategizing process is seldom found in practice. Instead, conceivable procedures range from a reversed procedure (i.e. actions initiate decisions that lead to small talk) to fluctuations back and forth between the different talk–decision–action stages. Thus, strategies are rarely (re)produced at one point in time or in a single or specific arena. No unique 'decision' produces a corporate path; rather it is the outcome of a stream of talk, decisions and actions carried out in more or less informal/formal arenas.[74] To be understood and accepted by the many, a strategy ultimately has to be sufficiently specific to communicate a desired path, and sufficiently general to allow for individual interpretations, flexibility and opportunism.

3.11 POSSIBLE CORPORATE PATHS

As explained earlier in this chapter, corporate paths emerge as a consequence of the efforts of individual and collective activity. In the extensive empirical studies presented in Part II, the focus is on the interactions between different kinds of institutions (primarily those linked to the national and industry levels) and among individual actors, particularly shareholders, directors and CEOs (stressing their various rationales and differing judgement capacities). The basic strategic paths that are available were described briefly above and are illustrated in Figures 3.2–3.4.

Operational risk-taking	Financial risk-taking: Low	Financial risk-taking: High
High	Industrialist strategy	Entrepreneurial strategy
Low	Reproduction strategy	Financialist strategy

Figure 3.2 Four ideal type risk-taking strategies

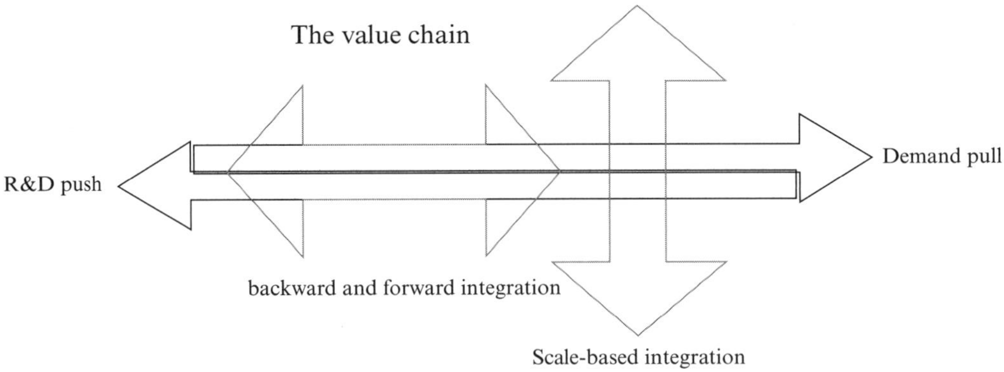

Figure 3.3 Two basic strategic expansion alternatives

	Current geographical market	New geographical market
New product (service etc)	Product differentiation	Diversification
Current product (service etc)	Market penetration	(Geographical) Market extension

Figure 3.4 Four different corporate paths

The first choice that shareholders (stakeholders), boards and CEOs usually face refers to risk, and it includes both the general risk level and the kind of risk taken (operational or financial). Basically, the different strategies linked to risk-taking could be described in the form of ideal types that comprise different governance rationales. Four of them stand out, namely those underpinning an 'entrepreneurial strategy', a 'heirloom strategy', an 'industrial strategy' and a 'financial strategy'.[75] An entrepreneurial strategy refers to the combination of high operational risk-taking and high financial risk-taking. If a corporation survives the entrepreneurial stage, it can evolve in three directions. In many cases, inheritors to the equity of such a corporation prefer a conservative, risk-averse heirloom strategy in which both the financial and the operational risks are kept low.[76] In many cases, however, a corporation abandons its initial founders for a more or less concentrated public shareholding. At that point two different alternatives emerge, namely an industrial strategy, where the financial risk is kept low and the operational risk high, and a financial strategy, where financial rather than operational risks are accepted. Obviously, the choice among these four strategic alternatives also influences what corporate paths will be pursued (cf. Figure 3.2).

Corporations' second strategic choice concerns their positions on various value chains reflecting different ways to expand/contract (the basic expansion alternatives are illustrated in Figure 3.3). One such path deals with scale advantages/disadvantages (vertical arrow), while another path addresses the merits of moving (expanding/contracting) along the value chain, backwards as well as forwards (horizontal arrow). It is also possible to expand the activities to more than one value chain.

A third strategic choice for corporations relates to market presence. Corporations could expand/contract their output of commodities, and/or reduce/expand their geographical presence. Corporations that stay in a chosen geographical market and basically offer the same commodities to their customers adopt a (market) 'penetration' strategy, while the addition of related products takes them along a 'differentiation/extension' line, as would an entrance into new geographical markets. Corporations that enter new geographical markets with new products/services take the biggest step, adopting what usually is denoted a 'diversification' strategy (Figure 3.4).

In the following part of this volume (Part II) the extensive empirical material will be presented as two industry descriptions (Chapters 4–5) and four (basically) chronological master cases each containing several subcases (Chapters 6–14). All master cases contain rather long and detailed descriptions to make it possible to discern the forces that have contributed most to the various outcomes, that is to say, whether and how natural occurrences and resources and individual and collective actors (coalitions/spheres, institutions, scientists/innovators and market demand) have impacted the formation of corporate paths. The rich empirical material focuses on the governance processes, that is to say, how actors in the operational and financial flows have interpreted those forces and acted upon them. Finally, the master cases also show what strategic choices have been made (cf. risk-taking, value-chain activities and product–market combinations).

NOTES

1. Downey and Slocum (1975).
2. Weick (1995 p. 91).
3. Sjöstrand (1997).
4. It is composed both of an operative and a financial idea.
5. Kallifatides et al. (2010).
6. Ansoff (1965), Allison (1971), Chaffee (1985), Shrivastava and Grant (1985), Johnson (1987), Schwenk (1988), Mintzberg (1990), Bailey and Johnson (1992), Eisenhart and Zbaracki (1992), Whittington (1993/2002), Rajagopalan et al. (1993), Nelson and Winter (1998) and Melander and Nordqvist (2008). Hitt et al. (1998), Hoskisson et al. (1999) and Faulkner and Campbell (2003) have all provided comprehensive reviews of the field.
7. E.g. input assets (employment), process assets (technology), channel assets (distributors), customer assets (e.g. reputation) and market assets (e.g. monopoly).
8. The open/public as well as the network-based (hidden) one.
9. North (1990).
10. MacIntyre (1981/1984).
11. Fisher (1989) even described human beings as homo narrans.
12. A tale is a story with a visible and intended moral (Ochs 1997).
13. A narrative is a description of a connected whole with a beginning, a middle and an end (Czarniawska 1998).
14. Gustafsson (1994).
15. Austin (1955/1980).
16. Guve (2003).
17. Track records are crucial for the impact of judgements. They are strong determinants of the status and power of an actor (at least for the 'opening balance' for an actor that enters a new constellation).
18. The wordings as such are also crucial, as is a person's rhetorical capacity and ability to use the 'cherished' terms of an audience to add power to the judgments given (Guve 2003). Thus the power of a judgement resides not only in its content but also in its form (aesthetical qualities).
19. According to Hamlyn (1987) rational decision-making theorists commit what Damasio (1994) denoted as 'Descartes' error'. They assume that individuals are able to separate their thinking self from their feeling self.
20. Guve (2003).
21. Sjöstrand (1997) and Kallifatides et al. (2010).
22. Kets de Vries and Miller (1984).
23. Kahneman and Lovallo (1993).
24. Like people in general.
25. Kahneman and Lovallo (1993).
26. Kallifatides and Sjöstrand (2011).
27. Rumelt (1974) and Melander and Nordqvist (2008).
28. Mintzberg and Waters (1985).
29. Stymne (1970) and Sjöstrand (1997).
30. Williamson (1975 and 1985) and Demsetz (1991).
31. Porter (1980).
32. Besanko et al. (2003).

33. Cool et al. (2002).
34. The classic industrial organization literature, e.g. Gort (1962), Berry (1971 and 1974), Markham (1973), Rhoades (1973) and Caves et al. (1980).
35. Besanko et al. (2003).
36. Economies of scope can also be exploited by licensing the use of the resource or capability to another firm. If a company has defined property rights in its trademarks and patents, licences with others could offer an effective way of acquiring the returns to these resources.
37. Schmalensee (1985), Duhaime and Stimpert (1991), Wernerfelt and Montgomery (1988), Chatterjee and Wernerfelt (1991) and Grant (2002).
38. Caves et al. (1980), Montgomery (1982), Pitts and Hopkins (1982), Jacquemin and Berry (1979) and Palepu (1985). Cf. also Rumelt's (1974) diversification categories.
39. Whittington and Mayer (2001).
40. Davis et al. (1994) and Stearns and Allan (1996).
41. Penrose (1959).
42. Gort (1962), Amey (1964) and Berry (1975).
43. Prahalad and Bettis (1986) and Grant (2002).
44. Grant (2002).
45. Prahalad and Bettis (1986), Ravenscraft and Scherer (1987) and Markides (2002).
46. Porac and Thomas (2002), Swedberg et al. (1987) and Whittington (1992 and 1993/2002).
47. Porac and Thomas (2002).
48. How to deal with customers, suppliers and authorities etc. Cf. Spender (1989).
49. Huff (1982), Spender (1989), Lyles and Schwenk (1992), Abrahamson and Fombrun (1994) and Porac and Thomas (2002).
50. Sjöstrand (1997) and Volberda and Elfring (2001).
51. Porac and Thomas (2002).
52. Caves et al. (1980) and Porter (1980 and 1985).
53. Venkatraman and Subramaniam (2002).
54. Alchian (1950 and 1979), Hannan and Freeman (1988) and Williamson (1991).
55. Pelikan (1989).
56. Cyert and March (1963).
57. Kallifatides et al. (2010).
58. Penrose (1959).
59. Wernerfelt (1984) and Barney (1995).
60. Resources developed over time or on a specific occasion are seen as semi-permanently tied to a corporation due to lower re-contracting costs and market imperfections (Teece 1986).
61. Williamson (1975 and 1985), Teece (1986), Rumelt (1987) and Peteraf (1993).
62. Prahalad and Hamel (1990).
63. Baum et al. (2000).
64. Kogut (2000).
65. Tsoukas and Knudsen (2002).
66. Ansoff (1965 and 1991) and Porter (1986 and 1996).
67. Weick (1990).
68. Volberda and Elfring (2001).
69. Stymne (1970) and Pettigrew (1973 and 1985/2011).
70. Mintzberg (1994) and Sjöstrand et al. (2001).
71. March (1976), Weick (1979) and Mintzberg and Waters (1985).
72. Lindblom (1959).
73. Quinn (1980).
74. Sjöstrand (1997 and 2000).
75. Kallifatides et al. (2010).
76. Emling (2000) showed that the doubly risk-averse attitude prevails in quite a few family-controlled corporations in Sweden. The use of the concept 'heirloom' was inspired by the work of Karlsson Stider (2000).

PART II

The empirical study

4. Before World War I

4.1 THE FOREST-BASED INDUSTRY BEFORE THE 19TH CENTURY

16 June 1288 was the day when a Swedish bishop, Peter, acquired about one-eighth of Kopparberget – an estate with mills, arable land, pastures, fishing-waters and forests. At the time, the Swedish aristocracy, including the King, owned Kopparberget, so all of them signed the sales agreement. The original document unambiguously describes the traded unit as a 'company', making Kopparberget (later renamed Bergslaget, Stora Kopparbergs Bergslag, Stora and Stora Enso) the oldest one still existing in the world.[1]

The use of the Swedish forests by private persons had been regulated at least since the 16th century by way of several regulations from the statutes of 1542 (during the era of the Swedish king Gustav Vasa) to the rather detailed legislation of 1734. Before that, far into the 16th century, any piece of land was 'owned' by the one who settled down on it and was able to defend the taking. The state's organized presence in the Swedish forest sector started in 1638, when its National Forestry Office (Riksjägmästarämbetet) was founded to watch over the crown forest areas and other public forests.

For ages, the Swedish state had been the dominant owner of the country's forests, but in the 18th century, in connection with land partitions, most of the forests were (at least initially) distributed to the farmers, who then – taken together – became a substantial landowner (thus, the state stimulated the colonization and cultivation of the northern parts of Sweden).[2] That distribution of property separated the land that was owned by the state from the land that was owned by the farmers (either individually or by village-based associations).

It was during that same century that small-scale production of paper gained some momentum in Sweden. Nature – both with respect to the presence of critical raw material and power resources (small rivers) – very much decided in what places and by what actors early forest-based industry was formed. Different kinds of permissions, which usually were provided by the state, had to be obtained. Also required were some form of entrepreneurship and manufacturing skills (i.e. an organizing initiative based on an understanding of the [potential] connection between a specific market and an offered commodity), as well as some wealth (i.e. actors with [at least] a small amount of capital). In the late 17th century forestry commissions were organized to establish borders for the commonages over which the state claimed supremacy.

Holmens Bruk, a forerunner of Holmen, one of the focal companies in this study, was one of the first paper producers in Sweden. Already in 1633, when the de Geer family bought the company, it became involved in paper production.[3] However, this was not for long – the mill was closed down after only ten years of operation, and paper production was not resumed again until 1807, when Trozelli inherited the business from his father.[4]

In between, the company went through several shifts of both ownership and core operations, and it was also hit by catastrophes (e.g. havoc [caused by a Russian fleet] and more than one bankruptcy). In 1836, Holmens Bruk launched Sweden's fourth paper mill.[5] Almost 40 years later a second paper mill was established (1874), and a third machine was also soon added (1876). At an early stage, the production was specialized on printing paper, from 1860 foremost newsprint, and later a change of the raw material source took place (from linen lump to wood/timber).[6]

Another early paper mill connected to one of the corporations in this study was the one that was built in Östanå in 1665, not far from Iggesund in the middle part of Sweden. Its output was intended for book manufacturing, a production initially triggered by a demand from the University of Uppsala, and made possible through an authorization from the state. The reason that state permission was granted was probably that the founders were most familiar with both the demand situation and the goods produced, as one of them was a master printer and the other represented the users. Soon, however, that output was sold throughout the whole region, including to customers in Sweden's capital Stockholm.[7] In 1722, Iggesund got a new owner, the company Abraham & Carlos Grill,[8] and about 50 years later that firm bought Östanå paper mill (1771).[9] Before that the company had experienced many problems ranging from another catastrophe caused by a Russian galley fleet[10] to unsuccessful attempts to manufacture paper from sawdust.

A third early paper production that ought to be mentioned is the one established around 1800 at Bergvik – a handicraft-based operation that flourished for several decades but was overrun when continuous paper machines arrived on the scene.[11] Bergvik would later appear as a minor part of another of the companies included in this study, namely Stora (Kopparberg).

Until the 19th century, Swedish paper production was almost exclusively based upon linen lump; thus a safe and steady supply of that raw material was an absolute necessity.[12] Moreover, the production of paper was a complicated procedure that required skilled workers. Together with other circumstances, that led to a rather expensive product. It was not until the end of the 18th century that machinery to a considerable extent could replace handicraft and add value and capacity to the production process. That industrial breakthrough opened up new uses of paper outside the classic book-publishing field, particularly for the new markets that the rise of the newspapers had created.[13]

The combination of an increased demand and a more efficient production technology exacerbated the difficulties in securing raw material sourcing. That problem became even more acute due to the growing shortage of linen lump that emerged already in the middle of the 19th century. That crisis both triggered and accelerated attempts to increase the market supply (the state actually organized collections of linen lump) as well as experiments with other kinds of raw material.[14]

At that time, most foreign capitalists still treated Sweden and the other Nordic countries very much as an underdeveloped region of Europe. What attracted them to the Nordic market was primarily the supply of low-priced raw materials in combination with cheap labour. Sweden (in particular) became regarded as a forthcoming main supplier of both metals (iron, copper and silver) and forest-based products. The first wave of foreign demand was for raw timber and wood, and that activity stimulated the establishment of numerous water-based sawmills in Sweden during the 18th and 19th centuries. In the middle of the 19th century grinderies were added, and a few decades later also pulp and paper plants.[15]

The state showed an early interest in preserving most forest resources for the emerging iron industry. The increasing competition for timber initiated a regulation of the factories' forest resources. From the 18th century each plant was entitled to the (potential) charcoal resources in its district. Eventually the state distributed some of its forests, and in those cases it received a yearly compensation for the ones the factories actually used. As the sawmills always had been regarded as dubious competitors to the cherished iron industry, they were only allowed localization at places where they did not compete with the factories for the timber. Consequently, before 1850, export of timber never became a noteworthy ingredient in the Swedish foreign trade statistics. However, when the sawing rights restrictions were abolished in 1842, the situation for the mills improved. That liberation stimulated several of the forerunners to this study's focal companies to return to the sawing business and invest. In the middle-northern region of Sweden, for example, Iggesund's major shareholder (von Stockenström) was one of the more renowned actors that made such operations grow again.[16]

4.2 THE FOREST-BASED INDUSTRY IN THE 19TH CENTURY[17]

It was during the 20th century that the forests became recognized as one of the most valuable assets of the Swedish territory, although the mechanical wood processing industry had had a long history in the country already before that. That rethinking took place because of the rapidly growing demand for wooden goods, which then to a large extent was met through an exploitation of the primeval forests in northern Sweden. The huge foreign demand had its roots in the emergence of industrial capitalism, the heavy investments in infrastructure (e.g. railways) and the growing freedom of trade between European countries.

At the time, the development of the Swedish forest-based industry was driven by both entrepreneurship and a growing presence of capitalists, and gradually also through substantial technological progress. However, that expansion of the Swedish forest-based businesses did not gather real momentum until the second half of the century, when it became technologically possible to use wood fibre to produce paper pulp (instead of the scarce raw material linen lump).[18] That technological breakthrough made the Swedish forests an even more valuable raw material source not just for the country itself but also for many parts of Europe. Eventually it allowed for large-scale production of mechanical wood pulp, sulphite pulp and kraft pulp (and somewhat later paper production). These rather dramatic changes taken together constituted a platform that made it possible for the Nordic pulp and paper industry to go on expanding (almost) continuously for more than a century.

Up until the middle of the 19th century most of the forest-based goods that were produced in northern Sweden were sawn timber and wood products. In the beginning it was the heavy timber that was exploited (i.e. the primeval forests). The crucial resources were water power, river-based distribution and a large supply of suitable timber. In the 1840s, the Swedish forest-based industry was still working in old-fashioned ways with a poorly developed technology. Lots of small paper mills based on manual production dominated the scene, and they were foremost located in the middle of Sweden. One of the more important firms that at the time was active in the northern parts of Sweden was James Dickson & Co, a company that early in the 19th century ran sawmills all over the region.

It is possible to trace MoDo, one of the focal companies in this study, back to 1759, and the small, water-based sawmill Mo located at Söderåfors not far from the coastal area of the middle of Sweden. However, it has also been generally accepted to date what was to become MoDo to 1823, when J.C. Kempe[19] and a partner developed the small Mo sawmill business and established Johan Wikner & Co.[20] In 1836 they decided to liquidate their joint company, and one result of that separation was that the Mo sawmill became J.C.[21] Kempe's personal property. The liquidation also provided him with other resources in and around the Swedish town Härnösand, and he started to buy more land, including the loading-place Domsjö,[22] a site that he rather soon expanded.[23]

In the early 19th century (1823), the Swedish state once again distributed land to farmers, who then – taken together – became substantial landowners. The state's intention was that the land reform would this time simplify timber-rights deals by facilitating direct connections between the sawmill industry and the producers of the raw material (timber). However, as a collective, the new owners did not take as good care of the forests as had been expected by the state. The government's belief in the merits of private ownership and in the capacity of farmers was turned on its head, as lots of complaints emerged regarding how the distributed forests were run. In 1859, a civil service department – the Swedish Forestry Agency (Skogsstyrelsen) – was established, which moved the authority over (foremost) the state's forests from the counties to a central unit. Here one could note that in northern Sweden there had been no regional or local forestry simply because of the absence of crown forest areas. That situation changed when the division of property between individuals and the state again took place in 1873. In 1883, the Swedish Forestry Agency was merged with the administrator of the state-run farms (Kammarkollegium's Domänbyrå) into a new constellation, Domänstyrelsen, a change that extended the state's responsibility since the new authority embraced all crown land (not just the forests).

In the 1850s, starting at the coastal districts of northern Sweden, steam-based sawmills were put into production. However, it took several decades before the new technology really began to make a difference. Before that, the expansion of exports was based on gradual improvements at the small water-powered sawmills. Between the 1840s and 1890s, however, exports increased tenfold.[24] The prime cause of that extraordinary expansion was the huge demand from the UK for wood products, but the demand also increased all over Europe for products for the building, infrastructure and carpentry industries. That trend lasted all through the 19th century. The large supply of heavy timber suitable for sawn products in combination with a safe supply of (cheap) labour and favourable conditions for timber transportation became a particular strength for the Swedish industry during that period. Entrepreneurship flourished in the second half of the 19th century, and particularly so around the Swedish town Sundsvall, thereby making that region the home of the biggest concentration of sawmills in the world.

The Swedish sawmills were often supplemented with grinderies and later, at the turn of the century, with plants for sulphite pulp production. The first paper machine in Sweden started its production in 1832 (Klippan), the first wood grindery in 1857 (Trollhättan),[25] the first sodium-based pulp plant in 1871 and the first sulphite pulp plant in 1874. Still, the sawmill industry was Sweden's predominant export business until the turn of the century when the pulp and paper businesses took the lead. Most production was carried out in comparatively small and scattered units, and, at the time, that industry fragmentation began to create efficiency problems. The way the sawmills had been localized also became a weakness, as they had been established in areas that were less suitable for large-scale export (i.e. far from harbours).

In 1905, the national governance of forestry was moved from the central state level and returned to the county level. The rising ambition to decentralize and deregulate business activity in general also materialized in many other ways, particularly in fields that were associated with industrial investments. The abolishment of restrictions regarding felling rights[26] (1842) and simplifications that addressed the legal opportunities to establish new sawmills (1863) were both important elements of the liberation process.[27] To these changes, specific for the forest-based industry, one could add the emergence of a more liberal legislation regarding economic activity and risk-taking in general. For example, the first Swedish Companies Act was introduced in 1848, legislation that significantly simplified the sourcing of capital to organized ventures. A similar argumentation was used during these decades when several commercial banks were founded. Moreover, the opportunities to carry out cross-border activities also improved, as, for example, both the Swedish export duties and the British import duties were lowered for wood products.

During the second half of the 19th century, the corporations began to buy the land that the farmers and the village associations previously had received from the state. The rapidly increasing demand for timber and other forest-based products almost forced the corporations to strengthen their long-term control of the raw material flow to reduce sourcing variations and make more reliable economic calculations possible. That control ambition was also encouraged by the new technological achievements that led production to become more capital intensive. Initially, the corporations bought felling rights to secure the sourcing of timber, but later homesteads became the primary buying target. That change of strategy was stimulated by a new law (1889) that restricted the time period for a felling right to a maximum of 20 years. The outcome of that legislation was that corporations bought huge areas of forests (real estate) from farmers, not always in decent and honourable ways. Such deceitful practices later (1906/07) brought about new legislation that prohibited corporations (i.e. limited companies and economic associations) from buying real estate in the countryside in large parts of the country. In 1925 that legislation became valid for the whole of Sweden.

Most of the forerunners to the four corporations focused on in this study were eager to buy forest resources to secure their raw material flows. For example, from 1876 to the turn of the century, Iggesund bought quite a lot of forests, thereby expanding its holdings to new areas outside its classic home ground. The dominating owner family at the time, the Tamm dynasty, followed that path, as they expected that Iggesund's wood goods businesses soon would expand considerably.[28] Like its forerunner 'Firma J.C. Kempe', MoDo, too, became an active purchaser of both felling rights and forests on crown land.[29] Also Holmens Bruk increased its forest holdings, but that effort did not gain momentum until the first decades of the 20th century, when the firm acquired substantial estates located close to its production units.[30] Thus, during those years, most (smaller) sawmills and firms connected to the forest-based industry sought to integrate backwards.

The sawmills and firms of the 19th century were generally small, and one or two families usually controlled each of them. However, there were also some exceptions to that situation. Svanö, for example, was an early example of an investment in a sawmill made by a co-operative (of farmers). Moälvens Träsliperi represented a similar effort, founding the first co-operative for pulp production. However, both of them rather soon ceased to be co-operatives, as the farmers were incapable of providing capital for the necessary investments. A Dutch consortium organized another kind of collective ownership that existed at the time – a capital-based one. Versteegh (39%) dominated that formation, and through acquisitions of other firms he soon became a major actor in the northern part of Sweden. Of particular importance was his purchase of Graningeverken (1899, 75%). Gradually, Versteegh strengthened his personal position in the grouping, making him the majority shareholder early in the 20th century. Francke established still another unorthodox ownership model in 1886, when he organized all his industrial assets in a special unit named Kungsgården-Marieberg.[31]

The entry of chemical pulp on the marketplace in the 1870s represented a significant technological breakthrough, although it is difficult to ascribe it to one or a few specific occurrences or actors. Instead, due to the achievements of basic research, that innovation tended to 'be in the air'. For quite some time there had been lots of more or less systematic thinking about a wood-based chemical alternative to linen lump and mechanical pulp. Like for many other innovations, the emergence of chemical pulp (various sulphate and sulphite methods) followed from many more or less co-ordinated contributions in a long scientific development sequence characterized by both incremental improvements and remarkable breakthroughs (and by setbacks).[32] However, like most new knowledge, the new pulp process also needed both an appropriate institutional context and dedicated actors (i.e. entrepreneurs) to be transformed into practicable production. The sulphate method, mainly developed in the UK, appeared on the scene first, and in Sweden Uddeholm became the pioneer in using it. The economic result of that effort, however, was rather poor mainly because of significant technical problems. Thus, the method lost credibility for some time.[33]

The situation for wood-based pulp production improved significantly when the sulphite method was put into practice. Once the remaining technical problems had been solved in the 1870s, it was not particularly complicated or arduous to establish such operations. The raw material for the chemical process was cheap and, unlike for the sulphate method, the colour of the sulphite pulp was pale, so it was easy to bleach white.[34] However, for some (potential) actors problems emerged. Eventually it became evident that the use of the new method demanded a large capital base because it brought in scale advantages and benefitted from a capacity to defray R&D costs. Over time, the need to exploit the potential scale advantages led to increased financial risk-taking in the whole forest-based industry. The operational risks increased, too, as pulp production was particularly sensitive to changes in demand and therefore was exposed to many of the difficulties associated with forecasting and planning.[35]

In the beginning of the 1870s, a British capitalist founded a sulphite plant at Bergvik, a small village situated in the middle of Sweden. Operations started in 1874 and it became the first commercial sulphite production unit in the world.[36] However, because the plant was small and had low profitability, it was rather soon closed down (1897). Thus, the innovative Bergvik effort did not catalyse a breakthrough for chemical pulp in Sweden. A second Swedish sulphite plant was established at Korndal (1881) that also produced paper, and soon the same engineering team also built a similar plant at Storvik (1888).[37]

In 1892 Korndal went bankrupt, but through efforts from a commercial bank,[38] a new paper mill was established at the same place, this time owned by Papyrus (later a part of Stora Kopparberg).

Holmens Bruk was another early producer of chemical pulp. The company established a sulphite plant in 1897 in a place named Loddby not far from the mid-sized town Norrköping situated in the southern part of Sweden. Other examples of early pulp production that later became linked with another of the corporations that are the focus of this study, namely SCA, were Frånö and Essvik. The former unit started sulphate production in 1896, and the latter launched sulphite operations four years later (and paper production in 1908). One could add that, during this period, there were also attempts to produce paper from straw-based pulp. Several units in southern Sweden pursued that path, for example Munksjö (1862), Katrinefors (1871) and Fiskeby (1871).[39]

However, it was not only the push from technological achievements during the second half of the 19th century that determined the development of Sweden's forest-based industry. There was also a strong demand pull from customers during that period. It was particularly strong (and continuously increasing) for printing paper (both for books and newspapers). It was impossible to match that rapidly rising call for paper with linen lump as the sole raw material source, so wood was brought in rather rapidly and in large amounts, and soon it was the dominant ingredient in pulp production. In the beginning mechanical wood pulp had a rather strong standing, but chemical pulp soon took the lead. The possibility of using wood as a raw material for paper production certainly strengthened Sweden's standing on the international marketplace, as its vast forests (after the pillaging of the heavy timber) contained large quantities of trees of smaller dimensions that so far had been used solely for the production of charcoal.[40]

However, it was not just growing demand, technological innovations, entrepreneurship, liberalized trade, and favourable geographical and natural circumstances (i.e. the presence of primeval forests, floating channels and water power) that explained the early development of the forest-based industry in Sweden. There was also a good supply of capitalists around financing its rapid growth. Some that became deeply engaged were trade capitalists from the involved regions, but there were also quite a few of the active capitalists that came from Sweden's trade centres in Gothenburg and Stockholm, as well as from the UK and continental Europe. Thus, there was a continuous flow of capital and capitalists to the middle-northern parts of Sweden adding resources to those already provided by the region's upper class. In that process towns like Gävle and Sundsvall became local metropolises for businessmen and shareholders. Basically, it was families that financed, controlled and led the rising Swedish forest-based industry of the 19th century – and many of them were of Swedish 'origin' (others like, e.g., the Bünsow, Dickson, Kempe and Versteegh families eventually became 'naturalized' Swedes).[41]

The Kempe family was particularly important for the development of the forest-based industry in northern Sweden during the 19th century. Several of the members were most active in the foundation and expansion of one of the focal firms of this study: MoDo. Over the years, the founding father of that dynasty, J.C. Kempe, became publicly known – and remembered – as an entrepreneurial businessman and energetic risk-taker, a combination that was regarded as a virtue by some – but certainly not all – of his descendants. In spite of that family discord, these attributes ascribed to J.C. Kempe were usually referred to as requirements for any Kempe aspiring to run MoDo. Thus, J.C.

Kempe not only left an economic legacy (the firm) to his heirs, but also guidelines regarding the preferred personality and rationality of future family heads.

When J.C. Kempe's company Johan Wikner & Co grew and became both large and diversified, he decided to involve two of his sons in the business (Bernhard Kempe and Wilhelm Kempe), and soon afterwards he transferred the firm to them (1858). However, he kept some of its parts under the name Firma J.C. Kempe, namely Mo sawmill and factory, the Domsjö-based shipping and a country house. The company's most important investment was the establishment of a steam mill at Domsjö (1865), creating a sister company to Mo. The two firms supplemented each other and constituted the basis for the planned expansion. When J.C. Kempe died in 1872, he left a rather prosperous firm and many children behind. Both Bernard and Wilhelm and their younger half-brothers Frans and Seth would go on to play prominent roles in the company.[42] In 1873, J.C. Kempe's 11 legal heirs finally decided to create the limited company MoDo.[43]

Frans and Seth Kempe had not expected to become the leaders of the new firm, but as time went by and as MoDo did not take off as expected, it became obvious to most of the stakeholders and family members that Frans and Seth were needed there. In 1879, they were appointed to the MoDo board, and five years later Frans Kempe became its CEO. As a consequence, he gradually phased out his partnership with his half-brother Seth. Frans and Seth were aggressive acquirers of (parts of) other firms during this period (e.g. Töre in 1983, Holmsund in 1896, Robertfors in 1897 and Gideå-Husum in 1903), and that expansion made the Kempe family and its companies deeply indebted to the banks. Thus, members of the Kempe family again practised the kind of risk-taking that J.C. Kempe was associated with, contributing to the emerging belief that MoDo had to have a family leader who possessed and executed that particular action rationale. Frans Kempe stayed as MoDo's CEO for 35 years (i.e. until 1917), and for an additional five-year period he was a member of its board.[44]

At the turn of the century there were also noteworthy merger activities in the northernmost part of Sweden. Olsson was probably the leading restructurer in that region. He also participated in structural deals further south in the Sundsvall region, and, for example, acquired Wifstavarf in 1906. Stockholms Enskilda Bank financed that and several other of Olsson's efforts. The bank also bought Kopparbergs and Hofors Sågverk and integrated Storvik in the same 'grouping'.[45] The Kopparbergs and Hofors Sågverk constellation was established in 1855 by an agreement signed by the board members of Stora Kopparberg, the owners of Hofors and five private individuals with the purpose to found a sawmill and buy forests in the middle part of Sweden.[46] Having Marcus Wallenberg the Elder as Chair and Knut Sundblad as CEO, Wifstavarf started a reconditioning of the plants and a rapid expansion. During the period 1907–14, the company built both a sulphate plant and the biggest sulphite plant in the country (at Fagervik).[47]

It is important to note that most of the families that owned forest-based companies in Sweden actually had no expansion ambitions, and very few of the bigger firms of the time could be characterized as large ones. Holmen and Uddeholm were the exceptions, but in neither case was pulp and paper the main business. In the late 19th century, the owners of these two forest-based companies (taken together) had the financial capacity to acquire most of the pulp and paper industry in Sweden, but nothing substantial materialized. The other major shareholders in the industry controlled only smaller companies, so they lacked the necessary capital. The path that remained was then to use capital from other industries or external actors in general. However, since buying and rationalizing pulp and paper companies in mid-northern Sweden was regarded as both risky and expensive, the external actors' interest was low. Moreover, at that time, such ambitions met institutional restraints, as the banks had not yet grown out of their regional thinking. The most important change in ownership just before the turn of the century was instead a disinvestment – the phasing out of the biggest sawmill constellation in Sweden, namely the Dickson group. There was neither a capable successor in the family nor a powerful coalition around to defend the constellation, so all its units were sold between 1891 and 1898.[48]

In spite of the lack of growth ambitions among the leading families, there was quite a lot of re-arranging of their shareholdings during the second half of the 19th century. Those changes might have been encouraged by the new opportunities provided by the Companies Act. It allowed for new ways to finance and change company control. Thus, for the focal firm Iggesunds Bruk, for example, several rather complicated ownership transactions occurred between 1851 and 1903. The major shareholder P.A. Tamm's last will from 1851 stated that Österby Bruk and Strömbacka Bruk 'had to be kept together for at least twenty years' (starting from 1856). When Iggesunds Bruk was acquired in 1869 by the shareholders of Österby and Strömbacka, the reorganization of the units had to wait until 1876. That year the units were divided into two separate companies – Iggesunds Bruk, which included Strömbacka Bruk and Hedvigfors Bruk, and Österby Bruk.

Iggesund established its articles of association in 1876 – a construct that strengthened the shareholders' standing and made the board a more powerful decision-making body (to the detriment of the CEO). Gustaf Tamm became its first 'CEO', followed by Lindman, who took on that role in 1878 and was replaced by his son four years later. The board included Hugo Tamm, the leader of the Tamm family, which continued to be the largest shareholder until the beginning of the 20th century. As most of the family-controlled shares were spread among – as Hugo Tamm saw it – too many hands, he decided to sell the company (in 1903; except Strömbacka Bruk, parts of Hedvigsfors Bruk and the mines) to Hudiksvalls Trävaru (later renamed Iggesund). Hugo Tamm sold in order to be able to concentrate the company's businesses in the forest industry and avoid future control problems. The buying firm Hudiksvalls Trävaru was formed in 1868, when it took control of Engelska bolaget's[49] resources (forests and sawmills).[50]

Thus, to briefly sum up this section: throughout the 19th century Sweden had a scattered and fragmented forest industry that was not always based on the best available technology. Moreover, at the end of that century the production of sawn timber began to stagnate in middle and northern Sweden, both because of the growing competition from other regions and countries, and because of the increasing demand from the pulp industry for wood. As a consequence, many sawmills had to go through troublesome structural changes that sometimes ended in liquidation processes, or experience painful technological transformations and dramatic adaptations to new market situations.

At the turn of the century most of the sawmills that were located close to waterfalls had been closed down and 'replaced' by steam-based sawmills. In the long run, the latter were superior because they did not have to be located next to a stream or river. The sulphite method dominated the pulp production but a comeback for the sulphate process was on its way. One advantage of the sulphate method was that it could use almost any kind of wood as raw material, while a sulphite plant had to rely on spruce of good quality. Another advantage was the sulphate-based paper's greater strength. Moreover, during the first decades of the 20th century, also plants using the sulphite method began to face high environmental costs, a burden previously placed only on the sulphate method.[51]

During the 19th century, and for many years after, most of the pulp production was sold as a standardized bulk good. Although there was growing ambition among the companies in the Nordic countries to include paper production in their operations, it was seen as inopportune to produce large volumes for export. At that time, the continental European and British companies had captured a dominating position in that part of the value chain and relied very much on Nordic pulp in their operations. There had emerged a kind of informal agreement – a kind of 'truce' – that the current division of the forest-based business ought to be preserved. Thus, as long as the continental and British firms did not invest substantially in pulp production, the Nordic firms would not integrate forward (invest in paper production) to such an extent that they would begin to seriously compete with their main customers.[52]

NOTES

1. The name 'Stora Kopparberg' will be used up until the company changed its name to 'Stora' (1984).
2. 'Avvittringen' (the division of property between individuals and the state).
3. Holmens Bruk was then basically a manufacturer of weapons.
4. Helmfrid (1954).
5. Holmens Bruk became a limited company in 1854.
6. A grindery was built in 1868. However, the use of grinderies in Swedish paper production started about twenty years before, i.e. in 1844 (Haslum 1993). Cf. also Helmfrid (1954) and Sjunnesson and Wahlberg (2003).
7. Valeur (2007).
8. Savalainen and Zacco-Broberg (1985).
9. Östanå was burnt down in 1841 (and was never rebuilt).
10. The Russians were active in those days and caused great devastation along the Swedish coast.
11. Valeur (2007).
12. Ibid.
13. Thus, in this case the demand was actually in place before the technological leap occurred.
14. Gårdlund (1951).
15. Croon (2005).
16. Savalainen and Zacco-Broberg (1985).
17. The first part of this section is to a large extent based on Pöyry and Ryti (1979), Andersson (1993), Haslum (1993), Valeur (2000 and 2003) and Croon (2005).
18. The method using wooden fibre instead of linen lump was developed in Germany in the 1840s (Glete [1987]).
19. J.C. Kempe = Johan Christoffer Carl Kempe.
20. J.C. Kempe got an offer to work in Härnösand for a sawmill owner (Wikner). Rather soon he married the owners' daughter, a wedlock that initiated his joining as a partner in the Mo sawmill (Unger [1967]).
21. Throughout this volume Christian names will only be used when several actors have the same family name (either because they belong to the same family or by pure coincidence).
22. The two first letters of Domsjö ('Do') together with the name of the sawmill 'Mo' then constituted the company's name: 'MoDo'.
23. Unger (1967).
24. Valeur (2007).
25. The grindery pulp was of a rather low quality when compared with those based on chemical cooking (Glete [1987]).
26. A certain maximum cutting of timber was determined for each sawmill.
27. The sawmill industry in Sweden had been surrounded for many years by detailed restrictions because of

the fear of excess cutting of (heavy) timber creating a shortage of raw material for the industry. That, in turn, would increase the output prices and thereby undermine the competitive power of the Swedish firms – not only the forest-based ones but also those active in the iron business. So, the basic regulation stated that new sawmills were only allowed in places where they did not compete with the ironworks or already existing mills.

28. Savalainen and Zacco-Broberg (1985).
29. Andersson (1993).
30. Helmfrid (1954).
31. Haslum (1993), Glete (1987) and Valeur (2000).
32. In 1866 an American (Tilghman) managed to produce sulphite-based pulp, although in a laboratory context. Between 1890 and 1930 lots of pulp plants (foremost sulphite-based ones) were established in northern Sweden. The pulp industry could then use the younger and more slender timber remaining after the felling of the heavy trunks in the 19th century (Glete [1987]).
33. Glete (1987).
34. Sulphate pulp was therefore often used for wrapping (brown) paper, kraft paper and carton.
35. Glete (1987).
36. Valeur (2007).
37. Gasslander (1956/1959).
38. Stockholms Enskilda Bank.
39. Glete (1987).
40. Savalainen and Zacco-Broberg (1985).
41. Glete (1987).
42. Unger (1967).
43. The board was expected to appoint a 'disponent' (i.e. someone who is not a COO/CEO but still head of a large business unit) among its members to take care of the operations. Bernard Kempe and Wilhelm Kempe were appointed board members together with the company's first disponent, Lindeberg.
44. Unger (1967).
45. Glete (1987).
46. Valeur (2000).
47. Sjögren (2005).
48. Glete (1987).
49. 'Engelska bolaget' = Hudiksvalls Steam Sawing Mill Co Ltd, founded in London 1857, financed by an international financial syndicate.
50. Savalainen and Zacco-Broberg (1985).
51. Valeur (1997).
52. Glete (1987).

5. The first half of the 20th century

5.1 NEW OWNERSHIP CONSTELLATIONS

5.1.1 Pulp Plant Expansion and the Initiation of Newsprint Production

The decades around the turn of the century saw significant technical breakthroughs and innovations in the forest-based industry, which brought about a substantial increase in its productivity. Those changes affected most parts of the value chain, from the cutting of timber to the transportation of the finished good to the customer. A road-based transport system was developed and soon replaced the one based on rivers. Moreover, the horse was removed from most forest work, as was sawing by hand. Instead, many kinds of machinery took over. The radical mechanization of the operational flow – that is to say, the introduction of tools, machines and systematization in the production processes – required significant capital, and therefore initiated a long period of steadily increasing economies of scale. It was during these years that pulp production more and more came to dominate the industry at the expense of timber and wood products.

The growing economies of scale put the firms' financial flows more into focus, which brought about changes in the requirements associated with corporate shareholding and – consequently – began to alter the distribution of ownership in the industry.

Over a very brief period – the last decade of the 19th century – a string of sulphate plants were established in northern Sweden close to the old primeval forests. That development brought no changes in ownership structures at the time. Indeed, the pattern of 'single family shareholdings' was still predominant, although several attempts were made to break that fragmentation and create jointly controlled companies.[1] During the same period, large investments were made in wood grinderies. The first plant of that kind appeared in the 1850s, but the bulk of the units were not established until the turn of the century, bringing the total to at least one hundred such plants (most of them small).[2]

The first decade of the 20th century was characterized by an immense leap forward for pulp production when sulphite production based on spruce gained momentum in the northern parts of Sweden. Some 15 plants were built during those years, beginning with Bergslaget's Skutskär plant (1900), which made Bergslaget one of the first Swedish firms that ran both sulphate and sulphite production. Bergvik & Ala established a new sulphite plant in 1902; Holmens Bruk founded Loddby (1897); MoDo built Domsjö (1902–03), Robertsfors (1904) and Hörnefors (1905–06); Utansjö's partners built Svanö (1906); Kramfors was established (1906–07); Forss put up Köpmanholmen; and the large Sundsvall-based companies built Svartvik (1905–07), Ortviken (1908), Nyhamn (1907–08), Söråker (1909–10) and Fagervik (1912). At Wifstavarf, however, the Wallenberg family invested in another technique and established a sulphate plant (1908).[3]

The Swedish Forest Service (Domänverket) conducted a study in 1907 that indicated a need to weed out many weak pine trees in the state-owned forests. Sulphate plants could make use of such thin trees. However, most new private investments during the first decade of the new century had been made in sulphite production, and the northernmost sulphate plant at the time was located as far south as in the Ådalen region in the middle of Sweden. Thus, the Swedish Forest Service decided to support the establishment of such plants also in the northern region of Sweden and offer cheap pulpwood.[4] As a result, during the second decade of the 20th century several sulphate plants were built in the region: Obbola (by Holmsund in 1913), Kalix (by Baltiska Trävaru in 1914), Wäija (by Strömnäs in 1914), Karskär (by Korsnäs in 1914), Nensjö (by Svanö in 1915), Husum (by MoDo in 1918) and Sandarne (by Bergvik & Ala in 1919). Iggesund distinguished itself from the other corporations by building a combined sulphite and sulphate plant (Hjälmåsen in 1914–16). Gunnar Sundblad, a legendary Swedish builder of pulp plants (and later Iggesund's CEO and Chair), was the driving force behind that investment. Outside the subsidized northern part of Sweden only one sulphate plant was established: Skoghall (by Uddeholm in 1917).

At the turn of the century Bergslaget was the newsprint pioneer in northern Sweden, phasing in such production at Kvarnsveden and integrating it with the production of mechanical pulp and sulphite pulp. Holmens Bruk became second in the newsprint race when it made its big investment in that business. Since the available nearby space could not accommodate its size, the new plant had to be located in Hallsta, a coastal village northeast of Stockholm, relatively far from the company's hometown (Norrköping). The site provided both an ice-free[5] harbour and regional energy sourcing. Holmens Bruk furnished Hallsta with a grindery, a sulphite plant and a newsprint mill. Its newsprint production started in 1915 and expanded almost immediately. The Hallsta and Norrköping plants made Holmens Bruk Europe's biggest producer of newsprint. Skönvik made the third big investment in newsprint in northern Sweden (1918) and Matfors the fourth (1919).[6]

Holmens Bruk expanded considerably over the first two decades of the 20th century, very much as a consequence of Carl Wahren's entry as new leader of the company. Of course, the establishment of Hallsta was not the company's only investment during those years: its cotton unit was modernized and merged with another firm, its power resources were expanded and a grindery was built. Moreover, substantial forest areas in the middle of Sweden were acquired and two additional firms were incorporated. Wahren intended to use the acquired power plants for sourcing an expanded and modernized Norrköping unit, and after a tough debate about where to locate the new investments, the board finally took a decision in 1927 in favour of the town (Hallsta was the alternative). The same year Holmens Bruk also acquired and integrated all of Förenade Yllefabrikerna (textiles) and built a new large power plant. During his many years as leader of Holmens Bruk (1907–38) Carl Wahren pushed for a rapid expansion of its two core businesses, textiles and newsprint, but he often met resistance from other members of the Wahren dynasty, who advocated a different path forward. Ernst Wahren, for example, who at the time represented the family ownership, preferred lower investments, a greater focus on textiles, and a board free of company managers. In the end, however, Carl Wahren's plan for Holmens Bruk won out, most likely because of his strong will and the strong support of the company's personnel.[7]

Another of the companies highlighted in this study, Iggesunds Bruk, became the mother company in a group led by Trävarubolaget, when the latter dissolved in 1916. Woodware was its main product, but pulp was a growing business and in the 1920s it became Iggesund's core activity. The company kept its larger sawmills but closed down the minor ones. When Iggesund was hit hard by the 1921 crisis, as were almost all other firms, the board stopped the company's hectic expansion activities. The same year its board appointed Gunnar Sundblad as the new CEO. To address Iggesund's forest-sourcing problems at the time, the new CEO tried to buy felling rights from its former partner firm Strömbacka. Eventually those talks led to a buy-back of that company (1923).[8]

5.1.2 MoDo: Frans Kempe's Era

MoDo emerged as a leading forest-based company already at the beginning of the 20th century. That prominent position was won during the period when Frans Kempe led the company. To give him credit for that development is easy, as he in many ways was a pioneer in the industry. Frans Kempe did most things his way and was not particularly sensitive to critique and protests. However, his autocratic management and leadership style could also be described as enlightened and progressive, as he really cared for his employees. Thus, like his father J.C. Kempe, he acted as a classic patriarch. Frans Kempe also showed many other qualities that were ascribed to his father, for example, a nose for business, entrepreneurship and risk-seeking behaviour. That heritage was compared with the one associated with his half-brother Seth, who was described rather as a careful, analytical and cautious person. These ascribed personality differences then lived on and served as important categorizations of most of the descendants of the Kempe dynasty, establishing a distinct image of two diverging family lineages, identities and affiliations – the Frans line and the Seth line. Both family arms would over the years play important – although different – roles for MoDo's development.

Also, from a social perspective, Frans Kempe made MoDo an exemplary company – in many such dimensions he was far ahead of his time. But 'for reasons of principle' he opposed the establishment of local unions as well as associations of employers, for he feared that such collectives would limit his freedom of action. His social ideals led him to establish pension funds as well as decent housing, churches, schools and shops (with fair prices) for the employees. That made MoDo an esteemed and respected company in the eyes of most stakeholders, especially among the workers in northern Sweden.[9]

Frans Kempe's ideas about how MoDo ought to grow often bore fruit, providing both innovative solutions and good economic results. He had studied the natural sciences at Uppsala University and become a member of a network of teachers and researchers active in the field, so he could often build his pioneering ideas and actions on scientific grounds. Thus, taken together, Frans Kempe had the theoretical grounding, practical experience, important scientific networks and economic resources to develop MoDo's forest-based businesses.[10] His truly multi-rational leadership made him a successful entrepreneur in (at least) two distinct fields, namely forestry and personnel, while he made the company grow in an impressive way.[11]

Frans Kempe's predilection for using scientific methods to improve MoDo's businesses led to the establishment of a unit for systematic R&D. That early initiative would influence MoDo's self-image and development for many decades.[12] He also initiated significant changes in MoDo's industrial structure. For example, a steam-based sawmill at Norrbyskären replaced the old water-based one at Mo (the plant that could be regarded as the origin of the company), and a sulphite pulp plant replaced Domsjö sawmill in 1902, as the demand for sawed timber was decreasing (new suppliers entered the scene and the primeval forests began to run out[13]). Instead, chemical pulp production began to take off, driven by the rapidly growing market for newspaper. MoDo also invested in a sulphite plant at Hörnefors in 1905.[14] Frans Kempe was highly active in all these new ventures. He even took on the role of plant manager at Domsjö (in addition to his position as CEO of MoDo) and became so heavily involved that the manager responsible for the building of the new plant felt uncomfortable.[15]

MoDo also expanded through acquisitions. From Dickson the company acquired Gideå & Husum (a steam-based mill and forest resources), and later – in 1915 – MoDo bought Sandvik Ångsåg (a steam-based sawmill). To facilitate expansion MoDo also bought both 'stand-alone' forests close to the company's existing businesses and later – after new legislation had been introduced – companies that owned such forests.[16] Furthermore, in connection with WWI, quite a lot of co-operation between actors in the forest industry and various authorities emerged. These discussions addressed a variety of issues: restrictions on production, interplant co-operation, timber regulations, subsidies to level prices and trade cycles, revaluation of the crown, export fees, regulations of export prices, and so on.[17] In 1912, the state also reorganized the Swedish Forest Service to create a special kind of public enterprise (affärsverk) with the instruction to administer its forests and agricultural estates. Because of that more commercial assignment, the Swedish Forest Service's function as a public authority was distributed to other agencies.

During WWI, MoDo's chemical plants delivered some one hundred different products, while its core businesses were kept at half speed. In that period, the viscose pulp and the forage pulp began to do well. However, the company's forest-based operations also provided, for example, dynamite, antifreeze mixture, detergent, soft soap, raw materials for cosmetics, electric fittings, film, glue, gramophone records and airframes. The company also produced pharmaceuticals, chloroform, acetic acid, artificial rubber, DDT and shoe soles. All these experiences during and after WWI caused the leading actors of MoDo to begin to think seriously about a business future in which forest-based chemicals might hold a prominent position.[18]

A sulphate plant at Husum was another important investment made during those years. Built between 1916 and 1919, it became a cornerstone in MoDo's operations all through the 20th century. Before that, however, the plant's construction caused a severe crisis between Frans and Seth Kempe. Seth Kempe complained loudly about the rising costs associated with its construction (which even ate up the dividends). For his part, Frans Kempe tried to deal with this critique. The situation certainly did not improve when both Seth Kempe and his brother-in-law Mauritz Sahlin suggested that Frans Kempe should resign as CEO – which he did, paving the way for his son Carl Kempe Sr to become the new CEO. Frans Kempe was instead appointed Chairman of the Board[19] and remained in that position until 1922. Seth Kempe (board member since 1879) succeeded Frans Kempe and was MoDo Chair for eight years.[20]

5.1.3 Financial Actors Begin to Dominate the Scene

During WWI, the ownership stability in the Swedish forest-based business came to an end. Inflation rose in those years, making the industry and its forests and power plants most attractive to many investors. Taking advantage of the situation, financial consortia and issuing syndicates bought several well-consolidated pulp and paper producers. After instituting bonuses, raising dividends and conducting mergers, they sent the companies on to the stock market and made considerable profits. Thus, since such ownership shifts were frequent and widespread, those years were a golden age for many financial actors.

The forest-based industry took on a somewhat different structure during the second decade of the 20th century when a sector of medium-sized, family-run companies gradually emerged (Strömnäs, Björkå, Kungsgården-Marieberg, Dynäs and Rö). In the northern regions, large structural changes were basically absent, as few owners were inclined to abandon the format of the family firm. There were, however, some exceptions. Handelsbanken's purchase of Bergvik & Ala in 1916 from a foreign owner was one of the more important structural changes during that time. The bank sold most of the stock it acquired, but kept some of it for 'future use'.

Another remarkable purchase took place when actors in and around Skandiabanken and the Wallenberg family acquired an influential position in Stora Kopparberg. That affair actually outmanoeuvred Handelsbanken. One could note that Wallenberg's formal shareholding position in that company was weak before the takeover – it ran up to about 3 per cent (divided between Investor, Caritas, Fiducia and Marcus Wallenberg the Elder's[21] private holding) – a situation that prevailed through the 1920s. The power was instead based on links to the company's top management, and from 1917 also on the control of the Chair position (Marcus Wallenberg the Elder, who stayed in that role until 1943).[22] Through that purchase and a growing engagement in several other forest-related businesses, the Wallenberg family gained unprecedented experience in such operations. At that time, they also invested in the Hofors factory, the sulphite producers Billerud and Storvik, the paper mill Papyrus and the sawmills Wifstavarf and Kopparberg-Hofors.[23] The actors in and around Wahren's Holmens Bruk were also active during the second decade of the 20th century although not through M&As. Instead, Holmens Bruk expanded organically and made substantial investments in its existing production facilities.

At the time, tentative attempts were also made to co-ordinate operations without accompanying ownership changes. This was often the outcome when attempts to buy, sell or merge companies failed. For example, three recognized producers of fine paper, Grycksbo, Klippan and Lessebo, tried to merge in 1902, but did not succeed. Ultimately, they founded a sales cartel in 1907.[24] That construct represented a first step in the Nordic forest-based industry's cartelization process – a development that would determine many of these companies' actions during the 20th century.

Many of the ownership changes that occurred in the forest-based industry during the early 20th century transformed family-controlled firms into corporations traded on the stock market. Some of the new constellations like Stora Kopparberg and Uddeholm had been listed for some time, but, by 1920, the forest-based category (that included corporations simultaneously running other kinds of businesses) had expanded significantly. Newcomers to the 'A-listing' (i.e. the most traded shares) were Bergvik & Ala, Axel

Christensson, Holmens Bruk, Kopparberg-Hofors, Korsnäs, Munksjö, Svanö, Wargön, Wifstavarf and Ytterstfors-Munksund. On the 'B-listing' one could find, for example, Fiskeby, Kramfors, Strömsnäs Bruk and Örebro Pappersbruk.[25]

At the time, the stock market was volatile, and it was easy to raise capital through new issues of shares. Rather often these issues were financed through loans, something that during these inflation years was advantageous. The rapidly growing public stock market also made it possible for 'all' owners of capital to become partial shareholders in corporations. Such investments also were made in sawmills, pulp works, paper mills, forest resources and power plants, that is to say, in many of the tangible assets that were linked to the forest-based industry. In this way, financial capital began to replace trade-based capital. It was not just used temporarily as a resource for restructuring activities, but also more and more as owner capital constituting the basis for corporate governance efforts.

After WWI, trading houses (or families with that background) were no longer the owner of most of the Swedish forest-based companies; instead, financial and industrial capitalists had taken control. Still, only a few nationwide M&As occurred. Moreover, several of the large family-controlled companies did not seek listing on the Swedish Stock Exchange (SSE), thereby missing the opportunity to use share issues to increase their capital bases (and the possibility to use that tool to acquire other firms).[26]

5.1.4 A Severe Crisis

Like many other countries, Sweden faced a severe economic crisis late in 1920. A deep international recession hit many economies, and it was usually combined with high deflation and mass unemployment. It eliminated most of the market demand and export opportunities for the Swedish forest-based industry. Many of the firms in the sector were struck hard, as the industry was capital intensive and foremost a producer of semi-manufactured goods (sawn timber and pulp), and therefore particularly exposed to demand fluctuations. The monetary value of the crown rose around 20 per cent each year, making the real rate of interest soar to previously unseen levels. That recession period lasted until 1922 – a year marked by bank crises.[27]

Many of the newer owners of firms failed during those years, mainly because they had not had sufficient time to establish stable business organizations. Some firms went bankrupt because of excessive borrowing and too much risk-taking (financial speculation). Already at the beginning of the crisis, it became obvious that even many well-established owners of Swedish forest-based corporations would fail in their efforts to maintain control of their holdings. The value of their real capital did not rise – because of the recession it tended rather to decrease. Instead, actual debts increased, and that unfortunate combination soon undermined the future for many corporations. Once assets were frozen, many banks had to enter as shareholders and company restorers, primarily by way of conversions of unpaid debt to equity (they could not sell the shares because of the poor market situation). That development both turned speculative shareholders with pledged stock into big losers and made some banks substantial owners of forest-based corporations. Handelsbanken was perhaps the Swedish bank that – at least in a longer perspective – benefitted most from all these ownership failures. Thus, like most crises of similar magnitude and kind, this one also shook up the market for corporate control and, in the end, it substantially changed the power balance in Swedish industry.[28]

Many families were hit hard by the crisis and lost their prominent positions in Swedish business life. A striking exception was the Kempe family that controlled MoDo. MoDo had survived the crisis mainly because of its different business profile and competent family heads (Frans Kempe and Carl Kempe Sr). That company was also one of the corporations that had invested heavily already before the crises and, in doing so, had managed to build up a stable business that made it possible for them to survive the deep recession. They had financed their operations during a favourable period (the war years, benefitting from inflation and a healthy stock market) and therefore made considerable profits and accumulated financial reserves for bad times.

Several corporations without ties to a particular family also suffered under the recession. Wargön and Ytterstfors-Munksund, for example, belonged to that category. Both were typical fragile creations from the boom years – swiftly put together, poorly organized, and highly indebted.[29]

In the early 1920s, while firm owners struggled to survive the economic crisis, forest owners began to worry about their own market situation, as they realized that the buyers of their timber had become more organized and powerful. Several forest owners revived the co-operative idea that had been practised for some years in the middle of the 19th century by farmers who established and ran their own production plants. Such a construct would ensure that the profits made in the later stages of the value chain would go to the forest owners – not to the 'capitalists'. Since they lacked the financial capacity to buy (or build) pulp plants, the new co-operatives focused on sawmills. However, even these more modest investments failed rather soon after they had been made, and it would take more than a decade before new attempts were launched to organize co-operative production in the Swedish forest-based sector.

The deep economic crisis severely shook people's confidence in the stock market for quite some time. A generation of shareholders saw their savings and investments lose most of their value. The banks had to accept their new role as major shareholders and the reality that the current situation might prevail for many years. The new ownership responsibility also brought about a deeper intertwining between the banks and many corporations, which contributed to the emergence of a more stratified and divided industrial structure. Handelsbanken was probably the most striking example of such bank activity, as it became heavily engaged in the forest-based industry both as substantial shareholder in companies such as Bergvik & Ala and Ytterstfors-Munksund and as 'controlling lender' in firms such as Holmsund, Nyhamn, Skönvik and Svartvik. However, Handelsbanken was certainly no newcomer to the forest-based industry – for many years it had acted as the principal bank for many other companies (e.g. Forss, Hylte, Korsnäs, Kramfors, Munkedal and Nykvarn), as well as for several industry owners (e.g. the Kempe and Versteegh families).

Thus, within a decade or two, Handelsbanken had become more than a large bank: it had begun to form one of the two industrial spheres that would dominate 20th-century economic life in Sweden – and that without a presence of wealthy capitalists. It developed into a constellation controlled by bank executives and managers of client firms (a power situation that also was reflected on its board), while the families or individuals owning most of the involved companies usually – but not always (e.g. Kreuger, cf. below) stayed in the background. During those years, banks other than Handelsbanken were also left with holdings or engagements in companies affected by the crisis. Skandiabanken, for example, 'inherited' Marma-Långrör and Wargön, Sundsvallsbanken got Essvik and was involved in the financing of Nyhamn and Svartvik, and Upplandsbanken was engaged in the crisis units Enhörningsbolaget and Sunds.[30]

The crisis hit certain kinds of corporations harder than others. Some of the less capable shareholders lost their fortunes and firms, as did those capitalists that took considerable financial risks. However, several large shareholders actually came out as 'winners', including families such as Bonnier, Broström, Dunker, Johnson, Kempe, Söderberg, Versteegh and Wallenberg. A number of them continued to be major shareholders for a long time. Among the forest-based corporations that benefitted from the crisis were the relatively large and financially strong units Bergvik & Ala, Billerud, Graningeverken, Holmens Bruk, Kopparberg-Hofors, Korsnäs, Kramfors, Mo & Domsjö, Papyrus, Stora Kopparberg, Wifstavarf and Uddeholm.

The Versteegh family continued their activity in the forest-based industry using Graningeverken as their platform. Arend Versteegh's son Gerhard was elected to its board in 1920, but a father–son conflict spurred Gerhard to take a position as CEO at Marma-Långrör. When he later came (back) to Graningeverken, first as member of its board in 1929 and then as its CEO in 1932, he quickly made the company profitable. His recipe was to use the profit (and some other resources) to make investments in power plants and waterfall rights. His ambitions for the pulp plants were instead rather modest and basically confined to maintenance and those modernizations that conservative calculations indicated would be profitable. Versteegh also took some very unorthodox steps such as making the company leave several Swedish industry and employer associations. He simply kept away from all organizations in which he did not have the final say. Versteegh also rabidly opposed the establishment of unions.

Gerhard Versteegh resigned from his post as Marma-Långrör's CEO when he became CEO of both Utansjö Cellulosa and Sandviken Cellulosa. These appointments occurred in spite of the fact that two years earlier (1930) he had obtained a truly bad reputation in many parts of Swedish society when he responded to a strike at Marma-Långrör by hiring strike-breakers guarded by the police. That provocation prompted Pappersindustriarbetareförbundet to arrange sympathy strikes at both Utansjö and Sandviken in 1931. There, too, Versteegh recruited strike-breakers, and the confrontations that emerged resulted in riots and even shooting fatalities among the workers.[31]

Many of the distinct boundaries between forest-based companies disappeared or faded when some of the owner families lost control. In a sense, that new ownership situation created an opportunity to engage in restructuring activities, but the banks and most of the financially sound corporations refrained from undertaking such efforts. In fact, most of the new major shareholders took care of their current holdings but showed very little ambition to expand their businesses through M&As. As the borders between the forest-based companies gradually became blurred, those between each bank sphere's holdings instead became increasingly sharp, a situation that probably contributed to the forest-based industry's inertia. Thus, most of the rationalizations and integrations occurred within rather than between spheres, and the result was not always optimal. The economic crisis had also severely reduced the number of capitalists capable of initiating structural changes, and as the banks were not allowed to buy company shares, they could not step in to fill the gap.[32]

From the mid-1920s one could talk about a new era, that of industrial capitalism, which replaced the classic trade capitalism that had dominated the 19th century (and long before that). Several researchers have used the 'industrial' label to identify the period that started sometime at the beginning of the 20th century and ended almost one hundred years later. That era saw innumerable applications of the outcomes of an unparalleled, continuous technological revolution. It is also possible to conclude that early in the 20th century another kind of capitalism, financial capitalism, set the tone, but the severe economic crisis of the early 1920s put an end to that.[33]

5.1.5 A New Boom Period

The Swedish economy began to recover already in the mid-1920s. The demand for both sawn timber and – particularly – pulp increased rapidly. Some of that demand originated from the US, a country whose industry needed sulphate pulp for its growing production of packing paper (cf. kraftliner). Thus, older plants were expanded, and many new sulphate plants were built: Karlsborg (established by the Swedish state, 1928–29, cf. below), Köpmanholmen (Forss, 1929–30), Marmaverken (Marma-Långör, 1927–28), Munksund (Handelsbanken, 1926–28), Norrsundet (Kopparberg-Hofors, 1923–25), Sandviken (the Versteegh family, 1927–28) and Östrand (SCA, 1930). In several cases, that wave of investment revived or rebuilt firms that had suffered from the economic crisis. Investments were made in (new) sulphate production because of its profitability, resulting to a great extent from the possibility of using lower qualities of timber. While sulphite plants also saw some expansion, only one new plant was built.[34] In reality, the 1920s marked the end of the establishment of new sulphite units. Instead, from the 1930s on, it was the sulphate process that developed, and eventually it became the dominant method for pulp production.[35]

It was Kalix Träindustri, established in 1928 mainly through state financing (but without state ownership), that invested in the new sulphate plant at Karlsborg mentioned above. The timing for that investment as well as an investment in its sawmill was not the best, as the Great Depression early in the 1930s hit the forest-based businesses hard, making the company's need for new state capital urgent. In 1934 the 'Kalix problem' became an issue for the Swedish Parliament and government, and a discussion arose based on a study about the general prospects for industrial activity in the northernmost regions. The conclusion was that the Swedish Forest Service (Domänverket) should run the Karlsborg site together with the other units in northern Sweden run by the Swedish Forest Board (Domänstyrelsen). As a consequence, the government decided that the company, Kalix Träindustri, should be liquidated (1937).[36]

Several mechanical grinderies were also added during those years. Investments were also made in kraft paper production with new units established at Billerud, Fiskeby and Uddeholm. Newsprint followed a similar course. For example, Stora Kopparberg and Holmens Bruk expanded their activities by installing new machines, and Matfors and Wargön, too, became important producers of newsprint. Almost all of these investments were carried out before any structural changes or ownership transformations had taken place. As a consequence, most of the expansions made the boundaries between the different ownership spheres even more rigid.[37]

It was not until the 1920s that the companies in the forest-based industry began to co-operate on a wide front, including engaging in price and market discussions on most kinds of pulp and paper products and developing a platform for production and sales statistics. An important step was the joint trade rule agreement that was concluded in 1925 by, on the one hand, the leading Finnish, Norwegian and Swedish producers, and, on the other hand, the British organization of wholesalers. That trade agreement also became a framework for the ones that were to follow, and its main principles held for a long time.[38] Under the agreement, British custom tariffs were set at a reasonable level for Swedish firms, and there were no quantitative limits. By contrast, most other European countries set higher customs rates and quotas, which almost stopped the Swedish forest-based industry's export to countries like France and Holland. Thus, the international market for forest-based goods was full of obstructions.

International co-operation became particularly popular in the newsprint sector. Many conferences were held during the 1920s, and the most important one took place in Copenhagen in 1928. At that meeting, delegates from Canada, Finland, Germany, Holland, Norway, Sweden, the UK and the US decided to establish a permanent committee (The International Committee on Newsprint), whose task was to promote the common interests of producers and consumers of newsprint. The ambition to create a similar body for the Swedish producers of kraftliner met with difficulties, although it was finally formed in 1927. The general idea behind these agencies was to ensure freedom for each corporation, at the same time as all of them were guaranteed certain sales and stable prices.[39]

5.1.6 MoDo: Carl Kempe Sr Takes Command

Carl Kempe Sr learned about MoDo during several years of work in many different positions in the company. In 1909 he became a member of the board of its sulphite company, in 1916 he was appointed to the same position in the mother company, and one year later he became its CEO. His promotion was not uncontroversial within the Kempe family. Quite a few relatives expressed doubts, particularly regarding his personality. They regarded him as a rather careless and superficial person with too much appetite for 'the good life' – they saw him as a 'bon vivant' with a limited inclination to seriously engage in important business matters. Other actors, however, described him as more of an epicurean than a reveller, that is to say, as a person who could control his 'extravagant habits' and keep them within socially acceptable limits. As a member of the 'Frans Kempe faction' of the MoDo dynasty, Carl Kempe Sr was also, in accordance with the emerging family legend regarding preferred leadership capabilities, characterized as a courageous and visionary leader ready to take economic risks based on both calculations and intuitive reasoning. He was also – in the same tales – ascribed a particular gift for business and a good head for making economic decisions.[40] His candidature for the CEO position was certainly strengthened by this type of characterization of his personality.

In 1918, not long after he had become MoDo's CEO, Carl Kempe Sr was elected to the board of Handelsbanken, thereby establishing a relationship that proved to be of particular importance for MoDo's development all through the 20th century. It was not an unproblematic linkage, in particular because Handelsbanken in the 1920s acted to create Svenska Cellulosa (SCA), a constellation that could eventually become a strong competitor to MoDo (particularly its pulp business).[41] At about the same time, Carl Kempe Sr was active in assembling and organizing the remaining family businesses in the forest industry in northernmost Sweden, so that they could continue to exist even if SCA expanded. Consequently, in 1926, Carl Kempe Sr decided to leave the board of Handelsbanken.

Husum's sulphite-based pulp factory was all set for production in 1919, a time when the recession had passed. The first few years of the 1920s, however, were highly volatile. They began with an exceptionally high demand for pulp and high prices, but already after a year or two an extraordinary decline squeezed the price down to around 15 per cent of that reached in 1920.[42] After that setback, prices and quantities rose again, and demand grew steadily (especially from the US). Carl Kempe Sr was quick to seize the opportunity and started to rationalize and expand MoDo's business. Thus, Hörnefors, Husum and Domsjö were all modernized and enlarged during the 1924–31 period.

Carl Kempe Sr also further developed MoDo's R&D capacity. An important step in that process was the hiring of Ulfsparre to the Domsjö site, and he was to a large extent the reason why R&D became a hallmark of MoDo. In addition to trying to develop a pulp quality suitable for silk production, he sought ways to recycle chemicals and economize on the use of energy resources. He also transformed the Domsjö site to more of a bulk-producing unit. However, what made Ulfsparre well known throughout the whole industry was his leadership in the development of a method for bleaching pulp (using chlorine dioxide).[43]

Another important step in securing strong R&D within MoDo was the establishment in 1930 of a laboratory building at Domsjö that contained equipment for boiling and bleaching, installations for the experimental production of viscose silk and acetyl cellulose, and so on. That investment was also motivated by the expected shortage of timber for pulp and paper production (cf. the need for a more effective use of the fibre).

MoDo's Ulfsparre was appointed Chair of a joint effort in the industry ('Cellulosaindustrins Centrallaboratorium'), where engineers tried to solve the problem of how to bleach brown pulp and, from that platform, get a strong white paper. Rather soon they discovered the merits of chlorine dioxide for that purpose. That method produced a whiter and cleaner pulp than the other methods accomplished. That improvement had the potential to put MoDo in a leading position in the pulp business. However, that method required that MoDo was successful in establishing an efficient, large-scale dioxide production. Its own laboratory solved the problem, but it was actually a competitor, Korsnäs, that obtained the patent. That move initiated a battle, and at an early stage MoDo expressed objections that were sent to the Swedish Patent and Registration Office. However, Ulfsparre realized that MoDo could only lose such a contest; a victory would permit everybody in the industry to use the method, while a defeat would make Korsnäs the sole user. So, MoDo suggested to Korsnäs's management that the two companies should co-operate regarding the utilization of the patent, and Korsnäs accepted the proposal.

During those years many companies in the forest-based industry developed a strong interest in R&D, partly triggered by the new challenges facing the industry, partly stimulated by the many scientific breakthroughs and successful innovations made in other Swedish industries. The state, too, invested heavily in research activities, and together with the industry it established both joint efforts and a division of responsibilities. The state provided resources and institutions for basic research, while the corporations primarily invested in applied research. The two sets of actors also created joint ventures, for example, in the forest-based sector, the Swedish Forest Research Institute (Svenska Träforskningsinstitutet, 1942). Most of these arrangements were successful, and many technical and commercial 'quantum leaps' took place during that time, including 'continuous cooking', chlorine bleaching, oxygen bleaching, defibration, 'free drying', 'the slalom wind' and many others. At the time, other kinds of collaboration and discussion between the Swedish forest-based companies and the state involved important topics such as regulations, export terms, forestry policies and pricing.

In his ambition to make use of as much of the timber as possible and to reduce the influence of demand/trade fluctuations, Carl Kempe Sr looked for possibilities to differentiate MoDo's existing product repertoire. Manufacturing wallboard represented one such path. Being one of the first Swedish companies that recognized the merits of the new application, MoDo decided in the late 1920s to establish 'Mo and Domsjö Wallboard Company' (later Treetex), which came to house the biggest wallboard factory in Europe (close to Domsjö).[44] The new plant was initially jointly owned with Handelsbanken (37.5%), something that again indicated the bank's linkage with MoDo, which also held 37.5 per cent of the shares in the new firm. The rest of the shareholding (25%) was distributed among a circle of MoDo-friendly investors. When preference shares were added in 1930, MoDo took 60 per cent of them, and only a few years later (1934) MoDo bought Handelsbanken's holding.[45]

SCA and MoDo were often described (and described themselves) as 'sworn enemies' in the Swedish forest-based industry – an antagonism that persisted (at least) for the whole century, although the direct clashes were few.[46] That they had the same bank connection (Handelsbanken) did not eliminate the rivalry. One possible reason for the hostility that had existed since SCA's founding in the 1920s was their competition to secure the dominant position in the northern part of Sweden. It did not take long for SCA to surpass MoDo's standing in many ways. MoDo's strong man Carl Kempe Sr did not like this situation and had difficulties accepting that SCA's Hèrnod had become a kind of 'number one' among the industrial bigwigs that regularly assembled to discuss common industrial issues. Carl Kempe Sr also disliked Hèrnod on a personal basis, something that made the rivalry between the two companies particularly visible. On the whole, Carl Kempe Sr seemed to look upon SCA's leading actors as some sort of parvenus that should be kept on a tight rein.[47]

However, some actors expressed a different view regarding the degree of rivalry between MoDo and SCA over the years. To describe the two companies as 'sworn enemies' was, according to Gunnar Sundblad (CEO of Iggesund 1921–56), to exaggerate the matter. However, he confirmed that 'substantial cultural differences' had existed between the two companies for a long time, probably very much emerging from the personalities and rationalities expressed by the company's leading actors. Some actors like Löf (MoDo CEO 1985–94) rather put the emphasis on the divergent forms of corporate governance practised in each of the companies. Löf saw MoDo as a family-based dynasty of 'physical' owners and top managers that handled all challenges that arose. Thus, in MoDo there was always a visible and dominant shareholder, who also led the operations. Lacking such a strong ownership structure, SCA was instead run by a CEO and board composed of actors that held only limited shares personally and that were mainly 'nominated' by the controlling bank (Handelsbanken).[48] Another difference stressed by Löf concerned the degree of focus on R&D and the allocation of resources to stimulate innovation. Unlike

SCA, MoDo had produced many technical and commercial breakthroughs – advantages that explained much of the success that the company experienced during the first part of the 20th century.[49]

5.2 THE FORMATION OF BUSINESS SPHERES

5.2.1 The Establishment of SCA

After the crisis years 1921–23 most forest-based corporations tried to increase their revenues by simultaneously rationalizing and expanding their plants, the latter to be able to utilize economies of scale for both sulphite and sulphate plants. At the same time, because several other European countries, particularly Finland, began to expand their forest-based industries, international competition gradually increased. The unprecedented technological innovations and dramatically shifting economic conditions (boom periods and deep crises) contributed to both the emergence of many new plants and the elimination of others that had functioned well previously. Svenska Cellulosa (SCA) was perhaps the most important new unit that emerged as a consequence of all these changes.

What became the holding company SCA could geographically be derived from companies located in northern Sweden. One of its more important building blocks was Bergvik & Ala, a profitable firm that was situated in the southernmost part of the northern areas. It was a listed, unspecialized forest-based company that held forests, sawmills and plants for sulphite and sulphate production. Several other firms that would be incorporated in the new SCA group were located a bit north of Bergvik & Ala. These firms, primarily Skönvik, Sunds and Svartvik, were heavily indebted. Although none was more important than the others, Skönvik became the central unit in the co-ordination efforts. Further north, Kramfors in particular was to become a significant unit in the process of building SCA. Even further north, SCA took over Holmsund (at the time a daughter company to Svartvik) and Munksund. A common feature of many of these firms was that they controlled rather modest forest resources in comparison with their respective production outputs, something that made integration with pulp production more difficult. However, the scales of their (non-integrated) plants were relatively large, although they were older than the competitors' units. Another shared characteristic among the firms that eventually comprised SCA was that most of them had Handelsbanken as their main bank connection.[50]

In the late 1920s, Kreuger carried out the biggest structural transformation that had ever taken place in the Swedish forest-based industry. His buying of several privately owned pulp-producing firms in northern Sweden led to a marked consolidation of the industry. That transformation was carried out in close co-operation with Handelsbanken and Sundsvallsbanken, with the former becoming the main bank for the emerging new constellation (SCA). Kreuger advocated market control through cartels, and industry consolidation through M&As. The basic idea behind the new creation was to make it big enough to be able to take the lead in such international price cartels, and make it capable of becoming a powerful force for restructuring the Swedish forest-based industry.[51]

SCA was founded during a difficult time period. Roughly at the same time as the corporation was established, the big crash occurred on the New York Stock Exchange

(October 1929), an event that triggered the Great Depression. Thus, for SCA's new management it was not just a question of getting the various units to form a coherent whole; it became of ultimate importance to form an efficient constellation that could survive the emerging global crisis. SCA's vision and role were decided in discussions among Handelsbanken, the owners of the various associated firms and the new SCA board. Ernfrid Browaldh at Handelsbanken developed the guidelines for those talks already in early 1929 (before the 'crash' and formal establishment of SCA).[52]

Eventually the relationship between Kreuger and Handelsbanken became less cordial. Nevertheless, co-operation was necessary as the bank had become the leading lender to the forest-based industry in northern Sweden, and also a major shareholder. The first renewed talks between Kreuger and the bank (through its CEO Stén) occurred by chance in an unplanned encounter on a ferry in 1929.[53] The two actors compared the way the American competitors were organized with the notoriously weak sales organizations in the Swedish forest-based industry and concluded that its fragmentation was the main problem. Stén suggested that Kreuger consider working towards a structural rationalization in the forest-based business to make export efforts more effective.[54]

Kreuger, who took the initiative to create the holding company that became SCA, and, in August 1929, Handelsbanken's CEO Stén, confirmed in a letter to Kreuger their preliminary agreement that all shares in the bank's daughter company Handion (later renamed SCA) should be sold to Kreuger & Toll (for SEK 40 million). Handion was the holding company in which Handelsbanken had concentrated all the holdings in the Swedish forest-based industry that it had been forced to acquire as creditor during the financial crises. Handion owned, for example, 42 per cent of Bergvik & Ala.[55]

In the end the SCA group, wholly owned by Kreuger & Toll, embraced Enhörningsverken, Essvik, Frånö, Holmsund, Kramfors, Munksund (later), Nyhamn, Salsåker, Skönvik, Strömnäs, Svartvik, Sund and parts of Ytterstfors. Due to the Kreuger crash[56] a few years later neither Bergvik & Ala[57] nor Marma-Långör became permanently integrated in SCA. Munksund was initially not included either, although the co-operation between the two companies was intense. Wallenberg's units Wifstavarf, Kopparfors-Hofors and Stora Kopparberg refused to participate in the industry's restructuring, as did Versteegh's and Francke's firms.[58]

It was not only the inefficiently divided export efforts, however, that motivated the forest-based companies in the Sundsvall area to co-operate. There was also a need for a sulphate plant there because the existing sawmills in the region left a large amount of wood waste that could be used to source pulp production profitably.[59] Moreover, such a plant would make the forestry more effective. Yet, none of the regional companies had the individual capacity to absorb such a big investment until SCA came along and in the early 1930s established a large sulphate plant at Östrand. The new plant was not only the biggest unit in the world, it was actually also the largest Swedish industrial investment made between the two world wars. Unfortunately, however, since the heyday of sulphate pulp ended around 1930 (and did not recover until after WWII), Östrand was established a decade too late from a market point of view. Instead, demand increased for processed commodities such as bleached sulphate pulp (offered by Bergslaget, Kopparberg-Hofors and Uddeholm).[60]

A fundamental issue in SCA's integration process was how to deal with the different company cultures that had evolved over time due to the varying geographical and operational circumstances. Another problem was that all involved companies except Bergvik & Ala were heavily indebted. Like the company's founders, Hèrnod, the SCA group's CEO, advocated the idea that SCA should be constructed as a holding company – not as an operative unit, as the diversities in the population of participating firms made such a solution too risky. Generally, the different firms were the important units in the eyes of most actors inside as well as outside the SCA grouping. The heads of the involved firms were not inclined to give up more of the independence of their units than was absolutely necessary (to be able to create value for the single firm). So, SCA became a rather loosely coupled constellation and a headquarters (HQ) with rather limited authority. It was Hèrnod who had the difficult task of trying to stimulate engagement for the new constellation as a coherent whole. One should note that Bergvik & Ala, which was in good shape economically, tended to take an even more autonomous position than the others.[61]

However, the competitors did not just passively watch the establishment of SCA. Several other forest-based companies in the north joined forces in 1931 and created a trading company, Nordsvenska Bruk, which primarily took care of the involved companies' pulp sales. Its total market capacity roughly corresponded to half of that of SCA. Basically, Nordsvenska Bruk involved family firms, among them MoDo and Robertsfors[62] that were owned by the Kempe dynasty. Nordsvenska Bruk also handled MoDo's and Robertfors's sales of wood products and sawn timber. However, the new company was not only a unit for sales co-ordination but also a defence arrangement against Kreuger's (assumed) further expansion attempts in the region. When that threat suddenly disappeared in 1932 (Kreuger's unexpected death) the new grouping split up.[63]

SCA and Nordsvenska Bruk were not the only constellations that tried to regulate competition in the early 1930s. A Nordic network (Scankraft) was established in 1932 with the purpose of creating a common pricing policy for the kraft paper business. It could make agreements both inside and outside the Fenno-Scandinavian countries and with both sellers and buyers. Similar informal organizations were formed a few years later in the wrapping paper sector and for newsprint (Scannews). Though Scannews was initially a group with little impact, it soon grew in importance, and after WWII other countries such as Canada and the UK joined. These cartels were rather successful and stabilized the market, which both producers and customers appreciated. At the time, (these) cartels were seen as legitimate constructs contributing to wealth in society by preventing economic crises (by making extraordinary price fluctuations less probable). In addition, cross-national co-ordination became indispensable because of the complicated export conditions that existed, and those arrangements remained in place for quite some time. New Swedish cartel-like associations were also established (i.e. Scanfin [fine paper], Scanpapp [packaging] and Scanpergamyn [printing paper]) – and an older one was revived (Scansulfit [pulp]).[64]

During the interwar period, the banks controlled a large part of the Swedish forest-based industry. The financial capitalists had also captured substantial holdings in other sectors of the Swedish industry. As major and often dominant shareholders, they replaced the many different families that each had controlled a (smaller) firm. Particularly in northern Sweden two identifiable spheres emerged that began to dominate the scene: on the one hand, the Wallenberg sphere that had acquired strong holdings in the middle part of Sweden since the close of the 19th century and, on the other, Handelsbanken (its holdings) and SCA, which together had taken control over many of the smaller firms located in the north.[65] At the same time, Handelsbanken sold its holdings in several sawmills to the Swedish state, something that became the basis for a new important constellation in the Swedish forest-based industry: ASSI (Statens Skogsindustrier).

During that period the embryo of a new (i.e. third) constellation appeared, comprising the forest-owning farmers and their associations, which already during the 19th century had attempted to establish their own production units, but failed because of lack of financial resources. In 1938 they launched a new effort to establish a pulp plant – Dala-Sulfit – but WWII put a stop to it.

SCA's first years of existence were shaky mainly because of the collapse of the Kreuger group and the negative effects of the Great Depression. The world prices for timber, wood products and pulp fell dramatically during those years, and it became commonplace to curtail or shut down operations. As Handelsbanken was the Kreuger group's largest creditor, it assumed the role as SCA's governing body. The bank was then SCA's most 'natural' buyer, since the main responsibility for the company's future lay in its hands. Moreover, the economic value for Handelsbanken of owning SCA was bigger than the value of the assets that the bankrupt's estate could expect from an agreement that did not involve the bank. Before selling to anybody, however, SCA had to restructure its finances. It had to write off a substantial sum for its claims on Kreuger & Toll and for the Östrand plant (the only one directly owned by SCA) and handle significant operational losses. In the end, the SCA shares were auctioned (1934), and, as expected, acquired by Handelsbanken. The bank then became the sole owner of SCA.

Handelsbanken's long-term strategy for its ownership of SCA was to establish regional subgroupings that could be sold as separate corporations. Not surprisingly, the bank intended to get out of its ownership of SCA in such a way that it regained its previous losses. Therefore, the bank (like the heads of the subsidiaries) opposed the creation of a more integrated SCA, which might have been a more effective construct. However, instead of the planned piecemeal selling of the company, Handelsbanken sold about 83 per cent of the SCA shares in 1934 to Wenner-Gren (however, on such terms that the bank maintained control). That sale was primarily a product of a coincidence. While in London, SCA's CEO Hèrnod happened to run across Wenner-Gren, who revealed that he had begun to consider phasing out his engagement in the global Elektrolux group and settling down in Sweden. Since he was interested in acquiring a new large undertaking that he could run from home, his attention had been drawn to SCA. After the acquisition of the majority of the SCA shares, Wenner-Gren became its new Chair and stayed in that position for four years.[66]

Eventually the rather loosely organized holding company SCA began to be more tightly integrated. In 1937, the decision was taken to follow up on CEO Hèrnod's suggestion that administration ought to be centralized, which resulted in the establishment of a new daughter company: 'Sundsvallsbolaget'. That new staff unit was assigned the planning and control of the various activities in the group, while responsibility for the running of the operations remained with each individual firm.

5.2.2 MoDo: Securing Family Domination

In the early 1930s, many prominent actors in the forest industry became concerned about the high degree of exploitation of the Swedish forests, and many ideas about restoration activities were proposed. In light of a general agreement that the cutting had been too extensive in the 1920s and early 1930s, a special committee was formed to deal with that problem. It concluded that the industry would face serious timber shortages if and when they tried to make full use of their production capacities. That particular understanding of the situation prevailed for quite a while and influenced many corporate decisions in the years to come.

In the 1930s, most of MoDo's production increases consisted of 'silk pulp' (i.e. an improved sulphite cellulose). Such production started at Domsjö in 1934 and seven years later also at Hörnefors. Other investments at that time included modernizations and expansions at both Domsjö (its bleaching capacity expanded in 1935) and Hörnefors, as well as a substantial expansion of the sulphate production at Husum (1935–37).[67] The philosophy of Carl Kempe Sr was to keep all plants modern and well equipped, as that was the best guarantor for success.[68] Of course, modernization almost always could be planned in such a way that a profitable production increase resulted.[69] Still, the plant that had taken MoDo through the years following the 1932 crisis was its Domsjö sulphite unit (due to the outstanding quality of its output) – the other plants yielded profit only in good times. That difference influenced the decision to add bleaching to the Hörnefors unit. However, it is also worth noting that Carl Kempe Sr rejected a suggestion made in 1937 by its site manager to build a paper mill at Husum, a decision that closed that path for many years.[70]

The 1930s and 1940s also saw the transformation of Domsjö from profitable small-scale production (e.g. customized viscose) to efficient[71] large-scale production (high-quality sulphite). That advantage was later strengthened when Husum (1946), Domsjö and Hörnefors introduced chlorine oxide-based bleaching – a method that produced a cleaner and whiter pulp quality.[72] The new process also made possible the use of deciduous forests, particularly birch timber, something that dramatically expanded the fibre resources available for pulp production. The combination of the novel method for bleaching sulphate with the use of birch as fibre base gave MoDo a competitive advantage. The new and unique sulphate pulp soon became a commercial success. As the patent for the bleaching method did not expire until 1955, and as Korsnäs (the other patentee) did not start its production until 1953, MoDo was the sole seller of a superior product for nearly a decade.[73]

In the early 1940s, MoDo's industrial portfolio included two sawmills (Domsjö and Norrbyskär), three pulp plants (Domsjö, Husum and Hörnefors), one wallboard factory and the newly established organic-chemical operations. During WWII MoDo concentrated on dissolving pulp, as it was suitable for the production of rayon-based commodities. Still, the basic strategy was to process the timber as much as possible. Therefore, not only Domsjö but also Hörnefors (and later Husum) housed bleaching processes. MoDo produced its own chlorine, which was a key resource not only for the forest-based industry, but also for the chemical industry in general.

The chemical sector's development in continental Europe and the UK, together with the company's own experiences, raised MoDo's interest in participating in some way. Generally, the chemical industry was expected to expand and play a significant role in industrial development throughout Europe. Carl Kempe Sr and other leading actors within and outside MoDo regarded the opportunities in that business as exceptionally favourable.[74]

Carl Kempe Sr's visionary capacity and openness to taking risks led MoDo to enter the growing chemical industry. Long before most other Swedish actors, he understood that fast-growing industry's enormous potential. So already in the beginning of the 1930s he asked the government authorities for the right to establish a plant for the production of sulphite spirit, a suitable raw material for a competitive Swedish chemical production. That request was approved only in 1939, and production began at Domsjö in 1940. Even before that, in 1936, MoDo built a factory for the production of chlorine potash.

MoDo was introduced at the SSE 1936. At that time, two important foundations were established with the sole purpose to act as shareholders in MoDo. The two foundations were named J.C. Kempe's Memorial Foundation (1936) and Seth M. Kempe's Memorial Foundation (1941) and were established by Bruzelius (daughter of J.C. Kempe and sister to Seth Kempe). Hwass (granddaughter to J.C. Kempe), too, provided capital to the former foundation. Together these foundations controlled 15 per cent of the MoDo stock, and they would play a prominent role in the late 20th century when serious control struggles broke out. The statutes stated that the foundations, through ownership of (solely) MoDo shares, should support the company's 'calm continuance and development' and 'contribute to a unification of the shareholders' interest' in the company, thereby securing the Kempe family's long-term control.[75] However, long before those conflicts, and for quite some time, Carl Kempe Sr's way of running the family foundations almost paralysed their meetings and activities. Eventually he had to leave as director and was replaced by Tore Browaldh (CEO of Handelsbanken), who was supposed to pour oil on troubled waters.[76] Still, Carl Kempe Sr's leadership was successful in reproducing the company's family-flavoured culture (i.e. a general feeling among employees that everybody in the company belonged to the same 'family'), and that despite MoDo's substantial growth and the decreasing presence of the Kempe name in its top positions.

MoDo's share price fluctuated a lot in those days, something that tempted several members of the Kempe dynasty to sell holdings during good times. However, the Kempe foundations were capable of buying most of the MoDO shares that the family members sold during the good times (but were incapable of buying back in bad times), so the Kempe dynasty kept control. Gradually, therefore, these foundations became the sole owners linked to the Kempe dynasty with the exception of Fanny Kempe's[77] son Carlgren's private shareholding in the company. However, despite all these share-price fluctuations, MoDo entered the 1950s in good economic health, and that status was strengthened during the consolidation that took place when Erik Kempe acted as the company's CEO.

R&D was also intensified in those days, particularly efforts to develop marketable organic-chemical products. Glycol became the first outcome of that effort and eventually a main product for MoDo. It also constituted a platform for other chemical-technical products. The investments in the chemical industry promoted by Carl Kempe Sr were probably the most important strategic decisions taken in the mid-1930s and early 1940s.

5.2.3 Iggesund: The Trygger Family Takes Control

Iggesund had planned to experiment with the bleaching of sulphate pulp soon after WWI, but the 1921 crisis stopped those plans. The experiments were revived at the beginning of the 1930s, however, and production of a semi-bleached sulphate pulp started in

1931, with a first-rate quality appearing by 1934. Two years later Iggesund was able to bring a fully bleached sulphite pulp to the market, thereby gaining the lead over its competitors. At the same time, many sulphate plants were built in the US, which dramatically increased that country's capacity to export pulp to Europe. Iggesund's CEO Gunnar Sundblad understood that it had become necessary to invest in the production of fully bleached sulphate pulp as well, but it took two decades before Iggesund finally got that bleaching capacity.[78]

By 1934 the Trygger family had obtained about 60 per cent of the shares in the companies controlling Iggesund, thereby indirectly becoming its major shareholder. The only other important shareholder was the Sundblad family. In the middle of the decade, Carl Trygger took over his father Ernst's leading role in Iggesund, with his appointment as Deputy Chair in 1937 and six years later, upon the death of his father, as Chair.[79]

At the end of the 1930s Iggesund's situation looked very promising, as the bleached sulphite pulp sold well in the US, prices on woodware were increasing, and large amounts of ironwork were exported to France. The company also expanded its sawmill and established factories for producing boxes, wooden houses and joinery products. The start of WWII put an end to that growth – 95 per cent of Iggesund's production was intended for countries that went into the war.[80]

5.2.4 Stora Kopparberg: A New Generation of the Wallenberg Family Enters the Scene

In the Wallenberg case one could note that the family's shareholding in Stora Kopparberg was as low as less than 5 per cent, but still Marcus Wallenberg the Elder dominated the company (exerting an extraordinary 'informal' influence that his successor Marcus Wallenberg Sr later reproduced in several companies). However, after WWII there emerged a power struggle between the Wallenberg family and the financial tycoon Kreuger regarding control over Stora Kopparberg. In 1929, the Kreuger group had 39 000 shares and the Wallenberg sphere 36 000 shares. The upcoming stalemate forced Wallenberg the Elder and Kreuger to meet and discuss the ownership situation in that company. At the first meeting the former claimed that Kopparberg-Hofors, Stora Kopparberg and Wifstavarf were 'Wallenberg companies'.

In December 1929 the two industrial leaders met again and made peace (they decided to consult each other when shares were put on the market and perhaps share the offered stock). Still, the contest went on until 1932, just before the Kreuger crash, and at that time the Wallenberg sphere controlled 12 per cent of the votes compared to Kreuger's 9 per cent.[81] Kreuger's crash simplified the Wallenberg sphere's possibility of controlling Stora Kopparberg (it did not have to increase its voting power in the company). Thus, from 1932, Marcus Wallenberg the Elder was able to firmly govern the company and control the recruitment of its directors and top management. Rather soon the company was regarded as one of the dynasty's core holdings, something that probably influenced their actions for the rest of the 20th century.

In the 1930s, a new generation of the Wallenberg family began to take charge in the sphere's industrial group. Marcus Wallenberg the Elder's sons Marcus Wallenberg Sr and Jacob Wallenberg Sr gradually took over his roles. Jacob was the one that advocated business ideals quite close to those of their father. For example, he disliked industrial conglomerates and large industrial groups and preferred moderate-sized companies that a CEO could grasp and manage. Moreover, he preferred low debt, high liquidity and low costs, that is to say, he was a risk-averse person. He considered it advisable to seek a high level of consolidation, for example, through depreciation of fixed capital, establishment of hidden reserves and low dividends. He preferred low dividends, as most dividends were anyway 'lost' as a sort of tax, while what stayed in the company at least benefitted the shareholders in the long run (by increasing stock value). Such a position made it easier for companies to survive bad times and created opportunities to invest in times when the competitors were incapable of doing so. Thus, in his eyes a low debt ratio made freedom of action possible, and high liquidity left room for investments in R&D, something for which one should not borrow.[82] One could also afford to take substantial operational risks, since the financial risk was kept low. Such a conservative financial strategy even made short-term speculation possible. Jacob Wallenberg Sr further stressed the need to offer well-prepared background material for board discussions, so that all directors could make up their own minds. He also tried to ensure that plenty of lead time was allowed for the truly important decisions.[83]

Marcus Wallenberg Sr's personality and action rationale were quite different to his elder brother's. Like Jacob, he was sociable, but much more active, energetic and always on the move. His tempo was extraordinary when he executed his monitoring and development functions in the sphere-run corporations including Stora Kopparberg (although it was one of Jacob's companies). He was a very active owner who made sure that all the important information reached him (almost) before it reached 'anybody else'. He took the liberty of contacting anybody anytime about anything. Furthermore, he was a tough, manipulative and demanding actor with a great need for control. At the same time, however, he was a most competent and dedicated developer of the sphere and its corporations, and his great interest in new technology was beneficial for the entire Swedish industry. He also worked to support the interests of his home country Sweden and eventually took on the role as the *pater familias*.[84]

Like Marcus Wallenberg the Elder both Jacob Wallenberg Sr and Marcus Wallenberg Sr were trained at Stockholms Enskilda Bank. Eventually they were appointed as the bank's Deputy CEO, CEO, Deputy Chair and Chair (one position at a time). Though they shared a similar education, their fields of interest differed significantly: Jacob Wallenberg Sr was a banker who took interest in industry, while Marcus Wallenberg Sr was an industrialist who by family tradition had become a banker. Eventually, the latter became the most prominent industrial leader in Sweden during the second half of the 20th century, combining the role as major (or at least dominant or most influential) shareholder with that of the intervening executive. In the Wallenberg sphere it became obvious that he had the final say regarding all the important issues in the family's industrial group.[85]

5.3 THE 1940s AND 1950s

5.3.1 The Post-War Period: Tentative Liberalization

World market demand for timber and pulp became massive when WWII ended. To prevent the rising prices from stimulating an inflationary development in Sweden, the

Social Democratic government of the time prescribed that exports of timber and wood products should be charged with a kind of price compensation fee. Moreover, licences for pulp export would only be provided if the price stayed below certain levels. Already in 1947, however, the pricing of export goods was liberated, as the government regarded it as important to have foreign currency streaming into the country. Instead, fees were introduced on the pulp and timber trade to neutralize major fluctuations. In 1950, the year the Korean War started, substantial shortages of raw materials emerged, particularly for pulp, wood products and paper, and prices increased dramatically. Once again the Swedish government intervened to stave off inflation, and solutions similar to those tried in the late 1940s were launched again, with the new fees removed in 1952.[86]

After WWII the world saw a more liberal economy emerge around the globe, although the initial steps were not overwhelming in magnitude. Strict protectionism was gradually abandoned, and Swedish companies, relatively unaffected by the war, began a rapid and massive internationalization. That meant that the companies kept or increased their specialization; they combined the benefits of in-depth knowledge (e.g. R&D) and scale economies by producing huge volumes for export. As a result, within a rather short time, many Swedish corporations made most of their sales abroad. The forest-based companies concentrated their efforts on selling products that continental firms had difficulties producing (i.e. kraftliner, fluting and newsprint).

Diversification of the operations on the Swedish home market could have been an alternative expansion path for the forest-based companies, but they saw that as less effective than international growth. The export-oriented approach required that they invested heavily to make the plants modern and scale efficient, and that they also invested in R&D to develop new pulp qualities, processes and applications.[87] One result of the R&D investments appeared in 1948 when it became possible to use continuous cooking (instead of batch cooking) in sulphate production. The international expansion also meant that many companies began to integrate forward and produce different kinds of paper, something that previously had been regarded as a dangerous path because it might mean head-on competition with customers. The growth in the size of companies and plants ultimately resulted in a halving of the number of pulp-producing units in Sweden between 1940 and 1950. It was primarily the small and medium-sized sulphite plants that closed (particularly those that produced unbleached qualities).[88]

Many of the tough restrictions surrounding the Swedish capital market that originated from the 1940s were kept for quite some time. They had been established by a Social Democratic government that did not believe that the market – the financial actors – would be able to satisfy certain basic societal needs (e.g. investments in electric power). That government also introduced specific monetary policy tools, including allocation rules, liquidity quotas, loan regulations, interest regulations and issue controls. Moreover, the exchange currency control introduced during WWII was preserved, although it abated somewhat over the coming decades. One example of the power of these regulations was that Swedish companies almost were obliged to go outside Sweden to get the financing for their foreign investments. That rule affected, for example, one of the big Swedish forest-based corporations, Stora Kopparberg, when it tried to finance its investments in Canada (Nova Scotia).[89]

After WWII three product groups dominated the Nordic forest-based industry: mechanical wood pulp, sulphite pulp and kraft pulp. The first two pulp qualities were relatively pale and could therefore be used as input for making fine paper and printing paper (without bleaching). Moreover, sulphite pulp was rather easy to bleach to a brightness (white colour) that matched pulp made from rags. At that time, however, there was no available technique for bleaching sulphate pulp. Therefore, that pulp was used to make wrapping (brown) paper. That difference regarding bleaching possibilities favoured sulphite pulp and mechanical wood pulp, although both of them could only be produced from spruce. The distribution of that kind of timber became a deciding force for where pulp-producing plants were established in Sweden. To a large extent, that distribution also explained why the forest-based industry grew so impressively in some of the Nordic countries during those years.[90]

During the 1940s and 1950s the Nordic export of pulp to North America decreased.[91] Some uncertainty also emerged surrounding exports to the region's biggest market: continental Europe and the UK. The Nordic companies were concerned that their (potential) American competitors would buy (shares in) European companies and thereby make Nordic companies dependent on the cost situation in North America. That worry was strengthened by the fact that some 80 per cent of the producers of corrugated cardboard in the US were integrated with producers of liner, and that idea was spreading to Europe, too.

The situation was different for more high-grade printing papers. Many forests contained several sorts of trees, not all of which were suitable for that kind of production, and sorting costs were substantial. Thus, in those segments, the circumstances were more favourable for the Nordic companies, which often were located in (or close to) homogeneous forests of spruce – a sort of wood that fit the production of wood-containing printing papers. Therefore, the Nordic forest-based companies concluded that they would face serious competition for chemical pulp, but remain strong in high-grade printing papers (including newsprint).[92]

Successful R&D achievements in the 1950s made it possible for several Swedish companies (especially MoDo and Korsnäs) to produce bleached sulphate pulp of good quality efficiently. The technological breakthrough also made birch an adequate new timber resource for the industry, beyond spruce and pine. That possibility allowed for an exploitation of forest areas that (because of lack of spruce) had not been used before, particularly those forests that were located nearby existing plants. Over time it also changed the criteria for the localization of new plants – they no longer had to be close to forests rich in spruce. However, the technical developments of the 1950s were not exclusively focused on making use of birch – a common tree in the Nordic regions. They also opened up options for making use of short-fibre trees in general. As a consequence of these efforts, two new product groups in particular appeared on the pulp market, namely bleached sulphate based on pine (demonstrating even better technical qualities than that based on spruce) and bleached sulphate based on hardwood (e.g. birch).

5.3.2 The Eroding Nordic Advantage

One consequence of the innovations of the time was that new forest areas around the world became suitable for pulp and paper production. Thus, in a rather short period of time, the Nordic advantage built on an almost exclusive access to long fibres (spruce) had eroded. Paradoxically, that turn of events was to some extent caused by innovations developed by two Nordic (i.e. Swedish) companies. Moreover, in the 1950s the mechanically produced pulp also became increasingly based on pine. Thus, technical developments radically changed the competitive landscape in a way that reduced the advantageous position of the Nordic countries.[93]

During the two decades following WWII most of the investments made by the Swedish forest-based companies concerned the establishment and expansion of their distribution channels in Western Europe. That path was complemented by sporadic acquisitions of wholesalers and paper companies. The global consumption of paper rose during the post-war years by about 5 per cent annually, so it was an ideal opportunity for investments and export efforts. That seemingly favourable situation posed a particular challenge for the Swedish firms,[94] which feared that their forest resources might prove to be insufficient. Therefore many forest-based companies began to search intensely for new ways of securing their long-term sourcing of timber. Without these sources, they would first gradually lose market shares and then the advantages linked to large-scale production.

Thus, around the 1950s, many global actors had understood that unexploited forests from, for example, Canada, the US and Brazil (plantations) represented excellent platforms for starting competitive pulp and paper industries.[95] In Sweden, Stora Kopparberg (Canada, Nova Scotia), SCA (Canada, British Columbia) and Billerud (Portugal) were the pioneers. They decided to broaden their insufficient and costly raw material bases and make direct investments outside Sweden. That was a risky path, however, as the Swedish investors lacked previous experience with such activities, and they soon learned that the conditions in these other countries differed significantly from those on their home ground. A basic problem was therefore how to manage such distant efforts – particularly such complex undertakings as establishing and running large production units (greenfield investments). The companies had to decide what activities their HQ should keep and what decisions ought to be decentralized to the various plant management teams. Examples of other problems – each of them manageable but taken together almost overwhelming – were the uncertain quality of the timber resources, the inexperienced labour forces, the unfamiliar customer traditions, the unknown business networks, the difficulties in interpreting the motivations of the local authorities, and so on. Encouraging investments, however, were the favourable conditions that the local (and/or national) authorities were offering investors, at least for an initial time period.[96]

5.3.3 The Start of Radical Structural Changes

Another important trend that took off in the 1950s was prompted by the Nordic corporations' ambitions to move away from standard bulk products to more differentiated and customized ones. Those goals made it almost necessary to switch from a sales system based on international agents to one based on foreign daughter companies. Through the latter, a company could better control the links to its customers and discuss and explain products being offered (and make adjustments to meet specific requests).[97] Getting closer to selected foreign markets was also a way of increasing the opportunities for future export growth. As the timber situation was interpreted at the time, the opportunity to export pulp was, if anything, declining. The expected timber shortage in Sweden was also one of the factors that stimulated the companies to gradually abandon the idea of not competing with its own customers (i.e. with the European paper mills). Instead, several of the Swedish pulp producers began to integrate forward to make better use of the scarce pulp resources, although the forward integration then usually took place in different business fields.

Thus, the Swedish pulp producers were still large and influential in the 1950s with substantial quantities of product for sale. At that time the biggest ones were Bergvik & Ala (controlled by an investment company [Industrivärden]), Billerud, Dynäs/Svanö (family [Ekman]), Forss (family [Hedberg]), Graningeverken (family [Versteegh]), Kopparfors (family [Wallenberg]), Korsnäs (family [Stenbeck and Klingspor]), MoDo (family [Kempe]), SCA (investment company [Industrivärden]), Stora Kopparberg (family [Wallenberg]) and Uddeholm (family and investment company [Johnson and Custos]). However, the establishment of free trade zones in Europe – the European Economic Community (EEC) in 1958 and the European Free Trade Association (EFTA) in 1960 – increased the uncertainty about how the European market would develop.[98]

The 1950s and 1960s saw the rather dramatic rationalization of the Swedish pulp-producing industry. All the above-mentioned changes created a need for transformations of various kinds. The larger companies that still had the financial resources to invest could – like their international competitors – benefit from the rapidly increasing advantages of scale and remain pulp producers (often in combination with paper production). After WWII there were around 250 pulp-producing sites in Sweden; already during the 1950s the number had been reduced to half that figure. As noted earlier, those that closed were the small and medium-sized producers of unbleached sulphite pulp, and by the mid-1960s there were only around 50 sites left. Although the idea was to deal with the environmental changes (technological innovations, international competition, a radically new global timber situation, etc.) by utilizing advantages of scale, only a few of the surviving units were large.

The other path taken was to concentrate on products for which the competitors on the European continent had limited capacities to produce (e.g. kraftliner, fluting and newsprint). The expansion in kraftliner and kraft paper was particularly strong in the 1960s, and some half a dozen new units were built (e.g. Wifstavarf [1960], Munksund [1960], Korsnäs [1961], Skärblacka [1963] and Lövholmen [1963]). Packaging, too, became a growth business (e.g. Papyrus's units for high-quality coated carton [1950 and 1956]).[99] SCA was one of the Nordic companies that became involved in the corrugated cardboard business on the continent (in Denmark and Spain).[100]

At the time, newsprint was a big Swedish export product. Holmens Bruk was the leading producer of that product, more than 50 per cent larger than Stora Kopparberg, which, in turn, was twice as big as SCA. Looking across the Swedish forest-based industry more generally, one could also note that three kraft paper plants (Gruvön, Munksjö and Skoghall) stood out as significantly bigger than any of the others, that MoDo's Silverdalen was the largest Swedish fine paper mill followed by Papyrus and Grycksbo, and that Korsnäs-Marma started Sweden's largest paper mill for liner and sacks (with sacks becoming the company's core business). During that period, Korsnäs also became a pioneer in the production of fluff pulp, which was intended for use in diapers and sanitary pads.[101] In 1960, Korsnäs merged with Marma-Långör forming Korsnäs-Marma, a new constellation that became Sweden's second biggest forest owner.[102]

NOTES

N.B.: When there is an 'i' inside a parenthesis below, that letter indicates that the note refers to an interview with the named person. All interviewees are listed in the Appendix. A complete listing of references is found at the end of the book.

1. Glete (1987).
2. The biggest ones were Matfors (1894) and Torpshammar (1871).
3. Glete (1987) and Haslum (1993).
4. Valeur (2003).
5. Most years.
6. Sjunnesson and Wahlberg (2003).
7. Glete (1994).
8. Savalainen, and Zacco-Broberg (1985).
9. An astounding example of this positive relationship between Frans Kempe and his employees was that the 'Great Strike' of 1909 did not affect MoDo at all.
10. Unger (1967).
11. Ibid.
12. Rydberg (1990).
13. Andersson (1993).
14. Unger (1967).
15. Gårdlund (1951).
16. Unger (1967).
17. Ibid.
18. Ibid.
19. The board was then reduced to three members – the third one being Treffenberg, who had entered the board in 1920 succeeding Seth Kempe as Chair in 1930, and left in 1947 to make way for Carl Kempe Sr (Unger [1967] and Croon [2005]).
20. Unger (1967).
21. Three different Marcus Wallenbergs will appear in this volume, namely the Elder (1864–1943), Senior (Sr) (1899–1982) and Junior (Jr) (1956–).
22. Sjögren (2005).
23. Glete (1987).
24. Finpapperbrukens Försäljnings AB.
25. Valeur (2003).
26. Glete (1987).
27. Rydberg (1990).
28. Glete (1987 and 1994).
29. Ibid.
30. Ibid.
31. Valeur (2000).
32. Glete (1987 and 1994).
33. Kallifatides et al. (2010).
34. Jössefors (by Billerud 1929).
35. Gaunitz (1979).
36. Valeur (2003).
37. Glete (1987) and Rydberg (1990).
38. Rydberg (1990).
39. Ibid.
40. Unger (1967).
41. SCA was established in 1929.
42. Svensk papperstidning (Vol. 61, No. 8).
43. Croon (2005).
44. Unger (1967).
45. Gårdlund (1951).
46. Nordstrand (2006i).
47. Lyberg (1984).
48. Löf (2006i) and Lars G. Sundblad (2006i).
49. Löf (2006i).
50. Gaunitz (1979) and Utterström (1979).

51. Glete (1987).
52. Valeur (2000).
53. Ibid.
54. Utterström (1979).
55. Haslum (1993).
56. By aggressive investments and innovative financial instruments he built a global business empire. Kreuger's financial empire collapsed during the Great Depression, and in March 1932, he was found dead in the bedroom of his flat in Paris.
57. From the start given a privileged status in the group.
58. Glete (1987) and Utterström (1979).
59. Such raw material could not be used in (the existing) sulphite plants.
60. Glete (1987).
61. Haslum (1993) and Utterström (1979).
62. An autonomous firm owned by Erik Kempe and Ragnar Kempe, their families and a few other relatives. The firm owned large forests in northern Sweden.
63. Glete (1987).
64. Rydberg (1990).
65. Glete (1994).
66. Utterström (1979) and Haslum (1993).
67. Unger (1967).
68. Lyberg (1984).
69. Pöyry and Ryti (1979).
70. Valeur (2003).
71. MoDo Domsjö was more efficient than its competitors, which substantially compensated for the fact that sulphite drew a lower price on the market than sulphate.
72. Unger (1967), Croon (2005) and Valeur (2007).
73. Valeur (2007).
74. Lyberg (1984).
75. Gårdlund (1951).
76. Browaldh was also appointed a board member of MoDo.
77. Frans Kempe's daughter.
78. Savalainen and Zacco-Broberg (1985).
79. Iggesund (1985).
80. Savalainen and Zacco-Broberg (1985).
81. Investor (1991).
82. Glete (1994) and Sjögren (2005).
83. Sjögren (2005).
84. Olsson (2000) and Sjögren (2005).
85. Glete (1994).
86. Savalainen and Zacco-Broberg (1985).
87. Rydberg (1990).
88. Ibid.
89. Sjögren (2005).
90. Valeur (2000).
91. Trotzig (1963).
92. Valeur (2000).
93. Pöyry and Ryti (1979).
94. Taken together the world's third biggest exporter of pulp.
95. Eventually the new kinds of fibre proved to be competitive and almost wiped out sulphite based on spruce from the market.
96. Sjögren (2005).
97. Gårdlund (1986).
98. Sjögren (2005).
99. Rydberg (1990).
100. Sjögren (2005).
101. Rydberg (1990).
102. Valeur (2007).

6. From Domänverket to Sveaskog: transformations and crises

6.1 THE FOUNDING OF ASSI

Domänverket's[1] forest-based industries were transferred in 1941 to a new state company named Statens Skogsindustri (ASSI). The main reason for that change was that Domänverket hosted two different kinds of operations, both of which would presumably benefit from a separation. One part of its operations, which essentially involved running (older) sawmills in several Swedish regions, was carried out in commercial (i.e. competitive) arenas. These units were moved to ASSI, which also got Domänverket's sulphate plant Karlsborg (located in northernmost Sweden close to Kalix). Most of the plants/machines within ASSI needed investments to become modern and competitive. Domänverket's other core activity – forestry – stayed where it was. Despite the 'carving up' of the commercial units and the formation of ASSI, the Swedish Forest Agency (Skogsstyrelsen) was to supervise also the new 'autonomous' joint-stock company.

ASSI's focus on sawn wood indicated that the addition of fibre production could be a fitting complement. Following that path, ASSI built two board factories (Piteå and Skinnskatteberg) in the late 1940s, and over the subsequent years it became Sweden's largest board producer. By 1950, the capacity of Karlsborg's pulp production had doubled, and a kraft paper mill was established there, which was supposed to reduce the company's dependence on the volatile pulp market. However, that expectation was soon dashed, as only a rather small share of the pulp was converted to kraft paper – a production that turned out to be unprofitable mainly due to intense competition, a situation that lasted the whole decade.[2]

In 1957, ASSI became an autonomous company subordinated to the Ministry of Trade.[3] By that time, the company had become so large that the government decided that it should be run wholly separate from Domänverket. Such clear autonomy would also make it easier for the state to exert financial control and balance its investments in ASSI against the ones in the other state-controlled organizations. Still, however, the two units' operative flows continued to be linked; ASSI (still) took more than 90 per cent of its timber from Domänverket, and a ten-year sourcing arrangement was agreed upon. There were also discussions about building a sulphate plant and a paper mill at Piteå in the northernmost part of Sweden close to the existing investments at Lövholmen. A substantial expansion at Karlsborg was considered, too.

One year later, the county administrative board in the northernmost part of Sweden informed the government that the region would like to see its forest-based industry expand. The triggers were an inventory of the regional forests that had revealed a large, unused (growth) surplus and high regional unemployment. At the same time, ASSI considered an expansion in the kraftliner segment, and Karlsborg was seen as the best location for such an effort, as it already housed a sulphate plant and a paper mill. But Domänverket did not have enough timber resources at its disposal in the Karlsborg area, so a new large liner unit placed there would face timber (i.e. transportation) costs that were too high.

However, there was a sufficient supply of timber suitable for pulp production near the Lövholmen sawmill. So in 1959 ASSI decided to build a new unit in that area destined to produce raw material for corrugated cardboard (sulphate pulp and kraftliner). The competitors (i.e. some of the larger privately owned companies) immediately complained and argued that the politicians had dictated that investment decision. They particularly disliked the localization of the new unit to Piteå, a town that already housed a kraftliner plant. One of the competitors, MoDo, even sent an official letter to the parliament, where it questioned the estimated size of the forest inventories that had guided the process. MoDo claimed that Karlsborg (Kalix) was a much better location, a place where ASSI's new investment also could benefit from the existing infrastructure (and the existing pulp and paper units). Another competitor, SCA, whose board already had decided to build a liner-producing unit at Munksund (Piteå), presented the government a counter proposition. SCA was willing to hand over all its forests in the district to Domänverket thereby making enough timber available close to Karlsborg for an expansion at that site. SCA expected to get a corresponding forest resource in return (one located close to its Munksund site). SCA also promised to build a large liner plant at Munksund.[4]

Despite the complaints and counterproposals, the government ultimately approved ASSI's investment in a new liner plant in Piteå. One important reason why ASSI's liner plant materialized was the position taken by its CEO Norlin. He had talked to a business colleague in the UK, who through close contacts with Reeds/Reedpack (a large producer of corrugated cardboard) was knowledgeable in the field. ASSI's new investment immediately triggered a race with SCA, which initiated a similar effort at Munksund to become first on the market and tie up customers. Paradoxically, SCA's investment in Munksund actually furthered ASSI's decision, as SCA's data and conclusions supplemented ASSI's superficial preliminary study (one page only).

ASSI started its new production in Piteå (Lövholmen) in 1962, and it became a big success ('the backbone of ASSI'). The reasons were partly a competent management, partly the installation of a second paper machine in 1972. The focus on paper with a white surface also contributed to the success,[5] as did the timing, which made it possible to ride on the extraordinarily good years 1973 and 1974. Another explanation for the success was the accelerating growth in the market for liner in Europe.

The large investments in Karlsborg (Kalix) and Lövholmen (Piteå) made it desirable to integrate forward to secure an outlet for the production of sacks and kraftliner. To refrain from such a move was considered to be too risky. So the new ASSI CEO, Rynell, bought Förenade Well from Ncb (a forest-farmers' co-operative; cf. below). He argued that a large producer of liner must have its own production of corrugated cardboard and also a sales organization for that product. He informed ASSI's board that on the US market 85 per cent of the liner companies were integrated ones. He also stressed that ASSI had the necessary management capacity for an expansion into corrugated cardboard, as the company could benefit from the extensive personal network that ASSI's Sales Manager Hamrefors had built both in his previous positions at Katrinefors as seller of fluting, and at ASSI as seller of liner.[6]

Late in the 1960s, ASSI started its expansion abroad by acquiring Flexer Sacks in the UK, and in 1970, ASSI became shareholder in the Swiss corrugated cardboard manufacturer Wellkarton (wholly owned as of 1976). At that time, Hamrefors became Head of ASSI Kraftliner and began to make that unit more market oriented. He also let everybody in the organization know that an effective large-scale production of few products (preferably one) was the best path forward, and that bleaching was not an option, as it would be impossible to get the necessary environmental permits. Later ASSI divided its kraft businesses into two units. That split was motivated by differing end uses. The liner managers could then focus on its particular markets[7] and, accordingly, change the distribution system.[8] At the beginning of the 1970s, ASSI had become an international company running sawmills and kraft businesses selling around 80 per cent of its production abroad (foremost in Western Europe).[9]

6.2 THE CREATION OF NCB

6.2.1 Rapid Growth

Two years after the establishment of ASSI, a second big Swedish forest-based cooperative was formed, namely Norrlands Skogsägares Cellulosa AB (Ncb). That establishment was inspired by a similar construct in southern Sweden established already in the late 1930s: Sydöstra Sveriges Skogsägareföreningars Förbund. It was founded in 1938 and followed in 1952 by Skogsägarnas Cellulosa AB (SCB), a farmer-owned pulp-producing unit. The southern farmers' association expanded and in 1964 it became Södra Sveriges Skogsägares Förbund (popularly known as 'Södra'[10]). That construct aroused interest among the forest farmers in the northern regions, and many of them bought shares in SCB. Voices were simultaneously raised that a farmer-controlled pulp production unit ought to be created in northern Sweden, too, but the national farmers' association gave priority to the southern one, because of the great timber surplus that existed in that part of the country.

For some time, the founders of Södra had considered acquiring Munksjö paper mill, but as that would not significantly increase the total consumption of timber in the region, that path was abandoned. Instead, they decided to invest in a new pulp plant at Mönsterås.[11] In the middle of the 1950s, the forest farmers also declared its interest in building another pulp plant in the region, this time at Mörrum,[12] which would double SCB's production capacity. At that point it became apparent to most actors that Södra's representatives on the SCB board were acting to take full control and squeeze out their colleagues from the north. Gradually, the tension between 'southern' and 'northern' forest farmers grew, and the 'northerners' decided to go their own way and establish their own production units. The poor chemistry between the two leading actors in the forest-farmers' sphere, Edström and Hedlund, also contributed to the split of the farmers' efforts.[13]

The founders (and owners) of Ncb were the regional associations of forest owners in the northern half of Sweden together with two national farmers' associations (LRF and Lantbruksförbundet). The *primus motor* in the process was the incoming leader of the organization, Hedlund (head of the political party Bondeförbundet [The Farmer's Party], which for many years had co-operated with the Social Democratic government). Like in the Södra case, 'Riksförbundet Landsbygdens Folk' (RLF) and 'Lantbruksförbundet'[14] together with all forest-owners' associations were invited to buy shares, but no associations south of mid-Sweden decided to participate. Instead, a swap of SCB shares between the northern and southern forest owners made the founding of Ncb easier, since the northerners held a substantial portion[15] of the SCB stock.

However, Ncb was not easy to organize, as there were rather strong tensions between several of the northern forest-owners' associations. Still, in 1958 a committee concluded that it would be advantageous for the forest farmers to form their own business corporation (i.e. Ncb). That conclusion was also supported by the findings of new research that indicated a substantial timber surplus (also) in the north, something that had squeezed the timber market prices, making the farmers' situation difficult. The creation of Ncb was also a deliberate attempt to participate in – and speed up – the structural rationalization of the forest-based industry in northern Sweden. As Hedlund saw it, that region contained too many small units, most of them incapable of handling the changing business conditions.

The basic idea behind Ncb was to further the interests of its owners (ultimately the forest farmers) by maximizing the selling price of their timber. It was a tool for breaking up the current unfavourable monopsony situation, which involved a weak market position for the sellers (the farmers) and a strong one for the buyers (buying cartels). Ncb's strategy differed from that of SCB in that it intended to achieve its purpose through acquisitions rather than through greenfield investments. But like SCB, Ncb wanted to integrate forward and broaden its output to retain the profit that often materialized in the later stages of the value chain.[16]

As noted above, RLF, Lantbruksförbundet and nine forest-owning associations in northern Sweden constituted Ncb. Hedlund was elected Chair in 1959 and the other Ncb directors were recruited from the founding associations' boards. Two years later, Hedlund was appointed CEO. Regardless of his formal position Hedlund was in charge of the company at all times. A central office was established in Kramfors (in Ådalen), but the HQ was actually located in Hedlund's own apartment in Stockholm. He ran the operations in a very hands-on manner and even intervened in many (minor) managerial issues. Several Ncb managers regarded that degree of centralization as absurd.[17]

Ncb started its operations by trying to find a suitable location for a new pulp plant. However, Hedlund's basic idea was that the company instead should acquire and modernize production units already running, as he thought that northern Sweden needed fewer plants.[18] He also wanted to make a quick acquisition so that it would be likely that Ncb could lead a restructuring process, and simultaneously compete with SCA for the 'hegemony' in the region. Such a purchase would also place him on an equal footing with his rival in the south, Södra's Edström. The fact that many family-controlled firms in the region were looking for new owners simplified his efforts. These firms had concluded that it was close to impossible for them to meet the demands that the technical development had put on the operative scales, financial resources and investments in R&D.

However, the competitors did not appreciate Ncb's entry on the northern scene. The owners of the larger corporations in the region even made an informal agreement to keep Ncb out. Some of them also regarded themselves as the most capable actors when it came to carrying out the necessary structural rationalizations, and some of them even regarded

Ncb's entrance as a threat to their timber sourcing. At that time, Sandviken (unbleached sulphate pulp) was the only plant for sale in the region that matched Hedlund's acquisition criteria. Therefore, when its owner Versteegh broke the informal pact and sold that plant in 1961, several other companies followed suit and sold some of their units to Ncb – particularly those that were dependent on timber from the forest-owning farmers. Unlike Versteegh, these other family-controlled firms handed over their units confident that Hedlund and Ncb would be a responsible owner. Versteegh, however, had at an early stage expressed his scepticism that a unit (like Ncb) that based its existence on promoting the price of its own raw material could survive in the long run.[19]

Versteegh was a controversial business leader who disliked the increasing concentration of the forest-based industry in northern Sweden. Therefore, he had demonstratively refused to engage in the timber-buying cartel that many of the other companies had established. Nevertheless, his relationship with Hedlund, a product of a long-term timber contract between him and Ådalarnas Skogsägareförening (where Hedlund was previously CEO), was good. That 'history' facilitated Hedlund's contact with Versteegh and their discussions about Sandviken's future. Actually, Hedlund had held informal discussions with Versteegh regarding all Graningeverken's plants over a rather long period. Because Versteegh had not invested much in Sandviken (he prioritized his power plants), the plant that Ncb bought for a relatively high price was not in very good shape. That premium was the price Hedlund (who led the negotiations) had to accept to get Ncb's acquisition process running, but – at the same time – it established high expectations among potential sellers and a corresponding price standard for future transactions (with an impact on the other buying opportunities that soon turned up). Hedlund had high-flying ideas regarding Sandviken. He immediately declared that Ncb intended to more than double Sandviken's production capacity. That statement prompted SCA to close down its Nensjö unit, as Ncb's planned investment ruined the opportunities to expand that site.[20]

At the same time, MoDo let Hedlund know that it considered selling Hörnefors (sulphite plant and fine paper mill) to get resources to expand its sulphate production at Husum. The sale was also supposed to strengthen MoDo's links to the forest-owners' associations, which would facilitate its sourcing of timber. MoDo Chair Carl Kempe Sr and Ncb's CEO Hedlund soon became friends, so it came as no surprise when Ncb acquired Hörnefors in 1961. Södra's leader (and Hedlund's rival) Edström, however, expressed a severe critique: 'It is not possible for the forest-owners' associations to carry out the industrialization of the private forest sector through taking care of misplaced units that structurally are doomed to failure.' Regarding Hörnefors, his prediction was right. In spite of large investments, it never reached an acceptable profit level.[21]

Rutger Martin-Löf played an important role in most of Ncb's acquisitions at that time. He was not just a board member of Ncb (1961–65; nominated by Hedlund); he was also head of Södra's pulp unit Mönsterås, and also (informally) Hedlund's chief adviser. Martin-Löf was later criticized for his evaluations of the target plants, judgements that were supposed to have contributed to the high prices paid. However, the prices Ncb actually paid were far above his recommendations. Hedlund claimed that it was necessary to pay those prices to get 'an admission ticket to the forest-based industry'.[22]

Ncb bought two additional family-owned companies in 1963–64, namely Hissmofors and Forss. Both SCA and Wifstavarf also tried to acquire Hissmofors, but Ncb won the contest by promising not to close down its sulphite plant. Hissmofors was one of the very few sulphite plants in the region that survived both the crisis in the early 1920s and the Great Depression. Because it was well located in the heart of huge forest resources, it would have been possible to expand the plant into a larger integrated pulp and paper unit, but neither the family nor ultimately Ncb was willing to take that risk. In its own investigations, SCA noted that the best place for processing the regional timber was at Hissmofors. However, SCA also had a unit (newsprint) at the coast that could use that raw material, and their analysis indicated that it was better to expand that unit than to invest at Hissmofors. SCA's fear was that somebody else would take control of Hissmofors, make it a timber-consuming unit, and thus create a sourcing problem for the company's coastal unit. To SCA, Ncb was the optimal buyer, since it was heavily indebted and not financially capable of expanding at Hissmofors.[23]

The purchase of Forss came about under quite different circumstances. The company faced both operative and financial problems: operationally, because Finland had established tough restrictions for its timber export, making the sourcing of the Köpmanholmen plant difficult, and financially, because the company was burdened by high interest payments. However, the initiative to sell did not come from the controlling family (Hedström) but from another of the larger shareholders, ship-owner Högberg, who played a leading role on Köpmanholmen's board. Högberg himself needed capital, so he was interested in selling. He contacted Ncb, as he was aware of Hedlund's great ambition to buy plants in the region. He offered the whole company confident that Ncb's ownership (also) would secure Köpmanholmen's timber sourcing. The sale was facilitated by succession problems in the Hedström family, with a CEO pursuing interests other than running the company.[24]

For Ncb, the acquisition of Dynäs in 1966 (sawmills, a sulphate plant and a unit for glazed kraft paper) was of particular importance. Already in 1956 the Ekman family that owned Dynäs had decided to invest in sack production to get a share of that rapidly growing market. That effort, however, brought financial strain to the company, as the coming decade's poor sack market made a profit-based financing insufficient. As a result, some of the necessary investments were not undertaken. Given that situation, the family concluded that Dynäs needed a financially more capable owner, and in 1965 the family started to negotiate with Ncb (i.e. Hedlund) and somewhat later also with SCA (CEO Mossberg). In May 1966, Dynäs Chair Mannerfelt made those discussions publicly known, and in a communiqué he stressed the need for co-ordination of the investments in the region (Ådalen). Ncb won the contest, to a large extent due to its ownership form, which was seen as a guarantor for the industrial development in the region. SCA was rejected, as its interest was to get hold of Dynäs's forests and use them at other plants. However, before the transaction was made, the forests and the power plant were moved to Svanö, a company that the Ekman family kept. Svanö's sulphite plant was moved to Dynäs, and both the family and Ncb agreed that it ought to be closed down. In that situation, SCA decided to halt expansion at Kramfors (paper mill), shut its sulphate plant and leave the Ådalen region.[25]

Dynäs was then transformed into a modern sack-producing unit, and rather soon it became Ncb's core business and one of the biggest sack producers in the world. Ncb also built a new machine there for the production of fluting. Those two investments indicated that most of Ncb's future activities would be in and around Dynäs. Consequently, that unit became one of the possible locations for a new journal paper machine, which should take up the remaining timber surplus in the region. However, the ubiquitous consultant firm Jakko Pöyry instead suggested that it should be located in Harg. To test the reaction among competitors, the idea was made public. Those reactions and the fact that Ncb still lacked a unit in the southern part of the region led to the beginning of discussions between Ncb and Korsnäs (controlled by Hugo Stenbeck). Hedlund was interested in buying a substantial holding in Korsnäs, but in the end (1968) Stenbeck instead offered Ncb the purchase of a sulphite plant, Vallvik.[26]

Ncb's plan was to make Vallvik one of the biggest journal paper producers in Europe. However, Jakko Pöyry informed Hedlund that journal paper required equal portions of sulphate pulp and mechanical wood pulp, and for cost reasons both had to be produced near the paper mill. Therefore, Ncb decided that the company's sulphite machine should be converted to a sulphate one. That decision was also facilitated by a decree from an environmental court that prohibited Ncb from running the plant longer than five years without extensive environmental investments, measures that were out of the question.[27]

In the late 1960s, Ncb had become one of the biggest pulp producers in Sweden, behind only MoDo and SCA. Ncb based its operations primarily on timber that was made available through the forest-owners' associations in the northern part of Sweden. Eventually the fast-growing Ncb incurred financial problems, and its special kind of shareholders did not simplify the situation. The ultimate ones, the private forest owners, were responsible for providing Ncb with the necessary capital, and most of them had never thought about that 'duty'. The banks, too, created difficulties for Ncb, as they first and foremost were loyal to their 'friends', colleagues and sphere allies – that is to say, to Ncb's competitors. So, in the end, the acquisition of Vallvik made Ncb's financial standing even more strained – later even precarious.[28]

In the early 1970s, Hedlund searched for somebody who could succeed him as CEO. Eventually, Westerlund was appointed. Hedlund knew his 'successor' well, as he had been his assistant at Ådalarnas Skogsägareförening. However, Hedlund kept most of his power, and his self-centred leadership style made Westerlund's CEO situation complicated. Hedlund had never been a friend of correct procedures, so as Chair he continued to act informally, handling most issues in unruly 'invisible' processes, taking the right to talk to anybody anytime about anything. Thus, he often ignored the organizational hierarchy and its formal decision-making procedures.[29]

Basically, the first half of the 1970s was a good period for the pulp industry, something that furthered Ncb's expansion. However, there was a certain market decline in 1971–72, so the pulp stocks increased, which made the business opportunities more uncertain. That ambiguity created passivity, causing Ncb to postpone its planned paper mill investment at Vallvik. Out of that situation also emerged the idea that a merger with ASSI could be advantageous for both parties. Contrary to those negative speculations and the growing passivity, 1973 and 1974 turned out to be true 'boom years' with almost fantasy prices on pulp and exceptional profits for many of the involved companies. Paradoxically, however, it was that success that also became the basis for Ncb's dramatic decline, as the company did not choose to consolidate. Instead, it continued its aggressive acquisition strategy both by integrating forward and by differentiating its products. Some of these acquisitions were first and foremost made for the benefit of different forest-owner groups without being particularly attractive from Ncb's perspective (Hedlund carried out these purchases without enthusiasm).[30] Most forest owners wanted Ncb to be strong in their own district, and in the exceptional boom times many of them had their way.[31]

Ncb concentrated its investments on areas that represented a further processing of its timber and pulp, and preferably they were made in a way that strengthened the company's positions on export markets. To guarantee part of Dynäs's output of sack paper, a Belgian sack producer (Saccalain) was acquired, and that company became an important platform for Ncb's further development in Europe. Since Hedlund wanted Ncb to secure its pulp sales by getting closer to the (end) customer, Ncb acquired the tissue producer Edet from Dutch Akzo in 1976. At the time, Edet controlled 35 per cent of the Swedish tissue market and had production units in four countries (Denmark, France, Holland and Sweden).[32]

6.2.2 A Severe Crisis

The good times disappeared already in 1976. Several units like the newly acquired Elementhus[33] and subsidiaries like Hannover Papier[34] made losses, and soon things got even worse and Ncb was in the red. The whole Swedish forest-based industry moved into a severe crisis, and undercapitalized companies like Ncb faced great difficulties. Ncb's solidity (percentage share of equity out of total capital) went down to 11 per cent in a situation in which the company lacked a main bank with an interest in assisting the company during its crisis. The CEO of PK-Banken (Danielsson) – the state-owned bank that had managed Ncb's international financial consortium – was reluctant to let the bank continue to shoulder the leading role.[35]

At that time, most forecasters expected that the forest-based industry would become the next crisis industry, following in the footsteps of steel and shipping. However, the post-devaluation situation favoured those Swedish companies that had invested in the further processing of the timber and pulp, as their dependence on the raw material prices had decreased. Ncb's crisis gradually deepened between 1975 and 1977, as personnel costs rose by about 70 per cent due to high inflation expectations. Like most competitors, Ncb had met the declining pulp demand by building stock. The surplus of pulp on the market pushed prices significantly downwards (even below the variable production costs),[36] to a 'disastrous' level, as most buyers learned about the large stocks and therefore waited for the inevitable pulp sale.[37]

Ncb, which had pulp as one of its core businesses, showed huge losses during the second half of 1977. It was not merely the pulp price collapse, however, that hurt (particularly) Ncb – the company also suffered from its low equity (≈ 1% [!]). The residual paid-in capital (≈ 5%) was in the form of 'industrial loans' from the shareholders. As the loans were issued in the form of convertibles, they could be counted as equity (although they were associated with interest payments). Many of Ncb's competitors could parry their losses with changes in the bookings of property (forests and power plants) or through support from their house banks. Neither of those paths was available to Ncb. Still, like the other companies it got support from the Swedish pulp trade association to finance the overstocking.[38]

The squeezed market situation for pulp triggered certain structural changes in the industry. These hit Ncb significantly, since the company recently had acquired several older units. One proposed way out was that Dynäs should expand and take over forests and personnel from Sandviken, which then could be closed. However, at that time (September 1977), when everybody knew that Ncb was in a severe crisis, Hedlund initiated investigations regarding the establishment of a new journal paper mill in Ådalen.

In November, Ncb got the authorities' permission to expand at Dynäs, which made a closing of Sandviken possible. However, that clearance was only valid for 'brown paper', so Hedlund informed the government that the market for (brown) sack paper had stagnated (due to the growth of plastic sacks), so production of journal paper had become a much better alternative.[39] He also reported to the Minister of Industry (Åsling, like Hedlund from the Centre Party [the renamed Farmer's Party]) that Ncb's situation was precarious. Every time Hedlund and Åsling met, the Ncb situation had worsened, so Hedlund and his team constructed a programme for a catastrophe. It included the closing down of several pulp units (Hissmofors, Sandviken and Hörnefors) and the sawmill at Dynäs, plus a reduction of the production at Elementhus.[40]

In February 1978, two auditors concluded that if certain steps were not immediately taken, Ncb would have to go into liquidation. So the first part of Hedlund's catastrophe plan was executed, namely the closing down of Hissmofors and Sandviken. Still, the losses exceeded equity on a yearly basis, so an extraordinary general meeting (EGM) was summoned, and at that meeting the financial year was prolonged to 18 months to earn time. However, that respite did not solve the problem – far from it. The losses continued to grow rapidly, and at the end of the period they were expected to reach half a billion Swedish crowns.[41] The situation was terrible, as a bankruptcy would hit the shareholding forest farmers (i.e. their associations) brutally. The Conservative Party actually recommended such a 'solution', but the other parties in the government instead worked for state support (like the Minister of Industry, Prime Minister Fälldin represented the Centre Party). The intense discussions in the government showed that there was an ideological split between, on the one hand, the Centre Party, and, on the other hand, the Conservative and Liberal parties regarding the benefits of co-operative and federative organizations. Soon, the government presented the parliament a bill suggesting that Ncb should receive a large loan with repayment under specific conditions.

Director Lyfors, who had been recruited to join Ncb's board by Hedlund, severely criticized the way the company had been run, claiming that he had treated Ncb almost as a 'personal business', and advised Hedlund to resign as soon as possible. However, before he took that decisive step, Hedlund wanted to attend some of the forest-farmers' associations' annual general meetings (AGMs) to listen to opinions and defend himself against the 'exaggerated and groundless' critique. When that strategy failed, Hedlund had to leave, which he did in 1979.[42]

In search of a replacement, the Minister of Industry (Åsling) asked the legendary Swedish industrial leader Marcus Wallenberg Sr if he was aware of any suitable candidates. Wallenberg returned with one name, Engman, who was at the time the head of Stora Kopparberg's sawmills.[43] When Engman started as Ncb's CEO in 1978, the losses were substantial. To lessen the financial strain and build a more stable future, Ncb embarked on a strategy that included combining its Fors unit with MoDo's plants around Alfredshem, inviting Stora Kopparberg to become a partner in Vallvik, and building a paper mill at Dynäs together with SCA.[44]

The same year Stora Kopparberg examined whether it could establish journal paper production close to its Sandarne site. When investigators discovered that a joint venture with Ncb in Vallvik would likely be both cheaper and in the long run more profitable, the Sandarne project was cancelled and a discussion with Ncb was initiated instead. Stora Kopparberg and Ncb looked into the possibility of establishing a new unit together with Papyrus, where the two 'Wallenberg companies' would take 70 per cent of the stock and Ncb 30 per cent. That unit would then buy Vallvik and build a light weight coated (LWC) paper mill at that site, all in accordance with Hedlund's visionary plan from 1968. Stora Kopparberg also opened discussions with Graningeverken with the intention to build a journal paper plant at the Utansjö site. There were also several other expansion ideas in the Swedish forest-based industry at that time; for example, there were talks between Ncb and SCA regarding a joint journal paper plant somewhere in the region (see below).

However, when Stora Kopparberg declared that there was an agreement with Graningeverken to build the Utansjö plant, all other similar projects in the region were stopped. Stora Kopparberg's CEO declared that their idea to establish a joint venture with Ncb at Vallvik was stone dead ('a messier partner than Ncb could not be found').

The new liberal minority government's handling of Ncb's crisis was heavily criticized by the previous government's Minister of Industry (Åsling). The company's top executives (e.g. Chair Lindqvist, Group CEO Engman and Deputy Group CEO Linde) presented a proposal that might have saved Ncb. The current Minister of Industry (Huss) intervened and advocated a sale of Ncb's best units. His idea was to sell Vallvik to Stora Kopparberg and Väja-Dynäs to SCA. In the latter case, one idea was to establish a new company in which Ncb would put Väja-Dynäs, SCA Östrand-Wifstavarf and the state fresh capital. The new unit would then build a LWC paper plant. That proposal was interesting for SCA, as the company then would return to Ådalen and be assisted by the state in its large investment at Östrand-Wifstavarf. However, at that time, Stora Kopparberg and Graningeverken's idea to build a plant at Utansjö became known, and that made SCA less interested in making a joint investment with Ncb. Ultimately, the political opposition to selling off Ncb's best units put an end to these discussions, and the state was compelled to take over all of Ncb.[45]

Hedström, the Director General (DG) of the Swedish Forest Agency[46] was appointed the state's negotiator in the process to save Ncb. The company had several issues that had to be resolved: lack of timber resources, weak points in its current restructuring plan (the board and the owners seemed to be reluctant to put it into practice) and discord among some of the owners. However, most important was that Ncb once again was facing bankruptcy, as the associations of the private forest owners had rejected CEO Rydbo's strategic plan. They were unwilling to shut down the pulp plants at Hörnefors and Köpmanholmen, and they also rejected the suggested write-downs of plants and subsidiaries. Moreover, they opposed the idea to co-operate with MoDo in the fine paper business, and, last but not least, they were unwilling to invest the necessary SEK 1 billion in the company.

It was associations of forest owners that had established Ncb, and they ran it as a core activity. As such, Hedström was not convinced that the state ought to take full control. Instead, he suggested that both the state and the forest-owners' associations should become shareholders in a reconstructed Ncb.[47] Hence, in May 1979, the state put in SEK 600 million and wrote off the recent loan (SEK 400 million). The forest-owners' associations contributed SEK 79 million. When all transactions were completed, the state controlled around 74 per cent of Ncb's votes. That new ownership situation made Ncb an organization without forest resources, as the forest farmers no longer controlled it. Moreover, soon thereafter, SCA made a sourcing agreement with Svanö, a company that for long had delivered timber to Ncb (Dynäs). Taken together, those 'timber losses' made it almost impossible to scale up any of Ncb's units to a profitable size.[48]

Two units constituted the basis for Ncb's future operations: Dynäs (unbleached sulphate pulp, further processed to kraft paper and sack paper) and Vallvik (bleached sulphite pulp; however, its production capacity was rather small, and its timber sourcing problematic[49]). Dynäs brown paper was used for sack production in France, Germany and the UK. The unit was regarded as an efficient one, and many competitors were expected to give up (and so they did). So, Ncb gradually increased its market share in several sack segments and successfully launched a 'super strong' sack paper on the market (1985). Vallvik's pulp was converted in Germany to wood-free coated paper. In both cases, the customers were rather small companies. By mid-1982 all of Ncb's pulp and paper mills and other units except Dynäs and Vallvik were either sold or shut down.[50]

6.3 THE TRANSFORMATION OF DOMÄNVERKET

In the 1960s, there was debate regarding the efficiency of the (Swedish) state's governance of its companies. Although Domänverket was far from the centre of that discussion, it became a target for some of that critique. In particular, pressure was put on rationalizations, and several reports on that topic saw the light of day. All these activities ended in a government proposal on 'how to make Domänverket more efficient, and how to co-ordinate the state-owned forest companies'. The general idea was that Domänverket ought to work like any joint-stock company and that its goal should be 'strictly economic'. As a consequence, the parliament decided in 1968 to make it possible for Domänverket to establish a joint-stock subsidiary to be able to (also) run businesses outside the forest-based sector.[51]

One of the leading actors behind the 'new Domänverket' was Rydbo, who also became its DG in 1970. At that time, individuals with a rather 'conservative' action rationale and limited experience from business environments populated Domänverket. A kind of 'forester management' was executed that produced an economically rather inefficient organization.[52]

In 1972, Rydbo presented his analysis of Domänverket's situation in a special report intended for the politicians. It indicated a pending crisis, if corrective actions were not taken in time. The problems that Rydbo stressed were: poor economic result, surplus of white-collar employees, shrinking business volumes (due to binding reductions of timber cutting) and low price expectations on the main product (timber/wood). The report also considered whether it was possible to use the existing personnel for new activities, and whether the fact that Domänverket managed around 20 per cent[53] of all forest ground in the country could be used as a platform for expansion. Rydbo recommended adding new businesses, including forestry on other owners' property, consultancy and machine service, as the company's best strategy.[54] However, such expansion and diversification were obstructed by Domänverket's legal construction. A company group with a limited company as parent is allowed to move capital from one subsidiary to another, but Domänverket's statutes made that kind of re-allocation practically impossible. However, Domänverket avoided that hindrance in 1975 by establishing a wholly owned subsidiary (Domänföretagen), which became the holding company for about 20 firms.

At the end of the decade, about 50 per cent of Domänverket's timber supplied the sawmill industry in Sweden; particularly the smaller privately owned ones. Domänverket also used some of its timber for its own processing activities, although as much as one third of the timber was bought by ASSI. Domänverket's leading actors claimed that in the future it would be difficult for the Swedish sawmill industry to use price as a competitive weapon. The manufacturing capacity far exceeded the possible timber supply, so acquiring substantial profits from huge volume increases was regarded as an almost impossible task. Instead, the special (and high) quality of a large part of the Swedish forests ought to determine the companies' product repertoire, although that would represent a difficult move, as the opportunities – the potential uses for quality trees – were almost unlimited. Such a wide-ranging product span had to be reduced to a manageable level. Thus, for each company it became crucial to develop a customized product repertoire, which in turn required a distribution system of a kind that Domänverket (among others) lacked. Traditionally, sawn woodwork had been distributed through agents and wholesalers, but that system was only effective for a standard retail assortment.

6.4 ASSI BECOMES PART OF STATSFÖRETAG

6.4.1 A Period of Expansion

Since its foundation in 1942, ASSI had expanded significantly, and its focus on sawed timber was gone. At the end of the 1960s, its biggest businesses were pulp and brown paper products. ASSI's organizational situation changed radically in 1970, when a state-controlled holding company was founded (Statsföretag). It took most of the state-owned companies, ASSI included, under its umbrella. At that time, the government had the ambition to expand the state-owned business sector in Sweden, and that effort also involved ASSI.

Statsföretag's CEO Sköld[55] contacted one of his friends, Bahrke, who currently worked at Uddcomb,[56] and appointed him CEO at ASSI. Bahrke was given a rather free hand and thought that he could work at ASSI the way he had worked previously in the private sector – that is to say, by applying a rather strict business rationale. Another reason for that approach was simply that he lacked experience working in a governmental environment. That background had provided Bahrke with certain preconceptions. For example, he believed that in a state-owned company like ASSI, it would be difficult to carry out rationalizations and structural changes. He also thought that the state's regional policy 'protected' the employment level in northernmost Sweden where many ASSI sites were located, thus making changes even more difficult. So Bahrke recognized that there was an implicit imperative linked to his appointment – he was not permitted to lower the number of employees.[57]

Bahrke soon learned that many issues were 'political', so he had to find out how that could affect his plans for ASSI. The government's regional policy favoured ASSI because of its location in the northern parts of Sweden, so it was difficult for its management to get clearance for larger investments abroad. Furthermore, the unions used ASSI and most other companies in Statsföretag as 'icebreakers' for certain demands, hoping that the outcome won with the state-owned companies would spread to the private companies in Sweden. Bahrke also soon learned that the state-owned group sometimes was used as a tool for politicians who wanted to show their voters various initiatives or 'reforms'. Added to all that, Bahrke found the company's decision-making structure very complicated, as there were several actor levels 'above' ASSI's board, meaning that he was answerable not only to all agencies that were part of or linked to the parent company Statsföretag but also to the various arenas that were linked to the Ministry of Industry. Bahrke also noted that Statsföretag was a most active 'parent' carrying out many investigations regarding its subsidiaries (including ASSI), some of them even addressing day-to-day operations.[58] Still, several actors claimed that CEO Bahrke's position was strong.

Bahrke declared that basically it was the employees that determined a company's chances of becoming successful in the forest-based industry, with the quality of the managers and the organization of human resources being key elements. He backed that statement by claiming that the limited number of machine producers that existed around the world offered most corporations similar technical solutions.[59] He acted on that firm belief in people as the decisive factor and reorganized ASSI's operations into divisions. One of the new units (the paper division) contained Karlsborg and Lövholmen (i.e. sack paper, sacks and kraft paper). That division had its production units located in the most northerly part of Sweden, while its sales were run from Stockholm. Initially, CEO Bahrke also took the position as head of the paper division and appointed Hamrefors as Head of Sales. However, in practice, ASSI's new organization turned out to be quite complicated, as the surroundings of the paper division contained a rather mixed timber composition, which made room also for sawmills, board manufacturing and sulphate production.[60]

In 1974, ASSI began responding to the state's implicit expectation and expanded its operations. Together with Domänverket it bought Örebro Pappersbruk and incorporated its industries (Domänverket got the forests). The enlarged ASSI made a more rational processing of the timber possible, as it could utilize the qualities of the surrounding forests better (they contained various kinds and sizes of trees suitable for many different purposes). Örebro Pappersbruk housed forest resources, unbleached pulp production and (small) kraft paper machines. Bahrke saw the purchase of Örebro Pappersbruk as an addition of crucial resources that made most pieces fall into place. The investment in chipboard production at Laxå was also made to better utilize the local timber variety. At that time, Örebro Pappersbruk was doing rather well. However, as Bahrke noted, most things worked because the circumstances were unusually favourable during that period (1972–74).[61]

6.4.2 A Crisis

Things changed dramatically for ASSI in 1975 when a severe crisis hit the forest-based industry in Sweden and several other countries. According to CEO Bahrke, the situation was worst for those industries that, like ASSI, had almost no forest resources of their own. ASSI and Ncb were the two Swedish companies whose timber sourcing lay in the hands of others (i.e. Domänverket and the forest-owners' associations). Thus ASSI and Ncb were hit harder than most of the others because product market prices fell drastically, at the same time as the raw material prices stood still. ASSI's situation was perhaps worst of all, since most of its operations were timber intensive (sawed wood products, building material, fibreboard and board). That disadvantage had been exacerbated when

Statsföretag was formed and ASSI had become its harbour for building material firms (most competitors did not engage very much in that kind of business). Added to all that, ASSI had in their accounts large loans taken on the international capital market, which had been easy to get because of the company's solid owner (the Swedish state). However, due to the falling value of the crown, the loans had become a tough burden.[62]

The circumstance that was the basis of most of ASSI's problems in 1975, however, was probably the propitious conditions that prevailed in 1974. That rapid upside paved the way for a sharp downturn. Everything went up in 1974 – costs (raw material and wages), volumes, prices, productivity, profit, and so on – but in 1975 the only thing that continued to grow was the costs. Despite this, Statsföretag asked ASSI to send money for use in other firms in the group. Furthermore, ASSI had to subscribe for Navigator shares (a state-owned consultancy firm). At that time, ASSI also was invited to buy 25 per cent of Rottneros (pulp) and 20 per cent of Broby industries (pulp and fluting). However, the board, at that time composed of Nordlander (Chair), Sköld (Deputy Chair), Edström, Manne Johansson, Sven Johansson, Rydbo, Sjöberg, Strömbeck and Bahrke (plus union representatives), rejected both offerings.[63]

For ASSI, 1976 became even worse than 1975, and the company's losses were massive (while the North American producers made record profits). The whole Swedish forest-industry lowered its prices and took losses to keep market shares, but basically they were unsuccessful in their efforts. While ASSI's corrugated cardboard and sacks made a healthy profit and wood products and plastic-coated paper showed a modest surplus, all the other businesses (chipboard, kraft paper, kraftliner, cardboard and pulp) presented more or less substantial deficits. Since the Swiss company Wellcarton (ASSI owned 45%) made losses, too, and was almost ready for liquidation, ASSI decided to become its sole shareholder to get the power to sort things out.

ASSI's strategy included an expansion of its profitable businesses and a continuous effort to improve the economic result for its bleached sulphate pulp. The strategy also addressed ASSI's complete dependence on others for timber and pulpwood. In 1976, the board discussed several new investment projects despite the current overcapacity in Sweden, for example, a factory for corrugated cardboard at Billingsfors and a paper mill project in Tanzania. The Minister of Industry, Åsling, liked the Billingsfors project and agreed to provide both a considerable localization grant (≈ 35% of the building costs) and a big localization loan (≈ 65% of the total investment). Statsföretag was also supposed to provide capital. However, in summer 1977 the Billingfors project was stopped, although a plastic producing factory was built there two years later. Somewhat later ASSI also discussed the establishment of a joint sawmill together with Domänverket (named Såginvest), and a further processing of the timber used at Seskarö sawmill. Ultimately ASSI bought a Danish brown paper company in 1976 (Dansk Kraftemballage; corrugated cardboard and solid board packaging). All those activities – planned and actually undertaken – produced a need for new equity capital; Statsföretag entered and invested SEK 100 million in new shares.[64]

ASSI's situation was still tough in 1977. Lyberg (former CEO of MoDo and ASSI director 1978–82) claimed that it was the divided governance that slowly but surely had hurt ASSI's financial position. The Swedish government, the parliament and Statsföretag each promoted their own ideas, which put an unco-ordinated pressure on ASSI, and even affected its daily operations. As if that were not enough, ASSI's board, too, was divided, with one faction from within ASSI and one from Domänverket. The disruption increased when Domänverket's DG Rydbo gradually began to transform Domänverket into a kind of 'mini-ASSI' ('Domänföretagen'), a construct that foremost was criticized because of the incompetent management of its Italian operations. Several ASSI actors also claimed that Rydbo's board membership in ASSI made it more difficult to achieve a fair timber sourcing solution.[65]

Lyberg had become a member of ASSI's board in a dramatic recruitment process. An important premise for that 'drama' was that the parliament in the 1960s had decided that ASSI and Domänverket ought to have overlapping board memberships (although the rule did not specifically refer to the Chair position). The CEO of Statsföretag, Sköld, offered Lyberg the position as ASSI's Chair, and according to Sköld that agreement implied that he also would become Chair at Domänverket. The Minister of Industry had informally approved that appointment unaware that the Prime Minister already had promised both Chair positions to Country Governor Lemne (former head of the Swedish Central Bank). The Prime Minister's decision upset Sköld, as Statsföretag's board was the (formal) arena for such an appointment, and he insisted that his candidate Lyberg should get both Chair positions. In that tense situation, Lyberg told Sköld that he was willing to accept entering ASSI's board as an ordinary director, but Sköld made him Deputy Chair (which, in turn, irritated Domänverket's Deputy Chair Rydbo). Rather soon, however, Lemne and Lyberg asked the ministry if they could each hold one Chair position, as there was a vicious discussion going on between the two organizations regarding various structural matters.[66]

ASSI's board was a rather passive entity more dealing with control issues (economic monitoring) than with strategic matters. It was also a rather weak agency, as it seldom criticized management despite ASSI's poor performance over several years. Instead, it was Statsföretag's CEO Sköld that acted (sometimes outside the formal arenas). For example, it was Sköld that contracted Boston Consulting Group to analyse various parts of ASSI, an effort that initiated an extensive discussion about ASSI's future. Still, to make the really important things happen, the ultimate owner, the Ministry of Industry, had to be engaged (though that agency seldom initiated anything).[67]

In 1977, ASSI recruited Carlsson from Obbola (SCA), who soon would become the company's Deputy CEO (1978), later CEO (1983–93) and finally director (1993–2002). He had lots of experience from the forest-based industry, especially regarding packaging operations, which was one of SCA's core businesses. Carlsson noticed that at ASSI it was the plant managers that ran the company, although the central market department had some influence, and ASSI's CEO chaired the plants' boards. Carlsson also noted that Karlsborg's environmental permits were set to expire and that it would be costly to adhere to the new requirements. Moreover, he learned that the demand for Lövholmen's kraftliner was decreasing and that the purchase of Örebro Pappersbruk was not as fantastic a business idea as had formerly been imagined. It was rather a simple sack and cardboard plant containing old machines that produced standard products for industrial buyers. Frövifors was also a problematic unit with its production of unbleached sulphate pulp and its three old machines manufacturing brown sacks.[68] Board production was troublesome, too; one way to solve that problem was to concentrate that production at its Skinnskatteberg plant.[69]

In 1977, ASSI's strategy for improving the situation contained six ingredients:

rationalizations, structural improvements (the selling or closing of certain units), development of closer co-operation with Domänverket (a new merger investigation was launched in 1977), restrictive attitude towards (new) engagement in the processing industry (although large investments were made at Frövifors, Lövholmen [liner] and Karlsborg [to maintain employment]), economic consolidation (ASSI was undercapitalized) and – lastly – aggressive product development including forward integration through acquisitions (e.g. the purchase of Dolan packaging [corrugated] and several minor companies). Statsföretag also transferred four companies to ASSI that used woodware as raw material (kitchen equipment, furniture, windows and stairways). ASSI had to match that expansion with forceful divestments, so assets that were only loosely connected to the core businesses were sold, thus lessening the need for further loans. For example, Hylte Bruk (newsprint) and Gullspång Kraft (power plants) went to the Wallenberg sphere, and the holding in Navigator (consulting) went to Statsföretag.

During springtime 1977, ASSI considered an expansion at Karlsborg – an investment that was so big that it had to involve Statsföretag. It was also necessary to get permission from several authorities. The government also became involved in the decision-making process because of controversies regarding the timber mix.[70] Statsföretag's CEO Sköld hesitated, as he regarded Karlsborg as a 'unit hard to cure', but the Minister of Industry did not want to see a closure. That position made it imperative for the state to provide a substantial amount of fresh capital to the company.[71] Eventually all crucial matters were resolved, so that in late 1977 the board took the decision to invest at Karlsborg and Lövholmen. However, that choice made it necessary to postpone the investments at Frövifors and Örebro.[72]

Despite the financial strain, management favoured a further processing of the unbleached pulp at Frövifors. Carlsson's analysis had convinced him and Bahrke that ASSI's future lay in liquid packaging paper and boxes, that is to say, in a 'free-riding' on Tetra Pak's market expansion. The latter company was ASSI's obvious partner/customer, although there were competitors for that role: Korsnäs and Billerud. A disadvantage for ASSI was Frövifors's problems with pollution, but Carlsson's technical competence and professional network once again saved the situation for ASSI. He found a solution to that problem in Finland at Tampella, which produced white cardboard from unbleached pulp. Carlsson concluded that a similar process and output might be a suitable path for Frövifors.[73]

Carlsson discussed the new production idea with Hans Rausing (one of the most influential members of Tetra Pak's owner family), while Bahrke, who had met Rausing several times before, instead concentrated on the ownership issue. That was actually the big obstacle, as Tetra Pak preferred not to own units that manufactured input material (e.g. carton for liquid packaging). Despite this, Rausing became very enthusiastic about Bahrke's conviction that ASSI could deliver eco-friendly white cardboard for liquid packaging purposes and even expressed flexibility regarding the shareholding issue. It was instead his father, Ruben Rausing, who objected: 'The Swedish state would become a too influential partner.' Despite that setback, ASSI continued to follow the 'liquid packaging strategy', not least because the only realistic alternative to that path was to shut down Frövifors.[74]

ASSI's board was gradually recomposed over the period 1978–80, and included Lyberg (Chair), Bahrke (CEO), Lemne (County Governor), Nydahl (Deputy Chair J.S. Saba[75]),

Redefelt (Head of Accounting and Control, Statsföretag), Schotte (DG Domänverket) and Wahlström (CEO SSAB[76]). The last took a leading role and stressed that ASSI's financial situation had to improve substantially before anything else was done. As long as the figures were strained, he saw an absolute necessity to concentrate the company's operations (both geographically and in terms of product). Like several other actors, he claimed that ASSI had to have its own forests and that it therefore was essential for ASSI to merge with Domänverket. Wahlström also emphasized that ASSI's strength lay in basic industry, and not in the later processing stages. He supported a kraftliner production at Lövholmen and a move into the corrugated cardboard business. The key question for Wahlström was whether ASSI had the financial capacity to acquire companies, or had to look for partners (e.g. Billerud or Korsnäs).[77] Due to all his engagements, Wahlström could not always participate at the board meetings (and had not always done his 'homework'), and that created some professional frictions with the CEO. However, Wahlström felt that the CEO and the board co-operated well, and that the CEO's standing was strong.[78]

In 1979, the board still discussed converting the production at Frövifors to liquid paper board (LPB). Wahlström hesitated because that path was new to ASSI, and it would put even more strain on the company's financial situation. His hesitation was also based on the market risk associated with such an investment. The strong position held by the intended customer Tetra Pak on a market with few other buyers represented too dangerous a path. Wahlström also remarked that it was impossible to add a second machine at Frövifors (something that usually was profitable) and that SCA's coated liner at Munksund might become a strong competitor. These arguments were so convincing that the board discussed whether it could make the investment together with somebody else. Carlsson (Head of Pulp and Paper), however, rejected some of Wahlström's arguments and claimed that SCA's product did not meet Tetra Pak's requirements. He also stressed the merits of having a nearby sulphate plant: such a combination could provide a competitive advantage that kept similar investments away.[79]

The joint-investment talks with Korsnäs were problematic, as the Ministry saw its owner Stenbäck as a 'difficult person', who – like Ruben Rausing – disliked partnerships with the state. However, there were other private actors who regarded the disdain of state governance as a sign of prejudice (they had not experienced any particular differences in management quality).[80] In its talks with ASSI, Korsnäs argued in ways that would spare the company a competitor and Billerud's CEO Engman voiced a similar strategy, so Bahrke's discussions with those companies led nowhere.[81]

In the end, however, Bahrke learned that the Ministry supported the planned investment, meaning that ASSI could take a business risk that its balance sheet did not justify.[82] Therefore, after a thorough vetting, ASSI decided to make the investment at Frövifors (1979, SEK 750 million) and change its production from unbleached pulp to unbleached coated cardboard. Capital from both Statsföretag and foreign sources was used to finance the undertaking, and the solidity goal was set to 20 per cent. ASSI's initiative surprised its competitors, foremost because they had thought that ASSI's financial status made such an enterprise impossible.

Also in 1979 director Rydbo suggested exploring co-operation with Billerud-Uddeholm.[83] Bahrke rejected the idea, arguing that such a constellation would be too weak on the carton market. Billerud-Uddeholm had technical/geographical problems, as

Gruvön sourced a carton unit located 40 km away (Skoghall). Instead, Bahrke preferred co-operation with Swedish Iggesund or German Feldmühle.[84]

At that time, Bahrke learned that Rydin, Chair of SCA, considered ASSI's corrugated cardboard business to be very successful. In a phone call Rydin asked for some kind of explanation. Bahrke was of the opinion that SCA had bought bad firms cheaply with the idea of improving them and making them profitable, while ASSI had bought healthy firms with competent management teams at higher prices and allowed them to continue as long as their economic results were satisfactory. He believed that corrugated cardboard was a bulky product that had to be produced and delivered in a very narrow geographical zone, and that such sales required an intimate knowledge about each local marketplace.[85]

6.5 DOMÄNVERKET IN THE 1980s

6.5.1 Domänverket + ASSI?

Once again a closer association between Domänverket and ASSI was brought to the fore, this time because ASSI experienced heavy losses (1981). Domänverket understood that the state wanted to make its total engagement in the forest-related businesses more effective. Still, however, Domänverket claimed that it ought to continue as an autonomous unit because of its crucial role as a reliable supplier (also) to all the small, independent sawmills. It also stressed that its employees' interests had to be respected, and that ASSI first had to finish its on-going restructuring and rationalization efforts in order to reach a decent solidity.

Bahrke knew that Domänverket's employees disliked the idea of a merger, since that meant that some of their 'down-to-earth benefits' (e.g. hunting rights) were threatened. Moreover, after a merger, the only selling task that was left was deal-making with one large internal customer (i.e. ASSI), and that was less challenging than negotiating with several minor external buyers. From ASSI's perspective, however, the situation was different. Timber prices had been discussed for a long time with Domänverket, knowing that its competitors continuously expressed a willingness to pay a higher price (for marginal quantities). Bahrke also noticed that Domänverket had begun to integrate forward and to use its best timber for that effort.[86]

Domänverket's DG Rydbo concluded that a merger with ASSI was unwise, but that other forms of co-operation could be considered since ASSI lacked forests and 60 per cent of its timber sourcing came from long-term contracts with his company. Complications at the very top of the two organizations also obstructed a merger.[87] The chemistry between Rydbo and Statsföretag's CEO Sköld was rather poor due to emotional 'sediments' from previous struggles. Sköld also disliked the industrial expansion that Rydbo was implementing. However, since that industrialization process did not materialize as fast as Rydbo wanted and since, at the same time, support for that path weakened, Rydbo decided to accept his appointment as CEO of Ncb (replacing Engman, who left for Billerud).

6.5.2 A Radical Transformation

Since the early 1970s, Hedström was acquainted with many actors and conditions in the forest-based industry, so it was not surprising that he was invited in 1980 to become DG at Domänverket. Hedström decided to turn down that offer and suggested instead Schotte for that position. Schotte was indeed appointed, but the state was not pleased with his performance, so only a few years later, the Minister of Industry, Carlsson, once again asked Hedström if he would take on the job. Domänverket's 'atmosphere' had become so bad that the Minister wanted him to start immediately. Hedström hesitated but promised to accept a short-term appointment (a few weeks), but was then told that the shortest possible period was six months. When the Minister explained to Hedström why he was the best candidate, the latter agreed to take up the post for one year (it ultimately lasted ten years).[88]

The atmosphere at Domänverket was dreary primarily because of its unsuccessful Italian operations. However, Hedström also identified 'a dysfunctional culture' in the organization that he wanted to change. Initially, however, he devoted his time to Domänföretagen (the recently formed subsidiary), whose activities in his eyes had strayed too far from Domänverket's core operations. Those Domänföretagen units that ran unrelated consumer businesses were sold. Thus, Domänverket should concentrate on its original core businesses (timber, sawmills and gravel) and expand in tourism, as the organization owned around 20 per cent of the Swedish forests.[89]

When it came to rationalizations and closures, Hedström was not free to act. Politicians – especially members of the Social Democratic Party (ranging from Ministers to local politicians) – now and then intervened. These politicians informed Domänverket that it was responsible not only for its own (current) employment level, but also for general employment in all its regions and districts.

Domänverket's task was then specified as 'running the state-owned forests including the adherent farm land, and running forestry and connected activities'. The ultimate owners (the Swedish people), represented by the parliament and the government, expected that Domänverket would deliver a 'decent' economic result. After having made comparisons with corresponding units in the industry, Hedström concluded that there were too many white-collar employees in the organization. To make the planned transformation of Domänverket visible and legitimate for all individuals in the organization, Hedström visited all regions, districts and sawmills and discussed the pros and cons of the existing ways of doing things. He also started the rationalizations from the very top of the organization, which built an acceptance for the upcoming radical changes. The entire time, the board chaired by Danielsson supported Hedström in his ambitions to modernize Domänverket.[90]

Hedström decided to carry out most of the rationalizations in summertime, as the parliament was inactive during that period. Although reorganization was a non-issue for most MPs, some of them had become active in similar processes and even tried to convince the government to intervene. Nevertheless, Hedström kept the Minister of Industry well informed so that the government would not be taken by surprise and obstruct his efforts. He also pushed the idea that Domänverket ought to be converted to a limited company and listed at the SSE. Hedström believed that it might become a truly 'popular stock', and that the shares would be of particular interest for Domänverket's employees.

He also suggested that the state ought to keep the majority of the votes. However, the Minister turned that idea down. For good reasons, the state was a big forest owner in many countries including several of the truly market-liberal ones.[91]

To sum up, during 1984–89 Hedström radically decentralized and transformed Domänverket: the (fewer) districts were given more power and made responsible for their (economic) results, while the upper echelons – the organization's HQ and regional offices – were cut back. Two divisions (one northern and one southern) were created to co-ordinate sales/deliveries and to support the districts. Domänverket's operational mix also changed – some businesses were abandoned (e.g. energy production) while others expanded (e.g. timber processing and gravel production). At the end of the decade, the organization contained five divisions, a 'holding company' construct and fewer but more powerful districts (the regional level had been removed). Thus, Domänverket had adjusted its structure to fit its new strategy. It implied a focus on running medium-sized companies that processed timber and made more customized products in regions where the state was a big landowner. The ambition was to integrate forward and become supplier to the carpentry industry, as well as a distributor of quality woodware to retailers.

6.6 ASSI IN THE 1980s

6.6.1 A Period of Restructuring

In the beginning of the 1980s, ASSI closed down or sold several units. Doing that it (almost) got out of the building material business – the unprofitable operations that had been foisted on ASSI by its parent company Statsföretag. What remained in that business area was ASSI Trä (five sawmills [which in 1984 were joined into a wholly owned unit, ASSI Timber]), ASSI board,[92] Töreboda Limträ (glue-laminated wood) and Etri Fönster (windows). In Sweden ASSI also included Karlsborg (bleached sulphate pulp and bleached coated kraft paper), Lövholmen (Europe's biggest unit for [unbleached and marbled] kraftliner), Frövifors (coated unbleached LPB), Förenade Well (corrugated) and Örebro Papperbruk (sacks, plaster carton, plastic coated paper and plastic sacks [sold in 1981]). Abroad ASSI contained FS-Karton (Germany), the Dolan Group (UK, corrugated), Flexer Sacks (UK), Dansk Kraftemballage (Denmark), Wellkarton Swisswell (Switzerland), Hamburger Wellpapper Fabrik Erich Siering (Germany), Lacaux Freres S.A.R.L. (France, carton), Gissler & Pass (Germany, packaging) and Gerro Karton (Germany; later ASSI Well Verpackungswerke).

ASSI considered adding companies to enhance its packaging business, primarily units producing corrugated. About one-quarter of ASSI's liner production went to its own packaging firms, and the ambition was to increase that share. Western Europe was the major market for ASSI's products, but there were no discussions about entering Eastern Europe. About three-quarters of the sales went abroad, and for some of its core products ASSI was a leading European actor. However, since ASSI's output at the time made it sensitive to market fluctuations, the company's goal was to move into more processed commodities (like paper and cardboard).

ASSI's economic performance was poor. Already during the years 1976–79 it had lost around SEK 750 million. That miserable result was explained mainly by relatively high[93] production costs attributed to the doubling of both timber prices and wages in just a few years' time. The losses had been 'handled' by loans on the global market. Interest payments and currency deficits (due to devaluations of the Swedish crown) had added another SEK 700 million in costs. At the same time, the investments had been huge – SEK 5 billion in total. All these facts indicated that ASSI entered the 1980s in rather bad financial shape. The company expected another loss in 1981, this time in the neighbourhood of SEK 500 million, and the prospects for 1982 looked even worse. The production of building material and the Frövifors unit were in bad shape. However, packaging and liner looked promising, so there were businesses on which ASSI could build its future.[94]

ASSI's directors regarded the situation as extremely awkward when it became evident that the company had to set up a liquidation balance sheet. However, the owner, that is to say, the state, did not find such a move acceptable (a state-owned company could not be allowed to go bankrupt). Thus, the board had to wait while the Ministry officials and the company discussed what steps to take.[95] Deputy CEO Carlsson described ASSI's situation as most troublesome, since its total capital was insufficient for the investments that were required (particularly in corrugated production to process the Lövholmen liner). The company had no resources to integrate forward through acquisitions, and it could not pay with its own shares. Carlsson's conclusion was that ASSI only could buy companies that could pay their interest, that is to say, firms in good condition. At the time, there were also credit restrictions linked to acquisitions abroad. However, as a state-owned company ASSI had no problems getting loans on the international credit market.[96]

In December 1981, the board concluded that the company needed fresh capital to survive. All investments were postponed, and management was asked to produce a programme for improved liquidity and solvency. A consulting firm concluded that most of the possible disinvestments were economically indefensible (ill-timed). To improve its balance sheet, certain revaluations were discussed. In the end, however, ASSI asked the Ministry of Industry for (more) financial support. The company needed SEK 1.4 billion plus a settlement with Domänverket. Its DG Schotte was then asked to look into the possibility of merging all state engagements in the forest-related industry. In spring 1982, the state increased ASSI's stock by SEK 300 million, and managers from the company Statsföretag were made adjunct members of ASSI's board. In addition, director Nydahl demanded a liquidation guarantee from Statsföretag, in which its responsibility as owner of ASSI was reiterated. That guarantee – together with another SEK 500 million capital infusion – calmed the banks. Still, since the actual need was SEK 2.4 billion, the board asked Statsföretag to provide that sum.[97]

In the second half of 1982, the government suggested that ASSI get SEK 2 billion, and that the interest and amortization payments linked to the Karlsborg site should be discontinued. The motive behind the large capitalization of ASSI was to reduce the debt burden, so that the investments needed to make long-term profitability possible could be made. The new capital should also make ASSI capable of withstanding the sizeable ups and downs on its output markets. In March 1983, the parliament finally decided that ASSI should get the capital injection. The six-month delay was explained by multiple factors including a dispute between the resigning Minister of Industry and Statsföretag, the change of government in 1982 and the incorporation of ASSI's request with other claims on Statsföretag.

The Swedish devaluation in 1982 helped ASSI to improve its competitiveness and regain market shares, but it was not enough to establish favourable conditions on all its markets. However, on the liner market, the devaluation made a difference. The American corporations produced about 15 million tons of liner, while their European competitors only supplied around 2 million tons. Thus, if the American companies sold just an additional 2–3 per cent of their output in Europe, the price would fall dramatically with tough consequences for ASSI. What stabilized the situation was that the leading actors on the global liner market knew each other well and acted in a long-term perspective. However, for ASSI's board production the devaluation only marginally improved the situation. When the European Community (EC) established fixed prices on such commodities, CEO Bahrke began to consider closing the Skinnskatteberg plant.

Åman became CEO at Statsföretag in 1982. Because of the continuing problems and current crisis in ASSI, Åman wanted to replace its CEO Bahrke. Several managers found the criticism of Bahrke unfair, especially since he had been forced to include certain firms in ASSI's kitchen and chipboard businesses that were in bad shape already when they were handed over. There was also a concern that ASSI could get a CEO that did not understand the forest-based industry.[98] Some managers had private connections both with leading politicians and the incoming ASSI Chair Persson, so they used those informal channels to influence the CEO recruitment process. Early in 1983, Bahrke left and Carlsson, then Deputy CEO, was appointed acting CEO. The new government also replaced some of the directors, installing Brandinger (Valand[99]), Hedström (Domänverket) and Johansson (SSAB) as new board members.

ASSI started to reduce its operations and concentrate on two businesses: packaging and building material. At the time, ASSI was the biggest packaging corporation in Europe, and its plants at Lövholmen (liner) and Frövifors (LPB) were large and modern units producing for growing markets. The plastic coated paper manufactured at Örebro pappersfabrik was also running rather well. ASSI Karlsborg had been modernized, and the corrugated business was profitable and used substantial kraftliner quantities from Lövholmen. ASSI's overall strategy was to integrate forward by expanding its packaging operations. In spite of its poor finances, ASSI had continued to buy units producing corrugated during 1982, and there was also a new issue of shares made in Förenade Well. Crucial for future success was secure and massive timber sourcing, and Domänverket was the strategic partner for that, as it supplied almost half of ASSI's timber use (the contract expired in 1983).

CEO Carlsson's plans for ASSI included investment in three areas: the corrugated cardboard business in Europe (an expansion led by Hamrefors in a unit named ASSI Packaging), the liquid packaging at Frövifors (cf. Tetra Pak) and the 'white' production at Karlsborg (bleached pulp and paper). Carlsson organized ASSI's operations into four groups: sawn timber, paper and carton for packaging, bleached pulp and liquid packaging (board). Liner and corrugated cardboard were kept apart, as they were regarded to be two different businesses. However, ASSI lacked the possibility to benefit from the cash flow generated by power plants and from profits based on forest ownership (Domänverket controlled those resources). Moreover, no progress was made in the discussions with Stora Kopparberg and Swedish Match regarding the problem-ridden building material business.[100]

Already by 1985, the Swedish forest-based industry's advantages from the devaluation had evaporated. At that time, all of ASSI's core businesses were exposed to huge cyclical swings, and once again there was a crisis at Örebro paper mill. In that situation CEO Carlsson wanted to get fresh capital from the owner without a 'doctrinaire attitude' regarding the ownership structure. As ASSI's economic performance was again unsatisfactory, the board[101] asked the CEO for a plan about how ASSI could become profitable.[102] The owner took no active part in those strategic discussions, and no 'genuine' state representative had a board seat. The Chair and the CEO conducted talks with the owner representatives (actors from Statsföretag and/or the Ministry). In those meetings the owner made clear that the restrictions regarding the board's right to close or rationalize units were still in force.[103]

6.6.2 Focus on Packaging

ASSI continued trying to free itself from the huge cyclical swings primarily by moving towards products that did not face competition from countries outside Europe. The favoured products addressed customers whose demand was rather stable and represented forward integration. Therefore, ASSI stopped its production of unbleached sack paper, increased its sales of quality carton and continued its expansion in corrugated. In the mid-1980s, packaging had reached 30 per cent of ASSI's total net sales, making a large part of the sales relatively unaffected by cyclical swings. ASSI continued along that path in 1987 by acquiring a rather big producer of corrugated, Thames Case (UK), while holding serious discussions with other firms. Deputy CEO Hamrefors[104] ran most of these activities, with strong support for his ambitions (including from the powerful unions). ASSI's state ownership also made the necessary borrowing rather easy. However, the balance sheet remained a problem, particularly when linked to the high growth ambitions. 'Everybody' understood that ASSI needed more capital, but nothing happened. The state's passivity was incomprehensible to many board members and made borrowing more expensive.

The corrugated industry used 50 per cent testliner and 50 per cent kraftliner in its plants. In order to find out how customers were planning to use such packages, Hamrefors launched an extensive investigation of that business. The most frequent answer involved the price dimension – such packaging should avoid 'excessive' quality to keep costs down. Once he was confident about what kind of product the customers wanted, Hamrefors decided that ASSI Packaging ought to focus on selected end-use segments and become number one on all markets entered. He was not interested, however, in seeing ASSI Packaging expanding its production into Eastern Europe. Like the board, he claimed that Eastern Europe lacked the production of commodities that required corrugated.[105]

At that time, Western Europe was home to around 250 manufacturers of packaging products, most of them small and only locally active. The 'big four' – ASSI, SCA (Sweden), SOCAR (France) and International Paper (US) – held 20 per cent of the market. ASSI's share was around 5 per cent (43 plants), roughly corresponding to half of its turnover. To secure the company's position as the leader on the technical front, Hamrefors established ASSI Packaging Development (which contained several of the competent employees that became supernumerary when Thames Board was bought).

At the end of the 1980s, ASSI closed or sold several of its sawmills, as the board did not like the idea that ASSI operated sawmills in competition with the (many small) private actors. ASSI also sold Smith, Stone & Knight, Örebro Pappersbruk[106] and Etri Fönster. However, Frövifors expanded and a new system for packaging beer and soft-drink bottles was introduced, which initiated the establishment of two new German companies. It was important to broaden the customer base and make sure that the major one, Tetra Pak, was satisfied.

In these years,[107] ASSI's board included Ametier, Carlsson (CEO), Danielsson, Flory, Hedström, Hägglund, Lindström, Lund, Pettersson, Rosén, Olof Rydh and Sprängare.

Flory had gained her experience mainly in marketing, a field that became more and more important for ASSI in the 1990s.[108] Lund[109] replaced Persson as Chair and he immediately took a more active role than his predecessor. Pettersson had worked at the Ministry of Industry during the 1970s, particularly with forest industry matters, and therefore knew many of its leading actors (staff as well as politicians). Furthermore, he was at the time CEO of Sweden's largest savings bank, which made him knowledgeable about financial matters. Lindström had a similar background, as he, too, was a bank CEO with experience from the forest-based industry (as Deputy CEO in SCA in the 1950s).[110]

ASSI continued to show poor economic results throughout the second half of the 1980s – both a loss (SEK 250 million) and a negative cash flow (SEK 1.5 billion).[111] Despite their poor performance, ASSI could not close its two chipboard plants because the Minister of Industry, Peterson, did not allow such a move. So, ASSI waited until Peterson was abroad to finally close the plants (!); a move for which Chair Lund was scolded.[112]

Some directors claimed that Karlsborg, another problem unit, ought to have been closed long ago, while the unions instead pushed for further investments.[113] It was particularly its sack production that was problematic, so eventually that machine was shut down despite its location in the most northerly part of Sweden, where the state always had been reluctant to reduce capacity. Moreover, whenever such moves were considered, the unions usually asked the (Social Democratic) government to intervene and stop most rationalization and shutdowns.[114]

ASSI Kraftliner's business idea was to source the European producers of corrugated with brown, marbled and white high-class kraftliner (including special qualities), although the expansion would take place solely in the 'white segment'. Another company aim was that a larger share of its output would be packages for consumer goods, although packaging solutions for industry still was the main road. All those efforts gradually transformed ASSI into a packaging company offering both liner[115] and corrugated cardboard. Notably, it was not regarded as a shortcoming that the company lacked fluting production, since no such producer had integrated into the corrugated business.[116] At the time, there were several acquisition ideas on the board's table, and the general understanding was that ASSI needed to double its volume in the packaging business over the coming decade to survive. ASSI also built up the necessary financial capacity for making modernization and expansion of its operations possible. One important ingredient in that effort was a large issue of new shares (SEK 1 billion), something that simultaneously made Domänverket one of its major shareholders (25%).

NOTES

N.B.: When there is an 'i' inside a parenthesis below, that letter indicates that the note refers to an interview with the named person. All interviewees are listed in the Appendix. A complete listing of references is found at the end of the book.

1. Domänverket is a Swedish 'affärsverk', which is a rather special construct. It is a state-run organization working very much like a 'central public administrative authority'. It is not organized as a joint-stock company, although its main purpose is to carry out business activity.
2. Valeur (2003).
3. From 1983 to the Ministry of Industry.
4. Valeur (2003).
5. Hamrefors (2007i).
6. Ibid.
7. Belgium, Denmark, Germany, Holland, Sweden and the UK.
8. Hamrefors (2007i).
9. ≈ 65%.
10. The name 'Södra' will be used throughout this volume.
11. Production started in 1959.
12. Production started in 1962.
13. Rydberg (1990) and Åsling (1996 and 1999).
14. In 1971 the two organizations merged and established the 'Federation of Swedish Farmers' (LRF).
15. 38%.
16. Åsling (1996 and 1999).
17. Åsling (1996) and Valeur (2000).
18. Åsling (1996 and 1999).
19. Valeur (2000).
20. Wallander (1998) and Valeur (2000).
21. Åsling (1996) and Valeur (2000).
22. Ibid.
23. Valeur (1997).
24. Valeur (2000).
25. Åsling (1996) and Valeur (2000).
26. Vallvik was established in the first decade of the 20th century when three sawmills (Marma, Ljusne-Woxna and Långrör) founded a company with the sole mission of establishing a sulphite plant that could take care of small timber. Later Vallvik became a part of the Marma-Långrör group, and that constellation was in turn incorporated into Korsnäs in 1960.
27. Valeur (2007).
28. Åsling (1999) and Valeur (2000).
29. Rydberg (1990) and Åsling (1999).
30. Ncb's acquisitions during the 1960s included Sandviken from Graningeverken (1961), Hörnefors from MoDo (1961), Hissmofors and Äggfors from the Nobell family (1963), Köpmanholmen from the Hedström family (1964), Väja and Svanö from the Ekman family (1966) and Vallvik from Korsnäs-Marma (1968). Source: Valeur (2000).
31. Valeur (2000).
32. Åsling (1999).
33. Producer of finished houses.
34. Hedlund bought 53% of that fine paper group in 1971 (later 75%).
35. Åsling (1999).
36. Valeur (2000).
37. Åsling (1996).
38. Åsling (1999).
39. Valeur (2000).
40. Åsling (1999).
41. Åsling (1996 and 1999).
42. Lyberg (1984).
43. Åsling (1996 and 1999).
44. Rydin's diary.
45. Åsling (1996 and 1999) and Valeur (2000).
46. 'Skogsstyrelsen'.

47. Hedström (2007i).
48. Valeur (2000).
49. Valeur (2007).
50. Rydberg (1990) and Valeur (2007).
51. Hofsten (1984).
52. Tegnér (2007i).
53. However, Domänverket merely carried out 10% of the country's total cutting. Lots of forests were located far away from mills and/or had poor productivity.
54. Hofsten (1984)
55. CEO 1971–82.
56. Uddcomb was a producer and seller of reactor tanks and other major components for the nuclear industry and other heavy industries.
57. Bahrke (2007i).
58. Ibid.
59. Ibid.
60. Hamrefors (2007i).
61. Bahrke (2007i).
62. Ibid.
63. Board notes cleared by Dockered in 2007.
64. Ibid.
65. Lyberg (1984).
66. Ibid.
67. Carlsson (2007i).
68. Ibid.
69. Board notes cleared by Dockered in 2007.
70. Ibid.
71. Carlsson (2007i).
72. Board notes cleared by Dockered in 2007.
73. Carlsson (2007i).
74. Bahrke (2007i) and Carlsson (2007i).
75. Parent company for retail businesses (food).
76. Swedish Steel, a large state-owned Swedish steel company.
77. Board notes cleared by Dockered in 2007.
78. Bahrke (2007i) and Wahlström (2006i).
79. Board notes cleared by Dockered in 2007.
80. Lyberg (1984).
81. Bahrke (2007i).
82. Ibid.
83. Uddeholm sold all its forest-related businesses to Billerud in 1978.
84. Board notes cleared by Dockered in 2007.
85. Bahrke (2007i).
86. Ibid.
87. Lyberg (1984).
88. Hedström (2007i).
89. Ibid.
90. Ibid.
91. In Canada the state owned 90% of the forests and in the US 50%.
92. In 1984 Swanboard-Masonite merged with ASSI's Royal Board and ASSI's holding then became 25%.
93. Compared to its American competitors.
94. Memo Statsföretag, 6 September 1982.
95. Lyberg (1984).
96. Carlsson (2007i).
97. Board notes cleared by Dockered in 2007.
98. Hamrefors (2007i).
99. A Swedish insurance company.
100. Carlsson (2007i).
101. Brandinger had left the board but Gehlin, Lindström, Lund and Karl-Henrik Pettersson had all become new members in 1986/87.
102. Board notes cleared by Dockered in 2007.
103. Karl-Henrik Pettersson (2007i).
104. From 1987.

105. Hamrefors (2007i).
106. Sold in 1988 to La Farge (France).
107. At that time, there were six European producers of unbleached kraftliner: SCA, ASSI, Cellulose du Pin (France), Kemi (Finland), Portucel (Portugal) and Nettingsdorfer (Austria).
108. Carlsson (2007i).
109. CEO at Gränges Nyby.
110. Karl-Henrik Pettersson (2007i).
111. Board notes cleared by Dockered in 2007.
112. Lund (2007i).
113. Board notes cleared by Dockered in 2007.
114. Lund (2007i).
115. Including a fitting pulp production.
116. Hamrefors (2007i) and Lund (2007i).

7. From Domänverket to Sveaskog: reviving the original core business

7.1 ASSI MERGES WITH DOMÄNVERKET

7.1.1 A Complicated Process

Back in 1978 a study had suggested certain minor changes in the relationship between ASSI and Domänverket (e.g. that most forests in ASSI's cutting areas ought to be transferred from Domänverket to ASSI). ASSI responded by calling attention to its 1977 proposal about a merger between the two organizations. However, nothing of significance materialized until 1984, when ASSI and Domänverket negotiated a new long-term timber agreement. A few years later (1987), the two organizations also agreed that Domänföretagen should take over some of ASSI's sawmills (Karlsborg [soon closed], Lövholmen and Seskarö). Domänverket was profitable during those years (1984–88) and delivered about SEK 800 million to the state. At that time, the conditions for the Swedish forest-based industry were favourable, and nothing indicated a downturn. Still, the investments were usually made abroad, which was explained by the relatively high cost for timber and wages in Sweden, and by growing uncertainty regarding future energy sourcing.

ASSI's timber deliveries continued to be a problem all through the 1980s. The company needed increased quantities, but Domänverket sent ASSI the message that it intended to cut back its sourcing, which could create a supply crisis for ASSI. Therefore, the board began to regard ASSI's lack of forests as a major problem, as it did not merely hurt the company's core businesses, but also made it miss a fair share of the industry's 'forest-generated' profits. So ASSI's board proposed that ASSI and Domänverket should establish a joint timber company, with Domänverket as its major owner (consolidating the economic result) and ASSI receiving a fair share of the new units' profits through dividends.[1]

As the buyers of timber became fewer and larger, the market situation changed to Domänverket's disadvantage. As it had no engagement in the pulp and paper industry, it became natural to respond by resuming the discussions with ASSI (its biggest customer). As a consequence, in 1989 Domänverket purchased a large part of a new issue of ASSI shares (SEK 1 billion; the state took 35% and Domänverket 65%), and ASSI's management expected that its new shareholding would result in a more secure and bigger timber delivery in the future. The Swedish Minister of Industry at the time, Nordberg, justified the state's investment based on ASSI's need to modernize and expand some of its existing plants over the coming years (at a total cost of SEK 5 billion). At the time, the state had no plan to link Ncb to the new constellation.

Domänverket's investment in ASSI bound the two organizations more closely together and strengthened ASSI's balance sheet. Hedström believed that something had to happen between the two organizations, as the complementarity of their operations was rather obvious. However, at that time, it was unclear what agency was best suited to govern the state's engagement in the forest-based industry.[2]

In 1991, Sweden voted in a right-wing government, and its Minister of Industry (Westerberg) endorsed a neoliberal ideology, which brought to the fore the idea that 'the time had come for privatization' (i.e. the selling of state-owned corporations).[3] Dockered, the Chair of the farmers' association LRF, described the government as almost 'dogmatic' in its neoliberal conviction.[4]

Even before the new government had taken office, parliament had already expressed openness to the possible transformation of Domänverket to a limited company, since civil service organizations were prohibited from being parents to subsidiaries.[5] In a technically complicated process, Hedström, in close contact with the Ministry, promptly transformed Domänverket into a limited company ('Domän'). Domänverket's union had changed its mind and approved the transformation. A significant side effect of Domän's new legal form was that it became more difficult for the state to extract capital from the company.

When in place, Domän stood out from most other companies in the forest-based industry in three ways: it was state-owned, forestry dominated and held major real estate. The CEO issue was easy to resolve – Ahlgren[6] was the obvious choice for what was soon to be AssiDomän, as Carlsson was retiring, and neither Lund nor Carlsson saw Hedström as a fitting candidate.[7] So the board of Domän hired Ahlgren, a manager with a strong track record (even awarded 'Leader of the Year' in Sweden).[8]

The new government that took office in 1991 organized a team that was to focus on the privatization and merger of ASSI and Domän. The team included two financial advisers, two actors from the Ministry (Ametier and Tegnér), and the chairs and CEOs from ASSI (Lund and Carlsson) and Domän (Danielsson and Ahlgren [appointed CEO of Domän in 1993]). Several Swedish competitors opposed the state's initiative; SCA's CEO Martin-Löf in particular objected intensely. The Minister of Industry had a tough time handling the unsparing critique that claimed that a joint AssiDomän would be a (too) strong competitor and make it difficult for other companies to acquire more forest resources.[9] Probably, the bad times intensified the resistance – global overcapacity existed in most of the forest-based industry, so many markets were weak. In addition, an unfavourable currency rate pushed prices down, particularly on white pulp.[10]

Under these difficult circumstances, ASSI closed down one of its machines at Karlsborg. At the same time, however, ASSI Packaging acquired Policarton in Italy (corrugated), and Örebro Pappersbruk bought Polycote in France (plastic coated paper for packaging). ASSI also added three new machines to its packaging business (in Belgium, Italy and the UK).

Because Sweden was experiencing a domestic bank crisis triggered by inflated prices on housing properties and needed capital, the state had taken out SEK 1.4 million from Domänverket already before Domän was created. So to keep it attractive on 'the market for corporate control', Domän was endowed with all of Domänverket's commercially interesting forests including 4.4 billion hectares of productive forestland, which, if privatized, would make Domän the biggest private forest owner in the world. The state retained those woods and fields that were located in vulnerable and inaccessible areas and those where cultural values or nature as such demanded special considerations. To take care of that land, the state established a new public authority, Fastighetsverket.[11] As would become clear later, however, the division of forest estates between the two units was not made in an optimal way, so that too few of the forests were reserved to make it possible to (continue to) source the many small private sawmills.[12]

In 1992, Sweden devalued its crown again, a decision that immediately changed the (short-term) competitive situation in the forest-based industry. Finland, which housed many tough competitors, had devalued already in 1991. These two Nordic devaluations provided a respite and an opportunity for their companies to make their business structures truly competitive also in a longer perspective. They had recently carried out dramatic cost-cutting activities and (eco-friendly) modernizations, which also built long-term strength. Consequently, almost all larger Nordic forest-based companies turned losses to profit in the period 1992–93. ASSI was particularly favoured by the new currency rate, as it had most of its production in Sweden. However, its plants and machines were rather small and not as technically advanced as those run by many competitors. There was also a slightly negative outlook for certain parts of its core business (corrugated). The use of waste fibres in that production segment increased steadily (approaching about 70% in Europe), and it was more and more based on testliner (not ASSI's major product kraftliner).[13]

The devaluation of the crown also led to Swedish companies falling in price. In light of the relatively low prices, several foreign competitors contacted ASSI, among them Jefferson Smurfit, whose owner Michael Smurfit met with Chair Lund. But Smurfit was only interested in acquiring ASSI's corrugated business and its kraftliner producing unit Lövholmen. However, since those parts were seen as ASSI's future, no agreement was made. ASSI also hesitated because of Smurfit's rather weak financial status (an Achilles heel for ASSI itself). Smurfit, for its part, vacillated because both Karlsborg and Lövholmen lacked forest resources. (As so often) ASSI also talked to SCA, and in 1992 those discussions addressed Munksund. There were also some meetings with Stora Billerud regarding Gruvön, and a dialogue with MoDo's leaders about its packaging company Iggesund. However, in the end no serious talks about structural changes materialized. ASSI also continued to seek a way to merge with Domän(verket) and even considered foreign investments such as the acquisition of Cellulose du Pin from St Gobain, which would provide ASSI with a 'cash cow'.[14]

In early 1992, two consultancy firms were hired to describe what a privatized ASSI might look like. They concluded that it could be successful if two conditions were met: Karlsborg had to be excluded and Domänverket had to be transformed to a limited company (that became a fact in March 1992). The AssiDomän merger was carried out finally in December 1993, soon after Domän's announcement that it intended to make a bid for Ncb. The general public was offered 49 per cent of a merged AssiDomän.[15] Its recently appointed (and first) CEO Ahlgren was given a favourable platform, as the new company was equipped with a very strong balance sheet (financial strength) and substantial forest resources (operational strength). Those initial conditions would make it possible for Ahlgren to launch large market investments and far-reaching structural and organizational re-arrangements.

Except for Chair Lund, Deputy Chair Danielsson, former CEO Carlsson (Ahlgren wanted him to stay as director) and former Minister of Industry Åsling (soon 'replaced' by Dockered[16]), the new board was composed of 'professional' directors, who all lacked deeper experience of the forest-based industry (Hagman [Tetra Pak[17]], Christiansson [Telia[18]], Nordmark-Nilsson [PwC[19]] and Tegnér [the Ministry of Industry]). Chair Lund claimed that the new board worked just like any other comparable unit in Sweden, that is to say, with close interaction between its Chair and the CEO (and more reactive directors). The board did not have the strength (or will?) to question the current Minister of Industry's instruction that AssiDomän ought to be privatized (49%) 'at any price'. As the government feared a loss in the upcoming general election, the planned privatization was to be carried out quickly.[20]

CEO Ahlgren was an impatient actor, who wanted to accomplish a lot in a short period of time. He had the necessary resources to act offensively, as the company had been provided with strong finances and lots of forests.[21] Ahlgren came from the CEO position in a family-dominated listed company (Korsnäs). There he had learned that its major shareholder (Stenbeck) was an 'interfering' person, and also that a delisting of the company from the SSE was considered, which would negatively affect his freedom. Ahlgren's unease with the situation at Korsnäs became quietly known, and Domänverket's Deputy Chair Danielsson, who knew Ahlgren, contacted him with the ambition to recruit him as successor to Hedström and as AssiDomän's first CEO.[22]

Ahlgren was not initially informed that AssiDomän was to be privatized. However, he was aware of the fact that the Minister of Industry, Westerberg, wanted to see Ncb[23] as a part of the new AssiDomän. That 'second' merger was necessary to keep the right-wing government together (the Centre Party advocated such a solution). Dockered, at the time Chair of the Federation of Swedish Farmers and a leading actor in the Centre Party, was the one that most forcefully pushed for that solution.[24] However, to integrate the two organizational cultures was difficult. They differed significantly, as did the power of their respective unions. A long tradition (and a northern location) had provided ASSI with particularly strong unions with 'direct' channels to leading politicians. Furthermore, although the new AssiDomän was constructed as a semi-privatized unit, it still worked very much as if it were a company wholly owned by the state. It would eventually prove to be problematic that Ahlgren lacked experience within such a politicized setting.[25]

7.1.2 AssiDomän Incorporates Ncb

In October 1993 AssiDomän publicly declared its intention to offer Ncb's shareholders the opportunity to exchange their shares against shares in AssiDomän. In April 1994, the Swedish state, controlling about 62 per cent of the votes in Ncb, decided to hand over its holding to AssiDomän on the same terms as the other shareholders in Ncb. After all those transactions had been carried out, the distribution of shares was as follows: the state held about 51 per cent, private individuals 32 per cent, institutions 13 per cent and former (non-state) Ncb shareholders 4 per cent.[26] This effective merger between AssiDomän and Ncb meant that the Social Democratic Party saved the 'darling' of both the farmers' movement and the Centre Party.[27]

The commercial reason for AssiDomän's purchase of Ncb was that it would strengthen its sacks and kraft paper operations. Ncb was a producer of brown paper qualities and manufactured sacks at Charfa-gruppen (one of the four biggest sack producers in France). That company group also owned close to 50 per cent of a Belgian packaging firm that contained three sack-producing units. Moreover, co-ordination of Karlsborg (AssiDomän) and Dynäs (Ncb) would provide AssiDomän with a 'complete' output of white and brown packaging papers. Karlsborg would also get access to Ncb's sack markets, and an enlarged AssiDomän would be a very significant player in the pulp business. Added to all that, the expectation was that the two sales organizations could be integrated and that the results of efforts in R&D could be used more effectively.[28]

AssiDomän's strategy was founded on an understanding of the forest-based industry as capital intensive and highly cyclical. It was also a business where currency fluctuations mattered and now and then turned competitive situations around. Thus, the operative risk was rather high, which in turn 'required' low financial risk, so the solidity goal was set rather high (> 45%). Operationally, AssiDomän planned to move from bulk products to more highly processed ones that were closer to the end user. Initially, all its core businesses were regarded as targets for that transformation, but soon that ambition was revised. AssiDomän decided to focus on three of them – packaging paper, packaging and woodware – and try to become one of the leading European companies in each of the fields. At the time, these three businesses represented 60 per cent of the company's turnover and 90 per cent of its profit. AssiDomän was number five in size among the European producers of corrugated – big enough to successfully participate in the concentration process underway on that fragmented market.[29] At that time, SCA was the biggest seller followed by Jefferson Smurfit, International Paper and Cellulose de Pin.

One thing that strengthened AssiDomän's position in the packaging business was its purchase of MoDo Packaging (1994), which contained Skärblacka, a Swedish producer of fluting, pulp and brown sack paper. AssiDomän was also already the second biggest kraftliner producer in Europe (next to SCA). Its plant in Piteå was the largest in Europe and one of the most efficient units in the world, so in a short-term perspective the investment needs were fairly small. The sacks market was mature with limited profit opportunities (however, better for white than for brown sacks), but it provided a stable cash flow. Paper producers controlled about 60 per cent of the sacks industry, although that percentage varied significantly between countries. For AssiDomän that figure had risen to around 30 per cent, as Ncb had been one of the bigger sack producers competing with, among others, Korsnäs, Stora Billerud, MoDo, Wisaforest (Finland), Frantschach (Austria) and Cellulose du Pin (France).

In terms of sack paper, AssiDomän was the biggest producer in Europe, and that production generated cash and had low operative risk. Ahlgren, with lots of experience from that business field, decided that the company should integrate forward, that is to say, acquire sack producers. A growth in sacks would also be a way to better integrate Dynäs (pulp and brown sack paper) and Karlsborg (white kraft and sack paper) in AssiDomän. Although it was a disadvantage that the (potential) customers for its products were so few (Elopak, PKL and Tetra Pak), Frövifors was another business on which AssiDomän could build its future, since it was the biggest and most modern liquid packaging plant in the world.

Örebro Pappersbruk was at the time Europe's biggest producer of coated cardboard. Its production units were located in Sweden (Örebro and Timrå) and France (St Omér-en-Chaussée and Gournay-en-Bray). Its customer base was diverse and plentiful, including paper mills and converters throughout Western Europe (none bought more than 6% of the output). Walki (part of UPM) and Wisapak (part of Kymmene) were the main competitors. Still, coated cardboard was not an obvious candidate for AssiDomän's journey into the future. Ahlgren drew a similar conclusion for the company's market pulp – the idea was to eventually phase it out through increasing internal deliveries. Consequently, the market pulp producer Vallvik was sold to Rottneros in 1994.

Asserståhl, Head of AssiDomän Forestry and Timber (and former manager at Domänverket), felt that several actors insisted on large investments, as the financial conditions for such a path had been established. Actors expected that the old plants would be re-equipped and also supplemented with new investments. Basically, the 'ASSI part' was underinvested, but the new constellation (AssiDomän) provided an opportunity for building really strong businesses.

Ahlgren accepted that challenge and became quite ambitious in his efforts. To get AssiDomän going, Ahlgren immediately argued for large investments in the existing plants, although that would not create instant positive effects on the profit and loss account – those were expected to materialize later. Investments were made both to rationalize production and to upgrade products. Rationalizing production, however, proved to be difficult to carry out, because the company had for decades been woven into the Swedish political sphere, meaning that jobs had to be protected to the extent possible. Still, all but one of the suggested rationalizations materialized. The Piteå site was the exception; the effort to reduce the workforce was abandoned foremost because of the resistance from the local unions.[30]

The company's merger with Ncb had contributed to its attainment of a strong position on the markets for sack paper and sacks. However, that position had to be defended, and Ahlgren claimed that the best way to build long-term profitability was by acquiring production capacity in Eastern Europe. Such a move would both make low-cost production available and secure a position close to the West-European (continental) market.

That idea induced a strong interest in the Czech company Sepap, which had both the right location (rather close to Berlin) and a fitting production. However, several other actors showed the same interest, so a struggle for control over Sepap began. To acquire that Czech company, AssiDomän also had to take a position in Russian Segheza, and although that would be a big step, it was not a particularly remarkable or unconventional one. At that time – when the Berlin Wall had fallen – many banks and industrial corporations in the Western hemisphere tried to take positions in Eastern Europe. Lots of once-only business offerings appeared, which all had to be addressed 'immediately', as similar opportunities never would appear again. Most capitalists (and politicians) advocated making such investments, and they often added that such efforts involved taking responsibility for a positive development within the former Soviet satellite states.[31]

As a consequence of these developments in Europe, AssiDomän's board began to discuss whether the company ought to follow an 'Eastern Europe path' and concentrate its expansion in that region. Many advisers were consulted and several analyses were made to establish a solid platform for a decision. Eventually, many politicians, particularly those representing the major owner, encouraged the CEO to pursue such a path (one could almost smell an 'aid spirit'). They liked that Swedish corporations took up their share of the Western countries' responsibility for the transformation and modernization of Eastern Europe. At the same time, a wave of privatization also flooded the Eastern European region, with the result that lots of firms were put up for ownership changes. Obviously, a (time sensitive) window of opportunity had opened, so it was urgent for

AssiDomän (and others) to try to take advantage of the offerings. As a consequence, many Western corporations acquired rather worn-out facilities. In fact, some of those investments represented pure speculation with buyers almost totally uninterested in the acquired firms' operations and future development.[32]

There were some problems linked to AssiDomän's rapid expansion. Its strong balance sheet made growth almost too easy for an energetic CEO, which necessitated a powerful board acting as a critical counterforce. However, the board did not always get high-class investment calculations, and seldom any follow-ups, so its influence gradually decreased. The emerging tensions between (some of) the directors and the CEO reinforced that tendency. The composition of the board with two members (Lund and Tegnér) standing particularly close to the company's major owner (the state) also created some strain, as the other directors sometimes became lesser (or at least later) informed about the owner's positions on important issues.[33] Added to that, one could note that the board seldom hosted strategic discussions, despite the fact that AssiDomän was a new, financially strong entity with rich expansion opportunities that almost made intense deliberations a must.

Most of the strategy was located inside the CEO's head – it was Ahlgren's thinking that governed the company. Soon it became evident that he disliked the strong state influence on the company. He saw state ownership as an impediment in international business affairs. Despite director Dockered's advice, Ahlgren continued to be outspoken on that matter, which irritated the board's state representatives.[34] However, in spite of those 'governance frictions', the directors unanimously and explicitly supported Ahlgren's idea to make sack paper and sacks one of the company's three core businesses (the two others were packaging based on corrugated and LPB).[35]

In 1995, AssiDomän bought Stora's (Billerud's) sack paper and sacks businesses, and one of its machines was shut down, which eliminated both one competitor and some of the overcapacity that existed in Europe. The idea was that AssiDomän would take over Stora's customers in these areas (but that did not happen). AssiDomän also bought Stora's Pacsac (Skoghall), its production of sacks in Scotland and Wales, and an option to acquire 10 per cent of Otor (a manufacturer of corrugated). At that time, it also finished its selling of Vallvik to Rottneros.[36]

7.2 A RUSSIAN CALAMITY

The most important step that AssiDomän took in the 1990s was the acquisition of Sepap from American investors.[37] The Americans had taken substantial positions in two of the companies that AssiDomän considered acquiring: Sepap and Segheza.[38] The Americans had in obscure ways bought Sepap under AssiDomän's very nose. Soon it also became clear that they had invested in Russia (Karelia), too – there they owned a part of Segheza, the biggest sack producer in the world. However, they were eager to get out of that investment because of their 'limited knowledge' about forest-based operations. Their message was that AssiDomän would be let in as owner of Sepap if it bought > 50 per cent of Segheza. Ahlgren negotiated with the Americans and with a bank to get a substantial credit commitment to lower the risk (he got an oral promise, but Chair Lund wanted to see the agreement in writing).[39]

Eventually Ahlgren's talks with the American investors resulted in a deal. AssiDomän bought 24 per cent of Sepap with a right to increase its holding to 49 per cent (its ambition was to reach > 50%). The remaining 51 per cent of Sepap was eventually bought, so in 1998 AssiDomän owned close to 100 per cent. That large investment equipped AssiDomän with lots of sack paper and sacks (and some other commodities), and a cheap production facility close to the company's major market: Western Europe. However, as alluded to above, its most important condition was that AssiDomän had to acquire the Americans' shareholdings in Segheza (57%).[40]

That was the start of a process through which AssiDomän via its board and CEO gradually slid into the Russian adventure without taking enough time to discuss some of the crucial issues.[41] Segheza was a gigantic corporation that produced sack paper and sacks (1 billion pieces), which almost single-handedly supplied the former Soviet Union and Eastern Europe with those products (≈ 75%). It ran four large machines that produced sack paper and 28 sack lines.[42] AssiDomän's executives saw Segheza's exceptional production capacity as a threat, since a substantial part of it could be placed on the European market at any time, and that would certainly destroy prices and hurt AssiDomän. The new political situation in Europe also made the Karelian company's entrance on that market more likely.[43] Thus, AssiDomän's taking control over Segheza was both seen as a form of self-protection and as a crucial ingredient in a domination strategy in a volume business.[44] The sack market was shrinking due to an increased use of bulk transports and new plastic materials. As such, there was no room for simple expansion investments – it was all about consolidation, restructuring (keep the large machines) and capacity reduction.[45]

AssiDomän's management supported Ahlgren's effort, although there were two factors that should have set off warning bells: first, the Americans were so-called 'Bahama-capitalists', and second, there existed significant legal and political risks in most deal-making in Russia. AssiDomän's board discussed this big investment proposal several times, and in the end it concluded that it probably was right to buy the shares offered in Sepap and Segheza.[46] The leading actors had been convinced that it was possible to run profitable operations in Russia; for example, they had noticed the forest-based company Mondi's many successful acquisitions in that country. They also checked the 'Russian situation' with the leading actors in the Swedish global packaging corporation Tetra Pak, who had extensive experience in running businesses in that country.[47]

One circumstance that raised the board's concern was Segheza's location. It was situated in the periphery of Russia in a town where the corporation and the local society had 'merged' in several important respects (e.g. the town got its heating from the company and was governed by its CEO).[48] So, AssiDomän's management analysed some of the legal and political risks involved in an acquisition of a large company in Russia, and concluded that CEO Ahlgren could go ahead and make the big investment.[49]

So, in 1996, AssiDomän acquired a 50 per cent interest in Stratton Paper Company, which in turn owned 57 per cent of the Russian pulp and sack paper mill in Segezha. AssiDomän acquired the remaining shares in Stratton Paper in July 1997 and became the majority shareholder in Segheza. Other major shareholders in Segezha were the Russian Karelian Republic through the State Property Fund (20%) and the Russian company UPAK (10%). A serious problem that emerged was that sales were very much carried out as barter affairs controlled by UPAK, an intermediate that took little risk but made substantial profit and severely hampered AssiDomän's expansion efforts (export to and penetration into Russia).

A Swedish managing director (Öberg) was appointed in January 1997, whereby AssiDomän took over operational responsibility for the paper mill. Work on a reconstruction of the company was initiated, and production started in August, with promising results for sacks but not for paper. At the end of the year, the Segheza project was still not profitable and its future was therefore uncertain. AssiDomän had invested SEK 575 million, but nevertheless Segheza lost SEK 15 million each week. Added to that, a visit from the International Finance Corporation (IFC)[50] and the European Bank for Reconstruction and Development (EBRD)[51] called for considerable environmental and social improvements at the site.

The reconstruction included the issue of outstanding taxes and pension liabilities, getting various permits from the authorities, securing long-term access to raw materials and acquiring external financing for necessary investments. However, the promised support from the authorities failed to turn up, and Segheza's management even became harassed through political actions and steps taken by various legal authorities. Moreover, all important measures and decisions taken by the company's management to develop operations and the competitiveness of the mill were questioned and subject to examination by the Karelian Parliament. So, three times in 1997 and 1998 Segezha's management was compelled to stop production, partly because of lack of assistance from the authorities, and partly due to the lack of working capital (its accounts were blocked by the tax authorities).[52]

However, the most serious strike against AssiDomän was when the public prosecutor in Karelia turned to the regional antitrust authority to have AssiDomän's ownership declared illegal, and to start bankruptcy proceedings and appoint a new (Russian) management at the mill. The final blow came when the Arbitration Court in Moscow annulled the permit that the Russian Antitrust Authority had given to Stratton to acquire shares in Segezha.[53] That also called AssiDomän's investment in Segheza into question. Basically, it was not clear that the Karelian Republic had had the right to sell Segheza to the Americans. Thus, the whole issue turned into an internal Russian struggle that involved many powerful interests. AssiDomän was completely unprepared for that intra-Russian fight and was incapable of influencing the actors involved. The uncertain ownership situation made it almost impossible for the company to continue the process.[54] The Russians also caused AssiDomän trouble in ways that its leaders not even in their wildest dreams had imagined (even threats existed). So the support AssiDomän had from the Karelian Governor was not sufficient to make it all work.[55]

All the directors had previously agreed that an expansion into Eastern Europe was a good idea, but in retrospect they regarded AssiDomän's entry into Karelia as a big mistake. The company's leading actors had believed that they could run Segheza in the same way as they were running Nordic units. However, that was certainly not the case. To run a business in Russia an investor really had to be familiar with that country's unique culture and institutions, and make sure that it had support from the involved Russians or risk trouble in many different ways. The Swedish ambassador had informed the board that it was of utmost importance that AssiDomän adapted its activities to the local context, but they had not acted upon that information. In retrospect, some board members in AssiDomän suspected that the company might have been more successful if it had engaged 'genuine' Russians to run the Karelian plant. Several directors also understood that Ahlgren's 'managerial profile' could have been less suitable for the Russian context. He was a classic honest and rational Nordic executive, who in Russia had been confronted with an almost inconceivable and unpredictable political context. AssiDomän had not got any help from actors in the Finnish forest-based industry either, although they had many years of experience doing business with their neighbouring country. The simple reason for that was that they, too, aspired to acquire Segheza.[56]

So, AssiDomän's board had obviously not been on its toes when it supported the company's Segheza investment, and the company's strong financial standing made the board less rigorous in its monitoring. Some of the directors also claimed that the board ought to have been more concerned about the fact that the attractive acquisition of Sepap was connected to the large, much more risky investment in Segheza. Notably, the directors never visited Segheza, and they met neither with the plant managers nor with other influential actors. Some of the directors were also unaware of the huge geo-political risk that AssiDomän took – they did not know that Russian institutions worked very differently from their Swedish counterparts. Thus, some of the leading Swedish actors were simply rather naïve. Chair Lund was particularly self-critical, as he had previously learned that the political context in Russia was complicated and that there existed incriminating circumstances that seemed to be relevant in the Segheza case. He was also uneasy about the way Segheza had been run and how it was 'integrated' with the surrounding town and the Russian and Karelian bureaucracies.

Still, there had also been strong arguments for making the investment. For one, Segheza was a large player in one of AssiDomän's three core businesses. In addition,[57] AssiDomän could allocate Segheza's sack machines all over Russia making sure that they did not enter and 'destroy' the European market (the pulp and sack paper production would be kept in Karelia). Furthermore, AssiDomän's financial situation was enviable. Finally, the company had a new ambitious CEO, who intensively, firmly and consistently pushed for the Russian affair. Therefore, the investment decision also had turned out to be a vote of confidence in the CEO.[58]

In that hopeless situation, AssiDomän's CEO suggested a termination of the engagement, and a withdrawal of all Swedish personnel from the plant (for security reasons).[59] After once again having analysed and evaluated all the circumstances, the board decided that AssiDomän should follow Ahlgren's recommendation, which meant that the unit would go bankrupt. The board and CEO also concluded that it would be impossible to sell the Segheza stock (as the ownership issue was unclear), so AssiDomän had to take a SEK 575 million loss.[60] The Russian fiasco seriously impaired the relationship between the directors and the CEO.

While all this was going on in Russia, AssiDomän invested SEK 400 million in Karlsborg (bleached sack paper) and bought the Italian firms Cartiera dell'Ania (corrugated) and Natrocellulosa (sack paper) in line with its sacks strategy. In seeking to grow in the liquid packaging business and become the sole deliverer to Tetra Pak, AssiDomän launched an investment project (SEK 1.1 billion) to obtain that position. Generally, demand for bleached surfaces increased on the sacks and packaging markets, a development that required some adjustments in the internal pulp production. AssiDomän also looked for new forest resources – foremost in the Baltic Sea region (not in Canada,

South America or Eastern Asia, as several competitors did). In line with its regional fibre strategy, AssiDomän bought Swedish Hasselfors, which held attractive forest resources. However, gradually more and more of AssiDomän's investments were made in the packaging and corrugated businesses – less in kraft products (although a SEK 225 million investment was made at Skärblacka [MG paper]). During these years, several purchases were discussed to strengthen the core businesses, and in 1997 AssiDomän bought three corrugated packaging units: Italian Demalena, Slovakian JCP Sturovo and French Lecoursonnois. However, AssiDomän failed in its attempts to acquire Otor (France), Intercell (Poland), Kuban (Russia) and Cochis (Italy).[61]

7.3 THE FOUNDING OF SVEASKOG

As AssiDomän's balance sheet was still strong in 1998, many of its leading actors discussed what the company should do once the Segheza calamity was behind them. Several crucial questions were raised. Should AssiDomän stick to its strategy? Continue to purchase companies? Launch a repurchase programme? Increase its dividends? Eventually the company decided to try to expand its forest resources and made a bid for a huge property (but failed to get it).[62] Still, the company had an 'unbalanced' balance sheet, as it owned a rather large portion of conservatively valued forests, which had resulted in a (too?) low share price. Therefore, the company faced the risk that it could be bought by any capitalist that had a strong financial position. So, if the state were to decide to sell (some of) its holding, it had to reduce AssiDomän's forest resources, but the state was simply not willing to reduce its control of that (type of) asset. The presence of strategic forest resources in the company also made it politically difficult (even for a right-wing government) to go below a 50 per cent shareholding. Thus, a project was launched to investigate the possibility of transferring about 20 per cent of AssiDomän's forest assets into a new unit initially named 'Vasaskog'.[63]

AssiDomän's position in forestry was strong. Its degree of self-sourcing was relatively high, although many of its forests were commercially useless. It was precisely those commercially weak areas that the state wanted to organize in a separate unit. Director Dockered was one of the leading backers of the Vasaskog project, and he realized that in the mid-1990s there existed a window of opportunity to re-establish something similar to the classic Domänverket. From that perspective he claimed that the investigators had furnished the new unit with both too little and too scanty forest resources.[64] Asserståhl, one of AssiDomän's managers, was picked to run the 'separation project', which was complicated and, for example, required approvals from several authorities. He completed his assignment early in 1999.[65]

The new Social Democratic Prime Minister Göran Persson criticized the former conservative-liberal government for its policy regarding state ownership in the business sector. He claimed that the former government had made the selling of portions of AssiDomän's forests part of an ideology-based sale of state holdings. So when Persson took office in 1994, the neoliberal path was abandoned. In his view, certain resources in a country ought to be state owned, particularly those that benefitted from an owner with a long time horizon and high risk-taking capacity. Persson used the examples of natural resources and manifestations of a country's culture and history. He regarded a substantial state ownership of a country's forests as particularly important, and especially in a 'timber country' like Sweden.[66]

The Prime Minister was also concerned about some of the Swedish private, forest-based corporations' current indecision regarding whether they should continue to treat their forests as strategic assets or not. He believed that a 'no' answer could create problems, since that might allow large-scale foreign owners with unknown intentions to be in control of a resource of great national and popular interest. Together with Dockered (AssiDomän's deputy director, LRF Chair [1986–95] and prominent member of the Centre Party), Persson sought a strategy for turning the classic Social Democratic forest-owning ambition into reality in the late 1990s. Like the Social Democrats, the Centre Party (including Dockered) also preferred a substantial state ownership of the Swedish forests. Its leading actors were truly concerned about how the Swedish forest resources would to be controlled and used in the future. As the Social Democratic Party was reluctant to consider a re-nationalization of AssiDomän, it became necessary to find another way to handle the ownership issue. Persson and Dockered even discussed whether it would be possible to reshape something similar to the former Domänverket, but that turned out to be too complicated.[67]

So there was a political majority in favour of the establishment of a new corporation with the sole task of managing state-owned forests. CEO Ahlgren, however, opposed the idea. Some actors claimed that his political conviction was behind that stance, others that the former conservative-liberal government had promised him a full privatization of AssiDomän.[68] Anyhow, in December 1998, the parliament authorized the government to establish Vasaskog (later renamed Sveaskog) – a unit that should hold some of AssiDomän's forests. Persson asked his Minister of Industry, Rosengren, to monitor the separation process.[69]

Several AssiDomän directors had negative opinions about the Sveaskog idea, but they did not oppose the owner's will. The board's proposal to the AGM involved a transfer of about 900 000 hectares of 'non-strategic' productive forests from AssiDomän to Sveaskog (valued at SEK 6 billion). Its shares were to be distributed to AssiDomän's shareholders (the state owned just above 50%), who were expected to swap them for shares in AssiDomän. The transaction would reduce the state's holding in AssiDomän to about 40 per cent.[70]

The board also investigated whether it would be proper to list Sveaskog on the SSE. One investment bank hesitated and stressed that there were too many restrictions connected to Sveaskog's operations to make it suitable for a listing. The same investment bank also thought that it was very difficult to evaluate the new company, and questioned AssiDomän's current stock-exchange price (too low). Still, Chair Lund and Deputy Chair Dockered gave the green light for both the distribution and the exchange of Sveaskog's shares.[71]

Dockered also mobilized political actors to get the separation process going. As a result Cabinet Minister Rosengren and his State Secretary Detter, together with Chair Lund, initiated the transformation process.[72] Their assignment was to establish a pure forest-owning company and to develop all its 'forestry-values' ranging from timber delivery to hunting and fishing. However, Sveaskog's forests were too dispersed to make the company a significant actor on the national timber market.[73] Early in 1999, Skogh became Sveaskog's first CEO soon followed by Lars Sköld. Sveaskog's top management also included Olofsson, who became Head of Forestry and a few years later CEO.

7.4 THE STRIPPING OF ASSIDOMÄN

7.4.1 Palme Replaces Ahlgren

In February 1999, a crisis – 'a workers revolt' – occurred at AssiDomän Kraftliner (Piteå). When Cabinet Minister Rosengren[74] visited the site, he received an 'open letter' undersigned by a Member of Parliament (MP) from the local community. The MP demanded that CEO Ahlgren should be replaced immediately. The letter was published as a reaction to announced personnel reductions at the Piteå site, and the MP claimed that Ahlgren was responsible for that downsizing. Ahlgren's alleged motive was to compensate for the sizeable losses the company had made in Segheza. Soon afterwards, the site manager was replaced (though Ahlgren was not involved in that decision since he had already been removed).[75] Still, several managers considered Ahlgren's downsizing ideas to be both appropriate and economically rational, although for political reasons difficult to implement (particularly in an election year).[76]

The state had been dissatisfied with AssiDomän's performance for a long time. The extensive investments and acquisitions (≈ SEK 25 billion) had not turned out as expected: in fact, the company's market value had decreased, and the privatization was more and more regarded as a mistake. The state had tried to intervene to improve the situation. For example, the former Minister of Industry, Sundström, had suggested that Ahlgren should be replaced, but the board had not carried out that wish (its Chair was not inclined to replace the CEO). One reason behind Sundström's suggestion was Ahlgren's refusal to implement the owner's will in certain important areas.[77] Another reason was Ahlgren's (too) strong confidence in his own ideas, even expressed in ways that created friction at board meetings.[78] The CEO was more of a 'loner' than a team player. Because that was something new for AssiDomän's management and staff, Ahlgren did not always win them to his side. Furthermore, he lacked experience in dealing with the type of complicated structures and extensive international operations that characterized AssiDomän.[79] The owner was also dissatisfied with Ahlgren's negative view regarding state shareholding in general. In light of all these factors, Cabinet Minister Rosengren decided to also involve director Dockered in the governance process and made clear to him that it was necessary to remove Ahlgren. So on 1 March 1999, Roger Asserståhl was appointed Acting CEO.[80]

7.4.2 A New Board

AssiDomän's owner had ideas about the company's future that involved substantial structural changes (including the sale of selected units). However, that vision was actually not far from what the former CEO had advocated already in 1998. At that time, Ahlgren – together with the consultancy firm Carta – initiated a review of the company's strategy. The main issue addressed was the relationship between the capacity to grow and the scope of the operations. The review resulted in a radically new strategy – the company ought to exit from two of its core businesses: sack paper and sacks. It was after that conclusion had been presented that the state replaced most of the directors and the CEO because it was convinced that implementing the 'new' strategy required executives with special experience and competencies.[81]

Initially, it was Chair Lund who got the assignment to find the new 'permanent' CEO, so he and the other directors began to discuss candidates. However, Lund could not proceed with the recruitment process since the government soon decided to also replace most of the board – including Lund. The new board would then recruit the new CEO.

Dockered was expected to succeed Lund as Chair, but instead the state recruited Magnusson for that position. Cabinet Minister Rosengren claimed that the coming structural transformation of AssiDomän required a Chair that had extensive experience in corporate restructuring. Magnusson, whom he knew rather well, seemed to match the recruitment criteria particularly well. In their initial talks, Rosengren informed Magnusson about the owner's ambitions in terms of AssiDomän, and as Magnusson was comfortable with the current vision, he agreed to become the new Chair.[82]

Magnusson was given the opportunity to choose 'his own board' (with one exception: Tegnér, who had years of experience in the Swedish political system, including its actors and rationales). The rush in combination with the complexity of the mission prompted Magnusson to ask individuals he already knew quite well. Thus, the board recruitment took him only a few days. Magnusson decided to keep Carlsson (an insider who knew 'all' the plants in the industry) but replaced all the others. He handpicked Björnsson (an experienced financial analyst), Duveblad[83] (an experienced IT manager), Helgesson (former CEO of Stora), Blomberg (from Mälarskog, another Swedish forest-based company) and Ros (CFO at Ericsson) as new directors in AssiDomän.

The setting for the restructuring process that the board was to execute was essentially owner determined, as it had a politically decided 'end product': a modern form of the classic Domänverket. Thus, the state expected that the new board would sell off all of AssiDomän's businesses except its forestry – and that at 'good prices'. However, as the ways to reach that 'simple' goal were numerous, the 'stripping' of AssiDomän developed into a difficult and complicated journey.[84]

7.4.3 The Chair Takes Command

The board was given a rather free hand regarding how to carry out the 'stripping' of AssiDomän. The only restriction was that it should not reduce the number of jobs in the company's northernmost plants. In all other respects the state acted as a classic capitalist, and its actors did not slow down the transformation process. When clearance from the state was needed, it was soon provided through the state secretaries (Detter and Rekke). Chair Magnusson and the board's representative from the state (Tegnér) carried out the necessary but irregular communications with the responsible Minister.[85]

Magnusson was certainly no newcomer to the forest-based industry, so he had a substantiated conception about the conditions he was about to face. When taking office he learned that AssiDomän had invested around SEK 25 billion in its operations in the period 1994–98. Still, the economic result had not improved. In reality, the whole forest-based industry had developed poorly during the 1990s, particularly if compared to listed companies in general. Magnusson's knowledge about the more important actors and companies made a quick start of the restructuring process possible. The carefully selected directors – their personal experiences and competencies – also contributed to that capability. New lengthy analyses were also unnecessary, as there existed lots of material based on recent strategic work.

Almost all the new directors were strong and self-confident individuals, who did not stay quiet during the numerous meetings. The discussions were usually intense, and as many of the directors were 'friends', they were neither afraid to state their opinions nor to express heavy-handed criticisms. For example, director Helgesson now and then voiced (unconventional) views that were contrary to the ones (initially) advocated by the Chair. However, it was an open-minded atmosphere, and the Chair really wanted to have thorough debates before important decisions were taken. Magnusson pushed many issues at the same time, but usually the others calmed him down – thus, the board provided the tough sparring partner he wanted. His drive made him function almost like a CEO, which forced the actual CEO to work a little more like a COO. For the most part, Magnusson's leadership produced unanimous decisions, although it often took several meetings (although not much calendar time) to accomplish that unity.[86]

The board decided that they ought to find the new CEO outside of AssiDomän in order to get someone who was unconnected to the company's recent performance and not too fond of the current operations (as almost all of them were on the selling list). Therefore, Asserståhl was not a candidate for that position, although he had done very well as Acting CEO. Magnusson was also looking for somebody who worked more like a COO, as the board would take a very active role in the strategic process and would become the 'hub' in the radical transformation of AssiDomän.

Soon Palme, Deputy CEO at Atlas Copco, was recruited for the 'COO-like' job.[87] As Palme's work was more of a general operative kind (he was supposed to execute the board's [strategic] decisions), his limited experience in the forest-based industry was of less importance. Moreover, Asserståhl, who decided to stay as Deputy CEO, complemented and supported Palme in that field. Instead, Palme brought the kind of international experience that the company needed in its new development phase, and the personal chemistry with the board members turned out to be excellent. He also accepted the board's active role in the restructuring process.[88] Palme knew that Magnusson believed that the intended transformation of AssiDomän might take some time, so the new CEO had time to learn the fundamentals and networks of the industry, as well as the specific operations of his new company. Palme took over as CEO in AssiDomän in September 1999.[89]

7.4.4 Selling Off Most of the Businesses

Chair Magnusson concluded that one important cause of the forest-based industry's low performance in the mid- and late 1990s was to be found in its combination of fragmentation and capital intensity. He also found its cyclicality problematic, particularly in the absence of regulating cartels. It had become more and more difficult to avoid periods of 'overexpansion', something that was accentuated by the entrance of new actors in South America and Asia equipped with modern, cost-effective plants. Magnusson further noticed that the technical rationale still dominated in most analyses and decisions and that the historically strong position of the unions persisted also in the new AssiDomän.

Magnusson's reputation among AssiDomän's employees was basically founded on his earlier efforts in Piteå as an SCA manager in a mill next to AssiDomän's unit. During that time, he had become acquainted with several of the local union representatives in that town, and those relationships helped him a lot also in his new role. Added to that, his dialect had a northern touch, and that, too, made both communication and confidence building a bit easier. As the assigned task implied extraordinary changes, Magnusson tried to build trusting relations with the union representatives by making sure that they always were well informed. He established 'full transparency' regarding all the important issues. As a result, for example, no board meetings were held without the presence of the union representatives. Thus, the unions were given the opportunity to listen to – and participate in – all the intense debates that were held.

Already at the AGM in June 1999, a few months ahead of Palme's arrival as the new CEO, Magnusson outlined what AssiDomän's shareholders could expect in the future.[90] Faced with a complicated restructuring (divestment) process, his lodestar became the currently popular catchphrase 'shareholder value'. He noticed that H&M's[91] stock value was larger than the corresponding sum for the whole Swedish forest-based industry, and that the share values in the industry had developed miserably. However, for AssiDomän, excellent forest resources, favourable market positions and large investments made an improvement of its current operations realistic, which in turn would lead to a better economic result. The Chair was convinced that companies needed 'competitive business structures' to become globally successful. Therefore, he wanted a more focused AssiDomän that increased its productivity with careful and controlled investments, and stimulated result-oriented behaviour throughout the organization. Thus, Magnusson made clear that structural changes were to come.[92]

At the time, AssiDomän consisted of six different business units (forestry, corrugated, sacks, kraft products, carton board, barrier coating and containerboard), and that was too many.[93] So in the second half of 1999, the board instructed CEO Palme to sell everything but forestry and 'packaging'. At that time, the executive levels were not informed about the owner's idea that AssiDomän should keep only its forestry. It should also be noted that the idea to sell the sacks and sack paper businesses was already in place – that path had been proposed when Ahlgren was still CEO.[94]

Magnusson governed the selling process together with the other directors, with Palme as executor. The board meetings were numerous because of the complexity of the selling process and the time pressure. Investment banks were invited to compete for the role as adviser to the board and the CEO, and Carnegie won the contest. So that firm began to provide calculations for 'every' possible strategic move (investments as well as disinvestments).[95] Although the directors did not know Carnegie's staff, they soon gained confidence in them (particularly in one person). Magnusson maintained that Palme and his team needed Carnegie, both because Palme lacked experience with AssiDomän and the forest-based industry and because its management was not accustomed to the kind of process that was to come.[96]

However, Palme expressed a slightly different view from that of Magnusson about how the restructuring process actually was to be run. He rather looked upon the directors as his (and Asserståhl's and Lundström's) 'sounding board'. Palme also maintained that he was the one who had initiated the use of Carnegie, as AssiDomän's management lacked the capacity to handle all aspects of the extensive changes that lay ahead. He simultaneously reduced the assignment for AssiDomän's current adviser Landsdowne to cover the sack business only. Basically, Palme interpreted his task as contributing to a rise in the company's share price. It should be accomplished both by improvements in the current operations and by changes in the company structure.[97]

Magnusson justified the high tempo in the restructuring work with the rather weak operative performances of many of the company's units – new owners or constellations were seen as possible solutions to such problems. Thus, every business field should be placed in the best possible context, and sometimes that could be outside AssiDomän. The Chair was also convinced that the two most important factors for success were capital intensity (scale) and relative market share (power).[98] Using that perspective, Magnusson concluded that AssiDomän was number one in Europe on the sack paper market and number two in sacks. Its market situation was acceptable for liner and fluting, where the company found itself in the second tier together with Kappa and Saica. However, all three lagged far behind the two biggest actors (Jefferson Smurfit and SCA). The same 'ranking' (three) applied to corrugated, although there it was Kappa and International Paper that occupied positions four and five. In the cardboard business the situation was much less favourable. Stora and Mayr-Melnhof Karton dominated that market with AssiDomän in a weak sixth position. The situation was similar for the woodware business but very different for forestry – AssiDomän was the world's biggest public owner of forests (followed by Weyerhaeuser and International Paper).

Magnusson claimed that the Swedish state had to reduce its shareholding if the intention was to expand AssiDomän abroad. Magnusson saw it as difficult to acquire or merge with other companies (or to co-operate in any significant way), if a state controlled a large part of the company stock. He also gradually recognized that there was another possible – and even more drastic – path ahead for AssiDomän, namely to sell all of it, only leaving the forests and sawmills. That path very much looked like the one that the owners – the leading politicians (Persson and Rosengren) – had in mind when the process initially was launched. However, Magnusson did not get that radical assignment from the owner (i.e. the government). Cabinet Minister Rosengren certainly expressed that it expected extensive changes, but not such metamorphosis.[99]

Chair Magnusson wanted to see a new structure for AssiDomän, and CEO Palme shared his view. The company had performed poorly in spite of all the investments that were made during 1994–99 – the only more apparent thing that had occurred was that the company's financial position had become less strong. Soon the board concluded that AssiDomän did indeed hold one or two healthy and promising businesses, but that it could become competitive only through simultaneous divestments. So the board and the CEO decided to keep the corrugated/containerboard businesses and sell off most of the others, that is to say, sacks and sack paper, LPB-Carton, Barrier Coating and Karlsborg together with Skärblacka. As preparation for the upcoming selling process the board asked management for in-depth analyses of all possible buyers/receivers of these four 'packages'. It should also cover companies for which an alliance or joint ownership was a feasible alternative. As all the larger corporations knew each other on these markets, it would be rather easy to conduct that investigation.[100]

During the board discussions about suitable merger candidates in the packaging field, Kappa (owned by the Private Equity [PE] firm CVC/Cinven) immediately turned up as an interesting option. However, that company was heavily indebted, so an integration of the two units (AssiDomän and Kappa) was judged to be too risky. The directors also seriously discussed two other candidates: SCA and Smurfit. However, eventually it became rather obvious that such a 'grand' acquisition/merger was a difficult path forward, as the general idea was to strengthen AssiDomän's core activities, not solve basic problems in the industry.[101]

For one of AssiDomän's major businesses, corrugated/containerboard, a merger soon became a feasible alternative. The company's profitability was poor in several important countries (France, Italy, Spain and the UK), although its general market share was rather high (but it varied significantly between countries). Most analyses indicated that there was an urgent need for a greater scale in that business. However, the high cost (around SEK 15 billion) to become 'big enough' was a serious obstacle. To be able to cross that financial threshold, the board decided to start the restructuring process from another angle, namely by first selling off all units that lay outside AssiDomän's core businesses and then investing in the prioritized field. So, in 1999 the board decided that AssiDomän should try to sell its sacks, kraft products (cf. sack paper) and LPB-Carton, and focus on corrugated/containerboard. The company also decided to expand in barrier coating (although it was a small business) and develop its woodware operations.[102]

Initially, the board hesitated somewhat regarding how to carry out the sales process. It decided to start with two of the businesses – sacks and sack paper and LPB-Carton (Frövifors). The latter unit was regarded as relatively easy to sell, while it was expected to be difficult to find a buyer for the sacks and the kraft products. Nevertheless, since Frövifors' operations were based on one machine only, the trade-off between scale economics and risk exposure was troublesome. Running a single machine also made it costly to switch between products. Moreover, it was almost impossible to expand at the present site, a path that otherwise used to be auspicious. Growth through acquisition was a difficult expansion method, too, as fitting units often were rare and expensive. For example, neither Stora Enso nor Korsnäs was interested in selling its corresponding units.[103] Moreover, Magnusson thought that the opposite path, a purchase by Stora Enso, would be stopped by the European Union (EU) authorities (the merged unit would obtain a too dominant market position). He was also concerned about the fact that Frövifors depended heavily on one customer (Tetra Pak: about 80%) – such a situation usually lowered the selling price. And finally, the board was keen to not sell anything too cheaply, as that could establish a 'sale' stamp on other parts of AssiDomän, and make it difficult to sell them at a decent price.[104]

There were some bids on Frövifors, but all of them below the lowest price the board could accept. For example, the bid from Mead was slightly below the board's limit for considering a divestment (SEK 2.6 billion). Still, the Chair made the bid an issue at a board meeting and asked each of the leading managers about their personal views about the offering. All managers expressed a positive stance except CEO Palme. After a lengthy discussion, his 'no' became the board's decision. Korsnäs's CEO Carlsund also showed some interest in buying Frövifors, because he needed its cash flow for investments in other parts of his business group (i.e. telecom), but the company's major owner (Stenbeck) did not approve.[105] Somewhat later (2000), the board began to put less emphasis on selling Frövifors. Its economic result had dropped, which required a revision of projections. Moreover, as the prices of all forest-based companies' shares had fallen, their capacity to buy 'each other' had decreased. Still, the current divestment failure also had an upside – it became evident to the competitors that AssiDomän was in good shape. The company was not forced to sell, but could wait for the 'right' investor, who (also) was willing to pay a decent price.

In 1999, AssiDomän also began to treat sacks and sack paper as divestment businesses. They were situated in markets where overcapacity existed, and where the total output level was hard to 'control'. There was also a general understanding that company size was the decisive factor required to become profitable.[106] The cash flow in the sacks and sack paper businesses was still healthy, but the outlook was rather dull – both businesses probably faced negligible growth and low profitability. AssiDomän's sacks and sack paper businesses were extensive, but unfortunately not very profitable. Therefore, the company asked its advisory firm Landsdowne to explore whether there existed any opportunities to acquire or merge with other companies to form sustainable operative structures. However, the shortage of buyers and merger candidates in the forest-based sector complicated the situation.[107]

Landsdowne had valued AssiDomän's sacks and sack paper businesses at SEK 4.5 billion (provided that expected synergies were shared equally and that the buyer paid a control premium). If the whole process instead would end up in a merger, the crucial issue would be the involved companies' shareholdings.[108] AssiDomän's main competitor in the sacks business was Frantschach (owned by Mondi), making that big and well-integrated company an attractive partner. At that time, Smurfit was not yet out of the picture.[109] Therefore, Palme and his team met Frantschach's leading actors. In those 'invisible talks' it became evident that they were interested in making a deal.[110] However, eventually it also became clear that Frantschach only considered purchasing – they were reluctant to merge or to sell its own sacks and sack paper businesses. That suited AssiDomän fine, as its owners and leaders wanted their company to get out of those markets. Still, it was very important to get a good price, particularly as LPB-Carton had failed to 'set the standard' (it was still unsold).

Unfortunately, the existence of a 'letter of intent' became known on the market for corporate control, and that weakened AssiDomän's position in the negotiations. Frantschach soon abandoned the initial valuations provided by advisers like Carnegie and Landsdowne. After implementing a traditional due diligence process, Frantschach started to haggle over the price and presented what was regarded as a poor bid.[111] In that situation, AssiDomän's directors discussed whether the negotiations should be terminated, but they decided that the talks should continue.

The price was not the only problem. Frantschach was determined to restrict its purchase to those units that contributed to a better 'balance' in its own business portfolio. As it already contained too much brown sack paper, both Skärblacka and Karlsborg (too much pulp) had to be excluded from a deal. On the other hand, Frantschach showed some interest in Barrier Coating, as it planned to expand in that business. At the time, AssiDomän's board was not interested in selling anything if Skärblacka and Karlsborg were excluded.[112] The last two units were actually known as the industry's 'black holes' – plants where lots of capital had been invested with negligible effects on profit. Some competitors even speculated that AssiDomän would be forced to close both of them.[113]

After some rounds, Frantschach bought AssiDomän's sacks and sack paper operations (the paper mills Dynäs and Sepap, and all the 15 sack manufacturing units) as well as Barrier Coating in 2000 paying SEK 4.5 billion (that sum was transferred to AssiDomän's owners through redemption of shares).[114] That divestment and the impending sale of LPB-Carton would make corrugated/containerboard AssiDomän's sole core business (together with forestry), although the well-invested plants at Karlsborg and Skärblacka would still – reluctantly – be kept (at least for a time). As the most significant actor in the Swedish sawmill industry, AssiDomän would also be a major actor in its unavoidable restructuring. The company also planned to make a 'strategic review' of its forest holdings.[115]

Several competitors were willing to solve some of AssiDomän's structural problems, and one of those was SCA. That company indicated an interest in discussing solutions for AssiDomän's corrugated/containerboard business. Therefore, Magnusson and Palme met with SCA's CEO Martin-Löf and Deputy CEO Bertorp during late 1999 and early 2000 and discussed a (new joint) packaging company and a separate woodware unit. Martin-Löf's idea was that SCA and Mondi should buy AssiDomän, and that SCA then would keep the forests and the corrugated/containerboard units, while Mondi would get the sacks and sack paper plants.[116] SCA wanted to buy AssiDomän with its own B-shares (low voting power), but such a construct would make the price for AssiDomän high, and that made Martin-Löf hesitant. Magnusson instead proposed a solution that presumed a dividing of SCA into two parts – a construct that seemed to be most profitable for both parties (SEK 3 billion in expected synergies). However, SCA's leaders were not interested in such a split-up.[117] Another actor, Custos, through its CEO Gardell, also proposed a new structural solution for AssiDomän. It was similar to the one Magnusson already had embraced, although with ingredients of a kind that only a financial actor could submit (and which the state and the unions never would even consider).[118]

During the early months of 2000, AssiDomän discussed Karlsborg and Skärblacka with both Rottneros and Stora Enso. Selling those plants would also facilitate an agreement in the concurrent discussions with Frantschach. Kappa, which AssiDomän had earlier considered as a merger option, suggested a price, but it was judged to be too low.[119] Palme believed that many actors ascribed Karlsborg close to a negative value, but he claimed that its bleached sacks could develop into a profitable business. He also noticed that Skärblacka produced a kind of fluting that Corrugated could use, so to keep it was at least of some value for AssiDomän. Therefore, the idea arose that the company ought to try to do something useful with each of the plants – not just sell them as a 'package' for a low price. At that time, Palme recruited Hans Pettersson from Holmen to run Kraft Products, but he also asked him to manage Karlsborg and Skärblacka.[120]

AssiDomän also established a specific project for its intended core business corrugated/containerboard. The company received a bid on that constellation from Kappa amounting to around SEK 10 billion. Mondi also offered a similar but slightly lower bid.[121] However, AssiDomän's board wanted to wait a while before deciding the future for corrugated/containerboard, as it expected improvements in that business field, which could raise a future selling price. Instead, the board decided to sell all the other more peripheral businesses before the future for corrugated/containerboard was determined.

Chair Magnusson believed that AssiDomän's corrugated/containerboard business was healthy, although its profitability was lower than the corresponding units at its main competitors (SCA, Smurfit and Kappa). One way to improve the situation was to expand in packaging and its raw material sources (fluting and liner). Kappa was the obvious alternative if acquisition were the chosen path. However, AssiDomän's financial status was not as solid as it was in 1994, so Kappa's price tag (SEK 15 billion) made the board hesitate (although such a 'big bite' would take AssiDomän's packaging business to the same level as SCA and Smurfit).[122] The major owner (the Swedish state) was not at all interested in a cash-based purchase, so the sole alternative was to pay with the company's own shares. That was not easy either, as actors on the M&A market seldom were attracted by possibilities to become large minority shareholders in state-controlled companies.[123] Moreover, if AssiDomän should buy Kappa, its main business would be reduced to owning a huge subsidiary. There was also concern about how the stock markets would react, and that was particularly important to Palme, as his basic assignment was to bring about a rise in the share price. Palme also found a merger between Packaging and Kappa problematic, because that would establish a most unorthodox owner mix (a state and venture capitalists), which could cause governance problems. So, eventually the selling alternative came into focus – but to whom?[124]

The merger alternative would have left AssiDomän a 50 per cent share, of which the Swedish state would own the largest part. Such a construct was not believed to be attractive for the intended co-shareholders (Kappa's owners), who were also concerned about how the Dutch stock market would respond to such a merger. Another reason for AssiDomän's decision to sell instead of buy was that management had difficulties with improving the packaging business' profitability, as 'invisible' political and union activities sometimes obstructed even well-motivated rationalizations. So at the last minute, AssiDomän's board changed its position and told Kappa that the whole deal could be done the other way around.[125]

The board carefully checked all other paths forward, but, finally, the Cabinet Minister Rosengren was approached to find out whether the state could accept a selling also of the corrugated/containerboard businesses, which (together with forestry) were intended to be AssiDomän's core activity for a long period of time. Rosengren informed the board that the state had no specific interest in running forest-based industries, but stressed that the situation was different for forestry. The state was firm on the point that AssiDomän had to keep all its forests.[126]

Since most of the analyses had already been completed when AssiDomän intended to buy Kappa, both actors knew the synergies involved. The buyer/seller swap was also facilitated by the great transparency that usually is present in businesses like this. Each corporation housed rather few – but big – machines that were 'concrete' and comprehensible for the other party. Such circumstances make it possible for the seller to reap some of the expected synergy effects as well. AssiDomän pressed Kappa with hints that SCA might be given the opportunity to make the acquisition,[127] but SCA's leaders were unwilling to pay in a form that would make them lose control of SCA's own packaging business and offered a lower price than Kappa. Kappa's higher bid was motivated in large part by the fact that AssiDomän's packaging business was its 'dream deal', which would bring the company to the same level as Smurfit and SCA.[128] Therefore, in March 2001, Kappa finally bought AssiDomän's corrugated/containerboard business for SEK 10.4 billion (without the forests). The sale included Lövholmen (kraftliner), plants for testliner and fluting, units for corrugated paper production, sheet plants and special paper units.

Kappa Holding had been established by two PE companies located in the UK, and AssiDomän's packaging operations were to be integrated with Kappa Packaging[129] (with its HQ in Eindhoven, Holland), which consisted of 54 operating units in 12 countries (turnover: SEK 17 billion).[130] Neither AssiDomän's board nor its top management was worried about selling AssiDomän's packaging businesses to a foreign PE company, as Lövholmen was a very strong unit in a segment that Kappa needed but lacked. The powerful unions up north learned that the buyer was both serious and well aware of the mill's competitive strength, so they did not obstruct the transaction.[131] When the deal finally was done, the Swedish state announced that an even larger figure than the purchase sum should be handed over to the shareholders, as AssiDomän's economic structure would have to be adapted to what a 'pure' forest company required.[132]

7.4.5 Establishing a New Billerud

After the sale of its core businesses, AssiDomän continued its efforts to create a new company together with Stora Enso that would include Karlsborg, Skärblacka and Stora Enso's Gruvön site. The politicians were more hesitant this time, as they believed that the three units were 'rubbish', and they suspected that Stora Enso's shareholders were trying to shirk their responsibilities as owners by transferring their debris units to the state (AssiDomän). That was true to some extent – both companies wanted to get rid of these plants – but they were actually in rather good shape.[133] A deal with Korsnäs was also considered, but a solution with Stora Enso was preferred, as it offered unique opportunities to make product switches and rationalizations. Stora had tried for years to sell Gruvön to AssiDomän, but each time Stora's offering had been rejected. This time the parties asked an investment bank to evaluate the three units. The bank suggested valuing Gruvön at 40 per cent and Karlsborg plus Skärblacka at 60 per cent, but Stora Enso pushed for 50:50. Stora Enso's two units Pak Enso and Heinola (fluting) were then excluded, as was AssiDomän's fluting in Sturovo.[134]

Asserståhl led the project that Pettersson earlier had initiated. The team also included Hägglund from Stora Enso, a friend of Asserståhl. Their relationship made the discussions easier, but what really decided the matter was the expected economic benefit from the integration of Karlsborg, Skärblacka and Gruvön. Together the three units reached critical sizes on certain market niches, which, for example, gave such a 'new Billerud'[135] a strong position in MG paper. Furthermore, the owners equipped that constellation with a strong balance sheet – the values of the incoming units were written down substantially. As a result, Billerud got fine machines for the booked sums. Other things that contributed to a nice start were currency hedging and luck with the timing.[136] Thus, Billerud became a successful construct; the company took over well-invested units (SEK 5 billion had been invested in recent years), and it immediately achieved a positive cash flow. Still, nobody at AssiDomän or Stora Enso had expected the high market value that resulted: SEK 5 billion.[137] AssiDomän had decided to distribute its Billerud shares to its owners (which established a dispersed shareholding), and, as it – before the listing – took a risk and acquired an option to buy Stora Enso's Billerud shares at what proved to be a very low price (50%), it also appeared to have made a very good bargain. So both parties severely misjudged the upcoming market evaluation of the new Billerud's shares.[138]

In November 2000, AssiDomän and Stora Enso announced that they had created a 50:50 company named Billerud, and that Ingvar Petersson (from Stora Enso's top management) and Östlund (from Stora Enso Pulp) were appointed its first Chair and CEO, respectively. AssiDomän appointed Björnsson (AssiDomän board member) and Tiveus (a former manager at MoDo who knew the forest-based industry from the inside) to board members. Billerud's listing on the SSE took place in November 2001.

By 2001, AssiDomän had sold everything except Frövifors (LPB), the forests and the sawmills. Fortunately those sales had taken place during a boom period. The board purposely utilized the positive atmosphere that prevailed in the forest-based industry between 1999 and 2001 (eager buyers). The concern about impending bad times was justification for the rapid pace of the divestment process, and already late in 2001 the good times were over.[139]

There was some criticism that the units sold were valued too low, and thus that the praise (and handsome compensation) for the board and top management was exaggerated.[140] Another weakness was that, through the sales, AssiDomän became tied to several sourcing contracts that moved future profits backwards to the selling moment – those deals later dampened AssiDomän/Sveaskog's economic performance. Thus, AssiDomän ultimately sold a part of its future to prices/contracts that later had to be renegotiated.[141]

AssiDomän also tried to bring the sawing business into shape. Stora Enso in particular showed interest in that idea, as it, too, was losing money in that field. However, because Stora Enso's units were booked high, the talks came to nothing. Similar discussions with Holmen, Korsnäs, SCA and Södra were also troublesome, and some companies, like SCA, regarded sawmills more as woodchip producers for pulp and paper operations.[142] The Minister of Industry supported the idea that something like 'Swedish Sawmills' ought to be created, but in the end nothing happened.[143]

7.4.6 Founding Sveaskog 2

In 2000, the AssiDomän board again began to discuss the establishment of a large, pure forest company through a transformation of such resources into a new company again named 'Sveaskog'. However, the state was unwilling to buy AssiDomän's forests, as such a separation would increase the value of AssiDomän's shares by SEK 10–15 billion, and thus inappropriately favour the company's current shareholders. To make such a division of AssiDomän possible, it was suggested that its forest resources should be valued sizeably higher.[144] Already in 1999, Sveaskog 1 had been created as an outflow of AssiDomän – 900 000 hectares of forests had been transferred to that unit. However, in 2001 AssiDomän still held 2.4 billion hectares of productive forests, so it was attractive to many competitors in the industry. As a consequence, Cabinet Minister Rosengren received several 'shameless bids' for the company, inter alia, from well-known PE activists.

Sveaskog 1's management wanted to buy more forests, and the state approved. Such an offer also soon appeared – Korsnäs wanted to sell some of its forests. Director Dockered consulted with the Ministry of Industry regarding the purchase, but, based on those talks, the board decided to refrain from a deal. The government did not want to take the risk that a political conflict would emerge and jeopardize the establishment of what was to become Sveaskog 2.[145] Sveaskog 1's CEO had actually come rather far in the negotiations with Korsnäs when the board intervened and stopped the process. He was not informed about the 'secret plan' for a new Sveaskog, which some powerful actors had outlined and informally also promoted. Another obstacle for a deal was that Korsnäs demanded a 15-year long timber-sourcing contract.[146]

At that time, Cabinet Minister Rosengren noted that some of AssiDomän's directors and its CEO Palme advocated the idea that the now stripped-down company ought to be transformed into a private forest-owning company. That worried Rosengren, who phoned director Dockered and informed him that the new strategy made it necessary for the state to intervene and execute the parliament's earlier decision.[147] Thus, for those who preferred a state-owned Sveaskog 2, AssiDomän would not survive much longer. In light of the situation, Chair Magnusson and CEO Palme worked hard to increase the value of AssiDomän by selling productive crown forest areas to financially strong buyers, thereby preventing Sveaskog 1 from acquiring the company. To forestall Magnusson and Palme, Sveaskog 1's board 'suddenly' (October 2001) decided to make a bid for AssiDomän.[148] It expressed Dockered's old vision to re-create Domänverket (a 100% state-owned forestry company). Dockered had found AssiDomän's mix between industries and abundant forestry resources troublesome. He preferred to see the state as owner of most of the Swedish forests (as was the case in similar countries).[149]

The government had concluded that Sveaskog 1's acreages were too small to make it possible for the company to fulfil the state's purpose with its establishment. The obvious solution was to merge AssiDomän and Sveaskog 1.[150] In the prospectus it was stated that the state has a long-term interest in owning forests, but that Sveaskog 1's resources were insufficient for the state's ambitions regarding efficiency, market presence and special obligations. Regarding the last, the state wanted a new Sveaskog that also contributed to better conditions for private forestry in sparsely populated areas. The total value of the offering amounted to SEK 280 per AssiDomän share (its current market price was SEK 223). However, the premium was actually higher (≈ 80%), as the state earlier had announced that it was to suggest a transfer of SEK 12 billion (≈ SEK 126/share) to AssiDomän's shareholders (redemption). That offering was now a part of the bid.

CEO Palme promoted AssiDomän as (becoming) a private forest company. He presented that idea on a capital markets day and got positive responses from almost all analysts. They were all interested in investing in such a corporation. AssiDomän's business would almost be unique in the world, and management expected that the company would become a buyer of forests from many pulp and paper companies, particularly as several of them were reconsidering their ownership of forests. However, the state did not want that such a large part of the Swedish forests (AssiDomän's estates) became available for purchase by 'anybody' on the market, since the forests could land in the hands of actors with a short-term perspective, who might either ransack the forests or create sourcing problems for the Swedish timber-based industry. New owners might also destroy recreation value and spoil forests close to the Swedish fjelds. Thus, AssiDomän's new core business had made the private part of its shareholding problematic.

Still, Palme was taken by surprise when Sveaskog 1's bid became public. He was unsure whether Chair Magnusson had been informed in advance, and assumed that it was the government – first and foremost through Prime Minister Persson and the Minister of Industry Rosengren – that together with Dockered stood behind the bid.[151] Because CEO Palme saw the Sveaskog 2 process as a strictly political move, he was opposed to selling AssiDomän to Sveaskog 1.[152] The state's bid also surprised AssiDomän's board including Chair Magnusson. However, he realized that the state was the only possible buyer of what was left of AssiDomän, as it contained lots of forests (≈ 10% of the Swedish stock).

Cederlund from the Ministry discussed the new situation with Magnusson, and those talks triggered a discussion about the pricing of AssiDomän. The high proportion of forest assets made it difficult to evaluate the company (those engaged in that task all suggested quite different values). The problem was solved in a pragmatic way. The board commissioned Chair Magnusson and director Björnsson to find a fair price. The two suggested that if two/three contracted evaluators came to a similar conclusion, that value would be accepted.[153] So, AssiDomän's board decided to offer the company's shares for (at least) SEK 280.[154] Alecta, SEB Funds and SEB Trygg Liv decided to accept Sveaskog 1's bid, so when it became public it had a backing of around 47 per cent of the votes (including the state's 35.5%). By December 2001 more than 90 per cent of AssiDomän's shareholders had accepted the bid, and by February 2002 that percentage had risen to 99 (the remaining per cent was redeemed compulsorily). Sveaskog 2's purpose was to concentrate on forestry, and therefore the plan was to sell Frövifors to a 'serious long-term owner'.

Cabinet Minister Rosengren appointed Sveaskog 2's[155] board and picked Dockered as Chair, as he was trusted by the government and shared its basic view regarding the future for the new constellation. The board also included Cederlund (from the Ministry for Industry), Domeij (The Green Party), Lena Johansson, Johansson-Hedberg (CEO of Lantmännen), Liffner and Söderberg. The board then appointed Sköld to be CEO of the new company.

The Head of Forestry,[156] Olofsson,[157] saw a future for Sveaskog 2 in the sawmill business, but not for all kinds of sawmills. He suggested that Sveaskog 2 should refrain from investing in industrial sawing, as that would lower the company's own raw material price. Moreover, he believed that the sawmills should not be regarded as a link in a 'fibre-chain' but as a core business. Thus, Sveaskog's subsidiary Setra should earn its money on woodware and a high fibre price.

NOTES

N.B.: When there is an 'i' inside a parenthesis below, that letter indicates that the note refers to an interview with the named person. All interviewees are listed in the Appendix. A complete listing of references is found at the end of the book.

1. Board notes cleared by Dockered in 2007.
2. Hedström (2007i).
3. Åsling (1996).
4. Dockered (2007i).
5. Rydberg (1990).
6. CEO of Korsnäs.
7. Carlsson (2007i) and Lund (2007i).
8. Tegnér (2007i).
9. Ibid.
10. 40% down in 18 months.
11. Åsling (1996).
12. Tegnér (2007i).
13. Lund (2007i) and Tegnér (2007i).
14. Carlsson (2007i) and Lund (2007i).
15. LRF Chair Dockered saw that as the first step – the right-wing government would not stop at that figure (Dockered [2007i]).
16. The owner claimed that 'one farmer was sufficient', so it had to be either Dockered or Åsling. The former was chosen because of better 'personal chemistry' with the current owner representatives and key directors. Dockered's position was also strong as Chair of LRF, while Åsling's career had passed its zenith (Åsling [1996] and Lund [2007i]).
17. A food packaging company.

18. A telecommunication company.
19. An audit company.
20. Åsling (1996).
21. Asserståhl (2007i).
22. Ahlgren (2007i).
23. The Swedish state owned 50%.
24. Ahlgren (2007i).
25. Dockered (2007i).
26. The company got around 600 000 shareholders and became a sort of people's stock (AssiDomän [1994a]).
27. Tegnér (2007i).
28. AssiDomän (1994b), Erbjudande till aktieägarna i Ncb (i.e. Offering to Ncb's shareholders).
29. It was comprised of 680 plants owned by 480 companies.
30. Ahlgren (2007i).
31. Ibid.
32. Asserståhl (2007i).
33. Dockered (2007i).
34. Asserståhl (2007i).
35. Woodware was dropped as a core business according to Dockered (2007i) and Tegnér (2007i).
36. Asserståhl (2007i).
37. Sepap's newsprint business was sold to Norske Skog.
38. Asserståhl (2007i).
39. Lund (2007i).
40. ASSI Annual Report (1997).
41. Carlsson (2007i).
42. Board notes cleared by Dockered in 2007.
43. Asserståhl (2007i).
44. Carlsson (2007i).
45. Tegnér (2007i).
46. Asserståhl (2007i).
47. Board notes cleared by Dockered in 2007.
48. Tegnér (2007i).
49. Asserståhl (2007i).
50. A member of the World Bank Group.
51. A bank that supported the transformation of the private sector in Central and Eastern European economies by issuing credits, guarantees and risk capital.
52. AssiDomän Annual Report (1997).
53. Ibid.
54. Asserståhl (2007i).
55. Tegnér (2007i).
56. Dockered (2007i).
57. Carlsson (2007i).
58. Lund (2007i).
59. Board notes cleared by Dockered in 2007.
60. Ibid.
61. Ibid.
62. Ibid.
63. Asserståhl (2007i).
64. Dockered (2007i).
65. Asserståhl (2007i).
66. Persson (2007i).
67. Ibid.
68. Dockered (2007i).
69. Persson (2007i).
70. Board notes cleared by Dockered in 2007.
71. Ibid.
72. Carlsson (2007i).
73. Olofsson (2007i).
74. Rosengren (Minister of Industry 1998–2002) had a higher profile than his predecessor Sundström (Minister of Industry 1996–98). Rosengren often personally expressed the will of the owner and pushed

certain issues. His actions were also sometimes influenced by local politics, and he usually listened carefully to the unions (Rosengren [2007i]).

75. Valeur (2003).
76. Asserståhl (2007i) and Tegnér (2007i).
77. Rosengren (2007i).
78. Tegnér (2007i).
79. Carlsson (2007i).
80. Rosengren (2007i).
81. Asserståhl (2007i).
82. Rosengren (2007i).
83. The major owner demanded that the board include at least one woman.
84. Magnusson (2007i) and Rosengren (2007i).
85. Ros (2007i).
86. Ros (2007i) and Tegnér (2007i).
87. Magnusson (2007i).
88. Carlsson (2007i) and Ros (2007i).
89. Palme (2007i).
90. Magnusson's transparencies for overhead projector (1999) and Magnusson (2007i).
91. A large Swedish global retail-clothing company.
92. Asserståhl (2007i) and Magnusson (2007i).
93. Asserståhl (2007i).
94. Valeur (2003).
95. Tegnér (2007i).
96. Magnusson (2007i).
97. Palme (2007i).
98. Magnusson's transparencies for overhead projector (1999) and Magnusson (2007i).
99. Magnusson (2007i).
100. Tegnér (2007i).
101. Board notes cleared by Dockered in 2007.
102. Ibid.
103. Ibid.
104. Magnusson (2007i).
105. Palme (2007i).
106. Board notes cleared by Dockered in 2007.
107. Palme (2007i).
108. Board notes cleared by Dockered in 2007.
109. Ibid.
110. Asserståhl (2007i).
111. Board notes cleared by Dockered in 2007.
112. Asserståhl (2007i).
113. Magnusson (2007i).
114. Valeur (2003) and AssiDomän Press release, 7 September 2000.
115. AssiDomän Press release, 7 September 2000.
116. Board notes cleared by Dockered in 2007.
117. Magnusson (2007i).
118. Ibid.
119. Board notes cleared by Dockered in 2007.
120. Palme (2007i).
121. Board notes cleared by Dockered in 2007.
122. Magnusson (2007i).
123. Ibid.
124. Palme (2007i).
125. Magnusson (2007i).
126. Tegnér (2007i).
127. Magnusson (2007i).
128. Palme (2007i).
129. Historically Dutch Koninklijke Nederlandse Papierfabrieken's (KNP's) packaging business.
130. Valeur (2003).
131. Asserståhl (2007i).
132. Magnusson (2007i).
133. Ibid.

134. Board notes cleared by Dockered in 2007.
135. The 'old' Billerud is described in Chapter 12.
136. Asserståhl (2007i).
137. Magnusson (2007i).
138. Palme (2007i).
139. Magnusson (2007i) and Ros (2007i).
140. Bahrke (2007i).
141. Olofsson (2007i).
142. Magnusson (2007i).
143. Palme (2007i).
144. Board notes cleared by Dockered in 2007.
145. It was important that the new construct would last for a long time, so it was essential to avoid moves that the Conservative and Liberal parties would oppose.
146. Dockered (2007i).
147. Rosengren (2007i).
148. Dockered (2007i).
149. Asserståhl (2007i).
150. Annual report for Swedish state-owned companies (2001).
151. Palme (2007i).
152. Tegnér (2007i).
153. Magnusson (2007i).
154. Alecta suggested SEK 310–330 per share, SEB Funds SEK 280–285, Carnegie SEK 270–290 and The Swedish Shareholders Association > SEK 300.
155. Together Sveaskog 1 and AssiDomän formed Sveaskog 2.
156. He was appointed CEO in 2004.
157. Olofsson (2007i).

8. From MoDo to Holmen: the building blocs

8.1 MODO

8.1.1 MoDo in the Driver's Seat

In the transformation of MoDo to Holmen two other larger corporations were added during the 1980s, namely Iggesund (1981) and Holmens Bruk (1988). Later MoDo, Iggesund and Holmens Bruk formed Holmen in a dramatic and complicated process (cf. Ch. 10). In this chapter the focus will be on Holmen's main building blocs, that is to say, on what took place in the three involved corporations before the controversial merger processes started.

The conditions for running forest-based industries changed rather dramatically during the late 1940s and 1950s. One serious problem addressed during the 1950s was the projected future shortage of timber. Already back in the 1930s, investigations had indicated a severe problem regarding timber supply, particularly as the industry as a whole was expected to grow substantially. This growth meant that the timber that the corporations could take out from their nearby surroundings (i.e. the geographical zone that offered a competitive timber price) would not be sufficient. To some extent this negative effect (the use of a more expensive [i.e. distant] resource) was moderated by technological improvements that made the timber use more efficient. However, that effect was also linked to the increasing economies of scale in the production processes, and as the competitors abroad invested heavily, too, it became a necessity for the Nordic companies to try to find new ways to counter the risk of timber shortage.[1] So, for some years, the sourcing problem severely restrained the expansion of the Swedish forest-based industry. The forest taxations also contributed to a development where several Swedish companies' considered diversifying their businesses and/or looking for timber abroad.

The difficulties in getting timber for a price that made the pulp production profitable became particularly serious for those companies that, like MoDo, partly supplied its plants with timber bought on the marketplace. To obtain lower prices, 15 of the larger forest-based companies in the region joined forces and founded Northern Swedish Timber Association ('Nordsvenska virkesföreningen') in 1947. That made them a bigger and co-ordinated buyer instead of a bunch of competing companies (cf. monopsony). It also meant that they divided the available timber among them based on what the various plants historically had used. So, to supply a new plant, one had to close down another one. When the exceptional pulp and paper demand that had existed in the early 1950s fell sharply, disputes arose among the member companies on how to carry out the reductions. As a result, MoDo left the association in 1952 and began to negotiate directly with the sellers.[2]

Later MoDo began to look south for timber and started to buy from that part of the country, too. Before that MoDo had invested in far-reaching programmes for silviculture, but those efforts were not sufficient to solve the problem. There were also discussions about whether MoDo should continue running its sawing mills or not. In the end, however, it was decided to keep the plants but be careful with new investments. The high price of timber certainly made it important to be fibre efficient.

For some other upcoming changes in the forest-based industry, MoDo itself was an important initiating actor, particularly as the company had had the ambition for a long time to be an innovative organization situated at the forefront of technological development. To keep its leading role, MoDo expanded its already impressive R&D efforts in 1961 by investing in a new large laboratory building. However, long before that MoDo (together with Korsnäs) had developed a method for bleaching pulp with chlorine, and the two companies decided to share the patent. MoDo moved fast and established the first industrial plant in the world for chlorine bleaching at Husum in 1946. Early in the 1950s, MoDo added the same process to its plants at Domsjö and Hörnefors, while Korsnäs did not start its pulp bleaching until 1954. The patent was challenged in a drawn out juridical struggle, but MoDo's lawyers were successful, so the 'monopoly' lasted to the mid-1950s. That meant that nobody else in northern Europe was allowed to use the method (another patent was valid in the rest of Europe and northern America).[3]

The new bleaching process made it possible to use birch-based sulphate pulp as raw material for fine paper and printing paper, although it was not strong enough for most other uses. It is worth noting that the dominating owner, Chair and strong man of MoDo, Carl Kempe Sr, did not support the idea that MoDo should try to develop a technique that made the company set to use birch. Instead, that development was initiated and run by Erik Diedrichs, site manager at Husum, without any involvement from Carl Kempe Sr. The new pulp quality soon became a big success for MoDo because its production cost was lower (birch was cheaper than pine and its 'yield' better) and the price to the customer higher. Later the competition forced MoDo to price its birch-based pulp slightly lower than the price for pine-based pulp. However, all in all, the rapid introduction of the new innovation gave MoDo two unique and profitable products to sell all over Europe – bleached birch pulp and bleached pine pulp – and that advantage lasted for many years, even after the patent had expired, as MoDo had already earned a worldwide reputation for its products and could profit from that more abstract 'capital'.[4] During that period MoDo also 'secured' its sourcing of electric energy by building and partly owning Harrsele power plant (49%; in use from 1957).

The possibility to use birch as the raw material in pulp production provided another advantage for MoDo (except for the bleaching as such): its own timber supply expanded considerably. At that time, it also became more and more evident that the projections regarding the total timber supply in the Swedish forests had been far too pessimistic. That finding, too, contributed to the general expansion that took place across the whole forest-based industry in the 1960s.[5] For MoDo, the development during the decade after WWII had made the company strong, and that state prevailed during Erik Kempe's term as CEO.[6]

For many years Husum, led by Erik Diedrichs, remained MoDo's most profitable unit. In reality he ran the whole pulp and paper business in the company on his own, and eventually he got what he wanted – bigger and more modern machines, continuous operations and forward integration. That made Husum one of the best sulphate plants in the world, both technically and economically. Diedrichs also pushed early on for an investment in a pulp and paper combine and made sure that MoDo in all its operations benefitted from all possible scale advantages.[7] His competence, status and importance for MoDo made it difficult for CEO Kempe and other family members to control him, and that unusual power situation continued when Lyberg later became CEO. Even Matts Carlgren, who became the true leader of MoDo in the early 1960s, had great respect for Diedrichs, and in retrospect Carlgren regretted that he had not made Diedrichs a board member.[8]

The interaction between the governmental authorities and the industry leaders was intensive in the 1940s, and it addressed many topics ranging from production restrictions, timber sourcing and co-ordination of operations to crown revaluation, export duties and regulation of export prices. During WWII (and in the early post-war period) MoDo's organic-chemical plants delivered around a hundred different products, but its core business, pulp production, was only running at half speed. However, certain qualities like viscose pulp were doing well. The timber also provided raw material for the production of dynamite, glycol, cosmetics, soap, film, glue, [gramophone] records, aircraft bodies, pharmaceuticals, artificial rubber, DDT, [shoe] soles, and so on. During the period that followed the war, most corporations focused on getting back on track, but they also expanded their pulp businesses and even entered into new business fields. In 1946, MoDo entered the manufacturing business by acquiring Jerfeds Mekaniska Verkstad (a boat and crane builder) and got a platform for what was to become MoDo Mekan (1972) – a unit for forest-related manufacturing.

A most important step was taken in 1949 when MoDo's board decided to build a fine paper mill at Hörnefors. That meant a substantial forward integration. However, the main reason for that step was not strategic, but it was a way of creating new jobs prior to the closing of a classic MoDo unit (Mo sawmill at Norrbyskär). That decision was fully in line with MoDo's long tradition of taking good care of its employees. Thus, in 1951 a fine paper machine was put into production – the first new investment in that business in northern Sweden since 1921. The choice of fine paper was foremost determined by the kind of pulp Hörnefors produced – bleached sulphite. That meant that the new plant would work like a 'combine' with its expected cost advantages (most competitors were non-integrated). However, the new unit did not become successful, so it was sold in 1961 to Ncb. That resulted in a concentration of MoDo's production of pulp into two units: Domsjö and Husum.

8.1.2 A New MoDo Generation Takes Command

Carl Kempe Sr replaced his uncle Treffenberg as MoDo Chair in 1947 but kept his position as CEO for two more years. His long period as leader of the company reproduced its character as a 'dynasty-based' organization (in spite of its rapid growth and the declining number of Kempe descendants in top positions). The MoDo character and 'spirit' referred to an attitude that both owners and employees held – a feeling that all involved individuals were part of one and the same history and shared a common (family-based) identity. Carl Kempe Sr was succeeded in 1949 as CEO of MoDo by his cousin Erik Kempe, the eldest son of Seth Kempe, and Lagergren became the new Deputy CEO. Erik Kempe earned a PhD in Policy Science from Uppsala and afterward devoted most of his time to the family businesses. In 1928 he replaced his father Seth as CEO of

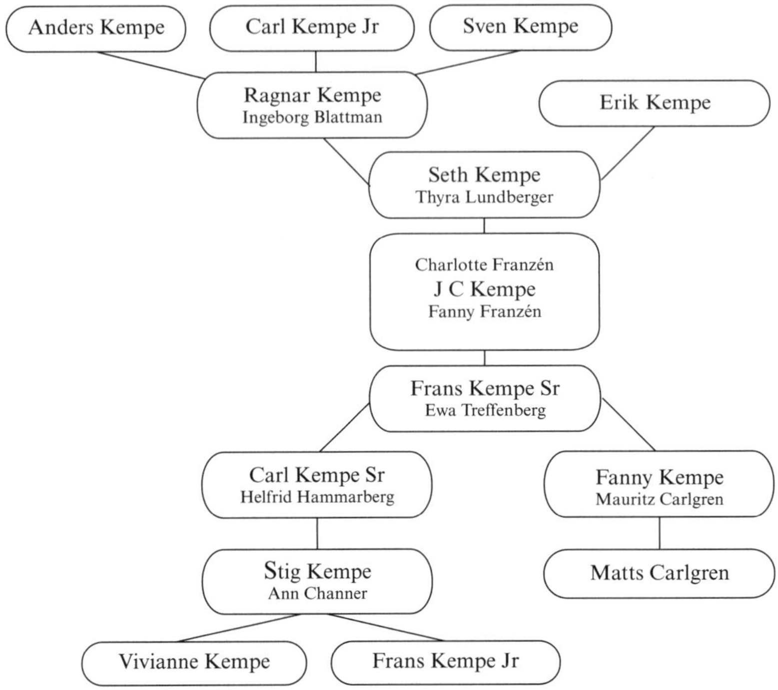

Figure 8.1 A selected part of the Kempe family tree (the Frans and the Seth factions)

Robertsfors. During the 1920s and 1930s, Erik Kempe had belonged to various boards in the MoDo group, and in 1940 he became the group's Deputy CEO (also Head of Forestry [1940–44]).[9]

However, it was not unproblematic to win support for Erik Kempe as the new CEO. To most people he was the obvious candidate, but at the same time it was clear that he lacked some of the qualities that were seen as particularly important for a MoDo leader. Except for his experience as CEO of Robertsfors, he had not engaged very much in commercial matters or international business activities. Thus, his knowledge of the European forest-based industry and sales management was rather limited. By contrast, his rival for the CEO position, Lagergren, was much more experienced in both those fields. Moreover, it was Carl Kempe Sr that had recruited Lagergren to MoDo and had given him the task of running 'Nordsvenska Bruk' – an organization that gradually faded and ended as MoDo's sales company for pulp. In that situation Lagergren looked for a greater challenge and offered himself as a candidate for the CEO position. In that race he benefitted from the on-going rivalry between the two arms of the Kempe dynasty, the Frans and Seth ones. Carl Kempe Sr (son of Frans Kempe Sr) and Erik Kempe (son of Seth Kempe) had different personalities and temperaments and certain difficulties in co-operating. There also existed memories of the times when Seth Kempe almost had acted as Carl Kempe Sr's guardian (Seth survived Frans by more than twenty years). As a consequence of all that, MoDo made a most unusual arrangement appointing Erik Kempe as CEO and Lagergren as Deputy CEO 'fully on par with the CEO and in some fields [sales] responsible directly to the board'. However, that construct first and foremost became a paper one – in practice Erik Kempe took charge in the traditional Swedish way.[10]

When Carl Kempe Sr stepped down as CEO in 1949, he wanted to take on the role of 'working Chair', which at the time was a relatively unknown arrangement in Sweden. To him such a position meant a formalization of his freedom to pass over Erik Kempe and Lagergren and discuss important issues directly with the responsible managers in the organization. However, neither Erik Kempe nor Lagergren allowed him to do so. At that time, Matts Carlgren, son of Frans Kempe Sr's daughter Fanny, engaged Chair Carl Kempe Sr in his activities at Wedevågs Bruk. By involving the Chair in this way, Carlgren laid a first stone in a trust-building process.[11]

8.1.3 Leadership Struggles

The period during which Erik Kempe took over the role of CEO from Carl Kempe Sr represented not only a switch from one family faction (the Frans lineage) to the other (the Seth lineage), but also a transformation of a medium-sized family firm to a large public company. This meant that it was increasingly difficult to run the company in a patriarchal way, a development that suited Erik Kempe's more modest leadership style well. However, it must be noted that Carl Kempe Sr still was MoDo's Chair, and thus the one that also formally had the ultimate power, particularly regarding the company's strategy.[12]

Erik Kempe immediately launched a consolidation strategy and cleaned up MoDo's somewhat untamed collection of businesses. He moved the company's headquarters to Örnsköldsvik, close to its core operations, and settled himself in Domsjö. During his period as CEO, a particular focus became keeping the pulp plants at Domsjö and Husum technically and economically effective. That became increasingly important, as new producers appeared on the market, particularly firms from North America but later also from Finland and southern Sweden. That new competition was mainly made up of plants that produced sulphate-based pulp.[13] It is worth noting that MoDo's modernizations and expansions of its pulp production actually put a rather limited pressure on its financial standing, and that the Korean War-based boom times added to the company's previous strong economic position.

However, Erik Kempe did not only keep the company's existing operations in good shape. It was during his time as CEO that MoDo took its first step into fine paper production by acquiring Hörnefors. MoDo also invested in power resources (Harrsele) and in the chemical industry (a purchase of an industrial estate at Stenungsund). The latter opened up opportunities for substantial investments in the fast-growing chemical industry. MoDo's founding of 'MoDo France' (1955) was another important strategic decision taken during that period.

MoDo's share price fluctuated significantly in the 1950s, something that tempted several Kempe family members to sell their private holdings in the good times. Unfortunately, they seldom could afford to buy them back in bad times, so over time that type of family ownership gradually decreased. Instead, the Kempe foundations kept buying shares to capture the dividends that, according to their statutes, should be added to the capital. In 1959, when Erik Kempe died, some problems arose regarding who should replace him, and those frictions also influenced the discussions at the boards of the family foundations. Since Carl Kempe's eldest son Frans had revolted and abandoned all plans to become an industrial actor, Carl's second eldest son Stig Kempe (board member since 1953, Deputy CEO since 1957) came into focus, particularly when Lagergren retired in 1956.

For a while Stig Kempe was regarded as the up-and-coming man in MoDo. However, several of the members of the Kempe dynasty were not that enthusiastic about him,[14] although in his father's eyes, he was an obvious CEO candidate. As Carl Kempe Sr saw it, Stig Kempe was clearly cut out for taking on such a responsibility, as he possessed the desirable qualities associated with the Frans faction of the dynasty. Thus, once again the tales about the characteristics of the actors belonging to one of the two factions of the Kempe dynasty rose to the surface and produced different opinions regarding how (and by whom) the company should be governed.[15] However, Stig Kempe never felt comfortable working in the family company, although he and Erik Kempe got along well almost from the start. It was Carl Kempe Sr's rough way of 'testing' candidates for top positions that put him off.[16] Years later, when Matts Carlgren became CEO, Stig Kempe was asked to leave his executive position in the company.[17]

Carlgren's mother was Fanny Kempe, a daughter of Frans Kempe Sr, and, consequently, Carl Kempe Sr's sister. Carlgren's father was Mauritz Carlgren, a certified forest officer who for several years had acted as MoDo's Head of Forestry. Matts Carlgren was quite ill when he was very young. Over time that and other experiences sparked his interest in sports.[18] He grew up to become a sort of 'clean-living man', as well as a person who never gave up and hated to lose. Carlgren earned his MBA at the Stockholm School of Economics, and soon engaged in concrete business activities. In his early 30s, he already owned several companies. By his mid-30s, he was appointed to the prestigious position of 'family auditor', and somewhat later he also became a MoDo board member.

The Frans Kempe family line led by his daughter Fanny Carlgren battled to have her son Matts appointed as the new CEO. The representatives for the Seth Kempe line, led by Ragnar Kempe, instead proposed MoDo's Deputy CEO since 1952, Lyberg. They regarded Carlgren as too inexperienced and not ready to shoulder such a heavy burden since his only qualifying experience was as CEO at Wedewågs Bruk – a minor manufacturing plant led by a professional COO. In the choice between Carlgren and Lyberg, Carl Kempe Sr, still actively involved in the foundations, finally changed his mind and decided to support his sister's candidate.

One could say that it was much of a coincidence that Lyberg ultimately attained the leading position in MoDo. In 1955 Carl and Erik Kempe received a visit from Uddeholm's CEO Danielsson, who was interested in recruiting Lyberg as his successor. That proposal brought up the question within MoDo about who should replace CEO Erik Kempe, who had held the position for six years, and Chair Carl Kempe Sr, who had reached the age of 70. To convince Lyberg to stay with MoDo, Carl Kempe Sr had told him that he would be a serious candidate to succeed Erik Kempe.[19]

To leave the company in the hands of a successor is difficult, especially so in a large family-controlled firm. To do so in an orderly and legitimate way, without frictions, requires planning. It is often necessary to train and 'cultivate' candidates and then single out a 'crown prince' without arousing destructive power struggles. Moreover, it is crucial that the one in command abdicates before he becomes too weak to be able to guide the process. Carl Kempe Sr was not particularly successful in managing the process of identifying Erik Kempe's successor. Maybe he waited too long to state his reasons and preferences, so that external occurrences more and more controlled his agenda and ambitions; or – perhaps – he simply changed his mind in the end. In any case, the Frans Kempe line gave in, and Lyberg was appointed. Carl Kempe Sr had preferred Carlgren, but since his and Lyberg's relationship had worked well, it was not a great loss.[20]

It was director Tore Browaldh who put forward the solution that opened up the family deadlock: MoDo should put on paper that Carlgren was the one that should replace Lyberg when he retired. All family members accepted that suggestion as a compromise.[21] However, since Carlgren really wanted to become CEO already in 1959, he had difficulties accepting defeat. He was given the unusual position as 'director on duty' with an undefined role. That arrangement provided him full information and considerable control, although Lyberg retained formal responsibility. During Lyberg's tenure as CEO, Carlgren continued to take many initiatives and push issues outside of the formal MoDo organization, a situation that created governance problems for the board, CEO Lyberg and other members of the MoDo organization.[22]

Carlgren was not unchallenged as the next head of the Kempe dynasty. The 20 years' younger Carl Kempe Jr was also a candidate for that position, although in the eyes of most dynasty members he did not have the same leadership qualities as Carlgren. Therefore, up until the 1990s, Carl Kempe Jr's role remained rather unclear even though he handled the Kempe foundations' shareholding in MoDo, a holding that actually was bigger ($\approx$ 25%) than the one controlled by Carlgren ($\approx$ 20%). In the 1960s, Carl Kempe Jr was not prepared to compete for the family leadership with Carlgren, who belonged to the 'right' faction of the dynasty (the Frans arm) and was supported by its grand old man Carl Kempe Sr. Carlgren was also favoured since he exuded a more 'CEO-like' managerial style. He used the broader strokes of the brush, while Carl Kempe Jr instead mastered the details. Those differences worked in favour of Carlgren, although both candidates had many similar gifts and qualities. Both were rather charming and were seen as equally talented. Both also expressed strong formal as well as emotional ties to MoDo and promoted the expansion plans that the company had begun implementing in the 1950s.[23]

8.1.4 Carlgren's Way of Thinking

CEO Lyberg had a good relationship with both Carl Kempe Sr[24] and Erik Kempe, something that worked as a kind of guarantee allowing him to act with vigour in his new position. Carlgren, however, did not forget that he had been sidestepped, and that emotionally flavoured memory later came to influence Lyberg's working situation.

Already in the late 1950s, Carlgren had begun to act strategically on his own, entering into commitments on behalf of the company, many of which had not been discussed or cleared with its CEO.[25] He had difficulties with the division of labour between himself and Lyberg, and he therefore did not always act in accordance with the way the Swedish Company Law distributed responsibilities and duties among the three principal governance agencies (AGM, board and CEO). Moreover, Carlgren did not always keep the boundaries clear between MoDo and his private companies. He regarded himself as free to act across these (juridical) borders. One striking consequence of this behaviour was that many leading actors were not as informed or involved in crucial matters as they, at least from a juridical perspective, should have been. Carlgren did talk to some actors about the most vital issues, but it is doubtful whether he was much influenced by what they said. Paradoxically, the bigger the issue, the less he tended to listen to others.[26]

Carlgren's way of thinking did not deviate significantly from that of several of his predecessors. Like them, Carlgren was backed by a dominating family shareholding, and he represented and promoted its traditions and dreams. To those like him it was natural to look upon a (non-family) CEO as a plain salaried employee, who had to carry out decisions taken on 'a higher level'. Moreover, if the head of the dynasty was 'an executive kind of personality', then it was also 'natural' that he directly intervened – even in the company's daily operations. Notably, however, when Carlgren was CEO (1971–81), most functions – strategic as well as executive – were linked to his position and not distributed.[27]

For the most part, MoDo's board had been a rather weak agency, particularly when somebody outside the family acted as Chair. Usually, the board was reduced to a formal arena that confirmed what was already decided and sometimes also executed. Thus, discipline in the early, informal and 'invisible processes'[28] was weak – everything circulated around Carlgren. He ran the company's strategic process not only partly outside the board meetings but also partly outside the board collective, in what seemed to be a rather haphazard way. However, one has to keep in mind that MoDo, to some extent, also was 'controlled' by Handelsbanken because of the high risk level and strained debt ratio. Therefore, it had become a custom that (at least) one of the bank's leading actors was appointed as a member of MoDo's board. From that platform that person could exert some influence on both Carlgren and the company's strategic path.[29]

Carlgren continued to dominate MoDo's development all through the 1960s, finally succeeding Lyberg as CEO in 1971. However, already by 1965 he had become 'working' Chair in MoDo, replacing Carl Kempe Sr (who left at the age of 80). At that time, MoDo's board consisted of seven members appointed by the shareholders: Carlgren (Chair), Browaldh (Chair of Handelsbanken; appointed in 1960[30]), Ragnar Kempe, Stig Kempe (Deputy CEO[31]), Peppler (married into the Kempe family) and CEO Lyberg. The Chair position provided Carlgren with a platform for his strategic ambitions and initiatives that had firmer legal standing, and his autonomy increased even more when Carl Kempe Sr died in 1967. As long as Carlgren was the Chair of MoDo, CEO Lyberg did not always feel comfortable. Most of the executive power had moved from the CEO level to the board level – and particularly then to its Chair.

Still, it was easier for Lyberg to accept Carlgren as Chair than as a director of the board with 'special duties'. The relationship worked rather well during the first years of Carlgren's chairmanship, but in the long run it could not be avoided that Carlgren's long-term ambitions interfered with the CEO's discretion. That occurred despite the fact that Lyberg allowed the Chair to 'star' at some of the big business deals that took place, for example, the acquisition of Bure and the forests owned by the Forss family. However, it was not until the late 1960s that Lyberg felt the ground trembling beneath his feet. It was then that Carlgren, supported by the newly appointed Chair of Cellulosaföreningen,[32] engaged in discussions regarding pulp business co-operation on an international basis.[33]

As described above, Carlgren began to dominate MoDo's development in the 1960s and would do so for about three decades, irrespective of what formal position(s) he held in the company. Like most people, Carlgren was a multi-rational person. At heart, he was a sterling fellow and honest person, but that was not always an advantage in the various situations characterizing business life. He was simply not a clever player, and his knowledge of finance was limited, certainly for his position, but particularly for the role he took on, a role that involved quite a lot of risk-taking. Unlike most other people he was born with a 'leader helmet', an upper class kind of self-confidence and a strong attachment to the Kempe family. Carlgren's major platform in MoDo was his support from that owner dynasty. Another source of personal strength was his spiritualism. He held séances in which he, for example, sought business advice from his predecessor Carl Kempe Sr.[34]

It is common that a founding family and its values, norms and attitudes often play a crucial role in how a company develops, and MoDo was no exception. In some of the families that have run a company for generations there frequently evolves a certain sense of responsibility for the company and its stakeholders (particularly its employees) and a duty to take the company to new heights. Usually that sense of responsibility is linked to the idea that only one or very few members of a dynasty are equipped with particular capacities to deal with that exacting task. Carlgren thought that he probably was the only one that had that especial talent, and many family members were of the same opinion. Then it is important to note that Carlgren was very much a loner, keeping his ideas, personality and emotions to himself. When it came to MoDo matters, therefore, he lacked trusted advisers and close friends, although he listened to some people in his extensive network.[35] One of them was Altbäck, Head of Accounting and Control, but he did not have the strength and authority to 'control' Carlgren. Häggkvist, who chaired MoDo during the 1970s, had some influence, and so did consultant Pöyry and Löf (MoDo CEO 1985–94). Not even director Wallander, who as Head of Handelsbanken was a very influential actor in the Swedish business society, could moderate Carlgren. One might have expected that Carl Kempe Jr, another leading actor in the Kempe dynasty, would work as an important sparring partner, but that was not the case since Carl Jr was rather Carlgren's implicit rival for control of the Kempe dynasty's shareholding.

So, in the end Carlgren tended to follow his own ideas and rationale. In several respects his approach also differed from that of his predecessor, Carl Kempe Sr. Nevertheless, belonging to the same Kempe faction (cf. Figure 8.1), his leadership style still reflected most of the classic 'Frans qualities', that is to say, he acted strategically, took substantial business risks and was most active in operative decisions and deeds. Like Carl Kempe Sr, Carlgren was determined to make MoDo a bigger and more powerful company.[36] The important challenge was to carry on the Kempe heritage and bring even more glory to the company, the family heirloom. Carlgren's strong will to fulfil the family tradition by making the company even bigger and eventually a leading company group in Sweden explains what happened between 1960 and 1990.[37]

From the 1960s, when Carlgren sat in MoDo's 'driver's seat', he was a powerful actor, who did not hesitate to take substantial risks. In the beginning his flair for making business was manifested in innovative initiatives addressing many different areas such as the forest-based and chemical industries, the fine arts, the hygiene sector, the medical technology field and the emerging opportunity (in Sweden) for commercial TV broadcasting. To stem that unfocused expansion, the actors that worked closest to him tried to function as dampers, although those who tried to do so often faced difficulties. However, Carlgren also had the patience to wait (a long-term perspective), and if matters turned problematic he usually kept a cool head. He was accustomed to the troublesome issues turning out his way for the most part. He expected banks to work as 'servants' to entrepreneurs and businessmen, a view that over time created problems in his relationships with the new generation of bank managers.[38]

The emerging financial strain arose from Carlgren's limited capacity to prioritize among the various ideas and ventures, and – linked to that decision agony – an inability to correctly evaluate both his own and MoDo's financial resources. He neither possessed nor controlled the capital needed for making all the investments linked to his many business ideas. Added to that, he had difficulties recruiting the most competent, clever and committed executives and staff to all the new ventures. One could also mention that a 'special rivalry' existed between MoDo and SCA, which explains to a great extent his and the company's actions (or passivity). Thus, it was of particular importance for Carlgren to keep up with SCA.[39]

8.1.5 Expanding into the European Continent

MoDo's ambition to move away from standard bulk products and engage more in differentiated and customized products made it almost necessary to switch from a sales system based on international agents to one based on subsidiaries established outside Sweden. Such companies could examine the specifications and qualities associated with each product and make adjustments based on particular customers' needs. Customizing had already begun at the Domsjö plant – a unit that during the 1950s became a supplier of high-value special pulp qualities. Such customer interactions created lots of new knowledge that made MoDo particularly capable of providing advanced service and development support to its customers.[40]

Against this background, MoDo's new CEO Lyberg regarded forward integration in Europe as the 'natural' way for the company to grow in the early 1960s. His ambition to establish a position in Europe was based also on the desire to join the group of continental European countries that co-operated regarding trade regulations and similar issues. That was particularly important, since it was not likely at the time that Sweden would become a member of the EC.

During the 1950s MoDo sold its pulp in France through a French agent, Lejeune. He, who spoke Swedish fluently, had been employed at Handelsbanken (1948) and was recruited as an assistant at MoDo's French sales company in Paris (1955). Eventually, he became head of that unit, and when MoDo's engagements in France expanded, so did Lejeune's activities. Carlgren and Lejeune became friends. That friendship meant that Carlgren supported Lejeune and permitted him to keep and develop his own private pulp and paper business. He even was appointed to an unusual position in the MoDo organization, reporting directly to Carlgren. Many MoDo managers found Carlgren's organizing inappropriate, but it was an outflow of his habit of disregarding juridical norms and boundaries when it came to corporate governance issues. Obviously, Carlgren had confidence in Lejeune, who had been successful in his own business activities. So, although efforts were made to grow also in Germany and the UK, MoDo decided in 1955 to move forward in France by way of a (sales) company that would be led by Lejeune.[41]

One of the reasons behind Carlgren's idea to appoint a Frenchman as the head of MoDo's French subsidiary was that he, like many other businessmen, believed that it was difficult for an outsider to successfully manage a business in that headstrong country. So, together with Carlgren, Lejeune ran the French operations, constantly telling the MoDo managers how they should act in that market. The pulp business in particular developed well under Lejeune's leadership. As a result he was also made responsible for the Papeterie de Pont Sainte Maxence (PPSM) plant, and later became head of all MoDo's activities in France. Carlgren underlined Lejeune's privileged position by making him a deputy member of MoDo's board (1985–91).

MoDo's initial internationalization strategy focused on purchases of smaller units located close to places where the consumption (of paper) was known to be high. Therefore, in the first half of 1960, MoDo decided to establish a special team for such initiatives located in Switzerland. Formally, the group – led by director Peppler[42] – was instructed to produce economic surveys, assist top management by generating and developing various long-term projects, and produce data and analyses for strategic decisions.[43] Peppler – supported by both Carl Kempe Sr and Carlgren – set an agenda that concentrated the team's efforts on internationalization matters. In practice, that meant carrying out analyses of MoDo's European business environment and coming up with suggestions regarding suitable companies and business systems that could or ought to be acquired. Through these activities, Peppler's group produced most of MoDo's expansion ideas. From the beginning they thought that it would be difficult to build up a market in a classic, organic way – it would not only take too long but also be both an expensive and a hazardous strategy. Instead, they wanted to build up a business either through some kind of joint venture with a well-reputed company or through the acquisition of a going concern.

It was often Peppler himself who picked and sought out 'suitable companies' and 'interesting projects' in Europe, that is to say, those firms and activities that he thought fit the strategy he had outlined. The first project carried out by the team was a thorough analysis of the outlook for products based on soft paper (tissue), but the following projects covered a broader spectrum of forest-based products. Generally, a business field was approached through a mapping of its producers and market opportunities. Then a period of reconnoitring began, where MoDo's investigators tried to identify possible acquisition candidates, particularly in France and Germany. However, on the whole, the target firms identified were not interested at all in engaging in joint ventures or selling. One reason for their disinterest was probably that MoDo was a relatively unknown company in most European business circles, although Peppler's many visits probably eliminated some of that anonymity.

However, Peppler's group did not solely look for a distinguished partner (or a firm to acquire) when it investigated ways that MoDo could become a major player in Europe. Like many other European forest-based companies, the Peppler team had come to the conclusion that, taken together, the European paper producers lacked sufficient timber resources for their planned expansions. Therefore, Peppler travelled widely to find out how the European forest-based industry best could tackle a coming shortage of raw material. His conclusion was that the sub-tropical and temperate areas in (particularly) South America were the most suitable and promising areas in the world for huge production and export of timber.[44] However, at the time, this insight did not materialize in the form of any new activities.

MoDo quickly concentrated its internationalization efforts on France and Germany. Assisted by Lejeune, many contacts were made, but unfortunately the more interesting and well-functioning units were hard to acquire. In the end, that made 50–50 solutions the only remaining path, although the actors knew that such arrangements often became problematic. After many discussions with various firm owners and top managers, MoDo decided to co-operate with a Swiss company, Holzstoff, which had paper mills in four European countries (France, Germany, Italy and Switzerland). That joint venture was limited to two mills, PPSM (outside Paris) and the Italian Cartiera di Carmignano (outside Verona). Peppler found Holzstoff through one of his bank contacts, who introduced him to the company's DG Zumstein. However, it took many rounds before an agreement was finally reached. The operative match was far from perfect, as Holzstoff's production repertoire did not match MoDo's pulp qualities particularly well. Moreover, Holzstoff was not willing to abandon its control of the plants, so MoDo was expected to become a minority owner only. In 1964, after many discussions, Holzstoff and MoDo decided to form a Swiss holding company, Intercelpa, in which the shareholding and voting rights were equally divided between the two founders. Intercelpa was composed of two of Holzstoff's plants, PPSM and Cartiera di Carmignano. MoDo rejected the inclusion of Papeterie de Versoix (outside Geneva). Initially CEO Lyberg was very pleased with that outcome.[45]

However, this joint venture did not turn out to be a particularly successful one. MoDo's payment never added to Holzstoff's equity – it went straight into its profit and loss account, something that made further expansion investments from the Intercelpa group difficult. Another complication was the 50–50 shareholding – a division of power that requires co-operation, transparent decision-making processes and joint actions. Moreover, there were culture clashes, as people from two different countries with different leadership styles were expected to work together, and there were also diverging opinions about the quality of the new machine that was installed in the French paper mill. Added to all that, calculations indicated that Intercelpa might face problems in terms of its profitability.[46]

Despite these difficulties, Lyberg worked hard to make the new joint venture function in a tolerable way. He talked frequently with Holzstoff's DG Zumstein, but experienced great difficulties in coming to an understanding. Both companies had expected greater degrees of autonomy. MoDo's ambition with its ownership was to 'fully' integrate the new unit and use it as a tool for further internationalization of its businesses. Holzstoff saw the joint venture as a way to secure the sourcing of raw material for its paper mills. These differing ambitions were known when the agreement was made, and there were reasons for believing that both companies' goals could be met. To a large extent it was the poor personal chemistry among the leading actors that created the problems. As a result, genuine distrust surfaced in the relationship rather early on, which made further co-operation impossible.[47]

Erik Diedrichs was the one that most intensively argued for a break-up of the Intercelpa agreement. It was rather easy to follow his advice, as both of the holding company's plants were rather unsuccessful, and the co-operation between the two owners had come to a standstill. In the break-up, Holzstoff was allotted Cartiera di Carmignano and MoDo PPSM. At the time, problems had emerged at the French unit. The main difficulty was that technological progress had made small-scale, non-coated fine paper plants less competitive. Other difficulties were connected to a mediocre management quality and rather poor employee relations. Yet MoDo was satisfied with that outcome, and CEO Lyberg was convinced that a modernized PPSM had a great future.[48]

8.1.6 Growth through Diversification

Since the late 1920s MoDo had been comprised of three core businesses – pulp, sawn timber and chemical products – and several minor ones including various kinds of manufacturing. Thus, MoDo was a relatively diversified company, although several of the businesses could be denoted as 'related'. Basically, Carl Kempe Sr was responsible for that development, although Erik Kempe had contributed in his way by not making more dramatic changes in any direction (neither diversifying nor concentrating the businesses), thereby consolidating the set-up formed by his predecessor.

Many of the decisions that MoDo took after WWII carried Carlgren's signature. However, they also had their roots in a long MoDo tradition manifested in its investments in people and plants. Of course, over the years new businesses had been established, too, particularly due to the very special conditions that the war situation had represented. However, although many of these differentiations and diversifications gradually were phased out, some of them survived and a few even prospered. That variety provided MoDo with an opportunity to grow along new lines partly away from its original business. Thus, MoDo was able to both follow its classic path developing its sawmill and pulp-based businesses and enter new, more venturesome paths, of which industrial chemicals stood out as the most important undertaking. At the time, MoDo's structure allowed for many possible futures. MoDo's director and family auditor Carlgren advocated a rather diversified strategy, supported by the company board with Carl Kempe Sr in the forefront. Obviously, MoDo's planning was loaded with optimism about its opportunities to operate in several different industries at the same time: the pulp business (developing new short-fibre qualities and expanding the machines to be the biggest ones in the world), forestry, the chemical industry and the entry into the continental European market through processing of pulp to fine paper and tissue.

As noted above, MoDo's growth strategy after WWII included diversification into the chemical industry. One reason for going in this direction was that MoDo expected a shortage of timber for its core operations. Furthermore, high expectations were associated with that fast-growing business field, and MoDo's leading actors wanted to seize the opportunity to become one of its large and profitable players, particularly as the company had incorporated a sizeable amount of chemical products in its business portfolio since the 1930s. Initially, that path might have been regarded as an entrance into a 'related business' (not a diversification), as some of its roots could be traced to chemicals used or produced in the forest-based industry. However, in the 1950s, the chemical industry instead became more and more based on petroleum, and the big multinational oil corporations were expanding their activities by building European crackers. Esso Chemicals, for example, made a large investment in Stenungsund (a small community on the Swedish West Coast).[49]

MoDo's use of alcohol to produce ethylene (oxide) at Domsjö became unprofitable when competitors started to use petroleum-based raw material for the same purpose.[50] So MoDo signed an agreement with Esso to buy certain quantities of ethylene, and that, in turn, implied the localization of a chemical plant to produce ethylene oxide to Stenungsund – a business that expanded substantially during the 1960s.[51] The profit from the expanding pulp production provided capital for that growth, and diversification at the company level became a viable option since it provided certain stability by spreading risk. At the time, businessmen in general saw diversification at the company level as an appropriate strategy for expansion. Soon, however, because MoDo needed to make large-scale capital investments in its core businesses, it began to concentrate on producing chemicals that required special know-how and lots of customer service.[52] During the second half of the 1960s, the chemical industry expanded substantially at Stenungsund. MoDo concentrated its production of ethylene oxide there, and its chemical operations (Domsjö, Mölndal and Stenungsund) were co-organized in a special unit named 'MoDo Kemi'.

8.1.7 Growth through Investing in a Related Activity: The Hygiene Business

In the late 1950s and early 1960s, MoDo considered, but decided not to enter into, brown paper operations, that is to say, into the sack and liner businesses. At the time, discussions were held between MoDo's CEO Lyberg and the American forest-based company St Regis regarding a plant for the production of liner for brown cardboard and unbleached sack paper at Husum. That development path was, however, blocked by the dominating shareholder in MoDo, the Kempe family, through its leading actor Carlgren, who did not like the idea of opening up MoDo to new shareholders – particularly American ones.[53]

In the latter half of 1960, MoDo carefully analysed another possible strategic path, namely to engage in the production of kraft paper and bleached cardboard at Husum. When Carlgren indicated support for the idea, MoDo, together with the British forest-based corporation Albert E. Reed, began to analyse that path. Initially, there was an understanding that MoDo would get a slight majority standing in the new joint company. Nevertheless, after the sale of Hörnefors in 1961, MoDo's attitude became tougher. They informed Reed that if a new plant for bleached cardboard were to be established at Husum, MoDo should have full control over the site. MoDo wished to remain the sole owner of the Husum plant and instead let the joint company hire the plant for a long period of time. Reed would then be linked to the project through a long-term contract that provided favourable prices, and the two companies would together own and run conversion plants in Europe. That reasoning was fully in line with MoDo's general scepticism towards 50–50 shareholdings. However, that was a solution that Reed could not accept. One should, however, notice that, in the initial negotiations with that company, MoDo seems to have accepted a large foreign shareholder in a core business venture, something that was considered inconceivable in the earlier discussions with St Regis.[54]

In the end, different opinions emerged about whether the proposed new output actually matched the kind of pulp that was produced at Husum. In any case, most actors rejected the bleached cardboard (paper) alternative, as they believed that the European market for such production was too small to justify an investment in a large-scale plant. There were also doubts about whether such an effort would be profitable even if decent demand materialized. These conclusions were crucial when finally, after long negotiations, the idea to form a joint venture with Reed was rejected. MoDo's decision not to enter the cardboard business came as a surprise to some actors, because bleached cardboard based on sulphate pulp ('foodboard') had been a tremendous success in the US during the 1950s. Many leading actors saw a combination of a sulphate-based pulp plant with the production of bleached cardboard as one of the most interesting ideas for the future. However, there was only one company that decided to follow that strategy and make it its main path: Iggesund (cf. section 8.2 below).

The first European tissue machine was not put into operation until 1961 (i.e. when the 'blocking' American patents had expired). For some time, there had been discussions within MoDo about whether the related hygiene business could be a profitable expansion alternative. Both Carlgren and Peppler pushed for such a development, and in the beginning they were supported by Carl Kempe Sr. Several companies were contacted, and eventually (in 1964) MoDo came across a Belgian producer, Mabelpap (located in Stembert close to Liège), that needed a partner to carry out its expansion plans. Mabelpap was discussing an investment in a new tissue machine with potential financiers including the state. The financiers requested that Mabelpap sought an alliance with an established company in the forest-based industry in order to secure the future delivery of pulp and further development of the operations. MoDo and Mabelpap soon agreed to a solution by which MoDo would invest a rather limited amount of capital but yet gain control over the company. MoDo also won an option to buy all the shares, and Peppler was offered the position as Chair.[55] That investment together with the acquisition of Satinex (UK) in 1966[56] represented crucial steps in MoDo's international hygiene business expansion. Carlgren and Peppler led that race, passively supported by MoDo's board.[57]

Through the acquisition of Paulistöm in 1965 MoDo – led by Carlgren – expanded into the hygiene business. Carlgren's move was made possible via a tip from MoDo's board member Browaldh, who informed him that the owner of Paulistöm, Wettergren, was interested in selling the company, which specialized in tissue-based products for the consumer market.[58] In the 1960s, Paulistöm and Mölnlycke were the two biggest diaper producers in the Nordic countries. Some core members of the MoDo staff, however, were critical of the Paulistöm acquisition. In their eyes, that firm contained 'a collection of rather rundown paper mills'. Others did not like the idea that an ancestral and prestigious company like MoDo was about to begin producing 'toilet paper and diapers'.

At the same time, Klippan bought Långasjönäs and Nyboholm, which together with MoDo's Paulistöm controlled the sales company Cellvaverken. That turned out to be an unstable construct, so in 1966 MoDo took over the whole sales organization. MoDo also bought a company in Norway (diapers), established a partnership in Denmark (together with Cederroths[59]) and started an activity in Holland (tissue). MoDo also made other attempts to enter new markets and sell their high-grade tissue-based products, but in the end these efforts were unsuccessful.[60]

Through these activities, MoDo entered the hygiene sector during the mid-1960s, but its position was – though not negligible – not big enough for a long-term capability. To achieve such a substantial presence in the sector, Lyberg discussed some kind of co-operation – or even merger – with its biggest rival on the Nordic market, namely Mölnlycke, a fast-growing Swedish producer of tissue-based products like disposable diapers and sanitary protections. The idea was discussed at MoDo's HQ, but Lyberg was dissuaded from such a path by several board members. However, that the discussions even took place could indicate that Mölnlycke's preferred partner at the time actually was MoDo and not SCA (later SCA bought Mölnlycke; cf. Ch. 13).[61]

MoDo's growth in the hygiene sector continued. In the late 1960s the company bought the diaper production machines and the corresponding product rights from Mab & Mya,[62] and transferred all those resources to Paulistöm.[63] There was also an attempt to enter Spain through co-operation with a Spanish family owning a company that produced pulp and paper. The idea was to move some machines from Mab & Mya to that plant, but MoDo soon found out that there was no market for such products in Spain at the time. There was also a failed attempt to establish a tissue-based business in France with a French partner. Instead, Mabelpap France was created with the understanding that MoDo's continental tissue-based activities (e.g. those in Germany) were to be run initially by Mabelpap Brussels through one of its former owners.[64]

The hygiene business expanded in a way that had a flavour of arbitrariness, although the path as such was followed with much enthusiasm. The new business area was expected to become a core business and a company flagship. Because of the pace, however, the material upon which decisions were based was not always of the best of quality, and neither was the negotiating skill. As a buyer, MoDo was a little bit too eager, a fact that the sellers soon used to their advantage. The fast pace also resulted in a rather fragmented and loosely integrated unit, although four 'separate' regions began to materialize (Scandinavia, the European continent, the UK and France).

In the beginning there was no head of what was eventually called MoDo Consumer Products ('MoDo Konsument[produkter]'), but rather soon (in 1968) Schollander was put in charge of that business area with the assignment to bring things in order and improve the economic result. Schollander had never managed a business unit before, and that, together with his friendly and emphatic personality, made it difficult for him to take the necessary measures to straighten things out. His successor Grünewald, however, was an experienced business manager, who had run profitable operations. He made the organizational hierarchy work and structured the product repertoire. Yet he also ran into trouble, as several managers and other employees were reluctant to follow and implement his ideas, basically because he had difficulty understanding the rationale associated with consumer products.[65]

Nordlund was appointed the new head of MoDo's hygiene business in 1972. He had worked as marketing manager and head of the Swedish hygiene business and from those positions learned about MoDo's aggressive expansion strategy. One of the first decisions Nordlund took was to replace the head of the poorly performing Satinex unit. That change upset some members of the board including Peppler, but, since Nordlund had checked the move beforehand with MoDo's strongman Carlgren, the critique soon stopped. However, Nordlund's assignment as 'head' of the hygiene business was unclear, as his relationship to the (hygiene) activities that Peppler ran on the continent was ambiguous.[66]

8.1.8 Growth through Investing in Another Related Activity: The Fine Paper Business

MoDo's most important strategic decision in the early 1960s was probably how it should expand its pulp plants, as larger scales and better qualities were necessary to make them competitive. The introduction of continuous production added to that capability. So, Husum expanded its production considerably both in 1963 and 1966, and Domsjö followed suit and was transformed into a cost-driven, scale-based producer of sulphite pulp. However, Domsjö's change away from smaller-scale customized pulp qualities generated problems, as it exposed the production to demand fluctuations (business trends) and delivered less profit (began to compete with sulphate-based pulp).[67] Overall, however, the new capacity built a platform for an expansion into fine paper through effective large-scale machines, and that, in turn, stimulated investigations of other paths forward. As a result, many trips were made abroad to learn about the production of fine paper, cardboard and newsprint.

MoDo, like most other forest-based companies, saw wood fibre as a scarce resource. Intense discussions focused on whether the company ought to integrate forward to gain more (profit) out of each unit of timber. The purchase of Hörnefors in 1951 represented a small start on a fine paper path, but it was seen as a risky one, as MoDo then would compete directly with its pulp customers. However, it still came as a surprise to many stakeholders when that plant was sold in 1961 to Ncb. Many explanations for the sale circulated, ranging from 'MoDo should not compete with its own (pulp) customers' to 'the scale of the Hörnefors plant is insufficient'.

To benefit from advantages of scale was the company's primary goal at the time, although MoDo also emphasized the need for continuous modernization and delivery of high-quality products. Those ambitions created a problem, however, when several different businesses (timber, pulp, hygiene, fine paper and chemical products) were to be run at the same time. Even if one disregarded the activities outside of the three 'core plants' (i.e. Domsjö, Husum and Hörnefors), the demand for both capital and timber seemed overwhelming. When it became necessary to give up one of the three core plants, Hörnefors was the obvious choice because it was small and not very profitable.[68]

Nevertheless, the sale of Hörnefors to Ncb could also be explained by a wish to avoid competition for resources with yet another timber user in the region (it was rumoured that Ncb had plans to expand there; cf. Ch. 6). Carlgren personally negotiated the sale, and MoDo got a favourable price. In spite of the 'rational' arguments provided for the sale of Hörnefors, it was at the time a tough decision and a sensational affair. It was a difficult choice because of the long-standing, almost personal relationship that had prevailed between MoDo's owner family and the citizens of Hörnefors. The municipality had been founded during the years when Frans Kempe Sr was in charge of the company. To sell was contrary to the Kempe family's tradition of keeping its units and caring for its employees. When Carl Kempe Sr announced the sale of Hörnefors in June 1961, he therefore stressed that the two main reasons for that move were to secure good conditions for future production (i.e. a sufficient supply of timber) and, thereby, to ensure stable employment.[69]

Later that decade MoDo also disinvested its wallboard business, Treetex. Attempts were made to further develop that business by moving away from the bulk segment, but even such a niche strategy proved to be a difficult path, as the whole wallboard industry was in crisis. The competition from particleboard and mineral fibre grew tougher, and most analyses addressing the possible future opportunities for Treetex did not bring much hope. Since MoDo's core business needed all the capital it could get to stay competitive, it was not too difficult a decision to close down the unit.[70]

In the 1960s the plant manager at Husum, Erik Diedrichs, got a leading role in MoDo's operative development. He mastered most of the current technical development in the industry as well as the technical matters and details linked to forest-based production. He was also a competent leader though not particularly impressed by the capacities of the board members. In his eyes, they 'did not understand very much of the technical matters and were only comfortable when it came to money counting'. As such, the proposals regarding new investments ought to be short so that technical details would not divert the board discussions.[71] Diedrichs was eager to make (lots of) marginal investments to remove those bottlenecks that continuously appeared in the production processes. The associated calculations almost always showed favourable results; the supplementary investments were portrayed as profitable and necessary to carry out. To most board members those computations were difficult to evaluate, so they were usually approved.[72]

Selling Hörnefors to Ncb was not the end of MoDo's fine paper efforts. It was not Diedrichs, however, that led MoDo to invest heavily in fine paper, although from his position as Head of Husum he advocated such a strategy. Back in the 1950s most leading MoDo actors thought that pulp production ought to be integrated forward into paper production. Ulfsparre actually recommended that path already back in the 1940s. In line with the ambitions of the internationalization team established in Switzerland (Peppler's group), that idea materialized in the above-mentioned joint venture with Holzstoff creating Intercelpa, a company that owned two fine paper plants. Though that collaboration ultimately failed, that investment provided MoDo's board and management with knowledge about a business that they seriously considered entering on a large scale.

If forward integration towards fine paper was to be the preferred path, it could be carried out in two ways: either through co-localization of the two production processes (a combine) or through localization of the fine paper production close to the customers. In the late 1960s Diedrichs pushed for a pulp and paper combine at 'his' Husum plant. He and several other MoDo actors considered a one-sided focus on pulp to be a too risky path that over time could also bring undeserved profits to those producers that already specialized in fine paper. Moreover, as the supply of timber for Husum's pulp production began to tighten, forward integration became attractive. To more seriously examine how to move forward, Diedrichs brought leading MoDo actors together to discuss fine paper production at Husum that would involve an effective large-scale paper machine (biggest in Europe). Making such an investment was regarded as a much better way to grow than buying small paper mills all over Europe. With MoDo's leading actor Carlgren's support for Diedrichs's recommendation, MoDo placed its focus and resources on the further development of the Husum site.[73]

However, fine paper was not the only alternative considered for MoDo's forward integration. At the same time (i.e. 1967), MoDo's CEO Lyberg revealed in an interview in a daily newspaper that MoDo was considering establishing a large newspaper mill close to either the Domsjö or the Husum plant. He also mentioned that substantial technical and commercial evaluations had been carried out to find out whether such an investment was feasible and fitted with MoDo's capability. The reason for making these internal discussions and analyses publicly known was to 'inform competitors and authorities in good time' in order to influence their plans and decisions. For example, MoDo's rival SCA had simultaneously applied for a location loan for building a newspaper plant at Kramfors, a plan that intruded upon what MoDo regarded as its territory. Not surprisingly, the CEOs of MoDo's major Swedish competitors (SCA's Mossberg and Stora Kopparberg's Sundblad) criticized Lyberg for MoDo's ambition to invest in a newspaper mill. Lyberg was of the impression that both competitors actually understood that operative circumstances spoke against an investment in a newspaper mill at Husum. However, at Domsjö such an investment could be defended considering the required mixture of pulp qualities (mechanical wood pulp [could be supplied from Bure] and sulphite pulp), but yet the total supply of fibre was insufficient.

In the end, MoDo decided to integrate forward into fine paper production, and that investment was to be carried out at the Husum site, as its pulp was almost perfect for wood-free fine paper (and cardboard, but that path had been abandoned). Moreover, due to MoDo's large investments between 1958 and 1966 and its innovative attempt to use oxygen for bleaching, the company had no other choice. Originally MoDo's experiments with the use of oxygen for bleaching were aimed at improving the efficiency of the production of bleached pulp (oxygen was cheaper than chlorine), but eventually the new environmental legislation made the investments even more profitable (and necessary).[74]

The fine paper strategy was also supported by a market analysis, although the lack of adequate statistics made that underpinning rather shaky. What may have tipped the scale in favour of a fine paper investment was a journey to Munkedal's fine paper mill (a MoDo customer). That educational visit made a strong impression on among others Diedrichs, and thus significantly contributed to MoDo's decision to invest in fine paper (a new, big machine, twice as big as the Munkedal one).[75] However, there were two substantial problems associated with the new path: there was no experience whatsoever in (fine) paper production at Husum and no machine of similar size around to study.[76]

A quite unexpected obstacle presented itself, however, when Marcus Wallenberg Sr pinched the new fine paper machine ordered for Husum for use at his Nymölla unit. It was Wallenberg's almost unparalleled standing among the Nordic business elite (including Finland, the country from which the machine was to be delivered) that made that 'capture' possible. Of course, Wallenberg's 'takeover' upset Diedrichs. Nevertheless, MoDo went on to win the race and started its production at Husum before the Wallenberg sphere got Nymölla going.[77] Once again MoDo showed its innovative capability, as the new combine could use wet pulp in the production process successfully without impairing the paper quality. Together with the accompanying advantages of scale, that innovation certainly made the company competitive.

Once again Carlgren showed confidence in the company's top management and specialists (R&D) by not intervening in the discussions about how to make the new paper investment. As major shareholder and board member, however, he made the final decision to invest substantially in a fine paper business, a path that never had been a main road for the company. MoDo's new core business matched Carlgren's ambition to have the company associated with innovation and operations in the technical forefront. Still, he was a risk-taker, a disposition that could further his interest in building a sizeable and flourishing MoDo – or could actually spoil such a development.[78] The risk he took in this case was to invest during a recession hoping to have the new machine ready for production when times changed for the better. Carlgren's action was built not only on the calculations that were presented to him and the other board members but also on his intuition and strong belief in the merits of the case.[79]

In the beginning MoDo believed that it could sell the fine paper from Husum as large rolls, which later could be converted into smaller ones or sheets. Thus, MoDo should stick to its two strengths: large-scale production and distribution. That was also in line with the expectations expressed by the bigger agencies and wholesalers in Europe. However, soon it became evident that MoDo's 'bulk and roll approach' did not work particularly well. Instead, Husum had to begin cutting its large fine paper rolls into smaller ones and sheets.[80] As a result, MoDo began to invest in a different, more ambitious marketing and sales approach. The company became particularly interested in co-operating with the Swedish fine paper wholesaler Svenskt Papper. MoDo took up discussions with Brusafors-Hällefors,[81] the majority shareholder of the potential partner company. Those talks ended in an agreement by which MoDo bought Svenskt Papper, which then also included Silverdalen (a producer of coated paper of high quality, usually used for printing), Mariannelund (a sulphite plant), forests and Herman Stenberg (a packaging company). Shortly thereafter Silverdalen began to use fine paper from Husum for some of its coated products.

Thus, MoDo's overall strategy beginning in the 1960s reflected the company's ambition to maintain its position as a modern, innovative and effective forest-based corporation. MoDo would continue to develop its forestry and sawmill businesses and control substantial power plant resources. The company would also continue to operate as a large-scale Swedish producer of high-quality pulp, but that output would to an increasing extent be further processed within MoDo – the net selling of pulp on the market was to be reduced. That reduction would basically come from two 'new' core businesses, that is to say, fine paper and hygiene, while less related businesses such as the chemical one would be sold off. The new core activities represented forward integration and were connected both to an ambition to expand internationally (particularly in Europe) and to get closer to the company's end customers. At the same time the new strategy broke an old taboo (and an agreement), as it turned MoDo into a competitor of some of its own (pulp) customers.

8.1.9 A New Core Business: Fine Paper

In spite of the rather radical change in the business mixture that occurred in the 1960s and took the company closer to its customers, MoDo still was very much a production-oriented company focusing on the early stages in forest-based operations. Since technicians still had a strong position in the company, much effort was directed towards securing the supply of timber and keeping the existing plants in good shape and running efficiently. Although MoDo, through its entry into the tissue business, had begun its long journey towards becoming more of a customer-driven corporation, it continued to sell its pulp and wood products in the traditional way. Sales were still very much a matter of an early 'outplacement' of pulp on the market for later delivery mostly to well-known customers, preferably in quantities that corresponded to the full capacities of the plants.

MoDo's investments in the pulp business were closely linked to the future of Domsjö (its sulphite plant). In June 1972, MoDo launched a study to develop ideas for making the site profitable on a sustainable basis. Three possible future paths were identified: expansion of the capacity to produce sulphite-based pulp, integrated production of writing paper and printing paper and closing the plant down. The second alternative was eliminated already in the first report since MoDo already had a paper mill at Husum, and it was more economical to add machines there than investing in a brand new plant. In the final report, it was proposed that Domsjö's sulphite production should be expanded in spite of the on-going 'sulphite-death' caused by the competition from sulphate pulp and the costs associated with getting environmental pollution under control. When the Swedish Environmental Protection Agency (Statens Naturvårdsverk) was established in 1967, and new extended environmental protection legislation was put in place in 1969, the situation for Domsjö became tough. As a result MoDo decided to phase out its viscose pulp production, but the question remained: could Domsjö survive over the long run? Considering MoDo's constant lack of capital, the only sensible answer seemed to be to close down the plant, but that did not happen.[82]

By the beginning of the 1970s, MoDo was one of the world's largest producers of pulp for sale, and that rather concentrated operational strategy had been profitable. However, there had also been problems due to pulp producers' vulnerability to the wide swings in economic trends. Thus, the pulp business was rather risky, and many corporations around the world had worked intensively to get out of that bulky market. In most of those efforts, forward integration was the preferred path, as it was for MoDo.[83]

MoDo's risky expansion during the 1960s, manifested in substantial investments and purchases of companies, had been carried out with an awareness that the chosen path implied that almost all possible means of getting capital were utilized. At the beginning of the 1970s MoDo therefore had the highest debt/equity ratio in the Swedish forest-based industry (> 50%). That was significantly higher than what most actors in comparable Nordic corporations regarded as an acceptable figure.[84] Nevertheless, the strained financial situation did not prevent Carlgren from considering the idea that MoDo should buy SCA, which faced several difficulties and was about to replace its CEO. Carlgren did not regard an alliance or a merger as an alternative to an acquisition.[85] Rather, it had to be a takeover, and MoDo had to get into the driver's seat to avoid the risk that MoDo (and the Kempe family) later would be 'swallowed' and marginalized. For some reason, Carlgren's acquisition idea was never vetted more seriously. It was never presented to prominent actors like the CEO of MoDo's principal bank (Handelsbanken) or any of SCA's leading actors.[86] The impression among those who were informed about Carlgren's idea was that it was a personal impulse that did not materialize in any serious discussions.[87] Altbäck, at the time Deputy CEO at MoDo, tried to talk Carlgren out of it because such a 'bite' was financially unrealistic. Since the family also opposed the idea, Carlgren gave up.[88]

At the beginning of the 1970s MoDo decided to build a large fine paper mill at Husum that would introduce substantial new quantities on the market. The decision to move to the right in the value chain was foremost a consequence of the fact that MoDo over time had built up a huge capacity for producing pulp. As noted above, concentrating solely on that bulky business was regarded as too risky, as it now and then was subject to dramatic price fluctuations that created financial strain for the company. The pulp business was also characterized by many of the other negative qualities traditionally associated with volume-intensive standard products (e.g. fierce price competition, regional tariffs and global overcapacity). MoDo wanted to reduce its heavy dependence on pulp, sell more processed products and enter a situation where the price represented only one of several competitive tools.

The choice of fine paper as the preferred path for the further processing of pulp could also – at least to some extent – be explained by the parallel activities carried out by MoDo's competitors. They, too, had begun to occupy the 'open spaces' that existed in the Swedish forest-based industry. Actually, at the time, almost all companies looked for ways to specialize their production and cut down their dependence on the bulky pulp business. MoDo's Swedish competitors had 'chosen' their main development paths: liner (ASSI and SCA), cardboard (ASSI, SCA and Iggesund) and newsprint (Holmens Bruk and Stora Kopparberg). These choices 'left' fine paper to MoDo, a commodity that in those days to a large extent was produced outside Sweden. The existing Swedish producers were all located in the southern and western parts of the country, and they used small machines and produced in short runs. Thus, at that point, fine paper was no bulk product, and its distribution was at least as fragmented as its production – many small independent wholesalers and retailers competed on the market. MoDo challenged that industrial structure and began to invest in large fine paper machines.[89]

The fine paper machine MoDo put into production in 1972 was the second biggest in the world, so it radically broke with the previous axiom in the industry that fine paper mills ought to be rather small and not run too fast. Due to the favourable economic trend, it was easy to find customers, and the huge success made a new sales organization and marketing approach necessary. Above all, however, the successful fine paper investment confirmed to the dominating shareholders and top management that MoDo's path forward had to be based on the further processing of its pulp production, particularly then into fine paper.

Thus, early in the 1970s, MoDo set its corporate path for many years. The period of 'free' search and investigations was over, and the main directions forward – fine paper and hygiene paper – were chosen. The company then expressed its goal to become an international and profitable giant in fine paper, and a leading actor in the forthcoming structural transformation of the hygiene business in Europe. Such a big challenge certainly stimulated MoDo's incontestable leader Carlgren. The fine paper part of that strategy became even more pronounced when a few years later a second large machine was built at Husum.

As the large investments in fine paper and other areas were planned and executed, it became vital to change the dominating company culture from one focusing on production and technical matters, to one with a greater emphasis on marketing, sales and business acumen. To implement this change, the two aspects were separated in 1973, and 'MoDo Paper' was formally established as a separate division. Both Carlgren and Peppler advocated that arrangement, although both were aware of the risk that the split could create a conflict, since the paper unit became a customer to the pulp unit. That would make the pulp price and the distribution of the economic result between the two units a controversial issue. However, because the board considered the benefits of a split greater than the drawbacks, it was executed.

In light of the difficulty inherent in radically changing the approaches of most managers, the new head of the fine paper business, Löf, decided to physically 'isolate' the group that ran its operations.[90] That would protect the customer-based fine paper business from the thinking and traditions of MoDo Cell (the pulp-producing unit). The controversial separation of the fine paper team from the rest of the company probably contributed to its success. The fine paper team could work without interference from other managers, who advocated a rather different approach. The team could also avoid lengthy and trying discussions with those in the company that were sceptical of the whole fine paper venture.

Shortly after the separation, the fine paper team presented a strategy for how its business ought to be developed. Their ambition was to establish MoDo Paper as one of the biggest actors in the 'office paper' segment. The new unit would base that development on its new, large fine paper machine at Husum, but also on specialization of the two smaller plants Silverdalen and PPSM. In reality, MoDo had considered closing those two minor units, but ultimately did not shut them down. Instead, the board followed the fine paper team's recommendation to continue production.[91]

One of the MoDo actors who pushed early on for the fine paper path was Peppler, who aspired to the position as head of such a unit. Sundberg, Diedrichs's successor as head of the combined unit, opposed dividing the pulp and paper units, and that, together with his rather poor 'personal chemistry' with Carlgren, forced him to leave MoDo. Löf replaced him as head of the fine paper operations.[92] Carlgren had approached Löf when there were changes in SCA's top management (of which Löf was a part).[93] When Rydin became SCA's CEO, replacing Mossberg, Löf began looking for a position in another company. In addition to recognizing the limited opportunities for advancement within SCA, Löf was less comfortable with Rydin than with the retiring Mossberg, who was the one that suggested Löf when Carlgren was looking for a manager for the fine paper operations.

Once appointed, Löf picked his own management team. However, it did not become particularly well liked inside MoDo, especially after Löf decided to physically separate the fine paper unit from the other parts of the organization, for the reasons mentioned above. Managers from other units saw members of the fine paper team as self-righteous 'know-it-alls', who ignored the 'old faithful servants'. Internally, that made MoDo a less open and less 'friendly' company than it used to be. Practically, that meant that Löf ran his unit mainly interacting with Carlgren, who in turn handled the other top managers and the board.[94]

Löf's competence profile and personality suited Carlgren well.[95] Carlgren had become rather tired of all the brilliant engineers that continuously came running with their improvement suggestions and investment proposals. In essence, it was R&D and technicians that ran MoDo, and Carlgren wanted to get out of that confining governance rationale. In Löf's case he got somebody that stressed the customer perspective – a person skilled in marketing. In Löf, Carlgren also had a person taken from one of MoDo's competitors, who with fresh eyes compared and evaluated the company's total business situation.[96]

When Löf entered in 1973, he was struck by the diversity of the company's business portfolio. MoDo contained a bunch of rather poorly related businesses in many different fields (i.e. the metal, chemical, pharmaceutical, hygiene, board, pulp and sawing sectors). Although it was not his assignment, he was one of the actors that tried to convince Carlgren that it was necessary to sell some of the units (first of all, the metal and chemical businesses). Löf considered it essential to make capital available for the company's new core business: fine paper. The heads of other business units thought along the same lines – they wanted resources for their operations and understood that MoDo could not go on investing in all current areas. The head of the chemicals operations (Agfors), for example, stressed that its further expansion required large amounts of capital. As a consequence, he did not oppose the sale of his unit to somebody with substantial financial resources, although that would be a technically complicated affair since some of the chemistry had been adapted to and hence was specific to the Domsjö plant. The head of the hygiene business, Nordlund, defended the hygiene business as part of MoDo's total repertoire, even though most of the top managers (but not Carlgren) expressed scepticism about whether MoDo would be able to provide the necessary investment resources. These two capital-intensive industries put heavy demands on the owners' capacity to provide financial resources. However, like the previous Kempe headmen, Carlgren was reluctant to sell the family's gems.[97]

MoDo's fine paper team visited Hallsta (part of Holmens Bruk) to look into a large-scale production unit. From that visit the company acquired its technical leader Nordstrand, who also became responsible for the new machine. The Husum investment became a major success in spite of all the prophecies that it would not be possible to produce quality fine paper from wet pulp. The two years following the installation of the new technology were boom times: demand was strong and prices high – the whole investment cost was paid during that short period of time, a result that was far better than even the most optimistic calculations indicated.[98] During those years Husum set an unrivalled profit record. The successful development of the fine paper business gave Löf a strong position among owners, directors and (most) top managers. He was the one that had understood the importance of marketing and made the investments from a customer perspective stressing 'office paper' and wholesaling.[99] The boom period convinced most of the leading actors at MoDo that large-scale fine paper production was the right path for the future. There were also promising forecasts for that kind of paper – steady growth was expected for the coming decade, so it was necessary to keep up with the others and defend the captured market shares. Later, however, the prices did not rise as high as expected, mainly because new fine paper capacities were introduced around the world.[100]

Internal competition was as tough as ever regarding the company's investment resources. The favourable outcome for the 'fine paper team' in that struggle was probably more a consequence of the tremendous success brought by the paper machine than a result of all the calculations presented. MoDo decided to plan for one or two additional fine paper machines, and for a considerable amount of related investments. In 1974, it was decided that the second machine should be built, thereby increasing MoDo's fine paper production to a level that matched half its pulp capacity. The expansion plan presupposed that MoDo would generate a substantial profit during the rest of the decade; it did not, however, turn out that way. Instead, 1975–78 turned out to be a recession period.

The second fine paper machine started commercial production in 1976, but the third one was postponed both because of market decline (partly explained by extraordinary customer overstock), and because of a heavy investment programme in the other core units (pulp and hygiene).[101] MoDo gradually abandoned its production of large and small rolls of fine paper and installed instead several machines that cut sheets (A4). Most R&D work was also redirected towards the fine paper field, and office paper became a speciality for which MoDo sought to be a leading producer and seller. Eventually cutting machines took care of all the fine paper that was produced at Husum. That development called for a new distribution strategy; MoDo's current system based on agents isolated it from its (final) customers.[102]

During the 1970s, the EC gradually phased out the forest-based industry customs duties for Sweden and other EFTA countries. That precipitated structural changes in the industry that cut across country borders. MoDo decided to make the most of the new institutional setting and formulated two principles that would guide it for the years to come. First, the scale of the machines would continue to be decisive for the company's competitive strength. Second, to be successful most operations had to be more market oriented and international in character. As a consequence, it had become necessary to invest in fully owned sales companies located in crucial countries/regions in Europe, and to abandon the old system with agents. For fine paper it was also necessary to obtain a strong position in the European wholesale business. That process had started in 1970 when Brusafors-Hällefors was acquired (it included the wholesaler Svenskt Papper).[103] For the European operations it took somewhat longer, with the major acquisitions materializing only at the end of the decade. MoDo bought several companies in France,[104] the UK, Holland, Italy and Germany. However, because of country-specific restrictions, it was difficult to buy customer-close firms in Germany; there MoDo had to add paper from competitors to its wholesale business.[105]

After the two fine paper machines at Husum had been built in the 1970s, most of the investments that followed during the decade became marginal ones, which improved production processes and matched the steadily rising demands for larger volumes. These investments were always presented as potentially profitable ones and consequently were approved by the board. In essence, the company's technicians produced the descriptions and calculations for all those minor investments – both those for expansion and those for reconstruction – leaving MoDo's board members very much in the hands of its top management and their ambitions and judgement. The technical arguments presented to the board were too complicated for most of the directors to evaluate, so it was difficult for them to challenge the conclusions drawn and to express well-founded criticisms that might impact the shape of the final decisions. That process, fully dominated by technicians, gradually turned MoDo into a fine paper producer.[106] In the end, the major investments at Husum during the 1970s became decisive for MoDo's strategy and long-term development path – probably much more than the actors at the time realized. That technically and economically successful venture kept MoDo from heading down other growth paths.

8.1.10 Leaving the Chemical Sector and Investing in the Hygiene Sector

Early in the 1970s, MoDo's leading actors became more and more convinced that the company's profitability – particularly in its pulp business – had not developed as expected, and the near future did not look much brighter. So, MoDo had to make (even) tougher decisions to prioritize the fields in which it should invest. MoDo's need for capital to allow it to remain a serious and profitable player in the fast-growing chemical industry, where large-scale operations were an absolute necessity, was almost overwhelming. That situation looked even more precarious for MoDo in light of the capital needs of its expanding pulp and paper businesses. Taken together, these well-underpinned requests for investment capital could not all be met by MoDo. Therefore, at the turn of the decade, the company had to make a crucial choice regarding its future strategy and business portfolio. A sale of the chemical activities then gradually emerged as the 'natural' choice for MoDo, as most of its business was in the fibre-based forest industry comprising sawmills, pulp plants and various kinds of hygiene and paper production. That had been the case for a century, and that tradition as such also mattered when the decision was taken.

The capital requirements for a future expansion in the chemical industry were of such a size that very few regional actors had the capacity to run such operations. The Swedish state, through its rather recently formed holding company Statsföretag, had the necessary financial muscle. Moreover, the Swedish government had signalled that it expected Statsföretag to play a significant role as a corporate owner in Swedish business life in the coming years. However, in 1968, MoDo still tried to ride on the growth of the chemical industry, and, as described earlier, the company established a special business unit named 'MoDo Kemi', which consisted of its organic-chemical operations at Domsjö, Stenungsund and Mölndal (Berol and SOAB).

MoDo's chemical operations grew fast, and as its pulp business was profitable, diversification was still regarded as an eligible path; the future looked bright indeed. But beginning in 1970 it became clear that the pulp business was unable to provide the needed – and expected – profit for running so many diverse businesses. It also became obvious that the chemical industry more and more used petroleum and not forest-based substances as its main raw material source, a development that was to MoDo's disadvantage, as its input base was attached to forest-based materials. So, in the forced choice between pulp and paper, on the one hand, and chemical production, on the other hand, the outcome was almost self-evident. Consequently, in 1973, MoDo Kemi was sold to Statsföretag. For the Kempe family, and for Carlgren in particular, that sale was traumatic, not least because it represented a lifetime achievement of the legendary former MoDo leader and dynasty head Carl Kempe Sr.[107]

However, the hygiene sector (one of the two more recently launched business areas) was still in focus. MoDo's leading actors regarded that business as more closely linked to the company's core than its chemical operations. As a consequence, a group was formed in 1969 to analyse the opportunities for establishing a large-scale production of tissue integrated with one of MoDo's existing pulp plants. The group concluded in 1970 that the conditions for such an effort were propitious, and suggested that the production plant should be located at Domsjö. Initially, that site seemed to be the best one, as almost all production of tissue was based on sulphite pulp. However, somewhat later, and after a deeper analysis, that conclusion was regarded as too hasty. New information indicated that pulp based on sulphite was becoming obsolete (also) for tissue production. Technological progress had made sulphate-based pulp applicable for tissue production – it had actually become a better base because of its superior strength and lack of rosin. Moreover, MoDo learned from several tissue producers that the type of pulp that was produced at Domsjö did not fit their processes.[108]

As mentioned above the continued focus on the hygiene business during the 1970s was manifested in the formation of a special unit for that sector 'MoDo Konsument' (MoDo Consumer Products), and Nordlund took office as its head. In that position he became close to Carlgren, who was a strong supporter of the hygiene path.[109] Like the huge investments in fine paper, the decision to expand into the hygiene sector reflected the goal to move MoDo's activities to the right in the value chain. It also represented risk spreading, as the markets for fine paper and for hygiene products basically were unrelated. Such diversification was seen at the time as a wise arrangement. The tissue business also represented a strategy that few Swedish competitors had adopted, and it was also a rather untrodden path in continental Europe. To establish a platform for the coming growth, Nordlund immediately divided his business unit into three subunits: 'Scandinavia' with paper mills in Paulistöm (the biggest diaper producer in Sweden) and Nyboholm and a HQ in Stockholm, 'the continent' with the Mabelpap paper mill and a HQ in Brussels, and 'UK' with operations in Hawarden (Satinex).

Rather soon MoDo acquired Stille-Werner (1974), whose main products were diapers and sanitary protection, although it also manufactured medical instruments and ran a retail chain. Nordlund's idea was to 'strip down' the acquired company and move the production of diapers to Paulistróm. While still alive, the CEO of Stille-Werner (Hessner) had opposed the sale to MoDo, but, after the CEO's death, Carlgren was able to convince the 'new' owner (Hessner's widow) that things would improve if MoDo took over. Thus, in the end the transaction materialized. However, in contrast to Nordlund, and convinced by Stille-Werner's current CEO's argumentation that the company was a particularly well-established brand in that specific field, Carlgren decided that MoDo should retain the company's production of medical instruments. As planned, MoDo transferred its production of sanitary pads and products for baby care to Paulistróms Bruk.[110] The purchase of Nyboholm in 1975 added products based on recycled fibres (toilet paper, towels and napkins) to MoDo's operations.

MoDo continued to expand its hygiene business by acquiring Klippan (in 1975), a paper mill controlling strong tissue-based brands ('Finess' and 'Fin'). That acquisition brought MoDo Konsument into the same 'league' as the market leader Edet. In fact, MoDo's CEO Carlgren had tried to purchase that company, too. He had negotiated with Edet's owner (Häger) and – according to Carlgren – the two had also shaken hands to confirm a deal. However, shortly thereafter upon his return from a trip abroad, Carlgren was informed that Häger had sold Edet to a Dutch actor, and that that company, in turn, had sold Edet to Ncb 1977. In light of this, MoDo started serious discussions with Ncb regarding some kind of co-operation between Edet and MoDo Konsument. These negotiations resulted in a prefatory agreement stating that MoDo's CEO had the board's permission to establish a rather far-reaching arrangement. The agreement described several strategic moves. For example, the pulp plants at Köpmanholmen and Hörnefors should be closed down, and a joint paper mill was to be built at Domsjö (all that added up to a restructuring of the regional forest-based industry). A merger between Edet and MoDo Konsument was also considered. However, rather soon it became clear that a paper mill at Domsjö would not be profitable, and Ncb and the Minister of Business were so informed. Later (in 1985) when Ncb ran into serious problems with its operations, Carlgren wrote a preliminary contract outlining the sale of Edet to MoDo. However, MoDo was not allowed to acquire Edet because of objections from the Swedish Competition Authority.[111]

Nordlund learned that the owner of Vereinige Papierverk had passed away, and wanted MoDo to buy that firm. However, once again MoDo was prevented from making an important acquisition – the tissue cartel that existed at the time (composed of Serlä, PWA, Scott, Kimberly Clark and others) stopped MoDo.[112] Instead, MoDo's Mabelpap unit expanded its continental activity by introducing a new big and modern tissue machine in Stembert. Because MoDo controlled insufficient production capacity to convert and export tissue, Carlgren, Nordlund and Peppler determined that such an expansion was required. That investment made MoDo Konsument more active outside Scandinavia. It entered both the BeNeLux market (through Mabelpap) and the UK market (through Satinex). However, all efforts to enter the French market for hygiene products failed.[113]

In the 1970s there also emerged a new product in the hygiene field, namely tampons, which were a rather complicated product that Paulistróm had obtained a licence to produce from an American company. After only three years, that production line was shut down, however, and, instead, MoDo increasingly invested in sanitary pads, which were produced all through the 1980s. In that decade, MoDo had become one of the biggest producers of tissue-based products, controlling around 40–45 per cent of the Swedish market of toilet and household paper. MoDo was also responsible for the marketing of Munksjö's hygiene products on the Swedish market (in a formal agreement with Klippan). Nevertheless, the competitors had caught up with Paulistrom, and the company began to lose market share.

In line with MoDo's general approach, MoDo Konsument's policy was to invest in the best available technology. Paper mills and converters were continuously modernized to be efficient units for tissue-based products.[114] However, there were some problems connected to that fast and somewhat 'wild' expansion. One problem had to do with the limited experience MoDo's top leaders held with respect to consumer businesses. There were few connections between that type of business and working with large-scale bulk production in the pulp and fine paper businesses. Too often discussions became superficial – far from the kind of analyses that could be expected from the board of a listed company. Particularly in the marketing area these shortcomings became visible and problematic.[115] Furthermore, MoDo Konsument wanted to buy (some of its) pulp outside of MoDo to get the market price. However, as MoDo was a net seller of pulp, such purchases were not allowed. Instead, MoDo Konsument got a 'MoDo average price' that lowered the unit's profitability and became a competitive disadvantage. Clearly, the pulp managers still sat in MoDo's driver's seat.[116]

MoDo's financial resources were not large enough to integrate all the company's (sometimes weakly related) acquisitions and expansion investments in the hygiene sector into a cohesive and efficient business unit. As a result, the company was not able to get a firm grip over the value chain. Its R&D, production, sales and marketing efforts, which should have addressed a large part of the European consumers of tissue-based products, were insufficient. Later (around 1980), MoDo considered selling Mabelpap and purchasing a French paper wholesaler (Davupap). Nothing materialized, but both ideas were kept alive during the coming years.

Despite these limitations, the strategic path that MoDo established in the 1950s and 1960s became a success. The consistent focus on volume and the heavy investment programme linked to the capital-intensive pulp business created a robust platform for the further changes that eventually were carried out. However, the success also bred a sense of invulnerability (and perhaps also a touch of *hubris*?), a feeling that might have contributed to the leading actors' financial optimism (expressed several times in the years to come). In that atmosphere, MoDo took crucial decisions that – added together – represented a significant strategic change that made MoDo a company that concentrated its efforts in three related core businesses: pulp, fine paper and tissue (hygiene).

8.1.11 Carlgren Becomes the New CEO

At the end of the 1960s, MoDo Chair Carlgren had begun to seriously worry about the disorder in MoDo Konsument and the emerging crisis in MoDo Kemi. Therefore, in 1971, he decided to take control and become CEO of MoDo and leave the Chair position to Häggquist, a 'docile' person proposed by MoDo director Browaldh. While that might look like a substantial change of command, in fact it formalized an already existing practice. Since the late 1950s, Carlgren had been in the driver's seat in all the strategic processes. He was also a much more operational actor than usually was the case for a Swedish Chair – a role that also differed from how the division of responsibilities and duties was formulated in the Swedish Companies Act.

All along, MoDo's CEO Lyberg had had difficulty defending his position, that is to say, not becoming 'reduced' to a COO. Already in the 1960s, Carlgren 'interfered' in the CEO's tasks by personally carrying out – also in practice – most of MoDo's acquisitions and (few) disinvestments. Carlgren also recruited personal favourites to top positions inside MoDo, and he spoke publicly about issues traditionally belonging to the domain of a CEO. Particularly in those situations, Lyberg had to calm several of the leading actors in the company. In the long run, all these activities created an impossible situation for the CEO, so Lyberg decided to leave when he was offered a position as County Governor.[117]

Back in 1969, Lyberg had tried to solve most of the organizational ambiguities by launching a new organizational structure for MoDo. Its profit-centre type units ('divisions') were transformed into relatively autonomous subsidiaries with considerable responsibility both for profit and loss accounts and balance sheets. Thus, MoDo was divided into MoDo Cell (pulp), MoDo Kemi (chemicals), MoDo Paper (fine paper), MoDo Konsument (tissue), MoDo Mekan (manufacturing) and MoDo Skog (forest and timber production). Moreover, an unorthodox executive committee was established composed of MoDo's Chair (Carlgren), CEO (Lyberg) and one of its directors (Peppler). That trio was supposed to function as the board in all larger subsidiaries (each subsidiary's CEO should also be a member of 'his' board). The MoDo group and its executive trio were also equipped with highly qualified staffs (i.e. units for accounting and control, law and finance).

When Lyberg summarized the most important steps taken during his 12-year period as CEO of MoDo (1959–71), he particularly stressed the following achievements: (1) the considerable expansion of pulp production at Husum and Domsjö, (2) the sale of the Hörnefors fine paper mill to Ncb, (3) the increase of the forest resources, (4) the acquisitions of new plants (Bure, Pauliström and Bruzafors), (5) the investments in the hygiene business, (6) the closing down of the wallboard production, (7) the establishment of the chemical operations at Stenungsund, (8) the acquisitions of paper mills on the European continent and (9) the decision to build a large fine paper machine at Husum.

8.1.12 Looking for Timber

Timber supply had become a particularly important issue in MoDo already back in the early 1960s. At that time, MoDo decided to invest further in Swedish forests, especially in its 'own region' in northern Sweden ('Norrland'). The company also extended its search for new fibre to the southern parts of Sweden. The latter meant increased use of the more expensive distant timber, but at the time, that cost could be partially compensated for due to the advantages following from Husum's large-scale technology.[118] Thus, in 1964, MoDo, together with Ncb, bought the Forss group and divided the company so that MoDo got the forests and Ncb the sulphate plant Köpmanholmen. During the following years MoDo bought Bure, Robertsfors Bruk and Paulistöms Bruk. Bure comprised forests, a mechanical wood pulp plant and a sawmill, but it was obvious from a 1966 memo from MoDo's CEO to the board that it was the forests that were the target – MoDo had to secure its supply of timber for the further expansion of its Husum plant. Management also calculated with a new user of the raw material processed in Bure's mechanical wood pulp plant, namely Domsjö's sulphite plant.[119] Already before the acquisition in 1968, Robertsfors was in the hands of the Kempe dynasty (the Seth faction) and that unit, too, contained forests, as did Paulströms Bruk.[120]

However, the domestic timber was not sufficient despite improvements of forestry techniques, development of fibre-saving pulp qualities and the introduction of birch for pulp production (sulphate). Moreover, the technology for using fast-growing short-fibre trees like eucalyptus in the production of pulp and paper had taken considerable steps forward. Thus, the Nordic 'spruce monopoly' era was over.[121] Fortunately, Chair Carlgren still was genuinely interested in forestry, and timber supply had been high on his and the company's agenda since the days of Frans Kempe Sr. The more prominent members of the Kempe dynasty had often feared timber shortage. Rather soon, however, more optimistic voices emerged regarding the possibilities to use timber/pulp from far-away places, particularly for further processing at Husum. The scale advantages were now supposed to offset the cost of long distance transportation, and it was expected that most other companies, too, would face increased timber costs.[122]

Carlgren was very fond of the idea that Brazil could become a future supplier of wood. He and some of the other leading MoDo actors saw there a possibility to create forest plantations of a sufficient size to be economical even when all the costs of transportation were included. Moreover, MoDo's leaders had learned that there had been a political decision made in Brazil in 1966 that the country should try to become a powerful actor in the global forest business. Added to all that, Carl Kempe Jr had also found a suitable partner (Battistella). However, that promising and innovative path was abandoned for the time being, because the unions – a most powerful grouping – acted firmly against such a strategy.[123]

Despite the difficulties in the late 1960s to get full internal support for increased timber sourcing (for Husum) from abroad, MoDo organized a new unit in Brussels for that purpose (1973[124]) – 'MoDo Inter'.[125] Croon led the new investigating unit, which also included Peppler and Carl Kempe Jr. The latter was particularly eager to make sure that MoDo supplemented its unreliable imports from the Soviet Union with timber from other sources. MoDo Inter was overseen by a prominent board that included Carlgren (who had by then become MoDo CEO and was Chair of the unit), Peppler (MoDo board member), Altbäck (Deputy CEO) and Gustafsson (Head of Accounting and Control).[126] For some reason, MoDo Inter was not integrated in MoDo's ordinary organization.

MoDo Inter's actors mainly sought possibilities to establish timber imports from new regions such as South America and/or Africa. Initially it was concluded that such transoceanic transports of wood and/or pulp for paper production in Sweden would be too expensive to be competitive, while those crossing the Baltic Sea still were regarded as practicable. The group was also inclined to suggest that MoDo – as birch supply was limited – focus on paper based on mechanical pulp using timber from long-fibred spruce.[127]

However, MoDo Inter soon reconsidered its hesitation regarding timber imports from long distances, and decided to proceed with a serious study about the political and commercial conditions for pursuing forest-based efforts in Brazil. Carl Kempe Jr was asked to look for potential partners for possible investments in pine and/or eucalyptus plantations.

One outcome of those efforts was the formation of MoDo Brazil (1973). Carl Kempe Jr, who had moved to Sao Paolo, began negotiations with Groupo Battisstella about forming the plantation company MoBaSa. MoDo had previously developed a birch-based technique at Husum (although birch supply was limited), so deciduous trees were the preferred kind. Competitors had also begun to think about importing timber from a long distance, particularly from South America (and even for fine paper production), but MoDo had taken the lead.[128] MoDo's idea was to start production and export of timber from (foremost) Brazil to an expanding Husum, and later build a Brazilian plant for pulp export to the continental paper mills. At the time, rather few competitors thought along these lines, so Carlgren was here a visionary. However, MoDo's unions still strongly objected to the proposed foreign investments (and they had a strong position in the company). That objection, together with the generally bad times in the industry and the weak support from many other leading actors in the company, decided the matter.[129]

Eventually, almost all actors in the industry became concerned about the supply of timber to their plants, and that worry grew during the mid-1970s crisis years. In the middle of Sweden that deep concern led to the foundation of Industriskog (1976), a company that had as its mission to supply timber to its owners Stora Kopparberg, Kopparfors, Korsnäs and Iggesund. A similar construct also materialized for southern Sweden: Sydved (1978). In addition to MoDo, the founders were Papyrus, Munksjö and Fiskeby. Basically, Industriskog and Sydved constituted buying cartels that acted to lower the price of timber by eliminating competition (cf. oligopsony).[130] Another rather obvious way to deal with the timber supply problem was to phase out some plants or machines and transfer the unused raw material to (expansive) superior units. Some of MoDo's minor plants were also shut down during the same period. However, these units were probably not closed primarily because of the need for timber at more prioritized plants – all of them (also) had profitability problems.[131]

Carlgren also tried several other 'innovative' methods to acquire timber to match MoDo's increasing needs. One such method was to buy run-down, forest-based companies that contained timber resources, as it was supposed to be cheaper than buying forests. Another alternative was to establish unorthodox alliances with companies outside the industry, where the target company had caught the interest of the alliance participants in different ways. MoDo also pursued the re-allocation of forest resources through barter agreements with other forest-owning companies.[132]

In general, the high raw material costs that prevailed during the 1970s made competition with the North American producers even tougher. This became a problem in particular for MoDo's Domsjö plant. Husum, however, was technically advanced and had a strong standing due to its scale, so it was not that much affected by the pricing of the timber. When the expected upturn of the world's general economic activity did not occur in 1978 (after two bad years), MoDo's overall situation began to be so problematic that a new and extensive strategic review had to be carried out.

8.1.13 A Strategy for the 1980s

MoDo entered the recession that took place in the late 1970s with a record-breaking investment programme. Due to certain time lags, the economic result did not change from profit to loss until 1977. That year, as well as in 1978, MoDo faced a considerable loss despite the Swedish crown's recent devaluation. The situation was so bad that the banks approached MoDo to discuss the company's debt situation (but no loans were terminated).

Indeed, MoDo's principal bank Handelsbanken decided to continue its support.[133] MoDo's crisis did not worry the Chair of Handelsbanken and MoDo board member Wallander, who noted that the bank had sufficient securities. What made him a bit concerned, however, was that moderating forces among the other family members did not check Carlgren's risk-taking. The executive bodies could not put a stop to the ambitions expressed by a united Kempe family.[134] However, the bank was not as supportive as most members of the dominating shareholder family had expected. What really mattered during the crisis was Carlgren's engagement (his strong and optimistic leadership).[135]

MoDo's crisis troubled Carlgren more than most other actors put in his position, as he was almost fixated on MoDo's relative size in the industry and really wanted to run an expanding company. As such, his 'invisible' assignment was not only to successfully administer the family heirloom; he was determined to leave an even bigger and more successful company to his descendants. To accomplish that he was prepared to take substantial risks. Despite that, one could note that the growth path Carlgren pursued for MoDo was far from unique. Most Nordic forest-based companies wanted to reduce their exposure to the volatility of the business trends by processing the pulp. For MoDo it was not enough to develop pulp into fine paper, as both businesses fluctuated in a similar way. Therefore, entrance into the hygiene sector had been both tempting and rational, because it represented a non-cyclic business and took MoDo closer to its end customers. There was also a cartel established in that field, which both simplified matters and increased profits. So, for Carlgren the solution was moving to the right in the value chain (together with making some investments in related businesses).[136]

In light of the crisis, MoDo Inter was asked to carry out an analysis regarding the company's future organization. Soon it became evident that most actors perceived the current organization as ambiguous. Most acted in ad hoc constellations that had one common denominator: everything was 'organized' around MoDo's main shareholder and CEO Carlgren. In addition, problematic relations existed between the top management in Stockholm and their colleagues in northern Sweden (in and around Örnsköldsvik). MoDo Inter's study resulted in a suggestion that MoDo's Group Management Team (GMT) ought to be strengthened and, together with certain staff members moved to Stockholm. It was also proposed that each major business area should be organized as a subsidiary, and that each of the CEOs ought to be a part of MoDo's new GMT. Such a change would alter the power balance to the advantage of the subsidiaries (thus, the leading specialists would lose power).

When he learned about the proposed new organizational structure, Carlgren's reaction was positive, but most of the company's staff managers were instead outright opposed to the suggested changes. In their view, it was better to base the GMT on the participation of the heads of Control, Finance, R&D and Technology; in that way they would function as a necessary counterforce to the heads of the powerful subsidiaries. The proposed structure would take away from the leading specialists their direct access to Carlgren – the key channel for having any influence in the company – and they were not willing to accept such 'degradation'. In light of the conflict Carlgren postponed the planned reorganization. At the same time, Martin-Löf, who had been recently appointed Head of Technology, left the company and went to MoDo's rival SCA (cf. Ch. 13).[137]

During the crisis, MoDo not only addressed its financial situation and considered a reorganization; the company also tried to postpone its planned investments and reduce maintenance. These saving efforts were so drastic that the responsible managers began to worry about the security of their plants. In 1978, the financial situation was so bad that MoDo began to sell some of its forests. Those located in the southern parts of the country were sold to the Swedish state ('Domänverket'; cf. Ch. 7).[138] In spite of all these steps, MoDo's debt ratio rose to a new height – in 1978 it reached 60 per cent.

However, it was not only the financial strain that put pressure on MoDo. Up until the 1980s, the forest-based industry had been full of well-organized cartels. Historically, there had been lots of (also legal) co-operation between forest-based companies, and that had made the leading actors colleagues as much as competitors. If somebody broke a price or quantity agreement, sanctions were applied. One example was MoDo's (and other forest-based companies') irritation over SCA's decision, together with PWA, to convert its Wifstavarf site to fine paper without considering the Nordic agreements regarding the future structure of the industry. That arrangement would allow a foreign competitor to establish a business on the Nordic market.

From the 1980s, the EC (and later the EU) began to act against cartel arrangements, a development that was inspired by US antitrust legislation and practice. One consequence of that change was that growth became even more important for the forest-based companies, as the cartels no longer 'protected' the older and mid-sized pulp and paper plants.[139] Thus, it is fair to say that before the 1980s, forest-related businesses were all about technology, production and cartels.

The collapsing cartels, the experiences stemming from the crisis in the late 1970s and the work carried out in MoDo Inter convinced Carlgren and MoDo's board that the company had to grow in order to continue to be successful. A stronger business core was necessary to be able to participate in the emerging globalization of the industry. Only those companies that were capable of buying others would survive. Carlgren was certain that such growth had to take place through the acquisition of Swedish companies, and he thought that time was running out. So Carlgren publicly declared that MoDo's ambition was to become one of the few large Swedish forest companies that would survive the coming decade. Thus, MoDo intended to expand both substantially and fast.[140]

However, there was one absolute restriction linked to MoDo's growth ambitions. The Kempe family had to keep its control of the company, that is to say, own the majority of the shares (voting rights). Therefore, the company could only marginally pay potential acquisitions with shares. Carlgren himself owned 22 per cent of the stock (votes), the Kempe foundations[141] 20 per cent, other Kempe family members 7 per cent and 'family friendly' shareholders 5 per cent. Together with MoDo's poor financial situation that control imperative created a severe problem in relation to the current growth ambitions. It also encouraged far too creative financial 'solutions' – it even stimulated unhealthy risk-taking.[142]

MoDo Inter's analysis presented three different development paths for MoDo. In the first, MoDo would house four related but different core businesses, namely MoDo Paper (pulp and fine paper), MoDo Konsument (tissue-based products), MoDo Iggesund (high-quality cardboard) and MoDo Holmen (newspaper and journal paper). As a platform for such a future, the investigators had identified substantial possible synergies between the three (envisioned) involved companies, that is to say, MoDo, Iggesund and Holmens Bruk. But they had also stressed that the realization of these synergies would demand a far-reaching integration – perhaps even a fusion – of the three companies. The group members also believed that certain paper qualities included in the suggested constellation would get closer to each other, creating synergies particularly in the sales and marketing fields. They also sketched a path in which the Husum paper mill would be redirected towards the production of coated qualities using the know-how from Iggesund, and there was also the option of installing a machine at Husum for producing an 'Iggesund-kind' of cardboard, which would make Husum a fully integrated mill. That solution would require the closure of Domsjö (because of lack of timber).[143]

Not surprisingly, shutting down Domsjö became a most controversial issue. Carlgren, Carl Kempe Jr and several other owners wanted to see Domsjö transformed into a business with a strong future. Like the family heads before them, they cared about that region and the unit's employees. Moreover, Domsjö's production had the advantage of being rather flexible, as it was based on both spruce and pine. Unfortunately there were divided opinions regarding its profitability (marginal timber pricing indicated losses, while average timber pricing indicated profits). An important drawback was that Domsjö competed with Husum for timber in the region, and, as a consequence, there were tough internal pricing discussions. Furthermore, Domsjö generated environmental problems that had to be solved. A main argument for continuing production there was provided by Carl Kempe Jr, who had suggested the production of fluff pulp (a path that later proved to be a mistake). However, not all leading actors backed Domsjö. For example, Löf (Head of Fine Paper), Sprängare (Head of Forestry), and Fahlin (Head of Technology) preferred to close Domsjö, as did board members Nabseth and Wallander. That option would also follow the mainstream rationale of the time – many competitors closed their sulphite plants.[144]

Thus, once again Domsjö was on the board's agenda as a problem unit. It continued to absorb not only financial but also managerial resources. However, as many times before, the preservation of the family name and reputation in the region carried a lot of weight. Particularly Carl Kempe Jr had a strong understanding of – and feeling for – MoDo's culture, and as a major representative for the family shareholding he was willing to let the foundation 'pay' for the reproduction of the core of their heirloom. To him Domsjö was a symbol for many of the important 'soft' values that were associated with the family and its industrial heritage. Thus, in the Domsjö case, Carlgren and Carl Kempe Jr were allies (and that was not always the case).[145]

In MoDo Inter's second proposal for MoDo's future, Domsjö was kept but rebuilt as an LWC plant based on CTMP.[146] In that alternative, Husum would be expanded to produce large quantities of coated paper. A thorough analysis showed that both the technical and the market conditions for making LWC at Domsjö were acceptable. The problem was that such a transformation of Domsjö required substantial amounts of capital; thus, it required a partner. There was also some uncertainty associated with sourcing (imported spruce). Gradually, Carlgren began to accept that MoDo might be forced to shut down Domsjö.[147]

The investigating team's third suggestion focused on the possibility of carrying out a merger with MoDo's rival SCA. From an analytical perspective, that alternative seemed to be promising. The two companies' forests were favourably located since they had common borders, and the product portfolios could jointly be developed to reach high-grade levels. Moreover, the companies could support each other in getting closer to end customers. The merits of such a constellation – MoDo and SCA – seemed to be so favourable that Carlgren contacted SCA's CEO Rydin, but he was not interested in discussing the matter.[148]

Thus, at the end of the 1970s, the crucial question was not whether MoDo should expand or not. Instead, it was in what way the company should grow, and whether and how such an expansion could be financed, as the company already from the beginning had a solidity that was regarded as too low by most actors in and around the industry. Except for the steps taken to lower the almost unavoidable debt increases that occurred during the crisis of the late 1970s, Carlgren made some private arrangements to try to counteract the financial strains expected for both himself and MoDo. It was an arrangement intended to preserve the family's control over a much bigger MoDo. To accomplish some of that, Carlgren began to build up his own company group (Sanna Holding). It included Stille Werner (bought from MoDo in 1981), Storliens högfjällshotell (a large, esteemed hotel located in the Swedish Alps), Bukowskis (a firm that traded fine art) and Nordic Channel (an unprofitable TV channel). He also used Sanna Holding for some of his shareholding in MoDo.

According to Frans Kempe Jr and Löf,[149] one or two of Carlgren's purchases were done primarily because it pleased him to own the units, while others were bought because he expected them to become profitable operations. However, when Carlgren bought the bleeding Stille Werner, he probably put it in his personal grouping because he had difficulties abandoning units that once had been under his control.[150] Taken together, Sanna Holding represented a true conglomerate constellation, and to Carlgren it was an arduous task to run those divided businesses in such a way that they generated a substantial profit. The general idea was to use the expected surpluses to finance future purchases of MoDo shares and increase its potential for expansion with the family still in control. Most actors in his environment were sceptical about that idea and sought to dissuade him from realizing it, but he did not follow their advice.

8.2 IGGESUND 1945–81

8.2.1 The Acquisition of Elektrokemiska (EKA)

During WWII Iggesund began to produce certain 'special products' that replaced previously imported commodities. The company also started to manufacture viscose pulp for sales to German textile companies that were short on raw materials. Soon that pulp quality also became much used in Sweden. To secure sourcing of a bleaching agent during those years, Iggesund initiated co-operation with Elektrokemiska (EKA), an alkali and chlorine producing company located close to Gothenburg. Eventually that relationship resulted in a purchase – Iggesund bought EKA (1951).[151]

Iggesund had been free from long-term debts since 1942, and that was a state that neither its major owner and Chair Carl Trygger nor its CEO Gunnar Sundblad wanted to abandon. Both had the experience of running a highly indebted Iggesund, and they

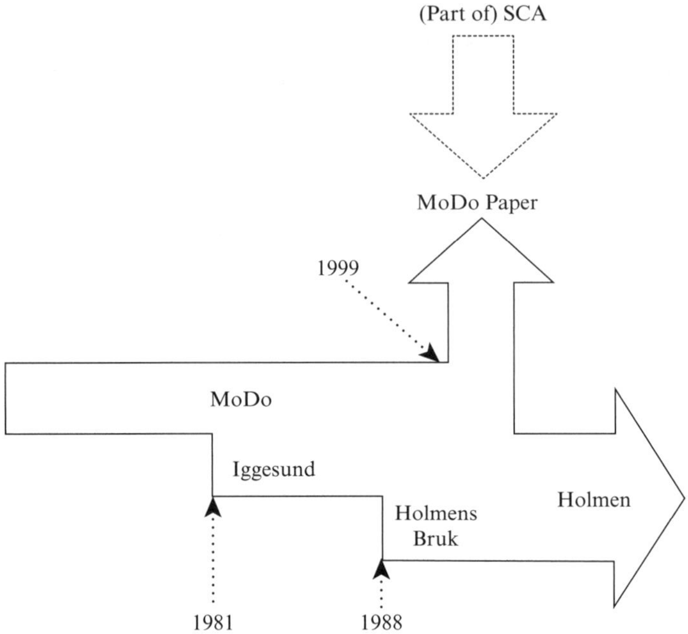

Figure 8.2 From MoDo to Holmen

did not want to go through that pain again. Therefore, no new grand investments were made, although there was certainly no lack of ideas. For example, there were discussions in 1941 about building a kraft paper plant, but that proposal never got off the ground. Instead, the board instructed the CEO to allocate capital in 'shares that were expected to become profitable investments'.[152]

The investment path was revived in 1947, however, when Sundblad asked his technical specialists for a description of what a machine for cardboard production might look like, and whether such a path might be worth following. The requested study also included an evaluation of the market opportunities for such a product, and the conclusion was that such an investment would be profitable for many years ahead. The investigators particularly referred to the recent developments in US retail, which were thought to be a strong indication of what later would occur in Europe.[153] However, just like back in 1941, nothing came of it this time either.

Due to such conservatism and risk aversion, Iggesund was in good economic and financial shape in the 1950s. It was almost debt-free (a solidity around 70%) and profitable (as most of the industry at that time), and had been very restrictive concerning new investments.[154] Like most corporations in the forest-based industry, the company had hidden much of the actual asset value in its books (they were booked far below their current market value).[155]

8.2.2 Lars G. Sundblad Replaces Gunnar Sundblad as CEO

Iggesund had no controlling shareholder in 1956. At that time, the Trygger family owned 22 per cent of the stock, while the af Ugglas family held 9 per cent. Three other families also had significant holdings: Sundblad 8 per cent, Westermark-Bexelius 5 per cent and Stackell 3 per cent. That year Gunnar Sundblad retired after 35 years as CEO, and he was succeeded by one of his sons, Lars G. Sundblad (to be replaced by a son was not unusual in those days). The new CEO was only 33 years old, but he had been involved in the forest-based industry for many years and had already spent some of them at Iggesund. However, the elder Sundblad did not leave Iggesund; he stayed on the board until 1962. Roughly at the same time, another son of Gunnar Sundblad (Erik) was appointed CEO of a competitor, namely Stora Kopparberg. That arrangement, that is to say, having two brothers simultaneously in the CEO position of two competing large public corporations, would later create delicate situations, particularly when Stora Kopparberg announced a hostile bid on Iggesund (1981; cf. below).

The Trygger family representatives continued to dominate the board. Carl Trygger acted as Chair and controlled the company by virtue of his formal position, large shareholding and long presence in the company. He was a complex person, hard to understand and rather capricious. He was also at loggerheads with his sons, which eventually produced a serious problem: they all refused to succeed him. In reality, Trygger did not have confidence in many other actors. CEO Lars G. Sundblad was one of the very few exceptions.

Ragnar Söderberg (Chair of Ratos[156]) was appointed board member and, together with director Stahle (CEO of Alfa Laval[157]), he became an important Iggesund actor. Board members in the late 1950s also included Carl Trygger (Chair and major shareholder), Bexelius (Deputy Chair), Gunnar Sundblad (former CEO of Iggesund, deputy from 1962), Jacob Wallenberg Sr (Chair of Enskilda Banken) and Lars G. Sundblad (ordinary director from 1962). Except for the Chair and Deputy Chair, few of these directors had any significant shareholding in Iggesund. Unfortunately, their experiences and competencies were also sometimes of only limited help to the company. However, at that time, that was not an unusual situation. Board membership was sometimes mainly a way of confirming and strengthening friendship relations.[158]

Lars G. Sundblad became Iggesund's CEO when the corporation was in a very strong position. Still, his basic assignment was to infuse fresh air into the company and make even better use of its 'slumbering' resources. Sundblad had to provide Iggesund with a business platform that could replace the previous one, which would become obsolete (aged pulp plants) in the coming decade. So he immediately initiated lots of minor investments and activities that, taken together, substantially increased production efficiency. However, Sundblad realized that Iggesund also had to expand to stay competitive in the current age of technological improvements and increasing economies of scale. He was also aware that with such growth raw material sourcing would become a problem.[159] In the middle of the 1950s, timber shortage was already a problem for most large forest-based corporations.[160]

Ever since Gunnar Sundblad became CEO of the company in 1921, Iggesund had not integrated forward and had instead stayed as (primarily) a producer of pulp for sale. As mentioned above, there had been discussions about entering the kraft paper business, but that idea never went anywhere. Lars G. Sundblad's first expansion project was directed towards the pulp business – he wanted to see an expansion investment in sulphate production. The board decided to follow Sundblad's recommendation and add a new production line in 1958 (bleached, partly birch-based sulphate pulp). That addition made it possible for Iggesund to make use of the fact that MoDo's bleaching patent had expired (1955), and to exploit birch wood found in the plant's surroundings.[161]

By 1960 most actors in the forest-based industry had recognized that the future for sulphite pulp production was uncertain mainly due to the environmental problems caused. Since Iggesund's own production of that kind of pulp was carried out in run-down plants, a decision had to be taken on a long-term solution. Once the sulphate production had been expanded and the huge investment in cardboard production had materialized in a new plant (1963), Iggesund's board finally had to decide what to do with its sulphite business. In autumn 1964 it became evident that the best solution was to gradually expand the sulphate plant even further, and then close down the sulphite production. That decision was to a large extent motivated by the fact that the sulphite plant's output did not suit the company's emerging core business: 'fine' cardboard. It was also a consequence of the technical development that had made bleaching of sulphate pulp possible – a method that in an economical way created superior raw material for most further processing purposes. By 1967, the new sulphate plant stood ready to produce bleached pine tree sulphate (which made it possible for the older sulphate plant to concentrate on birch pulp).[162]

8.2.3 Building a New Core Business: Cardboard

CEO Sundblad thought that Iggesund was too small and needed to grow in order to become competitive in the long run. One path forward was a further expansion of the pulp business, although problems with the sourcing of raw material would eventually arise. Therefore, like almost all other corporations in the forest-based industry during those years, Iggesund considered various ways to further process its pulp. The arguments were the same as for the other actors: Iggesund would then be less exposed to price fluctuations, and it would also – by getting closer to the end customer – become more profitable (better prices). Since Iggesund produced primarily bleached pulp qualities, its leading actors thought that the path forward ought to be writing paper, tissue or cardboard.[163]

To be better prepared for a decision regarding Iggesund's future strategy, the board asked Sundblad to take a trip to the US and find out what was going on there. The CEO was particularly instructed to learn more about tissue and cardboard production (writing paper was a more familiar business for a Swedish actor). What struck Sundblad the most was a rational handling of food using cardboard boxes ('foodboard'; both for dry and wet stuff). That product's fast growth in the US was driven by an accelerating expansion of supermarkets – a development that had not even started in Europe. However, Sundblad also understood that a transformation of the American kind would soon hit Europe, and that it would not only involve cardboard for foods, but also for other business segments. In addition, he noted that the American authorities neither accepted mechanical pulp nor waste-containing cardboard[164] as raw material; one had to use bleached cellulose as the basis. To supplement his own on-the-ground research, he asked his organization and consultants to examine the potential new path's technical demands, revenues/costs, market outlooks, and so on. After many informal discussions the issue was dealt with at a longer board meeting in 1959. In early September CEO Sundblad presented a blueprint for a cardboard plant. Later he also presented the board a report that described various ways to produce different qualities of tissue – both 'facial tissue' (handkerchiefs and napkins) and heavier tissue (kitchen paper and paper towels).[165]

In the second half of 1960 Iggesund's board got a report from an American consultancy firm addressing both businesses in question: cardboard and tissue. An advantage of establishing a tissue business at Iggesund was that the product was already well established on the market, and that it was expected to grow substantially in the coming years. A disadvantage of that path was that entry into that market called for a very extensive sales effort, as the barriers to entry in that industrial segment were high. For cardboard for foodstuffs (folding cardboards), by contrast, the market was limited (even if one calculated fast growth). However, there were only a few manufacturers of such high-quality, pulp-based cardboard: Billerud (Sweden), Enso-Gutzeit (Finland) and Container Corporation (US).[166] Sundblad soon discovered that a new production technique for cardboard had been developed at a company named Walmsley that increased machine speed substantially, thereby making the product segment more attractive. The timing could not be better, and Iggesund was a bit lucky, as its machine partner Beloit bought Walmsley.

Sundblad's standing within Iggesund had become rather strong, as almost all of his previously proposed 'moderate' investments had paid off well. Thus, it was not too difficult for him to convince the board that Iggesund should go ahead and focus on fine cardboard. Before that, however, Sundblad had to get – and got – approval from the company's major shareholder, Carl Trygger. All agreed that the company had to grow to stay competitive, and that it had the necessary financial resources to expand, but they all rejected expanding the pulp production – limited forest resources precluded that alternative. Like the CEO, the owners and the board considered further processing of the pulp as the obvious strategy to pursue. The only feasible alternative to the fine cardboard path was tissue, a segment that – judging from the development in the US – also seemed to have a bright future. However, the tissue volumes were projected to be rather small for quite some time, as a 'new' market had to be built and Iggesund lacked experience there (hotels, clubs, restaurants, etc.). Moreover, the raw material that Iggesund currently used did not fit tissue particularly well. So when the pros and cons were put together, the tissue path was judged to be both too risky and costly. Over time, Iggesund became number three in the fine cardboard segment, but the company had a stronger position than its ranking indicated, as the other two companies (one British and one Australian) used mechanical pulp and waste paper in their production processes, and that was forbidden in the US.[167]

In May 1961, the board finally decided that Iggesund should build a plant for 'fine' cardboard (i.e. wholly bleached stiff and homogeneous products of the highest quality), and in 1963 it started production. It was already a rather common product in the US, and the general expectation from the CEO and the board was that the European market would grow fast and in a similar way. However, the new strategy was not without risk – the heavy investment in fine cardboard production represented a new path and the promotion of a product that was almost unknown in Sweden and had only a limited market in the rest of Europe. Thus there were quite a few sceptical voices among the more prominent actors in the forest-based industry.[168] Nevertheless, demand grew fast, and Iggesund delivered record sleeves, boxes for frozen foods and cigarettes, book covers, and so on. Perfect timing made it a very successful launch. Thus, already in 1968 a second machine was needed, and the board decided to make that big investment. The tactics Iggesund used to stimulate demand from the 'inexperienced' and reluctant actors was to simultaneously work on the customers' customers – that is to say, the end users. Iggesund's message was that the new packaging solution made it easier for its customers to market – and sell – their products to their customers. To facilitate success, the company first picked the manufacturers of the most suitable goods for the new product. Another tactic was to turn to the graphics industry and sell the new product to publishers and advertising agencies.[169]

From 1963 onwards, Iggesund continuously developed its products starting with a non-coated kind for corrugated cardboard boxes, broadening its repertoire to include coated cardboard, and eventually introducing a CTMP-pulp-based layer to provide an attractive solution for the graphics industry.[170] When in 1968 it became necessary to invest in a second cardboard machine it was not evident that it should be located at Iggesund, as most of the customers were companies within the EC (of which Sweden was not a member). Thus, a continental location was seriously considered. Eventually, however, after careful calculations, the board decided to build the new machine at Iggesund next to the first machine (production started in 1971).

Iggesund also contained a subsidiary in UK, Thames board, which included a new plant in Workington with two machines. Although most of Iggesund's resources and managerial efforts were used in connection with the investments in the cardboard business, other steps were also taken to strengthen the company. For example, at the end of 1964, Iggesund had increased its shareholding in Boxholm to 35 per cent, and the following year it became 100 per cent. Boxholm was financially a rather strong company, which took care of its own investments and delivered both dividends and untaxed cash flow to Iggesund. However, Boxholm's most important contribution to Iggesund was its forest resources, which improved the timber-sourcing situation significantly.

Another example of Iggesund's activity during the 1960s was the acquisition of the listed company Ström-Ljusne, a forest-based company with fine old traditions that contained forests, a sulphite plant and a sawmill. In 1966, its major owner (the Lundquist family) was looking for new owners, as they suspected that, despite its good shape, the company would not be able to carry out the necessary modernization investments. An important catalyst for the ownership change was Wallander, a member of Ström-Ljusne's board, at that time CEO of Sundsvallbanken (and later a MoDo director). He worried about the company's future and asked Lars G. Sundblad to take a look at it. As Sundblad was on visiting terms with the factory owners in the region, he already knew the Lundquist family. On the basis of his positive impression of the company, Iggesund's Chair Carl Trygger and director Jacob Wallenberg Sr arranged that Iggesund would acquire Ström-Ljusne, while Bergvik & Ala got its subsidiary Ljusne-Woxna. That split suited Iggesund, as its part included the forests as well as the sulphite plant. However, Trygger obstructed the deal since he was reluctant to pay some of the purchase amount with a new issue of Iggesund shares, which would dilute his ownership position. The arguments that finally convinced him were that none of the other Ström-Ljusne shareholders would get any holding of importance in Iggesund, and that the deal as such was favourable for 'his company'.[171]

Soon Ström's sulphite plant became a problem. The intention had been to keep it running for some years, although its remaining economic and technical life was rather short. Sundblad, who had grown up in an industrial community, felt that he had an inherited responsibility for the people and the business activity in the region, so he and his management team started to look for a substitute industry. However, the analyses showed that there was one pulp plant too many for the region's timber supply capacity. In addition, new environmental legislation, launched in 1969, substantially increased companies' obligations to reduce their noxious outputs. Ten years later the plant was closed. Before that, however, Iggesund detached Ström's Kartongförädling and Ström's Tallriksfabrik and made them parts of Iggesund's division for pulp and cardboard.[172]

8.2.4 A Company without a Major Shareholder

In 1970 four families held around 34 per cent of the voting power in Iggesund: Trygger – including its family foundation – controlled 17 per cent, af Ugglas 9 per cent, Sundblad 5 per cent and Westermark-Bexelius 3 per cent. Institutional investors held 11 per cent and other families with 'an Iggesund history' had 6 per cent of the votes. Together these three categories of shareholders held the majority in Iggesund (51%). However, during the 1970s, the Trygger children, af Ugglas and several other relatively large private shareholders sold some of their Iggesund holdings. The Trygger family reduced its shareholding to 12 per cent, af Ugglas to less than 5 per cent, and the Sundblad family to below 4 per cent. In total that meant that these three families reduced their shareholdings over the decade by one-third (11%).

Instead, institutional investors like Handelsbanken Pension Fund (up to 6%), Skandia[173] (up to 5%) and SPP[174] (up to 4%) bought shares in Iggesund. These changes had a 'Handelsbanken flavour', but basically Iggesund became a company lacking a controlling constellation of shareholders.

Strangely enough neither Trygger nor any other board member or larger shareholder made attempts to try to establish an owner situation that would be sustainable in the long run. So when Trygger passed away in 1978 there was no unifying actor that could organize the shareholding and defend the company's interests. Thus, Iggesund – a well-trimmed company with a promising core business (quality cardboard) – became the perfect candidate for a takeover. The company was valued at around SEK 300 million, although its equity and free capital – if the value of the forests and power plants were included – together amounted to at least SEK 1.5 billion.[175] Up until that year Carl Trygger had been the dominant shareholder in Iggesund, but when he passed away his heirs preferred to put the shares on the free market. In that ownership vacuum and generally unstable situation, Iggesund's top management took command and determined the future path for the company.

In its strategic analyses, top management recognized that Iggesund was too small to handle the expected costs of capital, and also too small to successfully deal with the projected timber shortage. Therefore, in the summer of 1980, its CEO Sundblad approached the Swedish forest-based company Billerud with the intention to undertake a 'friendly' takeover. The leading actors in and around the two companies intensively discussed the idea. Among the ones most involved were Marcus Wallenberg Sr (although Papyrus's shareholding in Billerud only amounted to 2%), for the last few decades the Grand

Leader in Swedish business life in general and for the Wallenberg sphere in particular, Stahle (a distinguished member of the Wallenberg circle and also Deputy Chair at Iggesund), Lars G. Sundblad (CEO Iggesund), Henrikson (Chair Iggesund), Thunholm (Chair Billerud) and Engman (CEO Billerud). Most of these actors knew each other quite well.

Sundblad was aware of the fact that Iggesund had lost its major shareholder, and that the company needed to both belong somewhere and become a bigger unit. Cavalli-Björkman, one of the CEOs at SE-Banken (part of the Wallenberg sphere), took the crucial initiative and contacted Sundblad and Iggesund's Head of Finance Svensson and suggested that Billerud could be a suitable partner for Iggesund. Svensson was asked to carry out most of the crucial calculations, and the merger idea looked fine on paper. Almost all calculations supported Iggesund's proposed takeover of Billerud. Based on that classic rationale there was no doubt that a merger was a promising alternative. Billerud's business portfolio represented considerable further processing of the classic raw materials (timber and pulp). It had fluting,[176] cardboard for fluid products and also a kraft paper business, and the future for the last two products looked quite promising. In a possible takeover, Iggesund would transform the fluting operations to one that instead produced bleached cardboard. However, if Iggesund, a relatively small company run by managers, was to be successful in such a complex merger process, it was necessary that the leading actors linked to the target company also liked the idea. Four actors were more important than the others in that situation: Iggesund's CEO Lars G. Sundblad, its Head of Finance Svensson, Billerud's Chair Thunholm and its CEO Engman.[177]

Iggesund soon discovered that they faced a reluctant target company. Billerud's CEO was not especially enthusiastic about the merger idea (and he might have been concerned about his future position). Moreover, after having weighed the pros and cons of a merger, its Chair also expressed scepticism. As Iggesund's Chair Henrikson was not particularly used to larger business deals and was also a rather risk-averse actor, he did not push the issue.[178] Eventually, Iggesund's leading actors came to the conclusion that the suggested path no longer was on the target company's agenda.

Billerud's CEO had listed his and the company's strongest arguments against the proposed merger. He particularly stressed the problems associated with establishing a new strategy for the group, handling differing management cultures, solving possible regional conflicts (based on divergent emotional affiliations) and integrating incongruent company values. Another main reason against a merger was that Billerud recently had gone through a similar process with Uddeholm, and, as a consequence, many of the Billerud managers and other employees were rather fed up with such activities. Another important factor that worked against a merger was that in two years (1983) Billerud was planning to celebrate its centenary as an autonomous company. So rather soon the whole idea fizzled out, and the takeover idea was put back on Iggesund's bookshelves.

Some key changes took place in the composition of the Iggesund board during the 1970s. In 1972, Henrikson (Deputy Chair at Götabanken) was elected to the board, and when Ragnar Söderberg left the board in 1974, he became Deputy Chair. Of particular importance was that Chair Carl Trygger, who represented the largest shareholding in the company, left in 1977 after 54(!) years as a board member. Henriksson succeeded him as Chair, and Stahle (CEO of Alfa Laval) became the new Deputy Chair. Two deputy members became regular ones, namely Nils Trygger (he left in 1980) and C:son Bonde. In

1978, Dahlström (former CEO of AP4[179]) became a regular member, and he was later – in a turbulent period – elected Chair (1981).[180]

During the period when Iggesund's shareholding structure was changing, that is to say, the 1970s, the company continued to integrate forward and bought a smaller packaging company near Stockholm. It was not a very successful acquisition, so two years later it was sold to Esselte, a packaging company that was an important customer of Iggesund. A few years later (1975) Iggesund made another acquisition and bought 20 per cent of a Swiss packaging company (Rentsch) – a decision that was one of the few not supported by company Chair Trygger. He decided not to participate in the decision because of a linkage to one of its owners. Later Iggesund increased its holding to 48 per cent.[181] Iggesund also tried to acquire one or two competitors. For example, in early 1975, discussions were held about a purchase of Bergvik & Ala, but that path failed (instead Stora Kopparberg made the acquisition; cf. Ch. 11).[182]

8.3 HOLMENS BRUK 1945–88

8.3.1 Newsprint is Supplemented with Journal Paper

Just before WWII von Sydow replaced Wahrén as CEO of Holmens Bruk (1938).[183] At that time the company had become one of the leading producers of newsprint in Sweden, exporting most of its paper to Western Europe. In the middle of WWII Holmens Bruk decided to broaden its repertoire into the sawmill business and bought Backa-Hosjö. Still, however, newsprint was the company's dominant forest-related business.

The boom times in the early 1950s stimulated many companies to invest in newsprint production, bringing about a surplus on the market. Concurrently, a dramatically expanding journal market created a strong and rising demand for a 'new' kind of paper suitable for such publications. In light of this trend, Holmens Bruk decided to expand in that field by increasing its production of journal paper at the Norrköping plant. Thus, that site became specialized in such paper, while the growing Hallsta unit concentrated its production on newsprint. Holmens Bruk also introduced a new quality in the journal paper segment: non-coated super calendered (SC) paper. Rather soon the company became the biggest Swedish producer of journal paper. With the expansion putting pressure on the company's timber sourcing, Holmens Bruk continued to buy forest-owning companies in the region.

Von Sydow upheld Holmens Bruk's classic policy that its board and CEO should work independently of the shareholders – there should not be any major owner (coalition) in control of the company. However, that situation changed in the early 1950s, when two big shareholders entered the scene – the Bonnier and Söderberg families. They demanded a position from which they could influence the company's operations and future development. Therefore, to maintain the company's autonomy, the current board members tried to mobilize the other shareholders to hand over voting rights to them (with the 1954 AGM at hand). They were successful in their campaign; the board members' voting power turned out to be stronger than that of the Bonnier and Söderberg families. The majority also opposed transforming Bonnier's (i.e. Dagens Nyheter's[184]) large shareholding into board seats. The main argument was that other buyers might suspect that the

Bonnier-controlled firms received price advantages, thereby damaging customer relations more generally. The Söderberg family's request, however, was accepted, and the family head Ragnar Söderberg soon became a board member and later even Chair of Holmens Bruk.[185]

The rationale behind Dagens Nyheter's (i.e. Bonnier's) entrance in Holmens Bruk as a substantial shareholder was to secure the company's sourcing of paper. Actually, the Söderberg family was of the opinion that Dagens Nyheter's ownership in Holmens Bruk was questionable in itself (the customer argument), and that the family therefore should refrain from a board seat. However, Wallander (Chair of Handelsbanken and linked to the Bonnier family through Chair positions) pushed for a place on the board for Bonnier, and when Reuterskiöld was appointed the new CEO of Dagens Nyheter (1980) the directorship materialized.[186]

8.3.2 Investing at Braviken and in LWC

Holmens Bruk had for a long time contained two 'legs', that is to say, the paper and the textile businesses, but in the late 1960s the latter one was questioned, as it had done badly. The paper business was not that successful either, mainly because of aging machines. When Önnesjö was appointed CEO in 1968, he launched a thorough review of the company's strategy. Önnesjö had been recruited from a similar position in the Federation of Swedish Forest Owners (Sveriges Skogsägares Riksförbund). Holmen's new strategic path was to focus heavily on investments in the paper businesses, and a simultaneous divestment of the company's textile operations. The activities in the paper industry were to concentrate on wood-containing printing paper, and in that segment Holmens Bruk would begin to broaden its repertoire.[187]

The acquisition of Wargöns Bruk in 1969 was probably the most important offensive step Holmens Bruk took that decade. It brought the company a substantial production of coated journal paper. The main reasons for the purchase were that the Norrköping plant had hit the production ceiling for that kind of paper and that Wargön's production could be expanded. After that acquisition, Holmens Bruk controlled around 60 per cent of the Swedish market for journal paper and about 40 per cent of the newsprint market. One-third of the production was sold in Sweden – the rest mainly to Western Europe. The purchases of raw material that had intensified in the 1960s continued, so the company acquired several new forest estates.[188]

In the 1970s and early 1980s substantial changes were made at Holmens Bruk, particularly with respect to its portfolio of businesses. The textile operations were closed down, finishing off a 350-year tradition. That closure made Holmens Bruk a pure forest-based company. However, by that time, the location of much of the production at the rather big Swedish town Norrköping had become a problem because the site offered no expansion possibilities. Moreover, the authorities banned discharges into the river crossing the city. The continuous transportation of timber, pulp and paper within the town had also become a severe problem. As a consequence of the expansion and environmental obstacles linked to Norrköping, Holmens Bruk planned to make its future investments instead at Hallsta and Wargön.

The problems with the Norrköping location made it necessary for Holmens Bruk to develop a new strategy. After careful analyses CEO Önnesjö and his team concluded that it was best to replace the Norrköping site with a brand new paper mill to be located at Bråviken[189] outside Norrköping and close to the Baltic Sea. While the new paper mill was being built, the Loddby sulphite plant was closed down, and the production at Norrköping reduced. The latter site was to be shut down when the new machine at Braviken started production. Holmens Bruk also considered building a sulphate plant and a sawmill – a plan that local public opinion strongly opposed. At the same time, however, Södra discussed establishing a newsprint plant near its sulphate plant at Mönsterås (cf. Ch. 6). To avoid competition, the two companies entered into a structural agreement under which Holmens Bruk refrained from building a sulphate plant and Södra from building a paper mill. Moreover, Södra was to deliver wood and sulphate pulp to Braviken, where also a TMP[190] plant was to be built.[191]

The authorities gave their permission for the new industrial establishment at Braviken in 1975 – the same year as the board took the investment decision. Braviken would produce newsprint and TMP pulp, and the journal paper activities would be transferred to Hallsta, where suitable pulp was produced. The first Braviken line started in 1977 and delivered bleached pulp to the Norrköping paper mill. Braviken's launch initiated the phasing out of the Norrköping site, although for a few years the two units worked like a combine (the pulp was pumped through a pipe 8.5 km to the mill).[192] In 1982, the decision was taken to rebuild one machine at Hallsta, so that it could take over the production of non-coated journal paper from Norrköping. That conversion was not so problematic because there existed an effective cartel that 'organized' the paper sales when production interruptions took place. Holmens Bruk's second newsprint machine was to be built at Braviken in 1982, but due to bad business times, the board's decision to build it was postponed until 1984. That year Hallsta took over the non-calendered offset paper from Norrköping, and it was decided that the company should stay in the non-coated, wood-containing journal paper segment. Moreover, leading actors raised the idea that Holmens Bruk might also produce high-quality journal paper at Hallsta in the future.

In 1980 the board was composed of Chair M:son Mannerfelt, Douglas (replaced in 1982 by Reuterskiöld), Lars G. Sundblad, Erik Söderberg (Deputy Chair), Trolle-Löwén, Gripenstedt and Önnesjö (CEO). Mannerfelt was resolute when he engraved in the directors' minds that they all had to work for the best of the company – not act as some kind of representative for somebody/something (e.g. a large shareholder). He also wanted and got an affirmation from Reuterskiöld that Dagens Nyheter's holding would not be sold. If Mannerfelt was a strong Chair, so was Önnesjö as CEO. Still, the latter always checked his plans with the board and particularly with the representatives of the two major shareholders. When something was put on the board's table, it was always ploughed through carefully – very much as a consequence of that, the board was a demanding body. Sometimes, when issues were particularly important or delicate, an informal board presidium composed of Mannerfelt, Reuterskiöld, Söderberg and Önnesjö took the lead.[193]

In the early 1980s there were indications that Holmens Bruk's shareholder structure might not be carved in stone. A broker contacted Reuterskiöld and asked if Dagens Nyheter's holding was for sale 'at any price'. Reuterskiöld had answered that Dagens Nyheter would not sell at any 'reasonable' price, but added that there, of course, also existed an 'unrealistically high' price level for which even Dagens Nyheter might be inclined to sell. In spite of Reuterskiöld's refusal of the broker's feeler, rumours emerged on the market that Dagens Nyheter was ready to sell. That irritated Chair Mannerfelt until he was informed that the rumour was false.[194]

At that time, Holmens Bruk's production was to be found at Braviken, Hallsta, Hult (axes), Norrköping, Sparreholm (sawmill; on the 'for sale' list), Vrena fiber (building material; sold in 1983) and Wargön. To that, one could add power plants and forests. Contacts were taken up with Fiskeby about a merger or purchase, but that company was not for sale. The board also discussed purchases of companies producing lignin, but those ambitions never materialized. Interest in entering the non-woven business grew steadily, test selling took place with goods from the American corporation Crown Zellerbach, and Deputy CEO Zetterberg travelled to that country to learn more about the fiberweb field. For Holmens Bruk, those efforts resulted in a plant at Braviken – Holmen Fiberweb – that started its production in 1984 (but was sold already in 1988).

The broadening of Holmens Bruk's repertoire with investments in non-woven – and later in hygiene products – was not first and foremost an outcome of a rational and systematic analysis. However, the focus on further processing of the timber and pulp resources was not particularly surprising – at that time, everybody in the industry did just that. When the sourcing of raw material became problematic, the actors looked for products that used less wood or diversified their companies. The former path could take the company closer to the customers, and such a move at least eliminated some of the existing market uncertainty.

There were suggestions that Holmens Bruk ought to expand its product portfolio, that is to say, add 'one more leg', and then the related non-woven business might fit. The company's market managers also wanted to serve the customers with more products (particularly LWC paper). Taking into account the investments in lignin, the linkage to the current operations was of a technological kind. Basically, that path was initiated because of access to a usable waste product from existing operations.[195] So, Holmens Bruk, through its unit for chemical products, began to co-operate with a Spanish firm[196] and became the majority owner of its lignin unit. The Spaniards delivered the pulp, and Holmens Bruk carried out the sales. At the time, there were also discussions with Reed (its Canada unit) regarding joint efforts in the lignin business.

Önnesjö retired as CEO in 1984 and was succeeded by Deputy CEO Zetterberg. The two major shareholders were active in that promotion process through Reuterskiöld and Sven Söderberg (the new head of the Söderberg dynasty). They made sure that the candidate was a person they both trusted. They also considered it important that the new CEO and the incoming Chair Önnesjö could work well together. Önnesjö was the obvious candidate for the position as Chair both because of his track record as CEO, and because of all his other merits. His well-known integrity was another quality that suited a company that housed two major shareholders.[197]

At that time, Fredrik Lundberg had begun to buy shares in Holmens Bruk, and fairly soon it became a rather substantial holding. He had become CEO of Lundbergföretagen in 1981, succeeding his father Lars Erik. The latter had invested primarily in the building industry, but his son wanted to reduce the company's exposure in that sector, as he did not expect very much from it in the coming years. As a large investor, Lundberg had learned a lot about Swedish industry in general, so he was well prepared to move to new sectors. Initially he looked for small and medium-sized companies, but eventually he also began to look for bigger ones. Doing that, he discovered that the market had put a rather low value on Holmens Bruk, and as Norrköping was his home ground he had become rather familiar with its operations and knew the important people pretty well. That familiarity, together with a certain dose of local patriotism, made Holmens Bruk his first larger investment in a bigger company. Because of that fairly large holding (≈ 8%) Lundberg was soon (1984) appointed a board member. As he had almost no previous experience in the forest-based industry, several leading actors in and around the company became concerned about his intentions. He wanted to acquire a larger share, but neither the Söderberg family (Ratos) nor the Bonnier family (Dagens Nyheter) wanted to sell their holdings. When Holmens Bruk rather soon acquired Fiskeby from Kooperativa Förbundet (KF), the latter also got a holding in Holmens Bruk. So, eventually, the ownership situation became less interesting for Lundberg, and already in 1985 he sold his shares and left the board (1986) (Johan Jacob ['Joja'] Bonnier became the new board member).[198]

The new CEO Zetterberg wanted to put his stamp on the company and maintain its autonomy. Like most colleagues in the industry, he considered forward integration as the most promising path. By tradition, the CEO had a strong standing in Holmens Bruk, although Zetterberg had highly qualified board sparring partners in both Chair Önnesjö and director Lars G. Sundblad.[199] Zetterberg stated his and Holmens Bruk's goals for the coming years in the 1984 Annual Report. The company intended to invest in products that economized on the usage of wood and in those that represented a high degree of further processing (like newsprint and journal paper). That ambition required a radical restructuring programme. The expected outcome would be a company that had become a leading actor in the segment of wood-containing printing paper (i.e. newsprint, coated and non-coated journal paper, catalogue paper and 'special qualities' paper). That path did not demand substantial new investments except in the LWC segment. There, Holmens Bruk decided to make a significant push, as it was important to lower the company's concentration on the bulky non-coated newsprint. That meant that the production at the Hallsta site had to change to focus more on further processing and specialization.[200]

Zetterberg wanted to get Holmens Bruk away from its high dependence on printing paper by diversifying into fiberweb and chemical products. He also sought to secure Holmens Bruk's position as an autonomous listed company, and therefore it was important that both newsprint and journal paper remained competitive. To keep his and the company's autonomy, Zetterberg considered it crucial that the company should grow and become too expensive to buy for any competitor that might be interested in fitting Holmens Bruk's operations into their business structure. However, Chair Önnesjö tended to be more cautious than his CEO, so the expansion took place more slowly than Zetterberg had planned.

These changes were carried out in a market situation that (still) did not match the requirements of effective competition. In the forest industry 'everybody' knew each other's strategic plans rather well. Moreover, the super consultant firm Jakko Pöyry had a total overview, as it was involved in the planning, construction and building of most of the paper machines in the world. That firm had few if any serious competitors (perhaps with the exceptions of Ångpanneföreningen[201] and Celpap[202]). Thus, through that nexus, most investment plans were made known in one way or another. Industry transparency was also supported by the presence of long-term planning in most companies. At the time, such efforts were exceptionally 'fashionable' – everything had to be put down on paper and then preferably in the form of figures and calculations, although most of them had to be based on highly uncertain assumptions. All that taken together – the transparency of the strategies, the Jakko Pöyry 'monopoly' and the preference for long-term planning – contributed to a cartel-like behaviour that was more or less evident.[203] An example of such cross-company co-operation was Holmens Bruk's 1986 membership in Industriskog – the firm that co-ordinated purchases of timber in the middle region of Sweden.

8.3.3 Entering the Hygiene Business

For Holmens Bruk, 1985 turned out to be a year of transformation. The closing of the Norrköping plants was almost completed, and the new paper machine at Braviken was running. The latter addition had made the company the biggest producer of newsprint in Europe. Furthermore, negotiations had once again begun with KF[204] to acquire Fiskeby with its expansive hygiene operations. There was a link between that kind of production and Holmens Bruk's fiberweb unit at Braviken. Still, the basic reason was to broaden Holmens Bruk's product repertoire beyond its various kinds of printing paper. Another reason for the acquisition attempt was that the two companies' timber sourcing could be effectively co-ordinated. During the talks, it also became evident that KFIAB (KF's industrial unit) wanted to develop Fiskeby's cardboard business and therefore excluded that part of the company from a sale. Holmens Bruk had no problem with that proposal.[205]

CEO Zetterberg pushed the Fiskeby purchase really hard. Like almost all other forest-based companies, Holmens Bruk sought a way to further process the raw materials, and in that competitive race, hygiene had been his and the company's first choice. As noted above, Zetterberg regarded Holmens Bruk as a small company that needed to grow to remain autonomous. To do so, it needed one more business, and that new 'leg' should represent three things: growth opportunities, timber 'stinginess' and a high degree of further processing of the raw materials. From that perspective, Fiskeby seemed like the perfect acquisition candidate. That it controlled forests was perhaps the most important attraction for Holmens Bruk, which had the lowest degree (10%) of self-supply among all the bigger Swedish forest-based companies. However, Fiskeby also operated a hygiene business that matched at least two of Holmens Bruk's three criteria. Zetterberg had also noticed SCA's success with its acquisition of Mölnlycke (cf. Ch. 13) and used that thinking as a model. He wanted a Holmens Bruk capable of competing with Edet, the dominating player on the hygiene market in Sweden at the time.[206]

However, some directors were hesitant about the new hygiene path, among them Reuterskiöld, who expressed his doubts both during board discussions and in separate talks with director Erik Söderberg. Reuterskiöld preferred that the company instead concentrate its production on semi-processed products like 'big rolls' that would be sold to those corporations that manufactured consumer goods (e.g. toilet paper or diapers). However, he was 'overrun' by the other directors, and in 1986 Holmens Bruk bought Fiskeby (except its cardboard business) and paid KFIAB with 11 per cent of Holmens Bruk's B-shares and SEK 30 million in cash. That figure, above 10 per cent (a level that activated minority rights), indicated that Holmens Bruk regarded KFIAB as a 'friendly' partner.[207] KFIAB also signed a letter of intent expressing its intent to keep a substantial part of its shareholding. After the sale, Fiskeby Hygien was renamed Holmen Hygien.

However, Fiskeby not only provided a hygiene business (the tissue producer Katrinefors and the Sanetta plant) and forests. It also included pulp and sack businesses. Moreover, it represented a rather different company culture from that of Holmens Bruk, making the merger process more difficult. Fiskeby had a friendly and lively culture, while Holmens Bruk contained a tougher and more cautious one.[208] The CEO's handling of the troublesome integration process made the Chair somewhat concerned, although it did not alter his basic confidence in the CEO. Fiskeby's CEO de Verdier became Deputy CEO at Holmens Bruk. The enlarged Holmens Bruk was composed of Holmen Printing Paper, Holmen Coated Paper, Holmen Kemi, Holmen Cellkraft (Skärblacka's division for pulp and paper), Holmen Fiberweb, Herkules and Holmen Hygien.

Also in 1985 Deputy CEO de Verdier presented the board a letter of intent signed by Holmens Bruk, MoDo Konsument and Union A/S. It stated that the three corporations were interested in forming a joint company (Union Mykpapir) for their hygiene paper businesses in Norway. However, the expansion ambitions had to be kept rather modest, as all the investments in the early 1980s had put substantial financial strain on Holmens Bruk. However, the situation improved when the Swedish Central Bank gave Holmens Bruk permission to issue the needed long- and short-term credits, and when a new issue of shares for cash was implemented in early 1987.

When the Fiskeby acquisition was underway, the German family firm München-Dachau Papierfabriken (MD Papier) communicated its interest in some kind of co-operation with Holmens Bruk. MD Papier was Europe's biggest producer of coated journal paper with a special focus on LWC. Zetterberg liked the idea, as MD Papier's LWC operations would make it unnecessary for Holmens Bruk to build its own LWC plant, something that would be regarded as a 'hostile move' by the EU's established paper industry (cf. the presence of cartels). The idea was that Holmens Bruk would acquire 25 per cent, and that it would sell MD Papier's coated paper in the Nordic countries, while MD Papier would sell Holmens Bruk's non-coated paper in Germany. The CEO's suggestion was well received at the board, so Holmens Bruk bought the shares for half a billion SEK, with the intention of increasing its holding to 100 per cent.

At the time, the situation in the fiberweb business changed. Crown Zellerbach was sold to James River.[209] Fortunately James River wanted to continue its co-operation with Holmens Bruk in the non-woven field. During the first half of 1987, the two companies formed a joint venture that included Holmens Bruk's fiberweb plant at Braviken and James River's licences and technological know-how. The two companies even began to discuss the possibility of a future joint effort in the printing paper business. A few months before those talks, Holmens Bruk had also established market co-operation in another soft paper segment, that time with Duni-Bilå (napkins, etc.).

The establishment of hygiene as a core business brought scale considerations to the fore. When CEO Zetterberg looked around, he found that a combined Holmen Hygien and MoDo Konsument would be the best alternative. He initiated merger discussions, with the board's permission. Holmens Bruk considered two alternatives: a purchase of MoDo Konsument's Swedish operations either with or without an acquisition of its shares in Mabelpap. The seller – MoDo's major shareholder Carlgren – would accept only A-shares in Holmens Bruk as payment (i.e. shares with strong voting rights). However, Holmens Bruk's major shareholders and its board would accept nothing other than a cash-based transaction.

NOTES

N.B.: When there is an 'i' inside a parenthesis below, that letter indicates that the note refers to an interview with the named person. All interviewees are listed in the Appendix. A complete listing of references is found at the end of the book.

1. Croon (2005).
2. Andersson (1993).
3. Valeur (2000).
4. Valeur (2007).
5. Valeur (2000).
6. Gårdlund (1951).
7. Croon (2005) and Croon (2006i).
8. Harry Diedrichs (2006i).
9. Unger (1967).
10. Lyberg (1984).
11. Lyberg (1984) and Croon (2005).
12. Valeur (2000) and Croon (2005).
13. Valeur (2000).
14. Lyberg (1984).
15. During these years there were not many uniting social activities, so many members of the two family factions were rather unknown to each other (Frans Kempe Jr [2006i]).
16. Lyberg (1984) and Frans Kempe Jr (2006i).
17. Frans Kempe Jr (2006i).
18. Eventually Carlgren became a member of the prestigious International Olympic Committee.
19. Browaldh (2005i) and Peppler (2006i).
20. The same was valid for Lyberg's and Erik Kempe's relationship.
21. Browaldh (2005i).
22. Croon (2005) and Peppler (2006i).
23. Altbäck (2006i), Nordstrand (2006i) and Sprängare (2006i).
24. Lyberg was introduced to MoDo through his father's contacts with Carl Kempe (both were members of Handelsbanken's board) (Lyberg 1984).
25. Croon (2005).
26. Altbäck (2006i).
27. Wallander (2006i).
28. Sjöstrand et al. (2001).
29. Frans Kempe Jr (2006i).
30. Suggested by Erik Kempe. Peppler (2006i).
31. Two other Deputy CEOs were appointed at the same time: Altbäck and Ulfsparre.
32. Haglund.
33. Lyberg (1984).
34. Croon (2005) and Flodström (2006i).
35. Croon (2005).
36. Dahlgren (2006i), Flodström (2006i), Frans Kempe Jr (2006i) and Nabseth (2006i).
37. Sprängare (2006i) and Wallander (2006i).
38. Harry Diedrichs (2006i), Frans Kempe Jr (2006i), Sprängare (2006i) and Wallander (2006i); and a letter written by Frans Kempe Sr.
39. Harry Diedrichs (2006i), Frans Kempe Jr (2006i), Sprängare (2006i) and Wallander (2006i); and a letter written by Frans Kempe Sr.
40. Croon (2005).
41. Altbäck (2006i).
42. Peppler (2006). Peppler was married to Erik Kempe's eldest daughter Elisabeth, and in the eyes of several MoDo actors his ambitions were high already from the beginning and seemed to include an aspiration to secure a top position in the company. One of several indications of that was that the relationship between him and the incoming CEO, Chair and family leader, Carlgren, rather soon became somewhat strained. Another indicator was the self-directed way he guided MoDo's internationalization process.
43. Lyberg (1984).
44. Altbäck (2006i), Harry Diedrichs (2006i) and Peppler (2006i).
45. Lyberg (1984) and Peppler (2006i).

46. Lyberg (1984), Peppler (2006i), and Harry Diedrichs (2006i).
47. Lyberg (1984).
48. Peppler (2006i) and Nordstrand (2006i).
49. Lyberg (1984).
50. Gårdlund (1986).
51. MoDo acquired e.g. SOAB in 1963 (a semi-manufacturer to the growing plastics industry), according to Lyberg (1984).
52. Gårdlund (1986).
53. Valeur (2000).
54. Unger (1967) and Peppler (2006i).
55. Peppler (2006i).
56. 60% in 1966 and 100% in 1967.
57. Croon (2005).
58. Gustafsson (2002).
59. A medium-sized Swedish company offering healthcare products.
60. Croon (2005).
61. Lyberg (1984).
62. A small Swedish textile company.
63. A small Swedish pioneering company manufacturing paper-based diapers.
64. Gustafsson (2002) and Croon (2005).
65. Croon (2005). Grünewald left in 1972.
66. Nordlund (2006i).
67. Lyberg (1984) and Croon (2005).
68. Unger (1967).
69. Gårdlund (1986), Unger (1967), Lyberg (1984) and Croon (2005).
70. Gårdlund (1986).
71. Croon (2005).
72. Nordlund (2006i).
73. Croon (2005).
74. Unger (1967).
75. Valeur (2000) and Croon (2005).
76. Croon (2005).
77. Harry Diedrichs (2006i).
78. Nordstrand (2006i).
79. Trolle-Löwén (2006i).
80. Valeur (2000).
81. A Swedish family that lived abroad owned the company. They became concerned when MoDo launched its new fine paper machine, and for that reason they were open to sell their company.
82. Valeur (2000).
83. Gårdlund (1986).
84. Valeur (2000).
85. Carlgren (1994i) and Dahlgren (2006i).
86. Altbäck (2006i), Browaldh (2006i) and Wallander (2006i).
87. Carl Kempe Jr (2006i).
88. Carlgren (1994i) and Altbäck (2006i).
89. Gårdlund (1986).
90. Löf (2004i).
91. Gårdlund (1986).
92. Harry Diedrichs (2006i).
93. It was Browaldh who introduced Löf to SCA's CEO Mossberg, who asked him to talk to the head of SCA's management secretariat (Brändström). The outcome of that was that Löf began working at SCA (Löf [2006i]).
94. Löf (2004i), Harry Diedrichs (2006i) and Croon (2005).
95. Frans Kempe Jr (2006i).
96. Flodström (2006i).
97. Löf (2004i).
98. Croon (2005).
99. Fahlin (2006i) and Frans Kempe Jr (2006i).
100. Nabseth (2006i).
101. Nordstrand (2006i).
102. Valeur (2000) and Croon (2005).

103. Gustafsson (2002).
104. E.g. Grifo in 1978. At the same time, Lejeune bought another wholesaler Navarre. For some reason that unit was not offered to MoDo (Carl Kempe Jr [2006i]).
105. Carlgren (1994i) and Croon (2005).
106. Wallander (2006i).
107. Croon (2005).
108. Valeur (2000).
109. Carl Kempe Jr (2006i) and Nordlund (2006i).
110. Nordlund (2006i).
111. Carlgren (1994i).
112. Carlgren (1994i) and Nordlund (2006i).
113. Peppler (2006i).
114. Ibid.
115. Croon (2005).
116. Nordlund (2006i).
117. Croon (2005) and Flodström (letter written in 2014).
118. Andersson (1993).
119. Andersson (1993) and Valeur (2003).
120. Andersson (1993).
121. Ibid.
122. Croon (2005).
123. Ibid.
124. About the same time the Swiss team organized in the 1960s was dissolved.
125. Harry Diedrichs (2006i) and Nabseth (2006i).
126. Ibid.
127. Carl Kempe Jr (2006i).
128. Harry Diedrichs (2006i) and Nabseth (2006i).
129. Croon (2005). One could note that ten years later, in 1987, MoDo began to import pulp from South America.
130. Andersson (1993).
131. Ibid.
132. Croon (2005).
133. Dahlgren (2006i).
134. Wallander (2006i).
135. Carl Kempe Jr (2006i) and Löf (2006i).
136. Löf (2006i).
137. Croon (2005).
138. Valeur (2000).
139. Reuterskiöld (2006i).
140. Valeur (2000) and Croon (2005).
141. Ragnar Kempe was Chair of the foundations, and the other board members were Stig Kempe and Browaldh. Later Ragnar Kempe was succeeded by Carl Kempe Jr, Stig Kempe by his daughter Viviann and Browaldh by Carl Kempe's youngest brother Anders Kempe (1992). The smooth family co-operation in the foundations continued until 1990, the year when Carlgren had to sell all his MoDo shares.
142. Valeur (2000) and Croon (2005).
143. Croon (2005).
144. Fahlin (2006i), Carl Kempe Jr (2006i), Nabseth (2006i) and Nordlund (2006i).
145. Fahlin (2006i) and Nabseth (2006i).
146. Many actors in the industry regarded this type of pulp – chemi-thermo-mechanical-pulp – as an important one for the future. However, that view produced too many investments in CTMP plants.
147. Croon (2005).
148. Carlgren (1994i) and Croon (2006i).
149. Frans Kempe Jr (2006i) and Löf (2006i).
150. Löf (2006i).
151. Savalainen and Zacco-Broberg (1985) and Valeur (2007).
152. Iggesund (1985).
153. Valeur (2007).
154. Savalainen and Zacco-Broberg (1985).
155. Iggesund (1985).
156. A holding company for the Söderberg family's growing enterprises.

157. Alfa Laval is a large Swedish global industry company that focuses on the marine, energy and food industries.
158. Iggesund (1985) and Lars G. Sundblad (2006i).
159. Lars G. Sundblad (2006i).
160. Valeur (2007).
161. Iggesund (1985).
162. Savalainen and Zacco-Broberg (1985) and Valeur (2007).
163. Savalainen and Zacco-Broberg (1985) and Iggesund (1985).
164. 'Paperboard' is used in the US. It is also used in the name of Iggesund's unit for that production. However, in this book using British English, 'cardboard' is preferred.
165. Iggesund (1985), Valeur (2007) and Lars G. Sundblad (2006i).
166. Iggesund (1985).
167. Lars G. Sundblad (2006i).
168. Iggesund (1985), Savalainen and Zacco-Broberg (1985) and Rydberg (1990).
169. Valeur (2007).
170. Iggesund (1985) and Savalainen and Zacco-Broberg (1985).
171. Iggesund (1985), Savalainen and Zacco-Broberg (1985) and Lars G. Sundblad (2006i).
172. Valeur (2007).
173. A large Swedish insurance company.
174. A large Swedish savings and pension business.
175. Iggesund (1985).
176. However, some actors thought that some of those processes 'destroyed' birch-based pulp when it was converted to fluting.
177. Lars G. Sundblad (2006i).
178. Ibid.
179. The Fourth Swedish National Pension Fund (AP4) is one of several buffer funds in the national pension system.
180. Savalainen and Zacco-Broberg (1985).
181. Iggesund (1985).
182. Ericson (1991) and Sjöstrand (1997).
183. Von Sydow was replaced by Gabrielsson, who stayed as CEO until 1968.
184. A listed company controlled by the Bonnier family.
185. Glete (1994).
186. Reuterskiöld (2006i).
187. Sjunnesson and Wahlberg (2003).
188. Ibid.
189. In this volume Bråviken will be spelled Braviken, as that became the official name of the pulp and paper mills located there.
190. Thermo-mechanical pulp.
191. Sjunnesson and Wahlberg (2003).
192. Ibid.
193. Reuterskiöld (2006i).
194. Ibid.
195. Trolle-Löwén (2006i).
196. Sociedad Nacional Industrias Aplicaciones Cellulosa Español.
197. Reuterskiöld (2006i) and Zetterberg (2006i).
198. Lundberg (2006i) and Zetterberg (2006i).
199. Trolle-Löwén (2006i).
200. Zetterberg (2006i).
201. A medium-sized Swedish consultancy firm.
202. A medium-sized Czech consultancy firm.
203. Zetterberg (2006i).
204. KF is a federation of consumers' co-operatives.
205. Sjunnesson and Wahlberg (2003).
206. Zetterberg (2006i).
207. Reuterskiöld (2006i).
208. Lundin (2006i).
209. A US producer of industrial papers.

9. From MoDo to Holmen: a conflictual merger process

9.1 CARLGREN BECOMES CHAIR AND SPRÄNGARE CEO

In the beginning of the 1980s, MoDo launched a new strategy for the whole company. It entailed an emphasis on its core businesses, that is to say, a 'concentration path' involving investments at Husum, disinvestments at Domsjö and Bureå,[1] and the exploitation of economies of scale. Moreover, the further processing of basic resources was given priority, implying that the amount of pulp aimed for market sale had to be reduced. Regarding the hygiene business, the goal was to increase its capital base by acquiring Edet, Klippan and/or – preferably – Fiskeby (which had not yet been bought by Holmens Bruk). However, as MoDo was financially hampered, acquisitions of parts of companies were considered, too.

An opportunity to buy companies and/or plants emerged at the end of the 1970s, when Ncb collapsed and was taken over by the Swedish state with the intent to restructure its operations (cf. Ch. 7). Ncb's Hörnefors (sulphite pulp) and Köpmanholmen units (sulphate pulp and paper mill) were of particular interest to MoDo, which launched a joint investigation with the state to examine possible common development paths for Domsjö and Köpmanholmen, and to check whether a co-ordinated sourcing of timber to those units was possible. The study ended in an agreement that the two parties would build and jointly run a fine paper mill next to the Domsjö plant. Ncb, that is to say, the state, would be responsible for most of the investment costs and close down the pulp production at Hörnefors and Köpmanholmen. All this would allow the strained local timber market to recover and avoid increased pressure on MoDo's already high debt ratio. MoDo committed to postponing its third fine paper machine at Husum.[2]

Many leading actors in the industry were surprised that MoDo's current CEO and major shareholder Carlgren signed such a preliminary agreement with Ncb, as several investigations had shown that locating a paper mill at Domsjö was a rather bad idea. In June 1980, MoDo's board also concluded that the suggested investment did not seem to be the optimal way of using the company's scarce capital resources. Carlgren, however, defended the agreement as a way of securing the supply of timber in the region, and stated that MoDo would not be able to finance a third fine paper machine on its own. Moreover, as he saw it, a paper mill at Domsjö was what MoDo had tried all along to establish to be able to secure the plant's long-term survival. However, after further analysis, it became obvious that the profitability of the new machine at Domsjö would be rather poor. So, MoDo's board decided not to carry out Carlgren's plan. Rather soon after that decision, Ncb closed down both Hörnefors and Köpmanholmen.

MoDo continued to develop its fine paper business particularly through a concentration on office paper and a strengthening of its distribution network. In 1981, the wholesaling activities of Svenskt Papper and Klippan were merged into one unit, as a result of which MoDo got 55 per cent of the shares. At the time, Löf, the Head of MoDo Paper, began to explore the possibilities for a purchase of the French fine paper company Papeteries de Ruysscher. It was a tempting acquisition, but due to MoDo's financial strain, it was postponed (and never realized). MoDo also made some investments in forest resources, as it was less well equipped in that field than its competitors. To be able to do that, certain sell-offs and closures were executed. Thus, the metal manufacturing unit MoDo Mekan was sold to Karlstads Mekaniska Verkstad and Stille-Werner to Carlgren's private holding company Sanna Holding.

During the late 1970s Carlgren learned that occupying the CEO position was not an optimal solution for a head of a dynasty trying to develop its dearly loved heirloom. As he had no intention whatsoever of leaving his function as the leading representative of the dominating shareholder group, the role as CEO became more and more problematic. In a way Carlgren filled 'all' functions ranging from those associated with an AGM to those carried out by a COO. He was the key to everything in the company. Consequently, lots of people wanted – and needed – to meet with him to check all sorts of issues. Carlgren's ascribed omnipresence both created an overwhelming demand on his personal time and built organizational confusion.

An important ingredient in Carlgren's approach was his idealism – his activities were always 'clean'. He tended to put confidence in other actors, even in those he did not know particularly well. However, that 'scout-like' approach sometimes created problems and generated disappointments, as his business 'colleagues' and opponents sometimes exploited that gullibility.[3] So in the early 1980s Carlgren still ran MoDo as if it were his own company, although management had achieved some power in the late 1970s. The other important actors were Handelsbanken's board representatives Browaldh and Wallander, and to some extent also the board members Wettergren and Nabseth. Carlgren also trusted certain 'internal advisers'. One of them, Altbäck, worked like a 'spider in the MoDo web'. At an early stage Croon also played a relatively important role, particularly regarding structural matters. Carl Kempe Jr, however, worked more as Carlgren's 'company memory', calling attention to MoDo's history and culture. However, what really convinced Carlgren were not people's judgements but rather various kinds of analyses based on careful research. Thus, he was sensitive to figures, although he also put some emphasis on the more qualitative arguments that were provided along with them.[4]

At that time, many actors in his environment had come to the same conclusion as Carlgren himself – he ought to leave the CEO position. Carlgren seemed to lack the capacity to take care of – and express a serious interest in – quite a few of the everyday operative issues that a CEO was supposed to handle. Surrounding actors also noted that he had taken on quite a few other time-consuming assignments (e.g. he had become a member of the International Olympic Committee). So in 1981, Carlgren decided to step down as CEO and instead return to the Chair position he left in 1971. Doing that, he still kept the position as 'Head of the Company Group', a role that in Swedish business life usually was linked to the CEO position.[5]

Carlgren wanted a CEO that mastered the operations and had a COO-like ambition, leaving the strategic matters to him. Three internal CEO candidates were discussed: Fahlin, Löf and Sprängare. Sprängare was the most popular person of the three. He was an analytical, vigorous, independent and competent certified forester, who even had earned a doctoral degree in the field. One weakness was his rather limited knowledge of business administration (however, in that field CFO Dyrhage was a strong back-up). Löf's particular strengths were his successful management of the fine paper business and his competence in marketing; his weaknesses were that he had not been in the company very long, and that he – outside the fine paper unit – was regarded as rather headstrong, particularly after he established (and physically separated) the new fine paper unit in the late 1970s. One of Fahlin's advantages was that Carlgren saw him as the most docile candidate of the three – and that was at the same time his disadvantage, as the board, particularly Wallander, wanted a strong CEO. Fahlin also had a rather poor personal chemistry with some of leading actors. For those reasons he was the first to fall out of the race. Carlgren decided to discuss the remaining two candidates with Altbäck, who ultimately expressed no preferences. Carlgren preferred Löf but yet he leaned towards appointing Sprängare for a few years (and then asking Löf to replace him). However, it soon became obvious that such a solution would not work simply because Löf and Sprängare did not get along particularly well.[6]

Wallander's support for Sprängare was based on the hope that he as CEO would act as a countervailing power to the Chair – that he could function as a kind of moderator within MoDo. With this in mind, he called the other board members (including Carlgren) and argued for Sprängare as the new CEO; in the end they all agreed. So did the unions, which might actually have tipped the scales in Sprängare's favour. They saw him as a stable, likeable and socially competent person, whose leadership was plain, reliable and foreseeable, and executed 'closer' to the unions. Löf was described as a 'powder magazine', who kept his distance from the other organizational units (including the unions), and whose approach many actors therefore found difficult to fully grasp and follow. Although Carlgren preferred Löf to Sprängare, he did not take up the fight against both the board and the unions. Like most prior Kempe leaders, he listened carefully to the unions.[7]

Sprängare had been appointed head of MoDo's forest business in 1974. Like several other MoDo managers he was recruited from SCA, where he had built up a network in the forest-based industry. He was appointed CEO in 1981, although the way Carlgren offered him the position indicated that the Chair was not fully convinced that Sprängare was the best choice. What finally made the latter accept the promotion was the support from the other directors – particularly Wallander – and from many MoDo managers and employees (including the union representatives).

Löf was disappointed that he was not chosen as MoDo's new CEO, not least because of his impressive track record as Head of Fine Paper. He regarded Sprängare as a most competent head of MoDo's forest business, but thought that the new CEO lacked experience in those fields that really mattered: the pulp and paper operations. Moreover, he noted that Sprängare lacked competence in business administration, particularly regarding control and marketing issues, and that he was weak in the technological field, too. Löf was also critical of Sprängare because of his use of quite a lot of American consultants – Löf wanted to see them thrown out. Löf had also been accustomed to a situation in which the CEO – up to 1981 Carlgren – did not interfere in 'his' operations at MoDo Paper. Sprängare, as the new Chair of that subsidiary, instead insisted on being informed regularly about its operations and on being involved in the bigger decisions. Sprängare wanted Löf to stay, but as the two personalities did not match, Löf left for a CEO position at Södra (1983).[8]

However, in spite of the difficult governance conditions, Sprängare was rather active as CEO (1981–85). He started by picking his own GMT. Together they began to work on a strategy for MoDo that did not contain an acquisition of Iggesund.[9] That process eventually made Carlgren realize that as Chair he might actually become less involved in the crucial early discussions on many strategic matters. Still, while Sprängare had the strength to vigorously pursue his standpoints, in the end he always had to give in to Carlgren when their views differed. However, Sprängare persistently tried to assume the classic Swedish CEO role, that is to say, as somebody who acted as head of a whole company group, and who was heavily involved in its long-term development. Doing that, Sprängare challenged Carlgren's strategic leadership, something that Carlgren did not like at all, becoming more and more concerned about the CEO's governance aspirations. Carlgren had no intention of leaving the strategic issues to his CEO – he saw that as his territory. As such, Sprängare was not allowed any significant influence either on Carlgren's strategic thinking or on the employees' opinions, as he did not clearly communicate his alternative vision and future path for MoDo (but he certainly conveyed the company's financial position and its strategic consequences).[10] One thing that Carlgren liked, however, was that Sprängare kept Carl Kempe Jr at a distance from the strategic discussions.[11]

When Sprängare was appointed CEO, Carlgren made Fahlin Head of Technology, a position from which Fahlin was supposed to filter all incoming investment proposals and only furnish Carlgren with the 'best' ones. The underlying reason was that the technicians' increasingly strong position had become a growing problem for MoDo's board. When Carlgren took the Chair position, he became concerned about all investment proposals that were sent to the board by the heads of the business units (encouraged by their technicians). They wanted to invest everywhere, found countless possibilities for technical improvements throughout the plants and provided marginal calculations that always looked reasonable. With the company experiencing a severe shortage of investment capital and his admitted own lack of technical competence, Carlgren needed an 'investment police' who filtered the proposals, that is to say, a Head of Technology and Deputy CEO, who could hold back the technicians.[12]

Although Carlgren had agreed to appoint Sprängare, he wanted to keep Löf at MoDo: 'Things are going to go your way', he said to Löf when the latter was appointed Senior Deputy CEO. After Löf's MoDo exit, Carlgren maintained the relationship through many phone calls, a behaviour that indicated that his support for Sprängare was not wholehearted. After a while, Löf began to detect from Carlgren an increasing uncertainty regarding Sprängare's capacity to act as MoDo's CEO.[13] At the same time Sprängare, too, felt that Carlgren had some doubts regarding his appointment. Indeed, he wrote Carlgren a letter that suggested a division of assignments between the two (i.e. the Chair and the CEO). It also contained thoughts about MoDo's financial standing and operative situation, as well as about the company's future possibilities. However, Sprängare decided not to send the letter.[14]

Chair Carlgren and CEO Sprängare never became close; in fact, rather quickly they began to drift apart, mainly because Carlgren wanted to keep the big topics for himself: 'There is only one strategy for MoDo and it is the one that exists inside my head.' The relationship between the two developed contrary to the intentions in Swedish legislation and common practice, as the Chair acted expansively and pursued many things, while the CEO scrutinized suggestions and tried to activate the brakes. Carlgren also showed disrespect for Sprängare by allowing Löf to talk directly to him and thereby bypassing the CEO. That sort of behaviour made Sprängare lose some of his internal authority. During the difficult period when Sprängare's position became almost impossible, director Wallander was his main speaking partner.[15]

The tension between Carlgren and Sprängare was not only the consequence of a role conflict between a Chair and a CEO who both wanted to run MoDo strategically. It was also a question of the extent to which one should link the financial and operative strategies, that is to say, which perspective ought to be in the driver's seat. According to the CEO, MoDo's current financial situation and the company's opportunities to improve it had to be taken as the point of departure when the operative strategy was determined. By contrast, the Chair started from a view of what resources the MoDo business portfolio required to stay competitive and tried to find ways to finance such a path.

Thus, during Sprängare's time as CEO, there was an unresolved incompatibility between, on the one hand, MoDo's financial situation and capacity, and, on the other hand, the ambitions for the company expressed by the Chair and his associates. The dominating shareholder family had limited financial resources, and as it could not accept losing its control of the company, the necessary growth to keep the operations competitive could not be realized in all businesses in which the company was involved. Several actors realized that and argued for a concentration strategy that involved more processing and a move to the right in the value chain. It was also seen as important to act in a way that took into consideration the contemporary activities of the company's Swedish competitors.

It had become obvious to many leading actors that the structure of the Swedish forest-based industry had to be improved in order to preserve its competitiveness into the coming decades. However, initially these thoughts were not acted upon, partly because most of the bigger corporations like MoDo, Holmens Bruk, Korsnäs, Stora Kopparberg, Billerud, Papyrus, SCA, and so on were 'imprisoned' in separate owner spheres, but also because one did not engage in cross-national activities in those days. So all of them tried to pursue the necessary expansion without crossing either national or sphere borders. Growth was crucial, as bulk prices (e.g. on pulp) were slowly but steadily declining by about 1 per cent a year. Moreover, at that time, scale economies had become even more important than before, making it necessary for the companies to invest in larger machine (or plant) sizes, which usually was accompanied by further specialization. As a result, maintaining and developing a relatively broad repertoire of forest-based businesses became less and less feasible. Such an approach would be far too expensive both with regards to the financial resources needed, and when it came to the necessary management capacity.

Thus, at that time the solution for almost all Nordic corporations was to strengthen their core businesses and get closer to the customers (i.e. integrate forward). That was also something that Sprängare advocated for MoDo. His suggestion was that MoDo either invest more heavily in fine paper or acquire Iggesund – not both. Actually, he had a slight preference for the former alternative, if it could be done in a financially sound way. MoDo's strained financial standing also made him hesitant about the company's on-going investments in the hygiene sector. Expanding the business repertoire this widely called for new and different managerial capacity. Furthermore, it established a new production and marketing process that was complex and demanding. Basically, Sprängare considered MoDo to be too small for the necessary financial undertakings in such a diversified set-up. Each of the business areas would have access to too limited capital resources to stay competitive in the long run.[16]

The board supported Sprängare's goal of concentrating MoDo's operations. Several directors (e.g. Wallander) argued that MoDo could not invest heavily in more than one of its businesses and that ought to be fine paper. Moreover, in the beginning of the 1980s, most of the other fields of business were already 'occupied' by the other big Swedish forest-based companies. SCA had achieved a strong position in the consumer business through its acquisition of Mölnlycke, Stora Kopparberg had become dominant in the production of printing paper and ASSI had large plants producing liner and cardboard. All these competitors planned to continue along their already chosen paths. This meant that the only forest-based business that was 'free' was fine paper – an area MoDo had entered more than 20 years earlier. The two new paper mills established at Husum in the 1970s had consolidated that choice for a long time.[17]

However, Chair Carlgren was determined to make growth possible for all of MoDo's more or less related businesses to make sure that the company stayed competitive in all its activities. That feat should be carried out without sacrificing family control, that is to say, without paying with the company's own shares (that actually had a low value at the time) or undertaking a merger that had the same consequences. However, to make that high ambition a reality in an already heavily indebted MoDo required an almost unimaginable financial creativity.

The trade-off between the available financial resources and the growth ambitions was the main issue in the company during the first half of the 1980s. Several board members wanted to moderate Carlgren's plans to make MoDo bigger, but he initiated substantial investments and even put himself in debt to realize his vision. As he saw it, MoDo had to grow – the Kempe family had to be linked to a grandiose company, to one associated with lustre and honour. In pursuit of this ideal, he sometimes made decisions that exceeded the bank's opinion about acceptable risk taking.[18] As a consequence, management usually had to handle the financial side of MoDo's growth efforts on an ex post basis, that is to say, when the investments already had been decided. Thus, at that time, MoDo functioned like a boat drifting towards a waterfall with management desperately rowing against the current.[19]

To sum up: once again Carlgren's leadership had created confusion in the upper echelons of the organization. This time it had occurred primarily in four ways: (1) as MoDo Chair he continued to have direct conversations with the Head of Fine Paper (Löf) thereby bypassing the company's CEO Sprängare; (2) he kept the position as 'Head of the Company Group', a role usually attached to the CEO; (3) he made the board a relatively weak agency;[20] and (4) he still listened carefully to the unions (in some situations they even persuaded him to veto the CEO). Sprängare finally began complaining about his untenable managerial situation to a few outsiders, but he found no way to correct the situation. So, in 1985, after only a few years, he decided to leave MoDo for a CEO position at the Swedish insurance company Trygg-Hansa.

9.2 MODO ACQUIRES IGGESUND[21]

During the 1970s, MoDo's main competitors in Sweden, SCA and Stora Kopparberg, began to buy or merge with other companies, mostly ones that belonged to their own 'business spheres'. So, what looked like two 'blocs' emerged in those processes (one bloc was linked to the Wallenberg dynasty [Stora Kopparberg] and the other to Handelsbanken [SCA]). One should note that that restructuring of the Swedish forest-based industry occurred almost entirely within the nation's boundaries – nobody seriously considered making acquisitions abroad or expected foreign firms to bid on Swedish companies. For example, the Finnish companies were seen as bitter competitors, not as candidates for mergers or takeovers.[22]

In that domestic restructuring process Carlgren decided to take up the challenge and make MoDo the third major player in the Swedish forest-based industry, and through that process grow to a size that was competitive also in the European context. Carlgren feared that a passive MoDo would become secondary to both SCA and Stora Kopparberg. He was also afraid that the opportunities to expand in Sweden were rapidly decreasing, as competitors in the not-too-distant future could occupy most 'open fields'.[23] Several generations of achievements and expectations in Carlgren's 'genes' spurred him – it was his duty to develop the dynasty heirloom. So, he felt pressure to make MoDo one of the few big forest-based companies that would remain after the on-going restructuring processes on the Swedish market. He coined the label 'The Third Bloc' to make his vision more tangible and communicable. It was still a rather ambiguous label that left him lots of freedom to shape the constellation he was seeking.[24] His idea was to create a holding company where the current leading actors in the Kempe–Carlgren dynasty would focus on ownership matters influencing the company's path through the vertical governance flow. Operations would be left to the company's top management to handle. The holding company – The Third Bloc – would then include MoDo, Iggesund and Holmens Bruk.[25] While that constellation was Carlgren's own idea, Carl Kempe Jr also supported it, so the family was united.[26] Several of the directors and top managers, however, were hesitant, and others (e.g. CEO Sprängare) were totally against.[27]

Carlgren's Third Bloc was expected to spread out the business risk and at the same time moderate the volatility in economic performance. That would be achieved by building a corporation based on three relatively independent 'legs'. The intended building blocks were at least potentially available (i.e. not already parts of the Handelsbanken or Wallenberg spheres).[28] Carlgren was inspired by George Weyerhaeuser, head of a forest-based US company wearing his family name, with whom he had a good deal of contact. That company was equipped with what Carlgren sought: three 'legs'.[29] However, the economic calculations did not look very favourable for such a constellation. The idea to create a third bloc was financially unrealistic. The Kempe–Carlgren dynasty did not have the capacity to acquire both Iggesund and Holmen – such a purchase required around SEK 6 billion.

However, as Carlgren felt pressure from his ancestry to develop MoDo into something big and impressive, and as he wanted to become a recognized leader in the Swedish forest-based industry, he took on substantial private loans to keep his and the family's control over the new sizeable MoDo that materialized during the 1980s.[30] Despite the shaky calculations and risks involved, MoDo's board approved Carlgren's plan. To director Wallander it was probably (also) an appealing idea to add two additional companies (Holmens Bruk and Iggesund) as customers to 'his' bank (Handelsbanken).[31]

When Carlgren discovered that there were Iggesund shares available on the market, he started buying; thus, the journey towards a third bloc began. MoDo bought Iggesund shares through its stockbroker and reached 12 per cent by September 1980. Iggesund's CEO Lars G. Sundblad was informed that MoDo had the intention to obtain over 10 per cent in an attempt to block others from taking control of the company. Carlgren thought that such a holding would be a good thing, as it opened up the two companies for profitable interplay, at the same time as it allowed Iggesund to remain autonomous.[32] Sundblad did not see Carlgren's investment in Iggesund as something 'unnatural'. The two actors had a good, if not a close personal relationship. Sundblad stressed that the leading actors at Iggesund were very conscious about the company's autonomy, which was crucial to Iggesund's ability to develop its businesses successfully.[33]

When MoDo began to buy Iggesund shares in 1980, two things were of particular importance. First, Marcus Wallenberg Sr had become aware of that initiative and decided that the family needed to act. He was interested in incorporating Iggesund into the family's business sphere in order to extend its operations into quality carton. Second, he also wanted to prevent the competing Handelsbanken sphere, in particular SCA, Handelsbanken's 'flagship' corporation in the forest-based industry, from doing the same. So Marcus Wallenberg Sr made sure that two companies in the Wallenberg sphere began to buy Iggesund shares (about this 'struggle between the spheres' see below).

Thus, the process that failed early in 1980 was reversed later the same year – only this time it was Billerud (and Stora Kopparberg) that bought into Iggesund. As Carlgren was a most active buyer, the Wallenberg sphere was in a great hurry to acquire a significant holding. Carlgren had a similar perspective. He was afraid to lose Iggesund to the competing Wallenberg sphere, that is to say, to Billerud and Stora Kopparberg. To Carlgren it was crucial to control Iggesund to be able to establish his Third Bloc.

Carlgren received substantial support within MoDo for an acquisition of Iggesund (unlike a decade earlier when he suggested a purchase of SCA). The circumstances were more favourable this time, as Iggesund lacked a controlling shareholder that was of a reasonable size from a financial perspective. Geographically, MoDo and Iggesund fit well; together they constituted a coherent forest locale. Iggesund also provided an interesting path for the further processing of MoDo's pulp resources, and suited its growth ambitions as well as its need to reduce operative risk. At Iggesund were also many good friends and positive relationships to build on.[34]

The Iggesund contest became even more intense in April 1981 when the Wallenberg sphere's leading actors learned that two leading actors from MoDo were to be elected board members of Iggesund (on 5 May 1981). The candidates were MoDo's Chair Carlgren and its director Wallander (Chair of Handelsbanken). At that time, MoDo had gained control over about 25 per cent of the votes in Iggesund (MoDo 13%, its allies 12%). Marcus Wallenberg Sr became upset when, as he saw it, Handelsbanken, through MoDo and its leading actor Carlgren, took the lead and forwarded its position, by increasing its shareholding and taking seats on the board, in Iggesund (and in the restructuring of the Swedish forest industry). So he instructed the CEOs of Billerud and Stora Kopparberg to 'counterattack' and try to take control over Iggesund.[35]

Although both the Wallenberg and the Handelsbanken spheres were aware of each other's interest in Iggesund, it still came as a total surprise both for the market and the rival (Carlgren) that the Wallenberg coalition – through Billerud and Stora Kopparberg – on 29 April 1981 made a hostile bid for Iggesund. That the bid was hostile was also a big surprise, as that kind of behaviour was almost unheard of on the Swedish stock market. Because of the growing portion of Iggesund shares held by MoDo and its associates and the impending recomposition of Iggesund's board, the bidders acted in such a hurry that the bid was neither cleared with all of Billerud's and Stora Kopparberg's larger shareholders, nor with most of its top managers. It was not cleared with the leading actors of the target company either – with one important exception: Stahle (simultaneously Deputy Chair of Iggesund and a leading actor in the Wallenberg sphere). Moreover, the extreme rush had also made the underlying calculations rather sketchy, although the actors could base their opinions on experiences from Iggesund's recent attempt to merge with Billerud. Several actors looked upon – and described – the hostile bid as another instance of the on-going battle between the two dominating capitalist spheres in Sweden.

Stora Kopparberg was the leading unit in the acquisition attempt, with the goal of controlling up to 80 per cent of Iggesund's shares. Billerud was more of an 'appendage' in the process with an expected share of 20 per cent. However, it soon became obvious that the bid was far from an expression of the wills of the bidding companies' shareholders and boards. One proof of that became evident at Stora Kopparberg's AGM on 8 May 1981, when one of its largest shareholders, Graningeverken, through its leading actor and CEO Versteegh, showed great anger and complained that he had not been informed in advance about the bid but rather became aware of it through the media.

Thus, everybody (except for a very narrow circle of actors) was taken by surprise, and several of them became truly upset. That included many leading actors in the two bidding companies (Billerud and Stora Kopparberg), as well as most actors in both the target firm (Iggesund) and the rival company (MoDo). The informed exception, Stahle, became concerned about the negative reaction from Iggesund's board and management – they did not, as he had expected, perceive the bid as one that rescued them from MoDo. On the contrary, as nobody at Iggesund had been informed by Billerud and/or Stora Kopparberg, their reactions were outright negative. That firm refusal was strengthened after the so-called 'airport incident'. By coincidence, Iggesund's Deputy Chair and Wallenberg-associated actor Stahle ran into Iggesund's CEO Sundblad at Norrköping airport and informed him in passing that Billerud and Stora Kopparberg the very same day had made a bid for Iggesund. That incident made Sundblad the first actor in Iggesund who knew about the takeover attempt. He immediately tried to contact his Chair, Henrikson, and a few hours later, they met and discussed the matter. All others at Iggesund (including its directors) were informed through the media later the same day.

When the hostile bid from Billerud and Stora Kopparberg hit the market, the Trygger foundation was happy that MoDo had the intention to stop that takeover and thereby assist in keeping Iggesund an autonomous listed company. By then, however, all actors outside Iggesund understood that the company had to land somewhere – it was too small to survive on its own. Lacking a major shareholder (constellation), Iggesund had become a target company in the Swedish forest-based industry's restructuring process.[36]

Stora Kopparberg and Billerud justified their bid in a communiqué. Synergies were to be found and realized in four areas, namely regarding: (1) sales and distribution of cardboard, (2) the chemical business, (3) woodware and (4) the forestry business. For the more detailed arguments the companies' statement referred to a forthcoming prospectus (however, such a document never materialized).[37]

The bid was comparatively high (strikingly 'sweetened'). It represented more than a 40 per cent premium.[38] Moreover, as noted above, the calculations indicated that a merger between the three companies would be advantageous to all of them – there was a potential for realizing substantial positive synergy and scale effects. Many shareholders were therefore tempted to accept the bid, but the largest shareholder grouping in Iggesund, that is to say, MoDo with its associates, and some of the other bigger shareholders were not interested in minority positions (plus cash) in Billerud and Stora Kopparberg. That negative stand was taken although most actors understood that the scale and synergy effects between Iggesund and MoDo were much lower (if any).

However, in May Iggesund's board, top management, and employees concluded that the proposed scale and synergy benefits expected from a merger should not decide the matter, particularly not when these likely advantages were put in relation to the accompanying downsides they also attached to the hostile bid. Thus, to take a stand was complicated and delicate and not easily 'calculated' or quantified. In such a merger, Iggesund would lose its autonomy and then gradually its company culture. There was also an increased risk that parts of the company's operations later would be closed down, and/or that rationalizations would take away some of the staff functions from the region. Moreover, the Iggesund HQ would be shut down, and in future allocation and crisis situations, no strong voice would be left to defend a specifically Iggesund perspective.

Moreover, a lingering anger regarding how the hostile bid had been presented to Iggesund emerged – the 'airport incident' was perceived as an insult. The way the bid had (not) been communicated had raised strong emotions both in and around Iggesund. That indignation was easy to understand, as there had been a long tradition of co-operation between its stakeholders and most other actors in the region. Ever since Gunnar Sundblad's era as CEO, the company had made quite a lot of commitments to its employees and their families, as well as to many other people who showed an interest in the functioning of the surrounding community. Thus, Iggesund was famous for its social responsibility – for its good citizenship.

All that taken together made people in and around Iggesund inclined to favour a solution with MoDo as Iggesund's major shareholder. Operational issues aside, they saw more similarities with MoDo than with the two hostile bidders. That included everything from the company cultures to personal relationships. Regarding the latter, there were, for example, rather strong ties between MoDo Chair Carlgren and leading union members at Iggesund through their joint efforts to support the Swedish track and field movement. Thus, in the eyes of many Iggesund actors, Carlgren possessed substantial personal capital – he was a popular and trusted man.

For some years Iggesund had no major shareholder; the two big Swedish banks, Handelsbanken (MoDo's principal bank) and SE-Banken (Billerud's and Stora Kopparberg's principal bank), had thus competed to service its financial flows for just as long. One odd part in the bidding process was that the distinguished member of the Wallenberg (SE-bank) sphere Stahle, who was the messenger between the bidders and the target company, also was Deputy Chair at Iggesund. It was even more remarkable that he did not bring the issue to Iggesund's board for discussion before the bid was actually made (as noted above, such hostile bids were rare on the Swedish stock market at the time).

Another unusual factor in the process was that the CEO of one of the two bidding companies, Erik Sundblad at Stora Kopparberg, was Iggesund's CEO Lars G. Sundblad's brother. Gunnar Sundblad, their father, had been Iggesund's CEO for 35(!) years when Lars replaced him in 1956. These family relationships had made Erik Sundblad a bit hesitant regarding the bid procedure. However, in the end, the business rationale outflanked the one based on kinship – Erik Sundblad made the hostile bid without leaking information to his brother Lars about what was to come.

Soon after the bid had been made public, Lars G. Sundblad informed everybody at Iggesund about its content and consequences for the company. He mentioned that the bidders wanted a 90 per cent acceptance rate, so that they could force the remaining shareholders to sell their shares, thereby making Iggesund a wholly owned subsidiary. He further stated that he had not yet made up his mind. Instead, he asked the bidders to more thoroughly explain their true motives and at the same time describe the industrial rationales involved.

As planned, MoDo Chair Carlgren and MoDo director Wallander were appointed new Iggesund board members. The latter's situation was probably simplified by the fact that he had had good relations with both the CEO of Stora Kopparberg and the CEO of Iggesund for many years. He had also built confidence by assisting Iggesund 15 years earlier in its engagement in Ström-Ljusne.[39] For those reasons he became an important person for both MoDo and Iggesund. Still, the problem was that as Chair of Handelsbanken, he always had two additional perspectives in his head: that of MoDo's competitor SCA and that of the bank.[40]

Iggesund's Deputy Chair Stahle indicated that it could be a problem to have MoDo actors on its board, as that company was in some ways a competitor to Iggesund. At the same time (in 1981), there was a shift of Chair in Iggesund: Dahlström replaced Henrikson. Henrikson had become angry with Carlgren, because the latter had talked to Sundblad and not to him about Iggesund's board recomposition. When Henrikson visited Carlgren and asked him to remove Lars G. Sundblad as CEO, Carlgren refused. As a consequence Henrikson resigned and asked the other directors to join him in that decision, since all of them, with the exception of Stahle, had been sidestepped. However, the 'neutral' Dahlström did not bow under that pressure and, instead, accepted the offer to become new Iggesund Chair.[41]

After the board meeting at Stora Kopparberg, the two Sundblad brothers Erik (CEO of Stora Kopparberg) and Lars (CEO of Iggesund) together with Engman (CEO of Billerud) met to discuss the bid situation. The unions at Iggesund met, too, and opposed the bid. They even contracted an 'employee consultant' (Ekström) to give their position more strength. His conclusion was that Iggesund needed neither MoDo nor Billerud and Stora Kopparberg. Mainly on the basis of his conclusion and initiative, a savings fund was established that had as sole purpose to encourage the employees to buy Iggesund shares. The goal was to acquire 10 per cent of the Iggesund stock – a large enough share to obstruct a takeover. The company facilitated that process by providing favourable loans to the buyers. The savings fund grew – around 20 per cent of the employees bought shares (each employee invested around SEK 200/month). However, since the market price for Iggesund shares eventually exploded, the savings fund never reached even close to the target figure. When the new investments stopped in 1984, the savings fund held only about 1 per cent of the Iggesund stock.[42]

Iggesund's board took up an idea that the Chair of the Trygger foundation Haglund proposed at the AGM, namely that, in response to the hostile bid, the company ought to formulate a strategic plan for a future autonomous Iggesund. Such a plan would make it easier for the shareholders to make up their minds. The plan, which was presented in mid-June, contained a slight preference for MoDo as major shareholder of Iggesund. However, foremost it showed that Iggesund could make it on its own. The idea was that Iggesund should focus on fine cardboard and then use its own timber for most of the input. Furthermore, the intention was that EKA should expand and Boxholm be restructured. Both the Chair and the CEO signed on, supporting the conclusion that Iggesund would be capable of developing on a 'stand-alone' basis. That statement meant that Iggesund's board, top management and unions had declared that they opposed the hostile bid from Billerud and Stora Kopparberg.[43]

Carlgren (i.e. MoDo) did not place a counter bid on Iggesund. His way to counteract the bidders was through continued purchases of Iggesund shares, so the share price rose dramatically from SEK 180 up to SEK 350–400. After a few months' 'hoovering' of Iggesund shares, Carlgren and MoDo controlled 29 per cent, the Wallenberg sphere 23 per cent, and the Handelsbanken sphere and the 'original' major shareholder the Trygger foundation 9 per cent each.[44] Since the Chair of the Trygger foundation, Haglund, did not want to see Iggesund treated the way Stora Kopparberg earlier had dealt with Bergvik, the foundation had decided to support MoDo in the Iggesund contest. That position was also encouraged by the repeated statements made by Carlgren that MoDo would maintain Iggesund as a listed company on the SSE, thereby guaranteeing Iggesund substantial autonomy. Later in May, Carlgren met with Marcus Wallenberg Sr, who congratulated him for his successful acquisition of Iggesund and offered him an option to buy Stora Kopparberg's and Billerud's shares in Iggesund. On 23 May 1981, the Wallenberg sphere gave up and withdrew its plan to incorporate Iggesund into its sphere, although for tax reasons they did not sell their shares until late 1983. Thus, Iggesund had both formally and in practice got a 'helmsman'.

At a MoDo board meeting in mid-1981, CEO Sprängare presented MoDo's substantial holding of Iggesund shares, and Iggesund's CEO Lars G. Sundblad described the acquired company. The unexpected hostile bid from the Wallenberg sphere had forced MoDo to raise its holding to 32 per cent, and together with its allies it amounted to more than 50 per cent. An agreement was made to co-ordinate the interests of the co-operating bodies. Sprängare was the only person who expressed doubts regarding MoDo's increased shareholding in Iggesund. He stressed the need for immediate and substantial debt reduction and forest investments. To achieve that he advocated for an investigation of the possible synergies between MoDo and Iggesund to free some capital – something that the board approved, although it stated that it regarded Iggesund as a strategic holding to be kept for a long time. A further increase in MoDo's shareholding in Iggesund was at the time not important because of the particular voting rule connected to Iggesund – a ceiling at 25 per cent. So in December 1981, MoDo still controlled 32 per cent of Iggesund's stock.

MoDo's CEO Sprängare entered Iggesund's board in the first half of 1982. His entrance, as well as the presence of Iggesund's CEO Lars G. Sundblad on MoDo's board, irritated the Wallenberg sphere (it still controlled around 23% of Iggesund). They made it clear that as long as Iggesund lacked a majority shareholder, it had to be run as an independent company. In May 1982, they consequently nominated the new Chair of Stora Kopparberg, former Supreme Commander of the Swedish Armed Forces, Synnergren, for board membership. Synnergren was appointed, but left only one year later (1983), when Stora Kopparberg fulfilled his promise to Carlgren and sold its Iggesund shares.

Parts of MoDo's management preferred that MoDo bought the remaining Iggesund shares as well and incorporated it as a MoDo division. Such a move would make it possible to integrate its operations into the mother company, realize all the potential synergy effects, rationalize, and control all cash flows. Carlgren, and probably several other actors, instead preferred to run the integration between the two companies on a more voluntary basis. He saw the construct as a kind of strategic alliance. However, as time passed, it became clear that very few operative synergies were realized (that outcome did not come as a big surprise for most of the involved actors).

Carlgren saw one promising integration opportunity between MoDo and Iggesund: the latter company's poor birch-based pulp line could be shut down and, instead, Iggesund's cardboard production could be sourced with pulp from Husum. In that way, a large investment at Iggesund could be avoided, and Husum would be linked to Iggesund and its birch forests. In Carlgren's view, Iggesund's cardboard was a jewel in his planned Third Bloc. However, the original idea was that the cardboard operations were to be sourced by raw material that was produced directly at the Iggesund site – if pulp were taken from a distant producer (e.g. Husum), the additional cost was regarded to be too high to make the cardboard competitive. All investigations carried out showed that a geographically integrated production of sulphate pulp and cardboard was far better than all possible external pulp sourcing alternatives. When Carlgren finally gave up the idea at a board meeting in June 1986, decisions were taken to upgrade not only the birch line but also the whole plant.[45]

From late 1983 when Stora Kopparberg sold its shares, MoDo controlled more than 50 per cent of Iggesund – that was clearly not in line with Carlgren's promise to its stakeholders. At an EGM in Iggesund in November 1983, the Chair of the Trygger foundation, Haglund, raised his voice and, in a very emotional speech, demanded that Iggesund's autonomy be defended. He claimed that Carlgren had promised Iggesund unbroken autonomy. He added that that issue had become even more acute, as MoDo's intention was to repeal Iggesund's voting rights restriction (25%) later in the meeting (which also happened). Haglund was so upset that directly after the EGM he had a severe heart attack (from which he recovered). The solution to the majority problem became a reduction of MoDo's Iggesund shareholding to a figure just below 50 per cent (49.8%), and transfer of the 'excess' holding (5.1%) into another company (with a right of repurchase): Rang Invest (where Carlgren already was a board member). However, Carlgren continued to act as if he held a majority position and kept the two companies' operative leaders at arm's length from each other. In his view, it was the shareholder level that constituted the link between the two companies.

Once MoDo had won control over Iggesund, it was possible to make use of all its resources in the on-going expansion of the group. Rather soon Iggesund made about SEK 1.4 billion available – an investment sum that followed from a new issue of Iggesund B-shares and from the sale of two of its subsidiaries (Boxholm and EKA) and other minor businesses. In 1984, MoDo was doing rather well, although its debt ratio still was too high indicating greater risk-taking than most competitors. At that time, Iggesund CEO Lars G. Sundblad claimed that Carlgren had broken his promise to keep Iggesund independent and decided to leave the company. The board picked Nordin to succeed him. At Sundblad's last AGM as Iggesund CEO in May 1984, board membership was reduced from eight to seven directors when Stahle (former Deputy Chair) and C:son Bonde left and Carl Kempe Jr took a seat.

9.3 MODO EXPANDS ITS FINE PAPER BUSINESS

The Swedish crown was devalued in 1982, a government decision that favoured MoDo. In that situation, Brändström, the new Head of Finance, started to improve MoDo's balance sheet by tackling the company's huge debt and currency risk in a more active way than before. MoDo decided to establish a financial model where the company borrowed substantial amounts of short-term capital from Germany at about 6 per cent interest, and invested it on the Swedish market at about 10–11 per cent interest. Currencies and currency risks were much more actively handled, and various positions and trends were continuously analysed. The new financial strategy successfully cut the negative financial net result by up to 50 per cent.[46]

The possession of Iggesund shares opened up new borrowing opportunities for MoDo, but their activation resulted in increasing interest costs that soon became burdensome. At the end of 1982, MoDo's debt ratio was still far too high, and all new investments were halted. This resulted, for example, in the rejection of an offer to buy Håfverströms paper mill from Södra. So, MoDo's board held a special session to address the company's unsatisfactory financial position. The Kempe and Carlgren families were firm in their refusal to sell its Iggesund shares – they would rather sell the company's power plants (and actually that became the outcome). Selling was necessary, as the Kempe–Carlgren dynasty did not possess the financial muscle needed to solve the problem through a new issue of shares.

The decision to sell the power plants emerged in a more informal arena, that is to say, at Carlgren's home Brandalssund, where he every year conducted a well-prepared conference addressing strategic matters that involved both directors and top management. The 'accompanying' board meetings often served as a setting for formalizing decisions based on conclusions drawn at that site.[47] Eventually, MoDo decided to sell its power plants to Junkaravan with a right of repurchase. These activities brought MoDo SEK 1 billion and lowered its debt ratio substantially. Still, however, the financial situation was so strained that the board discussed taking out a major loan in USD – a loan that would provide liquidity, mitigate the need for disinvestments and make some growth possible.

MoDo's tough financial situation resulted also in modifications relating to several of its operations decisions. As usual, Domsjö was the focus in the never-ending discussions about possible structural changes. This time MoDo renewed its talks with Ncb and Graningeverken to try to secure reliable timber sourcing. Carlgren contacted the leading actors of the two companies to find out if a structural solution involving three plants in the mid-northern Ådalen region – one from each company – could be of interest for the others. At a press conference, MoDo's CEO stated that the three, Domsjö, Utansjö and

Väja, were one plant too many. While he did not make clear which of the plants he preferred to shut down, obviously it was not Domsjö, the most modern and rational of the three. MoDo was actually open for a joint ownership of that unit (if Utansjö and/or Väja were closed). However, actors in the Ådalen region, heavily hit by many closures, could not take another one. A reduction of one or two plants was a very delicate issue both politically and emotionally, and neither Ncb nor Graningeverken was inclined to phase out its pulp plants, so the suggested structural change did not materialize. In response MoDo, together with SCA, tried to gain control over Graningeverken, but that attempt, too, failed.

MoDo also returned to its earlier discussions about how to handle Mabelpap (Belgium). That effective site represented the core of MoDo's European hygiene business, but it was associated with two problems: it had no production based on recycled paper and outside Belgium it was a small player. To stay competitive, MoDo needed to expand its hygiene production, but lacked the necessary financial resources to make such acquisitions. Here was yet another reason to engage in serious attempts to improve the company's financial situation, which would also make MoDo capable of handling a possible declining market for its products and services. One problem was that MoDo's major shareholders (the Kempe dynasty) historically had proved to be both reluctant and slow when it came to disinvestments. Furthermore, MoDo was compelled to invest substantially in its existing plants and operations (such efforts were already in progress at Husum [fine paper] and Domsjö [CTMP pulp]).

When MoDo began seriously considering the production of CTMP pulp, the Domsjö site was on the agenda. Discussions started in 1983 in connection with research on possible fields of co-operation with Iggesund, which was developing a new kind of cardboard that had CTMP in its middle layers (to increase its stiffness). Iggesund hesitated, however, as the sourcing of CTMP was uncertain. By early 1984, when MoDo received authorization from the Swedish Board for Environment Protection to increase its production at Domsjö with a CTMP plant, it decided to move forward. While it may have been more rational to locate the plant at Iggesund, Carlgren had promised the unions new production at Domsjö to replace the sulphite plant that was planned for closure.[48]

In 1985, the Head of Finance expressed the opinion that MoDo was about to 'invest itself to death' if all plans were to be realized. In two to three years' time the debt ratio would rise to somewhere around 65 per cent, and then there would be no power plants to sell and no forests to revaluate (the latter had already been done). The Iggesund shares were all that would be left. Thus, the capital needs had to be covered by bank loans, and Handelsbanken provided a new large credit (some other reserves were also established). The gravity of the situation became clear when the decision to invest the modest sum of SEK 18 million at Mabelpap became a big issue. The board discussion even led to consideration of selling the Belgian company.

Due to the financial strain, MoDo created a special project company for the new MoDo–Iggesund CTMP investment with Carl Kempe Jr as its CEO. MoDo provided 50 per cent of the equity and the rest of the capital was acquired through a bond loan.[49] Half of the production was intended for Iggesund and the other half for MoDo Konsument. However, because the physical distance between Domsjö and Iggesund was considerable, the preferred solution was not an ideal one. It was also hoped that it would be possible to use CTMP pulp for printing paper, and if so, Domsjö could be supplemented with a paper mill.[50] As Domsjö was the family heirloom, such a development appealed to both Carlgren and Carl Kempe Jr.

Domsjö started CTMP production in 1985, but the investment turned out to be a mistake. For a long period, technical problems hampered production. By the time those problems had been solved, Iggesund began to reduce its manufacture of the CTMP-based cardboard. Thus, MoDo had to find new buyers on the market, but it was already a crowded field since many other forest-based firms had also invested in CTMP production. At the beginning of the 1990s, MoDo therefore stopped producing CTMP and later sold the equipment to Stora's cardboard plant at Fors.[51] Neither Carlgren nor Carl Kempe Jr wanted to close down Domsjö, but top management was convinced that such a move was necessary. Together with the Head of Fine Paper (Nilsson) Sprängare pushed for a solution that favoured the Husum site and its timber sourcing.[52]

Back in 1984, MoDo had decided to invest in a third fine paper machine at Husum. Nilsson and his team (including the Head of Technology) had several talks with Chair Carlgren and eventually convinced him that MoDo ought to go ahead. Nilsson was also the one who pushed the investment through the board,[53] even though Sprängare opposed such a decision mainly because of lack of financial resources (thus, the Senior Deputy CEO did not walk in step with his CEO). The major shareholders stood behind the huge investment, although it took up all the available capacity. This time Carlgren presented a financial solution that put the investment outside MoDo's balance sheet.[54] Again, a special project company was founded, and MoDo put in 45.5 per cent of the capital ('Svenska investeringsbanken'[55] provided 49.5% and interests associated with Götabanken[56] 5%). The remaining amount was borrowed from the two participating banks.[57]

MoDo was supposed to lease the machine from the project company and run it alone. Moreover, MoDo had the right to buy all the project company's shares at any time. Because of its minority position, MoDo did not have to consolidate that business in its balance sheet, so its equity ratio was not affected negatively.[58] The new investment represented a substantial increase in production capacity. Indeed, there were some doubts about the market's capacity to absorb that new output. Therefore, some of the production was to be coated at Silverdalen, and a new machine for that purpose was installed. The new paper machine's weakness (when compared with the existing ones) was that it did not represent a significant step forward – rather it was of a similar size, and its technical architecture was not particularly innovative. However, the new investment confirmed that fine paper was to be MoDo's core business for many years to come.

Many leaders of Western European paper mills expressed discomfort with the Nordic pulp producers' forward integration. They feared a situation in which the Nordic companies sold them pulp at a high price, at the same time as they lowered their paper prices to outcompete them. In turn, the Western Europeans reduced their purchases of Nordic pulp, and promoted EC-approved sanctions 'against the unfair Nordic competition'. As there were several new Nordic paper machines ready to start production, the EC asked MoDo to employ its third Husum machine at a later date.[59] However, the general Europeanization of the Nordic forest-based corporations had just begun, and MoDo believed that it should take the lead in that process. Here, too, Carlgren was the driving force, and rather soon an opportunity emerged in France: Alicel in Alizay.[60] The circumstances that triggered MoDo's European expansion were that the French and Italian paper mills, in particular, were regarded to be in bad condition, and several actors suggested that MoDo should expand through acquisitions of such worn-out plants.[61]

MoDo had been in the pulp business in France since the 1950s, led by Lejeune – a successful pulp seller and a driving, charming and socially competent person (cf. subsection 8.1.5). Eventually leading managers like Brändström and Diedrichs developed the impression that Lejeune rather 'directed' MoDo's GMT than followed its instructions (however, the slack reins could also be explained by language difficulties). In the 1980s, they thought that Lejeune had become 'too big for MoDo' – he and 'his' businesses became hard to control. Moreover, when MoDo's GMT discussed the French operations with Carlgren, he always stressed that Lejeune had 'free hands' and that he was placed outside the regular MoDo hierarchy.[62] CEO Sprängare found such a division of responsibilities remarkable.[63]

In the middle of the 1980s, the French plant, Alicel, which was based on deciduous forests and sold sulphate pulp to fine paper customers, had gone bankrupt. Lejeune saw that as a chance for MoDo to cheaply obtain a business that could be developed. It was generally difficult for a foreign investor to acquire the majority in a French company – the unions effectively prohibited that through strikes and riots – so Alicel represented a rather unique opportunity. Because the company was bankrupt, large state subventions were promised to whoever took over that worn-out plant and invested in it (and saved jobs). Peppler suggested that MoDo should buy all of it. As there had been discussions in MoDo since 1982 about finding a 'local' (i.e. French) pulp producer for PPSM, the offering fell onto good soil.

The French state promised MoDo 'favourable treatment', since, for some reason, it was interested in having the Swedish company involved. Still, as noted above, foreign ownership of French companies was restricted (≤ 35% shareholding). Thus, Carlgren and Lejeune agreed to establish a joint French consortium (Calanda) that should buy the majority of shares (about 65%) in Alicel, with MoDo as minority shareholder (≈ 17%) along with Feldmühle (≈ 17%). As noted above, Lejeune considered this deal an opportunity for both him and MoDo, and Carlgren was positive as well. CEO Sprängare, however, was decidedly opposed to it both because he saw no benefits for MoDo of (part) owning another pulp producing unit and because he found Lejeune difficult to control. Officially MoDo said no, but Carlgren and the 'fine paper gang' made sure that MoDo, through PPSM, bought 17 per cent for a modest sum (in 1985).[64] At the same time, they allowed Lejeune to build his consortium and incorporate Alicel.[65] Lejeune promised MoDo a good return in two years' time, and using the grants promised by the state, Alicel's modernization was soon underway. Lejeune became its CEO, Altbäck its Chair and Sprängare one of its directors.[66]

To gain better control over the market volatility of fine paper, MoDo decided to try to build its own European wholesaler business. As one component in that strategy MoDo acquired an option to buy the remaining 45 per cent of the Swedish wholesaler Svenskt Papper in order to close that channel to its competitors. That part of the value chain was growing in importance not only in Sweden but also abroad, and it was an increasing problem that 'uncontrolled' wholesalers kept stocks that the producers (e.g. MoDo), lacking contact with the end customers, did not see.

In 1985, Iggesund bought about 10 per cent of MoDo to show its stakeholders that the company wanted to maintain its autonomy over the long term. That holding was acquired from Björkegren, a Swedish capitalist, who with unknown financing had taken a corner position in MoDo. Björkegren offered that holding several times to Carlgren, but he said no thanks. Later, however, Iggesund offered to buy Björkegren's holding, and did so. Carlgren had realized that such a holding in MoDo could play an important role for the dynasty's possibility to pledge long-term control over MoDo. So when he announced Iggesund's purchase he said: 'Now MoDo's future and the family control over the company are secured.'[67]

During the same year, despite the on-going discussions about the company's precarious financial situation, MoDo began negotiations with the ambition to acquire a firm of extraordinary strategic interest: Svanö (attractive forest resources). However, since that 'titbit' went to MoDo's rival SCA, there was only one way left to secure more substantial forest assets in northern Sweden (outside what was owned by the state), and that was Graningeverken. That company had large forest resources that suited MoDo well and controlled several power plants. For these reasons Sprängare favoured that move and regarded the target company's size 'fitting'. However, this time, and to the surprise of many, Carlgren was not particularly enthusiastic, perhaps because Graningeverken had a unit at Utansjö that had to be closed (and that would be tough). Still, MoDo increased its holding in Graningeverken from 4 per cent to 10 per cent in 1987 (i.e. to a 'corner position'). As a consequence, the Chair of the Kempe foundations, Carl Kempe Jr, became a member of Graningeverken's board.

Eventually both Chair Carlgren and CEO Sprängare recognized that they did not get on well together. Carlgren thus started the search for a new CEO. He talked to people in whom he had confidence but – as usual – he took the decision himself. He liked the former Head of MoDo Paper Löf, who, as noted earlier, had left the company for a position as CEO of Södra. Löf was on Carlgren's short-list because he had a favourable track record in MoDo's core business (fine paper).[68] Ever since 1981, Carlgren had remained in contact with Löf. That gave Löf a strong negotiating position, so he ultimately won favourable terms. He also knew what he wanted to do, and – last but not least – he and the Chair understood each other's rationales.[69]

During one of the recurrent global industry conferences, Carlgren had confidential, informal talks with Löf regarding his possible return to MoDo as its new CEO. Carlgren told him that Sprängare was about to leave for Trygg-Hansa. Löf answered that such a solution was subject to certain conditions: (1) Carlgren should stay as Chair but Löf should become not only CEO but also head of the whole MoDo group, (2) MoDo's business structure should be open to changes, that is to say, MoDo Konsument was not to be seen as a sanctified holding, (3) it had to be possible to merge MoDo Cell (pulp) and MoDo Paper (fine paper) and (4) rationalization should be allowed. The last condition was necessary, since Carlgren, as a member of the Kempe dynasty, from his heart disliked such activities. Löf suspected, however, that there was a lot of 'slack' in MoDo's organization, so it was essential for him to have that freedom.[70]

Löf also talked quite cautiously to MoDo director Wallander about his possible entry as CEO of MoDo. Löf had the (false) impression that Wallander had recommended him back in 1981, but as the relation between Wallander and Carlgren at that time was rather 'cool' – although not frosty – Löf was uncertain about Wallander's opinion. Löf had learned that Wallander sometimes asked Carlgren tough questions during the board meetings, and he was not sure that Wallander thought Carlgren had the right skills for a Chair position. Löf also thought that Wallander at heart preferred MoDo's rival SCA and the way that company was run, a preference that could also partly be explained by the ownership situation – unlike SCA, MoDo had never been a part of the Handelsbanken/Industrivärden sphere.[71]

Carl Kempe Jr was also actively involved in the process of luring Löf back to MoDo. He even went to Löf's summerhouse to convince him to take the job. However, as Löf and his wife liked living at Växjö (Södra's HQ), it was necessary for Carlgren to sweeten his bid, and that also included offering Löf's wife an attractive job.[72] What spoke for a move back to MoDo was that Löf had learned that winning the trust of its shareholders in a forest-owners' co-operative like Södra was a most delicate and difficult task.

Carlgren did not actually remove Sprängare as CEO. As one of the directors in the Swedish insurance company Trygg-Hansa, he could use a vacancy in that company's CEO position. Carlgren's mission was simplified since his friend Dahlgren, a MoDo director, also was connected to Trygg-Hansa. However, it was Trygg-Hansa's Chair Åkerman that attracted Sprängare to the insurance company, so when Sprängare left MoDo in 1985, Löf replaced him. Löf immediately removed those managers that he saw as members of Sprängare's circle (potential opponents). Despite his proven integrity, Löf already from the beginning began to adjust some of his acting to Carlgren's way of thinking.[73]

A few weeks after Löf had taken office, he summarized his ideas about the problems MoDo faced. He listed six items that had to be addressed already during his first year as CEO: the tough competition in the pulp business, the big losses at Domsjö, the future status and opportunities for MoDo Konsument (which indicated that he saw Carlgren's 'three leg' strategy as problematic), the need for substantial investments in the existing plants, the management at MoDo Paper (its head Nilsson had recently left MoDo) and the strained financial situation. To handle the last item MoDo sold power plants for about SEK 1 billion but touched neither Domsjö – sacred unit for the Kempe–Carlgren dynasty – nor Bureå. The forests were also kept intact. Regarding the fine paper leg, the desire to expand was reflected in the third fine paper machine at Husum (decided before Löf's re-entry into the company), an investment that could be defended economically. There were also problems associated with the hygiene business, as the attempts to acquire Edet, Klippan and Fiskeby failed. MoDo could simply not afford the necessary sums – instead, competitors bought these three firms.[74]

In 1986, Löf re-opened the discussions regarding the future development of the fine paper business. The company's market potential in that field had increased well above Husum's limit. Thus, the idea to invest in a new paper mill in France was once again put on the board's agenda – and this time, too, the talks focused on the Alizay site. Both Alizay's Head Lejeune and MoDo's new CEO favoured a localization of the new unit next to Alicel. Through PPSM MoDo already controlled 17 per cent of Alicel, so there was a platform for further activities. In December the board got the terms for an Alipap investment in Alizay and they looked attractive. If it was carried out MoDo (through PPSM) was supposed to increase its share of Alizay (i.e. Alicel and Alipap) from 17 per cent to 34 per cent with an option to reach 51 per cent.[75] At the end of 1986, MoDo increased its focus on fine paper by exercising its right to acquire all shares in the third fine paper machine at Husum, thereby making it a subsidiary. At the same time, MoDo got more than 50 per cent of the shares in MoDo-Iggesund CTMP, making that unit, too, a subsidiary.

A summation of MoDo's situation at the end of 1986 indicated that many things remained to be addressed. The Domsjö site was still a problem, while Bureå's operations were acceptable, although the decision regarding the level of new investments at the latter unit was unsolved. PPSM was undercapitalized, so debt was converted to equity. In the hygiene business, it became obvious that MoDo was losing ground because of lack of capital. Instead, it was SCA that had bought Edet, and Holmens Bruk that had acquired Fiskeby. However, MoDo negotiated with Bonnier about acquiring its tissue producer Duni, because Carlgren wanted to create a large hygiene group composed of MoDo Konsument, Holmen Hygien and Duni. Therefore, there were also on-going talks with the leading actors at Holmens Bruk regarding some kind of co-operation. The Finnish producers, too, had at that time come up as possible partners.[76]

MoDo's hygiene business grew in the 1980s, but still it was too small. It also became obvious that the company's financial muscles did not allow for three different core businesses (economies of scale had increased dramatically in importance). The investments in the fine paper business in France and in the new machine at Husum became decisive for how many – and which – units could be kept. The Head of MoDo Konsument, Nordlund, was actually one of the actors who early on raised the issue of whether 'his' business perhaps ought to be sold to find a better setting for its future growth. As usual Carlgren was the key decision-maker when it came to strategic matters, and in this case the focal business was not close to the family identity, in terms of either its geography or the kind of operations involved. The will of the new CEO Löf probably also mattered, and he wanted MoDo to unambiguously focus on its strong fine paper business. Wallander shared his view.[77]

9.4 MODO ACQUIRES HOLMENS BRUK

The idea to build the Third Bloc by acquiring both Iggesund and Holmens Bruk had become Carlgren's vision for a highly respected MoDo (still) run by the Kempe dynasty. Korsnäs was in his mind, too, but its CEO showed no interest at all in discussing possible ways to co-operate. Carlgren had followed the development of Holmens Bruk and was impressed by its newsprint investment in Braviken. He noticed that the plant was profitable and believed that it had a bright future, so he began to meet with leading actors both inside and outside Holmens Bruk. Thus, as so often, he established a network of people both inside the 'target company' and among its shareholders. At the same time, he reassured Holmens Bruk's Chair Önnesjö that 'he would not touch the company'[78] – thus, he made the same promise as its two major shareholders (the Bonnier and Söderberg families) had given long ago.

Carlgren handled most of the Holmens Bruk discussions himself. He shared very little information with the other leading actors about his talks with the other party, and about how a possible acquisition could be carried out. He regarded it as his task to meet with the important actors for preliminary talks and to make the necessary initial deals – thus, big acquisition processes were something that he handled himself.[79] In his ambition to expand the heirloom MoDo to finally be on par with the two really big Swedish forest-based companies SCA and Stora, Carlgren became almost obsessed with acquiring Holmens Bruk. So, through Iggesund, he began to buy its shares as a 'capital investment'.[80] That was possible because Iggesund had substantial cash on hand after the sale of EKA and Boxholm. Moreover, both Iggesund's CEO Nordin and its Head of Finance Svensson – fully aware of Carlgren's strategic ambition – convinced him (and that was not difficult) that Iggesund ought to buy shares in Holmens Bruk with the freed capital. In the beginning, the purchases of Holmens Bruk shares were kept secret, but, by 1986, once the amount reached 11 per cent of the capital (15% of the votes), Iggesund made its holding publicly known.[81]

Once the news was out, one of the two major shareholders in Holmens Bruk, the Söderberg dynasty, through its investment company Ratos, expressed both surprise and discomfort and opposed the purchases ('Carlgren does not belong here').[82] The Söderberg family certainly did not admire Carlgren; it belonged rather with the Wallenberg sphere.[83] In fact, Söderberg and Carlgren could not be in the same room.[84] So the Söderberg family bought 10 per cent of the Iggesund stock in an attempt to block the situation. Moreover, they firmly opposed the appointment of Carlgren to Holmens Bruk's board.[85] The Söderbergs also supported the CEO of Holmens Bruk, Zetterberg, in his efforts to stop Carlgren.[86] In that tense situation the other large shareholder, the Bonnier family, through Reuterskiöld (CEO of Dagens Nyheter), stressed its intention to continue to act as a united front with the Söderberg family regarding all Holmens Bruk matters.[87] For his part, Carlgren persisted in his efforts to gain control over Holmens Bruk and fostered his long-time friendship with Joja Bonnier,[88] who saw his relation to Carlgren as a possible ticket to those bigger arenas he strived for. In return, Joja Bonnier could help his friend to realize his much longed for Third Bloc.[89]

Joja Bonnier's long-time friendship with Carlgren began to involve direct co-operation in business matters. For example, Bonnier owned the tissue producer Duni, which had problems with its operations at its Långsjönäs site. Carlgren stepped in to support the Bonnier family and instructed MoDo to acquire Duni. Through that transaction, a business relationship developed that involved the potential for a return favour from the Bonnier family.[90] Later, Carlgren, who at the time controlled about 7 per cent of Holmens Bruk, pushed for a board seat there for Joja Bonnier. Sven Söderberg (Ratos) took note of that effort and concluded that there seemed to be at least the seed of an alliance between MoDo and Bonnier, and that Ratos might well land in 'the back seat'. In that situation, Sven Söderberg informed CEO Zetterberg that Ratos might consider selling its Holmens Bruk shares.[91]

The leading actors in the Söderberg family were displeased with Bonnier's activities in Holmens Bruk mainly because of Joja Bonnier's weakness for Carlgren's Third Bloc vision. Joja Bonnier's endorsement of Carlgren's board candidature in Holmens Bruk led the Söderberg family to suspect that the Bonnier family, through Joja, was building a relationship with MoDo-Iggesund. Sven Söderberg feared an alliance between Bonnier and Carlgren that would put them in a squeezed ownership position in Holmens Bruk. Thus, the previously rock-solid tie between the Söderberg and Bonnier families was seriously threatened.[92]

At that time, Carlgren visited Albert Bonnier and informed him that he could buy two more holdings in Holmens Bruk, one containing about 7 per cent of the votes (offered by Lundberg) and another one representing about 1 per cent, all together endowing him with control of about 15 per cent of the votes.[93] Since Iggesund carried out these purchases, the 'MoDo group' had by January 1986 become a major shareholder in Holmens Bruk.

After a short time Carlgren asked for a seat on the board referring to 'sound business practice'. Albert Bonnier agreed and promised to try to convince the other major shareholder, the Söderberg family, about the reasonableness of his proposal. The Söderberg family, however, felt most uncomfortable, as they disliked the idea of being on the same board as Carlgren.[94] In reality, the Bonnier-controlled Marieberg board was divided regarding the appropriateness of appointing Carlgren director at Holmens Bruk. Albert and Joja Bonnier's stance was not supported by all of Marieberg's board members.[95]

Soon after the size of Carlgren's holding had become publicly known, Chair Önnesjö, referring to the stable ownership situation, declared that Carlgren's entry did not change anything for Holmens Bruk. For many decades Dagens Nyheter (i.e. the Bonnier family) and Ratos (i.e. the Söderberg family) had controlled the company (together they owned about 60% [votes]). In a letter dated in February 1986, Sven Söderberg (Ratos) wrote that he could not – from Holmens Bruk's perspective – find any synergies or operational advantages at all following from collaboration between the two companies.

In a letter to Holmens Bruk's Chair Önnesjö dated April 1986, Albert Bonnier suggested the appointment of Joja Bonnier as the new director at Holmens Bruk 'to solve the information problems' between shareholders and top management. Önnesjö refused, explaining that in such a case both Ratos and KF/Fiskeby would be entitled to ask for board memberships, and that would make the arena too big. In terms of the capital invested, Fiskeby was the largest shareholder in Holmens Bruk (16%).

After the transactions were completed, Carlgren explained the motivation behind the purchases of Holmens Bruk shares at an Iggesund board meeting. He stated that it was a long-term investment in a most interesting company. The price was high – 50 per cent above current market price – but that was something that Iggesund had to accept. Lars G. Sundblad did not register a reservation in the minutes, but was firm in his view that the Chair should not be allowed to buy more shares without explicit permission from the board. Sundblad made clear that it was the board's task to decide on the use of the capital available for investments.[96]

Almost a year later, that is to say, in March 1987, Zetterberg (CEO of Holmens Bruk) wrote a letter to Löf (CEO of MoDo) in which he expressed his concern regarding MoDo's (Iggesund's) intentions with its shareholding. He also mentioned that Holmens Bruk still wanted to buy MoDo Konsument. The same day Zetterberg also wrote to Albert Bonnier and asked him to publicly express that Marieberg had no interest in becoming part of Carlgren's Third Bloc. If he could not do that, there was a clear risk that actors in the environment would have the impression that Marieberg had accepted Carlgren's vision.[97] Therefore, a week later, Sven Söderberg (Ratos) and Reuterskiöld (Marieberg) signed a letter to Holmens Bruk's board that 'co-ordination benefits with other Swedish forest-based companies did not exist at the time', and that they intended to work for 'an incessantly autonomous Holmens Bruk'. That promise was repeated at the next AGM, and it became known as the 'declaration of independence'.[98]

In mid-1987, MoDo sold its hygiene business (MoDo Konsument) to Holmens Bruk. Holmens Bruk's CEO Zetterberg and its head of the hygiene business Persson were the ones that pushed hardest for that transaction, which ultimately made the company the third biggest producer of tissue in Europe. MoDo CEO Löf also supported the transaction because he did not consider hygiene to be a future path for his company. Carlgren had hoped to get the payment in stock, but Holmens Bruk did not accept it. In order to make the purchase, Holmens Bruk stretched its financial resources almost to the utmost limit. The board and top management felt like they had to act, since the possibility that somebody else was considering making the same acquisition could not be ruled out,[99] although SCA could not buy MoDo Konsument, as such a purchase never would have passed the Swedish Competition Authority. The two major shareholders in Holmens Bruk (the Bonnier and Söderberg families) particularly stressed that the transaction was a one-off affair, and that it did not point towards any further co-operation between the two companies. After the sale, Carlgren (again) asked for a seat on Holmens Bruk's board based on 'his' holdings (15% of the votes), this time with the justification that MoDo-Iggesund no longer held competing operations (i.e. no hygiene business).

Before a meeting with Albert Bonnier, Zetterberg wrote in a mid-September memorandum that Carlgren's manoeuvres worried him, even though the situation had improved after his and Ratos's public declaration of independence for Holmens Bruk. Still, Iggesund's request for a seat on Holmens Bruk's board was not without complications. To appoint Carlgren director – the symbol for the Third Bloc vision – would probably revive negative vibrations from the past two years and make things more difficult for Holmens Bruk's top management. Moreover, it could put doubt on the validity of the 'declaration of independence'.[100]

At this point, Carlgren exploited the friction between the Bonnier and Söderberg families. One complication was that the Bonnier representatives on Holmens Bruk's board did not report to Albert Bonnier, something that the other board members and the CEO took for granted. Therefore, the contacts between the two major shareholders were rather limited, and Holmens Bruk's Chair Önnesjö could not get Albert Bonnier and Sven Söderberg to sit down and talk things through. Albert Bonnier was also irritated that Zetterberg did not want to see Carlgren as director, although the latter controlled a substantial portion of the stock.[101]

Late in September 1987, Albert Bonnier wrote to Sven Söderberg regarding Carlgren's request for a board seat. Bonnier thought that the main obstacle had been removed, as MoDo had sold its hygiene business to Holmens Bruk. Furthermore, the Bonnier–Söderberg declaration ensured that the situation at Holmens Bruk would stay unchanged. Albert Bonnier also firmly rejected the other arguments against Carlgren's entrance: his age (70)[102] and the CEO's discomfort. So, at the 7 October EGM Carlgren was elected deputy director, as formalities made a regular seat impossible at this stage.

Sven Söderberg was not willing to accept a situation in which Ratos held 30 per cent of Holmens Bruk and an imagined alliance between MoDo and Bonnier controlled around 46 per cent. Such a move would tilt the power balance that the two long-time partners, the Bonnier and Söderberg families, had established. Söderberg also began to get the impression that the Bonnier family preferred to have Carlgren as a board member rather than somebody representing Ratos. Thus, Söderberg had become increasingly uncertain regarding the Bonnier family's commitment to uphold their joint declaration that 'Carlgren should be kept away from Holmens Bruk'.[103] With those concerns in mind, he initiated a general reappraisal of the family's overall holdings, and particularly its shareholding in Holmens Bruk. Söderberg had learned that even long-term agreements between individuals belonging to different families are fragile, as over time new family members enter the scene and elder ones leave.[104] Ultimately, the Söderberg family had grown tired of the Bonnier family, that is to say, especially of Joja Bonnier and his favouring of Carlgren. Sven Söderberg's trust in that family (company) was gone. So instead of facing a bitter conflict at the upcoming AGM, Ratos – in a crisis meeting – decided to sell its holding in Holmens Bruk to MoDo. Thus, one of Carlgren's great strengths – his staying power – had finally paid off. He had successfully used his 'wear-down tactics' in his efforts to realize his vision.

Since there was no agreement or clause stating that the Bonnier family had a pre-emptive right, Ratos could sell to anybody.[105] Thus, on 30 September Carlgren was contacted by a broker that offered MoDo the Ratos holding in Holmens Bruk at a price of SEK 725 per share (SEK 1.4 billion) plus Ratos's holding in Iggesund at a price of SEK 695 per share (SEK 400 million). The broker wanted a decision (yes/no) at the latest by 5 October 1987 and stressed that neither the price nor the number of shares was negotiable.

Ratos's decision to sell its holding struck many leading actors in and around Holmens Bruk like a lightning bolt from the sky. For example, Marieberg's CEO Reuterskiöld learned about the affair through the newspapers and, not surprisingly, became upset. Moreover, he could not even reach Carlgren for clarification, as it was 4 October, a day when many Swedish businessmen took part in demonstrations for private ownership of corporations. However, as Marieberg had no pre-emptive right, Reuterskiöld had no formal platform to use for taking action. Eventually it became clear that Carlgren and Joja Bonnier considered dividing the Ratos holding between them, but Reuterskiöld saw no strong reason why Marieberg should become more deeply involved in Holmens Bruk.

Holmens Bruk's CEO Zetterberg questioned whether Sven Söderberg had talked to the other major actors, that is to say, Albert Bonnier and Wallander, about his intentions before he went ahead and sold. Since the sale would provide Carlgren with a holding in Holmens Bruk amounting to around 47 per cent, he could easily acquire more than 50 per cent through classic market buying. That new ownership situation put the Bonnier family in a weak position and therefore – with the possible exception of Joja Bonnier – inclined to sell its holding.[106]

On 2 October, the SSE market price for Holmens Bruk A-shares was SEK 600 and for Iggesund A-shares SEK 590. Carlgren contacted Marieberg and offered to share MoDo's Ratos holding in Holmens Bruk with that company. He also informally contacted all MoDo board members and got their permission to acquire the shares offered by Ratos. However, Marieberg did not respond before the deadline (5 October). That silence was at least partly explained by the existence of a divided board. Marieberg's directors disagreed about the acceptance of the offering of half of the Ratos holding.[107] Therefore, on 5 October, MoDo decided to buy Ratos' entire holding (30%) in Holmens Bruk, and to give Ratos an option to sell its holding in Iggesund (10%) to MoDo or somebody else that MoDo put forward.[108]

In a letter dated 6 October, Holmens Bruk's CEO informed all employees that Ratos had sold its holding in the company (16%) to MoDo and that, as a part of the deal, MoDo had pledged to find a buyer for Ratos's holding in Iggesund, representing 9.8 per cent of the votes. He added that the transaction did not affect Marieberg's holding (16%). However, as other actors outside the MoDo group owned 75 per cent of the capital, there was no plan to change Holmens Bruk's path. At the same time, Chair Önnesjö 'publicly' welcomed MoDo as a new major shareholder and declared that he expected unchanged autonomy for Holmens Bruk in the future.

At the Holmens Bruk board meeting on 7 October 1987 the new director Carlgren stressed that MoDo did not intend to increase its holding. On the same occasion Joja Bonnier, the representative for the other major shareholder Marieberg, stated that the Holmens Bruk affair had not yet come to an end. Erik Söderberg, who would be leaving the board, justified Ratos's sell-off with the disadvantages that Holmens Bruk would face having three major shareholders. As long as the Bonnier and Söderberg families together had been in control things had worked well, but the situation had changed. The board decided to summon an EGM on 3 November, where a new board would be appointed. At MoDo's board meeting on 13 October, the Ratos deal was only briefly mentioned. According to the notes, the board was content with the purchase. The consequences of the new shareholding situation in Holmens Bruk were not discussed at all.

In a letter dated 16 October 1987 Zetterberg wrote that he had decided to leave the company.[109] He informed the board formally about his retirement at its meeting in connection with the extra EGM that was carried out on 3 November. At that time, Carlgren learned that other actors also had expressed interest in acquiring Marieberg's holding in Holmens Bruk, so he was eager to start the negotiations. The discussions between Carlgren and representatives for Marieberg resulted in a declaration, where MoDo and Iggesund jointly informed Marieberg that they were willing to pay SEK 725/share (a sale option; same share price as in the Ratos deal). It was also stated that Iggesund/MoDo had the right to match a possible competing bid during the lifetime of that option. Carlgren had tried to get a call option and thought he had received such an instrument from Wallander, who represented Marieberg (and at the same time was a member of MoDo's board). Indeed, Carlgren informed MoDo's management that, through his talks with Wallander, he had negotiated a call option for Marieberg's holding in Holmens Bruk. However, when MoDo's CEO Löf read the actual document, it became clear that it was the other way around – Marieberg had acquired a sales option, that is to say, MoDo had to buy the holding when it was called upon to do so at the share price of SEK 725 – the 'Ratos price' (although the market price had slipped considerably since that deal).[110]

Holmens Bruk's top management was surprised when they learned that soon there might be a bid for the whole company. They did not believe that such a purchase was possible. CEO Zetterberg had regarded it as quite inconceivable for financial reasons.[111] However, in Carlgren's view, the acquisition of Marieberg's holding in Holmens Bruk was also an act of defence. He was eager to prevent another large owner – particularly Stora – from entering Holmens Bruk and depriving him of a unique opportunity to create the Third Bloc. He had already experienced the downside of having a locked situation when he acquired Iggesund (1981–83).

The 19 October stock market crash made the Marieberg agreement even tougher for MoDo, although it did not affect the legal formalities. It did, however, give MoDo's top management greater incentive to check whether it was possible to declare the Marieberg deal invalid. Carlgren was kept out of these efforts, because he was content with the purchase and regarded MoDo as capable of handling the additional financial demands. The attempt to cancel the deal was based on the idea that it might be possible to claim that Wallander had acted in *mala fide*, that is to say, that he both ought to have known that Carlgren acted without a mandate from MoDo's board (of which Wallander was a member), and ought to have understood that Carlgren sought a call option for MoDo.[112] However, management's efforts to cancel the agreement were unsuccessful, and on 26 October, the option was extended to 1 December to allow Marieberg to resolve the internal differences of opinion regarding whether the company should remain a shareholder in Holmens Bruk.

In mid-November, Albert Bonnier wrote to Carlgren with suggestions about how to divide the Ratos holding in Holmens Bruk. Basically, these suggestions contained variations of Joja Bonnier's oral agreement indicating 37 per cent for each of the groupings. Carlgren turned all those proposals down. After those futile negotiations, the Bonnier family (i.e. Albert Bonnier) decided that Marieberg should accept MoDo's offer. Thus, on 17 November Marieberg informed MoDo that the company intended to use its option to sell its holding in Holmens Bruk, and on 22 December 1987 that sale was formally executed. The day for taking control of the holding was 8 April 1988, and payment was due on 29 April 1988.

Beginning on 17 November MoDo started to investigate how the Third Bloc could be established in the Swedish forest-based industry to compete with the other two big 'blocs' SCA and Stora. Before that date neither MoDo's board nor management had made any plans for a possible merger between MoDo, Holmens Bruk and Iggesund. According to MoDo's CEO Löf, the main reason was that the Chair and major shareholder Carlgren firmly had opposed such a high degree of integration among the three. Among MoDo's top managers, however, the opinions on that issue were divided.[113]

Carlgren had not yet decided how to organize the new Third Bloc when Marieberg triggered its call option. Before the acquisition of its holding, MoDo controlled 53 per cent of the votes in Holmens Bruk; afterwards, MoDo would hold 75 per cent of the votes. Still, since there were expensive 'millipedes'[114] left to acquire, it was difficult to reach the 'magic threshold' of 90 per cent. However, to buy the rest of Iggesund (35%) was not particularly costly.[115] Indeed, several advised Carlgren to abandon his ambition to control 50+ per cent of the votes in MoDo, and they drew parallels to how the Wallenberg sphere was kept together. These recommendations did not change Carlgren's view. Instead, the biggest loan in MoDo's history – SEK 1.2 billion – was signed. In that situation KFIAB expressed its concern for the future value of its holding in Holmens Bruk.

Formally, MoDo's board did not discuss 'the Marieberg deal' until 26 November 1987, although the directors, one at a time, had been informed about Marieberg's call option and its content. At that board meeting, from which Wallander was absent, the critique of Carlgren's deal was harsh, although everybody realized that it was formally correct, since the Chair was authorized to sign MoDo agreements. The deal meant another tough financial strain for a MoDo that recently had paid about SEK 1.8 billion buying the two Ratos holdings (SEK 1.4 billion for a stake in Holmens Bruk and SEK 0.4 billion for a stake in Iggesund). The fact that Carlgren had carried out such a big deal on his own without a preceding board discussion was also criticized. This time, again, the sum was SEK 1.4 billion, and that was certainly a sizeable figure. In this situation it was really crucial for MoDo to obtain a statement from the Swedish Securities Council that MoDo did not have to offer all other shareholders in Holmens Bruk the same price.[116] Fortunately, its decision was favourable for MoDo.[117] The Head of Accounting and Control, Dyrhage, had made several calculations of the financial consequences for MoDo of all these actual and potential payments and concluded that MoDo would have been confronted with a serious liquidity problem, as the interest payments would generate a sizeable negative cash flow.[118]

Once MoDo had acquired Ratos's and Marieberg's holdings in Holmens Bruk,

Dyrhage again checked the cash flow situation. It certainly did not look good. Therefore, and for tax reasons, top management insisted that MoDo had to control more than 90 per cent of both Holmens Bruk and Iggesund. They made clear that they did not want to see any part-owned companies organized in some kind of holding construction. MoDo was too financially weak for such a solution. Carlgren, however, did not perceive the financial risk high enough to be a deterrent. He was convinced that it all would turn out fine in due course. As he saw it, MoDo finally had its 'three legs' (fine paper, newsprint and fine cardboard), which moderated the troublesome trade fluctuations. Thus, MoDo had escaped its high dependence on the pulp market, and Carlgren saw that risk reduction as roughly equal to the increased financial risk. He also expected things to go his way – economic trends used to be on his side.[119]

At MoDo's board meeting on 9 December, Carlgren described his on-going work regarding the formation of the new forest-based industrial group (the Third Bloc). That was the board's first joint discussion that addressed that crucial topic, but the directors did not come to a conclusion on how to treat the three involved companies (MoDo, Iggesund and Holmens Bruk). A serious problem was the continuing decline in the stock market prices, which made a depreciation of MoDo's holdings in Holmens Bruk necessary. That, in turn, would create an extraordinary cost in the profit and loss account.

9.5 ARMOURING THE THIRD BLOC

On 1 January 1988, the biggest shareholders (voting power) in Holmens Bruk were MoDo with 34 per cent (capital: 17%), Marieberg with 31 per cent (16%) and Iggesund with 16 per cent (11%). KFIAB only controlled a negligible part of the votes (capital: 11%). The differences reflected the different types of shares issued by Holmens Bruk: A-shares (1 vote each) and two kinds of B-shares (1:1000 vote each).

In February 1988 Engman replaced Zetterberg as CEO of Holmens Bruk. Chair Önnesjö saw that as a temporary solution until the shareholding situation in Holmens Bruk was settled and its consequences clear. The board was recomposed and included Carlgren (MoDo), Joja Bonnier (Marieberg), Reuterskiöld (Marieberg), Sundblad (Iggesund), Gripenstedt, Trolle-Löwén, Löf (MoDo), Nordin (Iggesund) and two members appointed by the unions, with (among others) Carl Kempe Jr (MoDo) and Ahrsjö (Marieberg) as deputies.

At its meeting on 11 March 1988, MoDo's board decided to buy the rest of both Holmens Bruk's and Iggesund's holdings in the company. At that time in Sweden, there was no legal obligation for a bidder to make an offer valid for all shares in a target company when a holding exceeded a certain figure. However, as MoDo had a poor economic result that year, and Holmens Bruk and Iggesund instead showed healthy profits, MoDo needed (more than) a 90 per cent shareholding in both the other companies to establish a single integrated financial unit that could use its total resources without paying attention to the minority shareholders. The 'free' capital had to be available for all units in the group. Aside from this practical matter, Löf aspired to become Group CEO.

Still, the question was how to organize the new constellation.[120] For several reasons (including tax ones), it was difficult to use a holding company construction. Yet, the favoured idea was to maintain the three involved companies as subgroups with boards of their own. In the end, however, the choice was made for a consolidation type of solution, where MoDo was put at the top of the new construct, although that was a controversial and perhaps also unwise decision.

Carlgren asked investment banks for advice regarding how to form the new constellation. Carl Kempe Jr believed that the best strategy would be an 'upside-down' affair in which Holmens Bruk with its 'millipedes' bought MoDo; it would then be much cheaper for the family to keep control. That solution would have required Carlgren to sell his MoDo shares, but he hesitated to do that.[121] Svensson, Head of Finance at Iggesund, was asked for an opinion. He was trusted primarily because of his earlier advice to Carlgren to buy Holmens Bruk shares through Iggesund. He assembled an internal group to study Carl Kempe Jr's proposed alternative. Svensson also engaged Hägglöf and Ponsbach[122] for that task, as it had previous experience from a similar situation.[123]

Some leading actors thought that the solution with Holmens Bruk 'at the top' would be the best for Carlgren and the Kempe family. However, MoDo's chief adviser Handelsbanken claimed that 'the market' never would accept such a construct, and that such a path could be criticized on ethical grounds and perhaps even become a juridical matter. According to Handelsbanken, the time was over when one could build new structures against the will of the many and with the assistance of 'millipedes'. There were also other difficulties associated with that kind of solution. In such a case, Holmens Bruk's board would have to suggest that construct and actively promote a merger between Holmens Bruk and MoDo. Among the existing board members, only Joja Bonnier could be expected to do such a thing, as the other directors, with Chair Önnesjö at the head, were openly opposed to the proposed merger. So that path would require an EGM that had as its sole task the replacement of all directors except Joja Bonnier with actors that would support the new construct. Considering how actors in Norrköping felt towards MoDo, that EGM would likely become a contentious one.

Moreover, the new Holmens Bruk board would have to produce a prospectus addressing the merger, and the accompanying delay would give the financial world plenty of time to speculate in the respective shares (e.g. in a sharp rise in Iggesund's and MoDo's share prices). A long merger process also would entail risks for certain organizational disorder, if leading managers left the company. Several MoDo actors were also concerned that minority shareholders in Holmens Bruk could cause trouble at the EGM, and substantially delay – or even stop – the merger. There was also uncertainty about which minority shareholdings would emerge, and what approaches they would take. Thus, it was in such a messy and complicated situation that Holmens Bruk's new board would have to make the offer.[124]

To place Holmens Bruk 'at the top' and let that company acquire MoDo, taking advantage of the far-reaching voting rights differences, was also considered difficult to explain to many of the stakeholders. However, at this stage, Carlgren rejected the 'Holmens Bruk at the top' alternative mainly because of the increased risks associated with that path; his scepticism was an outflow of an assessment indicating that significant value might be lost if the takeover process took an extended amount of time. Moreover, Carlgren was a person who tried to avoid conflicts; taking up an open fight with Önnesjö and the rest of Holmens Bruk's board was not an alluring path.[125] He was now pleased – after 20 years of hard struggle, he had achieved his goal. Furthermore, he and MoDo had been under stress before, so he kept cool.

A second construct was the one denoted the 'PK path', which included the creation of a holding company – a new 'umbrella' for the three participating companies. However, that path was also soon crossed off the list. The third alternative, MoDo 'at the top', was supported by, inter alia, MoDo's CEO Löf, its Head of Legal Affairs Flodström and its Head of Accounting and Control Dyrhage, and by advisers linked to Handelsbanken. These actors did not see a dilution of Carlgren's dominance in the new MoDo as particularly problematic. Such a development might even allow for new structural solutions. Perhaps Handelsbanken saw a possible future in which MoDo and SCA became more tightly integrated? So, it was in a constellation of MoDo managers and expertise from Handelsbanken that the 'KVB solution'[126] emerged. That solution's supporters told Carlgren that such a construct would make it possible for him to maintain his control over MoDo, as it would be more favourable for investors to keep their KVBs than to convert them to MoDo shares. Carlgren saw the KVBs as temporary instruments, and he was convinced that the whole shareholding situation later could be 'corrected', bringing the family back into an unchallenged driver's seat.

Unfortunately for Carlgren, the chosen KVB approach rather soon weakened his standing – in fact, some actors suspected that the KVB solution was actually a way for some actors to gradually undermine Carlgren's control over the new MoDo. The KVB path diluted Carlgren's holding in MoDo to 30 per cent, while the Kempe foundations retained 18 per cent. By contrast, a construct with Holmens Bruk 'at the top' would have made it possible for the family to use the 'millipedes' as a rather cheap platform for control.[127]

In the end, MoDo's offering to the shareholders and owners of convertibles in Holmens Bruk and Iggesund became very complicated. The general ingredient was a combination of a cash component and one of two different KVBs in MoDo (A-KVBs, C-KVBs) – or cash together with a mix of the two kinds of KVBs.[128] One of the members of the owner family, Frans Kempe Jr, did not understand why MoDo offered A-KVBs for A-shares in Holmens Bruk and Iggesund. Since MoDo already had the voting majority in those two companies, their A-shares had become a kind of B-shares. Frans Kempe Jr thought that SE-Banken's[129] proposal to offer cash plus C-shares was the best one. In that way MoDo could act quickly and the family would keep its control – the guard against attacks from other capitalists would not be lowered. However, Carlgren had discarded that solution because it would be 'too expensive' since there was little cash left after paying both Ratos and Marieberg. Frans Kempe Jr was afraid that neither Carl Kempe Jr nor Carlgren, who merely had experiences from family firms, was equipped to handle the tricky stock market issues and financial intrigues in the highest 'league'. That constellation simply lacked the experience, competence and planning required in these crucial financial and control fields. The bad timing, too, pushed the controlling family in an unfortunate direction.[130]

Frans Kempe Jr stressed that nobody really knew what effects the KVB construct would have on the family's relative shareholding in the company. It started at the 50+ per cent level, but theoretically the family's stake could fall to as low as 25 per cent. However, Handelsbanken predicted that very few actors would actually choose A-KVBs, since the current price relationships made it favourable to take C-KVBs. The KVBs would run for 40 years and offered a better interest rate than the corresponding share dividend, so few would – still according to Handelsbanken – convert. Thus, family control should be secured for a long time. However, some actors, including Frans Kempe Jr, pointed out that such price–earnings relationships could suddenly change.[131] Even so, Carlgren and several other leading MoDo actors came to the same conclusion as Handelsbanken's expertise had expressed, namely that only a few shareholders would chose A-KVBs.[132]

So, despite these warnings Carlgren trusted his judgement and was full of self-confidence from earlier accomplishments. If the family shareholding became too diluted, he thought he would just have to buy more shares. Moreover, the banks had always helped him and MoDo out in the past, something he saw as their basic function: banks should support businessmen and healthy company groups. Later, however, lots of A-KVBs became available on the market, not, as was expected, C-KVBs, and that outcome was most unwelcome for Carlgren.

In April, Holmens Bruk's board discussed MoDo's bid for the whole company. MoDo Chair Carlgren described the motives for that step, and MoDo CEO Löf explained its expected effects. It was obvious to the board that Carlgren was responsible for the purchase – Löf was not powerful enough to launch such a big deal. MoDo's entry into Holmens Bruk was not particularly strong – the leaders of the target company questioned their strategic plans and governance capacity as well as their 'professionalism'. So, MoDo did not impress the top executives at Holmens Bruk when they described the merits of the combined operations. Moreover, Engman, who replaced Zetterberg as CEO, was more seen as a MoDo associate than as a Holmens Bruk leader.[133] Chair Önnesjö argued for the right for Holmens Bruk's shareholders to call back their approving votes if MoDo did not reach 90 per cent. Önnesjö also asked for calculations of the expected gains from the intended merger and a description of the value of the bid for the shareholders. He also wanted to see the planned organization structure.

Lundberg followed the Holmens Bruk contest with great interest. He had read the prospectus and looked carefully at the KVBs, and especially at the A-KVBs. That construct seemed to open up the situation. MoDo had chosen convertibles to 'guarantee' that Carlgren in the short run would keep his shareholding undiluted, but Lundberg could not grasp how it would be possible for Carlgren to handle the acquisition when he had not chosen Holmens Bruk as the buying company (with its possibility to use the 'extreme' voting differences between the A-shares and B-shares). The only reasons for Carlgren's reluctance that Lundberg could see were the 'heated atmosphere' at Holmens Bruk and concerns about some minority holdings in Holmens Bruk. Through Lundbergföretagen,[134] Lundberg bought quite a lot of Iggesund and Holmens Bruk shares, something that pushed the prices upwards and made the 'cash alternative' less attractive for MoDo investors. Seeing the opportunity, Lundberg also bought both KFIAB's B-shares in Holmens Bruk and other securities on the stock market, as lots of A-KVBs had become available.

Lundberg also offered a rather high price for those Iggesund's shares in MoDo that the company had to sell when it became a part of MoDo. However, Iggesund's board decided to divide those shares between Lundberg and Carlgren, and the latter actually got a larger portion (cf. below). Carlgren personally bought those shares that Iggesund owned (with strong voting rights), and took a loan abroad to carry out that purchase (SEK 370 million). That purchase became expensive for Carlgren, and it contributed significantly to his high private indebtedness. By late 1988, Lundberg had managed to get a 22 per cent holding in MoDo (votes) and approached Carlgren to discuss a seat on

MoDo's board (at the time Carlgren had 21%, the Kempe foundations 19%, Marieberg 17% and various actors close to Handelsbanken 6%).[135] There was also a pre-emption right established between Carlgren and Marieberg valid for the A-shares.

To strengthen the capital base in the new constellation, MoDo placed SEK 1 billion of Holmens Bruk shares among larger investors (who got KVBs in MoDo). At Holmens Bruk's board meeting on 3 May, Carlgren described the reasons for those sales. Marieberg's CEO Reuterskiöld also explained the motives behind his company's purchase of a larger holding, thereby again becoming a sizeable shareholder in Holmens Bruk (i.e. in the enlarged MoDo). Marieberg's re-entry as 'shareholder' took place when it responded to Handelsbanken's search for investors to execute the KVB solution. By bringing in additional investors, Wallander (Chair Handelbanken) sought to secure the bank's influence over the new and much bigger constellation. He had no difficulties convincing Joja Bonnier, who already had an informal agreement with Carlgren that Marieberg would enter the new MoDo.[136] Joja Bonnier had disappeared from the scene when Marieberg sold its shares in Holmens Bruk to MoDo in 1987, and, as he wanted to get back on stage, he tried to convince the family that a re-entry was a good idea. It was actually a good bargain for Marieberg to buy roughly the same stake in the larger and more interesting MoDo at a lower price. Wallander believed that purchase to be foremost a placement of capital, although Carlgren appreciated that it was Marieberg that bought MoDo stock since he regarded the Bonnier family as a friendly buyer.[137] All in all, the premium MoDo paid for the Holmens Bruk shares was around 30 per cent (the total price was SEK 6 billion).[138]

The big question was how Carlgren should maintain control of the enlarged MoDo group. His original idea was to organize MoDo into three subgroups (MoDo, Iggesund and Holmens Bruk). Löf, however, was hesitant, and he and Carlgren asked a professor at the Stockholm School of Economics[139] for an analysis of pros and cons and advice. During a long day at the HQ Carlgren came to the conclusion that making anything other than an integrated company group of MoDo would be too expensive – few or no synergies would be utilized, moving investment capital across such subgroup borders would result in complicated internal processes, and the company would be difficult to govern with such a ambiguous management structure. Thus, Carlgren changed his view completely, even though he previously had promised the staff/employees, the concerned county districts, the County Governors and the two CEOs a continuation of the autonomous standing of the acquired companies. Particularly in Norrköping (where the HQ of Holmens Bruk was located), that complete turnaround aroused strong critique that was expressed both in local media and by local politicians.[140]

In that somewhat tense situation Carlgren decided to assemble all the top executives from the three companies – more than 15 executives – at a residential centre outside Stockholm in an effort to establish an integrated MoDo group out of three basically autonomous companies (i.e. Holmens Bruk, Iggesund and MoDo). That retreat took place in the beginning of September and was run by an advisory team of professors linked to the Stockholm School of Economics.[141] During those sessions over three days and nights the crucial decisions were taken. That included the governance principles, a new organizational structure and the appointment of Löf as Group CEO, who would manage the enlarged MoDo.

Chair Carlgren had promised the two acquired companies a continuation of their autonomy in relation to MoDo, so Löf understood that it would be hard to realize group synergies. His plan was to organize six relatively autonomous businesses: newsprint, fine paper, pulp, cardboard, forestry and woodware. However, as expected, he faced resistance across almost all the organization. At the very top only the division heads were outright positive. In that difficult situation, Carlgren and Löf established a committee that was supposed to govern the integration process (Carlgren, Carl Kempe Jr, Lundberg, Braun [CEO Marieberg] and Löf). Reluctantly Holmen and Iggesund Bruk helped the process while ensuring that neither their companies nor personnel were disadvantaged. As a result, many synergies were lost. The only operations that were relatively easy to organize were the non-overlapping ones. It was merging the others that became troublesome.[142] Löf's efforts also included selling off businesses in areas where MoDo was expected to have difficulties in competing successfully. One such big disinvestment was the selling of the subsidiary Holmen Hygien to the Finnish forest-based company Metsä-Serla (SEK 1.3 billion). Holmen Hygien was simply not in the very best shape and was regarded as too small to be competitive. Furthermore, MoDo lacked both the financial and the managerial capacity to carry out the necessary expansion of that business.[143]

In 1989, MoDo also sold its remaining 50 per cent in HJR Fiberweb to James River and Holmen Ligno Tech to the Norwegian company Borregard Industries. At the same time, MoDo continued to invest, and for the first time in a North American pulp business. MoDo bought 25 per cent of Slave Lake Pulp, a company that was building a large CTMP plant in Alberta. Its pulp was intended for the production of printing paper and was to be marketed solely by MoDo. The costs for timber and energy were estimated to be half of those in Sweden (production started late in 1990). MoDo also made a substantial investment in Bureå's groundwood mill in Sweden that year, and in a cardboard plant in the UK.[144] In addition, MoDo showed interest in buying the French Chapelle d'Arblais but could not bid high enough. All the big deals forming the Third Bloc and the investment in Alizay described above had left MoDo 'financially paralysed'.[145]

During 1988, MoDo, together with AGA[146] and SCA, tried to acquire Graningeverken. MoDo had gradually bought shares in Graningeverken since 1984, and by early 1988 the company had reached a 10 per cent holding. In March, the co-operating 'trio' presented a bid for acquiring all shares and convertibles in Graningeverken (SEK 5.7 billion). The main argument for the purchase attempt was that Graningeverken's resources would be better utilized in bigger industrial contexts. AGA would incorporate the water power plants in its subsidiary Uddeholms Kraft, while MoDo and SCA would divide the forest resources 60:40. MoDo, with its 10 per cent holding in Graningeverken, stood behind the bid, and so did Skanska[147] with its 30 per cent block. However, most of the other shareholders were outright opposed, as were most actors and people in Graningeverken's local environment. The Nordin family, the second biggest shareholder (24%), refused to sell at any price. That refusal created an unsolvable problem, as the consortium had attached a condition to its offering: a 90 per cent acceptance rate. As that figure became impossible to reach, the whole takeover attempt failed.[148]

In mid-1988, a 'partnership financing' of Holmens Bruk's power plants was executed. The plants were sold with a repurchase right to a new company, Holmens Kraft, in which a consortium of Swedish insurance companies and pension funds became large shareholders. However, MoDo held the dominating position, owning 51 per cent of the votes (13% of the capital). The agreement provided MoDo with a right to buy back the power plants every year from 1998 up to 2010. The sales freed SEK 700 million for MoDo.[149] In August 1988, MoDo owned 90 per cent of Iggesund, at the same time as Iggesund owned 10 per cent of MoDo (the 'Björkegren holding'). Therefore, the latter shares were available for sale.[150] As described previously, that stock had been acquired back in 1985, when MoDo was on the offensive, to calm people at Iggesund. Carlgren regarded that 10 per cent share as crucial for the family's future control of MoDo. So, the rumour[151] that there was an internal proposal that the holding should be placed with a long-term investor that was 'friendly' to the Kempe–Carlgren dynasty did not surprise anybody; however, the rumour also was that Carlgren was not entirely comfortable with such a construct. When Iggesund's board discussed the matter, both Carlgren – who wanted to buy the holding – and Carl Kempe Jr were challengeable, so they had to leave the meeting.

Carlgren claimed that he had a promise from Iggesund that he could buy its MoDo shares. He thought that by buying them, he could prevent other, perhaps unfriendly, investors from doing so. Iggesund's CEO Nordin considered that to be an excellent arrangement, as it protected the company from future 'corners' belonging to hostile shareholders. Nordin also supported Carlgren's claim to have pre-emptive right to the holding, although there was no formal document indicating such a status. He believed that Carlgren's participation in the long MoDo-Iggesund process had been based on an acknowledgement that he had 'a right before everybody else' – a call option.[152] Board member Wallander noted that Iggesund's former CEO Sundblad did not agree, but nevertheless tried to persuade him, as well as other actors, that Carlgren should be allowed to buy the holding. He was also convinced that Carlgren had informally been given a call option right, and emphasized that such an arrangement created a stable shareholder situation for MoDo.[153] Sundblad's opposition was based on his goal to keep MoDo in check. In that case, he thought, it would be better for Iggesund if Lundberg, too, entered as a shareholder. Having two large shareholders would provide a better opportunity for Iggesund to function reasonably independently from any of them.[154]

Before the board meeting, Sundblad had met with Iggesund's Chair and learned that the current idea was to let the Kempe–Carlgren group buy the holding to secure a lasting majority and that several directors had discussed such an arrangement. Sundblad rejected that solution, and in a letter he informed the board about his talks with the Chair. His arguments for opposing Carlgren's purchase were that the initiative to purchase the shares from Björkegren was taken by Iggesund's top management, and that the deal was approved by the board without any mention of any priority for somebody to (later) acquire that holding.[155] Sundblad also claimed that the whole matter ought to be moved to the mother company MoDo, as it controlled more than 90 per cent of Iggesund. In his view, the fact that Iggesund had become a subsidiary to MoDo had altered the decision-making level regarding such large issues. As Sundblad could not attend Iggesund's board meeting on 12 October when the matter was due to be decided, he wrote a letter to Carlgren and told him that there was no call option right – if so, that should have been mentioned in both the minutes and the prospectus. Sundblad also added that if Carlgren went ahead and bought the shares, he would leave Iggesund (and so he did).[156]

In the end, the board decided to ask CEO Nordin to start negotiations with Carlgren regarding the sale. After the board meeting, Nordin checked the market price for MoDo A-shares and suggested a price based on that figure plus 5 per cent. Thus, there was no bidding process. Afterwards, however, it became clear that the price Carlgren paid actually was 5 per cent below the current day's rate. Carlgren put his shares in his private company Sanna Holding. Moreover, he did not purchase all the available 'Björkegren shares'[157] – Nordin made it possible for Lundberg to get a part of the holding for the same share price as Carlgren had paid.[158] To Carlgren's consternation, his main bank Handelsbanken refused to lend him the necessary amount. Carlgren regarded the bank's refusal as 'treachery'.[159] To be able to carry out the deal, Carlgren, assisted by SE-Banken through one of its CEOs (Palmstierna), took out a loan basically in Swiss Francs, which meant a low interest rate but also a currency risk. He also had to leave Bukowskis as a pledge[160] – a company that was worth around SEK 200–250 million.

Soon thereafter, Sundblad learned that the board on 12 October had decided that the so-called 'Björkegren holding' was to be sold outside the market to the Kempe–Carlgren group. He was most surprised that his letter – delivered to the Chair (Wallander) the day before the board meeting – never was distributed to the other directors, nor was it read aloud. In a new letter to the board dated 24 October, he criticized that procedure and announced his retirement.[161] Wallander looked up Sundblad on 29 October and asked him to reconsider his decision to leave Iggesund, and instead participate in the forthcoming board meeting scheduled for 22 November, where the final decision regarding the 'Björkegren holding' was to be taken. However, the following day Sundblad told Wallander that he would stick to his earlier decision.[162]

At about the same time (October 1988), Önnesjö declared that he wanted to leave Holmens Bruk. Carlgren was then appointed as the company's new Chair, and two new board members were recruited: Lundberg and Måberg (Marieberg, replaced in 1989 by Braun). The CEOs of Holmens Bruk (Engman) and Iggesund (Nordin) continued as directors. By that point, several shareholders had acquired substantial holdings in MoDo. Marieberg had bought such large blocks in MoDo A-shares that it had acquired roughly the same voting power as Carlgren.[163] Joja Bonnier and Carlgren were close friends with a shared concept of how family-owned corporations should be run, so they co-operated. That collaboration even resulted in a formal long-term shareholders agreement by which Marieberg, the Kempe foundations, Sanna Holding and Carlgren all received prior option of purchase regarding their MoDo shares.[164]

9.6 CARLGREN'S DEBACLE: THE KEMPE FAMILY LOSES CONTROL

Early in 1990, Carlgren worked to get 'full' control over the enlarged MoDo. He had achieved his current dominant position at the price of high indebtedness, both personally (including Sanna Holding) and for MoDo. However, the control contest was not yet over. This time, too, Carlgren needed the support of healthy trade conditions, and some luck as well. He had a strong competitor among the shareholders – Lundberg (through 'Lundbergföretagen') – that had both strong financial capacity and the possibility to use cash flow from other businesses to strengthen his position in MoDo. The Kempe–Carlgren faction had to rely on MoDo's achievements (i.e. its dividends) and support from Bonnier/Marieberg.

Carlgren's Sanna Holding was originally established to function as a complementary financial source to keep him in control of MoDo, but his holding company did not develop as well as he had expected. Bukowskis had shown excellent economic results in the late 1980s, providing capital both for its interest payments to SE-Banken, and for its own investments and operations. However, in 1989 the situation changed: Bukowskis's economic performance dropped, and neither Stille-Werner nor Storliens Högfjällshotell generated profit. In this rather strained situation, Carlgren, to the surprise of many actors, decided that Sanna Holding should invest in a new venture, Nordic Channel,[165] a business that seemed to have an excellent future but currently was far from profitable. Thus, the intended 'cash cow' Sanna Holding did not live up to its main purpose – it even had to take additional loans to run its own businesses.[166] So, instead of supporting Carlgren's (and the Kempe family's) ambition to control the family heirloom MoDo, Sanna Holding began to be a problem in itself. That development made Carlgren's total financial standing even more vulnerable.

However, Carlgren had been in tough financial situations before. Previously, he had managed to survive due to periods of good economic conditions, creative financing and sheer luck. For a long time, it looked like he was going to make it this time, too, as enduring boom times had supported all his risky transactions in the 1980s. For 1989, MoDo even made an all time high profit amounting to SEK 1.2 billion (after having paid all interests), so the company's debt burden was lowered from SEK 8 billion to SEK 6.6 billion. Thus, at the turn of the decade things were looking good for Carlgren.[167]

As Lundberg's shareholding in MoDo gradually grew, Carlgren began to seriously worry about how to keep the family in control of the company. One example of what that control struggle looked like is illustrated by the time when KF, as previously mentioned, sold Fiskeby to Holmens Bruk. KF received a substantial holding of B-shares as part of the payment. When MoDo later bought Holmens Bruk, KF's board refused to accept the offered share price. Instead, Lundberg solved the problem by acquiring the shares. Eventually he informed Carlgren that his intention was to reach 25 per cent in MoDo to get the tax benefit linked to that percentage. Carlgren listened politely, although he never thought that Lundberg would reach that level. He also did what he could to prevent such a situation from occurring.[168]

For his part, Frans Kempe Jr had become more worried about Lundberg's true long-term intent and capacity. He was convinced that capitalists always looked for good investment objects, and that Lundberg had become interested because Carlgren, together with the Kempe foundations, did not have safe control of MoDo. Frans Kempe Jr had also noted that Lundberg's track record had developed in a way that he stood out more and more as a serious, long-term industrialist. Lundberg had started his business career with rather modest activities and then gradually increased the 'stakes'. Frans Kempe Jr claimed that Lundberg had learned 'the rules of the game' and was ready for big things. He was looking for a large, listed industrial company in which he could make long-term investments and gain a strong position.[169]

At the beginning of 1990, Carlgren's idea was to develop MoDo into a financially sound, international forest-based company that had a leading role in selected business fields and geographic areas. At that time, internationalization was a hot topic, not least because of the emerging strong interest for changes in business structures that crossed national, regional and continental borders. However, the ability to participate in such developments presupposed a capacity to make large investments and to make full use of scale economies. Such a path made it necessary to focus on relatively few production sites. For the new MoDo, priority was given to Husum (pulp and fine paper), Iggesund (cardboard), Hallsta (magazine paper) and Braviken (newsprint). To keep and develop these core businesses, MoDo needed to free around SEK 4 billion. However, in those days Carlgren began to question whether the family would be able to maintain control over such a large MoDo group even in a medium-term perspective. His optimism that still prevailed as late as 1989, reinforced by the economic success that year, gradually began to erode. For 1990 the profit was down from SEK 1.2 billion to SEK 225 million, and for 1991 there was a loss of about SEK 1.7 billion. Sanna Holding also suffered from the bad times, so a severe financial crisis materialized for Carlgren personally, which obviously weakened his capacity to ensure full family control of MoDo.

Given the crisis situation, it was not surprising that the relationship between Carlgren and Carl Kempe Jr became a bit strained. Carl Kempe Jr – and some other members of the Kempe family – began to take tougher positions against Carlgren. There were confrontations on 'invisible' arenas, but signs of friction became visible also in more public situations. Carl Kempe Jr had the impression that Carlgren had kept him away from the position as his 'natural' successor, and, according to several leading actors in MoDo, that was probably true. Over time, they had heard Carlgren making comments regarding the strengths and weaknesses of the potential candidates in the family, and his message had always been that nobody had the necessary qualities for the position as MoDo Chair or CEO. So, if Carlgren left MoDo, there appeared to be no capable family member around to replace him.[170]

At the turn of the decade MoDo, its Group CEO Löf (with backing from Carlgren), SCA's CEO Martin-Löf and SCA's Chair Rydin gathered to discuss possibilities for co-operation.[171] The idea was to merge the two companies' printing paper units and establish a new 50–50 company. Fulfilment of that idea could also be seen as a first step towards a full merger of the two companies. However, when the first step, a plan for the integration of the printing paper businesses, was presented at the MoDo board meeting in January 1990, it was not applauded. Both Lundberg and Carl Kempe Jr were of the opinion that MoDo's plants were in much better shape than the matching ones belonging to SCA, and Lundberg was also sceptical about a 50–50 construct.[172]

Despite these concerns, the discussions between some of the leading actors of the two companies continued, with the talks concentrating on possible co-operation in the fine paper area and on ways to integrate the sawmills. MoDo's efforts were somewhat uncoordinated, as, on the one hand, Chair Carlgren reassured SCA that he was genuinely interested in starting some kind of co-operation, while, on the other hand, CEO Löf began to abandon the SCA path. Carlgren was influenced by the advice he got from the distinguished Finnish consultancy firm Jakko Pöyry that a structural solution merging the two companies was the best path forward for MoDo. As noted above, it was not only Löf that was hesitant – there were also mixed opinions on MoDo's board.[173]

In mid-1990, two large Swedish banks, SE-Banken and somewhat later Handelsbanken, contacted Carlgren and declared that they regarded his personal economic standing as too fragile. These meetings represented serious warnings. SE-Banken asked Carlgren to take strong measures to reduce his total debt. With Sanna Holding included, Carlgren had outstanding loans amounting to around SEK 750 million.[174] Carlgren then looked for 'bridging loans', but none of his old friends supported him. That was not surprising, as Carlgren's financial problems coincided with a domestic financial crisis in Sweden.

All bank actors feared great losses on housing mortgages and stopped most risk-taking activities. Maybe some actors even had expected – and waited for – a Carlgren debacle? Maybe some actors actively acted to create that personal tragedy? There were several 'bigwigs' on the capital market that did not see Carlgren as particularly capable of sitting in the driver's seat in such a large public company as MoDo.[175]

Carlgren neither listened to warnings nor advice from the family (e.g. Frans Kempe Jr) or from his management (e.g. Altbäck). He believed that the banks – as always before – would support him. He expected that his old friends on the Swedish business scene still would be influential when the banks finally made their decisions. Moreover, he had always looked upon banks as service organizations assisting businessmen and industrialists like himself. However, this time Carlgren was confronted with a new generation of bankers that lacked personal relationships to him and his friends, and acted in a more strict, calculating way.[176]

Carlgren had bought MoDo shares up to the price of SEK 700, so when the MoDo share price fell dramatically during the general stock market decline in the second half of 1990, the price fell far below the one that had been set when he had used them as security. In that situation SE-Banken demanded the immediate payback of a loan for which the interest payments amounted to SEK 20 million. Carlgren went into a meeting at the bank full of confidence, but it did not turn out as he had expected. The bank assumed an unresponsive attitude when listening to Carlgren's explanations of the situation and expectations for the future. If he did not pay back in time, the bank would liquidate its securities.[177] According to Carlgren himself, a Finnish bank had provided a guarantee that made it possible for Sanna Holding to pay the demanded amount, but for some reason SE-Banken did not accept that bank security. Carlgren also looked up MoDo's former Head of France, Lejeune, to get a loan mediated by him, but that path, too, failed.[178]

By the second half of 1990, the larger shareholdings in MoDo were distributed as follows (percentages of votes and of capital): Lundberg 25 (30), Carlgren 21 (11), the Kempe foundations 19 (10) and Marieberg 11 (21). In that situation the banks, starting with SE-Banken, demanded liquidation of Carlgren's securities. The loans with interest due for payment were so large that Carlgren had no choice but to sell his block of MoDo shares.[179] MoDo's main bank Handelsbanken was rather unaffected by the Swedish bank crisis, but still it did not treat Carlgren particularly well (many leading actors described the bank's acting as 'indecently rough'). Handelsbanken's interests probably did not fully overlap with that of the Kempe–Carlgren dynasty and MoDo, since the bank also had MoDo's rival SCA as one of its most important customers. Moreover, the Handelsbanken sphere had a dominating ownership position in SCA (but not in MoDo). Added to all that, several leading Handelsbanken actors had had difficulties over the years understanding Carlgren's approach and saw him therefore as a person associated with high business risks. So, by November 1990, Carlgren was forced to give up his and, with it, the family's control over MoDo.

Due to the pre-emption agreement, Carlgren first turned to the Kempe foundations and offered his MoDo shares (including those held by Sanna Holding). He also offered the foundations some time for consideration.[180] However, according to some actors, that process was halted. There were voices claiming that the Kempe foundations actually refrained from buying the offered shares due to regulations limiting their right to incur large debts and high risk.[181] However, some family members claim that Carlgren sold his holdings without even asking the Kempe foundations. Instead, in his negotiations with the leaders of SCA, he had promised them that he could convince the Kempe foundations that they, too, ought to sell their shares to SCA. He also mentioned that – if necessary – he could replace the foundations' current Chair Carl Kempe Jr.[182]

CEO Löf had for some time worked towards helping Lundberg become a new major shareholder in MoDo. Lundberg had bought quite a lot of KVBs and, in spite of poorer returns, converted them to MoDo shares, with the result that he controlled a large portion of that company's capital. So with permission from Carlgren, Löf contacted Lundberg and asked if he was interested in making a bid for Carlgren's MoDo shares. Lundberg gave a positive answer. MoDo's directors took different positions regarding what buyer to favour: Lundberg or SCA. Some of them, for example Nabseth, based their stance on the calculations that spoke for a merger between MoDo and SCA. Director Wallander remained neutral, probably also because he did not want to lose Lundberg as a Handelsbanken customer.[183]

Carlgren could not present a complete picture of his own financial situation, and neither Frans Kempe Jr nor the old retainer Altbäck could help him with that. It was particularly difficult to get an overview of Carlgren's total debt burden.[184] Löf therefore asked Harry Diedrichs (MoDo; Head of Legal Affairs) to join the Swedish investment bank Öhmans (Carlgren's adviser) to calculate what share price Carlgren needed to 'survive' the crisis – calculations about which Lundberg was informed. When the calculations were finished and the conclusion drawn, Löf got Carlgren's permission to call Lundberg and tell him about the suggested share price.[185] Lundberg arrived in Stockholm from Zürich the same evening and met Carlgren the following day. Lundberg had the impression that they were close to an agreement, that is to say, that he would be the buyer of Carlgren's MoDo holding.[186]

Lundberg offered SEK 550/share – a figure that was far above the current stock exchange price of SEK 325.[187] That was close to the share price that Carlgren needed to escape the crisis situation unscathed. He needed an additional SEK 50 per share, and tried using Löf as middleman to convince Lundberg to raise his already generous bid – but that attempt failed.[188] Then SCA entered the scene and offered the same price as Lundberg. In that situation Lundberg decided not to raise his bid, partly because he was uncertain about how far SCA was prepared to go. Moreover, Lundberg was of the opinion that he and Carlgren already were close to a deal. However, Lundberg noticed that the buying process was dragging on, so he began to think that there might be a catch somewhere – that somebody else was involved as well. He delivered his proposal on Friday 6 December with a time limit set to Monday 9 December at 18.00; such a long period for consideration was in his eyes generous – almost 'adventurous'. It was at the end of the time limit, at 17.59, that Carlgren called Lundberg and told him that he had sold his MoDo holding to SCA for the same price that Lundberg had offered.[189] At 19.30, SCA Chair Rydin called Lundberg and confirmed the deal with Carlgren.[190] There was also a rumour that a new long-term agreement had been made that secured a mutual pre-emptive right between SCA and the Kempe foundations.

It was an emotionally loaded moment for Carlgren when he had to give up his control over MoDo, the heirloom of the Kempe dynasty. It disappeared as an integrating symbol for the family. However, the holdings of the Kempe foundations remained, representing around 12–15 per cent of the votes, with Carl Kempe Jr as its leading actor.[191]

So, after some thinking and discussions with advisers, Carlgren had decided to sell his MoDo shares to SCA. He was of the opinion that a constellation of MoDo plus SCA was industrially sound, and he also found the price acceptable. Like several distinguished business actors at the time, Carlgren was sceptical regarding Lundberg, who (still) had a reputation as a short-term financial capitalist rather than as a long-term industrialist.[192] Carlgren's scepticism was foremost built on his experiences from Lundberg's earlier buying into Holmens Bruk, something that had 'irritated' his friend Joja Bonnier as well.[193] Several actors saw Lundberg as unthinkable as Chair of MoDo both because he lacked experience within the forest-based industry, and because he was regarded to be an opportunistic financial player. However, it was actually during this period that his reputation grew, and a decade later Lundberg was described rather as a serious industrial capitalist with a low-risk profile and staying power.[194]

Carlgren also believed that the Kempe foundations would have a better position in an SCA constellation, as it was run by executives and not by a dominant long-term shareholder. In due time, SCA's structure might create an opportunity for the Carlgren–Kempe dynasty to get back into the driver's seat. Carlgren also began a 'comeback' attempt by trying to replace Carl Kempe Jr as Chair in the Kempe foundations. Thus, to Carlgren the SCA path contrasted favourably to one where Lundberg took over the helm in MoDo, as the latter outcome would marginalize the Kempe dynasty's influence 'forever'.[195]

In that situation, Marieberg, too, decided to sell its MoDo holding to avoid being put in an awkward position. It offered their MoDo shares to Lundberg, but he was not interested. He had already offered a high sum for all of Carlgren's MoDo shares, so he was not willing to pay a similar market price (SEK 330) also for Marieberg's holding in MoDo.[196] SCA, however, bought the 'Marieberg shares' for that price, as its top management had included MoDo in its strategic vision for decades. They saw great advantages to closer cooperation between the two companies, particularly regarding printing paper.[197] For half a year, SCA had analysed the possibilities for entering MoDo as a major shareholder. Thus, it can be said that the purchase of a substantial holding in that company was no passing fancy, although the whole process moved very quickly in the end. Through this step, SCA sought to make both companies better without tying up lots of capital; buying Lundberg's MoDo holding as well was, therefore, not an option.[198]

With short notice, SCA's Chair Rydin summoned the company's board, and at its meeting on 9 December 1990 the formal decision was taken to carry out the acquisition of the Carlgren holding in MoDo on the same terms as Lundberg previously had offered. SCA also bought the block that Marieberg had offered. Thus, in this new shareholder situation, SCA controlled around 30 per cent of the votes, Lundberg 25 per cent and the Kempe foundations around 19 per cent. The result was a deadlock situation, as none of the shareholders were able to form a working majority.

On 11 December, SCA's leading actors held a press conference announcing the purchase. Many of its participants interpreted the situation as one where SCA in principle had acquired – taken control of – MoDo. For example, there was quite a lot of talk regarding coming changes on MoDo's board. However, SCA Chair Rydin declared that SCA had asked Carlgren to stay as MoDo Chair as long as he was capable and suitable to hold that position.[199] Carl Kempe Jr had been invited to appear at SCA's press conference, mainly because of the agreement between the Kempe foundations and SCA regarding a mutual pre-emptive right for their MoDo shares. When Lundberg had learned about that agreement, he called Carl Kempe Jr and explained to him why such an ownership situation would be disadvantageous for MoDo's future development. He also mentioned that lots of small talk in the Swedish business community indicated that SCA intended to split up MoDo. Carl Kempe Jr was influenced both by Lundberg and by the on-going discussions among other leading Swedish businessmen. When Carlgren once again tried to convince him to join forces with him and SCA, Carl Kempe Jr refused. Instead, the Kempe foundations joined forces with Lundberg. Consequently, Carl Kempe Jr decided not to attend the press conference. As a result, Carlgren asked MoDo's CEO Löf to participate, which he did.[200] It was probably during all those discussions that a sense of mutual trust began to materialize between Carl Kempe Jr and Lundberg.[201]

As Carl Kempe Jr saw it, SCA's intention was to integrate and improve the two companies' printing paper businesses, and then sell out the fine paper and cardboard operations. Therefore, to get over the crucial 50 per cent voting power in MoDo required to pursue these actions, SCA needed the MoDo block controlled by the Kempe foundations. However, the foundations' shares were not for sale.[202] Still, SCA's CEO pushed this matter hard – he really wanted to carry out his vision, as a process that made SCA a majority shareholder in MoDo would permit a restructuring of all its businesses, including the sale of certain units. However, in the current situation, when SCA was 'only' a very large shareholder, it had interests that obviously did not coincide with those of MoDo. For example, SCA did not want to see a new printing paper machine in Braviken, that is to say, a competitor with another agenda making things difficult for SCA's own plants. That was a tricky situation for SCA's MoDo directors to handle. In dealing with such potential conflicts, Rydin was regarded by most MoDo actors as behaving in a more 'statesman-like' manner (he did not favour SCA), whereas Martin-Löf sometimes could be more partial.

According to several members of MoDo's top management, SCA's purchase led to a bad atmosphere in MoDo, since, from that moment, the long-time rivalry took place on the board where SCA was represented by its two most distinguished actors, namely Chair Rydin and CEO Martin-Löf. That entrance almost paralyzed Löf in his role as CEO of MoDo – he did not appreciate the new split shareholder situation, although he tried to stay loyal to both factions. Löf stressed that it was important to keep in mind that no merger had occurred. The whole situation was not improved by the fact that Löf got Martin-Löf as one of the directors, since the personal chemistry between the two had been rather poor for quite some time.[203]

Looking at possible integration effects between MoDo and SCA, one could note that their locales overlapped, which previously had created a competition regarding timber sourcing that now could be put to an end (solved by hierarchy). SCA was still foremost a hygiene and packaging company, although with both fine paper and newsprint businesses. MoDo's core business was fine paper, but it also produced fine cardboard and newsprint/journal papers. So there were substantial overlaps in certain of the business fields, and therefore opportunities both for restructuring and rationalization.[204]

The significant cultural differences that existed between the two companies were a major obstacle. SCA was mainly a 'motley crew of companies' stemming from the Kreuger epoch, while MoDo instead had grown organically. Moreover, MoDo had always been linked to the upper class (the Kempe family) and long time horizons, while SCA instead was associated with highly qualified, salaried professionals.[205] Added to all that, one could note that Löf was sceptical regarding the merits of joint ventures ('joint failures') primarily because of the associated lack of control of the cash flows.[206]

On 14 December, Carl Kempe Jr, Lundberg and Martin-Löf met and came to an agreement regarding the principles for composing a new MoDo board and the procedure for finding a new Chair. Lundberg was eager to have a neutral and independent person at that position, and that proposition was approved by both Rydin and Carl Kempe Jr. MoDo CEO Löf asked an adviser[207] for candidates that matched that criterion, and he suggested the current Chair of Ericsson, Svedberg, a name that Löf decided to bring up for discussion with Lundberg and Rydin. To SCA's leading actors, however, the treatment of Carlgren had become embarrassing, as they had given – and even made public – a promise to Carlgren that he was to continue as MoDo Chair. Later, during New Year's Weekend, Carlgren met with Martin-Löf at a Swedish winter resort and was informed that Svedberg would be elected to serve on the MoDo board and be appointed Chair by that body. Carlgren was also told that he was not to become a member of that board, although SCA intended to nominate him for an Honorary Chair position.[208]

Thus, on 1 January 1991, MoDo's board was recomposed and five new members were appointed, namely Larsson, Martin-Löf (CEO SCA), Rydin (Chair SCA), Svedberg (Chair) and Welin. Larsson and Welin were rather closely linked to Lundberg and – obviously – Martin-Löf and Rydin to SCA. At the same time, Braun, Engman, Karhola-Wettergren and Nordin left MoDo's board. At the following AGM, Mårtensson, CEO of Handelsbanken, joined the board, replacing Wallander, who retired because of his age.[209]

Although Svedberg was well known in the Swedish business society as former CEO and current Chair of Ericsson, his connection to both the forest-based industry and its leading actors was weak. He knew only some of MoDo's major shareholders and directors. Moreover, he had never met MoDo's CEO Löf and only a few times talked to SCA's CEO Martin-Löf. Actually, it was only director Wallander that knew Svedberg well. As he had moved from the position of CEO to Chair at Ericsson, he had time available for the new task as MoDo Chair (and he was also a person who liked 'new challenges'). When Svedberg decided to accept the appointment, he was aware of the unusual situation that existed on the board, namely that two of the directors were affiliated with SCA, a tough competitor to MoDo. However, as he saw it, that was not a big problem, because the clashes of interest foremost stemmed from operational issues – not the strategic or financial ones. Svedberg did not know the intentions of the major owners, but he observed that both factions acted cautiously – despite several talks, not much happened at that level. What he also noticed was that SCA was particularly anxious about the company's relationship to Carl Kempe Jr and tried to make a good impression on him.[210]

Almost immediately after his sell-out to SCA, Carlgren made clear that he intended to make a comeback in MoDo through the Kempe foundations. In the early 1990s, the boards of the two foundations were composed of four members each. Three members were family members, and they had a seat in both foundations. The fourth member in each of the foundations was appointed by the state (Dau and Köhler, one in each foundation[211]). Carl Kempe Jr had the Chair position (with a casting vote) with his wife Margareta as deputy,[212] and the other two regular members were Viviann Kempe, with her brother Frans Kempe Jr as deputy, and Anders Kempe with Sven Kempe as deputy (cf. Figure 8.1).

In the beginning of January 1991, Carlgren replaced Frans Kempe Jr as deputy for Viviann Kempe. From that platform he expected that he – as the 'headman' of the dynasty – soon would be able to take control of the foundations and make them co-operate with SCA. Carlgren had informed SCA about this plan during the negotiations that took place before his sell-out to SCA, and it appealed to them. It might also have contributed to their promise to Carlgren that he could become MoDo's next Chair.[213] Carl Kempe Jr opposed that switch, but Frans Kempe Jr put forward several arguments for why Carlgren ought to be appointed. First, in the current situation, the foundations needed as much knowledge and experience of the forest-based industries as possible and all the international networks that were available – and Carlgren possessed these crucial qualities. Second, the pre-emption right was still valid for SCA and the Kempe foundations, and that agreement ensured that the foundations were not run over by some new majority, because then the A-shares – in practice – would be deflated to B-shares and lose value. The foundations had the opportunity to make arrangements if SCA wanted to sell, and in such a situation either buy the holding or place them somewhere else. Due to all his contacts, having Carlgren as a board member would improve the foundations' opportunities to develop favourably. Third, and finally, to appoint Carlgren the new deputy director would also show that the dynasty stood united – something that protected both the dynasty as such and the foundations' capital.

When appointed, Carlgren sought to oust Carl Kempe Jr from the board, as he did not side with the same major shareholder in MoDo as Carlgren did. Carlgren's intent was to join with SCA to push Lundberg out of MoDo.[214] Already a few days after completing his deal with SCA, Carlgren had worried about the rules stipulating how the Kempe foundations had to vote on MoDo AGMs. After a consultation with Browaldh (former Chair of Handelsbanken), he believed that there was a regulation that stipulated different voters for each of the foundations. However, when he was shown the minutes from March 1990, where the voting rules were written down, he concluded that the rules instead had been changed so that the family factions should vote jointly.

SCA's proposals regarding closer co-operation with MoDo, common industrial plans, acquisition of the Kempe foundations' shares in MoDo and a merger between the two companies were all rejected by Carl Kempe Jr using his casting vote on the board of the (divided) Kempe foundations. He was reluctant to even discuss these issues at its meetings.[215] Carl Kempe Jr, supported by his wife Margareta, had come to the conclusion that it was best for the dynasty that the Kempe foundations sided with Lundberg. Viviann Kempe and Anders Kempe, however, preferred SCA. They thought that the industrial structure and the identity as 'a Norrland company' would benefit from a solution where SCA took the lead.

The family antagonism grew as it became obvious that the Chair, Carl Kempe Jr, supported by the directors appointed by the government,[216] advocated Lundberg as the best harbour for MoDo. The divided family view regarding MoDo's future broke several generations of unity, and eventually the remaining SCA-friendly ancestors on the foundations' boards were squeezed out.[217] Thus, in the end, the Kempe foundations decided to support Lundberg,[218] and, for the first time ever, leading actors of the Kempe dynasty had become antagonists in a fight for control in which the family heirloom was at stake.

New Chair Svedberg noticed that Carlgren had ambitions, and that he kept an office space at MoDo's HQ (now and then Carlgren contacted Svedberg and explained how MoDo ought to be run). Svedberg was not particularly fond of that arrangement, so Carlgren had to leave his office. However, the new Chair did not solve Löf's difficult position of having to serve two large owners that did not always express similar views, and Svedberg had the impression that Löf was somewhat uncomfortable in that role. Löf's situation was certainly difficult – earlier Carlgren had limited his freedom of action, and Löf had also been encircled by Carl Kempe Jr, who had a strong ownership position (the Kempe foundations). However, in spite of the radically changed ownership situation, Löf still paid attention to Carlgren's views, although Svedberg encouraged him to go his own way and take a firmer grip. In that situation, Svedberg even pondered whether Löf ought to be replaced. However, Svedberg's stay with MoDo was brief (he left in April 1992), as he got an offer to become CEO of a large Swedish bank in severe crisis (SE-Banken, part of the Wallenberg sphere). That made it necessary for him to leave MoDo, since that company belonged to the competing business sphere (the Handelsbanken one).[219]

At the beginning of 1991, SCA was the largest shareholder in MoDo controlling about one-third of the votes and 16 per cent of the capital. To get strong voting power in MoDo and the most from SCA's large investment, SCA's CEO Martin-Löf kept working hard to convince the directors of the Kempe foundations that it would be best for MoDo if they swapped their MoDo shares for SCA ones. Such a move would make it possible to take advantage of the potential integration effects that existed, and make SCA's investment in MoDo shares worthwhile. In SCA's opinion, substantial synergy returns could be expected from a co-ordination of the two companies' printing paper businesses, sawmill plants and fine paper operations.[220] Viviann and Anders Kempe met with Martin-Löf and agreed that he should address the foundations in a letter (with a copy to each director) and make his case. Chair Carl Kempe Jr immediately and preliminarily answered the letter stressing that it was MoDo's CEO and board with its new Chair that were responsible for the discussions on how to co-ordinate MoDo's efforts with SCA. Several leading actors – including MoDo's board members – had raised their eyebrows when they learned that SCA's CEO had written that letter to the Kempe foundations stating that MoDo's current strategy was inadequate; they were surprised because SCA's CEO was himself a board member and consequently also responsible for the 'poor MoDo strategy'.[221]

Martin-Löf also invited the board members of the Kempe foundations to a seminar where he intended to give a detailed presentation of the future positive effects of an integration and rationalization of the two companies' overlapping businesses.[222] There were calculations showing synergy returns amounting to SEK 1–1.5 billion.[223] Martin-Löf also talked to the directors one by one. All of them indicated afterwards that they might be interested in allying with SCA rather than with Lundberg.[224] However, in the end, after a board meeting, the Kempe foundations declared that they had turned down SCA's invitation.[225] Consequently, SCA's top management's frustration increased. The company's expensive holding in MoDo did not provide the integration benefits that they had promised their own board. The MoDo share price sank like a stone, and SCA tried to regain some of the lost value by trading in options. At that time (May 1992) there were articles published in the Swedish business press[226] that Lundberg had tried to get MoDo CEO Löf replaced by Zetterberg, the former CEO of Holmens Bruk.

9.7 STRENGTHENING THE FINE PAPER PATH

During the shareholder stalemate period (1991–93) there were several attempts to establish some kind of co-operation between MoDo and SCA, regarding both the newsprint and the fine paper businesses. The main idea was to establish co-operation in the printing paper business. SCA foremost wanted to get hold of the relatively modern Holmens Bruk and offered in return Wifstavarf, an old fine paper mill, and Ortviken, an old newsprint mill. In terms of operations, MoDo was stronger in the overlapping fields, but from a shareholder perspective SCA was the stronger part because of its large ownership in MoDo, and it was from that position SCA's leading actors pushed for further co-operation.[227]

Both CEOs tried to find projects that provided either synergies or structural benefits. Regarding sawmills, the talks turned into concrete actions, but as MoDo and SCA had differing views on most crucial matters, attempts in all other areas failed. For example, seeing the need for substantial investments in Husum, MoDo Paper's head Roland Martin-Löf (brother to SCA's CEO Sverker) suggested increased co-operation with SCA's Östrand plant including linked export transports, but that idea never went far.[228] There were also rumours within MoDo that the company would be split up if SCA got control – the grapevine conveyed that Roland Martin-Löf advocated such ideas. However, both Löf and Lundberg opposed such a division of MoDo.[229] Making matters worse was the long-standing difficult relationship between the CEOs of the two companies. The strain between them intensified as a consequence of the familial relationship between Roland and Sverker, which cut across the two companies.

It was also rumoured that Roland Martin-Löf had aspirations to succeed Löf one day as CEO of MoDo. There were indications that the former now and then talked to Carlgren about Löf's performance (and not always in an appreciative way), and things did not improve when Roland Martin-Löf hinted that substantial personnel changes ought to be carried out at MoDo's top executive levels. When that view became known Löf fired him both because of his critique of MoDo's management, and because he had sided with his brother Sverker and supported SCA's vision rather than the one promoted by Lundberg and most of MoDo's executives. While the principal reason for that discharge was unclear to many actors, it was obvious that lots of emotions were involved (particularly) between, on the one hand, Löf, and, on the other hand, the Martin-Löf brothers.[230]

The year 1991 was a tough one for MoDo. CEO Löf had a long list of potential divestments: Workington, Wargön, Silverdalen, Domsjö, Skärblacka and Bureå.[231] The Domsjö site was once again in crisis, and a closing down of the CTMP plant was discussed at the board. Bureå was shut down, but Wargön was allowed to continue. As there was no longer a need for the Graningeverken holding, it was put on the sales list. As almost always, various ways to release capital were talked about, and Skärblacka, sacks and certain forest resources were brought up for discussion. The board also expressed concern that the investments in some of the existing plants were neglected. Some more expansive issues were also considered, such as acquiring the remaining 75 per cent shareholding in the newsprint producer MD Papier and/or the Spanish fine paper wholesaler Commercial Paper Aldi. There were also discussions within the board regarding the relationship between the total plant capacity and the available forest resources. Director

Welin was rather critical and claimed that MoDo's capacity was built out far beyond the possible local/regional timber sourcing, making import of distant timber necessary (even from as far away as Chile). Later Lundberg tried to handle that problem by trying to acquire the Boxholm forests, which were perfectly located with respect to the investments in Braviken. However, another actor outdid MoDo in the bidding process.[232]

Lejeune and his partners were interested in selling their shareholding majority in Calanda in 1991 (the Alizay site), and Löf argued for an acquisition, which then included both Alicel and Alipap. MoDo also began to negotiate with Lejeune, who indicated a price of SEK 1.5 billion. There was an earlier agreement giving MoDo the right to acquire Calanda's holding, but the price Lejeune now suggested was far above the level that Carlgren claimed previously had been agreed. Carlgren was of the opinion that a fair price was around SEK 0.5–0.75 billion, but as he was no longer part of MoDo operations, that figure did not come up in the negotiation process. In that situation, Lejeune also asked a French bank to look for other purchasers.[233]

Aside from the proposed price level that Carlgren in particular found to be impudent, there were other concerns regarding dealing with Calanda. The MoDo actors remembered how Calanda had commissioned a contractor a few years earlier to manufacture a fine paper machine (Alipap) next to Alicel in Alizay on a turnkey basis. That project was a disaster that had ended up in court.[234] The current proposal to MoDo from the shareholder consortia that Lejeune headed was 'buy it all or sell the 17 per cent holding'. The situation was complicated because there were probably other buyers around – MoDo believed that (at least) Finnish Enso Gutzeit was interested.[235] To put less pressure on its already strained financial resources, MoDo considered acquiring Alizay together with a partner. Roland Martin-Löf, at the time the new Head of MoDo Paper (that also contained MoDo Cell[236]), believed that the Chilean company CMPC would be the most suitable partner (MoDo had co-operated with CMPC for some time) since it produced the kind of pulp that Alizay used. However, as CEO Löf was sceptical towards joint ventures – and particularly towards those with actors from 'the other side of the planet' – that path was rather soon abandoned. To him, such distances were not merely a matter of geographical distances or divergent time zones. There were also cultural and institutional differences that tended to create problems and particularly so in 50–50 constructs.[237]

However, MoDo continued its acquisition attempt, as the calculations in French currency looked good (but soon the price began to slip upwards). Moreover, the vision to become the leading fine paper company in the European office market seemed right, and that presupposed both a market presence and a production capacity on the continent. To MoDo, it was important to have a substantial share of the production within the EC, as it was supposed that Sweden would not enter that constellation. Alizay represented a possibility for MoDo to become an inside actor and avoid both customs duties and French protectionism.[238] Most top executives were tempted by the opportunity to increase the company's shareholding in the group from 17 per cent to full control. CEO Löf could also provide strong arguments for the purchase, and his track record and reputation gave these motives extra weight. As usual, the main problem was that MoDo's financial situation was strained, and that made many board members hesitate. However, Löf put his personal capital 'in the pot' and eventually had his way, very much because the board was a rather weak reviewer,[239] the shareholder situation was troublesome (a stalemate situation) and the Chair was a newcomer in the industry.

The Head of Finance (Svensson) saw two possible paths for the future expansion of MoDo. One was to increase its newsprint business (both production and market share) through an acquisition of the remaining 75 per cent in MD Papier; the other was to strengthen the fine paper business and develop the plants in Alizay and Pont St Maxence. Löf wanted to see MoDo as the buyer of Calanda, but at the same time he also wanted to increase MoDo's holding in MD Papier (so that it exceeded 50%). His deputy CEO Engman favoured the MD Papier path. The SCA directors on the board were probably interested in acquiring MD Papier for SCA, so they preferred an Alizay investment for MoDo.[240]

The top management team and several of the board members were divided on how to handle the Alizay site. Chair Svedberg stated that he knew too little about the industry to make judgements wholly on his own, and asked the CEO whether MoDo had any commitment to go beyond PPSM's current 17 per cent shareholding in Calanda. Unfortunately, none of the directors were able to answer clearly (Carlgren was probably the one that possessed the best information on that topic). Svedberg then invited each member of the top management to explain individually and confidentially what path forward they favoured. All of them supported the investment, which moved Svedberg's decision towards a 'yes'.[241] Welin was one of the hesitant directors, but as he was a newcomer to the board, he did not act with authority. As 'everybody else' in the industry bought companies (e.g. MoDo's Swedish rivals SCA and Stora), top management wanted MoDo to grow, too, and Welin did not object to such a strategy. Moreover, a 'no' would implicitly also mean a step towards replacing the current CEO, with all the extra uncertainty such a move would bring about.[242] Lundberg, another relatively new director, was not particularly enthusiastic about an acquisition either, but despite his current strong minority position, he decided not to act. Yet, his neutral stance contributed to the outcome, as did SCA's reluctant 'yes'. Thus, in reality the board's decision was very much based on faith in the judgement of MoDo's top management.

In May 1991, the board finally decided that MoDo should attempt to buy the remaining shares in Calanda (83%) to become the sole owner of the company, and in July the acquisition was formally made for an estimated FRF 1.5 billion.[243] One month before the deal was final, there was a rumour that Lejeune had been about to sell the Alizay plants to Metsä-Serla, and that information might have influenced the price. MoDo's successful French wholesaling activities were simultaneously handed over to the sellers (that was necessary to be able to finance the purchase). One of MoDo's top managers, Nordstrand, found it problematic that MoDo bought the Alizay unit at such a high price before Alipap had even been put into production. Nordstrand believed that the price level showed that Lejeune had defrauded Carlgren completely – Carlgren had believed that Lejeune's previous purchase of the major holding in Alizay (i.e. Alicel) was done on his behalf as his 'front', and that MoDo would be able to buy it back later on easy terms.[244]

Some time after the deal, Sweden unexpectedly devalued[245] and the crown fell about 20 per cent, which made Swedish pulp and paper producers very competitive. However, the strengthening of the French currency in relation to the Swedish one, together with the depressed trade conditions in 1991–93, wiped out the benefits of the Alizay purchase for quite a long time. However, the timing was a catastrophe,[246] and according to director Mårtensson, it meant an extra cost of around SEK 1 billion for MoDo. Moreover, those who had advocated the purchase lost internal prestige and also some discretion. The badly timed acquisition also increased the tensions among the already divided directors (the SCA faction vs the Lundberg one).[247]

An alternative strategic path was also still on the table: to invest further in newsprint by purchasing the remaining (75%) stock in MD Papier. The Head of Newsprint Lundin worked hard to make that deal, and he had been successful in lowering the price. MD Papier suited MoDo well, as its medium weight coated (MWC) was a good complement to Wargön's LWC. If the financial resources were lacking, he instead suggested a sale of MoDo's 25 per cent holding, as he had found it difficult to work from a minority position in Germany. However, a Finnish competitor outmatched the company's bid for 'the rest' of MD Papier, leaving MoDo still with its minority holding.[248]

Together, that acquisition failure and the large investment in Alizay 'armoured' MoDo's strategy for the coming years – fine paper would continue as MoDo's core business. However, Nordstrand found it remarkable that the acquisition of MD Papier did not occur, considering Lundberg's strong position in MoDo and his care for Holmens Bruk and its (newsprint) businesses.[249] Lundberg had visited MD Papier and was exposed to hard selling of newsprint as an alternative to fine paper. So, CEO Löf would have to work extra hard for his fine paper vision, especially since Lundin and his newsprint management team physically were placed near Lundberg in Norrköping.

After the acquisition of Alizay, MoDo's strategic decision-making process took on a new turn. The dissatisfaction with the current procedure was widespread among MoDo's directors. It was foremost Lundberg that in the second half of 1991 initiated more systematic strategic discussions at the executive levels (and made the board work as an active sparring partner for the CEO and his team). The outcome of those discussions was a business structure that lasted for several years. It stressed that the company had to concentrate its activities. It had become possible to follow that path as many of the emotional ties to the 'old' MoDo simultaneously weakened.[250]

MoDo's strained financial standing in 1992 resulted in the sale of its Graningeverken holding (10%). Still, MoDo made a substantial loss that year. As noted earlier Chair Svedberg had to leave because of his appointment as the new CEO of SE-Banken. Lundberg did not support SCA Chair Rydin's idea of a co-chairmanship, so Carl Kempe Jr, Lundberg, Löf and Rydin together asked Önnesjö if he would accept the Chair position at MoDo. He agreed, although he realized that it meant that he had to Chair MoDo during a most difficult period. His track record and his deep knowledge of the forest-based industry infused the Chair position with power and prestige, particularly in relation to the company's top management. Önnesjö came to preside during a period when MoDo, foremost because of Lundberg's efforts, moved from being a heavily indebted company to becoming a financially healthy one. Former Holmens Bruk's Chair Önnesjö's strong support of MoDo's ambition to invest in a third newsprint machine at Braviken also made a difference, a move probably no Chair from northern Sweden would have advocated with such enthusiasm. Instead, such a person would most certainly have invested rather in the surroundings of Iggesund and/or Husum (i.e. in cardboard and/or fine paper).[251]

In 1992, the board informed the employees that the pulp plant at Bureå was to be closed in one year's time. Nonetheless, MoDo continued to buy wholesalers in Europe, this time Spanish Commercial Paper Aldi (up to 95% [1994]). MoDo also increased its holding in the Swedish wholesaler Svenskt Papper to 95 per cent, and even considered a large investment at Hallsta (printing paper). During the 1992 discussions about new business and structural opportunities, Chair Önnesjö claimed that Sweden's recent membership application to the EU (in 1991) had made European corporations at least as interesting as the domestic rival SCA.[252] Moreover, when he familiarized himself with the MoDo–SCA issue, he became convinced that the expected synergy-based returns (SEK 1–2 billion) had no place in current business reality – they related to the days when the companies were expanding and building new paper machines. In such a situation the two companies could have co-ordinated their investments and benefitted substantially from a joint effort. Under current circumstances, however, Önnesjö saw finding ways of weeding out excess capacity as the crucial strategic issue.[253]

9.8 LUNDBERG BECOMES MODO'S NEW MAJOR SHAREHOLDER

Like several other leading businessmen MoDo's CEO Löf publicly criticized the crisis decisions taken by the Conservative government and the actions of the Swedish Central Bank. In October 1992, Löf claimed that the discontent with the currency and interest handling was of such a magnitude that leading representatives from the forest-based industry ought to approach the Prime Minister to try to bring about changes. Löf argued (1) that the Swedish crown was overvalued, (2) that the interest rate had to be lowered to below 10 per cent, (3) that a trade boom would not solve the (underlying) problems, (4) that most economists do not know what they are talking about (because they have never seen a production site) and (5) that those economists that have suggested that Sweden should tie its crown to the German mark must be totally incompetent. Löf added that the industry's (public) acceptance of the government's crisis response could be explained primarily by the fact the government was a 'bourgeois' one – not a Social Democratic one (as it used to be).[254] However, as mentioned above, Sweden abandoned the fixed currency rate in 1992, and that action substantially devalued its currency. All actors in the forest-based industry welcomed that decision.

The newly appointed MoDo director Mårtensson noted that the relationship between MoDo and SCA was tense. The situation was unstable, and, particularly for MoDo's sake, it had to be resolved immediately. Despite their careful preparations SCA might have acquired the MoDo holding more on intuitive grounds and then tried to take advantage of the resulting situation in a better-thought-out way, but that ambition encountered difficulties. The year 1992 was miserable for the Swedish forest-based industry, and particularly so for MoDo. The company's economic performance was poor, and the debts overwhelming – MoDo simply fought for its survival. However, the serious crisis 'united' the major owners and top executives in a joint effort to save the company. The situation was actually so bad that several previously 'impossible' decisions were taken, such as the sale of Bureå and Domsjö (and that without a 'veto' from Carl Kempe Jr). Even power plants and forests were sold.[255]

During a break at MoDo's board meeting on 7 September 1992 SCA's Chair Rydin informed MoDo's Chair Önnesjö that SCA had decided to develop its businesses separately from MoDo. As a consequence, SCA's CEO had to leave his board position at MoDo.[256] Önnesjö welcomed that decision, as the previous board situation had been problematic. The presence of a top manager in a competing company's board usually hinders effective work processes, because information that might be of value for that competitor could be neither revealed nor discussed in that arena. However, Önnesjö saw no problem with a continuous presence on MoDo's board for Rydin, as he worked at the shareholder level (and since SCA was a major owner).[257]

The year 1993 began almost as bad as 1992. The investment in Alizay was still close to a catastrophe, although the uncertainty regarding ownership had been sorted out. The equity in Alizay had to be increased, and around SEK 1 billion was therefore put in to stabilize the situation. Moreover, there was a need for a write-down of SEK 2 billion. However, one has to keep in mind that much of the bad result in the expanded French business emanated from the huge change of value of the Swedish crown. Media speculated about a bid for MoDo from a consortium consisting of SCA and International Paper, but it did not materialize. Even the controversial issue of splitting up MoDo was discussed, but it was regarded as impossible to carry out in the current situation. Another 'classic' issue was what to do with the 25 per cent holding in MD Papier. Due to the stretched financial standing, the board appointed a special task force that would analyse the liquidity situation and suggest necessary actions. It was composed of the major shareholder's most distinguished representatives, namely Carl Kempe Jr, Lundberg and Rydin. Their conclusion was that MoDo needed a capital infusion amounting to about SEK 1.2 billion.

In March 1993, Lundberg initiated renewed informal discussions with Rydin. The two industrial leaders agreed that the strategic discussions had to be revitalized and established a working group for that purpose selected from the two shareholder factions. The group was composed of Zetterberg, Enander, Löf and Carl Kempe Jr. All possible paths, that is to say, operative and financial strategies, would be analysed and presented to the board. Among the topics to be explored were a possible co-operation with SCA and the question of whether Holmens Bruk or Iggesund was the best unit to keep. However, that group never made any substantial impact, as the ownership situation soon changed and made the constellation obsolete.

Lundberg experienced the atmosphere in MoDo as rather bad during those days and began thinking about what to do. At the same time, Rydin gradually became fed up with the messy situation, as MoDo had rejected all proposals regarding operative co-ordination. As a final attempt to solve the situation, SCA had suggested that MoDo should be divided in such a way that SCA should take control of Holmen Paper (printing paper), fine paper should be sold and Lundberg should get Iggesund (cardboard). However, most other actors that were involved in the governance of MoDo turned that proposal down. As a result of this refusal (and other obstructions), MoDo had almost become an ugly word in SCA. SCA's CEO Martin-Löf had left the MoDo board, and on the whole SCA merely seemed interested in getting out of its engagement in MoDo in an honourable way.[258]

During the first half of 1993, the company lost around half a billion SEK, so at that time MoDo really needed a capital infusion – it was heading for a collapse. Otherwise the board would be forced to split up MoDo (e.g. sell the Holmen units to SCA), and that in a weak bargaining position. SCA actually might have believed that MoDo's poor financial situation would force the company to sell its newsprint business to them – something that SCA had wanted for a long time. However, gradually Rydin discovered that Lundberg had serious and long-term ambitions for MoDo, which became obvious when Lundberg advocated the idea that the company needed a large new issue of shares to solve its high indebtedness and liquidity problems. MoDo manager Nordstrand speculated that a personal reason for Lundberg's risk-taking might have been that he – as local patriot – disliked selling a Norrköping-based company (Holmens Bruk) to one located in Sundsvall (SCA).[259] In any case, Lundberg guaranteed his company's full participation in the new issue of shares (SEK 1.5 billion), and he actually even bought more shares in MoDo. That commitment to invest made the MoDo organization happy – especially Chair Önnesjö and CEO Löf, who both understood the seriousness of the situation. Reluctantly, SCA joined Lundberg and subscribed. The Kempe foundations eventually subscribed for shares, too, although that was perhaps not fully in accordance with their statutes.

CEO Löf described the new issue of shares as a necessary move. To him, it was the only alternative, as there was nothing MoDo could sell at a decent price. Löf became a bit concerned when SCA tried to excuse itself from the new issue, and even tried to stop the whole thing by questioning the right for the Kempe foundations to participate (referring to its statutes).[260] Instead, SCA preferred to wait for the prospectus before taking a stand. In the end, however, SCA did subscribe, although some of its leading actors made trouble even during the final stages of the process. For example, some of them wanted to see bids from other buyers, and they also tried to influence Carl Kempe Jr in his efforts to mobilize the foundations for a quick relinquishment decision.

So, once again the Kempe foundations settled the issue, since Lundberg would only subscribe under the condition that the foundations guaranteed that they would not sell either A-shares or subscription rights (so that SCA could acquire them). On 12 October 1993, the foundations decided that there was no obstacle to subscribing (and even borrowing capital, if that was required). At that point, SCA played its last card and asked the foundations whether they wanted to make use of their right of first refusal for the MoDo A-shares that SCA got when they purchased Carlgren's holding. On the basis of a negotiated offering from Lundberg, SCA also considered exchanging A-shares for B-shares. At the request of Viviann Kempe, an adviser from SE-Banken gave an account of other Swedish actors' interest in SCA's MoDo holding. He concluded that there were no other buyers around.[261] The problem was that SCA had bought the MoDo holding for SEK 550/share, and that the current price was not even half of that. So nobody was interested in paying something even near what SCA originally had paid. In that situation SCA decided to give up, and declared also publicly that its holding in MoDo was for sale.

Before the new shares were issued, the voting power in MoDo was distributed roughly in the following way: SCA 32 per cent, Lundberg 26 per cent and the Kempe foundations 19 per cent. The issue of new shares was decided at MoDo's board meeting in September 1993. Rydin regarded the sum as a little too high, but since Lundberg was prepared to subscribe to his part, SCA went along as well. SCA soon sold its holding to Lundberg, acquiring a significant number of B-shares that they would sell when the market was right. After all transactions were completed, Lundberg controlled 47 per cent of the votes, the Kempe foundations 18 per cent, actors close to Handelsbanken around 10 per cent and SCA 4 per cent.[262] SCA's board and top management were disappointed that their investment in MoDo had failed to create shareholder value, but in the end SCA had not lost any money (but time and energy). The payment they received for their

MoDo holding covered (with a minor surplus) what they had paid for Carlgren's and Marieberg's holdings.[263]

SCA's failure to take control over MoDo and/or obtain the benefits from business restructuration did not create any major problem for Handelsbanken. It was also MoDo's main bank, although the company was not a part of the bank's industrial group. Handelsbanken's CEO and MoDo director Mårtensson had good relations with Lundberg, so the tensions that had existed between, on the one hand, Lundberg, and, on the other hand, Rydin and Martin-Löf faded away.[264] Lundberg's initiative and his new standing as MoDo's major shareholder started the company's journey from being a high-risk company to becoming a low-risk one.[265]

NOTES

N.B.: When there is an 'i' inside a parenthesis below, that letter indicates that the note refers to an interview with the named person. All interviewees are listed in the Appendix. A complete listing of references is found at the end of the book.

1. The union representatives registered a reservation and Carl Kempe Jr a comment in the minutes.
2. Valeur (2000).
3. Löf (2004i).
4. Löf (2004i) and Fahlin (2006i).
5. Carl Kempe Jr (2006i) and Nabseth (2006i).
6. Carlgren (1994i), Altbäck (2006i), Sprängare (2006i) and Wallander (2006i).
7. Carlgren (1994i), Dahlgren (2006i), Harry Diedrichs (2006i), Fahlin (2006i), Flodström (2006i), Nabseth (2006i), Nordstrand (2006i) and Wallander (2006i).
8. Löf (2004i).
9. Dahlgren (2006i).
10. Harry Diedrichs (2006i), Fahlin (2006i) and Lars G. Sundblad (2006i).
11. Carlgren (1994i).
12. Fahlin (2006i).
13. Löf (2004i).
14. Sprängare (2006i).
15. Dahlgren (2006i), Flodström (2006i), Carl Kempe Jr (2006i), Nordstrand (2006i) and Sprängare (2006i). Sprängare actually asked the author of this book to accept an assignment to try to 'straighten out the executive situation', but that offering had to be turned down because of the author's concurrent engagement at a competitor.
16. Sprängare (2006i).
17. Nabseth (2006i).
18. Wallander (2006i).
19. Fahlin (2006i).
20. In 1980, MoDo's board was composed of Wegerfelt (Astra; Chair 1978), Altbäck, Dahlgren (Trygg-Hansa), Häggkvist (Handelsbanken, left in 1981), Nabseth, Wallander (Handelsbanken) and Stig Kempe (during a part of 1980). In 1981, Lars G. Sundblad (Iggesund) and Sprängare entered the board. Sundblad left already in 1982, six years after Karhola-Wettergren had been appointed. Carl Kempe Jr and Frans Kempe Jr were deputy members.
21. The Iggesund contest is extensively described and analysed in Ericson (1991) and Sjöstrand (1997).
22. Nabseth (2006i).
23. Carlgren (1994i).
24. Flodström (2006i).
25. Carlgren (1994i).
26. Carl Kempe Jr (2006i).
27. Harry Diedrichs (2006i).
28. Nabseth (2006i).
29. Carlgren (1994i) and Carl Kempe Jr (2006i).
30. Dahlgren (2006i).

31. Nabseth (2006i).
32. Lars G. Sundblad (2006i) did not confirm that Carlgren had mentioned that figure.
33. Lars G. Sundblad (2006i).
34. Altbäck (2006i), Nabseth (2006i) and Wallander (2006i).
35. Lars G. Sundblad (2006i).
36. Nabseth (2006i).
37. Iggesund (1985, Part II).
38. Three Iggesund shares could be swapped for two new shares in Stora Kopparberg, one Billerud share plus SEK 150. The value of the offering then became 2x SEK 235 + SEK 117 + SEK 150, a total of SEK 737. For each Iggesund share that meant SEK 245, as compared with the market price at the SSE 172 (a premium of 42%).
39. Wallander (2006i).
40. Carlgren (1994i).
41. Lars G. Sundblad (2006i).
42. Iggesund (1985, Part II).
43. Ibid.
44. Together with investors linked to the Handelsbanken sphere MoDo controlled the majority of the Iggesund stock. Stora Kopparberg controlled 22% and Billerud 3.5%.
45. Valeur (2007).
46. Frans Kempe Jr (2006i).
47. Nabseth (2006i).
48. Valeur (2007).
49. Andersson (1993).
50. Valeur (2000).
51. Valeur (2000).
52. Sprängare (2006i).
53. However, Nilsson was not alone. In the eyes of other members of the top management at the fine paper unit, Andersson and Sjölund, too, were most active in promoting the third machine.
54. Flodström (2006i), Nordstrand (2006i) and Sprängare (2006i).
55. A state-owned bank designated to support the development of the nation's business life.
56. A Swedish commercial bank.
57. Andersson (1993).
58. Ibid.
59. Valeur (2000).
60. Wallander (2006i).
61. Nordstrand (2006i).
62. Harry Diedrichs (2006i).
63. Sprängare (2006i).
64. MoDo and Feldmühle shared the allowed 35%.
65. Flodström (letter written in 2006).
66. Sprängare (2006i).
67. Croon (2005).
68. Nabseth (2006i).
69. Harry Diedrichs (2006i).
70. Löf (2006i).
71. Ibid.
72. Carl Kempe Jr (2006i).
73. Flodström (2006i), Larsson (2006i) and Wallander (2006i).
74. Dahlgren (2006i).
75. Harry Diedrichs (2006i) and Carl Kempe Jr (2006i).
76. Carlgren (1994i).
77. Nabseth (2006i).
78. Carlgren (1994i). Cf. also a private CD provided by his son Anders where Önnesjö talks about how Holmens Bruk became a part of MoDo.
79. Altbäck (2006i).
80. A private CD provided by his son Anders where Önnesjö talks about how Holmens Bruk became a part of MoDo.
81. Svensson (2006i).
82. Carlgren (1994i) and Sven Söderberg (2005i).
83. Altbäck (2006i) and Lars G. Sundblad (2006i).
84. Croon (2005).

85. Reuterskiöld (2006i).
86. Sven Söderberg (2003i).
87. Reuterskiöld (2006i).
88. Carlgren (1994i). Joja Bonnier was sometimes characterized as that family's 'enfant terrible'. He was seen as a person keen on making business deals – a passion that was not always appreciated by the actors in his environment, since they did not give him credit for having a particular standing, track record or skill in that field.
89. Zetterberg (2006i).
90. Nordlund (2006i).
91. Zetterberg (2006i).
92. Ibid.
93. Croon (2005).
94. Ibid.
95. Svensson (letter written in 2006).
96. Lars G. Sundblad (2006i).
97. Zetterberg (2006i).
98. Reuterskiöld (2006i).
99. Löf (2006i) and Trolle-Löwen (2006i).
100. Zetterberg (2006i).
101. A private CD provided by his son Anders where Önnesjö talks about how Holmens Bruk became a part of MoDo.
102. Albert Bonnier was 80 years old.
103. Dagens Nyheter, 7 October 1987.
104. Sven Söderberg (2003i).
105. Svensson (2006i).
106. Zetterberg (2006i).
107. Dagens Nyheter, 7 October 1987.
108. Swedish Securities Council (1988, p. 4).
109. Zetterberg (2006i).
110. Flodström (2006i).
111. Nordstrand (2006i).
112. Flodström (2006i).
113. Löf (2004i).
114. Holmens Bruk had shares with 1 vote (A-shares) and shares with 1:1000 vote (B-shares [millipedes]).
115. Svensson (2006i).
116. Flodström (2006i).
117. Swedish Securities Council (1988, p. 4).
118. Croon (2005).
119. Frans Kempe Jr (2006i).
120. Svensson (2006i).
121. Carlgren (1994i) and Carl Kempe Jr (2006i).
122. A banking firm.
123. Veckans Affärer, 26 November 1987.
124. Ibid.
125. Svensson (2006i).
126. KVB ('convertible proof of share of profit') = Stock without voting rights offering a larger dividend than ordinary stock; could be converted to ordinary stock (usually) at a price set in advance.
127. Flodström (2006i).
128. For five Holmens Bruk A an owner got one A-KVB, one C-KVB and SEK 111 cash *or* two C-KVBs and SEK 172. One could also get one C-KVB for two Holmens Bruk A. For thirteen Holmens Bruk B an owner got four A-KVBs and SEK 384 cash. One could also get three C-KVBs and SEK 52 in cash for eight Holmens Bruk B. For five Iggesund A an owner got four A-KVBs, four C-KVBs and SEK 553 cash. One could also get five C-KVBs and SEK 411 in cash for three Iggesund A *or* two C-KVBs and SEK 23 in cash for one Iggesund A. For three Iggesund B an owner got five C-KVBs and SEK 396 cash. One could also get two C-KVBs and SEK 18 in cash for one Iggesund B. Those who owned convertibles in Holmens Bruk (nominal value SEK 200) got convertibles in MoDo (nominal value SEK 402) plus SEK 114 in cash. Those who owned convertibles in Iggesund (nominal value SEK 530) got convertibles in MoDo (nominal value SEK 545) plus SEK 192 in cash.
129. The Swedish bank SE-Banken was later renamed SEB (in 1998).
130. Frans Kempe Jr (2006i).
131. Ibid.

132. Lots of calculations and simulations were carried out where MoDo's A-, B- and C-shares, Iggesund's A- and B-shares, and Holmens Bruk's A and B-shares were compared internally and put against various bid combinations including A-KVBs, C-KVBs and cash.
133. Lundin (2006i).
134. An investment company controlled by Lundberg.
135. After full conversion the Kempe–Carlgren dynasty would have 33% of the votes (of which the Kempe foundation would have 15%). Cf. MoDo Annual Report 1988 and Lundberg (2006i).
136. Carlgren (1994i) and Svensson (2006i).
137. Carlgren (1994i) and Wallander (2006i).
138. Andersson (1993).
139. The author of this book.
140. Löf (2006i).
141. The author of this book was in that team.
142. Löf (2006i).
143. Svensson (2006i).
144. Andersson (1993).
145. Rydin's diary.
146. A Swedish world leading gas company.
147. A Swedish world leading construction company.
148. Andersson (1993).
149. Ibid.
150. According to the current Swedish Companies Act a company was not allowed to own its own shares.
151. Croon (2005).
152. Carlgren (1994i).
153. Wallander (2006i).
154. Lars G. Sundblad (2006i).
155. That statement corresponds fully with the minutes from Iggesund's board meeting on 25 August 1985.
156. Lars G. Sundblad (2006i).
157. Lack of capital?
158. About 10% according to Carl Kempe Jr (2006i). However, Frans Kempe Jr (2006i) claimed that the holding was equally divided between Carlgren and Lundberg.
159. Carlgren (1994i), Harry Diedrichs (2006i), Lars G. Sundblad (2006i) and Svensson (2006i).
160. Carlgren (1994i).
161. Lars G. Sundblad (letter to the Iggesund board written in 2006).
162. Lars G. Sundblad (document from 2006).
163. Carl Kempe Jr (2006i).
164. Croon (2005).
165. A Swedish commercial television channel.
166. Carlgren (1994i) and Croon (2005).
167. Valeur (2007).
168. Carl Kempe Jr (2006i).
169. Frans Kempe Jr (2006i).
170. Carlgren (1994i) and Croon (2005).
171. Carlgren was not a member of this constellation because he had problems relating to Rydin.
172. Carlgren (1994i) and Croon (2005).
173. Ibid.
174. Ibid.
175. Flodström (2006i).
176. Frans Kempe Jr (2006i).
177. Carlgren (1994i), Valeur (2000) and Croon (2005).
178. Carlgren (1994i).
179. Valeur (2007).
180. Carlgren (1994i).
181. Stated purpose: 'Through owning and administrating shares in Mo and Domsjö AB (i.e. MoDo) further that company's continued existence and development.'
182. Kempe (2006).
183. Carlgren (1994i) and Nabseth (2006i).
184. Flodström (2006i).
185. Harry Diedrichs (2006i).
186. Lundberg (2006i).
187. Croon (2005).

188. Löf (2004i) and Croon (2005).
189. Lundberg (2006i).
190. Ibid.
191. Carlgren (1994i)
192. Ibid.
193. Croon (2005).
194. Mårtensson (2006i).
195. Nabseth (2006i).
196. Löf (2006i).
197. Croon (2005).
198. MoDo's press service.
199. Rydin's diary.
200. Carlgren (1994i) and Löf (2004i).
201. Lundberg (2006i).
202. Carl Kempe Jr (2006i).
203. Altbäck (2006i).
204. Löf (2006i).
205. Altbäck (2006i).
206. Löf (2004i).
207. The author of this book.
208. Carlgren (1994i) and Harry Diedrichs (2006i).
209. Mårtensson (2006i).
210. Svedberg (2006i).
211. Dau was a politician active in the Conservative Party, and Köhler had a similar role in the Social Democratic Party.
212. A personal deputy was customary, but Carl Kempe Jr changed that tradition in March 1991 through a revision of the foundations' statutes. From that date the entrance of a new director (or deputy director) required the consensus of three board members, making it possible for the Chair together with one director to block a decision. However, that change of the statutes was made too late to prevent Viviann Kempe's election of Carlgren as her deputy.
213. Harry Diedrichs (2006i).
214. Frans Kempe Jr (2006i).
215. Ibid.
216. The reason for Dau's and Köhler's alliance with Carl Kempe Jr is unknown.
217. Croon (2005).
218. Carlgren (1994i) and Frans Kempe Jr (2006i).
219. Svedberg (2006i).
220. Croon (2005).
221. Harry Diedrichs (2006i) and Svedberg (2006i).
222. Ibid.
223. Veckans Affärer, 20 May 1992.
224. Croon (2005).
225. Harry Diedrichs (2006i).
226. Veckans Affärer 20 May 1992. Zetterberg was at the time a member of Lundbergföretagen's board.
227. Löf (2006i) and Svensson (2006i).
228. Dagens Industri, 15 October 1992.
229. Löf (2006i) and Svensson (2006i).
230. Croon (2005), Löf (2006i) and Flodström (2006i).
231. Löf (2004i).
232. Welin (2006i).
233. Carlgren (1994i).
234. Croon (2005).
235. Flodström (2006i).
236. The two MoDo units had merged.
237. Löf (2006i).
238. Löf (2006i).
239. Several board members were new in 1991, and many of them had their experience from other industries.
240. Svensson (2006i).
241. Svedberg (2006i).
242. Welin (2006i).
243. That figure is from the board minutes.

244. Nordstrand (2006i).
245. Sweden implemented a floating exchange rate.
246. Löf (2006i) and Larsson (2006i).
247. Mårtensson (2006i).
248. Lundin (2006i).
249. Nordstrand (2006i).
250. Larsson (2006i).
251. A private CD provided by his son Anders where Önnesjö talks about how Holmens Bruk became a part of MoDo.
252. Dagens Industri, 15 October 1992.
253. Ibid.
254. Dagens Nyheter, 7 October 1992.
255. Mårtensson (2006i).
256. Croon (2005).
257. Dagens Industri, 15 October 1992.
258. Croon (2005).
259. Nordstrand (2006i).
260. Löf (2006i).
261. Margareta Kempe (2006).
262. MoDo Annual Report (1993).
263. Croon (2005).
264. Ibid.
265. Mårtensson (2006i).

10. From MoDo to Holmen: a consolidation period

10.1 A NEW CEO

Already by mid-1993 there were rumours spread by the Swedish business press that MoDo's CEO Löf was to be replaced. One could read that one of the three major shareholders demanded his retirement. However, in a meeting with Löf, SCA's Chair Rydin made clear that the rumour was false, and that the journalists' articles were plain speculations not founded on facts. In that situation, MoDo Chair Önnesjö wanted to see a denial from the board in the form of a communiqué. Rydin sought wording by which MoDo refuted both a change of CEO and discussions addressing that topic, and accepted – considering the on-going equity offer – also a sentence confirming full confidence in Löf.[1] However, rather soon after that public denial, circumstances changed and the search for a new CEO began.

Ten years as MoDo's CEO had made Löf rather jaded (he had reached the age of 60) not least because of the company's troublesome shareholder structure. Moreover, he was first and foremost a strong supporter of fine paper capacity, and that business was not unchallenged any longer as the preferred path into the future.[2] Added to that, the problems with Alizay had not strengthened his position. So, gradually his authority weakened both within the board and in the top management group.[3] SCA was repeatedly critical especially because the expected benefits from inter-firm co-operation projects were dashed time and again, and Löf was seen as responsible for that failure.[4] Furthermore, Lundberg and Löf did not work particularly well together – their focus differed somewhat. Lundberg stressed the financial flow and aspects related to effectiveness and efficiency, while Löf was more familiar with the operational flow and especially marketing issues. As the CEO did not place priority on financial matters, capital rationalization went rather slowly and intended divestments lingered on unimplemented; as a result the old situation remained.[5] Lundberg eventually came to the conclusion that it was time to replace Löf and initiated a search process in which Chair Önnesjö was particularly active. A head-hunter was contacted to help them, and to a large extent he ran the process himself; thus, Önnesjö and Lundberg did not meet with the final candidate until a rather late stage, actually close to a planned appointment.[6]

Önnesjö happened to know the main candidate,[7] Bengt Pettersson, well from his work at Stora and Uddeholm (and had even tried to recruit him already back in the late 1970s and 1980s to a position at Holmens Bruk). As he preferred a person with experience from the forest-based industry, Önnesjö asked Pettersson if he was at all interested. Lundberg was open to recruiting somebody not only outside of MoDo but also outside of the industry, but Önnesjö convinced him that they ought to look for an industry 'insider'.[8]

It was actually a conflict at the very top of Stora's organization that stimulated

Pettersson's interest in changing company and position. Pettersson was 54 years old, so MoDo's offer was – as he saw it – his last chance to do something new and challenging. Becoming MoDo CEO offered an opportunity to go from merely dealing with operational matters to (also) handling some of the strategic challenges – something he thought would suit him well. The division of responsibilities between Lundberg (Chair) and Pettersson (CEO) was that the former would focus on the need to establish a stronger capital structure in the company, while the latter would spend most of his time trying to get the business 'palette' in order. Pettersson's management approach was to combine calculations and other kinds of figure-based and text-based material with intuition. To him calculations established the platform and course for action, while intuition made the intended things happen.[9]

Lundberg liked Önnesjö's candidate Pettersson's track record and personality, so the final outcome was that Pettersson replaced Löf in 1994. The CEO entered into a new uncomplicated ownership situation, and he pushed for the same ideas as the major shareholder. Pettersson saw his assignment as a difficult one. MoDo was in crisis and quite a lot of changes were necessary, so he saw it as a five-year job. Pettersson was first and foremost an industrial man, without much experience in marketing and finance. This, however, was regarded as an advantage in the current situation in which MoDo had to get its operations in order – the new CEO had to sort out, divest and invest. When he arrived, the economic turnaround had not yet occurred. However, he was lucky – it happened soon, at the same time as he began carving out MoDo's future core businesses. Pettersson immediately recognized that MoDo ran too many different businesses and noticed in particular the weakness in its northern activities, where the fine paper business faced tough competition. Pettersson also found that Holmens Bruk was in good shape, and he helped Lundberg discover Iggesund's qualities. The 'classic MoDo', however, had difficulties – the fine paper operations in Alipap were still a problem business.[10]

Lundberg became MoDo Chair in 1995, and he was much more active in that position than both his predecessors Svedberg and Önnesjö – in that way the situation had become similar to the one that prevailed when Carlgren was in charge. Lundberg even became involved in the operative flow, because he really wanted to learn about the forest-based business and understand its rationale. So, from that platform, he was able to govern both organizational flows, that is to say, the financial and the operative ones. However, Lundberg had great respect for Pettersson's judgement, so in practice he backed most of the CEO's proposals.[11]

Pettersson was a cautious general who also acquainted himself with details, especially operative and technical ones. He then knew what details were important for the bigger decisions. Based on personal experience from the industry – its operations and actors – Pettersson was able to deliver his own qualified judgements. Soon Pettersson's sorting, scrutinizing, disinvesting and investing were found to be both insightful and reliable. The directors put faith in his assessments; he was convincing and created the kind of relationship between a board and a CEO that they wanted to see. However, he was not the obvious choice in the eyes of everybody. He was picked from outside of MoDo, and some managers saw him as a person who lacked vision, charisma, media impact and 'luminosity'.[12]

As main shareholder Lundberg was anxious to secure a healthy capital structure for the company. Regarding the businesses as such, he saw structural deals as an overrated path since they usually involved tough processes that often failed; Lundberg preferred organic growth. He was also firm on the issue that before making any investments at all, a company has to have everything in order, and that was not the case in MoDo in 1994 and 1995. However, from 1996 on, most aspects looked much better. Lundberg also stressed that the size of the company was not the crucial matter – instead, he saw the size and composition of the plants as the important dimensions when a forest-based company tries to establish efficient operations.[13]

From his recent Stora position Pettersson knew MoDo's (Iggesund's) cardboard operations quite well, and he found that business to be in good shape. However, all in all, he considered MoDo to be a company in crisis not far from bankruptcy – the company was heavily indebted and had a poor financial situation. At the same time, MoDo had several operational problems such as an unprofitable Alizay, an impaired Domsjö, a Husum in need of a coating capacity, a problem-ridden MoDo Packaging (e.g. Skärblacka) and an inefficient Silverdalen. Pettersson also saw some similarities between MoDo and Stora. The capital base and managerial capacity in both companies were spread across too many business fields: packaging, newsprint, fine paper, sawmills, pulp, sacks, and so on. Like Stora before its acquisition of Swedish Match (cf. Ch. 12), MoDo consisted of three core businesses, namely fine paper (classic MoDo), newsprint (Holmens Bruk) and fine cardboard (Iggesund). Already during his years at Stora, Pettersson doubted whether it was possible to have three 'legs' without having a much larger capital base. Over the years he had also learned that if a forest-based company was not the biggest one in a certain business area, it had to be among the very best.[14]

In 1994 the recently closed CTMP plant in Domsjö was sold to Stora Billerud. In the next year MoDo Packaging[15] and two other holdings were sold (Rentsch [a Swiss company] and Slave Lake Pulp Partnership [Canada]).[16] CEO Pettersson believed that the latter two holdings (also) existed to provide opportunities for executives to take seats on foreign boards and get low-taxed fees. He also claimed that the holdings generated lots of meaningless and costly travel. Pettersson's removal of these managerial benefits was unpopular, but they had to be carried out, as those minority shareholdings did not fit MoDo's planned business mix.[17]

Pettersson took a different stand regarding MD Papier. There, MoDo faced a controlling shareholder (75%), who wanted to sell his holding. Making that purchase would mean that MoDo seriously entered the high-quality LWC segment of the newsprint market. MD Papier's LWC was of such a good quality that Pettersson saw that as a promising path. He regarded the present 25 per cent shareholding as too small (even when considering the [legally unsecure] option to reach 50%) for the successful development of such operations.[18] The financial situation in late 1995 actually would have allowed for such a large acquisition (SEK 2 billion), but still Pettersson said no, and the board followed his proposal. According to Pettersson, the problem was MD Papier's Dachau unit (not its LWC plant), a site that was in really bad shape, but at the same time the heirloom of its main owner (and MoDo would have had to buy both units). Because of Dachau's status and history, it would have been difficult for MoDo to rationalize its operations (and in Germany it was always difficult to do such things).[19] An alternative to stay as owner together with Norske Skog was discussed at a board meeting in October 1995, but since neither the Chair nor the CEO was particularly fond of 50–50 constructs, and for other reasons, the idea was dropped. In the end, MoDo sold its 25 per cent share in MD Papier in 1996 to Metsä-Serla for SEK 0.5 billion.

The Chair was concerned about the composition of MoDo's foreign activities – it was a 'straggly' mix with an uncertain contribution to the totality. To address this concern, the board decided to concentrate (and lower) the production at Silverdalen to supply only the profitable markets, that is to say, the UK and Sweden, where MoDo sold straight to its own wholesalers. Husum's need for Silverdalen had also gradually decreased, as the former site faced an increasing market for its non-coated fine paper. The suggested disinvestments that Pettersson implemented confirmed to the board that he was the right person for the CEO position. Thus, eventually he became quite powerful and respected although not always liked by everybody in the organization.[20]

Pettersson also changed MoDo's classic and almost 'holy' R&D organization by splitting it up and distributing the parts to the three core business units. The arguments were that the central unit had concentrated its efforts too much on research and too little on development, and that it had focused too much on fine paper projects. Basically, Pettersson had found rather few synergies between the three business areas, so why keep an integrated R&D unit? His decision also strengthened the positions of the business areas and made operations more driven by customer demand. Another reason for the R&D split-up might have been that it would simplify a future disinvestment of one or two of the current core businesses. That idea had already begun to evolve in the minds of several leading actors in the company, and it was the fine paper business that was the prime target. However, there was one leading actor that certainly would oppose such a move, namely Carl Kempe Jr, the spokesman for the second largest shareholder in MoDo (the Kempe foundations). He was expected to intensely defend that classic part of the new MoDo.

The year 1994 represented the start of a turnaround, not only for MoDo but also for the whole forest-based industry. Two key factors made it possible for MoDo to move from losses amounting to about SEK 1 billion to large profits in just one year's time: the devaluation of the Swedish crown in late 1992, and the strong return of market demand.[21] Director Larsson added Lundberg's leadership to that listing. He particularly stressed Lundberg's focus on profitability, and his initiation of the substantial new issue of shares that took place in 1993. Lundberg showed the organization that he was in charge, and he restored the employees' belief that there was a future for the company.[22]

In 1994, MoDo's indebtedness was (still) far too high (0.81), but it was dramatically reduced (to 0.41) already in the course of 1995 due to devaluation effects, divestments and an improved market situation. That successful development made it possible for the company to once again act more proactively and not just focus on disinvestments. So, the board decided to invest SEK 1 billion in improving Husum, SEK 900 million to modernize Iggesund and SEK 2 billion in a new newsprint machine at Braviken. The latter meant that the old plan to establish a third machine finally was implemented. The investment also included an expansion of Braviken's recycled product-based pulp production, as it had become obvious that recycled paper actually improved the quality of the newsprint. Even Alizay began to improve, and an analysis presented in early 1995 indicated that it would be best for MoDo to keep it.

The new newsprint machine was discussed already back in 1991, because demand looked good in a long time perspective, and because MoDo's scale of operations in that business still was too small – at least to influence the prices. Top management had strong support for that investment from Chair[23] Önnesjö, who also had the establishment of the Braviken site as one of his great achievements. When director Lundberg also backed the idea, it eventually became reality. It might also have simplified things that these two key actors were Norrköping patriots.[24]

Thus, the new machine was up for consideration already when Pettersson entered MoDo. He discovered that it was a promising project in many ways. The infrastructure was in place; it was the right time to buy a machine (recession); and the financial situation was improving, as the sale of Skärblacka to AssiDomän for an attractive price was underway. AssiDomän's CEO Ahlgren was keen to buy Skärblacka, and therefore not particularly price sensitive. In the end, that sale gave MoDo around SEK 1 billion, which significantly improved MoDo's investment capacity. Moreover, most leading actors believed that boom times lay ahead and that the company would benefit from the weak Swedish crown.[25]

MoDo also considered a new investment in its A4 paper operations and decided that Alizay was a better target than Husum. The arguments for Alizay were its better sourcing of timber, its lower transportation costs and its better opportunity to integrate a new line with an existing pulp production. Alizay was also more propitiously located, that is to say, more closely situated to 'southern Europe', which represented one-third of the European customer demand. Regarding Alizay, MoDo had received SEK 140 million in indemnification for the problems that the turnkey contractor had created when Alipap was built. To this series of successes one could add, however, at least one major setback: a SEK 200 million fine caused by the unmasking of a cardboard cartel, of which MoDo (Workington, UK) was judged to be a part.

10.2 DISINVESTING THE FINE PAPER BUSINESS

As noted earlier, when CEO Pettersson entered MoDo, his experience at Stora told him that three core businesses were one too many – it was difficult enough to be outstanding in one or two business areas. That conclusion was based not only on financial considerations but also on market expectations. When he evaluated the operational side of the three businesses, Iggesund came out as rather exceptional. The company had a leading position in a profitable business with relatively price insensitive customers. Though Iggesund's Workington plant was not in the best shape, Pettersson believed that it could be developed into something better. He regarded the Braviken site as a pearl and found Hallsta's performance satisfactory. Both the latter sites housed bulk production, so it was crucial to reap the benefits from scale economies.

At the time, MoDo focused its fine paper operations on A4 paper, and that segment was growing. One possible path that Pettersson identified for fine paper was increasing the production of coated qualities, and many actors including most board members found that a 'natural' way forward. However, as Pettersson saw it, coated paper, too, needed large volumes to be profitable, and that meant that the scale economies of Husum's non-coated qualities gradually might decline. MoDo would then face the risk of becoming only mediocre on both market segments.[26]

Pettersson considered Husum to be an excellent fine paper unit, while Alizay – particularly its Alipap plant – still performed rather poorly. Moreover, Alipap only housed one machine, and that was too little to reap the benefits of large volumes – at least one machine had to be added to make that site profitable. Pettersson also stressed that competition from Asia was a great risk; fine paper was relatively easy to produce, and Asians could do it at a lower price, which would hurt the market. So, although all the three legs basically looked fine, he pointed to the fine paper leg as the weakest one. He had the impression that both the major shareholders and the directors had come to the same conclusion.[27]

Eventually the board officially concluded that three 'legs' were one too many, and that fine paper was the one MoDo should abandon. As the Kempe dynasty had become weaker, it became possible to sacrifice that family 'heirloom'. The preference for keeping newsprint was foremost based on the conviction that demand and prices would continue to be relatively stable. Long-term agreements were common practice in that industry, and mutual interests among sellers and buyers kept (price) fluctuations down. So, the board expected a stable growth for newsprint, although new market channels might develop. Still, the business was seen as regional – an offensive from Asian producers was regarded as unlikely, at least during the coming decade. Instead, the board worried about the (rising) price for electricity and what impact that the IT revolution would have on demand for newsprint and related products. The conclusion was that the latter would take time, so MoDo could continue its investments in that area. The Braviken unit was complete with a well-utilized infrastructure, so future investments there were less likely. It was probably the best site in the world of its kind. For Hallsta, with its less modern equipment and structure, the board also thought that a new machine ought to be considered. However, the Wargön site was a problem, as it was too small and not fully modern. At that time, the board also had to handle the European Commission's cartel accusations that foremost addressed the European printing paper market.[28]

For high-quality cardboard, the fluctuations were even less volatile, and the calculations even better, so the future for MoDo's third 'leg' looked fine. It was a profitable global market that was expanding, particularly in Asia and the Americas, and the only strong competitor in Iggesund's segment (high-quality cardboards for end-use consumers) was Westvaco. Moreover, the threat from potential new entrants on the market was low, as there were barriers to entry that made it difficult for newcomers to become profitable: it took a long time to become an efficient producer and to build well-functioning customer relations.

In September 1996 the board discussed MoDo's strategy at a lengthy meeting. The company's financial status was excellent due to a combination of successful disinvestments and good operative results. That meant that the board faced fewer restrictions when it was to decide about the company's future. At the meeting, a growing concern for fine paper in general emerged, although long-fibre-based qualities were still regarded as promising, particularly if they were used for special papers. However, the future for the more 'bulky' qualities of non-coated fine paper was questioned, as many new actors were entering those segments, and most of them with large modern machines. The newcomers were low-price producers located in, for example, Indonesia and Malaysia. They expanded because it was possible to use more and more short fibres in these products. Basically, that expansion was unco-ordinated, which meant that one could not expect that some kind of stabilizing 'price leadership' would emerge.

From a journey in Asia, CEO Pettersson got the impression that new large fine paper plants already were materializing (with its low cost for both raw material and labour). That new production of (mainly) low-cost, short-fibre-based fine paper could then rather soon reach the European market. So, if there was to be a future for MoDo in A4 paper and other kinds of cut fine paper, it had to be based on strong branding and effective distribution (the business based on large rolls was decreasing and unprofitable). In such a situation, MoDo would need its three plants: Husum, Alizay and PPSM (unfortunately PPSM was not profitable). The production at Silverdalen was of a good quality, but it was difficult to extend the operations there. Domsjö's sulphite pulp was rather successful on the market, but to continue its specialization strategy would demand substantial investments in the near future, so it was far from evident how that unit should be handled.

MoDo's strategy discussions raised several questions that were connected to the company's fine paper operations. Should the French businesses (PPSM and Alizay) be sold? Should Husum be converted to a cardboard producer? Should the wholesaling business be even more decoupled from production? As MoDo Merchants was a rather small player outside of Norway and Sweden, one could be concerned about its future capability to make a substantial market impact in Europe (not to mention globally).

Regarding the possible sale of Alizay, there were doubts about whether it would be possible to get a decent price, as several other sellers also were active in the same market. Alizay had cost MoDo quite a lot of money (and was still unprofitable), so selling it for an acceptable price would certainly not be easy. One could also question whether MoDo (fine) Paper could do without its French business, that is to say, whether the total volume and market presence otherwise might become too small. It also offered substantial accumulated loss deductions that would become available in 1997–98 (due to the very poor results of 1992–93). A continuation of the operations there required a strengthening of the capital base of MoDo France, and huge sums reaching SEK 5 billion were mentioned. In that situation, MoDo France's shareholding structure was discussed, as was the idea of establishing a MoDo-controlled French holding company that would own Alizay and PPSM, making it possible for MoDo to sell (some of) its shares in that holding company on the stock market.

The general conclusion from the strategic discussions was that MoDo should keep and develop two of its businesses, namely newsprint and cardboard. For fine paper the future was seen as more uncertain, although MoDo had to invest carefully there, too, until that path was completely abandoned. However, no expansion investments in fine paper were to be carried out. More generally, Chair Lundberg stressed the importance of financial stability and low indebtedness. That position indicated a cautious and conservative strategy – an organic path by which the company took a more passive role in the industry's structural discussions, and instead focused more on the status of its own machines (no merger/acquisitions initiatives were to be taken, although preparations were made if something would turn up).

In 1996, CEO Pettersson suggested that MoDo should expand its Husum sulphate plant significantly. To secure the sourcing of wood to support that new capacity, it would be necessary to close down the Domsjö sulphite plant. For MoDo and Pettersson that was not a new idea. The CEO had actually suggested that move rather soon after he had begun his work, but the board was not ready for such a decision – the directors were divided in how they valued the pros and cons of a closure. As a decision to shut down

Domsjö would be particularly difficult for the members of the Kempe dynasty, Lundberg decided not to pursue the case.

Pettersson's statement that Domsjö's plant ought to be closed down sounded already very much like a decision in the ears of several of the involved parties. His suggestion aroused strong feelings among the employees, and created a wave of protests from the unions and the local community. It even spread outside the region and became a national issue, and most leading media expressed their discontentment with how the Domsjö unit was treated. Even the Prime Minister was approached, and he had a conversation with MoDo's major shareholder Lundberg. Objections towards a closure were raised also in the Swedish Parliament.[29]

Several arguments were put forward for why MoDo ought to keep Domsjö running. Some actors claimed that Domsjö had been underinvested and mistreated for at least a decade. The unions stressed that Domsjö's investment in viscose pulp still had not had enough time to prove its long-term profitability. That investment had represented a step into a non-standard market with a less well-known demand structure, so the big challenge was to find the right buyers for the new customized pulp qualities. The argument was that such a matching would take a few years. It was also claimed that competition in that area was decreasing, as several viscose plants recently had been shut down (mainly because of high environmental costs), while MoDo's investments at Domsjö had made that plant almost unique in the world among viscose producers in limiting emissions. Another argument against closure was the plant's far-reaching integration with two other companies in the municipality Domsjö, namely Akzo Nobel[30] and Sekab[31] (regarding steam, process water and cleaning of waste water). Moreover, the nearby town Örnsköldsvik was dependent on Domsjö for its heating. MoDo's leading actors seriously considered all these arguments, and eventually the decision regarding the future for the Domsjö site was postponed for two years (until 1998).[32]

MoDo offered both Rottneros[33] and Borregaard[34] the opportunity to acquire Domsjö, but both rejected the offer. However, at the time, a small group of investors had been organized that considered taking over plants that did not fit into the large actors' core businesses, when they decided to concentrate their efforts on fewer 'legs' and large-scale activities. Norlin, one of the leaders of the investor consortium, and his colleagues discussed several potential purchases, for example, Billingfors Bruk, Wargön, Gruvön and Domsjö – and the last soon emerged as a serious acquisition candidate. Norlin and his associates created a financial formula that they hoped would make MoDo interested in starting negotiations. The Norlin consortium was composed of actors with supplementary competences, and MoDo's former Head of Forestry, Erkén, was one of its key members. He knew Domsjö well and was highly regarded in the local community, qualities that proved to be indispensable both before and after the takeover.[35] So, in the first half of 1999, when MoDo together with SCA established a new fine paper company ('Modo Paper', see below), it was declared that the Domsjö plant did not fit into any of the remaining core businesses of MoDo and that the plant therefore was to be sold. That also happened in 2000, when the plant was sold to the Norlin consortium, which decided to continue its operations in a 'new' company named Domsjö Fabriker.

MoDo's board continued to discuss the future for its various businesses all through 1997. The financial circumstances were excellent, making room for well-prepared investment plans amounting to around SEK 11 billion. Still, it was important to rank the needs of – and demands from – the various businesses and evaluate all the opportunities that appeared. In the short run, most operations were doing well, but in a longer time perspective there were strong doubts regarding the fine paper business. It represented a rather 'bulky' one, as even MoDo's (former) flagship A4 paper had moved in that direction. Moreover, for most companies working on the fine paper market, profitability had been rather poor during the 1990s and, as a consequence, some of them had initiated consolidation processes. However, both Husum and Alipap were strong units, and PPSM was rather successful in the special papers segment (but otherwise it performed rather poorly). Basically, four possible paths were available: (1) grow organically and through modest investments try to become the market leader in office paper, (2) sell the fine paper business and face the risk of strengthening a competitor (making synergies available), (3) grow globally and utilize scale economics and international financing and (4) split MoDo into two units, one containing a 'dressed up' fine paper business, and the other the two core businesses. The former unit could then be introduced at the SSE or run together with a partner. MoDo's board preferred the first and the fourth alternatives.

The board also discussed what to demand from an acceptable fine paper partner. It would be optimal if it had a focus on office paper, ran plants with efficient machines and complemented MoDo's market presence. As always, most things would be simplified if the partner's company culture resembled that of MoDo. Considering those criteria, CEO Pettersson provided a listing of potential European candidates that were regarded as suitable for exploratory activities. Chair Lundberg stressed that it was important that the financial standing of the companies approached became a crucial part of the judgement when the final candidates were selected. The board instructed the CEO to start informal discussions with certain companies. The contacted companies were not unresponsive, but nothing concrete materialized.

MoDo's (fine paper) merchant organization was keen to continue its growth, foremost through acquisitions in Denmark and Belgium, and later also in the UK and Spain. However, at the time most efforts were put on trying to expand the company's cardboard business. Many paths were discussed. One way to grow was by acquiring a European niche company, another by purchasing an American company (not necessarily a niche actor). A third way could be to invest in a new machine that added substantial capacity to the market. However, that path entailed a long phase-in time, and the sourcing of raw material and energy could become a problem. The unions expected that a third machine would be located at Iggesund, but CEO Pettersson hesitated. He was not convinced that the market could 'absorb' the new volume.

Regarding newsprint, Pettersson was convinced that existing machines could be improved and generate significantly larger volumes. However, there was still a need to invest at Hallsta, and if so, that would mean larger volumes of special papers and journal papers. Pettersson supported such a development, but Chair Lundberg hesitated to make another huge investment in an energy-consuming production process. Pettersson stressed that, after the sale of its holding in MD Papier, MoDo lacked LWC on its repertoire. Instead, it had a possibility to cover some of that market through a 'new' kind of high-quality non-coated paper – something for which customers already had indicated interest. However, such an investment was not yet a burning issue, and it was not obvious that it should be located at Hallsta.

Many forest-based companies sold out their forests during the 1990s. In MoDo's case, however, that would only be done if the company faced serious financial trouble. The company believed in securing the sourcing of timber for its own production; therefore, in the second half of 1997, the board decided that MoDo in (almost) all circumstances should own substantial forest resources. The directors also believed that energy prices would rise, so the board decided that MoDo should control that resource, too. These two convictions were very much a product of the rationale associated with MoDo's major shareholder and Chair Lundberg. As so often, he did not simply imitate the actions of the majority in the industry – he established a rather unique long-term path for MoDo, and resisted the external critique that emerged. For example, he was not impressed by the analyst's arguments that forest ownership usually was associated with low returns. Lundberg was distinct and explicit regarding his governance approach – his engagement as major shareholder was high, he wanted to achieve a productive balance between the board and the CEO, the company's time perspective should be long, its financial status had to be healthy and operations had to be the focus.[36]

MoDo's strategy to merely own forests that fitted its operations was tested when a large forest holding located near its Braviken site was put up for sale. If acquired, it would significantly increase MoDo's self-sourcing. The board favoured the purchase, so MoDo decided to bid up to SEK 1.3 billion for that forest. However, another bidder (not a forest-based company) raised the price to SEK 1.4 billion. Opinions were divided on whether MoDo should try to abandon its limit and match that price, or give up. The board decided to follow the CEO's recommendation, and MoDo left the bidding process.

At about the same time, it became known that Stora was to merge with Finnish Enso-Gutzeit. For a while the implications for MoDo of the establishment of that new formation topped the board's agenda. That merger caused MoDo to reconsider its strategy of being rather passive (but well prepared) in the restructuration processes that were going on. It would have to take into consideration the risk associated with not participating in such structural deals, as scale economies had become more and more crucial in most forest-related businesses. The board reaffirmed that MoDo should carry on with cardboard and newsprint as its core businesses and try to divest its fine paper operations. It also stated that no M&A activities should be allowed to threaten the company's financial strength, so in all such contacts it was particularly important to carefully check the quality of the other party's plants and machines before starting more serious discussions.

In late 1997, the major shareholders and the directors began to focus on the possibility of separating out fine paper and distributing the new unit (MoDo Paper) to the shareholders. The forests would then stay in MoDo, as would Domsjö and the wholesale business; what would be partitioned off were Husum, Silverdalen, PPSM, Alizay (Alicel and Alipap) and the sales companies. The problem with such a solution, however, was that it did not bring about any synergies, and therefore it created no additional value. Moreover, since the new separate unit was considered to be too small to qualify as a listed company, an industrial deal or a merger with somebody else would be required – at least before going public. At that time, MoDo was financially sound, so it did not have to act immediately – it could wait for a 'window of opportunity'.[37]

A partial merger with SCA – combining the two companies' fine paper operations – could be a first step. Therefore, MoDo investigated the possibility of creating a new '50–50 corporation' that later could be brought to the stock market – a path that was judged to be a better one than just a separation of MoDo Paper from MoDo. During the November 1997 board meeting, the Chair unexpectedly received a message that SCA might be interested in participating in such a joint venture and scheduled an extra meeting for the following day. It was a complicated matter, as it entailed a partial merger with the long-term 'rival' company SCA that had a very different history, governance tradition and company culture. Sooner or later that kind of co-operation tended to fail. Still, MoDo thought the idea was worth considering, so talks started – discussions in which MoDo made clear that it was uninterested in ownership of the new unit. MoDo wanted cash, but that was not acceptable for SCA.

Early in 1998, MoDo developed a stable platform for the discussions with SCA regarding fine paper. First of all, it was important to have the responsibility issue clarified, if a joint effort of some kind were to materialize. As MoDo was in good shape both financially and operationally, it ought to get at least a 50 per cent shareholding in a 'merged' unit and appoint its CEO. Such a large combined fine paper company would then have a satisfactory market share (≈ 20%), although it covered several segments (e.g. 'large rolls', sheets and coated qualities). MoDo's board members also discussed the possible consequences of a development by which SCA, at a later stage, got (or took) the leading role in the new fine paper unit, placing MoDo in a minority position. In such a situation, it was important that MoDo could leave, and that made it necessary to have the new unit listed on the SSE. However, that 'phasing out' option presupposed that SCA was the more competent actor of the two when it came to running the new company, and MoDo's directors were sceptical about that supposition. Because of all the uncertainties surrounding a possible partial merger with SCA, it was decided that the fine paper issue should be put 'on ice' for a while.[38]

In the latter part of 1998, MoDo's board carried out its yearly strategy meeting, carefully scrutinizing the company's operative and financial status. Regarding MoDo Paper, for which the merger discussion with SCA had been put on hold, the strategy still was to concentrate on high-quality office paper and long-fibre sulphate. In addition to technical upgrading of certain machines, MoDo Paper's management pushed for expansion investments at Husum and Alizay amounting to SEK 3–4 billion (in the 'usual' three years' perspective). The European fine paper market had improved, primarily through structural rationalizations that made the big firms even bigger and more dominating. Regarding newsprint and journal papers, the important task was to make MoDo (Holmen) strong on standard qualities in Europe – special qualities should be treated as 'supporting' businesses. The suggested investments amounted to around SEK 3 billion, most of it intended for the Hallsta site. For MoDo's successful cardboard business, the investment demands were more modest, adding up to SEK 0.7 billion.

Throughout the second half of the 1990s, MoDo worked to concentrate its business portfolio and strengthen the company's financial position. With a debt/equity ratio of 0.2 at the end of 1998, and a profit after net financial items amounting to SEK 2.3 billion, the company's position was regarded as stronger than necessary for the development of its business, making room for substantial dividends (even redemptions). MoDo's target for its long-term debt/equity ratio was 0.5–0.7.

CEO Pettersson kept stressing that it was difficult to run three core businesses in an optimal way, as they all needed to expand to stay competitive. After a careful analysis, he suggested that investments amounting to SEK 7 billion ought to be carried out in 1999–2001. Most of the capital should be invested at Hallsta, Husum and Workington. By contrast, investments at the pulp and fine paper units at PPSM, Alizay and Domsjö were to be relatively modest. As before, Silverdalen and Wargön were discussed as potential divestments.

Early in 1999, MoDo made its strategy public. In its press release, the company stated that it had decided to invest in cardboard (cf. Iggesund) and newsprint and journal papers (cf. Holmen) – areas where MoDo was judged to be competitive (now and so also in the future). Regarding its third main business, fine paper (MoDo 'classic'), the company declared that it intended to continue its concentration on office paper, and was open to all forms of co-operation (including joint ventures).

Back in late 1998, new contacts were taken up between MoDo and SCA, and both MoDo Chair Lundberg and SCA CEO Martin-Löf concluded that a partial merger between the two companies could be a wise structural move.[39] However, MoDo discussed a merger of its fine paper unit with other companies as well. For example, there had been discussions with Enso-Gutzeit before that company's merger with Stora, but as the Finnish company wanted to create a 'MoDoEnso' the whole idea was dropped. Chair Lundberg did not like such a construct – he wanted to continue to be majority shareholder (Enso-Gutzeit was more successful in its parallel discussions to merge with Stora; cf. Ch. 12).

Lundberg really wanted to get MoDo out of fine paper, so he did not close any doors to SCA (or to other actors). His idea was to merge the two companies' fine paper operations without including the forest resources – a delivery agreement had to do. He also purposely pushed for 'Modo[40] paper' as the name of the new company, because then it would be identified with its classic core business, but still distinct. Lundberg's (and MoDo's) idea was to distribute the new fine paper company's shares to MoDo's shareholders, while SCA wanted to sell their Modo Paper shares (to use the capital for SCA's further development).[41]

One foreseeable problem with a merger between the two companies' fine paper business was that it would be a joint venture involving the two 'sworn enemies' of the Swedish forest-based industry. An aggravating factor was the recent struggle between Lundberg and SCA to gain control over MoDo (cf. Ch. 9) – a process that had left unpleasant memories in the minds of several of the leading actors. Some insiders described the relations as 'frosty and imbued with negative emotions'. SCA's conception of MoDo was that it was 'a generally inferior company', while MoDo typecast SCA as 'a villainous company'. In spite of the rather poor relationship between the two companies, talks regarding a partial (i.e. fine paper) merger started again early in 1999, involving among others MoDo's CEO Pettersson and SCA's CEO Martin-Löf.

Through these talks, six issues had to be resolved: (1) the valuation of each company's units, (2) who should be appointed CEO of the new unit, (3) how the new board should be composed, (4) how the exit opportunities should be constructed, (5) what should be done with the Domsjö site and (6) how the sourcing of timber/wood to the new unit should be handled. The last issue – a crucial one – was solved when an agreement was reached that Modo Paper should not own any forests. Regarding the first issue, MoDo claimed that it had all its fine paper plants in good shape, although for Alizay only a short healthy period could be claimed. MoDo regarded SCA's plants generally to be inferior to MoDo's, making a shareholding distribution 55–45 in favour of MoDo reasonable. Not surprisingly, SCA came to the opposite conclusion: 45–55. So, Pettersson had to convince MoDo's board that 50–50 was OK and Martin-Löf had to do the same at SCA.[42]

During the early part of 1999, the idea of merging MoDo's fine paper business with SCA's gradually won out. The equal distribution of the shareholding was accepted with great reluctance. Indeed, discussions continued within MoDo's board until the last minute about whether a way might be found to achieve, for example, a 52 per cent share. The reason for the dissatisfaction with a 50–50 solution was that MoDo's own fine paper business was judged to be in good shape, while there were still significant problems associated with SCA's contributions, particularly stemming from the fact that the Wifsta and Hallein plants had been added as parts of the deal. Wifsta was linked to Östrand – not an optimal combination – and Hallein was facing a most difficult environmental situation. So, MoDo still considered other alternatives to joining forces with SCA to accomplish a divestment of its fine paper business. Therefore, deals with, for example, Neusiedler[43] and Soporcel[44] were considered, but rejected.

Despite all these doubts, MoDo and SCA announced on 28 April 1999 that they planned to merge their fine paper businesses into a new unit named Modo Paper, in which the shareholding would be equally divided. The Modo name was chosen because that brand was the stronger of the two on the fine paper market. At the same time, MoDo changed its name to Holmen.[45] The agreement also stipulated rules for each party's exit: the two founders' disposition of their respective shares was restricted until 2003.

The purpose of the partial merger was ultimately to establish a unit with great status and impact on a market characterized by overcapacity. Significant returns were expected to come from rationalizations and/or synergies in administration, marketing, sales and R&D. It was thought that the new unit would be strong in two fine paper segments, namely office paper and coated sheets, and weak in two other fields, namely rolls and large sheets. Still, there was uncertainty regarding whether its lack of forest resources might make it less attractive in the eyes of potential investors. All had to live with this uncertainty, however, because Lundberg insisted that MoDo (Holmen) kept its forest resources.[46]

For many years, European fine paper producers were convinced that structural changes had to come. The returns were low in general, and 'bulky' fine paper was expected to face strong Asian competition in the future. Still, almost no M&As took place, due mainly to diverging opinions among sellers and buyers about fair transaction prices. As mentioned before, the idea was that Modo Paper should either be introduced on the stock market or be distributed to the shareholders. MoDo made it publicly known that it would not even consider owning a large portion of a company over a long period without being in full control (in a press release one could read that the goal was to go public in two years' time). MoDo's Chair stressed that, before going public, the new unit would have to show a strong balance sheet (i.e. equity around SEK 10 billion) and would have to demonstrate that it was in good shape and had a promising future.

As MoDo's board still regarded its own company as the more competent operator of a fine paper business, it insisted on seeing somebody from MoDo in charge of the new constellation. There were two strong 'internal' candidates at the time: Hans Pettersson (MoDo, who had competed with Bengt Pettersson for the CEO position [cf. above]) and Åström (the latter currently working for SCA, but with a track record also at MoDo). In the end, MoDo 'gave in' and Åström was appointed CEO of the new company (and Hans Pettersson left MoDo). Each of the founders was allowed to appoint three directors to the new Modo Paper board and had to agree on the choice of the seventh member, a neutral Chair. Despite the acceptance from MoDo's owners and board, Åström's appointment aroused negative feelings among some of the managers in MoDo and Modo Paper, but that scepticism never materialized in any significant actions.[47] Together with the new board the new CEO immediately established a strategy for Modo Paper, organized its operations and started its journey towards becoming a powerful and effective business unit expected to capture a leading position in Europe.

At the time, MoDo's board was concerned about what they described as 'SCA's short-termism'. They claimed that SCA had 'dressed up the bride' and, for example, not made efforts to make improvements at the problem unit Wifsta. Although the new Modo Paper first and foremost represented a merger of complementary business segments, it also constituted a platform for further structural initiatives that could add those substantial synergies that the new formation basically lacked. At the same time, it was expected that the value of both MoDo and SCA would increase because of the more concentrated business repertoire and the divestment of a low-margin business. In the final agreement, MoDo furnished Modo Paper with Husum (Sweden), Alizay (France), PPSM (France), Silverdalen (Sweden) and MoDo Merchants. SCA Fine Paper provided its units at Hallein (Austria), Stockstadt (Germany) and Wifsta (Sweden), as well as its sales unit SCA Paper Trade. Taken together the new constellation obtained a wholesaling presence in 20 countries.

MoDo and SCA now had three alternatives in terms of Modo Paper: go public with the new company, sell it or distribute the shares to its shareholders in the founding companies. As mentioned above, MoDo was inclined to use the third path, while SCA seemed to prefer the second one. However, the new Modo Paper decided to pursue the first path – a stock market introduction, so management went on a 'road show'. To their great surprise there was almost no interest at all for the new stock. At the time, there was a global 'IT hype', so the venture capital went elsewhere.[48] This made the third path again more interesting for MoDo, while SCA stuck to the selling alternative. In either case the shareholders would benefit from the synergies that in a few years' time were expected to materialize. MoDo thus had to co-ordinate the distribution of most of its Modo Paper shares to its shareholders with SCA's selling of most of its holding. Initially each company was to keep 15 per cent of the total Modo Paper stock. However, in March 2000, due to a weak stock market, SCA was no longer willing to introduce the Modo Paper shares on the SSE, so MoDo had to postpone its planned share dividend.

10.3 THREE CEOs IN FOUR YEARS

In June 1999, not long after the deal with SCA to create Modo Paper was announced, CEO Pettersson declared that he intended to leave his position no later than at the forthcoming AGM scheduled for spring 2000. As usual, there was discussion about whether his successor could be found among current top management, but the CEO doubted that was the case. One manager that would fit the CEO position was Lundin, but he was regarded as too old to represent a long-term solution (he was two years younger than Pettersson). So, MoDo looked outside and contracted a head-hunter, who together with the Chair and the CEO managed the recruitment. The top candidate was Per Ericson, who had a strong track record, although not within the forest-based industry (he was head of Sandvik's[49] steel business). Ericson was a bright person with strong merits as an executive, and he was indeed familiar with industrial operations and rationales. All board members supported the idea of recruiting him. Pettersson was asked to stay as a board member and assist Ericson, in case the latter needed advice based on experience from the forest-based industry.[50] So, in October 1999 Ericson was appointed as MoDo CEO. He took charge formally on 15 February 2000 just a few days after MoDo had changed its name to Holmen (but before the agreement to sell Modo Paper to Metsä-Serla, cf. below).

Initially, Holmen's board gave the new CEO three assignments: the Workington plant had to be improved, the sawmill business needed to gain momentum and a renewal of top management was needed. However, other than addressing the third of the listed tasks (e.g. replacing the Head of Group Finance and the Head of Group Human Resources), Ericson basically started from another angle and went in a different direction. He applied his industrial experience and concluded soon that quite a lot of what his predecessors had done had to be changed – substantial operative improvements topped his agenda. His conclusion did not fall on good ground.

Holmen's top management accepted the appointment of Ericson as the new CEO. However, even before the board had finally decided to offer him the position, one or two of them raised doubts regarding his aptitude for that position. Most managers soon came to believe that Ericson's recruitment was a mistake. Already at an early stage, the CFO had tried to call the board's attention to the emerging lack of harmony in the top management group, but for some time that information did not get through. Basically, Ericson managed the company with indirect methods ('Excel-sheet management'), and that neither fitted Holmen's team-oriented management culture nor built confidence. Thus, Ericson preferred to work 'alone', and to a large extent his actions were based mainly on his own calculations and conclusions. Therefore, top management had difficulties understanding his core ideas, and what development path for Holmen he advocated – and why. Thus, his social and communicative skills seemed to be not as strong as his analytical and calculative abilities. His lack of experience within the forest-based industry also made him rather dependent on the quantitative figures as such – his background provided him with a limited capacity to add more qualitative and experience-based judgements to the calculations, making several of his propositions only weakly linked to specific forest-industrial settings. Moreover, since he came from another industry, Ericson needed some time to gain acceptance in the relevant business networks, to learn their ways of thinking ('business recipes') and to understand the on-going interpersonal processes. However, that kind of learning did not have enough time to materialize.

As an externally recruited CEO, Ericson interpreted the situation as one where change was expected. That was, however, a misjudgement. When he entered Holmen, current top management did not anticipate any radical changes at all. Thus his interpretations of the state of affairs differed from those of the people around him, and that dissonance soon produced uncertainty in the organization regarding what path Holmen was about to take.[51] Ericson's (short) stay as CEO did Holmen no harm, although the company might have lost some time and speed.[52]

In the first years of the new millennium, Holmen began to discuss an acquisition of Frövifors (LPB) with AssiDomän (a Swedish state-owned company; cf. Ch. 7), but decided not to pursue the issue. There were also discussions regarding the merits of following the decided strategy and making a new large investment in the newsprint business. The board had identified two alternatives: a third machine at Braviken and an acquisition or establishment in Spain.

Since the beginning of the 1980s, Spain had lacked significant production plants in the printing paper business, and Holmen (i.e. MoDo) had sold substantial quantities of newsprint there. In addition, since it was a country that was not yet 'claimed' by some other producer, investing there would probably discourage others from doing the same. At the millennium, only three countries in Western Europe had substantial imports of newsprint, namely the UK, Spain and Portugal, and among them Spain was seen as the most interesting growth market.[53]

Soon Papelera Peninsular in Madrid emerged as an acquisition target, and an agreement to buy that unit was reached in April 2000 (with Unipapel, a family-run company listed on the stock market). Holmen already had Frölander in place working in Spain – he had been there since 1988 and had built a growing business. Thus, he knew that country's forest-based industry, and was well integrated in its business networks. However, it was actually the Head of Newsprint, Lundin, who initiated and carried through the acquisition. A rapid purchasing process was possible since Holmen was well prepared in the event that opportunities like the current one should appear.

On markets where the company had an established business, Holmen regularly tried to acquire all permissions and authorizations in advance, and learn about the context, so that its leading actors – if necessary – would be prepared to act quickly. Like other potential buyers, Holmen was aware of the drawbacks of purchasing Papelera Peninsular, but its leading executives also – and perhaps better – understood the opportunities involved. Holmen had learned that running a domestic production plant was a great advantage politically, as well as in terms of transportation costs and sourcing. Its leading actors also knew that the major shareholding family was inclined (perhaps almost forced) to sell. The target unit, Papelera Peninsular, contained a modern paper mill (1998) (though not especially tailored for newsprint production) and two partly owned companies running waste paper businesses. The mill was sourced by recycled paper from Spain and Portugal and was located close to Madrid. Over the long run, the mill's location could make the water sourcing problematic. However, a particular strength of the site was that its infrastructure would allow for at least one more machine investment. Holmen went through with the transaction (the price: SEK 1 billion plus a takeover of debts of a similar size). The purchase was fully in accordance with CEO Ericson's idea that to further develop its newsprint position in Europe, Holmen (also) had to grow through acquisitions.[54]

At that time, Metsä-Serla (and particularly its new CEO) began to show interest in acquiring Modo Paper from MoDo and SCA. A rather unexpected proposal from the Finnish company threw a different light on the planned (but postponed) introduction of Modo Paper on the SSE. Metsä-Serla's CEO, who came from the car industry, envisioned making the company the biggest fine paper unit in Europe. His lack of familiarity with the forest-based industry might explain why Metsä-Serla paid so much. Including the debt that accompanied the purchase, Metsä-Serla paid around SEK 19 billion.[55] SCA found the first serious bid equivalent to SEK 17 billion more than satisfactory, but MoDo's Chair Lundberg considered it too low. Metsä-Serla then raised its bid by SEK 2 billion, and, finally, both sellers accepted that sum, which was at least 25 per cent higher than what they would have got by going public.[56] The transaction was concluded in August 2000, once the European Commission had approved it. SCA made a SEK 2.7 billion capital gain, and Holmen earned around SEK 1.8 billion. Thus, the sale provided Holmen with a strong financial position. Its debt/equity ratio was down to 0.16, so SEK 6–8 billion was available for investments. The balance sheet was so strong that a repurchase of shares was on the agenda at the August EGM (it corresponded to 10% of the stock, i.e. SEK 2 billion), as there was also a large extra dividend. So, the sale of Modo Paper was certainly a favourable deal for the sellers, while it also made Metsä-Serla Europe's biggest producer of fine paper.

Director Carl Kempe Jr – representing the heritage of the Kempe dynasty – expressed some concern when the sale of Modo Paper to Metsä-Serla was proposed. He was hesitant since Holmen had committed itself to taking the new company to the stock market and distributing its shares to the shareholders (i.e. to the Kempe foundations). In his view, breaking that promise could be interpreted as a deceitful action. However, the sale of Modo Paper was in fact a powerful manifestation of the new Holmen strategy decided by MoDo's board in January 1999. Its basic idea was that Holmen should reduce its core business to two: newsprint and quality cardboard. CEO Ericson also expected that Holmen would grow further in these areas, and that it now had sufficient financial resources for such efforts.

Thus, paradoxically, the 'Third Bloc' that Carlgren had created in 1988 to 'guarantee' the Kempe dynasty's long-term control over MoDo both sold out its classic core business (fine paper) and replaced its original name with Holmen. The 'new' company contained two main business areas, cardboard (Iggesund) and wood-containing paper (Holmen), but also forestry, power plants and sawmills. A global consultancy firm that Holmen commissioned to investigate the future for the various kinds of printing papers that existed (or were expected to reach the market soon) described the future for that business area as promising even in a long-term perspective. That conclusion convinced Holmen's board that the chosen path forward would work. However, one could add that, at that time, the European Commission was investigating a suspected cartel in the European newsprint business, and the board regarded the likelihood for conviction as rather high.

The year 2001 became a very good year for Holmen. For example, Holmen Paper alone made a SEK 2.5 billion profit. The company also initiated substantial investments that year, including the SEK 1.85 billion destined for the Hallsta site. Holmen's intention with that decision was to make the company one of the leaders in magazine paper. CEO Ericson saw it as a promising growth area, where new products 'continuously' would be developed to satisfy new customer requirements. The large investment fit in well with Holmen's strategy of achieving organic growth in areas where the company already had a strong niche position and close customer relations. In Europe overall, the level of investment in new production capacity within magazine paper was low, and it was expected to remain so for the foreseeable future. Therefore, Ericson expected that the new machine soon would operate at 'full' capacity.

When Holmen had taken the decision to rebuild one machine at Hallsta and started that project, the market for journal paper unexpectedly collapsed, and that in a situation where prices were high. It was the advertising market that fell through, and that debacle hit the company hard. However, due to the new investment, Holmen was lucky to have planned a work stoppage during that market decline, so the company could continue serving its customers.[57]

In spite of the good economic result of 2001, CEO Ericson had to leave his position and Holmen (co-operation difficulties). Soon an experienced internal actor replaced him: Lundin. He had been passed over when Ericson was recruited because he was considered to be too old. There was also an up-and-coming young man around (Magnus Hall), but to promote him to CEO at that time was seen as a bit too early. It was Chair Lundberg who convinced the recently retired and respected Lundin to return for a few years as CEO.[58] He had worked at Holmen for a long time and had been Head of Holmen Paper back in the 1980s. Thus, Lundin was a man who really knew the forest-based industry, and particularly its newsprint sector. Like Ericson, he changed the composition of the top management. Among other things, he appointed Hall new Head of Holmen Paper and Kvick new Head of Iggesund Paperboard. He also installed new people as heads of Personnel and Accounting/Control.

According to Holmen's strategy, it was important for the company to control the crucial input resources (i.e. timber and energy). So, to own substantial and well-located forests and power stations was given high priority. Therefore, Holmen used its (MoDo's) option from 1983 to buy back hydroelectric power assets for SEK 1.7 billion (in 2002). The strategy also stated that Holmen should keep its production resources efficient and invest continuously when needs were identified or competition made such efforts necessary. Therefore, in 2003, large investments were made at Braviken, Workington and Iggesund, in all cases primarily to improve product quality.

Holmen's good result at the beginning of the millennium contributed to the board's readiness to discuss new large investments – for example, a new machine for newsprint. Since it was not considered feasible over the long run to keep the Madrid paper mill in its present shape (one machine only), the preference was to locate that new investment in Spain. However, the board wanted to have a comparison with another realistic localization alternative, so the Braviken site became the internal competitor in the evaluation process.[59] Still, it was never treated as a serious contender – all through the evaluation process the leading actors believed that an investment in Spain was the best choice, since it was assumed that Holmen should take the opportunity to consolidate its position as a dominating European supplier of newsprint from that market.[60]

Eventually, after many investigations, analyses and discussions, the Spanish alternative was chosen. Several circumstances supported that path. For example, a two-mill site was usually much more economical than a one-mill site, primarily due to benefits that normally followed from a sharing of infrastructure. Localization outside Sweden also implied fewer currency problems and energy price risks, and generally production costs were expected to be lower and the sourcing of timber better. However, the decisive argument was that the Spanish alternative was associated with a stronger market potential. Demand was growing in that country, and the competition was still weak. Through the new large machine, Holmen could almost 'close' Spain for newsprint investments from other actors.[61]

In 2002, all preparations for the establishment of a new newsprint machine in Spain had been carried out successfully – that included everything from required permissions and authorizations, to the securing of sourcing of raw material and energy. However, the board hesitated as a result of a decline in demand. Moreover, at the end of the preparatory process, the environmental costs had increased (i.e. due to new EU instructions and regulations). The competitors (Stora Enso and Myllikoski) increased their output too, so there was a largely unforeseen substantial net addition on the market. That unexpected development led Holmen to postpone the investment until the business trends began to improve again. Thus, the board began to discuss a later start of the machine (2004 or 2005). The board also came to the conclusion that Holmen should avoid investing in the biggest machine available on the market, a move that would have been too expensive and risky. So, the budget for the new machine was cut from around SEK 4 billion to SEK 2.8 billion – that is to say, Holmen tailored the effort to suit the expected market structure.[62]

On 3 February 2004, the board met and finally decided to go ahead with the building of a recycled-fibre-based newsprint machine at Papalera Peninsula in Spain. The investment cost was estimated at SEK 2.7 billion, and production was planned to start in 2006. The primary market for its products was to be southern Europe, where the high rate of growth in consumption was expected to continue. The competitiveness of the project was also based on low transport costs and superior service. A particular advantage with the new investment was that it created an opportunity to produce more quantities of highly processed products on other machines, particularly to raise the output of lightly coated magazine paper on the existing machine in Spain, as well as increasing the share of special products at the Swedish mills.

At the same board meeting, Lundin formally informed the directors that he wanted to retire at the latest by 31 March 2004. His resignation was accepted, but he was asked to stay on the board. The board also decided to appoint Hall as the new CEO with 1 April as his first day of duty.

At that time, the Workington site (again) had indicated profitability problems that would make new investments in its existing machines necessary. Also the successful Iggesund site needed substantial investments in the years to come (SEK 1 billion). However, the latter unit's position was strong, although European production figures indicated a certain overcapacity on the market. That surplus was currently handled through considerable export from Europe to Asia.

The board also spent quite a lot of time discussing the problems with the Wargön site (coated printing paper). There were a few interested buyers around, but no agreement was reached, usually due to disagreements among the (potential) buyers' leading actors (shareholders, directors and CEOs). To try to improve the situation, an action programme – a reorganization – was later launched to address Wargön's poor result and overcapacity, as well as its insufficient product quality. There were also some problems at Braviken and Hallsta regarding product mix and efficiency (SEK 1 billion was needed), but in those cases, too, long-term profitability looked to be satisfactory.

NOTES

N.B.: When there is an 'i' inside a parenthesis below, that letter indicates that the note refers to an interview with the named person. All interviewees are listed in the Appendix. A complete listing of references is found at the end of the book.

1. Rydin's diary.
2. Carl Kempe Jr (2006i).
3. Larsson (2006i).
4. However, many actors instead regarded Lundberg as the one that stopped SCA from realizing its ideas regarding MoDo.
5. Larsson (2006i).
6. Pettersson (2006i).
7. There was only one serious internal competitor: Hans Pettersson.
8. A private CD where Önnesjö (inter alia) talks about his time as Chair at MoDo, and Lundberg (2006i).
9. Pettersson (2006i).
10. Ibid.
11. Flodström (2006i).
12. Mårtensson (2006i).
13. Lundberg (2006i).
14. Pettersson (2006i).
15. To AssiDomän for SEK 1 billion (cf. Ch. 7).
16. Croon (2005).
17. Pettersson (2006i).
18. Flodström (2006i).
19. Pettersson (2006i).
20. Svensson (2006i).
21. Lundberg (2006i) and Welin (2006i).
22. Larsson (2006i).
23. Chair 1992–95.
24. Lundin (2006i).
25. Pettersson (2006i).
26. Ibid.
27. Ibid.
28. Mårtensson (2006i).
29. Valeur (2000) and Croon (2005).
30. A Dutch multinational active in the fields of decorative paints, performance coatings and specialty chemicals.
31. One of Europe's leading ethyl alcohol producers.
32. Valeur (2000).
33. A supplier of high-quality paper pulp.
34. Norwegian Borregaard produced advanced and environmentally friendly biochemicals.
35. Croon (2005).
36. Larsson (2006i).
37. Larsson (letter to the author written in 2006).
38. Larsson (2006i).
39. Croon (2005).
40. The spelling was M*odo* – not Mo*Do* – to distinguish the new fine paper company from the elder one that carried the same name.
41. Lundberg (2006i).
42. Pettersson (2006i).
43. An Austrian fine paper producer.
44. A Portuguese pulp and paper company.
45. There had actually been three alternatives on the table: a new name, Holmen and Iggesund. The major shareholder Lundberg and most directors favoured Holmen, and Iggesund had to accept that choice.
46. Instead, a seven-year delivery contract was set up.
47. Larsson (2006i), Lundin (2006i) and Pettersson (2006i).
48. Pettersson (2006i).
49. A Swedish global high-tech manufacturing company.
50. Larsson (2006i) and Pettersson (2006i).

51. Hall (2006i).
52. Svensson (2006i).
53. Lundberg (2006i).
54. Holmen Press Release 2004-04-06, Hall (2006i) and Svensson (2006i).
55. Lundberg (2006i).
56. Pettersson (2006i).
57. Hall (2006i).
58. Larsson (2006i) and Lundberg (2006i).
59. Hall (2006i).
60. Hall (2006i).
61. Lundberg (2006i).
62. Hall (2006i).

11. From Stora Kopparberg to Stora Enso: in search of a strategy

11.1 THE POST-WWII PERIOD

11.1.1 A Divided Family

The Wallenberg sphere had reached a dominating position in the Swedish industry by the middle of the 20th century. In the forest-based sector, the sphere controlled five large corporations, namely Stora Kopparberg, Wifstavarf, Kopparfors, Papyrus and Hylte. After WWII, the Wallenberg sphere had redefined its business rationale from one under which individual companies were built and developed organically, to one under which industrial restructuring, mergers and acquisitions dominated the expansion efforts. The family had also slowly but surely obtained the competence to govern large and operatively diverse corporations. To achieve that capability, they had developed skills in recruiting qualified managers and furnishing them with various kinds of resources including inspiring networks. Over time, several of these managers achieved top positions in the Wallenberg companies, ready to exchange experiences with their colleagues in the sphere, something that made continuous innovation and reorientation possible.[1]

Jacob Wallenberg Sr and Marcus Wallenberg Sr tried to establish the best possible market positions for all 'their' corporations, although Stora Kopparberg was a particularly cherished unit. That goal was not pursued solely through traditional business activities, but also through active participation in all relevant social and political arenas. Thus, the Wallenberg brothers also tried to influence the external conditions for the sphere's corporations. Moreover, the traditional clear-cut division of functions between owners and executive bodies was relaxed, as several of the leading members of the family also were appointed to the latter kind of positions. Thus, although listed, the Wallenberg companies were run very much like most other large family businesses.[2] However, the ownership structure was rather unique, as the Wallenberg sphere's shareholding was handled primarily through three different kinds of units: the Wallenberg Foundations, the investment companies (Investor and Providentia) and the 'family bank' SE-Banken.

The Wallenberg family's ambition to act as a leading industrial restructurer in the forest-based sector soon materialized. In that process, Stora Kopparberg became the hub, but eventually the efforts revealed that the two leading actors of the dynasty did not get along particularly well. To limit conflicts they had divided the sphere into two rather separate parts – up until the 1960s there was rather little co-operation between them – each of the brothers ran 'his' companies. Still, to most external actors they represented the core of one integrated business empire. The prestigious Stora Kopparberg positions were divided as follows: Jacob Wallenberg Sr entered the board in 1941 and became its Chair in 1950, and Marcus Wallenberg Sr got a board seat in 1944 and acted as Deputy Chair

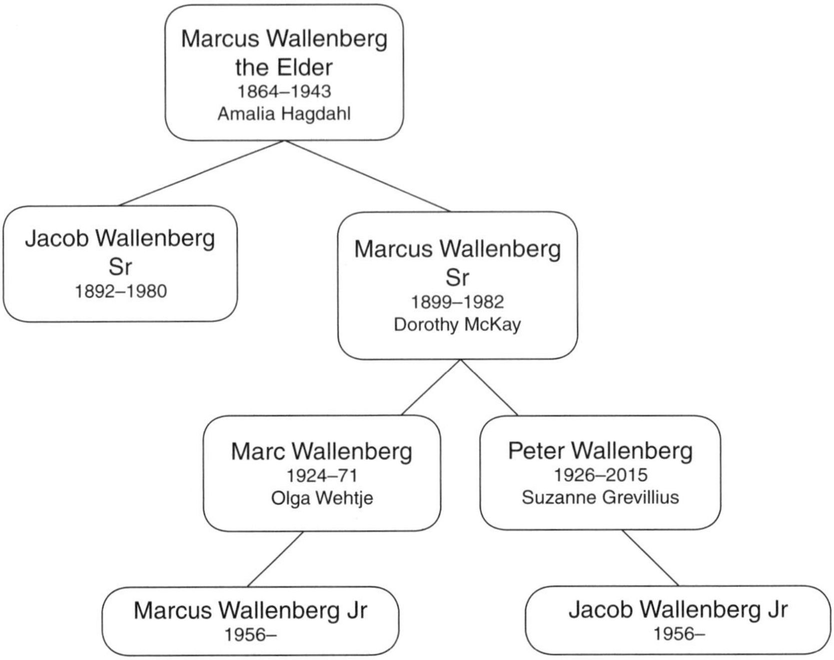

Figure 11.1 A selected part of the Wallenberg family tree (only family members mentioned in this volume are included)

for many years before he was appointed Chair in 1976. Stora Kopparberg's unique standing in the Wallenberg family sphere was acknowledged by the fact that it was the sole industrial company in which both Wallenberg brothers held board seats simultaneously.[3]

The two brothers' leadership styles differed significantly (cf. Ch. 5), but they had the same ambition: to keep the sphere together and to make it even stronger for the coming decades. Both shouldered the role as controlling shareholders, and continuously reviewed and reshaped 'their' corporations by bringing new technological, financial and managerial achievements to the global marketplace. As almost all of the 'Wallenberg companies' were listed and thus only partly owned (usually $< 50\%$), sphere governance and integration also had to be based on something other than plain shareholding, in this case on the presence of a particular 'atmosphere' and culture where competence, trust-like relations and responsibility were key ingredients. It was also important that the strategic paths that were decided on were beneficial not only for the corporations but also for the sphere and its key individuals.[4]

Jacob Wallenberg Sr had a circumspect and analytical turn of mind that often was accompanied by caution and a rather passive image. However, that wait-and-see attitude that occasionally surfaced was founded in a respect for both current actors and efforts made by previous generations.[5] He was also often ascribed a personality that resembled that of a scientist and in many circles supposed to qualify for such a career. Yet his brother also expressed a similar interest for research – Marcus Wallenberg Sr was truly fascinated by the industrial opportunities that modern high-tech provided (although that attitude did not come out strongly in his leadership style). Both of them regularly discussed findings with scientists looking for new ideas that eventually could be applied somewhere in their company group. Actually, the sphere had been involved in the scientific sector for a long time, as early members of the family had established a group of foundations that, in addition to holding substantial amounts of stock in the sphere's companies, also financed a non-negligible part of 'the Swedish research budget'. Thus, Jacob Wallenberg Sr and Marcus Wallenberg Sr had inherited an extensive national and international network of scientists that also included many leading politicians.[6]

Both Wallenberg brothers were person-oriented actors but in different ways. Jacob Wallenberg Sr basically governed 'his' part of the sphere through the involved CEOs and concentrated his efforts on ownership matters and strategic discussions. He also acted as a most respected international financier. Marcus Wallenberg Sr communicated even more with 'his' CEOs, but he also built a personal network that included many actors on the lower corporate levels and used them to control performance and – if 'necessary' – intervene. At the same time, he scouted for new management talent that later could be used in top positions in the sphere group. Thus, Marcus Wallenberg Sr participated in many concrete business discussions, and he even tried to master many of the details in crucial investment decisions and other operative matters.[7]

Håkan Abenius was Stora Kopparberg's CEO from 1948. He was a timid, serious and upright man who seldom raised his voice. His low profile was accompanied by a reluctance to talk to the press. The journalists were not that eager to meet with him either, as he was an uncontroversial person dedicated to making sure that the company was profitable and could expect a bright future. Basically, Abenius's role was to administer a company group in good health during a long period of growth. Despite the huge cultural differences between Falun (Stora Kopparberg's HQ) and New York (the world's financial centre) and his shy appearance, Abenius won great respect among the American bankers in the Nova Scotia discussions in the mid-1960s (cf. subsection 11.1.2), foremost because he had done his homework and could express his ideas and thoughts well.

After WWII, product development regained momentum in Stora Kopparberg. A new method for producing sulphate pulp was put into full-scale production at the Skutskär site (1955), and soon (1959) a chlorine-bleached product was marketed to challenge MoDo's and Korsnäs's innovation in that area. Skutskär also began to produce 'fluff' – a sort of pulp that for some time had been used as a raw material for various kinds of hygiene products. During this period Stora Kopparberg also bought Strömsnäs Bruk (1955), which housed the biggest sack production unit in Sweden. In that way, Stora Kopparberg had added three new businesses to its repertoire (bleached pulp, fluff pulp and sacks), something that strongly influenced the company's strategy in the early 1960s.

During the 1960s, Stora Kopparberg worked consistently to strengthen its forest resources by acquiring some of the minor mills 'belonging' to Jacob Wallenberg Sr's part of the sphere (Sternfors-Ställdalen, 1961; Wikmanshyttan, 1966; Grycksbo, 1966; and Mackmyra Sulfit, 1969).[8] When Mackmyra was acquired, Jacob Wallenberg Sr did not inform his brother until after the transaction had been completed. The reason was that Stora Kopparberg's CEO Sundblad suspected that his company otherwise would have to share Mackmyra's forests with Kopparfors (a firm that Marcus Wallenberg Sr governed), as it had started a parallel expansion process by acquiring Bollnäs Skog[9] and Kilafors Jernverk.[10] These unco-ordinated expansion efforts soon brought about speculations regarding which brother would engulf the other. At that time, Marcus Wallenberg Sr also advocated that Kopparfors should acquire Bergvik & Ala. However, such a merger would be tough economically, as the gap between Bergvik & Ala's stock market value and its net asset value made such a deal unlikely. Once again the rivalry between the two brothers became apparent, as Jacob Wallenberg Sr's Stora Kopparberg also investigated a possible purchase of that company (which also soon materialized).

In 1965 something unusual happened: straightforward barter between companies. The Wallenberg-controlled Wifstavarf was transferred to Svenska Handelsbanken's business sphere, and in return Bergvik & Ala was obtained by the Wallenberg sphere (its bank [SE-Banken]). The exchange came as a total surprise to most actors, but it had been prepared for in confidential talks during the autumn of 1964 involving Ernfrid Browaldh (Chair of Handelsbanken) and Jacob Wallenberg Sr (Chair of Stora Kopparberg). However, Bergvik & Ala's Deputy Chair, Francke, who represented a minority shareholding, instead expressed a preference for a merger with Iggesund, so he was not satisfied with the outcome.[11]

In spring 1967, Bergvik & Ala bought Ström-Ljusne, which soon was sold to Iggesund.[12] In that situation most actors thought that everything was settled for a grand merger between the adjoining corporations Stora Kopparberg, Kopparfors and Bergvik & Ala. However, mergers in the Wallenberg sphere did not always follow a straightforward business rationale. Instead, the rivalry between the two Wallenberg brothers sometimes determined what was possible (as each of them defended 'his' part of the sphere). Both of them also hoped that they could buy forest-based companies outside the sphere, and at the time their focus was on Iggesund and Graningeverken.[13]

11.1.2 A Disastrous Investment Decision: SFI in Nova Scotia

Swedish forest-based corporations' interest in investing abroad was largely sparked by concerns about an impending shortage of timber in Sweden. The estimated forest resources limited the future production volumes. For Stora Kopparberg, for example, it would not be possible to supply an expansion of its operations at Skutskär (pulp) and Kvarnsveden (paper) with local timber. After extensive research and a long planning process involving divided and ambiguous actors (owners, directors and managers), the board finally decided to build a new pulp mill in Nova Scotia (Canada).[14]

Stora Kopparberg was at that time already active in North America through a subsidiary. Its head (Clausen) understood the situation; his job was to find new sources of raw material on that continent rather than to act as a traditional pulp seller. So when Scott Paper gave up its option for certain crown forests in Nova Scotia to instead invest elsewhere, Clausen saw an opportunity for Stora Kopparberg. Geographically, the Nova Scotia location was excellent as it offered a deep, ice-free harbour and an auspicious supply of timber, which according to tests was suitable for both sulphite and sulphate production. The former method was given precedence, as its yield was higher. However, such an investment also required the active support of Canadian politicians (e.g. a long-term contract to secure timber supply and guarantees regarding the water and power sourcing). As the Nova Scotia project competed internally for investment resources, its financing became a crucial issue, too. However, in 1956 Marcus Wallenberg Sr declared his support for the Nova Scotia investment, although to be fully convinced he needed certain additional data and calculations.

At that stage it was time to inform the local government in the region and Stora Kopparberg's Chair Jacob Wallenberg Sr about the Nova Scotia project. However, the Chair was far from convinced by the information that had been collected. As he saw it, the demand for sulphite was poor, the risk of a drop in the pulp price high, the test of the Canadian timber too sketchy, the problem with the recycling of alkali unsolved and the financial stress too high. CEO Abenius could not refute Jacob Wallenberg Sr's objections regarding the Nova Scotia project, so he returned to the US and informed Clausen about the Chair's position. Clausen then suggested that Stora Kopparberg's North American subsidiary should house the project, possibly together with some other party, and with only limited involvement from its parent company. As a consequence, Clausen was permitted to establish a new unit, Nova Scotia Pulp, where he became both Chair and CEO. However, 'Stora Kopparberg' was not permitted to be a part of its name, as that would indicate a considerable engagement from the ultimate owner.

While Jacob Wallenberg Sr continued to express scepticism and to stress the financial difficulties and the market uncertainty, his brother Marcus Wallenberg Sr refused to give in, as he was eager that Stora Kopparberg, like MoDo and SCA (cf. Ch. 9 and Ch. 13), should run operations in North America. Fortified by a personal visit to the planned site and a positive report from his forester, Abenius expressed support for the project. He informed the board that all infrastructural matters could be resolved and that the directors' concern about the unattractiveness of the product as such (sulphite pulp) was unwarranted. However, the financing of the project was still a problem. One idea was to offer a contract under which the North American customers had to commit themselves to a certain quantity over a ten-year period and to buy shares over that same time. Such a procedure would simultaneously secure sales and attract partners (up to 50%). To sell Koppartrans[15] to free capital was another possibility, but initially it was rejected.

Stora Kopparberg had to take a decision soon, as the Nova Scotia project needed support from the Canadian government, which had to pass certain legislation during spring 1959 to make the investment possible (tax and expropriation matters as well as clarifications regarding the sourcing of water and power). Since the project involved around 10–15 per cent of the forest area in the province, it was a major regional issue. To start the process, Abenius provided the shareholders and some of the other leading actors with four reasons why Stora Kopparberg should start to build the plant: it was strategically right – if Stora Kopparberg did not invest some other actor would, and that could create problems even on the European market; a favourable option existed to buy a large forest area containing timber suitable for pulp production; the mill would be located in the middle of the forest and close to an ice-free harbour; and the company's new competitive technology for producing high-quality sulphite pulp would be used on a large-scale basis.

Marcus Wallenberg Sr still supported the project, while his brother Jacob Wallenberg Sr continued his resistance. In that struggle the elder and more experienced directors sided with Jacob, while the younger and greener directors stood behind Marcus.[16] Later, a meeting between Clausen and the two Wallenberg brothers 'crashed' – emotions ran high and insults were frequent. Clausen even threatened to resign, and that made both brothers both upset and suspicious. However, Abenius restored the damaged relations pretty well, and the outcome became that they all agreed to ask the Canadian Prime Minister for more time. They also authorized Stora Kopparberg's management to buy the necessary property. Those two decisions represented the first crucial steps towards an investment in sulphite production in Nova Scotia. Soon thereafter the Canadian Prime Minister, in his 'speech from the throne', suggested certain legal changes, and asked the parliament for resources for infrastructure improvements. However, the financing of the planned investment still was not brought to a successful close.

Carl De Geer began to explore the possibility of mobilizing funding for the Nova Scotia project in Canada and the US, but the actors in those countries were not particularly optimistic regarding the future of sulphite pulp. Another possible obstacle to the deal was the opinion of the Swedish Foreign Exchange Control[17] regarding the intended export of capital and/or lending from abroad. While that agency expressed no objection, it demanded that Stora Kopparberg should hold the majority in the upcoming joint venture. Abenius then thought that a formal board decision was all that remained before the project could be launched. However, Jacob Wallenberg Sr still refused to support the investment. He wanted better terms from the Swedish Foreign Exchange Control and demanded that the project should be shared with an equal partner. He believed that if it was as good as its advocates asserted, then it would be rather easy to find a suitable (American) co-investor. St Regis also soon announced its interest in some kind of joint effort with Stora Kopparberg but not on equal terms, something that the Chair had required. Eventually, Jacob Wallenberg Sr abandoned that condition, because of the good reputation of St Regis and because of the decision taken by the Swedish Foreign Exchange Control that Stora Kopparberg had to be in control of the joint venture. The concurrent selling of Koppartrans also facilitated his decision. However, the whole thing took a new turn when Clausen came to the conclusion that St Regis was an unfit partner, mainly because it lacked an apparent need for sulphite pulp. Scott Paper then emerged as a new possible partner and decided to join the project with a 20 per cent share.

The problems that immediately materialized at the Nova Scotia site involved the construction of the plant, unforeseen legal expenses, unfavourable currency exchange rates, inexperienced personnel, strikes, poor management, technical deficiencies and weak demand. Since Stora Kopparberg had to cover all the unanticipated costs alone, the project became an economic catastrophe, something that the board did not fully understand until the annual report was in production. Many actors described the Nova Scotia establishment as an almost 'irreparable calamity' – large amounts of resources were channelled to that site with almost no accompanying benefits for Stora Kopparberg. Thus, the decision to invest there was wrong from the very beginning, and neither Abenius nor (later) Sundblad was able to repair that mistake.

As Abenius saw it, the setback in Nova Scotia seriously hurt the parent company. The large capital injection that was needed to build and run the new plant worried him. He also noticed that the company's partner Scott Paper had gone behind his back and decided to build its own plant in Nova Scotia. Having learned from Stora Kopparberg's failure, Scott Paper had decided instead to produce sulphate pulp, something that several Stora Kopparberg managers had advocated from the very beginning.

During 1965, Stora Kopparberg carried out extensive research to explore the best way to tackle the Nova Scotia problem. For example, for some time the company considered investing in the production of fluting (for corrugated cardboard), as suitable forests (birch and maple) comprised around 30 per cent of the timber resources – tree types that sulphite production could not use efficiently. Abenius claimed that the future for fluting looked bright with a steadily increasing demand, and that the production costs at the Nova Scotia site seemed to be the lowest in the industry. So instead of competing with planned and existing large plants on an uncertain market for pulp, the new (cheaper) machine would bring new capacity to a growing fluting market. At the same time, there were also serious discussions about expanding the existing sulphite plant. Such a larger plant would effectively absorb the large infrastructure investments already made. That path also became the company's first choice, but when the leaders of Scott Paper informed Stora Kopparberg that their company was not interested in participating financially in such an expansion, the project fell through.

Clausen left in 1965 when the discrepancies between his 'American business style' and that of most of Stora Kopparberg's actors became overwhelming. For some years, many HQ managers had looked upon him with great suspicion, although he had proved to be a successful salesman with an excellent network in North America. To many of them it was a mystery that Abenius had been so fond of Clausen – no one but Clausen had made him take such big risks.

When Abenius left as CEO in 1966, he described his experiences from Nova Scotia as basically negative. The main problem with the pulp mill was that its cost of capital was too large in relation to its production capacity. The only possible solution was to expand the plant in some way so that a larger volume could carry the high initial investment costs. Abenius also claimed that the decision-making process had been influenced too much by intuitive judgements and actor personalities; something that at least partly could be explained by the many interpretations made possible by the available information. It was not feasible to merely rely on traditional calculations and a well-known technology.[18]

11.2 ERIK SUNDBLAD BECOMES THE NEW CEO

The appointment of Erik Sundblad as the new CEO of Stora Kopparberg had been prepared for a long time.[19] Abenius informed Jacob Wallenberg Sr already in 1964 that he intended to retire in spring 1966. Ingmar Eidem's name immediately arose, but Abenius thought that the company needed somebody that was at least ten years younger.[20] Wifstavarf's CEO Erik Sundblad was a candidate that met that criterion, and as Chair (also) in that company, Jacob Wallenberg Sr had noticed Sundblad's leadership qualities. When Wifstavarf was sold, Sundblad became available for new positions, and Jacob Wallenberg Sr recruited him to be the new CEO at Stora Kopparberg[21] with the special assignment to sort out the Nova Scotia project.[22]

Generally, the CEOs were the 'locomotives' in Stora Kopparberg, and Sundblad was no exception. Jacob Wallenberg Sr, who was a conservative, careful and 'decelerating' actor, was always more supportive than interventionist – not the company's leader. Marcus Wallenberg Sr, however, was indisputably a commanding person. As such, he tried to get inside Stora Kopparberg's businesses from all possible angles – he installed auditors, consultants and employees (loyal to him) in the company so that they could keep him up to date about what was going on. However, sometimes these informants misled him, which could put 'unorthodox ideas in his head'.[23]

Erik Sundblad was one of Gunnar Sundblad's sons. As the undisputed leader of Iggesund for a quarter of a century, the latter was a living legend. Another of Gunnar Sundblad's sons, Lars, had replaced him as CEO at Iggesund (cf. Ch. 8). Taken together 'the Sundblads' had a strong position in the Swedish forest-based industry. Erik Sundblad was rather young when he became CEO (37 years), but he had a solid education, a family that was deeply rooted in the forest-based industry, and a talent for running large organizations, so many leading actors expected great things from him.[24] Initially, however, his relative youth created some difficulties in his relations with several of the other (and elder) managers in the company. To emphasize that he was the new leader of Stora Kopparberg, his behaviour sometimes became rather brusque.

Sundblad was a powerful CEO – an authoritarian centralist with an ambition to know almost 'everything'. When he had made up his mind, he often forced his way through. Thus Sundblad's more imperial managerial style[25] certainly changed the scene (his predecessor Abenius had run the company with rather slack reins), and not everyone appreciated it, although Sundblad's reputation continued to grow.[26] He was an extrovert who liked to talk to the press, often expressing his thoughts in rather drastic wordings. Among outsiders he was perceived as a rather snooty person, but, according to those who knew him well, that attitude was foremost a cover-up for his sensitive nature. Thus, like most people he was a complex personality combining a modern innovative bent with an old-fashioned kind of appearance. Marcus Wallenberg Sr did not like Sundblad's vices, but since Chair Jacob Wallenberg Sr valued him, Sundblad could continue to run the company his way. Eventually he became more comfortable in his CEO role, and his leadership became more relaxed and generous.

Over time Sundblad's ties to Jacob Wallenberg Sr deepened, and they developed almost a father–son kind of relationship. Sundblad began to submissively admire Jacob Wallenberg Sr,[27] at the same time as his connection to Marcus Wallenberg Sr became much more distant. That could partly be explained by the strained relationship between the Wallenberg brothers, but also by Sundblad's imperial style, which Marcus Wallenberg Sr regarded as his privilege to exert.

After the (student) revolts in 1968, the fear of socialism (and with it a stronger position for the unions) was greater than ever. With this in mind Marcus Wallenberg Sr urged Sundblad to adjust his behaviour to better match the spirit of the time. The former claimed that the autocratic attitudes and hegemonic rules that those in power enacted had to be revamped. Marcus Wallenberg Sr's impression was that Sundblad did not understand the current societal trends. In 1969 his discontent was of such a magnitude that he wrote a letter to Sundblad (and informed his brother Jacob) that he would resign from the board, so that he would not have to sign the company's annual report.[28] That threat made it necessary for Sundblad to travel to Stockholm and avow subservience to Marcus Wallenberg Sr, who then decided to withdraw his resignation.[29]

The Sundblad era contrasted with that of his predecessor Abenius. It became a period marked by restructuring and painful shutdowns. He had to take many difficult and unpopular decisions, and with the gradually stronger positions for the unions in these radical days, the negotiations often developed into veritable battles. The tradition in Wallenberg-controlled companies that no employee should be dismissed certainly did not make Sundblad's already difficult job easier. However, he stayed unswervingly loyal to the company and its interests, and upheld without hesitation his opinions on the most crucial matters. Some of Sundblad's rather controversial views made him suspect in certain circles, but his straightforward and honest actions also created respect and made his strategic leadership visible and distinct.

The most important structural change that Sundblad launched was the breaking up of the company into two main groupings: one steel-based, the other forest-based. In addition, so that Stora Kopparberg would have a direct link to many of its ultimate customers, he replaced the sales agents in many foreign markets with wholly owned sales companies. Sundblad also tried to broaden the company's business repertoire, but lacked the necessary capital for such activities (most of it was locked into the Nova Scotia project). He also considered establishing production in South Carolina (USA), buying the big German forest-based company Haindl,[30] and acquiring the Swedish Vallvik site (from Ncb; cf. Ch. 6), but none of these ideas materialized. However, Sundblad's promotion of a partnership with German Feldmühle[31] at the Hylte site in which Feldmühle bought a 25 per cent stake in 1970 turned out to be important in the long run. Another move that mattered for Stora Kopparberg's strategic development was his establishment of a link to a Finnish LWC mill.[32]

During the Sundblad era, Stora Kopparberg also bought a small paper mill in the US (Newton Falls), intending to make it a supplier to the Nova Scotia operations, but that plan did not materialize, as the mill's pulp turned out to be too expensive.[33] In this case, however, it was not Sundblad that had pushed for that purchase. Instead, it was Marcus Wallenberg Sr's son Peter Wallenberg who had promoted such a step. He got the idea from actors in his extensive network. Since the board agreed, the investment was carried out despite the scepticism of some of Stora Kopparberg's directors and managers, who had bad experiences previously from situations where acquisition ideas not stemming from operative actors had been endorsed by a large shareholder.[34] Unfortunately, the sceptics turned out to be right, as most things went wrong with Newton Falls (the mill was in bad shape and almost 'inaccessible').

When Sundblad entered Stora Kopparberg as its Deputy CEO in 1965, Nova Scotia was by far its greatest problem. However, unlike his predecessor Abenius, Sundblad was very enthusiastic about Nova Scotia and claimed that no other site could be better for expansion of forest-related operations, particularly with the existing forest-sourcing agreement in mind. He immediately took his place on the board of the Nova Scotia subsidiary and started to investigate possible futures for that unit. With Clausen out of the picture by then, Sundblad had rather free hands to act.

The planned Nova Scotia mill was an important part of Stora Kopparberg's long-term industrial strategy that included an operational presence in North America so that it could expand its raw material sourcing and increase market shares. The platform for the expansion was the parent company's high technical knowledge, strong cash flow and well-developed contacts on the capital market (through the 'family bank'). Sundblad's main conclusion was that the Nova Scotia mill was too small to reap the benefits of the large investments made in infrastructure (i.e. the factory area, roads, harbour, power and water supply, housing, workshops and offices). During the construction of the plant, technology also had taken a significant step forward, which made twice the size of the initial investment a necessity. Thus, the new mill had to be enlarged substantially and that rather soon. Moreover, the subsidiary's debt/equity ratio was unfavourable, which made interest payments and amortizations a heavy burden. In spite of all this, Sundblad still regarded an investment in producing more pulp and/or expanding into fluting as a promising path for Nova Scotia, and even seriously considered investing in newsprint. The problem was that the co-owner Scott Paper was totally uninterested in any expansion plans. As a consequence, that company was bought out in 1969.

After three years of investigations, discussions and negotiations Stora Kopparberg's directors had made up their minds. The board decided that the company should both invest in an expansion of the current pulp mill and add a newsprint machine. The sourcing of timber would not be a problem as it suited newsprint, too. Moreover, as a well-tested technique was to be used this time, no problems were expected.

The board's decision to invest in a newsprint mill surprised the head of the site (Lundqvist). He claimed that such production required significant amounts of (cheap) electric power but not that much timber – something that did not correspond particularly well with the conditions in the plant's surroundings. He also stressed that a well-educated and motivated staff had to be present – such a big and complicated effort could not be governed from a distance (from the Swedish HQ). Moreover, the price for the electricity was uncertain, as it was in the hands of the local government (which currently subsidized it). Once again, problems emerged on the pulp side regarding both the building process as such and its costs. In particular, the actions of the workforce (stalling, disloyal behaviour, strikes, etc.) resulted in major difficulties. Moreover, some loans put pressure on the subsidiary's balance sheet, so the negotiations with the financiers continued. In the end, the new investment turned out to be most expensive – it ran up to four times the budgeted cost.[35]

By 1971, even though Stora Kopparberg put its own employees in at the Nova Scotia unit, several serious problems remained (e.g. the output quality, the low price, a market downturn and import customs). So, in a Christmas letter in 1971 to Jacob Wallenberg Sr, Sundblad wrote that the plant still was a 'tough business' both economically and operationally, although the situation was gradually getting better (the newsprint mill was running well). Sundblad also wrote that the Nova Scotia investment had affected Stora Kopparberg's liquidity negatively, and that over the long run, it could hurt the company's strategic position and capacity.

In 1972, the board started to discuss whether the sulphite mill could be converted to a sulphate one, but that path did not materialize. However, 1973 became a turnaround year, as the economic reports indicated an operating profit for Nova Scotia Forest Industries[36] (SFI) for the first time. Still, however, the investment was a burden for Stora Kopparberg (negative cash flow, net losses, etc.) – break-even was actually not reached until the late 1970s.

Jacob Wallenberg Sr regarded his (reluctant) decision to support the project as his greatest mistake. As he saw it, Stora Kopparberg lacked the necessary knowledge about the people and conditions in Nova Scotia to have a fair chance to be successful. Moreover, the intended investment was made too far away (Canada) from the company's leading actors (Sweden), and most company actors knew too little about what economic and other resources such an effort actually required. He concluded by claiming that the opinions of CEOs too often won out. Former CEO Abenius felt seriously insulted by those words, although Jacob Wallenberg Sr comforted him by making clear that the (implicit) target for the critique was his brother Marcus – nobody else. Nevertheless, several rather 'profitable' years followed, so when retiring as Chair in 1976 Jacob Wallenberg Sr praised

Sundblad for his (North American) achievements, a homage that several leading managers regarded as too generous. In their opinion Lundqvist, the Head of SFI, was the real hero.

In the mid-1970s Marcus Wallenberg Sr wanted to concentrate all of the sphere's forest-based companies into one strong unit, but his brother Jacob Wallenberg Sr opposed such a move. As the latter was the dominating actor in Stora Kopparberg, the former had to confine his activities to mergers between, on the one hand, Kopparfors, and, on the other hand, the units connected to Papyrus, Nymölla and Hylte. So in 1975 Papyrus bought almost all outstanding shares in Ry and sold its new fine paper mill to Nymölla, where Papyrus owned 49 per cent of the stock. Papyrus also acquired Kopparfors the same year – a corporation that owned large forest resources and produced bleached sulphite pulp at Norrsundet, pulp and cardboard at Gästrike Hammarby and cardboard at Fors. Taken together, these changes established Papyrus as one of the largest cardboard producers in Europe.[37]

Stora Kopparberg also bought Bergvik & Ala in 1975, partly paying with shares. The deal was facilitated by the fact that Jacob Wallenberg Sr held the Chair position in both companies. Sundblad regarded that acquisition as the most important improvement of Stora Kopparberg's structure since WWII. Bergvik & Ala controlled large forest resources, power plants, Sandarne (sulphate pulp), Bergvik (sulphite pulp) and Ljusne (board and plywood factories [and chain production]). However, the acquisition was complicated by the rivalry between the two Wallenberg brothers. Kopparfors (where Marcus Wallenberg Sr held the Chair position), too, had explored the possibility of acquiring Bergvik & Ala, but lost the contest. At that time, Stora Kopparberg also made substantial changes in its own internal structure, foremost a radical concentration of its pulp production. While the sulphate production at Skutskär was expanded, all its sulphite-based units were closed.[38]

11.3 DIVESTING THE STEEL BUSINESS

Up until the mid-1970s, Stora Kopparberg was a traditional combined mill and works corporation where the steel part accounted for slightly more than half of the turnover and the forest-based part about 40 per cent. The Wallenberg sphere was the controlling shareholder, although its voting power was as low as 15 per cent. However, the integration among the company's forest-related businesses (Skutskär, Grycksbo, Kvarnsveden and Nova Scotia) was rather weak, and that 'open situation' influenced Stora Kopparberg's strategic action. Investor was the important link between all the forest-based corporations in the sphere, as it was the biggest owner in several of them: Stora Kopparberg, Bergvik & Ala, Papyrus and Kopparfors. Jacob Wallenberg Sr chaired the first two companies and Marcus Wallenberg Sr the last two.[39]

The international iron and steel crisis of 1975–77 hit Stora Kopparberg hard. It was the worst setback in that industry since the Great Depression in the 1930s. As the company's two core businesses (steel and forest-related business) recently had been reorganized in separate groupings, the losses in the steel business were even more striking. At an early stage, Marcus Wallenberg Sr was prepared to give up the steel business and concentrate Stora Kopparberg's operations in the forest-based sector alone.[40] Several members of top management agreed with him and supported his ambitions. His main argument for that great transformation was that both core businesses were capital intensive and the company's size and capital base were insufficient to successfully house both. However, since Jacob Wallenberg Sr held the steel business very close to his heart, he did not support its divestment. As a result, Marcus Wallenberg Sr almost had to force that radical change through, and that effort even included the removal of his brother from the company's chairmanship.

Stora Kopparberg's steel operations included special steel (i.e. stainless steel, tool steel and high-speed steel) and commercial steel produced at the Domnarvet site. Jacob Wallenberg Sr felt that Domnarvet's strategy to meet the increasing costs for producing standard qualities with increased volumes was a mistake; in such a race the large continental plants would drive it out of business. He preferred a strategy by which Domnarvet would specialize its production on the basis of careful profit and loss calculations. Although top management gradually began to suspect that he might be right, their understanding came too late to save the steel operations. Thus, the board decided to try to divest its steel business as quickly as possible.

Peter Wallenberg[41] entered Stora Kopparberg's board in 1974. He was well acquainted with his uncle Jacob Wallenberg Sr's way of running things. The latter was careful and cautious, although the board meetings were not always constructive. Not much free range was given to the younger or more recently appointed directors, and sometimes the board materials did not arrive until the meetings began. Peter Wallenberg learned that the discussions generally focused on the technical aspects of the mills and machines, while debates about markets, sales and customers were basically absent. As he saw it, the exclusive focus on production had to change. He also sided with his uncle regarding the problems associated with running two separate core businesses, and preferred that Stora Kopparberg sold all its steel operations.[42]

At that time, Bo Berggren was Deputy CEO and managed the special steel plants at Söderfors and Vikmanshyttan, both of which were rather run down and hardly profitable (if at all). He participated in many of the on-going talks about the structure of the sector in the future. For example, Stora Kopparberg discussed with Fagersta whether their respective speed steel operations could be better off if they were integrated. Berggren supported that merger idea, but his Chair, Jacob Wallenberg Sr, rejected it partly because Fagersta belonged to another ownership sphere, partly because the forecasts for special steel operations looked bright at that time (summer 1974; just a few months before the severe crisis hit the steel industry). Stora Kopparberg and Oxelösund's Jernverk also held meetings regarding a possible merger, but those discussions did not progress to action either.[43] Berggren had two explanations for those failures. One had to do with the two leaders of the Wallenberg sphere, who often showed reluctance to push for or support radical structural changes. The other was Domnarvet's opposition to such a change, given that one of its consequences would be the closure of its ore metallurgy (which was to be concentrated to Oxelösund).[44]

The production of stainless steel was yet another problem. The first two production stages (melting metallurgy and hot rolling) were located at Domnarvet, while the further processing (cold rolling, pickling and annealing) took place at Söderfors (although hierarchically subordinated to Domnarvet). At the height of the steel crisis, the leaders of Stora Kopparberg decided that the company could pursue one of three alternatives for its stainless steel operations: invest SEK 200 million, close down or merge with another firm.

Stora Kopparberg concentrated its efforts initially on the third alternative and contacted Gränges,[45] suggesting a joint venture. However, due to the need for additional capital, the discussions were cut off. Instead, Stora Kopparberg contacted Avesta Jernverk[46] and Outokumpu,[47] neither of which showed any interest. They expected that Stora Kopparberg would close down its stainless steel operations anyway; as the closure would reduce capacity in that sector, it would in fact further their interests. When Stahlwerke Sudwestfahlen (Germany) was approached, they initially agreed to co-operate, but those negotiations, too, collapsed. With no alternative in sight, Stora Kopparberg decided to shut down all its stainless steel operations in 1977.[48]

Starting in springtime 1976, the Swedish Steel Producers' Association (Jernkontoret) initiated a large investigation regarding the future of the Swedish special steel industry. The appointed commission recommended a merger between Stora Kopparberg and Uddeholm's special steel businesses, and as both CEOs were present at the presentation of the study, they immediately made contact and started discussing whether the suggested path was a practicable one. Initially, a joint venture was discussed, but soon another path emerged as the favourite, namely that Uddeholm should acquire Stora Kopparberg's special steel operations (for a low price). That deal, however, would then exclude Vikmanshyttan (speed steel) and Domnarvet (hot and cold rolled strip steel).[49]

That same year the state launched a thorough investigation of the Swedish trade steel industry. Stora Kopparberg co-ordinated that state-led investigation with the above-mentioned one conducted by the Swedish Steel Producers' Association. The business situation of the three companies involved (Gränges, NJA[50] and Stora Kopparberg) differed significantly. Stora Kopparberg housed a poor steel business but also healthy forest-based operations, Gränges was making major losses and wanted the state to take control of its Oxelösund plant, and NJA had never delivered a profit but could – for several reasons – count on continuous state support. In terms of trade steel, the study recommended that Oxelösund should (continue to) be the sole producer of thick sheet iron, Stora Kopparberg (the Domnarvet plant) should concentrate its operations on hot rolled strip steel and cold rolled sheet metal, and NJA should manufacture bar steel.

Wahlström was appointed CEO of NJA in 1976 after leaving the position as Deputy CEO at SCA, where he had learned how to build new business structures (cf. Ch. 13). Soon Wahlström made contact with his old friend Lars G. Sundblad, Iggesund's CEO. That company, too, had problems with its steel business (Boxholm, cf. Ch. 8). Stora Kopparberg was also drawn into those talks through its CEO Erik Sundblad (Lars's brother). Although the discussions did not lead to immediate action, they became important for what was to come. For example, Erik Sundblad and Wahlström learned a lot about each other's companies and built trust. Rather soon the situation for both NJA's and Stora Kopparberg's steel businesses became acute (losses were 'gigantic'). Therefore, in early 1977, discussions started that ultimately resulted in the founding of SSAB.[51]

Stora Kopparberg's CEO Erik Sundblad and the manager of its steel business Deputy CEO Berggren were its representatives in the negotiations, although it was Chair Marcus Wallenberg Sr who took the crucial decisions. Initially, CEO Åkerman spoke for Gränges, but soon the new CEO Abrahamsson and Chair Werthén replaced him. CEO Wahlström represented NJA. All actors recognized the need for co-operation and for a new structure for the Swedish trade steel industry. They also understood that the state was the sole actor that had the financial resources to capitalize the new construct. That circumstance made NJA the strong and assertive actor. As such, it initially tried to solve its own problems without regard for the needs of the other two companies. When NJA's intentions became clear to Stora Kopparberg, its Chair Marcus Wallenberg Sr reacted furiously and contacted NJA's Chair to make his company change its course and begin to co-operate.[52]

To resolve the difficult issue of how to evaluate each of the companies' steel businesses, independent consultants were contracted to examine them and provide advice. In the end, the actors reached a compromise and ascribed all three companies similar worth. The problem then was that Stora Kopparberg's assets were booked about SEK 300 million lower than the corresponding assets of the two other companies – and an outcome of that difference could be that Gränges would be declared bankrupt (could not take the required write-downs). The state then decided to save Gränges by paying separately for its railway company (an asset that already was included in the original deal). Another problem was that Sundblad did not want to relinquish Stora Kopparberg's power-generating resources to the new organization (something that Wahlström demanded if NJA was to include its mines). However, Marcus Wallenberg Sr convinced the Minister of Industry (Åsling) that Stora Kopparberg should be allowed to keep its power plants.[53]

SCA's CEO Rydin criticized both the final agreement and Wahlström's efforts. He claimed that the state through NJA (and Wahlström) in an unfair way had saved a competitor (i.e. Stora Kopparberg). In reality, though, it was first and foremost Marcus Wallenberg Sr's extraordinary status in the Swedish (business) society that made the state support Stora Kopparberg – not Wahlström's contributions to the process. Sundblad and Berggren's efforts were regarded by most actors to be of minor importance. Although the two participated in most of the negotiations, they continuously had to check all the important issues with Marcus Wallenberg Sr.

In December 1977, the agreement to establish SSAB was signed. It was to be owned by the state (50%), Gränges (25%) and Stora Kopparberg (25%), and had an equity amounting to SEK 2 billion. Marcus Wallenberg Sr wanted to see Berggren as CEO of SSAB, but Wahlström was appointed instead.[54]

Berggren left his position as Deputy CEO at Stora Kopparberg in summer 1978 to become CEO of another Wallenberg company (Incentive[55]), as Marcus Wallenberg Sr did not want Berggren and Sundblad 'to step on each other's feet' in a split Stora Kopparberg. Still, Berggren was appointed deputy director in Stora Kopparberg's board and continued as its representative on SSAB's board.[56]

Stora Kopparberg did not remain a minority owner in SSAB for long. Already in 1981, SSAB needed an infusion of capital. This situation prompted discussions within Stora Kopparberg's board about the company's future role in SSAB. A deal was suggested whereby Stora Kopparberg would buy shares for SEK 125 million, provide debentures amounting to SEK 150 million (redemption in 1990) and continue to be shareholder until 1990, when its SSAB holding would be acquired by Statsföretag (paying SEK 375 million). At the time, however, the forecast for SSAB worsened, indicating greater losses than originally predicted. That prognosis implied that SSAB later would need yet another new infusion of capital. Despite this, Stora Kopparberg's board was inclined to participate in the further capitalization of SSAB, a disposition that was strengthened when it became clear that the state (through Vattenfall[57]) was prepared to buy Stora Kopparberg's holding in its power company Bergslagens Gemensamma Kraftförvaltning for SEK 228 million – a sum four times that expected by Stora Kopparberg.[58]

Stora Kopparberg's directors were divided regarding the company's future involvement in SSAB. Peter Wallenberg registered his dissent in the board minutes. He was afraid that many other states would subsidize their steel industries in the coming decades, something that would reduce SSAB's competitive edge. He also stressed that there was no real obligation for Stora Kopparberg to participate in a new capital injection in SSAB.[59] Moreover, he saw its future performance as a threat to Stora Kopparberg's forest-based businesses. Capital that was urgently needed for those operations might end up being channelled to unproductive uses (i.e. to SSAB). In addition, the discussions regarding SSAB swallowed precious management resources that were needed elsewhere. All in all, involvement in SSAB could delay the necessary structural changes in the Swedish forest-based industry (particularly for the companies belonging to the Wallenberg sphere).[60]

SSAB presented a new forecast about a month after the Stora Kopparberg board meeting at which Peter Wallenberg had tried to make his case. The report indicated a loss for 1981 of SEK 750 million. Moreover, poor liquidity and growing uncertainty regarding the expected future redemption of Stora Kopparberg's SSAB holdings did not improve the situation. As a result, Stora Kopparberg shifted gears and refused to participate in the forthcoming SSAB share issue. Instead, it sold its SSAB holding to Gränges for a symbolic sum (SEK 1). That transaction halved Stora Kopparberg's turnover to about SEK 3 billion, and made it a 'pure' forest-based corporation.

11.4 CONCENTRATING ON THE FOREST-BASED BUSINESSES

11.4.1 Board Turbulence

Stora Kopparberg's acquisition of Bergvik & Ala (described above) strengthened its position in the forest-based industry. Together with the divestment of all its steel operations, that purchase started a concentration of its business portfolio, a process that continued, although with an ambition to grow in a rather novel but very expansive product field: LWC paper. Early in 1978, it was clear that Stora Kopparberg intended to build a mill for production of non-coated, wood-containing printing paper close to its sulphate plant at Sandarne. Production of mechanical pulp and a unit for bleaching were planned, too. However, before that investment had materialized, Stora Kopparberg saw an opportunity to participate in a similar project at Vallvik (Ncb; cf. Ch. 6), where the circumstances seemed to be much better. As a result, management had to lower the newly raised expectations at Sandarne, and by 1981 it had become obvious that the site was out of the picture (the planned mill at Vallvik did not materialize either).[61]

For the same reason – the ambition to expand in wood-containing printing paper – Stora Kopparberg intended to buy 50 per cent of the Utansjö plant from Graningeverken (sulphite pulp and mechanical wood pulp). However, two problems arose: unclear timber sourcing and uncertainty about the possibility of using the existing infrastructure for an additional machine.[62] So that path, too, was abandoned.

Stora Kopparberg was also determined to participate in the development of the European journal paper market, as its machines were in better shape than many of those run by its competitors in the EC (with the exception of those run by Finnish companies). Therefore, Stora Kopparberg decided to move ahead already in 1981 and, at the same time, deter (particularly the Finnish) competitors from further investing in journal paper production. The same year, the company also invested in a sawmill in the US (Canal Industries, South Carolina).[63]

During the first years of the 1980s, Stora Kopparberg made radical changes in its board composition. Jacob Wallenberg Sr left as Chair in 1976 and was succeeded by his brother Marcus. Eidem replaced him in 1980, and at the same time Peter Wallenberg was appointed Deputy Chair. Eidem was a former CEO from another 'Wallenberg company', and he had some experience in the pulp industry.[64] Nonetheless, the change in the Chair position certainly did not mean that Marcus Wallenberg Sr's influence was reduced; in fact, there was a memo from the board that stipulated that he had to be consulted in all 'important matters' (budgets, investments plans, financial matters, closing of the books, M&A ideas, liquidity issues, etc.). The same year Palmstierna entered the board, a person who characterized himself as an 'ally of Marcus Wallenberg Sr'. That standpoint was of some importance, as the two Wallenberg brothers had come to loggerheads (although they did not show that to the general public).[65] At that time, director Lundvall, CEO of Ericsson and a rising star in the Wallenberg sphere, left the board (and was succeeded by Turesson).

Already in 1981 Synnergren replaced Eidem as Stora Kopparberg's Chair. That appointment was certainly a surprise to most actors (including Synnergren himself). He was a former Supreme Commander of the Swedish armed forces, and had no experience holding a Chair position of that magnitude and no track record in the forest-based industry. Marcus Wallenberg Sr, who in reality was the one who appointed Synnergren, did so because of the latter's strong societal network, which extended even into the heart of by far the largest political party in Sweden, the Social Democrats. However, Synnergren soon felt uncomfortable in his new role, a feeling that gradually grew stronger both during the formal board meetings and in the informal talks connected with them. Therefore, after only one year as Chair, he made clear that he wanted to leave.

Peter Wallenberg then replaced Synnergren in 1985. One might have expected that Marcus Wallenberg Sr would have installed his son Peter as the new Chair already in 1980, when he stepped down. Instead, he had doubts about his son's capacity to govern large business organizations and shoulder the responsibility for the family sphere. Thus, this was no classic father–son relationship – Marcus Wallenberg Sr even went behind his son's back and entered into an agreement with Gyllenhammar (CEO of Volvo), which the public interpreted as a sign of who he really wanted to see as his successor.[66]

Marcus Wallenberg Sr's sidestepping of his son Peter as his replacement could be interpreted as evidence that the family governed its sphere 'professionally' exercising 'rational' criteria, that is to say, that friendships, antagonism, emotional ties and kinship did not count. However, in many cases the dynasty's leading members had violated that kind of rationalism through 'irrational' behaviour, being governed by feelings, intuition and (even) aesthetics. Moreover, several sphere leaders had also regarded matching personal chemistries as important in recruitment and promotion processes. In such cases, they had sometimes shown a weakness for both the (old) nobility and the self-made men (and scepticism towards academics). Thus, the ambition – and ability – to establish close links with powerful social actors (politicians, scientists and businessmen) inside as well as outside Sweden has been a main ingredient in the family rationale throughout generations. In that way, the Wallenberg dynasty had gradually and assiduously built a unique global family 'capital' that opened up opportunities for many national and global business activities.

11.4.2 The Iggesund Contest

Early in 1981, the so-called 'Iggesund contest' took place (cf. Ch. 9 for an in-depth description).[67] However, it was already back in the 1970s that the Swedish forest-based companies began to buy (or merge with) each other, although primarily with companies from within their own business sphere. MoDo was not part of any sphere, but stood close to the Handelsbanken/Industrivärden one, as the latter was its major bank connection (and the bank's Chair was a member of MoDo's board).

MoDo's Chair Carlgren was one of the actors that decided to participate in the restructuring of the Swedish forest-based industry, and through that effort make MoDo grow to a size that would be competitive at least in a European perspective.[68] In early 1980, when Carlgren discovered that a significant number of Iggesund shares were available on the market, he started buying. Thus, MoDo's journey towards a third bloc had begun, and by September of that year its Iggesund holding had reached around 12 per cent. However, MoDo's buying of these shares did not take place without reactions from the Wallenberg sphere. When its leading actors found out about Carlgren's initiative, they immediately began to consider some kind of countermove. Earlier in that same year, Billerud had held merger talks with Iggesund and discovered the merits of integrating the two companies' cardboard businesses. If such a constellation were established, the Wallenberg sphere expected both economies of scale and synergies. There were also rumours that its 'Great Leader', Marcus Wallenberg Sr, intended to crown his unrivalled life achievement in the Swedish business society by building a more effective structure for the country's forest-based industry. So he made sure that Billerud and Stora Kopparberg began to buy Iggesund shares, too. As Carlgren was a most active buyer, the Wallenberg sphere was in a great hurry to acquire a significant holding. Carlgren had a similar perspective. He was afraid to lose Iggesund to a competitor, that is to say, to Billerud or Stora Kopparberg.

The race to gain control of Iggesund became intense in April 1981, when the Wallenberg sphere learned that MoDo's two leading actors were soon to be elected board members at Iggesund. By that time, MoDo had won control over about 25 per cent of the votes in Iggesund (MoDo 13%, its allies 12%). Marcus Wallenberg Sr became upset when, as he saw it, Handelsbanken, through MoDo and its leading actor Carlgren, took the lead and forwarded its position in the forest-based industry. So he instructed the CEOs of Billerud and Stora Kopparberg to make an effort to take control of Iggesund by making a joint bid for it.[69] Erik Sundblad, too, was active, particularly at the beginning of the process. He visited Dahlbäck to discuss the acquisition idea, but the latter showed no enthusiasm. Despite that, and impelled by Marcus Wallenberg Sr, he also contacted Iggesund's Deputy Chair Stahle (a person close to the Wallenberg family) about the acquisition idea, but Stahle, too, expressed surprise that such a purchase was seriously considered.[70]

Stora Kopparberg had earlier shown interest in Iggesund's cardboard business and its well-situated forests and therefore bought shares amounting to a few per cent of its stock. However, Stora Kopparberg's primary concern then was preventing its rival SCA from moving its operations south towards 'their' part of Sweden. Thus, the Wallenberg sphere was not that much afraid of MoDo at that time, but that attitude soon proved to be a mistake.

When they watched a soccer game in the Swedish top division, Marcus Wallenberg Sr, Engman (CEO, Billerud) and Erik Sundblad (CEO, Stora Kopparberg) drew up the scheme for a consortium that would stop MoDo's plan to control Iggesund. After that meeting they acted very quickly.[71] In their haste, the bid was built on rather superficial analyses – it was primarily based on the calculations and judgements made one year earlier when Iggesund tried to buy Billerud. This time, the leading actors decided that Billerud (20%) and Stora Kopparberg (80%) should form a consortium that should make a bid for all outstanding shares in Iggesund. For three Iggesund shares, the consortium offered two shares in Stora Kopparberg, one share in Billerud and SEK 150. Thus, the bid was a generous one – far above the current trading price.

However, several actors connected to the Wallenberg sphere questioned the construction of the bid. One of Stora Kopparberg's directors, Palmstierna, noted that MoDo could exchange its Iggesund shares for shares in Stora Kopparberg and ultimately become the largest shareholder of that corporation. Thus, as he saw it, the bid was not properly thought out; in fact, it was a veritable threat to the Wallenberg family's control over Stora Kopparberg. Thus, Palmstierna phoned Erik Sundblad, who in turn phoned Marcus Wallenberg Sr and discussed the bid again. However, no immediate actions were taken to stop it.[72]

The arguments for taking control of Iggesund were basically the same as those that had been put forward in 1980 to promote a merger between Iggesund and Billerud (with the addition of some benefits linked to Stora Kopparberg's entry on the scene). Wallenberg saw it as necessary to acquire Iggesund if the sphere's companies wanted to be serious actors on the cardboard market. Iggesund would provide such a business – bleached high-quality cardboard – which supplemented Billerud's cardboard machine (for liquid packaging). Co-ordination of Iggesund and Stora Kopparberg's forests could also bring synergetic effects.[73] Erik Sundblad expected that the broadening of the company's raw material base and the addition of a promising business segment (bleached cardboard) would open up a new expansion path for Stora Kopparberg.[74]

None of Stora Kopparberg's board meetings addressed the bid issue until the very same day it was made public – something that confirmed the board's subsidiary position. At its meeting, it was asked whether those that constructed the bid had taken into consideration that, if it became a success, the rival sphere (Handelsbanken/Industrivärden) would gain around 20 per cent of the votes in Stora Kopparberg. That tough question aroused nothing but silence. At the end of the meeting, the board concluded that Carlgren's ambition and current holding would make it difficult for the bidders to reach even close to 90 per cent of the Iggesund stock.

The hostile bid triggered strong negative reactions both among actors in the target company and among some of the leading actors in the bidding companies. Neither the Iggesund board nor its top management was contacted in advance (with the exception of Deputy Chair Stahle, who belonged to the Wallenberg sphere). At Stora Kopparberg's next board meeting held just before the upcoming AGM, an irritated large shareholder, Atmer (CEO, Graningeverken), raised questions about the Iggesund bid, which had been constructed and launched with such a great haste that it was not even mentioned in the summons. However, his questions were dismissed on formal grounds since the bid was not on the agenda.

So it was not until at the AGM on 5 May that the conflict between Versteegh, the main owner of Graningeverken, and the Wallenberg sphere, Stora Kopparberg's dominant shareholder, became acute. At the meeting, Versteegh openly criticized the board's handling of the Iggesund bid, noting that important steps had already been taken to make way for it even though no formal decision had been taken yet. He also questioned whether it would be possible to make that acquisition profitable. Versteegh pointed out that only two years earlier Stora Kopparberg had decided that wood-containing papers would be its core business, and that the current bid for Iggesund implied an entirely new course. He wondered when that radical strategic change had been decided and by what agency. What made the bid particularly objectionable in Versteegh's eyes was that Stora Kopparberg intended to (partly) pay with its own shares, a move that would not only dilute the positions of the present main owners but also have a negative impact on the share price. He also noted that it had been possible to buy Iggesund shares much cheaper in 1979–80. To underline Graningeverken's critique, Versteegh neither granted the board discharge nor took part in the election of its directors.[75]

Stora Kopparberg's bid process had started with an extraordinary board meeting on 29 April, at which the offering was discussed (and later the same day made public). Then the unions in both bidding companies were contacted for the mandatory 'MBL-negotiations' (MBL referring to the Swedish Co-determination Act), and after that, the bid proposal was brought back to the board for a formal stance. When the board confirmed ('decided') that the bid should be made, all shareholders would be informed and called to an EGM. At the same time, there would be a prospectus distributed, so that Iggesund's shareholders could decide whether to accept the bid or not.[76]

The hostile bid triggered an intensive trade in Iggesund shares. A 'buying race' emerged that involved the consortium (Billerud and Stora Kopparberg) and MoDo. Soon the Iggesund share price even outdid the most generous bid level, and in a short period of time about 20 per cent of its stock changed hands. At their next meeting, Stora Kopparberg's directors learned that Iggesund was most unwilling to become a part of a larger company group. Iggesund's CEO Lars G. Sundblad made clear that the company wanted to remain an independent corporation. However, Iggesund did not turn down invitations from other companies to co-operate if the proposals were based on rational business considerations. Iggesund's CEO stated that the company actually welcomed joint efforts between equal partners.[77]

At Stora Kopparberg's accompanying EGM several large shareholders questioned the bid construction. In light of this, the CEO suggested that the company should wait for Iggesund's upcoming board meeting (scheduled for mid-June) before any further action would be taken (e.g. a reconstruction of the bid). At Stora Kopparberg's next board meeting director Palmstierna declared that the economic reasons for an acquisition still held true, but that the situation was problematic, as both Iggesund's management and unions had rejected the proposal. He maintained that Stora Kopparberg would be a better choice for Iggesund than MoDo. The directors noted that Iggesund's share price had risen so high that the current bid would no longer be attractive. To complicate matters, MoDo had by then obtained control of 30 per cent of Iggesund. However, at that time, there was no indication from Billerud's leaders that the consortium ought to give up the contest.[78]

At Iggesund's AGM, it was decided that the company should first make a thorough analysis of all its operations and then consider both the current shareholder situation and a possible merger with Stora Kopparberg and Billerud. After two weeks of intensive work, the investigators concluded that Iggesund was capable of running a profitable business also as an autonomous company.[79] That outcome gave Stora Kopparberg reason to hesitate. When its leading actors also learned that MoDo and its associates controlled more than 40 per cent of Iggesund's shares and that Billerud and Stora Kopparberg could reach only 28 per cent at most, they refrained from pursuing the bid. Both MoDo and Stora Kopparberg then decided to stop at the current levels (31% versus 28%), figures that provided both contestants with tax-free dividends. At that point Peter Wallenberg met with Carlgren and discussed the situation. To Wallenberg it became clear that there was no place for Stora Kopparberg/Billerud in Carlgren's plan for MoDo.[80]

In 1982, a year later, MoDo announced its intent to buy Stora Kopparberg's holding in Iggesund – at least so much that it would reach the 50 per cent level (offering SEK 350 for each share). Stora Kopparberg's directors discussed that proposal in May 1982, the first board meeting that Volvo's CEO Gyllenhammar attended (cf. subsection 11.5.1 below). Peter Wallenberg (Deputy Chair), Berggren (director) and Erik Sundblad (CEO) all declared that the price offered was too low. Gyllenhammar agreed, but stated that Stora Kopparberg ought to divest that holding in the near future (as it was overvalued and the yield was too low). Due to Swedish taxation rules, however, the sale was delayed for one year. The price was finally set at SEK 380, which landed the sellers a considerable profit.

At that point, Stora Kopparberg was no longer entirely occupied with the Iggesund contest. Instead, the company continued its efforts to expand in the fine paper segment and explored possibilities in Austria (a minority holding in Neusiedler), Germany (Papierfabrik Scheufelen) and Italy (a possible majority in Cartiere del Garda). Given the last company's strong position in its home market (20%), which would give Stora Kopparberg a much better position in southern Europe, the original intention was to buy the whole company. However, in 1984 Stora Kopparberg's newly appointed CEO (Berggren) put a halt to that and other fine paper deals, as he initially preferred to make the most of Stora Kopparberg's new investments in the printing paper business.

Up until the early 1980s, Stora Kopparberg had a 'low-processing' profile, something that stimulated the new management's effort to find new paths for the company's future development. Stora Kopparberg was also heavily exposed to the market swings in the forest-based businesses, because its 'pulp for sale' accounted for around 25 per cent of its total turnover. That was not in line with the industry trend towards more integrated mills. In that situation, the board preferred growth based on acquisitions rather than expansion through investments in new machines at existing sites. Another reason for the board's stance was the presence of global cartel agreements, which firmly regulated investments in new capacity.

11.5 LOOKING FOR NEW WAYS TO EXPAND

11.5.1 Volvo Becomes a Major Shareholder

Early in the 1980s, a new shareholder appeared on the Stora Kopparberg scene: Volvo. Its entrance as a large owner in that company was to a great extent precipitated by an unexpected succession problem in the Wallenberg dynasty. The sudden death in 1971 of Marc Wallenberg, Marcus Wallenberg Sr's eldest son and the presumed incumbent family head, had generated a leadership problem in the sphere because several actors – including Marcus Wallenberg Sr – questioned the capacity of his other son, Peter Wallenberg, to fill the gap. The succession problem came to a head at the beginning of the 1980s when both Jacob Wallenberg Sr (1980) and Marcus Wallenberg Sr passed away (1982).

However, a few years before that occurred, Marcus Wallenberg Sr had been talking to Volvo's CEO Gyllenhammar, a business leader who had greatly impressed him. They discussed, among other topics, the future of a core company in the Wallenberg sphere, namely Atlas Copco.[81] Marcus Wallenberg Sr invited Volvo to become a new, major shareholder in that company (25%), and soon after his death, Atlas Copco issued new shares exclusively intended for Volvo.

In fact, it was Marcus Wallenberg Sr who had initiated contact with Gyllenhammar. Peter Wallenberg suspected that his father had identified Volvo's CEO as a potential successor to him, and that their 'secret' meetings had produced an agreement that Volvo and the Wallenberg sphere should find ways to co-operate. Peter Wallenberg was surprised that his father had not informed him about these talks. The secrecy, together with other manifestations of his father's lack of confidence, made him doubt his own capacity to shoulder the huge responsibility linked to the peak position in the family's large business group.[82]

Gyllenhammar claimed that he also had an agreement with Marcus Wallenberg Sr that Volvo should become a new, substantial (25%) shareholder in Stora Kopparberg. Unlike with the Atlas Copco deal, that agreement was unknown to all other actors including Peter Wallenberg, who nevertheless decided to take Gyllenhammar at his word and accept the existence of such an agreement.[83] Some actors thought that Peter Wallenberg accepted the deal because his capability was questioned and he needed time to prove his competence and build up a strong and respected position.[84] Still others supposed that the main reason instead might have been that Stora Kopparberg's leading actors thought that the company needed a large capital injection.[85] Marcus Wallenberg Sr was worried about the capacity of the family-controlled investment companies Investor and Providentia to provide all the corporations in the sphere with sufficient capital; thus, he was seriously concerned about the future of the whole Wallenberg group.[86]

Peter Wallenberg was appointed Chair of Investor and Providentia in 1982 and used their combined shareholding as a base for his governance of the Wallenberg group. By including the investment companies' CEOs Dahlbäck and Lundberg, he formed a leadership trio that replaced his father's one-man show.[87] The two companies, Investor and Providentia, however, had a rather poor track record. In response to Wallenberg's request to find a way to improve their performance, Dahlbäck suggested the addition of trading – a field unfamiliar to Wallenberg. It nevertheless became quite successful over time.[88] In addition, Wallenberg asked his cousin Bonde, Head of Banque Scandinave en Suisse at the time, to accept the position as Deputy Chair in both investment companies. Bonde was then also appointed Deputy Chair in Stora Kopparberg.[89]

In 1982, Volvo made it publicly known that it had bought 9 per cent of the shares in Stora Kopparberg (from Graningeverken). Volvo also stated that it intended to bring its shareholdings to 25 per cent. It was furthermore agreed that Volvo should bring around

SEK 500 million to Stora Kopparberg in the form of a debenture loan that could be transformed to shares before 1984.

By virtue of the size of its shareholding, Volvo merited a seat on the board, and it was suggested that Gyllenhammar should be elected at the upcoming EGM. Stora Kopparberg's board stated in a communiqué that it regarded a significant Volvo shareholding as propitious – its financial resources and industrial know-how were expected to contribute to the company's stabilization and further development.[90] As soon as he was elected Gyllenhammar took a conspicuous role at Stora Kopparberg's board meetings – something that irritated the leading members of the Wallenberg sphere. Gyllenhammar also expected that CEO Sundblad visit him regularly at Volvo's HQ in Gothenburg.[91]

Peter Wallenberg did not want to share the sphere leadership with Gyllenhammar. Among the reasons was that Wallenberg's experience was foremost from the manufacturing industry (particularly Atlas Copco), while Gyllenhammar had his experience foremost in a big insurance company (Skandia). Moreover, their upbringings, educations and personalities differed as did their appearances, manners, bearings, rhetoric, and so on. Wallenberg also felt that Gyllenhammar's ideas sometimes strayed too far into politics.[92] The growing conflict between the two actors impeded the proper functioning of the board. The atmosphere at meetings became tense, and the other directors began to watch to see whether Wallenberg could stand up to Gyllenhammar (that was not always the case). Berggren and Dahlbäck in particular sided with Wallenberg in that struggle.[93] Wallenberg soon concluded that he and Gyllenhammar were not able to co-operate particularly well, and moved to end the agreement between, on the one hand, Atlas Copco and Stora Kopparberg, and, on the other hand, Volvo.[94]

Thus, Volvo's shareholding in Stora Kopparberg did not last long. By 1983, there were already many indications that top management was dissatisfied with the situation – to serve two different non-co-operating wills was difficult, particularly when the clashes pertained to crucial issues like the company's mission and strategy.[95]

In that situation Wallenberg instructed the sphere companies to buy shares in Volvo (at first a few per cent, later a bigger percentage [7%]). The latter holding was acquired when Investor and Providentia each bought 25 per cent of a family-controlled firm (Forsinvest).[96] Wallenberg saw the Volvo investment as a part of his father's agreement with Gyllenhammar. However, when Gyllenhammar learned about Wallenberg's entrance in Volvo, he was enraged, and the conflict between the two escalated. According to Gyllenhammar, it was an emotionally trying fight where great values were at stake – two different governance ideas and value systems had clashed.[97] He claimed that an agreement existed between the former Volvo CEO and the Wallenberg family that the latter would not include Volvo in its restructuring and expansion plans. In response, Wallenberg stated that the buying of Volvo shares only represented a 'friendly capital investment', and the sphere continued its Volvo purchases, rather soon reaching close to 20 per cent. By then, Gyllenhammar realized that Wallenberg did not intend to try to take over Volvo – he only wanted Volvo to get out of 'the Wallenberg companies' (i.e. Atlas Copco and Stora Kopparberg).

So early in 1984 Gyllenhammar and Wallenberg met to settle the conflict. They asked Dahlbäck (Investor) and Lindén (Volvo) to solve the ownership issues.[98] Volvo offered favourable terms if it was allowed to acquire Stora Kopparberg, but Wallenberg refused because he wanted to keep both companies in the sphere.[99] Volvo also proposed buying (substantial parts of) other companies in the Wallenberg group (i.e. Alfa Laval and Ericsson), but those propositions were rejected as well.[100] Ultimately, what remained was to try to find a price for Volvo's holdings in Atlas Copco and Stora Kopparberg that both parties could accept. The result was presented in April. Through Patricia, a new company founded by Investor and Providentia, the Wallenberg sphere paid SEK 3 billion for Volvo's holdings in Atlas Copco and Stora Kopparberg.[101]

At the same time, Gyllenhammar and Peter Wallenberg also competed for the position as the new Chair of SE-Banken, a bank that for a long time had been regarded as part of the Wallenberg sphere. In the end, neither Wallenberg nor Gyllenhammar got the position. Instead, a 'neutral' candidate, Olsson, was appointed. That perhaps unexpected outcome resulted from the conclusion drawn by some of the leading actors in and around the bank that the appointment of one of the two major candidates (Gyllenhammar and Wallenberg) could hurt the bank's businesses irreparably. Thus, in that troublesome situation, certain actors decided to be loyal to the bank rather than to the Wallenberg family – and that was something that Wallenberg never forgot.[102]

11.5.2 Attempts to Diversify

Cartels – both legal and illegal – were rather common in the forest-based industry and had existed for a long time in many of its segments (particularly in the pulp and newsprint businesses). They were actually legal in (for example) Sweden up until the middle of the 20th century and were usually run from high up in the organizational hierarchies, upheld by tacit consent from leading corporate executives and major shareholders.[103]

The strong and continuous presence of cartels had its 'rational' explanations. First of all, demand for paper was rather stable, showing only a small increase each year, while the supply varied considerably. Unco-ordinated investments in new large-scale production plants repeatedly generated large price variations and output fluctuations that created substantial sourcing, sales and planning problems for the companies. To establish more stable and predictable industry conditions, the corporations had decided to make an agreement that contained quotas for every product type. Each company's sales and production for each geographical market was noted in a matrix. Thus, the volumes and prices were put on paper, and a 'peak co-ordinator on duty' was appointed, who should monitor that all involved corporations complied with the agreement (i.e. output and sales restrictions).[104] That industrial 'truce' lowered the investment risks, which were sizeable due to the huge costs associated with the building of new paper machines. These kinds of cartels continued to play a significant role in various forest-based businesses even during the 1970s, when they finally had been declared illegal.

Basically, cartels 'eliminated' competition, so prices could be kept high. Thus, in a short-term perspective, most producers and sellers benefitted from the regulations, but in the longer-term perspective the more efficient ones lost (not to mention the customers). Cartels tended to favour small and medium-sized companies, as the output and price regulations tended to slow down the development of more effective production and market structures (inefficient, i.e. older and undersized machines were not scrapped). However, there were also always those companies that did not 'follow the rules' – small firms that ran at full capacity, as well as large ones that concealed their matrix deviations. However, in general, the cartels 'worked well', although the 'inflated' profitability tempted some corporations to make new investments, which almost 'guaranteed' continuous market overcapacity.[105]

There was also another – although much subtler – 'regulation' in the global forest-based industry: the leading position that the Finnish consultancy firm Jakko Pöyry had captured as adviser to corporations (including Stora Kopparberg) that considered investments in machinery. There were probably not many actors who understood that firm's impact on the organization of the forest industry. As the value of customer knowledge usually is low on cartel markets, most focus is put on the production side, which in this case made knowledge about the machines (types and capacities) that were running around the world strategic. Jakko Pöyry had most of that information, since its staff provided advice to numerous companies about what machines they ought to buy and why. At the same time, Jakko Pöyry learned a lot about each customer's market estimates and strategic considerations.[106]

As mentioned above, Stora Kopparberg was looking for ways to expand and at the same time reduce or eliminate its dependence on certain parts of its forest-based operations. Thus, the company also examined opportunities that were not directly linked to its current operations, although some kind of connection was preferred. In mid-1983, CEO Sundblad summarized Stora Kopparberg's problems and opportunities in a memo. He regarded the hygiene business as the sole growth sector in the forest-based industry. Outside the Nordic countries it was a tough field dominated by four big American corporations: Kimberly-Clark, Scott Paper, Johnson & Johnson and Procter & Gamble. However, in Scandinavia there was still the potential to secure a substantial market share, but that required acquisitions (Lilla Edet, [part of] Klippan and Duni Bilå). To add MoDo Konsument to that list was desirable but not possible, as MoDo refused to abandon the hygiene business. For Stora Kopparberg's current core businesses, Sundblad saw purchases of minority shares in continental units as the preferable path. In that same memo he also addressed the company's Nova Scotia investment, writing that a review of the paper industry in the US finally had produced a possible acquisition candidate, namely the fine paper producer Penntech. His proposal was to add Grycksbo's know-how regarding coated paper qualities to the US company, and then try to build a market for that segment in northern America. In his report Sundblad expressed hesitation regarding the company's ambition to invest in a newsprint plant in South Carolina (together with Canal Industries), as the market outlook for that product was poor.[107]

In 1983 CEO Sundblad became interested in acquiring Esselte. That company would add a new entry point in a relatively familiar field and substantially contribute to Stora Kopparberg's internalization ambitions. It also provided a less capital-intense and more profitable business than the ones Stora Kopparberg ran at the time. Furthermore, the profits could cover some of the costs of Stora Kopparberg's coming expansion. Sundblad concluded that the benefits of a merger would take time to materialize, but that it ought to be easy to explain its merits both to shareholders and employees. In the end, however, these plans never reached the board (and Peter Wallenberg was never involved).[108]

Already back in 1980, Stora Kopparberg's leading actors had talked about a possible merger with Swedish Match, but Marcus Wallenberg Sr had rejected that idea.[109] However, a few years later (spring 1983) such a merger was once again discussed, but this time more seriously. The initiator of these new talks was Dahlsten, CEO of Swedish Match. He saw one particular benefit of a merger of the two companies: in such a constellation the cash flow from Stora Kopparberg's operations could be used for more profitable purposes than further expansion investments in pulp and paper. Instead, the cash could be used to launch an international home furnishings group, build an international consumer business and expand trading operations.[110] At the time, Sundblad thought that he needed a 'big achievement' to keep his CEO position, so he argued in favour of a merger. His reasoning was quite similar to that in the Esselte case.[111] However, a complication was that he and Dahlsten disagreed about which company should be on the buying side – Stora Kopparberg or Swedish Match.[112]

When Berggren, Gyllenhammar and Wallenberg met in April 1983, Berggren was asked to find out if a merger between Stora Kopparberg and Swedish Match was as good an idea as Dahlsten and Sundblad claimed. He returned after two weeks with the conclusion that since the companies differed significantly, a culture clash was highly likely. The possibility of conflict should not, however, be considered a decisive argument against the move. Berggren was convinced that the circumstances favoured a positive outcome despite the potential cultural costs and negligible synergy effects. He admitted, however, that he was uncertain regarding the profit potential for Swedish Match's divisions. Nevertheless, if further analyses showed that their total profit could be expected to exceed a certain figure, he would recommend a merger. At the end of his memo, Berggren once again expressed concern about the two companies' cultural differences and wrote that it was of utmost importance that integration was carried out with great respect for both companies' special traditions and values, because otherwise, the costs of the merger could become devastating.[113]

After a careful study of Berggren's report and additional materials, Stora Kopparberg 'finally' decided to give up the idea to merge with Swedish Match (however, cf. Ch. 12). One important reason not mentioned in the written reports was that the leaders of the Wallenberg sphere considered both Sundblad and Dahlsten to be incapable of carrying out such a large-scale merger. Moreover, Wallenberg was not particularly fond of Dahlsten. He saw him as a peculiar person, an 'ego-boy' with rather limited business talent, and as an individual he just could not trust. The fact that Swedish Match's current Chair Thunholm supported Dahlsten was certainly no plus point in the eyes of Wallenberg. There was also a problem with the timing: Stora Kopparberg's organization was considered to be too immature for such a big step. First and foremost, the company needed to sort out its forest-based businesses and establish well-structured units and efficient operations.[114] However, the cancelled merger had important consequences for Stora Kopparberg's strategic actions, because the analyses, feelings and understandings related to the unrealized merger left a 'sediment of experiences' that later was re-activated when the 'same' merger issue surfaced a third time in 1988 (cf. below).

However, already in 1984 Stora Kopparberg's board began to discuss whether it would be possible to integrate the company's window manufacturing business with the corresponding one at Swedish Match and establish a joint window company. The idea was that the latter company a few years later should be offered control over the new unit. However, Wallenberg disliked the construct and claimed that it was better that Swedish Match bought Stora Kopparberg's window operations straight away, as the plan anyhow was to give that company full management responsibility from the start. The board agreed and took the decision to sell, but eventually the Swedish antitrust authorities did not approve that effort.[115]

11.5.3 A New Leadership

Berggren, CEO of Incentive since 1978, was open to accepting a leading position in another company. One important reason was that he did not get along particularly well with current Chair Gustafsson, who had replaced Marcus Wallenberg Sr in that position.[116] Thus in the early 1980s several actors contacted Berggren regarding different CEO positions, but he turned them all down, with the exception of a proposal from Holmens Bruk. Its Chair Mannerfelt and CEO Önnesjö discussed the matter thoroughly with him.

Berggren made clear that he did not intend make such a decision behind Marcus Wallenberg Sr's back and thus informed him about the current offer from Holmens Bruk. Wallenberg clarified that his intention was that Berggren should succeed Sundblad as CEO of Stora Kopparberg.[117] Berggren in turn met with Stora Kopparberg's Chair Synnergren, who on behalf of Wallenberg (whose health faltered) 'formally' asked if he was ready to shoulder the position as the new CEO of the company. Berggren told Synnergren that he would accept such an offer, and the Chair took on the task of informing the company's current CEO Sundblad about the coming change.

However, before Synnergren had the opportunity to follow up, Marcus Wallenberg Sr passed away (September 1982). That occurrence dramatically changed the situation for the Wallenberg sphere, putting issues other than corporate ones into the forefront. So the 'CEO-talk' with Berggren was not brought up again until January 1984, when Peter Wallenberg, the new head of the Wallenberg family, informed him that Stora Kopparberg's board had decided to replace Sundblad, and that he was the preferred successor.[118] Other candidates had also emerged, including, for example, Sprängare, the CEO of MoDo, who had a rather strained relationship with the company's main shareholder and Chair Carlgren (cf. Ch. 9).[119]

Already late in 1983 Sundblad had felt the tide turning against him at the board meetings and contacted director Palmstierna to ask for his support. Palmstierna listened to Sundblad but soon came to the conclusion that it probably was best for the company to replace him, both because the company's businesses had begun to 'tread water' and because the CEO himself had adopted an 'imperial' leadership style that precipitated problems both inside and outside the organization.[120] At the same time, Gyllenhammar and Wallenberg began to doubt Sundblad's capacity to handle the upcoming expansion period for the company. Sundblad was regarded as a solitary being, not a team player, and teamwork would be necessary to be able to deal with the current acquisition ambitions and structural transformations. He was also blamed for a mistake in connection with an attempted acquisition of the Dutch corporation Schoenmacher, and for the failed mergers with Esselte and Swedish Match.

As a consequence of all the succession talks and rumours, Sundblad paid an unannounced visit to Berggren in February 1984. Beforehand, he had talked to retiring Chair Synnergren regarding Berggren's whispered future as the new CEO. All through the following day Berggren and Sundblad discussed matters linked to Stora Kopparberg. During those talks, Sundblad asked whether he could have the position as Group CEO ('koncernchef') if Berggren became CEO. However, 'koncernchef' was a fictitious position not regulated in the Swedish legislation, and, because of that, as well as because of the dysfunctional practical implications of such a construct, Berggren turned that proposition down.[121] Erik Sundblad passed away a few days later (15 February) after being informed by Synnergren that he soon would be replaced as CEO of Stora Kopparberg.[122] Director Gyllenhammar had also somewhat earlier hinted to Sundblad about what was to come.[123]

On 8 March Stora Kopparberg's board appointed Berggren as the new CEO of the company. In the beginning Wallenberg had some doubts about whether he was the right choice – maybe because Berggren also was his father's favourite candidate – but that feeling soon disappeared. At that time, Wallenberg formed a team that assumed responsibility for governing Stora Kopparberg. In addition to Berggren and Wallenberg himself, it included Investor's CEO Dahlbäck, mainly because of his financial competence. Wallenberg trusted these two persons, and later he added Ingvar Petersson, Stora Kopparberg's Head of Control and Finance, to that inner circle.[124]

The team's strong position meant that Berggren had moved a bit closer to the family and also to Investor, and simultaneously established a certain distance to his own top management. That change had a decisive impact on Stora Kopparberg's development during the 1980s and 1990s. The team regularly discussed strategy matters including various more or less fitting combinations of companies, and was supported in those discussions by Investor's staff with its expert resources including calculative skills. The team researched almost all possible combinations of units and companies in the forest-based industry and identified (positive) synergies – at least on paper – in many of those more or less realistic constructs. Petersson also contributed to these discussions, as he had a recognized capacity to combine strategic reasoning with concrete figures (but he never competed for the CEO position because he did not see himself as a 'frontline' personality). The team also considered Hagelin, another member of Stora Kopparberg's top management, as a judicious actor.[125]

By the mid-1980s, Stora Kopparberg had become a company where the leaders walked in step. That situation contrasted favourably with the previous era during which the two Wallenberg brothers Jacob and Marcus often expressed divergent opinions on important matters.[126] In this new situation, Berggren took the role as initiator and developer, while Peter Wallenberg and Dahlbäck acted as careful examiners of all propositions.

To make things happen Berggren had to convince Peter Wallenberg first and foremost. As controlling shareholder, Wallenberg's task was to pave the way for top management by providing crucial business networks and exclusive ('inaccessible') information. As Wallenberg had inherited considerable social capital in the form of prestigious consanguinity, a well-reputed family name and an unparalleled international network, his capacity to carry out that arduous mission was excellent.[127]

Some actors also regarded director Marcus Wallenberg Jr as an influential actor in Stora Kopparberg. He was the late Marc Wallenberg's son, the grandson of Marcus Wallenberg Sr and, consequently, Peter Wallenberg's nephew and Jacob Wallenberg Jr's cousin (cf. Figure 11.1). So it was the Wallenberg family that governed the company, although a few leading actors[128] actually saw Dahlbäck as the leader (from his position as CEO of the Wallenberg-controlled Investor). All this meant that Stora Kopparberg was run very much like a family firm, where the executives had to obtain – and maintain – positive connections to the leading family members to be able to work successfully. That situation did not represent any dramatic changes in the basic governance system – various family members had run Stora Kopparberg for ages. Still, the board tried to act professionally and critically review all proposals, but, since Peter Wallenberg and Dahlbäck beforehand decided the most important matters, the board was in practice a rather weak body. Some directors were nevertheless active in certain fields, for example, Palmstierna (finance), Mogren (R&D and international marketing) and Persson (production).

Berggren radically changed the way Stora Kopparberg was managed. His predecessor Sundblad had run operations in a centralized way, but Berggren, inspired by his years as CEO of the industrial conglomerate Incentive, instead launched an opposite approach – 'radical decentralization'. Moreover, like in Incentive but unlike Sundblad, Berggren did not establish a GMT to consider and make the important decisions. Instead, the 'sphere level' handled most of the truly important issues, particularly by Peter Wallenberg in his discussions with Berggren and Dahlbäck. However, there were also meetings that involved Stora Kopparberg's CEO and top management, but those sessions primarily consisted of information exchanges and 'vertical' reporting – seldom in-depth, 'all-channel' discussions addressing crucial questions.[129]

One of the top managers, Grafström, described Berggren's management style as diametrically opposed to Sundblad's. Berggren practised a sort of decentralization by which, for example, acquired units simply were added to the existing organization without any more advanced integration efforts. His decentralization allowed most divisions and subsidiaries a high degree of autonomy with their own boards, staffs and in several cases also balance sheets (with the exception of finance and forestry, which remained highly centralized). Berggren was of the opinion that many of these units were as big as ordinary listed companies and that they therefore deserved to be treated as such. Some actors claimed, however, that Stora Kopparberg then missed many opportunities to rationalize and take advantage of cross-unit synergies. Resources could also become too dispersed; for example, the sales staffs were spread across several hierarchical levels (at mills, divisions and regional companies). However, because the corporation's focus was mainly production oriented, most employees did not see the dispersed sales responsibility as a problem. In the mid-1980s, Wallenberg began to stimulate a more sales and market-oriented way of thinking – even among the company's top ranks – but he was not particularly successful initially, mainly because top management was fully occupied with expansion plans.[130]

11.5.4 Looking for Ways to Grow

When Stora Kopparberg had divested its steel operations, its major owner Peter Wallenberg began to explore ways the company could expand as a 'pure' forest-based company. As the current organization was too small to qualify as one of the leading players in that industry, Stora Kopparberg had to adapt its expansion ambitions to the paths laid by some of its larger competitors. Moreover, because of its relatively small size, it was also at the mercy of its customers, who had the power to 'set' the prices by threatening to go to other companies (substitutable products). Thus, the companies' possibilities to influence market prices were to a large extent determined by its relative market sizes.[131]

Wallenberg regarded the homogeneity of most of the inputs intended for further processing as a problem. He opposed the idea that had dominated that industry for years, namely that the input material ought to be (roughly) the same almost regardless of its intended further use. He noted that standardization had gone so far that there actually existed a product named 'Swedish pulp' and 'everybody' seemed to produce similar bleached sulphate. The buyers seem to have accepted that situation, even though the pulp they received often did not fit their needs as well as more customized qualities would have done. Recognizing an opportunity, Wallenberg wanted Stora Kopparberg to get to know its customers better and, based on this knowledge, differentiate its pulp output (and be able to ask for better prices). He expressed similar concern regarding the situation in the woodware business, where the focus on the production side led to more interest in the percentage of sawn timber one got from each log than in the economic value each log could provide to the company. To address these concerns, Wallenberg wanted to reorient Stora Kopparberg's R&D policy from one focused on production efficiency to one concentrated on finding out the needs of each individual customer and making those customers willing to pay for concomitant product modifications. As he saw it, the main emphasis ought to move from process R&D to product R&D.[132]

The prevailing emphasis on production in the forest-based industry could be understood as a consequence of the powerful cartel arrangements that imbued many of its segments. The efficiency of these informal contracts between 'competitors' made marketing efforts less of a priority.[133] Cartel arrangements were dysfunctional constructs for those companies like Stora Kopparberg that had the ambition to differentiate their customer offerings. Because of that and his earlier experiences at Atlas Copco, Wallenberg disliked that form of 'industrial organization'. It tended to shift focus away from price to other dimensions and conditions such as credit terms, various kinds of 'services', fringe benefits and peripheral equipment. Wallenberg wanted to break up the 'deadlock' that the governing cartels had created, and establish a more complex competitive context in which customer preferences became the crucial driving force. He claimed that cartel-based standardization for a (too) long time had hurt the effectiveness of the whole industry, making it possible for certain smaller, outmoded, less innovative and unproductive firms to survive.[134]

In line with that new spirit, Wallenberg asked CEO Berggren to travel to Brussels (EEC) and declare openly that there were cartels in the industry and that, like Stora Kopparberg, other corporations were prepared to 'show their hands'. Once that new path was blazed, all companies had to invest in sales and marketing. Stora Kopparberg met that requirement by building up an internal sales organization worthy of that name. Not surprisingly, the move made both Stora Kopparberg and its CEO unpopular among many colleagues in the industry. Still, like several other companies, Stora Kopparberg had to pay substantial fines. The upside was that it had become possible for everybody to act freely and compete on the various markets. Thus, a basic condition for corporate growth had been established that corresponded with Stora Kopparberg's new ambitions.[135] The first expansion path that it considered was into fine paper. Berggren launched the idea that the company ought to acquire Papyrus (cf. Ch. 12), and then leave Grycksbo,[136] Newton Falls[137] and its 50 per cent holding in Pegenova (a sales company) to Nymölla.

11.5.5 Sphere Disharmony

Papyrus, which produced and sold fine paper and cardboard, originated from activities back in the 17th century and had acquired a prominent position in the Wallenberg group since its founding in 1895. The reason for its favoured status was that it was the first big industrial holding for one of the founders of the Wallenberg dynasty, namely Marcus

Wallenberg the Elder (cf. Figure 11.1). The 1940s marked the start of a period of expansion that made Papyrus a relatively large forest-based company.

In 1959 Marcus Wallenberg Sr was appointed Chair of Papyrus, and he soon made clear that he wanted to establish a large pulp mill at Nymölla in the southern part of Sweden to supply Papyrus operations with appropriate material. He had learned about a new method for production of bleached sulphite pulp that promised lower operating expenses, more easily handled waste and easy switching between softwood and hardwood. That method fit the forests in southern Sweden, where the share of hardwood (birch) was high. Furthermore, it could partly solve the timber shortage problem.

Wallenberg's forest-based industry in southern Sweden was dependent on timber from privately owned forests (i.e. 'forest farmers'). Therefore, the Wallenberg sphere faced a problem when the forest farmers decided to expand their own industrial activities in that region, thereby creating a new unit that also needed timber supply. The forest-farmers' association decided to build a sulphate pulp mill only 20 km from Wallenberg's Nymölla. That move initiated a race between the two spheres to offer the most attractive terms for the farmers' timber (and obtain long-term contracts). Edström, the pugnacious head of the federation of forest owners in southern Sweden, argued vigorously against Wallenberg's establishment of pulp production at Nymölla and encouraged the forest owners to unite in the fight against that new competitor.

Ultimately, the leaders of Stockholms Enskilda Bank (the Wallenberg family's bank) inaugurated Nymölla in 1962, and soon it became a subsidiary of Hylte Bruk (in which Wallenberg's Papyrus owned 60%). The new plant was built to meet the rising demand that was expected to follow from the merger of the two Western European trade blocks, the EEC and EFTA. However, by the mid-1960s it became obvious that the Nymölla investment had become a debacle.[138] An important cause of its severe technical problems was that the new sulphite method still was not ready for large-scale use.[139] Since Marcus Wallenberg Sr had promoted the new method, he became even more engaged as the problems grew. Several actors around him had become sceptical of the new method, particularly as no profits were being generated to finance the venture; instead, loans and new equity supported the expansion. Nymölla soon became the family bank's worst customer.[140] Because of Nymölla's poor performance, the company's top management was inclined to instead introduce a more proven sulphate process. Although the company Chair Jacob Wallenberg Sr favoured that idea, it still did not materialize.[141]

Despite Nymölla's poor performance, Marcus Wallenberg Sr's hurry and his ambition to build 'his own' strong forest-based company group (separate from that led by his brother Jacob) drove him to pursue its growth. The expansion was supported by an unusual financial construct – a new issue of shares linked to loans creating debt/equity 'units'. Both the Swedish authorities (the Central Bank was at that time obliged to control all new issues of shares) and Jacob Wallenberg Sr disliked the construct. Because of Jacob Wallenberg Sr's opposition, Investor and Providentia refrained from participating in the subscription; as a result, Marcus Wallenberg Sr had to rely exclusively on Papyrus. Thus, once again, the conflict between the two Wallenberg brothers became publicly visible. It prompted Marcus Wallenberg Sr to build a forest-based company group outside Stora Kopparberg based on Papyrus that besides Nymölla also included Hylte Bruk.

It took until 1969 before Nymölla became a stable part of the growing Papyrus. At that time, Papyrus's board declared that it intended to build a paper mill next to the existing

Nymölla plant and use its pulp for fine paper production. Papyrus also had ambitions for Hylte Bruk, which had been run at a loss for several years and whose plant had become rather run down. In 1970, Marcus Wallenberg Sr declared that Europe's biggest newsprint plant was to be built at that site. In total, the Papyrus group invested more than SEK 1 billion, and as Jacob Wallenberg Sr firmly opposed the expansion, the required capital was raised without any assistance from Investor and Providentia. Eventually, all these investments became profitable – even the controversial sulphate-based pulp became a real hit. As a consequence of the success, two more newsprint machines were eventually built at Hylte Bruk. These new investments were accompanied by important changes in that company's ownership. A new 'Hylte Bruk company' was created, which was equipped neither with forests nor with power plants. The remaining part of the 'old' Hylte Bruk (renamed 'Ry') controlled 37.5 per cent of its votes, Feldmühle (the biggest newsprint and cardboard producer in the EEC) acquired 25 per cent, ASSI 20 per cent, Stora Kopparberg 10 per cent and Papyrus 7.5 per cent.[142]

NOTES

N.B.: When there is an 'i' inside a parenthesis below, that letter indicates that the note refers to an interview with the named person. All interviewees are listed in the Appendix. A complete listing of references is found at the end of the book.

1. Glete (1994).
2. Sjögren (2005).
3. Brantingson (1994).
4. Gustafsson in Investor (1991).
5. Lindgren (1994).
6. Investor (1991).
7. Glete (1994).
8. Lindgren (2007).
9. A small Swedish forestry firm.
10. A small Swedish company with a sawmill and (later) ironworks.
11. Lindgren (2007).
12. Valeur (2007).
13. Glete (1994).
14. Sjögren (2005).
15. A Swedish petroleum-based company.
16. Lindgren (2007).
17. Valutakontoret.
18. Lindgren (2007).
19. Sjögren (2005).
20. Eidem was 56 years old.
21. Sundblad actually joined the board as deputy member of the Canadian subsidiary when he still held the CEO position at Wifstavarf.
22. Wallander (1998).
23. Haegerstrand (2005i).
24. Lars G. Sundblad (2006i).
25. The 'King of Dalarna' (the region where Stora Kopparberg resided) became one of his nicknames.
26. Haegerstrand (2005i).
27. Lindgren (2007).
28. Letter from Marcus Wallenberg Sr to Sundblad dated 28 December 1969.
29. Lundqvist, quoted in Sjögren (2005).
30. G. Haindl'sche Papier Fabriken.
31. A large and expansive German company that ran operations in Arnsberg, Flensburg, Hillegrossen,

Lülsdorf, Oberlahnstein, Reisholz, Uetersen and Wesseling. In 1959 Feldmühle acquired Kabel and in 1960 the majority of Dynamit Nobel. In 1962 it became a part of the Flick group.
32. Haegerstrand (2005i).
33. Ibid.
34. Palmstierna (2004i).
35. The second half of the paragraph builds on an interview with Haegerstrand (2005i).
36. Its new name.
37. Investor (1991) and Althin (1945).
38. Brantingson (1994).
39. Investor (1991).
40. Palmstierna (2004i).
41. A son to Marcus Wallenberg Sr.
42. Brantingson (1994).
43. Ibid.
44. Berggren, in Brantingson (1994).
45. A large Swedish steel company.
46. A Swedish producer of stainless steel.
47. A Finnish producer of stainless steel.
48. Brantingson (1994).
49. Ibid.
50. A Swedish state-owned steel company.
51. Wahlström (1999).
52. Ibid., p. 123.
53. Ibid., p. 126.
54. Olsson (2000, p. 403).
55. A Swedish high-tech industrial conglomerate.
56. Brantingson (1994).
57. Sweden's biggest energy company (owned by the state).
58. Brantingson (1994).
59. Ibid.
60. Palmstierna (2004i).
61. Valeur (2007).
62. Haegerstrand (2005i).
63. Dahlbäck (2004i and 2007i).
64. Ibid.
65. Palmstierna (2004i).
66. Palmstierna (2004i), Peter Wallenberg (2005i) and Investor (1991).
67. Except from being based on the specific material collected for this extensive study, this section also builds on Ericson (1991) and Sjöstrand (1997).
68. Carlgren (1994i).
69. Brantingson (1994) and Lars G. Sundblad (2005i).
70. Dahlbäck (2004i and 2007i).
71. Haegerstrand (2005i).
72. Palmstierna (2004i).
73. Dahlbäck (2004i and 2007i).
74. Brantingson (1994).
75. Dahlbäck (2004i and 2007i).
76. Ibid.
77. Ibid.
78. Ibid.
79. Brantingson (1994).
80. Ibid.
81. A manufacturer of compressors, construction and mining tools and equipment, power tools and assembly systems.
82. Peter Wallenberg, in the TV documentary 'Wallenbergs' (Swedish Public Service Television, 2007).
83. Peter Wallenberg (2005i).
84. Palmstierna (2004i).
85. Berggren (2004i and 2005i).
86. Dahlbäck, in the TV documentary 'Wallenbergs' (Swedish Public Service Television, 2007).
87. Investor (1991).
88. Peter Wallenberg, in the TV documentary 'Wallenbergs' (Swedish Public Service Television, 2007).

89. Investor (1991).
90. Brantingson (1994).
91. Dahlbäck (2004i and 2007i).
92. Peter Wallenberg, in the TV documentary 'Wallenbergs' (Swedish Public Service Television, 2007).
93. Palmstierna (2004i).
94. Peter Wallenberg, in the TV documentary 'Wallenbergs' (Swedish Public Service Television, 2007).
95. Brantingson (1994).
96. Investor (1991).
97. Gyllenhammar (1991, p. 91).
98. Brantingson (1994) and Lindgren (1994).
99. Dahlbäck in Brantingson (1994).
100. Brantingson (1994) and Borgström and Haag (1988).
101. Borgström and Haag (1988).
102. Palmstierna (2004i).
103. Knuts (2005i).
104. Helgesson (2004i).
105. Knuts (2005i).
106. Hagelin (2004i).
107. Brantingson (1994).
108. Ibid.
109. Ibid.
110. Ibid.
111. Memorandum from Sundblad published in Brantingson (1994).
112. Brantingson (1994).
113. Memorandum from Berggren published in Brantingson (1994).
114. Brantingson (1994).
115. Ibid.
116. Berggren (2004i and 2005i).
117. Brantingson (1994).
118. Berggren (2004i and 2005i).
119. Haegerstrand (2005i).
120. Palmstierna (2004i).
121. Berggren (2004i and 2005i).
122. Brantingson (1994).
123. Gyllenhammar (1991).
124. Palmstierna (2004i) and Peter Wallenberg (2005i).
125. Marcus Wallenberg Jr (2005i).
126. Peter Wallenberg (2005i).
127. Jacob Wallenberg Jr (2006i).
128. Hagelin (2004i).
129. Grafström (2006i).
130. Ibid.
131. Peter Wallenberg (2005i).
132. Ibid.
133. There are 'rational' explanations for the existence of cartels linked to the perceived importance of media for the society's democratic functioning (newsprint), and for many decades they were perfectly legal in Sweden (although they had to be 'registered' by the authorities).
134. Berggren (2004i and 2005i).
135. Peter Wallenberg (2005i).
136. Acquired by Stora Kopparberg in 1966.
137. The idea was that the company should take 30% of the pulp from that produced at Stora Kopparberg's plant in Nova Scotia.
138. Sjögren (2005).
139. Olsson (1986).
140. Sjögren (2005).
141. Olsson (1986).
142. Ibid.

12. From Stora Kopparberg to Stora Enso: towards a grand merger

12.1 FOUR LARGE ACQUISITIONS

12.1.1 The Acquisition of Billerud

In the early 1980s, Stora Kopparberg gave priority to its expansion into fine paper. As noted in Chapter 11, CEO Berggren had proposed that the company make a non-cash acquisition of Papyrus, while Nymölla would get Grycksbo, Newton Falls and a 50 per cent holding in Pegenova from Stora Kopparberg. Nymölla would then change its name to Papyrus and continue as a listed fine paper company. Berggren noted that such a 'new Papyrus' would thus have the strongest marketing and distribution organization for fine paper in the region and would be capable of developing a unique and broad product repertoire without arousing conflicts of interests inside the family sphere. A larger and more focused Papyrus would possess the necessary resources for extensive product development and expansion abroad. All in all, the company could become one of the strongest units on the European fine paper market.[1]

Wallenberg hesitated, as he was not convinced that the suggested re-shuffling of units would work in practice. However, Dahlbäck supported Berggren, and the two convinced Wallenberg to change his mind. In those talks, Berggren suggested even more far-reaching structural plans for the Wallenberg family's forest-based industrial group with Stora Kopparberg as the hub. He wanted to see Stora Kopparberg acquire (in turn) Papyrus, Billerud and Swedish Match.[2] Berggren proceeded to calculate what a purchase of Papyrus would entail and showed his figures and analyses to some of the leading actors in the family sphere.[3] Berggren also discussed the acquisition idea with Persson (CEO of Papyrus) and learned that he also was in favour of such a path. However, the key decision-maker was Peter Wallenberg, and he was still not convinced that Stora Kopparberg should go ahead. As late as 1985, he asked Berggren to 'take it easy'.[4]

Several of Stora Kopparberg's managers worried about the company's almost exclusive focus on expansion and believed that the company would be better off if it began its 'new journey' by making substantial disinvestments. At that time, Stora Kopparberg comprised numerous small units, and – according to several top managers – some of them ought to be sold immediately. However, they also noted that Berggren did not pursue growth 'at any price'. He had turned down Italian Garda, and his talks with German Scheufelen also did not result in any actual purchase. Berggren also focused on how Stora Kopparberg could secure a continuous supply of 'cheap' timber to its expanding operations. He was particularly concerned about the investments that several competitors made in eucalyptus fibres (and similar woods).

When Stora Kopparberg was unexpectedly presented with the opportunity to acquire

Billerud from Uddeholm and Tresor (a constellation led by the Swedish financier Wall, who controlled 56% of the Billerud shares), the leading actors hesitated, because such a purchase was not part of the current strategic plan. Furthermore, they did not want to impair Stora Kopparberg's possibilities of acquiring Papyrus. However, eventually the calculations showed that Stora Kopparberg was able to do both, so the company went ahead with the Billerud acquisition, although it would take lots of managerial costs to co-ordinate the operations of the two companies.[5]

It was Dahlbäck who got a tip from a stockbroker that Wall wanted to sell Tresor's holding in Billerud.[6] That company had already in the 1960s expanded beyond Sweden and got the Portuguese authorities' permission to build a pulp plant (Celbi) in the middle part of the country with the idea of making use of the fast-growing[7] eucalyptus tree. Celbi, which was jointly owned by Billerud (71% of the shares) and a Portuguese investor (29%), soon became one of the most successful producers of eucalyptus-based pulp in Europe.[8]

In 1978 Billerud acquired a large part of Uddeholm (its forests, forest-based industry and chemical business) to shore up the two companies' forest-based operations' combined losses of SEK 350 million during the previous year. At the same time Engman – a person with a solid track record in the Wallenberg sphere (Kopparfors and Bergvik & Ala) – was recruited from Ncb to become CEO of Billerud.

By the late 1970s, when Billerud's situation had become even more problematic, its leaders began to look for possibilities to co-operate with other firms. During the summer of 1980, Iggesund's CEO Lars G. Sundblad contacted Billerud's Chair Thunholm and discussed his company's ambition to acquire Billerud. However, CEO Engman firmly argued against such a step, and the whole effort quickly petered out. One year later, however, the reverse process took place when Billerud, together with Stora Kopparberg, made an unexpected and 'hostile' bid for Iggesund. As described earlier in this chapter, that spectacular attempt failed, too, as in the end MoDo won the contest and bought Iggesund (an extensive description of both processes was presented in Ch. 9).[9]

In 1983 Billerud celebrated its centenary as being one of the biggest forest-based corporations in Sweden, comprising two large integrated pulp and paper mills (Gruvön and Skoghall), one special paper mill (Billerud), four sawmills, three packaging plants and one chemical industry. Outside Sweden, Billerud ran one pulp mill in Portugal (Celbi), corrugated cardboard plants in France, Germany, Austria and Malta, and sack producing units in Belgium and the UK.

The Celbi success prompted the Brazilian corporation Aracruz to ask Billerud whether it was interested in managing the establishment of the biggest eucalyptus-based pulp mill in the world. In this way Celbi also indirectly brought Billerud a minority share in a Brazilian unit (7%).[10] The Aracruz connection had important consequences for Stora Kopparberg as well. Aracruz received a Marcus Wallenberg Sr award for its forestry operations. The prize motivated CEO Berggren to go there, where he 'discovered' the cheap Brazilian eucalyptus timber. Because of the potential for cheap timber sourcing and possible future pulp production, he thought that Stora Kopparberg ought to establish a significant presence in that region.[11]

Billerud continuously tried to become the market leader in Europe for several of its products and had achieved such a position for sack paper, LPB, semi-chemical fluting, eucalyptus-based pulp and certain special products. The company had also invested heavily to become one of the most efficient producers in the industry.[12] At the end of 1983, Billerud discussed a share issue exclusively directed to Tetra Pak, its major LPB customer, which would in exchange have received 20 per cent of the votes in Billerud. Despite initial interest, Tetra Pak's leaders ultimately decided to turn down the offer. In spring 1984, Billerud's CEO Engman contacted Papyrus and its CEO Persson, as he thought that the two companies would fit well together. Engman proposed that Papyrus should buy Billerud, but Persson was not interested, most likely because of the expected price.[13]

Engman had carried out a major restructuring in Billerud, so the company was in rather good shape, although perhaps somewhat underinvested (the dominating shareholder Uddeholm was a financially weak company).[14] After being rejected by Iggesund,[15] Wall (the controlling shareholder) got a new opportunity to sell his majority position in Billerud when he quite accidentally met Peter Wallenberg in Stockholm. During a stroll Wall asked Wallenberg[16] if Stora Kopparberg might be interested in buying his holding in Billerud. Wallenberg was rather surprised, since Wall had stated publicly that his ambition was to be a long-term controlling shareholder in Billerud.[17] However, many business leaders doubted Wall's statements: they believed that his primary goal was to build a private fortune – not to take long-term responsibility for a group of corporations.

Dahlbäck regarded the acquisition of Billerud as an opportunistic move. The chance to buy 'suddenly surfaced', and Stora Kopparberg took it. Neither Investor nor Stora Kopparberg had formulated any distinct goal for such a purchase, so it was not easy to argue 'rationally' that the step should be taken. It did not expand the sphere's bank business, and it would not bring Stora Kopparberg significant synergies or other business strengths. It became a question of 'why not' rather than 'why'.

Despite the favourable price, Wallenberg hesitated. He was concerned about the large size of a combined constellation and uncertain about Berggren's capacity to handle such a complicated merger.[18] However, he also understood that Stora Kopparberg by making such a purchase could take its first step towards a size that made it possible to influence market prices. Dahlbäck and Berggren were the ones that carried out the negotiations with Billerud, which was represented by Wahlström (Deputy Chair) and Johansson (CEO).[19] The initial idea was that Stora Kopparberg would pay with a combination of cash and convertibles. Nevertheless, since Wall was not interested in becoming a minority shareholder and Wallenberg was not particularly eager to let Wall inside the company, the convertibles never materialized.

As mentioned above, it was not easy to justify an acquisition of Billerud, as there were both a limited rationalization potential and few positive synergies between that company and Stora Kopparberg. SE-Banken and Investor provided the calculations and other kind of inputs necessary for decision-making. Four things favoured a purchase: Berggren was eager to make Stora Kopparberg a bigger company so that it could compete internationally, Billerud would bring considerable forest resources connected to Stora Kopparberg's own estates, the bid was 'friendly' (cf. Iggesund's attempt to buy Billerud 1980, described in Ch. 8) and Stora Kopparberg had the capacity to handle an enlarged constellation.[20] However, the 'mistimed' purchase of Billerud would force Stora Kopparberg to re-write its strategic plan since the order of the planned acquisitions had been switched. It would have been easier for Stora Kopparberg to instead justify a purchase of Papyrus, as it was obvious to most observers that those two companies would do well together. Moreover,

Billerud would fit well in such an enlarged constellation – much better than with Stora Kopparberg alone.[21]

The acquisition of Billerud was not only hard to explain to the actors on the stock market – it also required certain authorizations from the County Administrative Board. That procedure was simplified by the fact that the leading actors in the county had been critical of the way the former majority shareholder had run Billerud. To make Stora Kopparberg's intentions in the region clear, Peter Wallenberg and Berggren met with the County Governor at his summer residence. He knew Peter Wallenberg's father well, and that family 'capital' – a reputation for staying power and decency – made things easier. Eager to have a new owner that worked with a long-term perspective, the County Governor was pleased when he heard about Stora Kopparberg's ambitious investment plans for Skoghall and Gruvön. Not too long after, Stora Kopparberg received the necessary authorization.[22]

In September 1984, Stora Kopparberg decided to go ahead with the purchase of Billerud. The board announced an agreement with Uddeholm and Tresor that included an obligation to buy the two companies' holdings in Billerud (56% of the total stock). Stora Kopparberg also publicly declared its intention to make the same offer to all other shareholders in Billerud.[23] The total cost for the acquisition of Billerud amounted to SEK 3.6 billion.

However, economic journalists, analysts and (potential) investors expressed scepticism, mainly because of the fundamental disparity between the two corporations' product mix. Stora Kopparberg's core businesses were printing paper and fine paper, while Billerud focused on packaging and cardboard. That made their businesses complementary (which opened up several strategic paths) rather than synergetic (which generated opportunities to specialize and rationalize). One could note, however, that the new constellation would become a global pulp player with plants located in many places around the world (Sweden, Portugal, Brazil and Canada) and a market presence in 12 countries.

There was some public criticism regarding the financing of the acquisition – the purchase represented a substantial strain on Stora Kopparberg's balance sheet that might require the sale of, for example, the power plants. Berggren did not disagree with the critics but stressed that the merits of the merger were to be found in other dimensions. He particularly emphasized that the acquisition made Stora Kopparberg a truly international corporation and created a very strong R&D resource. The purchase also made it possible to use both kinds of fibres – the more expensive long Nordic (spruce) one and the cheaper short foreign (eucalyptus) one – in the fields where they had their particular strengths. However, Berggren also recognized that the new rather heterogeneous constellation would be difficult to integrate. Two regional 'jewels', each with its own realm and high status, were to be merged. There were even signs that it was two 'sworn enemies' that were to become one unit.[24]

Thus, the acquisition of Billerud brought about a broadening of Stora Kopparberg's business repertoire, as well as a strong position in a new, growing field: cardboard. The well-located forests also offered possibilities for utilization of economies of scale and rationalizations. However, two of the other operations that Billerud ran (sacks and fluting) were not particularly attractive businesses for Stora Kopparberg. As such, there were thoughts about selling these 'superfluous' units to either AssiDomän or SCA. It soon became evident that these 'remaining parts' of Billerud (e.g. Gruvön) actually (also) were quite unattractive to most other actors.

In the new 'integrated' organization, Billerud's forests, power plants and sawmills became part of Stora Skog, Stora Kraft and Stora Timber, respectively. Celbi became part of Stora Cell together with the pulp-producing units at Skutskär and Sandarne. What then was left of Billerud was combined into a separate Stora Billerud unit, and what remained of Stora Kopparberg was organized into four units (Kvarnsveden, Grycksbo, North America and 'the Rest').[25] Billerud further contributed to the new constellation by boosting R&D and international thinking in Stora Kopparberg. Former Stora Kopparberg CEO Sundblad had not acted on the global scene, so the acquisition of Billerud had turned a former weakness to a strength. The Billerud acquisition also forced Stora Kopparberg to improve its own structures and processes.[26]

All in all, the acquisition of Billerud turned out to be a splendid affair. Among the more striking contributions were three years of healthy profits and the sale of Billerud's power resources to AGA. In retrospect, Berggren regarded the purchase of Billerud as the company's best undertaking during his time as CEO of Stora Kopparberg.[27] It moved Stora Kopparberg to the right in the value chain, which reduced trade fluctuations. There was also a substantial lessening of exposure to cyclical pulp qualities. Moreover, pulp production increased much less than paper production, which almost doubled (if 'special qualities', Celbi and Aracruz were disregarded). Thus, newsprint, magazine paper, coated fine paper, liquid packaging board and other packaging papers became the new constellation's core businesses. All in all, however, the exposure to price fluctuations still existed, although the qualitative improvements of the products mitigated that problem.[28]

Soon after Stora Kopparberg had acquired Billerud the name of the new constellation was discussed. It was decided that (legally) it should continue to be 'Stora Kopparbergs Bergslag', although the shorter name 'Stora' should do for everyday use. One of the directors (Palmstierna) registered a reservation at the decisive board meeting pleading for the name 'Kopparberget', but all the other board members supported the 'Stora' proposal.[29]

When Synnergren left as Chair in 1985, Peter Wallenberg was the favourite to replace him. However, Wallenberg actually did not want to take the position at that time. Wallenberg's explanation for his reluctance was that he did not want Johansson, a director of Stora and former CEO of SKF,[30] to become Chair in SKF; his plan was to stay as Chair in SKF and nominate Johansson as Chair of Stora. However, both Berggren and Dahlbäck preferred to see Wallenberg as Stora Chair, since it had a particularly prominent standing in the family sphere. The regional Social Democratic politicians also acted to promote Wallenberg as Chair. That indeed became the final outcome of the process.[31]

As the newcomer in that position, Peter Wallenberg showed that he was eager to get all directors involved in the work of the board. From the very beginning he made clear that he expected the active participation of every director including a declared opinion on every important issue. This required all directors to take more active responsibility for the company's development.[32] Thus, Wallenberg's approach to the Chair position broke with that of his ancestors, who themselves handled most of the crucial company matters and only involved the board when formalities so required.

The forming of Stora did not eliminate the need for new large investments. To obtain the capital needed for these investments, Stora sold not only Billerud's power plants but also Stora's holding in Finnish Kaukas.[33] However, the crucial capital came from the selling of Stora's power resources (with a right to repurchase) to a consortium of Swedish insurance companies and pension funds. Together with the buyers, Stora then established a new unit – Kopparkraft – that should serve as the owner of the hydropower resources. Stora Kraft got 51 per cent of the votes in Kopparkraft, and Stora provided 10 per cent of its equity. That agreement substantially increased Stora's net assets (added SEK 6 billion).

The investment decisions for the coming four years (1986–89) included a new newsprint machine at Kvarnsveden (SEK 1.3 billion, 1988), an expansion of the fine paper operations (SEK 900 million, 1988), the building of a newsprint machine at Hylte (SEK 1.2 billion, 1989), a possible expansion of the Nova Scotia programme (another newsprint machine was discussed) and a broadening of Billerud's product repertoire (multilayer packaging paper and CTMP pulp). Despite the new capital inflow, the financial strain caused by these investments prompted Stora to organize a special finance committee with a rather unusual composition – a mix of actors from Stora and its main shareholder Investor (14%[34]), which included Jacob Wallenberg Jr (Peter Wallenberg's son), Berggren (CEO, Stora), Petersson (Deputy CEO, Stora), Haegerstrand (CFO, Stora) and Harrison (Deputy CEO, SE-Banken). A large new issue of B-shares was also carried out (1988).[35]

When the Billerud acquisition was a fact, Stora's board resumed its discussions about the company's future business structure. The new constellation still did not resolve three of Stora's long-standing problems: the lack of timber, the high exposure to trade fluctuations (pulp and woodware) and the presence of too many unprofitable products. Furthermore, there remained the problem of how to handle the operations at Skoghall, which produced LPB, and Gruvön, which was moving towards manufacturing non-coated, wood-free fine paper based on birch. Basically, Stora intended to invest in fields with market growth, limited demand fluctuations and long-fibre advantages. Thus, in due time, Stora intended to get out of sack paper and industrial paper.

At that time, the board also discussed a partial shareholding in Danish Forenade Papirfabrikken (controlled by Dansk Sukker) and in Mohawk Paper Mills (a US family firm). The majority of Mohawk Paper Mills (51%) was acquired in 1986, later an additional 29 per cent and still later the remaining 20 per cent (total cost: SEK 500 million). That purchase took some time, as the holding in Newton Falls had been sequestrated because of a dispute from the 1970s.[36]

12.1.2 The Acquisition of Papyrus

Soon after the Billerud merger, Papyrus once again came up as a hot acquisition candidate. It had expanded its operations substantially during the 1970s, particularly through the purchase of Kopparfors in 1976 (which contained two pulp plants [Norrsundet and Gästrike-Hammarby], one cardboard unit [Fors] and sawmills and forests). In 1981, the large German corporation Feldmühle entered as a shareholder in Norrsundet (50%). Feldmühle was at that time already a partner to Stora with its involvement in Hylte.

Papyrus had always been a family favourite, as it was the first industrial company in which Marcus Wallenberg the Elder had been deeply engaged. He and his successors had promoted what eventually developed into a special Papyrus culture characterized by low-cost thinking, small administration, plain offices and the like.[37] Investor, Providentia,

Export-Invest, and several Wallenberg dominated foundations held 29 per cent of the votes in Papyrus. Its second biggest shareholder (9%) was another family-owned investment company (Ratos, controlled by the 'friendly' Söderberg dynasty).[38]

Ingvar Petersson became Deputy CEO of Stora in 1986. Berggren recruited him from Kopparfors, where he had been CEO since 1981 (and a member of Papyrus's board).[39] At one of his first top management meetings at Stora, Petersson was asked to take a look at Berggren's earlier analyses of the implications of a merger between Stora and Papyrus. However, very soon Berggren regretted that special assignment, as he recalled that he had promised Wallenberg two years ago not to touch Papyrus. Thus, he told Petersson to forget the whole idea, but did not simultaneously inform his top management team about that counter-order. That circumstance could explain why Stora's interest in Papyrus leaked to the business press and became front-page news.[40]

Just a short time later, when Berggren and his wife were out sailing with Peter Wallenberg, Wallenberg said out of the blue, 'now it is time for Papyrus'. Wallenberg's sudden 'green light' for that purchase had several explanations: Berggren and his team had successfully handled a large purchase (Billerud), Stora's financial standing had improved significantly and Stora's new organization was in place. And – last but not least – Papyrus's CEO had reached retirement age.[41]

Thus, in mid-1986, actors in the Wallenberg sphere began to discuss Papyrus, although – as always – other alternatives were analysed, too. Such a situation with on-going parallel investigations was nothing unusual. Wallenberg's investment company Investor, for example, had had close contacts over the years with several broker firms, which identified and suggested many more or less realistic structural options. In that way Investor obtained valuable information (news, rumours, analyses, etc.) and became a kind of 'slop basin' for business opportunities that, after being evaluated, were handed over to suitable companies in the Wallenberg group.[42]

This time when Papyrus was in focus, Berggren (CEO, Stora), Persson (CEO, Papyrus), Dahlbäck (CEO, Investor), Petersson (Deputy CEO, Stora) and Söderberg (Deputy Chair, Papyrus) participated in the negotiations.[43] Wallenberg – Chair in both the involved companies – was challengeable, so he could not take part in the talks. Because it was important for the Wallenberg family that all shareholders were treated correctly, Nicolin, Chair of ASEA,[44] was engaged as an impartial 'mediator', ensuring that everything was done according to best practice.[45]

Current share prices made the timing of the Papyrus purchase propitious.[46] By and by, Stora's directors became informed about the negotiations, and in late September the board took the formal decision to make the bid. The directors regarded improved timber sourcing, a stronger position on the newsprint market and increased internal pulp sales (to Papyrus) as the strongest arguments for the merger. In addition to forests, Papyrus contained Hylte (newsprint),[47] Nymölla (pulp and fine paper), Fors (cardboard) and Norrsundet (pulp). It became a friendly and smooth acquisition process that ended in an unusually short agreement contract (ten pages).[48] However, the price was regarded as high ([part of the] financing was to be done with the company's own shares).[49] At an EGM in November 1986, Stora's shareholders decided to carry out the acquisition of Papyrus (at a total cost of SEK 6 billion).[50]

Stora's Deputy CEO Petersson saw six motives behind Stora's acquisition of Papyrus: (1) Hylte was owned by both companies (and by Feldmühle; ASSI had sold out its holding), (2) the new constellation had a coherent forest zone in the middle of Sweden, (3) the combination of Hylte and Kvarnsveden represented a substantial consolidation of the Swedish newsprint business, (4) a merger would solve some of the governance problems for the jointly owned wholesaler Pappersgruppen (the divided control had furnished its CEO with too much autonomy), (5) Nymölla and Grycksbo would have the same owner and (6) the merger would 'secure' a better long-term future for Papyrus.[51]

Petersson suggested that the acquisition be made in two steps. First, Papyrus would make a bid for Nymölla (of which it already owned 49.75%), and then Stora and Papyrus should merge. That would make it a merger between 'equals', something that was expected to simplify the integration process. Stora indeed followed that path, and Petersson was put in charge of the transformation process.[52]

In the Papyrus prospectus, Stora justified its bid for Papyrus with four statements about the new constellation. First of all, around 80 per cent of Papyrus businesses were in fields already prioritized by Stora's management. Second, a merger would also build an industrial base that could make use of the expensive high-quality Swedish fibre on products/markets where its advantages really made a difference (which indicated investments in newsprint, magazine paper, fine paper, cardboard, packaging paper and high-quality sawn timber). Third, the merger would bring more stability to operations by lessening the company's involvement in products facing strong price and volume fluctuations. And, finally, it would create a better balance between 'natural assets' and 'industrial assets' to improve profitability. When Berggren in 1986 summarized the Papyrus acquisition, he noted that businesses exposed to huge price and volume fluctuations had reduced their share of total sales from 24 per cent to about half that figure. The more processed products (newsprint, fine paper and packaging paper) had instead gone up from 30 per cent to 55 per cent of total sales.[53]

Early in 1987, Berggren presented his plan for how Stora should develop over the coming years. The share of total sales attributed to businesses that were exposed to heavy market fluctuations should be reduced from the current 26 per cent to 20 per cent, while the more processed ones instead should increase their share to 60 per cent. Berggren had become optimistic about the future for the long-fibre pulp market – global overcapacity had been eliminated, and there seemed to be a steady increase in demand (2% per year). He regarded Stora's position on the fine paper market as solid, as both Grycksbo and Nymölla were among the most effective mills in Europe, and as the market was growing particularly in the fields where Stora was active. A similar situation prevailed for both newsprint and magazine paper. The prospects for packaging paper and cardboard diverged – for some products like fluting, white liner and liquid packaging board, strong growth was foreseen, while for other products like sacks and boxboard a stagnant market was expected. For woodware, the future looked gloomy because of the huge overcapacity (in Europe about 25–30%). In that business Stora planned both rationalizations and changes in the assortment (a focus on high-quality products).[54] By that time, the Aracruz investment in Brazil had become a problem, as several crucial issues remained unsolved (including the management issue). However, for the time being (1988) Stora kept its 5 per cent shareholding, board membership (one director) and the opportunity to buy pulp at a reduced price.[55]

12.1.3 The Swedish Match Adventure

In 1988 Stora was fully occupied with the first two of its three planned acquisitions (Billerud and Papyrus). Still, the third one – that of Swedish Match – was brought forward, as the Wallenberg sphere had begun to doubt the competence of its top managers, as well as the path they had chosen. Therefore, Wallenberg pushed for a change, and – rather quickly – Stora bought Swedish Match.[56] One should remember that a few years earlier (1983) Swedish Match had approached Stora Kopparberg and suggested a merger, in which Swedish Match would be placed in the driver's seat. At the time, however, Stora Kopparberg was not particularly interested, so Swedish Match's initiative soon petered out.[57]

As Investor was a major shareholder (40% of the votes) in Swedish Match, it felt particularly responsible for the increasing management costs and the weakening link between the board and top management.[58] In those days Swedish Match bought lots of companies on the suggestion of management, and it was not always easy for the directors to keep up with things. That development worried Peter Wallenberg, who eventually intervened on the basis of his rather long experience as director in the company (1977–82).[59]

Over time, Wallenberg became more and more concerned about the true capacity of Swedish Match's CEO Dahlsten, and began to question how Swedish Match was managed. For example, he regarded several of the corporate deals as 'strange'. Despite his position as largest shareholder, Wallenberg did not feel that the other directors (including Chair Thunholm) and top management (including CEO Dahlsten) took his views into account. As a result, he decided to leave the board and make way for Nicolin to take his place. That decision was also prompted by the fact that Wallenberg at that time was to replace his legendary father Marcus Wallenberg Sr as family head, and therefore reconsidered all his assignments.[60]

However, Nicolin did not operate as the Wallenberg sphere had anticipated and hoped. He preferred to chair a Swedish Match that was kept intact, that is to say, as an integrated subgroup within Stora – at least for a few years – and his opinion became Stora's official stance, which also was expressed in the prospectus. Nicolin thought that Swedish Match was in a propitious development phase, and he was confident that the new CEO Larsson and his team could handle that process well.[61] He stuck to that position in spite of the many attempts made by the Wallenberg sphere to persuade him to change his mind. They blamed Nicolin for not acting hard enough to get a grip of how each of the businesses contributed to the collected economic result, something that made it difficult for Swedish Match's board to decide about various matters, including the strategy for the company. However, Nicolin did not exclude the possibility that Swedish Match in a long-term perspective might benefit from a merger with Stora.

When Wallenberg's appointment of Nicolin to the board did not solve the control problem, he decided to take further steps to get a firmer grip on the company. But before his plans materialized, CEO Dahlsten resigned from the company when he understood that he would not follow Thunholm as Chair. As a result, a successor to Dahlsten had to be found. Two candidates competed for the CEO position: Electrolux CEO Bystedt, nominated by the Wallenberg sphere, and Swedish Match's Deputy CEO Larsson, proposed by Chair Thunholm. Since the Wallenberg sphere held only a minority position on Swedish Match's board, it could not decide the matter. Ultimately the sphere lost the 'CEO struggle' – Larsson was appointed. However, that setback rather triggered the sphere to buy more shares in Swedish Match. Within a brief period of time, the sphere's holding grew to 47 per cent (Custos then had 33%). So at an AGM shortly thereafter (1985), the Wallenberg sphere took control of the board by appointing Dahlbäck and Bystedt as new directors and Nicolin as the new Chair.

It was not until the end of the 1970s that the Wallenberg sphere (Investor and Providentia) had become a dominant shareholder in Swedish Match. By that time, the sphere had acquired 40 per cent of the stock, while the second biggest shareholder Custos[62] had a 30 per cent holding. However, even before this situation occurred, Thunholm had anticipated that there was a 'risk' that Stora would try to buy the company. To make a Wallenberg takeover more difficult (due to ownership dilution and a higher price for a majority position), he wanted to undertake a new issue of B-shares. Thunholm justified his proposal citing Swedish Match's need for capital for its coming acquisitions, but Wallenberg turned down that suggestion.[63]

As evident from the discussion above, a major obstacle all along was that both Thunholm and Dahlsten were at odds with the Wallenberg family and wanted to see Swedish Match decoupled from the Investor group entirely. Thunholm did not like 'strong shareholders' that intervened in operations and ran over executive bodies. In his view, the shareholders should use the AGM for their governance efforts. He stressed that large shareholders had no special function or responsibility above and beyond that of the legal corporate bodies and no right to ask for exclusive information.[64]

In early 1987 Swedish Match's shareholding situation changed dramatically. Nobel Industries[65] got a call option regarding Custos's 33 per cent holding.[66] The leaders of Nobel Industries (Penser et al.) raised the idea that it should merge with Swedish Match. Custos actually sold that call option without informing Wallenberg, the other major shareholder in Swedish Match. The CEO of Nobel Industries, Carlberg, contacted Wallenberg and told him that Nobel Industries wanted to buy Investor's and Providentia's Swedish Match holding, too, but Wallenberg was not interested in selling. Instead, the tables quickly turned, and the Wallenberg sphere ended up buying the Nobel Industries' call option on Custos's holding. Then, with control of more than 80 per cent of the votes (later over 90%), Investor and Providentia sold their holdings in Swedish Match to Stora in 1988.[67] The offering to Swedish Match's shareholders and owners of convertibles amounted to almost SEK 6 billion. Stora's bid[68] was the biggest cash offering ever at the SSE, and it ended the company's series of large purchases, which taken together amounted to SEK 15 billion.[69]

The acquisition of Swedish Match was another important step that was carried out without really involving Stora's board, which was informed after the fact and took the legally required decisions. Thus, some of the distinguished directors were less well informed about both how the process had started and how it proceeded, and about which actors were the most important for the final outcome. It even happened that neither Stora's Chair Berggren nor its Deputy CEO Petersson attended executive meetings during 'the acquisition period'. Dahlbäck, CEO of Investor (1978–99) and member of Swedish Match's board (from 1985), supported the takeover idea, but Swedish Match's CEO Larsson and his team were more sceptical, as was its Chair Nicolin.[70] At the time of the takeover, Swedish Match contained six business units: (1) Tarkett (one of the biggest floor producers; turnover SEK 5.7 billion), (2) Consumer Products (matches and related products [the company's world famous original business]; turnover SEK 4.7 billion), (3) Kitchen Products (turnover SEK 1.7 billion), (4) Åkerlund & Rausing (packaging; turnover SEK 1.7 billion), (5) Swedoor (door manufacturer; turnover SEK 1.2 billion) and (6) Alby (a sodium chlorate producer; turnover SEK 0.4 million).[71]

The six motives for the purchase of Swedish Match that Berggren presented to Stora's board in March 1988 were: (1) Stora was still too exposed to trade fluctuations; (2) Stora's huge need for capital ought to be matched with more market-oriented investments; (3) Stora still lacked capability to act on the international scene (despite the Billerud purchase); (4) the financial strength of the new constellation could be used in Swedish Match's product and market development; (5) there were strong links between Stora's production of woodware and Swedish Match's kitchen and door businesses; and, last but not least, (6) Åkerlund & Rausing, one of Swedish Match's business units, was a substantial customer of Billerud.[72]

One of the directors was of the impression that the actual motive for acquiring Swedish Match was to make it a new 'hub corporation' – some kind of nexus – within the Wallenberg group.[73] However, director Palmstierna warned of potential negatives in the offering, as Stora had to pay attention to the goodwill issue, face the risk that it might become classified as a conglomerate and cope with the heavy burden that a large corporation with a considerable business scope puts on top management.[74]

Dahlbäck stressed that the purchase (also) was made to make sure that the Wallenberg sphere's heavy investment in Swedish Match could be defended – it was necessary to get that company in order. From the very beginning the plan was to sell off its 'classic' business activities (e.g. matches), so Investor had carried out a kind of a 'slaughter calculus' before even making the bid.[75] Right after the acquisition, Berggren stated publicly that Stora had no intention of splitting up Swedish Match and selling the parts. Nevertheless, shortly thereafter he did precisely that. This sharp strategic turn upset many actors including several influential business journalists and analysts. As a consequence, some of Berggren's later declarations were scrutinized with considerable scepticism.

Certain economic journals[76] published rather critical pieces about the Stora–Swedish Match affair, claiming that it was done to strengthen the Wallenberg sphere rather than to improve Stora's situation. To some extent Berggren confirmed that view when he stated that Wallenberg had been eager to find 'someone that took care' of Swedish Match – a company whose performance the family had been dissatisfied with for a long time.[77] Hagelin, member of Stora's GMT, regarded the merger agreement as 'a typical Dahlbäck construct', and maintained that it actually was Investor that had pushed for the acquisition. To some actors, the purchase of Swedish Match was seen as an essential element in a reorganization of Investor's company group. Knuts, another member of Stora's GMT, described the acquisition as 'inexplicable from a Stora perspective' and as an outright result of the Wallenberg family's long-term ownership strategy.[78] In the end, not very much happened between the two 'merging' companies – the conditions for a successful integration between the two were not particularly favourable, and the vast inter-company differences did not make things any easier.[79]

From the very beginning it was decided that Stora's CEO Berggren would continue as CEO of the newly enlarged Stora. However, the choice of Deputy CEO was a more complicated matter, as Larsson, the CEO of Swedish Match, was interested in being appointed to that position. For merging companies of comparable sizes it was common practice in the Swedish business society to retain the CEO from the buying company and recruit as Deputy CEO the CEO from the target company. Thus, Larsson's ambition was a most traditional one. However, for both Berggren and Wallenberg that solution was out of the question because the previous power struggles in Swedish Match left a deep impression on them. Still, Berggren found it appropriate for Larsson to become a member of Stora's GMT and did not plan significant changes in Swedish Match's organization. He intended to run the new Stora (i.e. Stora plus Billerud, Papyrus and Swedish Match) in very much the same way as he had run the large Wallenberg-dominated investment conglomerate Incentive, that is to say, in a very decentralized way that allowed the various units extensive autonomy.

Finally, Stora's new GMT included six managers from Stora but only one from Swedish Match (Johnsson, CEO of Tarkett). Its HQ remained in Falun, which also housed the CEO, the GMT and most other leading group functions. Swedish Match's units Tarkett, Kitchen, Swedoor, Consumers Products (renamed to Swedish Match) and Åkerlund & Rausing were put on the same (hierarchical) level as Stora's own subsidiaries. Kvarnsveden, Hylte and Stora Forest Industries (Canada) formed a new company, Stora News and SP-Snickerier became part of Swedoor. The chemical operations Alby, Billerud Chemistry, Diacell (a 50% holding) and Stora Kopparberget also became the core of a new company named Stora Chemistry.[80]

Initially, Berggren had declared that Swedish Match should remain an integrated subgroup within Stora, but, like the earlier promise that Swedish Match would not be split up, this promise was also broken rather soon, when Stora's top management discovered that such a structure brought about a tremendous waste of resources. When Berggren changed his organizational model, he lost the confidence of several of the former Swedish Match managers.[81]

Berggren presented his strategy for Stora at a board meeting in June 1989. There, he claimed that the consumer products (i.e. the Swedish Match units) could prosper only in a context dominated by other consumer products. Since consumer products were almost absent in Stora, the sale of those units would therefore place them in a better environment and contribute to a more concentrated business repertoire for Stora. Berggren mentioned that the decision to change course was a tough one, because of both his previous promises and the emotional ties to Swedish Match. The sale also implied that some of the stated merits of the acquisition, for example, the incorporation of a business with a different capital structure and business cycle, were lost.[82] Regarding the internationalization effect, however, Berggren claimed that Stora, despite its selling of Swedish Match units, could continue to be active in all the new countries. Indeed, one positive outcome of the very short 'Swedish Match period' was strengthened positions in South America, the Far East, West Germany and Italy. Furthermore, Stora had also become more of a 'two-legged' company, consisting of both a forest-based business, which was highly capital intensive, and a building material business, which was much less capital intensive and almost countercyclical.[83] Director Palmstierna, however, maintained that the Swedish Match purchase did not bring Stora the expected synergy effects. In fact, Swedish Match turned out to be a 'constellation of entrepreneurs', all of them running their own 'boxes'. It soon became obvious that Stora's large-scale-based management processes could not handle such a straggly organization.[84]

Stora's initial idea with its acquisition of Swedish Match was to sell off the 'match business' and floor products (Tarkett), but keep most of the other businesses. However, the newly enlarged Stora soon ran into trouble because of clashing company cultures and frictions between leading actors. Top management described the cultural difference in the following way: Stora's leaders behaved like 'chess players' (they thought first and acted later), while Swedish Match's leaders resembled 'hockey players' (they acted first and thought later).[85] However, it was not merely the cultural differences that drove Stora and Swedish Match apart. In fact, the business logic in Swedish Match's building material markets was of a small-scale type that differed significantly from Stora's large-scale-based forest businesses – a difference that was underestimated at the time of the merger. Moreover, the quality and fit of the packaging unit Åkerlund & Rausing was overrated; thus, that company instead became a severe problem, and its CEO had to leave (and finally the company was sold).[86] Moreover, in Stora it was the major owner that occupied the driver's seat, while in Swedish Match top management decided the course. These and other differences between the companies created considerable co-ordination difficulties.[87]

However, the main problem with the merger was probably that all the integration efforts would 'lock up' Stora's management for several years. For that and other reasons Stora resolved to make substantial disinvestments, and Petersson and Grafström were the ones that were assigned to sell off parts of the new constellation.[88] Stora decided to keep Swedish Match's packaging business, its chemical business and most of its building products. The 'classic' parts of Swedish Match were sold in 1989 (cf. below), but it was difficult to find buyers willing to pay the expected prices. What was left of Swedish Match after the sell-off resembled a 'B-formation', and those units never caught the full attention of Stora's leaders. Thus, 'rest-Match' ended up in a rather subordinated role in the new formation.[89]

Stora's ambition had been to sell Swedish Match's core business as one coherent unit, and first and foremost it looked for a Swedish buyer. By the end of 1989, Stora had 12 bids on the table for that unit, and Gillette's proposal was initially preferred (although it was not a Swedish corporation). However, those negotiations soon broke down, and instead a Dutch consortium came to the fore bidding SEK 4 billion.[90] In 1990, the Swedish government gave Stora permission to sell the match business to a foreign owner. Stora also successfully sold several other former Swedish Match units. Ultimately, in a longer-term perspective, Swedish Match principally served as a financial tool for Stora's expansion.[91] Berggren also admitted that the purpose of the acquisition never was a structural one – Swedish Match was to be disintegrated and its parts transferred to better homes.[92]

12.1.4 Expanding into the EC/EU

In the late 20th century, national borders in Western Europe began to lose importance, as deregulation within and between countries opened up for the (relatively) free movement of commodities, capital (permission from the Central Banks was no longer required) and labour. That development was based on a neoliberal ideology that had grown strong in the late 1970s, promoted by many US economists and practised on that continent. The failure of the planned economies in the late 1980s also stimulated market liberalization, and spread the US kind of capitalism over large parts of Europe. The opening up of most intra-European markets was supposed to provide better opportunities for corporate restructuring processes, which in turn would lead to more competitive business constellations. Thus, from the 1980s, the US kind of capitalism seriously challenged the European form(s), and financial rationales took the lead, placing the operative ones in the backseat.[93]

In the middle of the 1980s, many leading Swedish actors again began to discuss whether the country ought to try to become a part of the European integration (EC later EU[94]) or not. Most of the business elite favoured full membership. Wallenberg, Chair of both Stora and the Federation of Swedish Industries, was convinced that the current most important task for Swedish industry was to work for full EU membership. As long as the government declared that Sweden 'never will join the EU', it forced industry to find its future partners inside that constellation, he concluded.[95] Berggren was of the same opinion – he did not believe that Sweden would enter the EU, but suspected that Finland (that housed tough competitors) soon would send in a membership application. Therefore, to do something on the continent – and fast – became Stora's first priority.[96]

The European Commission's 1985 white paper on 'completing the internal market' marked out the path towards 'a free European market', and when announced it added a new dimension to Stora's internationalization process. It made a substantial acquisition within the EU almost a necessity. The white paper became the starting shot for an extensive investigation of possible acquisitions inside the EU (and a ranking of them). Leading managers were also asked to provide suggestions on how Stora should handle the disadvantage of being run from a non-member country.[97] Hagelin, a member of the GMT, noticed that the commitment to expand within the EU drove Stora's strategic activities during those years.[98] However, another GMT member, Knuts, expressed a different opinion. He claimed that the EU membership issue was both exaggerated and politicized, and stressed that Sweden already had a satisfactory agreement that worked well for business activities on the European continent.[99]

The 'EU-ropeanization' of Stora started in 1987 when it bought 25 per cent of the Danish fine paper company De Forenede Papirfabrikker (Denmark was an EU member) and soon thereafter the remaining shares. For SEK 630 million Stora got a 'EU company' with a SEK 1.7 billion turnover. However, the acquisition did not result in success. The rather poor economic outcome could be explained by Stora's eagerness to 'get inside the EU', which had substantially affected the quality of the pre-purchase calculations. However, Stora also made several other purchases inside the EU at that time: French Moyet Perrin, Italian Veneta Cucine (80%), French Espalux (10%) and German Bischof & Klein (40%).

Stora completed its investigation of potential acquisition objects (or joint venture partners) in late 1988. The resulting report contained an analysis and ranking of about 20 European corporations. Feldmühle (Germany), KNP[100] (Holland), Burgo (Italy), Haindl (Germany) and Wiggins Teape (UK) were at the top of that listing. Two of these corporations became the focus of Stora's efforts: Feldmühle (well known as partner in Hylte and Norrsundet) and Wiggins Teape (a large cross-European producer of pulp and fine paper, also housing a sizeable wholesaler business). Berggren soon contacted Feldmühle, KNP and Burgo, and all of them recognized the merits of a merger, but none was interested in taking action. Some of that reluctance could likely be explained by their positions as 'crown jewels' in their respective countries.[101]

While Knuts (head of Stora's pulp business) tried to make a coherent unit of Celbi

(Portugal) and Aracruz (Brazil), Stora also began to look outside the EU. He claimed that Stora's pulp business ought to seek most of its growth in certain regions in South America and Asia because of the much better timber situation (both supply and prices). Knuts got support for that strategy but there were also problems with the Aracruz site, as the Brazilians began to act (too) nationalistically. It was agreed that Stora should be the exclusive seller of Aracruz's pulp in Europe, but eventually that understanding was violated. Its limited holding (5%) made it impossible for Stora to act forcefully, so it gave in and left the Brazilian investment (but returned later).[102] At that time (1989), Stora also considered investing SEK 4 billion in a new pulp line at its Celbi unit and reorienting the production at Skutskär to concentrate on fluff and birch-based short-fibre pulp.

Stora News was eager to increase its use of recycled paper, make the fibres and the paper qualities fit better together and add LWC to defend its market position in Europe. It had entered LWC a few decades ago through a joint ownership with Kymmene. Stora also discussed with Graninge (the Versteegh family) doing something similar, but those talks never materialized. Berggren suggested that Stora should convert its Skutskär site to LWC and tried to renew the board's interest in an acquisition of Feldmühle (something he had proposed already back in the 1970s). In spite of the on-going co-operation with Feldmühle at Hylte and Norrsundet, the board rejected a new acquisition move because it would be impossible to implement.[103]

Stora's board also considered three new large investments: (1) at its Nova Scotia site (SEK 4 billion), (2) in forest projects in Chile (SEK 3 billion) and (3) in Ireland (SEK 3 billion). GMT member Knuts had recommended the forest projects, but his colleagues Hagelin and Petersson were sceptical and hoped that Berggren would stop those proposals.[104] Furthermore, purchases of Italian Cartiere del Garda (SEK 1.6 billion), French Chapelle-Darblay (SEK 1.5 billion), Irish forests (owned by Coillte) and the remaining shares in Danish De Forenede Papirfabrikker (SEK 0.5 billion) were considered, too. The board concluded that Celbi, Chile (forests), Cartiere del Garda and De Forenede Papirfabrikker (75%) were the most interesting investment alternatives. Acting on these ideas, the remaining shares in the Danish company were soon acquired. Regarding Chapelle-Darblay the plan was to buy the corporation in co-operation with Kymmene (50–50).[105] Stora's board approved the idea. Both Knuts and Guy Ehrnrooth (Kymmene) were enthusiastic because such an acquisition would bring newsprint to Stora and LWC to Kymmene (although the intention remained joint ownership of the acquired unit). However, after the Feldmühle Nobel acquisition a few months later, Stora had to sell its part to Kymmene (but got a buy-back right).[106]

The ambition to make further investments at Celbi involved many talks with the Portuguese government. In its current shape Celbi had a satisfactory timber supply, but to increase pulp production substantially would require the purchase of additional forests to secure enough timber.[107] The uncertain timber supply and the Portuguese government's ambiguous attitude led Stora to instead consider a paper mill. Wallenberg confirmed that such an investment could be a possible growth alternative for Stora, but that it should not be undertaken until the market situation had improved. As expected, the Portuguese domestic competitors opposed Stora's planned investments. For that and other reasons, it was not advisable (although possible) to start investing without a green light from the politicians. Stora broke the deadlock by promising the government to (also) invest in a paper mill (which then had to be in production by 1998 at the latest).

Based on that agreement, the Portuguese government authorized Stora to carry out its planned pulp investment. However, the acquisition of Feldmühle Nobel described below interfered in that process, too. Since Stora's balance sheet could not support both projects, the pulp investment was postponed.[108]

At that time, Wiggins Teape suddenly offered its 43 per cent holding in Soporcel[109] (SEK 1–1.5 billion) – a corporation in which the Portuguese state owned 55 per cent and the general public 2 per cent. Soporcel resembled Stora Celbi, but it also held a large fine paper unit. Furthermore, Soporcel produced more pulp than Celbi, and as only half of that production was used in its own fine paper production, it could supply another machine. The Portuguese government was initially favourable to Stora's interest in buying its Soporcel holding, although a merger between Celbi and Soporcel would put the state in a minority position. Stora believed that the possibility to obtain more than 43 per cent of Soporcel was low, but attempted to win a clause stating that it would receive an 'offer of first refusal'. Stora's GMT member Knuts negotiated with Wiggins Teape, and the two companies reached a preliminary agreement. However, that settlement was conditional upon the approval of Stora's CEO and board. When Knuts phoned Berggren to inform him about the preliminary agreement, Berggren decided not to give it his blessing. That was a big disappointment for Knuts, who had to take the bad news back to Wiggins Teape. To his surprise, Knuts learned that the government, too, opposed the preliminary deal.[110] Instead, Stora was offered the state's[111] 29 per cent holding in Celbi.[112]

Stora's current timber partner in South America was Auraco, a subsidiary of the large Chilean corporation Copec Chile. Auraco in turn owned a forest-owning subsidiary named Pedro de Valdiva. With the idea to establish a large pulp plant in Chile that could be in full production at the turn of the millennium, Stora decided to buy 50 per cent of Pedro de Valdiva.[113] Tussiat, Auraco's CEO, was in favour of an agreement with Stora, since his company needed support for its expansion plans. Therefore, Knuts went to Chile several times to discuss the matter (often accompanied by Westergren, Head of Forestry, and/or Alsholm, Head of R&D). Similarly, Angelini, the major shareholder in Auraco, visited Stockholm and met with Wallenberg and Berggren. Forestal Valdiva was to be launched as a joint venture (50–50) focusing on afforestation, with the vision of establishing a pulp plant in less than a decade's time. Stora's entry into the Chilean market was made with 'pomp and circumstance', as it involved both the country's President and its most prominent business dynasty.[114]

Stora also considered buying Coillte's Irish forests. The aim was to build a CTMP plant in that country together with Smurfit (the size of the intended investment made a partnership necessary).[115] It was Peter Wallenberg who had got the idea while discussing forest-based businesses with some of his friends. Berggren, however, regarded Wallenberg's suggestion as commercially unrealistic. As he saw it, Wallenberg had been misinformed – the intended output (TMP) required not only cheap fibre but also cheap electricity, and that was simply not available. Berggren also regarded an investment in Ireland as too modest a step in the company's attempt to acquire fast-growing forests.[116] Here, too, the upcoming acquisition of Feldmühle Nobel postponed a decision. There was also growing doubt regarding the merits of investing in pulp production. As a result, in 1991, the Irish project was dropped.[117]

Stora also had the opportunity to buy a substantial part of Korsnäs (15%) from Patricia (another Wallenberg company). Korsnäs was a large Swedish forest owner and producer of forest products (foremost LPB). Korsnäs was in many ways the Swedish company that fit Stora's current operations best, but another reason for an acquisition was that the Wallenberg sphere was afraid that it otherwise could end up as part of a competitor. Its major shareholder (51%) was the Swedish investment company Kinnevik (controlled by the Stenbeck family). Stora even wanted to purchase a larger share than Patricia already held, but Korsnäs's leading actor Jan Stenbäck stopped that attempt. His resistance had its roots both in a sceptical attitude towards the Wallenberg family and in a differing view regarding the appropriate price for the company.[118] Later (in 1992), when Stenbäck wanted to merge Kinnevik with Korsnäs, Stora renewed the discussion about the strategic value of its holding. The board concluded that Korsnäs held certain businesses that Stora was abandoning anyway, and therefore decided to sell out.[119] However, some actors claimed that Korsnäs's businesses still fit Stora well (the forests, the pulp sourcing and the cardboard operations), and that it rather was the strained financial situation that led Stora to divest.[120]

At that time, Stora's interest in other Swedish forest-based companies was limited. In fact, the company looked almost exclusively outside Sweden. For example, AssiDomän was not even mentioned, and to approach Södra would mean that Stora, contrary to its current strategy, would move backwards in the value chain. Moreover, Ncb was in bad shape, and in the rather diversified SCA only fine paper was attractive. The family-controlled MoDo was not for sale, although there was at least one circumstance that motivated a joint effort: both companies were heavy indebted and (therefore) concerned about staying competitive in their fine paper operations. However, since Stora did not find MoDo's large French fine paper unit Alizay particularly interesting, nothing came out of the informal talks between the leading actors.[121] Finally, to make acquisitions in the neighbouring country Finland was considered 'too difficult', as the business culture in Finnish companies was 'different', and, as Berggren put it: 'Why go east when we can go south?'[122]

12.1.5 The Acquisition of Feldmühle Nobel

Marcus Wallenberg Sr had known Feldmühle's large shareholder, the Flick family, since the 1950s, and their relationship had materialized in Stora and Feldmühle's joint operations at Norrsundet (its pulp suited Feldmühle's LWC production) and Hylte (the shared ownership improved Stora's balance sheet). Like most other families, the Wallenbergs regarded the establishment of personal networks – based on either weak or strong ties – as essential for doing business. The stronger tie then usually implies that the actors actually meet and perhaps even share hobbies and leisure-time activities. That makes 'secret' meetings and (lots of) small talk possible, which provides rich opportunities for testing passing fancies as well as more elaborated ideas.[123]

New family head Peter Wallenberg stressed from the very beginning that the owners and top management of a company should (re)produce strong (personal) ties to the potentially most important actors in society (businessmen as well as politicians). He also emphasized that such efforts usually take a long time, sometimes several generations.[124] Wallenberg had for several years met with Feldmühle's leading actor Geginat, Chair of its 'Vorstand' (i.e. executive board). Berggren had also built rather close relationships to leading actors in Feldmühle (including Geginat), and already in 1987, he and GMT member Petersson brought up the question of whether the two companies might benefit from a merger. However, Geginat hesitated,[125] and Feldmühle's Vorstand and the owner's legal representative opposed a sale to Stora.[126] However, Berggren obtained Geginat's promise to be contacted if Feldmühle later considered selling.[127]

Feldmühle was the biggest paper manufacturer within the EU. First and foremost, it produced various kinds of printing papers (LWC and journal paper) as well as packaging paper, fine paper and tissue. Thus, most of its operations did not compete with Stora's businesses. Moreover, there was another interesting complementarity: Feldmühle was one of the biggest buyers of pulp, while Stora instead was one of the biggest sellers. So there were several reasons why Stora was interested in buying Feldmühle.

At the time, however, the latter company had become part of the larger business group Feldmühle Nobel, a holding company that had been formed in 1986 when the Flick family integrated Feldmühle with Burderus[128] and Dynamit Nobel[129] and put it on the stock exchange. Feldmühle Nobel had a complicated shareholding structure that included tough voting rights restrictions,[130] repurchase clauses and stock options.[131] However, Stora thought that it would be possible to acquire around 80–85 per cent of the stock, although permission from the German authorities (Bundeskartellamt) first had to be obtained. Until then only 25 per cent of the stock was available.[132]

The leaders of Stora and Feldmühle continued their discussions, and in 1989 they decided to conduct a joint study that would include the description of a possible future strategy and structure for a merged Stora-Feldmühle. It soon became obvious that the two companies – at least on paper – fitted well together. Feldmühle would get a safe and adequate pulp supply and be able to focus on the expansion of its LWC and fine paper businesses. It would also gain the opportunity to develop its wholesaling operations.[133] A merged Stora-Feldmühle would be one of the strongest printing paper corporations in the world: Feldmühle's strong LWC position would be combined with Stora's solid position in newsprint, and both companies had strong positions in the journal paper business. Moreover, the expected number one position on the European printing paper market would constitute a solid platform for reaching a similar standing globally. Stora's major owner and Chair Wallenberg also claimed that the EU presence that would result from such a merger was of utmost importance for Stora, as was the possibility to exert price leadership, which would follow from the new constellation's large production capacity and extensive market shares.[134]

At the time of the talks with Feldmühle's leading actors, the Flick family offered Stora out of the blue a 30 per cent holding in Feldmühle Nobel. Stora had to respond immediately (i.e. in a few days). As a consequence, Berggren and Dahlbäck went to Düsseldorf to negotiate. However, since the time pressure was too intense and the available information not complete enough to make a deal, Stora decided to reject the offer. Instead VEBA[135] bought the 30 per cent offered by Flick and soon increased its total shareholding to 51 per cent[136] of which the Flick family had a right to buy back 38.5 per cent (given certain conditions). The Flick family still controlled about 30 per cent (they owned 5% themselves, 20% through options and 5% ['the SCA holding'] through a buy-back clause). The general public, finally, owned about 20 per cent (of which the Flick family indirectly controlled 5%).[137]

In January 1990, less than a year after the previous offer, Stora got a new opportunity to acquire Feldmühle Nobel stock. This time Stora was offered a 5 per cent share in

Feldmühle Nobel with an option to buy an additional 20 per cent. Once again Stora's top management went to Düsseldorf – and once again they returned without shares. Feldmühle's management defended its autonomy, and Stora promised to respect that position as long as no other company tried to buy Feldmühle Nobel shares. The situation soon took a dramatic turn when Stora's Swedish rival SCA suddenly bought a 5 per cent holding in Feldmühle Nobel – the one that Stora had just turned down. Soon it also became evident that SCA had no intention to stop at 5 per cent.[138] The US forest-based corporation Scott Paper also indicated an interest in buying shares in Feldmühle Nobel.[139]

In response Stora informed VEBA and Feldmühle Nobel that it opposed its rival's (SCA's) presence in Feldmühle Nobel because of the strong operative linkages between Feldmühle and Stora (at Hylte and Norrsundet).[140] Berggren immediately told Feldmühle Nobel's major shareholder and top management that SCA's purchase of shares had made the agreement in which Stora refrained from buying Feldmühle Nobel stock invalid. The leading actors in Feldmühle Nobel recognized that and stated that they preferred Stora as (one of its) shareholder(s) (rather than SCA).[141] That preference was based on their experiences from the co-operation at Hylte and Norrsundet. Another motive was an impression that SCA (and Scott Paper) were trying to exclude all units in Feldmühle Nobel outside Feldmühle from a deal. Flick got his way, so this time the Vorstand's task was reduced to trying to influence the choice of buyer.[142]

Stora's motives for acquiring Feldmühle Nobel were all connected to the Feldmühle part of the holding company. They included improving pulp operations (increasing the scale), becoming the leading printing paper corporation in the world (with a complete and well-balanced product repertoire in that business area), creating a strong fine paper unit (which included a competitive wholesaling business), making it possible to double the capacity in the cardboard business, providing new opportunities to rationalize production, making more efficient distribution possible, making co-ordinated investments across the two merging corporations possible and being able to invest more in R&D (because a larger size could absorb a higher development cost). The total synergy effects were estimated to reach SEK 670 million.[143] However, it was not obvious that Stora's financial situation made such a big purchase possible. There were also doubts about whether Stora possessed the necessary management capacity to handle such a large-scale acquisition.[144] The board also discussed Kymmene's strong negative reaction to the acquisition plans, as Stora's purchase would make the new constellation Kymmene's largest competitor on the market for its core business (LWC). Kymmene was an important actor for Stora, as it currently was a 50–50 partner in Chapelle-Darblay (journal paper).

The Feldmühle Nobel purchase was carried out through three units. Patricia (one of the Wallenberg-owned investment companies) and Stora would each buy 25 per cent, and Deutsch-Skandinavische Bank 5 per cent, which made up a total share that roughly corresponded to the holdings that Flick controlled. VEBA's 51 per cent would be put in a depot awaiting a go-ahead decision from the authorities. The total price for the purchase would amount to around DM 4 billion. The resulting financial strain would make divestments necessary, and Stora planned to sell off some of the businesses in Feldmühle Nobel, particularly those that were weakly related to forest-based operations.[145]

The Feldmühle Nobel contest was settled in April 1990. Representatives from SCA, Scott Paper and Stora were all in place in Düsseldorf to negotiate with the German owners. Their respective corporate jets were placed next to each other at the airport.

One negotiation session followed another in an intensive process that lasted for several days and nights. The talks were carried out at a hotel, so the different delegations could not avoid running across each other. The competition was tough, and Stora was clearly disturbed by the fact that SCA as new shareholder participated in the competition.[146] The Berggren and Dahlbäck duo ran Stora's negotiation process, and that was certainly not the first time they represented the Wallenberg sphere in such circumstances, having led Stora's recent purchases of Billerud, Papyrus and Swedish Match.

To be part of the Wallenberg sphere was usually regarded as a competitive advantage, as it provided an extensive and exclusive national and international network of both businessmen and political leaders. Lots of communication took place in that web in which Peter Wallenberg occupied the hub position. Thus, innumerable informal contacts between the major shareholders and board members of Investor and Providentia offered possibilities to exchange information, discuss upcoming matters and take important decisions – all on a continuous basis. Such 'invisible'[147] activities took place wherever the Wallenberg actors met, for example, at formal meetings, conferences, journeys, dinners, sailing events, hunting parties and golf clubs. Not even the most 'private' arrangement was spared business talk.

Thus, in the Wallenberg sphere, corporate governance was executed on a daily basis, and it rather often also involved the major shareholder in person. Even when it came to large acquisitions (like Feldmühle Nobel), big issues were more seldom settled at the board meetings – they had been prepared beforehand in extensive informal processes so that the board's decisions were usually a formality. Peter Wallenberg always had the final say, and now and then he interposed his veto (but not in the Feldmühle Nobel case).[148]

However, the sale of Feldmühle Nobel was instead conducted as an auction, a bidding form that disregards existing networks and ties between the seller and one or several of the competing buyers, and it also usually produces a rather high price. Winning the contest despite those conditions made the Wallenberg team very pleased, particularly as Feldmühle (Nobel) was their 'dream acquisition'. They also found the (rather high) price 'acceptable'.[149] However, it was actually rumoured that the day after the handshake between Stora and Feldmühle Nobel, SCA's Chair Rydin should have looked up the latter company's negotiators and indicated to them that SCA might raise its bid. Stora's actors took that (unverified) rumour as an indication that Stora's final bid was indeed reasonable.[150]

However, several German actors had difficulties accepting that it was Stora that had bought Feldmühle Nobel and not the other way around. Therefore, Stora put the experienced Deputy CEO Knuts in charge in Düsseldorf in 1991 with the assignment to take control. One crucial component in the acquisition plan was that Investor should take care of most units outside Feldmühle, and organize them as a PE unit. Unfortunately that arrangement became impossible, and because Feldmühle Nobel's Vorstand vigorously influenced in what way and to whom Stora was allowed to sell the acquired subsidiaries, the prices became much lower than Stora had expected.[151]

The Feldmühle Nobel group offered Stora a significant presence inside the EU, which was seen as very important for the company's future development. Since the Feldmühle part – the forest-related businesses – was number one in that market, Stora had become a truly continental corporation. Stora also got its longed-for LWC business. Furthermore, the purchase facilitated its operations at Hylte, Norrsundet and Kabel.[152] As a large buyer of Stora's pulp, the last was a real 'jewel'. The acquisition of Feldmühle (Nobel) also strengthened Stora's identity as a 'pure' forest-based company (i.e. once all unrelated businesses had been sold). Another consequence of the purchase was that Stora became a corporation based on large-scale operations.[153] Stora's new structure was also supposed to make the company more robust against recessions.[154]

However, there were also some critical voices raised in Stora. Director Palmstierna claimed that the timing for the Feldmühle Nobel purchase was unfortunate: the company was acquired in a boom period making the price high, and that created financial strain. However, as Palmstierna saw it, it was first and foremost Wallenberg's ambition to make Stora an important player inside the EU that impelled Stora to carry out the acquisition.[155] Hägglund, CEO of Stora Forestry (1991), also found the purchase ill timed, but still he thought that it looked like the right thing to do. He believed that the high price was a consequence of the competition with SCA, an 'intrusion' that irritated Stora's leading actors.[156] Deputy CEO Knuts also expressed scepticism ('the purchase was a mistake'). He was convinced that the sheer size and expected financial consequences of the acquisition ought to have made Stora more careful in the buying process, and that Stora should have, for example, carried out due diligence. Knuts also claimed that several of Stora's negotiators had exaggerated the quality of the target company. However, as SCA had acquired a 5 per cent share, and as there were reasons to believe that its leaders intended to try to increase that holding, the time pressure was intense.[157]

When Stora's board met in September 1990, they decided that the new organizational structure should be comprised of four main businesses, namely Feldmühle (Head: Geginat), Papyrus (Head: Helgesson), Billerud (Head: Bengt Pettersson) and Stora Cell (Head: Torbjörn Pettersson). The Feldmühle unit would include newsprint and SC journal paper (Kvarnsveden, Hylte, SFI [Canada], Langerbrügge and Reisholz) as well as LWC paper (Hagen-Kabel and [part of] Corbehem) and carbonless paper (Hillegrossen and Flensburg). Papyrus would comprise all Stora's fine paper operations (Nymölla, Grycksbo, Mölndal, Newton Falls, Maglemølle, Dalum, Silkeborg and Uetersen) and all wholesaling units. Within Billerud would be included packaging paper, liquid board and cardboard (Gruvön, [part of] Skoghall, Fors, Newton Kyme [UK], Baienfurt, Arnsberg and [part of] Corbehem). Finally, Stora Cell would consist of the pulp businesses (Skutskär, Sandarne, Norrsundet, [part of] Skoghall, Celbi and Forestal Valdivia [Chile, 50%]). Stora also contained Stora Kraft (power plants), Stora Forests, Stora Timber, Stora Kitchen, Åkerlund & Rausing, Burderus and Dynamit Nobel.

12.1.6 Taking Care of the Balance Sheet

Already in the second half of 1990, Stora's board began to discuss how to sell off the rest of Feldmühle Nobel (e.g. Burderus and Dynamit Nobel). Both Wallenberg and Berggren pushed hard for these and other divestments.[158] Berggren was particularly concerned about Stora's balance sheet. Thus, it became urgent to sell off these units as quickly as possible, even if the prices would not be as high as initially calculated. He even considered hiring external assistance in the selling process (but that idea never materialized).[159] At that time, Patricia informed Stora that it did not wish to remain a shareholder in Feldmühle Nobel, so Stora took over its 24.9 per cent paying SEK 3.6 billion. That purchase strained Stora's financial situation even more.[160]

At the same time, problems arose with some of the key actors in Feldmühle (some members of its Vorstand). Stora's purchase was one of the biggest foreign acquisitions in West Germany since the 1920s, and it was made by actors that lived far northwards – even outside some of the German maps. The purchase was almost seen as an offence, so many actors – from the unions to Deutsche Bank – did what they could to stop the whole thing. As a consequence, it became politically impossible to sell the rest of Feldmühle Nobel piece by piece, as Stora had planned. Instead, it was sold as a package in 1991 to Metallgesellschaft[161] for a rather low price – about the equivalent of SEK 5.3 billion. That lowered Stora's net debt by SEK 7 billion (down to SEK 25 billion). From that time, Stora owned 98 per cent of Feldmühle Nobel (there was no legal possibility to force the remaining shareholders to sell).[162] In the midst of all these efforts to sell off units, Berggren bought a rather 'shaky' Danish paper producer, Forenade Papirfabriken (without having consulted Stora's GMT).[163]

In 1991 Stora sold Finess[164] to Duni and left the Irish project.[165] It also left its Chilean operations, although most of Stora's top managers certainly did not applaud that move. Despite all these divestments more had to be done, so Berggren announced a plan to lower the debts by SEK 5 billion. Yet, Stora's financial standing remained acceptable because of the presence of a premium over the book (power plants and forest resources).

However, the strained financial situation was not Stora's sole weakness, although it was by far the most important one at the time. Director Mogren, for example, thought the company's R&D was underdeveloped, despite the fact that all its businesses incurred high raw material costs and were capital intensive. He also claimed that the technical knowledge in the company was far from the best in the industry. Moreover, Mogren regarded the company's long and glorious history as a drag on its capacity to innovate. Stora had developed norms and institutions that (re)produced inertia, and those structures tended to squeeze out many new business ideas. There was also a rather weak marketing and sales organization – perhaps an inheritance from the 'cartel days'.[166] In 1991, the EU actually accused those corporations that produced and sold cardboard of operating a cartel, and Kopparfors and Feldmühle were among the companies charged (Stora was among the companies fined).

After a five-year period characterized by huge investments (SEK 20 billion was used in acquisitions and upgrading of plants), Stora eventually returned to a more 'normal' activity level. Its turnover had risen from SEK 6.5 billion (1981) to SEK 50.4 billion (1991), and the company had developed into a corporation that ran 40 per cent of its operations outside Sweden. Stora's forest-based businesses amounted to 75 per cent of the turnover, while products connected to the building industry made up the remaining 25 per cent. Still, Stora was weak in 'the European Sun Belt' (Greece, [Southern] France, Italy, Portugal and Spain). The use of recycled fibres also lagged behind. That new raw material source 'grew' in large European cities, not in the Swedish forests.[167]

An important occurrence that 'saved' Stora from lots of problems was Sweden's change from a fixed to a floating exchange rate in 1992. That 'devaluation' of the Swedish crown improved Stora's economic result by around SEK 1.5 billion in 1992, and again made its Swedish units competitive.[168] Although its effect on profits was significant, the devaluation of the crown only marginally contributed to an improvement of the company's market shares. They were basically stable, very much as a consequence of a century of divided markets (i.e. cartels).[169]

12.2 A PERIOD OF CONSOLIDATION

12.2.1 Helgesson New CEO

When it comes to corporate governance, 1992 became a very special year for Stora. For health reasons, Wallenberg left both the board and the Chair position, and was replaced by Berggren, who in turn was succeeded as CEO by Helgesson. However, Berggren stayed as Group CEO of Stora ('koncernchef'), and as such he kept the Chair position in the bigger subsidiaries (e.g. Feldmühle). Essentially, Berggren continued to run Stora alongside Investor, and top management seemed to understand the rationale behind that arrangement (but they did not like it). The board remained a less important agency, although it continued to take the mandatory formal decisions.[170] Berggren soon began to spend more and more time as one of two stand-ins for Peter Wallenberg (the other was Anders Scharp). Both Berggren and Scharp were appointed Deputy Chair at Investor and were assigned different Chair positions in the business group. Berggren also worked as mentor to Marcus Wallenberg Jr, who represented the family's next generation. All those responsibilities made Berggren a serious candidate for succeeding Peter Wallenberg as Chair of Investor. He also moved his office to Stockholm, although he kept his family and private life in Falun.

Jacob Wallenberg Jr, together with his cousin Marcus, represented the new Wallenberg generation, which gradually began to take on the responsibility for the sphere's companies. He regarded the board as a useful arena for discussions and tests of various ideas and proposals. Yet he claimed that the important decisions emerged through iterative talks within a narrow circle of actors who analysed all issues that arose from their different experiences, positions and perspectives. When populating that circle, Jacob Wallenberg Jr added two persons to the troika his father had used, namely Stora's Deputy CEO Petersson and himself (although he regarded his own influence on the group's decisions as relatively modest).[171] The composition of the governing circle made it clear that it was the major shareholder (the Wallenberg family) that ran the company (in this case through the Chair). The new CEO Helgesson, who was accustomed to the old Swedish tradition with strong CEOs, tried to modify Stora's governance mode, but his effort was met with opposition. Thus, already from the beginning a latent conflict was established between the two top executive levels (board and CEO) regarding how the company ought to be run.[172]

Helgesson was Berggren's favourite to succeed him as CEO. While CEO of Incentive, Berggren had met Helgesson who worked as head of a subsidiary (Garphyttan).[173] In 1987, they met by chance when they sat next to each other on a flight, and during their conversation Berggren suggested that Helgesson should join Stora's top management. However, the latter was not particularly interested in working in the forest-based industry, but since he had lived before in Gothenburg (the HQ of Stora Papyrus) and had enjoyed that town, he did not immediately turn down the offer. The main obstacle was that Papyrus recently had recruited a new CEO, Höglund, which meant that that position seemed to be 'booked' for quite some time. However, to Helgesson's surprise Berggren returned again half a year later (1988) and offered him the CEO position in Papyrus (as things did not work well with Höglund).

As CEO of a listed company, Helgesson had been used to having rather free hands.

In addition, he had observed that the former Chair of Swedish Match had secured such autonomy in Stora for some of the heads of the acquired businesses. Therefore, Helgesson expected that something similar would apply to him in his new position. He also told Berggren that his hesitation to take the job was driven primarily by the fact that he had never seen a paper mill before. However, Berggren did not see that as an insuperable problem – sometimes such 'greenness' could even be an advantage, as it could bring fresh ideas to ingrained structures and processes.[174]

After about one year (1990), Helgesson already had the impression that it would not be possible to run Papyrus as independently as he had expected. The acquisition of Feldmühle with its extensive fine paper operations aroused his doubts. That purchase increased the risk that Papyrus would become a subunit (division) in 'something bigger', so Helgesson phoned Berggren to discuss the developing situation. Helgesson's ambition was to get another CEO job inside the Investor group – he was not interested in being 'demoted' to division manager. Berggren then surprised Helgesson by telling him that he was intended for the CEO position in Stora when Berggren left. Helgesson had expected that either Knuts or Johnson would be Berggren's successor.[175]

However, there were several other CEO candidates in the field.[176] Since Berggren began to spend more and more time at Investor, Deputy CEO Petersson had carried the heaviest burden, so many regarded him as the leading candidate. He always formed his own opinion and was recognized at Investor for that, and like Berggren he discussed many things with Peter Wallenberg and Dahlbäck.[177] However, Petersson was not inclined to act as a number one in a large corporation (cf. doer) – he was more comfortable working as a number two (cf. adviser). He had come to that conclusion in spite of the fact that he had Peter Wallenberg's ear, and most of the qualities that the major shareholder wanted: Petersson was an autodidact and his character was built on thrift, loyalty, reliability, integrity and cleverness. Like most controlling shareholders, Wallenberg feared being misinformed by the executive actors. He disliked managers that 'held their cards close to their chests', and Petersson was one of those managers who never withheld anything important from his principal. In addition to Helgesson and Petersson, there were two other strong candidates for the CEO position: the GMT members Knuts and Hagelin.[178]

Some of Stora's leading actors regarded Knuts as too independent an actor, who might not function well as a team player, a quality that particularly Berggren was eager to get.[179] Knuts thought that Dahlbäck – for the same reason – was sceptical about having him as the new CEO.[180] Obviously, the major shareholder (Peter Wallenberg) did not support Knuts's candidature either, even though he was the one who earlier had wanted to see him as Deputy CEO of Papyrus.

Since Berggren saw his own future role in Stora as that of 'the strategist', he wanted a new (team-playing) CEO, who concentrated his efforts on operative matters (i.e. worked more like a 'COO').[181] Helgesson was thought to be the candidate that most easily could accept such a more restricted role, as he previously had worked with Berggren in a similar relationship.[182] There were also expectations among Stora's top management that Helgesson's recruitment would bring back power from Investor to Stora (and its top management).[183]

Still, several actors saw Knuts as a strong CEO candidate. He was regarded as a person with many executive qualities. For example, he had handled the Feldmühle constellation very much on his own and had been successful in his previous positions. However,

Knuts's own experience was that when a prestigious position is at stake (e.g. as CEO at Stora), it is important for any contender to have caught the eyes of a powerful actor, who then could promote one's case. Knuts supposed that there might have been such an actor pushing for Helgesson, which might also explain his appointment as CEO of Papyrus back in 1988 – a position that Knuts had been interested in as well.[184]

Hagelin, the other strong contender, came from Garphyttan,[185] where Berggren had been one of the directors. He had soon become a GMT member and initially worked as Billerud's CEO, but had in more recent years primarily focused on strategic issues. However, the board saw him, like Knuts, as too much of a 'senior actor' in the organization. Furthermore, the directors found it difficult to pick one of the two. They concluded that it was both better and easier to choose somebody outside the current GMT.[186]

In reality, it was Berggren who recruited Helgesson to the CEO position, although not without Wallenberg's consent. The latter agreed, as he saw no serious alternatives within Stora and had the impression that Helgesson had done a good job at Papyrus.[187] However, some actors claimed that Wallenberg was a bit hesitant about Helgesson, but that Berggren eventually convinced him.[188] Still others claimed that it was the former CEO of Papyrus Persson that had advocated Helgesson as a fitting new Stora CEO and got Wallenberg's and Dahlbäck's approval of the idea, and that it actually was their pressure that made Berggren go for Helgesson.[189]

In the view of some leading actors in Stora, Helgesson's appointment was made to put in place someone who could run the daily operations (i.e. act as a COO). There certainly was a need for somebody who would release the synergies that existed across many of the acquired units and ensure that modernizations and rationalizations were carried out all over the organization. More order and clarity were needed in Stora's internal governance processes, and the new CEO was expected to carry out such reorganization.

However, Helgesson himself preferred to act more like most other Swedish CEOs, that is to say, also engage in strategic matters. So rather soon the Chair and the CEO began to discuss what the most appropriate and well functioning role for the new CEO could be.[190] Helgesson wanted to be in the driver's seat and was not interested in being curtailed by either the Chair or by other leading actors inside and around Stora. In that way he tried to both decentralize (bring the momentum back to Stora) and centralize (work as Stora's peak co-ordinator). However, because of that high ambition, it became a problem that he never moved to the company HQ in Falun[191] – and that was something that irritated Chair Berggren (who still had his home in that town).[192]

Thus, Helgesson tried to function as a classic Swedish CEO by keeping a certain distance from both its major shareholders (in this case Investor/Wallenberg) and from its board (including its Chair). However, when he took office he found it difficult to obtain that customary executive power. That was made 'publicly' visible when Berggren decided to stay as Group CEO ('koncernchef'), something that confused the GMT members. He also wrote his own text ('the Chair's report') in the annual report and placed it before the traditional CEO statement. Berggren kept the position as Group CEO for 18 months. Nevertheless, he did not always participate at the GMT meetings. That, too, contributed to top management's uncertainty about Helgesson's role – they were never sure about who decided what. Gradually, that ambiguity undermined Helgesson's legitimacy to act. However, in their relations with the more formal Germans, Berggren and Helgesson agreed that Berggren should step down as Chair of Stora Feldmühle; otherwise the

Germans would only listen to Berggren's opinions and orders, and not take Helgesson's proposals seriously.

Helgesson discussed his executive dilemma with his friend director Mogren, who had a similar situation in Astra, where he was CEO and Berggren Chair. The big difference was that Berggren's track record and standing in the pharmaceutical industry was much weaker than his corresponding merits and reputation in the forest-based industry. Helgesson also brought up the Chair/CEO issue with the major shareholder (Wallenberg), but did not receive any support.[193] Thus, Helgesson never succeeded in building a Stora that could work fairly 'independently' from Investor; it never became the autonomous listed corporation that he had tried to establish. It even became difficult for Helgesson and his GMT to attain the necessary operative authority, as the GMT was composed of staff members only and the powerful operative managers were not part of that group.[194]

12.2.2 A Period of Rationalizations and Massive Sell-Offs

The new CEO wanted to produce synergy effects through centralization and conducted a thorough investigation of all the plants and (larger) machines – something that was not appreciated by all operative managers. Berggren was also hesitant, as Helgesson's conclusions could be interpreted as a critique of his actions while he was CEO.[195] The relative standstill regarding operative matters in the early 1990s could also be explained by the fact that the board did not function particularly well after Peter Wallenberg left – the new Chair, Berggren, was regarded by some directors as too dominant at least before Söderberg and Mogren became new board members.

Several circumstances made Helgesson's initial period in Stora even more difficult: the bad times in the industry (recession), the post-acquisition situation (Stora's operational and financial strain) and the obstacles linked to the capturing of cross-unit synergies.[196] Things were not simplified by the relative ambiguity of Helgesson's formal position in dealing with all these issues. Nevertheless, he accepted the challenge and tried to transform Stora from an organization primarily based on acquired legal units (e.g. Stora Feldmühle) to one instead based on core product areas (e.g. Stora Publication Papers). The current structure contained loosely coupled and very decentralized subsidiaries, which continued to run their operations very much in the same way as before their incorporation in Stora. The extent and speed of the growth had made it difficult to run an effective integration process, but by 1992 the time had come for such efforts. It was accompanied by a renaming of the major units, which was intended to strengthen the 'Stora' label as the key corporate identity for all units and actors in the group, and, at the same time, devalue the status of the previously highly autonomous sub-companies.

Thus, Helgesson's proposals were to play down the autonomy of the large subgroups, break them up and reorganize several of their plants into new integrated product/output-based units, and then reap synergies and rationalize. That was easier said than done. His operative subordinates were used to taking orders from Investor/Wallenberg actors (including Chair Berggren), and that tradition resulted in authority problems for Helgesson. Thus, his power in the vertical flow was limited, and the fact that his team (still) was composed primarily of staff managers did not improve the situation. His difficulty to take charge immediately upon entering as CEO also contributed to his rather weak position at the time. When he – after some time – attempted to assert his authority, it had become too late. Thus, the initial period of role uncertainty (CEO/COO) both delayed his initiatives and eroded his formal position. Furthermore, since Berggren kept the position as Group CEO, many top managers turned to him instead, particularly if Helgesson did something they disliked. So, for some time, Stora basically continued as a 'collection of forest-based activities', that is to say, as a company without effective horizontal processes.[197]

Although Berggren had engaged heavily in lobbying during the recruitment process, his successor was a very different kind of leader. Helgesson was not used to working in such a 'political' environment as Stora's, with its elements of direct shareholder intervention. He preferred to have well-defined responsibilities and authority lines in his organization, and wanted to see the executive levels in control of the operations. He was also determined to get timely reports from the subunits to be sure that he always knew how things were developing. However, not all his subordinates appreciated that approach, as many of them were used to slack reins.[198] However, Helgesson persisted and tried to centralize several of the internal governance processes, for example, investments, capital allocation and marketing efforts. The Chair, however, had a different opinion on what degree of centralization was the most appropriate, and that divergence remained all through Helgesson's stay as Stora's CEO.[199]

In the early 1990s Jacob Wallenberg Jr became Deputy Chair in Stora, but his role in Stora was rather limited all through that decade. He was not as interested in the forest-based industry as his cousin Marcus Wallenberg Jr, who had worked in Stora Feldmühle as head of its newsprint sales. Marcus Wallenberg Jr was also considered for a board seat, but at that time he was not inclined to succeed his uncle Peter Wallenberg. However, from his position as CEO of Investor, he still played an important role in Stora's development, and eventually he also became a board member.[200]

At the end of the 1990s, Investor was Stora's major shareholder (28% of the votes) followed by Trygg-Hansa[201] (7%), and AP4[202] (4%). Stora's statutes contained a paragraph stating that foreigners were not allowed to own more than 40 per cent of the capital and 20 per cent of the votes in the company. However, since the EU did not allow such restrictions, they were discarded. Still, Stora maintained its two kinds of shares – A-shares with the relationship one share to one vote and B-shares with the proportion ten shares to one vote.

Once again management had to focus on SFI (Canada), this time because of its large losses. The situation was actually so bad that the board even considered closing it entirely or ending the pulp production and concentrating on paper (a new SC machine would cost about SEK 3 billion). The necessary timber and power resources were available for the latter alternative, and an investment in a paper machine in North America would also make Stora less dependent on the SEK–USD exchange rate. The Deputy Chair even raised the question of why such an investment had not been proposed earlier, as SC paper was a growth business in the US, and as several customers had expressed a wish to change its input from LWC to SC. Chair Berggren and GMT member Knuts were particularly eager to see that investment materialize, and soon the board decided to approve the project.[203] However, Knuts's interest faded when Helgesson created a new position in the organization – that of Head of Stora North America.

Stora's long and bad experiences of SFI were clear indications of the large risk the new investment entailed. Historically obstructive unions, small machines, tough environmental restrictions, mediocre markets, and so on, had caused the company substantial losses – the unit had been a serious problem from the start. As if all that did not make the investment risky enough, Stora had decided to use a new production technique and to be first on the US market with the new SC product.[204] SFI had also tied up significant management capacity. Berggren, for example, had been forced to visit the site many times to sort out problems.

Deputy CEO Petersson claimed that since WWII Stora had had an 'idée fixe' that the corporation had to be present in North America. However, the reason behind the fixation was unclear. Nevertheless, once SFI had been established, Stora tried to expand further in that region through acquisitions of Mohawk (did not materialize) and Newton Falls (soon sold) and new (risky) investments at SFI. Once Feldmühle Nobel was acquired in 1990, Stora's North American situation turned for the better. Feldmühle had sold quite a lot of its output on that market, so it knew the competition rather well. The enlarged Stora also had the advantage of facing a domestic forest-based industry with a rather obsolete set of machinery. As a consequence of all this, CEO Helgesson decided to increase his engagement in the company's North American businesses and particularly in SFI's expansion. Its prospects were excellent, as the new machine's standard was positioned sky-high above those of its North American competitors. Added to that, Stora had a strategic forest-use agreement that spanned 50 years.[205]

In contrast to Helgesson's enthusiasm, some leading Stora actors were hesitant. For example, the Head of Forestry, Hägglund, was concerned because he regarded the quality of the forests as rather poor. Moreover, he was not convinced that those who took the investment decision were aware of his assessment. The planned SC investment also competed internally with applications from Kabel, and Hägglund found it particularly strange that one of the main arguments for preferring SFI over Kabel was SFI's better timber supply. It was also hard for him to evaluate the preparations that had been made before the decision.[206]

At the end of 1991, Helgesson established an agenda for his first years as Stora CEO. It represented a concentration and rationalization strategy – due to the financial strain only minor supplementary acquisitions were to be accepted. It was actually Investor that had stressed that tough path by demanding a substantially improved solidity and debt situation. Investor also had its own challenges, so it was not equipped to issue larger amounts of capital to any corporation. That fact, too, contributed to Helgesson's strong focus on internal efficiency, that is to say, on the performance of each plant and on how the available capital was used. Each quarter he also reported to the company's major shareholder on how the rationalization efforts advanced (the Chair had approved such a procedure). Helgesson was then a bit worried that Berggren would perceive his efforts to streamline Stora as a critique of the latter's previous achievements as CEO, but he saw the situation as a rather typical one for a corporation that had made a series of large acquisitions.[207]

The cost-savings programme Helgesson launched was ambitious with a 15 per cent target figure. He also planned to make substantial disinvestments to improve Stora's financial situation. In two years' time one could already see the marked effects of Helgesson's efforts. A cost reduction of SEK 4.5 billion had been achieved, and the company's net debt was halved. Moreover, production and product quality improved, at the same time as productivity increased throughout the company. Stora also restructured its operations into four business groups: basic products (power plants, forests and pulp), graphic papers (publication papers, fine paper, North America and merchant papers), packaging (cardboard) and 'other' (e.g. financial services). In addition, Stora created joint functions for sales (i.e. national or regional sales companies), R&D, purchase and transport.[208] The rationalizations were supplemented with new investments, foremost to improve productivity, utilize scale advantages and modernize operations.

Stora's ambition was to operate specialized and highly efficient plants and machines. The company invested only in units that also seemed to be able to deliver profit in the future, and that meant an emphasis on large-scale efforts and – consequently – the sale of smaller units. One reason for that strategy was that many of the products in the forest-based industry were difficult to differentiate both technically and on the markets. Therefore, the main road to profitability was to run a cost-efficient production (provided that the product quality was adequate). The rapidly falling prices[209] on most forest-based products also reinforced such a strategy.[210]

Helgesson soon identified quite a lot of problems with the general condition of the plants and their capacity to generate future profits. Compared to the Finnish competitors, Stora did not come out particularly well – its machines were generally much older. For printing paper, where Stora was number one in Europe, the situation was particularly shaky. At the Hylte site three out of the four machines were older, so its paper quality was lower than the European average (but Hylte could at least use substantial percentages of waste paper in its production). One of the machines at Kvarnsveden was also in poor shape (and it could not use waste paper) and produced paper of a too low quality and with an inappropriate width. Reisholz and Langerbrugge's[211] machines were both too small (and the former actually produced substandard quality). The situation for SC paper was also rather precarious, even though Stora had a 25 per cent market share in Europe. On the whole, many of the production units were rather mediocre and Stora's market shares had also begun to fall. However, in the LWC field Stora was competitive (and second biggest in Europe). All in all, this meant that Stora needed to invest at Hylte (SEK 300 million), Kvarnsveden (SEK 400 million) and Reisholz (SEK 100 million), and the board approved those proposals from the CEO.[212] That endorsement was simplified by the fact that Stora had turned a SEK 1.3 billion loss in 1992 into a SEK 8 billion profit by 1995.

In 1994 Helgesson provided a classification of all production units into three categories: strong, average and problematic. He used the figures from 1990–94 and focused on both capital employed and returns on capital employed. In the 'problematic' group he put Langerbrugge, SFI, Flenburg, Gruvön, Mölndal, Dalum, Silkeborg, Maglemölle, Skutskär and Norrsundet. Reisholz, Newton Kyme, Aronsberg and Baienfurt were placed in the 'average' category. The strong units were Kvarnsveden, Hylte, Hagen-Kabel, Corbehem, Hillegossen, Skoghall, Fors, Nymölla, Ueterden, Grycksbo and Celbi. One could note that some of the problematic plants actually showed losses (and that most of them were former Feldmühle units).[213]

There were also several external circumstances that supported adopting a concentration strategy. Helgesson particularly highlighted the overcapacity in the industry, the consequences of deregulation, the recession-like times and the currency exchange rates (SEK versus USD). It was also generally difficult to influence some of the key production costs, for example, those for energy and timber.[214] The current overcapacity followed from the good times in the second half of the 1980s, when demand was high and steady, profits were high and it was easy to raise capital. Those favourable circumstances tempted companies to invest heavily in new plants and machines. Each investment was probably rational in a narrow company perspective, but taken together in an industrial perspective they caused lots of problems. Moreover, deregulation enhanced cross-national competition and put pressure on many product prices. That outcome obviously benefitted the consumers (which also was the EU's and the national governments' ambition), but at the same time it threatened many forest-based companies' profitability.

The recession struck early at some of the important markets for Stora, particularly the UK and the Nordic countries, and that, together with a falling USD rate, increased the competition on the European market. So the 1990s seemed to become 'the decade of competition' in the forest-based industry. Factors like the rapid internationalization, the general overcapacity, the disintegration of the cartels and the new environmental legislation all contributed to the tougher competition. Helgesson also noticed that non-European companies had begun to set up businesses in Europe and that, consequently, cheap pulp from countries in Asia and South America was offered globally.[215]

In 1992, Stora asked the other shareholders in Kopparkraft to convert their debentures, so that Stora's share would fall to just below 50 per cent of the votes (and just below 10% of the capital). That move made it possible to deconsolidate Kopparkraft from Stora's balance sheet. Helgesson also wanted to write down certain Stora assets, but the Chair stopped that idea.[216] As he saw it, that would eliminate some of the shareholder's capital.[217] However, a write-down would also reduce some of the financial stress that made the rationalizations and selling of units necessary. On the selling side Stora made what several actors saw as a mistake – it sold its 50 per cent holding in Forestal Valdiva to Aranco (SEK 1 billion). The critics believed that the sale eliminated the potential for large future values and destroyed Wallenberg's strong link to one of Chile's leading business families. Supporters of the sale countered that Stora was forced to choose between keeping Celbi (Portugal) or Forestal Valdiva (Chile). Moreover, Peter Wallenberg also had to accept the selling of one of his favourite investments, that of Ireland. However, the divestment of the consumer products (the building material units) had to wait, as the prices offered were considered to be too low.[218]

Thus, the Forestal Valdiva holding was sold together with several other units when Stora and the Swedish forest-based industry in general were in severe financial trouble (many companies – Stora included – showed losses in 1992). In that crisis situation Helgesson acted cautiously and rationed new investments and stopped most of the expansion plans. He found many of them too big and risky and advocated a Stora that once again focused on Europe.[219] The above-mentioned sale of Forestal Valdiva was probably the most controversial divestment of them all, and it engaged many Stora actors. One reason for the disunity was their differing views about what balance sheet quality the current situation required. Both Berggren and Helgesson favoured a relatively strong balance sheet, and particularly Helgesson became a driving actor[220] in the sale process. Berggren also called attention to the fact that the long-fibre qualities that existed in Chile did not possess full spruce quality, which made them less interesting for Stora. Peter Wallenberg had no decided view on that issue, so he did not object when Helgesson suggested a sale. The board also unanimously supported that proposal.[221] Helgesson and GMT member Grafström got the tedious assignment to terminate Stora's Chilean involvement.

Helgesson also wanted to sell off everything that did not belong to Stora's core operations. That included Tarkett, Åkerlund & Rausing, all units producing and selling building products, the sacks business and the SAS[222] holding. Consequently, Tarkett was sold in 1994 for SEK 3.5 billion to a consortium. The same year, half of Åkerlund and Rausing was sold to the Finnish Ahlström group with a clause (option) making the sale of the remaining half possible during the coming two years (it took place already the same year). Stora then deconsolidated that company, thereby lowering the net debt significantly. The 50 per cent holding in WM-Data Stora was also sold (to WM-Data[223]). Moreover, the Sandarne site was closed down, although former Stora CEO Sundblad once had promised that the company should defend that unit's operations to the very last.

Helgesson could conclude that the effect of all the sell-offs and rationalizations was a significantly stronger balance sheet. During 1994 the net debt had been reduced by SEK 8 billion, and the solidity had risen from 33 per cent to 41 per cent. The latter figure indicated that Stora finally had reached its financial goal (which took into account the cyclical and capital-intensive character of the forest-based industry).[224] The sell-offs continued through 1995 when sacks and sack paper (Pacsac and Robert Fleming) were sold to AssiDomän, and the Swedish PE firm Industri Kapital bought Stora's unit for building products. In 1996–97 Stora continued its divestments by selling Arnsberg, Bishhof-Klein, Enveltec and Newton Falls. During the same period several capacity reductions were made, too: in Corbehem (one paper machine and one cardboard machine), Langerbrugge (one paper machine), Skoghall (one CTMP-fluff machine and one MG-paper machine) and Port Hawkesbury (pulp production). Together those reductions took away around 600 kilotons of basically non-competitive products.[225]

12.3 GLOBALIZATION TRIGGERS NEW EXPANSION

12.3.1 A Globalization Strategy Emerges

Once again – in merely a decade's time – the institutional setting changed profoundly. Most of the cartels that had dominated the industry during the majority of the 20th century had died out, and in 1994 the General Agreement on Tariffs and Trade (GATT) treaty was signed. Those two circumstances created a new competitive situation for most industrial corporations. The GATT treaty, for example, represented a radical lowering (or even an abandoning) of the European customs fees for most kinds of paper products, which implied that the European mills had to be efficient not just in a European context but also in a global setting. Market liberalization forced many of the larger corporations to reconsider their overall strategies. Instead of looking for cheap fibre, they began to discuss the global potential for their current products.

One consequence of market liberalization was that substantial product volumes began to move between continents. For Europe and the US, it was primarily SC paper that was imported/exported, while for South America and Asia it was mostly pulp. Fine paper, too, had begun to cross the seas. However, the forest-based industry was still rather fragmentized – the companies that aspired to stay competitive had to scale up their units substantially. To do that, substantial amounts of capital were needed. Despite all the acquisitions in the late 1980s, Stora's capital base was too small (and too fragile) to constitute a basis for such global activity. The capital demands on those companies that aspired to be in the forest industry's 'Ivy League' were exceptional (e.g. merely to invest at Veracruz required SEK 10 billion). Thus, Stora found itself at a crossroads – should it try to dramatically increase its size and become a global actor, or should it continue as a regional player? If Stora chose the former path, it had to find a large partner. One fact that spoke for the 'Ivy League ambition' was that many of the American forest-based companies had for many years failed to invest at home. That omission produced a current window of opportunity for their European (and Asian) competitors.[226]

Thus, Stora was once again ready for expansion, but this time the company aimed for a leading role on the global scene. That journey began with the ambition to invest around SEK 20 billion over the coming years.[227] Despite the recent sell-offs, however, the scope of Stora's business was still too broad, and that worried CEO Helgesson. To stay at the top in several different businesses was no longer possible, as each of them needed extensive investments on a continuous basis. Thus, the crucial tasks for Stora were to decide in what business areas it should concentrate its efforts and to find out how it could stay competitive in those selected fields on a globalized market. To accomplish that, Stora launched a comprehensive analysis both of its own strategic situation and of the future for the whole forest-based industry.

In 1994, when the crisis had been overcome, Helgesson organized a systematic analysis of possible acquisition candidates.[228] As a result, the family firm Haindl (a producer of newsprint, SC paper and LWC) came into focus. That company was number four in Europe on the printing paper market (right after Stora, UPM and Norske Skog). It had four plants in Germany, one in Holland and one in Canada (sacks and sack paper).[229] Deputy CEO Petersson regarded Haindl as a most interesting acquisition target for Stora, but in the end the asking price was too high.[230] Stora had once before paid 'a lot' for a large German corporation (Feldmühle), and that was not to be repeated.[231]

The board also discussed the acquisition of French Papeterie de Condat. It had a strong market position in the fine paper field and ran a solid packaging business. The company was already in the midst of a selling process in which Jefferson Smurfit (Ireland) was the intended buyer. However, since Jefferson Smurfit lacked fine paper operations, there was a window of opportunity for Stora to purchase that part. Stora had long been interested in acquiring a large fine paper unit within France. However, in the end Papeterie de Condat turned out to be too expensive.[232]

Scott Paper's American fine paper business S.D. Warren was a third acquisition candidate. It was unusual that such an extensive business unit was up for sale. It had around 25 per cent of the US market for coated fine paper, but also non-coated fine paper and chemical paper. Since Stora was only interested in buying the plants that produced coated paper, no deal materialized.[233]

Berggren described the new competitive situation as one in which ownership, investments and trade – all at the same time – would soon involve players that acted globally, showing no consideration whatsoever for national borders or traditions. He expected that such a development would be almost 'too much' for a fragmented industry like the forest-based one. The present globalization process also opened up opportunities for new products and services, as the need to transport large quantities of products across long distances would increase, something that ought to stimulate the demand for various kinds of packages, boxes and wrappings. Berggren further predicted that quite a few new actors would appear on the global scene that based their competitive capacities on cheap raw material, on their presence in fast-growing (home) markets and on modern and large-scale plants and machines. He saw emerging tensions between large, mature markets with slow growth (Europe and North America) and small, virgin, fast-growing markets (South America, East Europe and [parts of] Asia); between slow-growing natural forests and fast-growing forests from plantations; between older, well-consolidated corporations and younger, highly indebted corporations; and between high-cost areas (Europe and North America) and low-cost areas (South America, East Europe and Asia). Berggren also wondered whether the IT revolution underway might replace many uses for paper, but took no stand regarding its effects on the world's total paper consumption.[234]

In the company's mapping of possible futures, the main conclusion was that Stora's focus ought to be on graphic papers, particularly journal paper, and on high-quality cardboard. Both product areas were expected to grow, and they were based on a 'Nordic' raw material (long fibres). In the Annual Report 1995 CEO Helgesson stressed that to be successful in the core businesses, it was an absolutely necessity for Stora to have modern and effective production plants and make sure that they stayed that way – additional investments to keep the machines productive had to be carried out on a continuous basis. The recent investments at Skoghall (liquid packaging) and Nova Scotia (journal paper) were consistent with that new strategy. Furthermore, the company's forests, power plants and pulp should principally be treated as input for the targeted production repertoire, and therefore adjusted to internal needs. Stora's acquisition that year of the remaining 29 per cent in Celbi (pulp) from the state-owned corporation IPE represented a diversion from that path, but it had its reasons (cf. section 12.1).

The new focus on graphic papers and high-quality cardboard led to a less prominent standing for newsprint and fine paper. That 'ranking' of the core businesses was based on the market developments at the time, the relative efficiency of the plants, the sizes of the market shares and the competition. Regarding newsprint, a product for which Stora was one of the five biggest producers in the world, its relative internal 'demotion' was explained by expectations of declining demand in the early 21st century due to the growth of electronic distribution and multi-media products. Furthermore, there was also a reduced difference between certain sorts of paper, for example, between coated journal paper and coated fine paper (rolls). Therefore, soon a part of the fine paper operations came to be treated as a subsection of the graphic paper business.

Stora was one of Europe's largest producers of fine paper. The focus was on office paper where the order volumes were small, time to delivery short and the production located close to the customers. Consequently, Stora had concentrated its fine paper business within the European market. Still, the company saw that product area as a less attractive one for the future. Fine paper had become a problematic business for many corporations, so many of them had become active on the market for corporate control trying to find new structural solutions. Taken together, the European forest-based corporations had an inefficient structure that had to change in the long run, particularly as intense price competition was expected from (new) producers in countries with much lower fibre prices and employee costs (e.g. Indonesia and Brazil).[235]

Partnerships with other companies, particularly in the fine paper field, were also pursued as part of the growth strategy. So Berggren (sometimes together with Dahlbäck and/or Helgesson) contacted the leading actors in MoDo, SCA and Norske Skog and tried to rouse their interest in structural re-arrangements. In MoDo's case, he met

Chair Lundberg and CEO Löf, but nothing came out of those talks. In the discussions with SCA's Chair Rydin and CEO Martin-Löf, Stora suggested that the forest resources ought to be included in a joint solution, but failed to convince SCA on that point. Another obstacle was that Stora did not want SCA to be one of its (major) shareholders. The discussions with Norske Skog were rather successful at the executive level, but the principals of the company, the Norwegian forest owners, showed no interest at all.[236]

Stora's idea had been to create a new, jointly owned 'independent' fine paper company, but as 'everybody' wanted to get out of that business, the establishment of such a new unit was rejected.[237] Another obstacle was a lack of confidence between the negotiating parties. All of them were afraid that an agreement would be advantageous to one/some of the others, or that they would be deceived. In such settings details tend to become insuperable barriers, and actor prestige also begins to play an important role in the negotiations. In such situations probably only a severe crisis could make something happen (or if some of the actors identify really striking profit opportunities [or the like]).[238]

As part of its expansion strategy, Stora looked for new ways to secure its fibre sourcing. The efforts involved both the integration of recycled fibres in parts of its paper production and the guarantee of a steady flow of cheap short-fibre timber. Berggren was convinced that forest owning in itself was a key factor for long-term success. He regarded the locations and varieties of the forests as decisive for the profitability of most investments. Actually, most pulp plants that were established around the world looked roughly the same. Thus, the plants as such did not determine the competitiveness of its output. In line with that reasoning, Stora bought cutting rights in Russia and started timber-buying units in Estonia, but those steps were primarily taken to secure the supply of timber for the company's Swedish sites – not to promote global expansion. Instead, that more ambitious goal was addressed in 1995 by a group led by the Head of Forestry, Hägglund (the team also included the CEO of Stora Cell and three more junior managers, and had a link to GMT-member Knuts).[239] Hägglund et al. were asked to find out 'where in the world forests grew best'. More precisely, their task was to look for the best location for a pulp plant, and, at the same time, establish where trees grew that were suitable for newsprint and magazine paper production in Southeast Asia.[240]

The globalization process forced Stora's leading actors to decide whether the company should grow (also) outside Europe and become a respected player on the international arena or remain a major regional actor in Europe (which currently accounted for about 90% of its sales). As mentioned above, Stora adopted the more ambitious global path, a decision that immediately raised two new questions: on what businesses should Stora concentrate, and in what parts of the world should Stora compete. One important reason for the preference for the global path was that the regions outside Europe and North America were expected to be the source of most of the market growth for pulp and paper products. CEO Helgesson further noted that each continental market had its distinctive features, particularly in terms of raw materials. Long fibres and electric power were scarce resources in Asia, so the newsprint and cardboard plants that were built there were usually based on recycled fibres. That scarcity also made it almost impossible for Asian firms to invest in the production of wood-containing journal paper, as well as high-quality cardboard and LPB. Instead, the circumstances were much more favourable for the graphic sector (e.g. fine paper). Helgesson also noted that in many Asian countries it was almost impossible to buy land for tree plantation – something that complicated market entries on that continent. The South American situation differed in that respect – the possibility to acquire forest estates existed in several of its countries.[241]

In 1995, Stora's board formulated the company's strategy for the coming years. It decided that the company should concentrate on graphic papers and high-quality cardboard. Towards that end, the emphasis should be on large-scale operations, which, in turn, required an expansion that primarily had to take place outside Europe (particularly in Asia). Long-fibre-based products sourced from the Nordic countries, Russia, Canada, Chile and New Zealand would also remain a priority. For journal paper the ambition was to stay among the top three in the world,[242] and for cardboard the goal was to remain among the top ten in the world and focus on LPB. The target was set lower for newsprint, where the company was already number three in the world and not particularly eager to climb higher. This new strategy implied a focus on hardwood that led to further efforts to secure that kind of timber from Brazil or Indonesia. Thus, the company planned to maintain internal sourcing of the key inputs (forests, power plants and pulp).[243]

At that time, many European and US actors talked about the Asian forests (especially those in Indonesia) as a possible future fibre source for their industries, but Stora's investigating team also considered South America. As Stora's primary ambition was to produce and sell fine paper in Asia, it had a preference for establishing its new pulp production in 'nearby' Indonesia, but that country turned out to be too corrupt. So South America was chosen. Because Stora previously had spoilt its reputation in Chile with its dramatic withdrawal from a joint venture (described earlier in this chapter), it focused instead on Brazil, Argentina and Uruguay. Ultimately, Brazil was chosen, actually very much by coincidence. Hägglund suddenly came across an investment made by the Brazilian building company Odebrecht: the Veracruz project. As a consequence of that 'finding', Hägglund's group suggested that Stora should produce pulp in Brazil, and then convert it to fine paper in China.[244]

Since the early 1990s the Brazilian Veracruz company had bought land, raised eucalyptus and received an environmental permit from the authorities to establish a pulp plant in the Bahia region sourced by cheap (planted) eucalyptus trees.[245] The pulp production was supposed to start in 2001, and the total investment was estimated to amount to about SEK 10 billion. The pulp was then not just intended for Asia (China) but also for Europe and North America. However, the financing of the gigantic project was a problem. Both Wallenberg and Dahlbäck had reservations regarding whether Stora ought to engage in the proposed mezzanine loan.[246,247]

The leading actors in the Wallenberg sphere (Barnevik, Dahlbäck, Jacob Wallenberg Jr, Marcus Wallenberg Jr and Berggren) were all enthusiastic about the business potential they saw in many Asian regions (e.g. China and India). They also regarded such a geographical spread of the activities as a way of moderating risks, handling economic trends and establishing new markets for many of the products/services provided by the sphere's companies. For Stora, particularly fine paper came into the forefront. One could note that Peter Wallenberg, the 'doyen' of the family, at that time was unable to govern the expansion process because of failing health. However, the family had built relations in Asia over a long time, which facilitated many of the sphere companies' activities on that continent. Those early Asian experiences also provided support to Stora's current efforts, as its leading actors could benefit from some of the already existing networks and friendships.

Marcus Wallenberg Jr was one of the family members who repeatedly had visited Asia – and particularly China – and those journeys had both established linkages to important Chinese actors and paved the way for later efforts. Already in the 1980s the family had become acquainted with Ronnie Chan, who became a key person for Stora in its efforts on the Chinese market.[248] Both Marcus Wallenberg Jr and his cousin Jacob Wallenberg Jr stressed the importance of building friendship-like relationships before starting discussions about concrete business matters. They had also invited Chan to Sweden and showed him parts of the family sphere's business sector. One of the journeys was actually made to Stora – a visit and a connection that later turned out to be crucial.[249] In 1996, Stora entered into an agreement that combined its ambition to give focus to its business repertoire with its aspiration to establish a network in parts of Asia. The settlement involved a takeover by Mitsubishi of 20 per cent of Stora Spezialpapiere (Germany). The idea was that Mitsubishi gradually should increase its holding, which later on could open up opportunities for joint projects in Japan. At that time, Stora's board also discussed the current structural re-arrangements that were taking place in the forest-based industry in other parts of the world. Several things happened in the US, but in Europe there was almost a standstill, with a fine paper unit at KNP and a LWC plant (Lanaken) as the sole larger units available for takeover.[250]

Back in South America, the planned Veracruz mill was expected to produce very cheap pulp. Hägglund regarded its location as the best in the world for such a plant. Both Berggren and Knuts approved the project, and Knuts, in particular, contributed with both important domestic contacts and strong support for the establishment of a joint paper mill in China.[251] At this stage, Dahlbäck, too, backed the Veracruz project, and despite some hesitation from other directors, the planning for a new large pulp plant was launched in 1997 (Veracel: a joint venture together with Odebrecht [50–50]).

Eventually, the Hägglund group became convinced that it was in China that Stora ought to process the Veracruz pulp to fine paper. As a consequence, Stora bought the majority of the fine paper producer Souzho Paper Mill, although this time the whole board hesitated. Therefore, Knuts was asked to contact Investor's Chair Barnevik and tell him about the project and get his judgement. The presentation to Barnevik was made in the presence of directors Berggren and Dahlbäck. In the end Barnevik gave the China investment his blessing (somewhat later the board took the formal decision).

The decision to invest in Brazil and China reduced Stora's ambitions for North America, which was no longer as important for Stora's future development as previously stated. As a global corporation, Stora had to invest in those regions where demand was growing and where the basic inputs were cheap.[252]

12.3.2 Looking for a Partner

From 1994 to 1998, Berggren and Dahlbäck worked together with Helgesson to figure out how Stora could become a leading global actor in selected parts of the forest-based industry. That high ambition required a much bigger balance sheet and a sizeable 'corporate body'. The idea was to utilize the strong European home base with its large production units and substantial sales as a platform for activities on three other continents. For North America, Stora's investments would be both concentrated and large enough to become profitable but, at the same time, also made to 'irritate' its global American competitors on their home ground. South America would be the basis for an extensive supply of timber and pulp, and (parts of) Asia would be the arena for rapid growth. That new strategy meant that Stora would have to give up its sole focus on long-fibre-based businesses (printing paper and cardboard), because such a concentration would have halved its turnover (from SEK 70 billion to SEK 35 billion). Since the new strategy did not allow such a reduction of the 'corporate body', attention would also need to be paid to short-fibre-based fine paper.[253]

At that time, there were basically two possible growth paths available for Stora. The first one involved a focus on printing paper; in that case, a merger with the Finnish company Kymmene was a rather obvious path. The second one involved a business future that stressed packaging – LPB and high-quality bleached cardboard – and for that path a merger with Enso-Gutzeit (also Finnish) was preferable.[254] However, the latter path was soon abandoned, primarily because of Enso-Gutzeit's ownership situation. It was state controlled, and its ownership share was not allowed to go below a certain percentage without a decision by the Finnish Parliament. Still, Enso-Gutzeit's CEO at the time, Härmälä, had such connections to the Finnish Prime Minister that it was not totally unrealistic that efforts to eliminate that obstacle could be successful. Nevertheless, Stora's first serious analyses focused on the first path, which led toward the 'Swedish-like' Finnish Kymmene. The two companies fitted well together both culturally and operationally. Their major shareholders – Ehrnrooth (Kymmene) and Wallenberg (Stora) – enjoyed a good relationship, which made a constructive dialogue easier.[255] The companies also had operational overlap, for example, both were active in Germany, and Stora even owned a small part of Kymmene's Kaukas[256] unit. Some of the leading actors had actually discussed the idea as early as 1993, but at that time nothing happened, mainly as a consequence of internal problems and poor markets.[257]

This time the situation was different. Stora's intended acquisition of Kymmene had the full support of Berggren and Dahlbäck, and most leading actors on the Finnish side also favoured the deal. However, some of Stora's top managers were hesitant as they anticipated a future in which a Finnish colleague would become CEO of the new grouping (as tradition required that one country should get the Chair [and that would most certainly be Stora's Berggren] and the other country the CEO position). Furthermore, many Stora managers were exhausted by the recent Feldmühle integration, and therefore not yet ready for a new 'big bite'.

In the background, Berggren and Helgesson secretly met with Kymmene's Chair Ehrnrooth and CEO Pihl. All were agreeable to some kind of co-operation, so two investigators were appointed (each company's Head of Technology). Their task was to estimate the possible synergies that would follow from a merger. The outcome of that study came as a surprise – a merger would only generate minor operational improvements. Both companies had already rationalized their plants, leaving only financial and market synergies, but such effects were not regarded as particularly important. Thus, since the executives could not show the shareholders that a merger would bring substantial improvements, the whole idea lost momentum for the time being.[258]

However, only a few years later (1995) Stora went back to Kymmene, which by that time had merged with Finnish United Paper Mills (UPM). These resumed talks took the merger issue much further than the previous efforts. Both Stora's Chair and its major owner thought that each of the firms was too small to be able to compete successfully in the global arena. This time, some parts of the two companies' management accepted a merger. Stora's CEO (once again) was reluctant, primarily because he doubted whether the company was ready yet for another large merger. As he saw it, Stora's new structure was not functioning well enough, and in several units the productivity was (still) not satisfactory.[259] Moreover, UPM-Kymmene was fully occupied with its own on-going merger, which made its managers sceptical about a new integration effort. Another complication was that UPM-Kymmene's board did not solidly back its director Ehrnrooth, one of the main promoters of the merger.[260]

The resistance could not be explained solely by bad timing and/or a lack of operational and cultural fit – motives could also be found elsewhere. For example, several board members supposed that one key obstacle was their intention to recruit the merged company's CEO from outside of both corporations (a 'neutral' person[261]). It soon became obvious to them that neither of the two management teams applauded such a solution. So, despite the owners' preference for a merger, the resistance from the executives blocked that path, as the owners regarded it as too risky to force their will on a reluctant organization. Publicly, 'cultural differences' was presented as the main reason for cancelling the merger.[262]

There were also some actors that were doubtful about a merger for a quite different reason – they suspected that the new constellation would be too big on the market, particularly in the printing paper business. That would make it difficult to get (most of) the merger accepted by the European Competition Network (ECN). The fine paper integration would probably be the only part of the merger that ECN would accept. However, fine paper was the business field that both companies wanted to leave: like most experts and competitors, they saw a clear risk that Asian producers soon would dump lots of it on the European market.[263]

At that time, SCA, too, was regarded as the best remaining alternative for some kind of co-operation or partnership, while, for example, Enso-Gutzeit still was regarded as an 'impossible' case. SCA had actually been an attractive alternative for Stora throughout the later decades of the 20th century (SCA had simply been 'number one' for Stora), so feelers were regularly thrown out. Now that Stora aspired to become a major global actor, its interest in SCA was stronger than ever. Expected large synergies in the printing and packaging businesses made a Stora–SCA combination most attractive. For Stora there was also a 'bonus' of bringing the hygiene business into the imagined new constellation – something that perhaps made Stora more eager to collaborate than SCA. Industrially, a straightforward merger between the two companies was seen as the most rational construct, but the 'unbridgeable' problem was the ownership situation. Two rival spheres were involved: Wallenberg/Investor (controlled Stora) and Handelsbanken/Industrivärden (controlled SCA). Each of the companies also had a strong Chair – Berggren (Stora) and Rydin (SCA) – and that, too, contributed to the negative outcome of the talks.[264]

UPM-Kymmene was still seen as one of the strongest candidates for some kind of partnership or merger, but there were concerns about the new constellation's exposure to cyclical variations. Another candidate, Norske Skog, ran an interesting graphical business, but Stora was uncertain about its future engagement in that field. On the European continent Stora regarded Burgo (Italy), Haindl (Germany) and Mayr-Melnhof (Austria) as the most interesting candidates for purchases/mergers/partnerships. Companies like

Soporcel (Spain), Saffa (Italy) and Sarro (Spain) either were regarded as mediocre and/or did not fit Stora's current strategy.

Above all Stora was interested in M&As in emerging or fast-growing markets (e.g. in parts of Asia and Eastern Europe).[265] Thus, at that time Stora's board discussed a substantial investment in China in the Shanghai area through Suzhou Papyrus Paper. Deputy CEO Knuts had been active in those talks, and the Finnish consultancy firm Jakko Pöyry had conducted feasibility studies for such an investment. Berggren and Dahlbäck, too, became interested in that project, as it could be seen as 'a ticket to the future' – they also had confidence in Stora's partner Morningstar (i.e. Ronnie Chan). Jacob Wallenberg Jr stressed that such an investment would be congruent with Stora's strategy to enter fast-growing markets. However, board members Söderberg and Mogren hesitated and questioned whether such an investment really was the best use of Stora's relatively scarce capital resources.[266]

The idea to enter the Chinese market was originally proposed by Knuts and director Madsen. Stora's ally in China was Chan, who ahead of most other actors had invested in Chinese paper mills. Most of Stora's leading actors wanted to make an investment in China, even if it was in the fine paper field, which the company – like many of its competitors – had considered leaving. However, CEO Helgesson was one of the sceptics regarding the suggested investment, as the calculations did not deliver the required economic return. So, at an unusual board meeting in 1997, he registered his dissent in the meeting minutes. Shortly thereafter Suzhou Papyrus Paper (later the name of the unit) more than tripled its production of coated fine paper, and in 1998 Stora bought the company. Before that, Stora's board had produced a 'letter of intent' (to buy 60%).

KNP was also a target for Stora's growth ambitions because it represented the focus on fine paper advocated particularly by Helgesson. In order to discuss future possibilities, Berggren and other leading Stora actors visited KNP's top executives in Holland. From the very beginning though, Berggren had expressed doubts about whether an acquisition of KNP really would contribute to Stora's new global strategy. Those doubts, together with the fact that the Dutch company was not in the very best shape, made Stora finally abandon that path as well.[267]

By the end of 1997, the friction between Berggren and Helgesson became so apparent that it became a serious problem for the company. Berggren had been regarded as a very good CEO, particularly when times were good. He was seen to have both the energy and intellectual capacity to deal with complex growth matters in a visionary way. Helgesson was regarded as a competent CEO, too, particularly in difficult times. He was considered to be a cautious, formal, controlling and systematic leader.[268] Some actors also described Berggren as more of an intuitive and emotional manager, while Helgesson more resembled a classical 'rational' actor. Thus, the two leaders' executive rationales certainly differed.

Practically speaking, the main problem was that both the Chair and the CEO wanted to develop the company's strategy. In Swedish industry it was common practice (although with exceptions) that the CEO acted as the initiator and driver of a company's strategic path, while the board (including its Chair) primarily acted as a sounding board, critic and ultimate decision-maker. For some time, the major shareholders and directors in Stora had noticed that the Chair and the CEO had contrasting views about how to divide their responsibilities,[269] which, for example, could make GMT meetings and board discussions rather uncomfortable. That tension tended to slow down Stora's development. Eventually Chair Berggren suggested that Helgesson ought to be replaced as CEO. The board supported its Chair and decided to appoint Stora's current Head of Forestry, Hägglund, who was at the time the company's leading internal candidate.[270] The candidates that had competed with Helgesson back in 1992 were regarded as 'too old', and several of the 'up-and-coming men' had already left the company (partly because of the ambiguities resulting from the friction between the Chair and the CEO). Hägglund's personality differed markedly from that of both Berggren and Helgesson. Basically, he was regarded as more of an academic – a thinker and analyser – not as a traditional 'hands-on' CEO.

The replacement of Helgesson did not occur without complications. His unwillingness to resign forced the Chair to execute the board's decision to discharge him.[271] The way Berggren handled the public process resulted in dramatic consequences for him, as well. In the end, it forced him to leave his Chair position not only in Stora and Investor, but also in all other 'Wallenberg companies'. Since Helgesson was discharged, he was entitled to a 'golden parachute'. But because Berggren wanted to be kind to him, he described the situation to the press as one in which Helgesson himself had chosen to resign. The problem was then that if Helgesson had in fact resigned, he would not qualify for the 'golden parachute'.[272] That inconsistency badly damaged Berggren's long-term credibility.

Berggren's commendable ambition to protect the other involved actors (i.e. major owners and board members) did not improve his standing. That was partly due to the competition for the Chair position at Investor, but also partly to the unexpected lack of support from the Wallenberg sphere.[273] In fact, that nobody from the sphere stepped in and backed Berggren really surprised the Swedish business community. It was a remarkable situation since for a long time Berggren's sphere position had been exceptionally strong, being one of two substitutes for Peter Wallenberg during the latter's long period of convalescence, not to mention the unparalleled impact he had had on Stora's development since the mid-1980s. Berggren's influence as CEO and later as Chair far exceeded what was regarded to be 'normal' practice in Sweden. Indeed, Marcus Wallenberg Jr[274] emphasized that the major shareholder was not dissatisfied with the way Berggren had run Stora – the problem was rather the way he had handled his relationship with its CEO.

Several top managers in Stora speculated that the Wallenberg/Investor sphere's treatment of Berggren was more likely a consequence of a power struggle between him and ABB's CEO Barnevik over the Chair position in Investor – a fight that Barnevik, at that time an international executive superstar, was about to win. Barnevik described Stora as a low-performing corporation and criticized Berggren for that. Berggren countered that ABB was not in particularly good shape, and that its official figures represented a 'coloured' description that concealed a mediocre result. Berggren's calculations[275] actually showed that Stora had done better than ABB over the last decade. However, at that time, the ABB bubble had not burst, so it was Barnevik's view that won out.

Peter Wallenberg also supported the recruitment of Barnevik to the prestigious Chair position in Investor (1997) – a decision that was easy to justify at that time. Wallenberg thought that Barnevik had all the necessary qualifications that an Investor Chair needed – international renown and a global network that included both political residences and business palaces. He was simply capable of opening many prominent doors, and that rather unique quality gave him the edge. However, when it later (in 2002) became evident that ABB was not the success that had been assumed, and Barnevik's managerial capacity and remuneration publicly was questioned, he became a burden as Chair of Investor. In that situation the Wallenbergs took the lead and replaced him with Dahlbäck.

From his position as Chair of Investor, Barnevik asked Berggren to leave Stora. That decision was supported by (among others) Dahlbäck and Marcus Wallenberg Jr. Rather soon, Barnevik removed Berggren also from his other positions in the Wallenberg/Investor sphere. An undesired side effect of that exclusion was that the long and close relationship between the 'radar pair' Berggren and Dahlbäck was spoilt. To Berggren his exclusion from the sphere was a heavy blow, as he had invested most of his professional life trying to make its corporations flourish.

Soon after taking up his duties, the new CEO Hägglund announced his strategy. His priority was to develop Stora's engagements in Brazil and China and make its current European plants more productive. He also presented an extensive analysis of Stora's competitors, covering everything from capital structures to machine qualities and suggested a future path for Stora based on this analysis. That long-term vision included more down-to-earth elements like vast write-downs for certain less productive units (Hillegrossen, Dalum, Mölndal and Newton Kyme), which were simultaneously put on the selling list.[276]

During the first half of 1998 Stora's board composition changed significantly. Deputy Chair Jacob Wallenberg Jr left and was succeeded by his cousin Marcus Wallenberg Jr. At the same time, Berggren was forced to leave as Chair (cf. above) and was replaced by Dahlbäck. Directors Söderberg, Wachtmeister, former CEO Helgesson and Marcus also vacated their seats on Stora's board. Marcus resigned because he was upset about how his friend Berggren had been treated by Stora's leading actors.

12.4 A MERGER WITH FINNISH ENSO-GUTZEIT

Already in 1996, an American investment bank contacted Stora and informed some of its leading actors that the Finnish state was looking for a partner for Enso-Gutzeit. That early informal contact led nowhere. By 1997, however, Stora Chair Berggren took up the idea again and began to talk about it inside the company.[277] Despite these tentative efforts, it came as a big surprise that Stora soon afterwards contacted the one company that it all along had most decidedly put aside as a potential partner. It was Berggren who approached Enso-Gutzeit's CEO Härmälä, and who later asked Knuts to go to Helsingfors and try to estimate the potential synergies of a merger.[278] At the time, both the major shareholder and the board opposed a merger between the two companies. One important reason for that resistance was that they still saw Enso-Gutzeit's state ownership as an almost insuperable obstacle. However, after some time, Berggren learned that the state ownership in Enso-Gutzeit might be removed and informed Dahlbäck about that unexpected possibility. That opening made it possible to recommence the investigations concerning what a merger would mean for both of the involved corporations.[279]

Some actors saw the explanation for the surprising signal that the Finnish state was open to abandoning its shareholding in Enso-Gutzeit in the Wallenberg family's favourable reputation in that country. In fact, Marcus Wallenberg Jr was soon asked to present the family's well-documented staying power in the Finnish Parliament. Like the whole

Wallenberg family,[280] Investor Chair Barnevik supported the merger, but he took no leading position in the subsequent discussions. It was instead the experienced dealmaker and new Stora Chair Dahlbäck that replaced Berggren as Stora's chief negotiator.

Stora's main actors saw two problems with a merger with Enso-Gutzeit. The first obstacle was that Enso-Gutzeit was a state-controlled company. The second one was that its corporate culture was 'super-Finnish'.[281] Thus, it was not primarily business mismatches that created doubts and reluctance. Nevertheless, Enso-Gutzeit was seen as a 'somewhat odd' but well-invested corporation that, because of its state shareholding, had been ascribed for a long time a (too) low value. The latter fact 'favoured' Stora and ended in a 60–40 valuation (yet the voting rules were set to 50–50). The merger was expected to generate SEK 2–3 billion in synergy effects foremost through more effective production, improved logistics and purchasing and better marketing and administration.

The Finnish state insisted upon certain provisions when the merger talks began. Enso-Gutzeit's CEO Härmälä had to be the new constellation's CEO; without this, the government was reluctant to go to the Finnish Parliament and ask it to unlock the shareholding situation. Härmälä's position was particularly strong both because of his impressive track record in Enso-Gutzeit and because state-owned Finnish corporations lacked the board level. He was also an able 'amateur politician', who often got the Finnish Prime Minister 'on his side'. Barnevik, one of the two obvious Swedish Chair candidates, also favoured the appointment of a Finnish CEO, as he thought that such leadership would be good for the 'low performing' Stora units. However, as Barnevik prioritized his assignment as Chair of the Swedish–English pharmaceutical corporation AstraZeneca, he was not a candidate for the same position in Stora.[282] So, the other Swedish candidate, Dahlbäck, became Stora Enso's first Chair (and Härmälä its first CEO).

Moreover, Enso-Gutzeit management was in a most advantageous situation, since Stora recently had forfeited much of its forest-based industry experience, when Chair Berggren, CEO Helgesson and several 'up-and-coming men' had either left or been dismissed. Added to that, Enso-Gutzeit's managers had noted that Stora Enso's new Chair Dahlbäck was primarily a financial strategist and that Stora Enso's new Deputy CEO Hägglund only had been Stora's CEO for a short period. While it was recognized that Hägglund knew the forest-based industry very well, he was regarded as too 'green' to take the lead in such a demanding management situation. Therefore, it was not particularly surprising that the Finnish managers favoured the merger – they saw lots of opportunities for themselves. Since Härmälä recruited basically a Finnish top management team to Stora Enso, Stora had to console itself with the pricing of its shares. Former Stora Chair Berggren, the actor who had initiated and promoted the whole merger project, finally ended up completely outside the new constellation.[283]

The idea to merge Stora and Enso-Gutzeit arose after Hägglund's informal appointment as the new Stora CEO in September 1997, but before that promotion was made public in December 1997. In the meantime neither Hägglund nor Deputy CEO Petersson were informed about Chair Berggren's discussions with Enso-Gutzeit's CEO Härmälä. At the same time as the merger idea materialized, the influence of its originator and strongest promoter Berggren rapidly weakened, and Barnevik intervened and asked Dahlbäck to take over the negotiations. Hägglund and his Deputy CEO were not involved in the merger talks until about three months before Hägglund's formal entrance as the new Stora CEO (March 1998).[284] Hägglund's acceptance of the merger was probably very important; otherwise Stora might have faced severe difficulties in carrying out the whole idea.

Barnevik and Dahlbäck convinced Hägglund that a merger with Enso-Gutzeit was a good idea, and despite the fact that his acceptance meant that he lost his new job as CEO of Stora, Hägglund decided to support the merger project and 'step down' and accept becoming Deputy CEO of the new constellation.[285] On 2 June 1998 both corporate boards confirmed 'the merger of equals', which made Stora Enso the largest forest-based corporation in the world and the leading actor in Europe in its core areas. The company consisted of 48 plants (94 machines) and 40 000 employees and had a turnover that exceeded SEK 90 billion. However, the five largest forest-based corporations in the world together only produced 15 per cent of the global output, so Stora Enso's leading position was on a fragmented market.

The formal merger procedure included, inter alia, a decision in the Finnish Parliament to delete the clause that specified that the state should control (at least) one-third of the votes in Enso-Gutzeit. It also foresaw an application to the EU to obtain clearance for the merger. An EGM then confirmed the full integration of the companies (given that certain conditions were fulfilled). Enso-Gutzeit was to acquire all Stora shares, and it offered Stora's shareholders the chance to exchange each of their B-shares against 0.50829 Enso-Gutzeit A-shares and 1.45142 Enso-Gutzeit R-shares. At the end of the exchange period (December 1998), Enso-Gutzeit had acquired 96 per cent of both the votes and the capital in Stora.

In November 1998 the EU approved the merger although with certain stipulations. In December the company name was changed to Stora Enso, and the same month it became listed on the Finnish and Swedish stock markets. In January 1999 the outstanding shares were redeemed.

NOTES

N.B.: When there is an 'i' inside a parenthesis below, that letter indicates that the note refers to an interview with the named person. All interviewees are listed in the Appendix. A complete listing of references is found at the end of the book.

1. Olsson (1986).
2. Ibid.
3. Stora (1994) and Berggren (2004i and 2005i).
4. Ibid.
5. Hägg (1987).
6. Brantingson (1994).
7. Four times a Nordic birch.
8. Paues (1998) and Sjögren (2005).
9. Cf. Ericson (1991) and Sjöstrand (1997).
10. Höök and Kihlström (1983).
11. Grafström (2006i).
12. Höök and Kihlström (1983).
13. Engman, quoted in Brantingson (1994).
14. Hägg (1987).
15. In early 1984, Wall approached Iggesund to find out if its major owner was interested in buying half of his Billerud holdings.
16. However, some sources claim that it instead was Wallenberg who asked Wall if he wanted to sell.
17. Brantingson (1994).

18. Dahlbäck (2004i and 2007i).
19. Brantingson (1994).
20. Ingvar Petersson (2004i).
21. Brantingson (1994).
22. Peter Wallenberg (2005i).
23. For two shares in Billerud, Stora Kopparberg offered a convertible debenture (SEK 250; 8%) and cash (SEK 400).
24. Berggren, quoted in Berggren et al. (1985).
25. Brantingson (1994).
26. Berggren (2004i and 2005i) and Dahlbäck (2004i and 2007i).
27. Ibid.
28. Berggren, quoted in Brantingson (1994).
29. The name 'Stora' had already been suggested back in the 1960s, but Jacob Wallenberg Sr and Marcus Wallenberg Sr turned down the proposal.
30. A large Swedish ball bearing company.
31. Brantingson (1994).
32. Peter Wallenberg (2005i).
33. A pulp and paper producing company.
34. Two other Wallenberg companies controlled 22% (Providentia 12% and Patricia 10%).
35. Brantingson (1994) and Dahlbäck (2004i and 2007i).
36. The dispute was resolved in 1989.
37. Persson, quoted in Brantingson (1994).
38. Brantingson (1994).
39. Ingvar Petersson (2004i).
40. Brantingson (1994).
41. Ibid.
42. Hägg (1987).
43. Berggren (2004i and 2005i).
44. A large Swedish industry company. In 1988 it merged with the Swiss company Brown, Boveri & Cie (BBC) to form ASEA Brown Boveri (ABB).
45. Peter Wallenberg (2005i).
46. Dahlbäck (2004i and 2007i) in Hägg (1987).
47. Hylte started its first newsprint machine in 1972 and two more followed in 1974 and 1979. That made Hylte one of the biggest newsprint producers in the world, and it was at the time the most profitable forest-based company in Sweden.
48. Berggren (2004i and 2005i).
49. Dahlbäck (2004i and 2007i).
50. Papyrus's shareholders were then offered three alternatives: (1) for each share in Papyrus they would get one share in Stora and one convertible debenture (nominal value: SEK 160; 8.5% rate); (2) for each share in Papyrus they would get one share in Stora, one convertible debenture (nominal value: SEK 80; 8.5% rate) and SEK 144 in cash; and (3) for seven shares in Papyrus they would get thirteen shares in Stora.
51. Ingvar Petersson (2004i).
52. Ibid.
53. Brantingson (1994).
54. Ibid.
55. Dahlbäck (2004i and 2007i).
56. Brantingson (1994) and Grafström (2006i).
57. Dahlbäck (2004i and 2007i).
58. Peter Wallenberg (2005i).
59. Brantingson (1994).
60. Peter Wallenberg, quoted in Brantingson (1994).
61. Dahlbäck (2004i and 2007i).
62. A Swedish investment company.
63. Peter Wallenberg (2005i).
64. Thunholm (2005).
65. Nobel Industries was created in 1984 by a merger of the Swedish chemical firm KemaNobel with the Swedish weapons maker Bofors.
66. Brantingson (1994) and Lindgren (1994).
67. Brantingson (1994) and Berggren (2004i and 2005i).
68. SEK 150 was offered for each A-share (free as well as restricted) in Swedish Match, and SEK 137 for

every free B-share. Stora was also willing to pay SEK 145.25 for the convertibles (nominally set to SEK 83). The day before the offering, the A-share price was SEK 120 and the B-share price SEK 107 (thus, the premium was 20–25%).
69. Brantingson (1994).
70. Brantingson (1994), Berggren (2004i and 2005i) and Ingvar Petersson (2004i).
71. Brantingson (1994).
72. Ibid.
73. Mogren (2004i).
74. Palmstierna (2004i).
75. Dahlbäck (2004i and 2007i).
76. E.g. Affärsvärlden.
77. Berggren, quoted in Brantingson (1994).
78. Knuts (2005i).
79. Hagelin (2004i).
80. Brantingson (1994).
81. Mogren (2004i).
82. Brantingson (1994).
83. Stora Annual Report 1989.
84. Palmstierna (2004i).
85. Hagelin (2004i) and Ingvar Petersson (2004i).
86. Ingvar Petersson (2004i).
87. Hagelin (2004i) and Ingvar Petersson (2004i).
88. Source: interviews with leading actors in the merging companies.
89. Ingvar Petersson (2004i).
90. Dahlbäck (2004i and 2007i).
91. Brantingson (1994).
92. Palmstierna (2004i) and Berggren (2004i and 2005i).
93. Kallifatides et al. (2010).
94. European Community (EC) until November 1993, when the European Union (EU) was established.
95. Peter Wallenberg, quoted in Brantingson (1994).
96. Berggren (2004i and 2005i).
97. Ibid.
98. Hagelin (2004i).
99. Knuts (2005i).
100. Koninklijke Nederlandse Papierfabrieken.
101. Brantingson (1994).
102. Knuts (2005i).
103. Berggren (2004i and 2005i).
104. Hagelin (2004i).
105. Dahlbäck (2004i and 2007i).
106. Knuts (2005i).
107. Ibid.
108. Dahlbäck (2004i and 2007i).
109. Sociedade Portuguesa de Cellulose SA.
110. Knuts (2005i).
111. Investimentos e Participacões Empresariais.
112. Dahlbäck (2004i and 2007i).
113. Ibid.
114. Knuts (2005i).
115. Dahlbäck (2004i and 2007i).
116. Berggren (2004i and 2005i).
117. Dahlbäck (2004i and 2007i).
118. Dahlbäck (2004i and 2007i), Hägglund (2005i) and Ingvar Petersson (2004i).
119. Dahlbäck (2004i and 2007i).
120. Ingvar Petersson (2004i).
121. Ibid.
122. Berggren (2004i and 2005i).
123. Sjöstrand et al. (2001).
124. Peter Wallenberg (2005i).
125. Berggren (2004i and 2005i).
126. Ingvar Petersson (2004i).

127. Berggren (2004i and 2005i).
128. A manufacturing company (heating products).
129. A chemical and weapons company.
130. 5%.
131. Brantingson (1994).
132. Dahlbäck (2004i and 2007i).
133. Brantingson (1994).
134. Peter Wallenberg, quoted in Brantingson (1994).
135. A German state owned energy company ('Vereinigte Elektrizitäts- und Bergwerks AG').
136. Brantingson (1994) and Investor (1991).
137. Brantingson (1994).
138. Ibid.
139. Investor (1991).
140. Dahlbäck (2004i and 2007i).
141. Brantingson (1994).
142. Ibid.
143. Brantingson (1994).
144. Dahlbäck (2004i and 2007i) and Berggren (2004i and 2005i).
145. Ibid.
146. Investor (1991) and Grafström (2006i).
147. Sjöstrand et al. (2001).
148. Berggren, interviewed in the Swedish business weekly 'Veckans Affärer', quoted in Investor (1991).
149. Dahlbäck (2004i and 2007i).
150. Grafström (2006i).
151. Dahlbäck (2004i and 2007i).
152. A German paper mill.
153. Ingvar Petersson (2004i).
154. Berggren (2004i and 2005i).
155. Palmstierna (2004i).
156. Hägglund (2005i).
157. Knuts (2005i).
158. Brantingson (1994).
159. Grafström (2006i).
160. Brantingson (1994).
161. Metallgesellschaft was one of Germany's largest industrial conglomerates.
162. Berggren (2004i and 2005i) and Ingvar Petersson (2004i).
163. Grafström (2006i).
164. A tissue producer.
165. Grafström (2006i).
166. Mogren (2004i).
167. Investor (1991).
168. Ingvar Petersson (2004i).
169. Knuts (2005i).
170. Helgesson (2004i).
171. Jacob Wallenberg Jr (2006i).
172. Helgesson (2004i).
173. Berggren (2004i and 2005i).
174. Helgesson (2004i).
175. Ibid.
176. Berggren (2004i and 2005i).
177. Grafström (2006i).
178. Berggren (2004i and 2005i).
179. Source: managers in the Stora organization.
180. Knuts (2005i).
181. Berggren (2004i and 2005i).
182. Source: managers in the Stora organization.
183. Hägglund (2005i).
184. Knuts (2005i).
185. Garphyttan developed and manufactured advanced spring wire.
186. Mogren (2004i).
187. Peter Wallenberg (2005i).

188. Palmstierna (2004i).
189. Hagelin (2004i).
190. Dahlbäck (2004i and 2007i).
191. Due to family reasons (source: Helgesson 2004i).
192. Hagelin (2004i).
193. Helgesson (2004i).
194. Grafström (2006i).
195. Ibid.
196. Hägglund (2005i).
197. Source: managers in the Stora organization.
198. Hägglund (2005i).
199. Helgesson (2004i).
200. Knuts (2005i) and Marcus Wallenberg Jr (2005i).
201. A large Swedish insurance company.
202. A large Swedish state-controlled pension fund.
203. Source: board minutes (publication of the content approved by Dahlbäck in 2007).
204. Dahlbäck (2004i and 2007i).
205. Ingvar Petersson (2004i).
206. Hägglund (2005i).
207. Helgesson (2004i).
208. Source: the CEO's overhead material and other similar documents.
209. Down 20–25% (1991–92).
210. Helgesson (2004i).
211. It could use 50% waste paper.
212. Source: board minutes (publication of the content approved by Dahlbäck in 2007).
213. Source: board minutes (publication of the content approved by Dahlbäck in 2007) and slides from Helgesson (2004i).
214. Helgesson (2004i).
215. Source: Helgesson's text in Stora's Annual Report 1992.
216. Hägglund (2005i).
217. Helgesson (2004i).
218. Hägglund (2005i).
219. Dahlbäck (2004i and 2007i).
220. Some actors claimed Knuts was the one that pushed for the sale, but he claimed that he was ordered to execute the pull-out (Marcus Wallenberg Jr [2005i]).
221. Berggren (2004i and 2005i).
222. Scandinavian Airlines.
223. A Swedish IT company.
224. Part of Helgesson's statement in Stora's Annual Report 1994.
225. Source: Helgesson's slides.
226. Marcus Wallenberg Jr (2005i).
227. Among other things, that figure included a rather spectacular investment (SEK 3 billion) in an advanced cardboard machine at Skoghall foremost intended for beverage cartons. That product segment had shown healthy growth numbers particularly in parts of Asia.
228. However, Helgesson himself did not regard that list as particularly important (Helgesson [2004i]).
229. Source: board minutes (publication of the content approved by Dahlbäck in 2007).
230. Later the Finnish forest-based company United Paper Mills (UPM) bought Haindl.
231. Ingvar Petersson (2004i).
232. Source: board minutes (publication of the content approved by Dahlbäck in 2007).
233. Ibid.
234. Stora Annual Report 1997.
235. Low timber costs due to plantation forests where eucalyptus trees grow ten times faster than 'corresponding' Nordic trees.
236. Helgesson (2004i).
237. Berggren (2004i and 2005i).
238. Ingvar Petersson (2004i).
239. Knuts (2005i) claimed that he led the group.
240. Berggren (2004i and 2005i).
241. Helgesson's text in Stora's annual report.
242. Stora was at the time no.2 in LWC and no.3 in SC paper.
243. Source: board minutes (publication of the content approved by Dahlbäck in 2007).

244. Grafström (2006i).
245. Ibid.
246. A claim on a company that is placed after a loan but before equity.
247. Roughly at the same time, Stora also invested substantially in property and rootstock in the Azores, an effort that was intended to support a new production line at Celbi, but those purchases turned out to be unprofessionally made (the estates were difficult to locate and there were restrictions regarding felling, etc). Source: board minutes (publication of the content approved by Dahlbäck in 2007).
248. Marcus Wallenberg Jr (2005i).
249. Jacob Wallenberg Jr (2006i).
250. Dahlbäck (2004i and 2007i).
251. Hägglund (2005i).
252. Knuts (2005i).
253. Helgesson (2004i).
254. Berggren (2004i and 2005i).
255. Berggren (2004i and 2005i), Hägglund (2005i) and Ingvar Petersson (2004i).
256. LWC; it was bought long ago by former Stora CEO Erik Sundblad.
257. Berggren (2004i and 2005i).
258. Helgesson (2004i).
259. Ibid.
260. Ibid.
261. Lillius was the main candidate.
262. Berggren (2004i and 2005i).
263. Ingvar Petersson (2004i).
264. Dahlbäck (2004i and 2007i).
265. Dahlbäck (2004i and 2007i).
266. Source: board minutes (publication of the content approved by Dahlbäck in 2007).
267. Berggren (2004i and 2005i) and Ingvar Petersson (2004i).
268. Grafström (2006i) and Hägglund (2005i).
269. Marcus Wallenberg Jr (2005i).
270. Dahlbäck (2004i and 2007i).
271. Ingvar Petersson (2004i).
272. 'The Helgesson case' also had a broader impact within the Swedish business society. From then most discharges had to be more brutal, because it had become apparent that a board had to be very explicit in stating its dissatisfaction with a dismissed CEO; otherwise the 'golden parachute' could not be released.
273. Berggren (2004i and 2005i).
274. Marcus Wallenberg Jr (2005i).
275. Berggren (2004i and 2005i).
276. Dahlbäck (2004i and 2007i).
277. Grafström (2006i).
278. Knuts (2005i).
279. Dahlbäck (2004i and 2007i).
280. Marcus Wallenberg Jr (2005i).
281. Berggren (2004i and 2005i).
282. Dahlbäck (2004i and 2007i).
283. Ingvar Petersson (2004i).
284. Berggren (2004i and 2005i), Ingvar Petersson (2004i) and Hägglund (2005i).
285. Hägglund (2005i).

13. SCA: the search for a new core business

13.1 STRENGTHENING SCA

13.1.1 Organizing Activities

As already introduced briefly in Chapter 5, SCA's development from 1929 to the 1950s was largely influenced by its attempts to integrate a dozen independent organizations. The process had to be carried out in two steps: first, the establishment of regional groupings and then the formation of an integrated corporation. SCA's leading actors were supportive, and initially they wanted to see strong subsidiaries that dominated their regional markets; later they intended to exploit the potential scale advantages inherent in the grouping as a whole. The controlling bank (Handelsbanken) also backed that two-step strategy because it would simplify a future sell-out of (units of) SCA. In a memo, Ernfrid Browaldh (Deputy CEO of the bank) addressed the organizing issue, providing both a description of the merits of the suggested grouping and a sketch of an imagined holding company. His organizational chart for SCA also outlined a possible division of responsibility between the mother company and the rather independent subsidiaries.[1]

Apart from the efforts to co-ordinate the mother company with its relatively autonomous subsidiaries, there were also strong forces that favoured rationalization of the central units and the idea to move the group's HQ from Stockholm to Sundsvall. The HQ re-location would put top management in closer contact with the company's everyday operations. Local patriotism also played a role in the discussion. Once the decision was finally made to re-locate the HQ, Hèrnod, one of the founding fathers of SCA, could focus his efforts on making SCA a cohesive unit.[2] However, he had to face the fact that the juridical form chosen (a holding company with subsidiaries) indicated that SCA was thought of more as a 'pooling' of companies than as an integrated unit. Still, however, the 'classic' central functions (purchase, production and sales) had a strong position in the grouping.[3]

Hèrnod left SCA in 1947 and was succeeded by Göransson, who had worked as CEO in one of the subsidiaries. At the same time, the HQ finally was moved to Sundsvall, leaving 'only' the sales unit in Stockholm. Axel Enström became the new Deputy CEO at SCA (leaving the same position at subsidiary Holmsund) and CEO of its central administrative unit. Together the HQ re-location and Enström's appointment speeded up the transformation of SCA towards an integrated corporate entity. That change occurred when it became obvious that the presence of many highly autonomous subsidiaries had created problems for the company as a whole. The far-reaching decentralization had produced tough internal competition regarding raw material sourcing, customers and investments (the last did not always find its way to the best plants). The mother company also found it problematic to grasp the subsidiaries' economic results, as their accounting systems differed.[4]

SCA's new integrated character manifested in many forms, including the way it recruited and used its personnel. For example, in 1948 the company introduced works councils, and in 1951 it began to employ forest workers on a more continuous basis – a general agreement guaranteed employees 240 days of work annually. Also in 1951 SCA launched certain social funds that offered the employees compensation that lay outside the 'standard' benefits.[5]

13.1.2 Ownership Changes

All through the 1930s and during the first half of the 1940s, SCA experienced substantial economic problems. As such there was room for neither grand investments nor bold ventures. Profit was low, and some years SCA even showed a loss (but that was basically due to heavy write-offs made to consolidate the company). SCA sought to improve its financial situation by selling several power plants to Sydkraft.[6] Despite the tough economic situation, SCA decided to try to escape its strong dependence on bulk production. It had already taken a first step in that direction in 1929 when it began to bleach its sulphite pulp at Essvik (both Svartvik and Ortviken followed suit). The second step taken much later was the introduction of sulphate pulp bleaching at Östrand in 1943. The selling of bleached pulp improved the company's economic result, partly because it was possible to add timber of a lower quality and partly because prices were better and more stable.[7]

Wenner-Gren took control of SCA in 1934 and acted as its Chair 1935–39 (cf. Ch. 5). He stayed as its dominant shareholder until 1947, when Handelsbanken bought him out. However, he had lost both ownership share and influence already in 1943, when SCA's equity was written down by two-thirds. That year SCA also transferred both (most of) its holdings in Bergvik & Ala and its shares in a large power plant to Handelsbanken. At the time, Hèrnod's ambitions for SCA did not fully correspond with those of Handelsbanken's CEO Ernfrid Browaldh, who was eager to separate the bank from SCA and have the bank's SCA shares placed on the market. However, Handelsbanken's board was reluctant to sell – most directors claimed that SCA had not yet reached its optimum size as a company group. They also saw a risk that a new controlling owner could split up SCA, and that would take the company even further away from an effective size. So, finally, Browaldh gave up and called off the planned sale.[8]

Encouraged by Browaldh, the bank moved both Bergvik & Ala and Hammarforsens Kraft to a new holding company named Industrivärden (later SCA's biggest shareholder). At the same time, Handelsbanken also used its right to convert a debenture loan to stock, thereby becoming SCA's majority owner (80%). Wenner-Gren disliked that change in control, so in 1946, in a letter to the bank, he offered a 25 per cent premium for all SCA shares – not just for those controlled by Handelsbanken. The bank, however, was far from interested. Instead, it decided to reject all upcoming private bids for SCA, and guaranteed the current shareholders (i.e. foremost itself) preferential rights in all future issues of shares.[9]

SCA's financial status improved significantly during the second half of the 1940s. In 1946, its solidity had gone from bad to good. The Swedish devaluation in 1949 also favoured the forest-based industry, and post-WWII the boom times released SCA from its financial linkage to Handelsbanken. That move made it possible for SCA to work more independently and explore ways to get out of its strong dependence on pulp.[10] In practice, that path had been closed for about 15 years, although SCA had considered possible ways to further process its production as early as 1931. CEO Hèrnod had suggested forward integration towards (fine) paper and/or cardboard, but the board had hesitated. It was not until 1943 that he could take such an initiative. He also commissioned a study to find out whether newsprint might be a lucrative path for SCA. However, the sales department opposed it claiming poor profitability, so nothing happened during that decade either.[11]

When SCA's economic standing improved around 1950, it became possible for Handelsbanken to sell its SCA holding on the market. The bank controlled 99.8 per cent of the shares, so only 0.2 per cent was in other (private) hands. Rather soon, it also became possible to introduce SCA shares on the SSE. Its new issue of shares covered 75 per cent of the stock, and the holders of the bank's preference stock bought most of the available shares. Substantial portions were also placed at Industrivärden, the bank's Pension Foundation and at a bank-friendly consortium (to secure the business link between the bank and SCA).[12]

13.1.3 A Grand Merger

Enström, who became CEO in 1950, was the one that established the more integrated SCA. Although he was the driving force, he listened carefully to other people and considered their advice. His own modest background and upbringing probably contributed to his social engagement and genuine care for all employees. That together with his personal action rationality won him respect in most circles, including among union leaders. One of his successors in SCA's top management, Wahlström,[13] was told by Enström that it was the company that should be rich – not necessarily the shareholders or its top management. According to Enström, a rich company could make big, well-thought-out, and concentrated investments that could generate a bright future. Then the shareholders would get decent dividends, the management respectable salaries and the employees both fair wages and job security.

Enström started his tenure as CEO by presenting the board an investment plan that would make SCA a more integrated unit. According to the plan, a company group perspective had to replace the existing radical decentralization among 'autonomous' subsidiaries.[14] Enström's ideas won the support of both SCA's board and Handelsbanken's leading actors – they, too, saw it necessary to make one cohesive organization out of the many unco-ordinated units. So, in 1954, the mother company and the subsidiaries formally merged. At the same time, Enström moved the important entities from Stockholm to Sundsvall – including the high-status sales unit.[15] The merger also included a transformation of the central administrative company ('Sundsvallsbolagens Gemensamma Förvaltning') into a timber-sourcing unit (SCA Timmerförvaltning).[16] At the time (1955), SCA also added timber resources by acquiring Kungsgården-Marieberg. Moreover, most power resources were collected in a separate company (later named Bålforsens Kraft [BÅKAB]), and a manufacturing unit was also created (Sunds Verkstäder).

13.2 THE TRANSFORMATION OF SCA

13.2.1 A Focus on Paper

Until 1935, SCA's units basically produced and sold various qualities of unbleached pulp. Bleaching eventually became important, but otherwise very little happened, basically due to SCA's poorly integrated organization structure. One exception during the 1940s, however, was SCA's establishment of a new centralized R&D organization, which was composed of three units: The Technical Council (composed of the CEOs of SCA's subsidiaries), The Technical Bureau (a kind of secretariat) and the so-called 'TIF-operations' (housing both research initiatives and laboratories).[17] These three units became part of the 'Industrial Unit' at SCA's HQ. That centralization was made to stimulate co-operation between all technical specialists in the company.

However, the new R&D organization's greatest impact did not become evident until the 1950s, when Ortviken was established (cf. below). The investment in Ortviken was a consequence of SCA's ambition to expand, based both on technical progress and on ideas about the merits of scale. At the time, SCA had to adapt to the more differentiated product mix and to the new ways of selling forest products that had evolved in Europe. Moreover, each new venture had become more risky, as the competitors' investments had increased dramatically. That, in turn, stimulated a planning rationale and an active interest in what the other actors in the industry prepared and implemented. Thus, strategic thinking and acting required much more investigation of possible future markets and emerging production opportunities than ever before. One consequence of all these changing circumstances was that longer time horizons and advanced business plans saw the light of day.

Although all of SCA's sulphate plants were regarded as too small by the end of the 1940s, very little had happened during that decade to change the situation. Suggestions to build a unit for kraft paper at Östrand and a unit for fluting at Munksund were never realized.[18] Still, it was during that period that SCA seriously began to review the opportunities for large-scale paper production of some kind. That path was motivated both by the lack of timber for increased pulp production and by the cost advantages following from a combine (an integrated pulp and paper unit). Of course, there were also drawbacks associated with entering the paper market. It might be dangerous to compete with one's own pulp customers, particularly as the European paper producers began to worry about such a development. Therefore, SCA concluded that a new paper investment had to be concentrated (i.e. covering a limited range of qualities and executed within a brief period of time), and done on a relatively large scale. Otherwise, there was an increased risk that some European countries would introduce new customs and/or other trade barriers (pulp was duty-free).[19]

The crucial question was on what kind of paper SCA ought to concentrate its efforts. Thorough investigations were conducted to seek an answer, and as half of SCA's pulp export before WWII had gone to the other side of the Atlantic Ocean, the US market and its leading corporations were included in the analyses. SCA was actually one of the few really big Swedish pulp exporters during the decade after WWII.[20] However, already early in the 1950s, the situation began to change – the Swedish pulp export to the US declined, and rather soon the US's exports to Europe surpassed the quantities that went the opposite way.[21] That development was to a large extent explained by the low timber price in North America, but also by efficiency advantages following from the fact that several US pulp and paper plants became organized as 'combines'.

SCA identified newsprint as a particularly interesting path. That product was already produced at its Matfors unit, and the market was considered expansive. The political risks were seen as low – import restrictions were regarded as less likely than for other kinds of paper. Newsprint was also attractive for another reason: the producers were rather few and foremost Nordic. They also co-operated regarding technical and commercial matters, and ran a cartel-like system for regulating market output and prices.[22] So, rather soon after WWII a study was launched to find out if an investment in a new newsprint plant could be profitable. The idea was to add one to four paper machines next to Kramfors's sulphite plant and thus take advantage of its existing infrastructure.

Initially (November 1951) the board approved the idea, but shortly thereafter it reversed its decision as a result of a comparison between the newsprint path and a modernization of Kramfors's sulphite plant.[23] The modernization issue also involved a decision about SCA's total future output of unbleached and bleached pulp ([price] competition had increased dramatically for the latter product). The fact that market forecasts indicated much better growth for kraft paper than for newsprint, journal and fine paper ultimately decided the matter. These analyses and comparisons also produced a listing of general criteria for how to rank investments. They should: strengthen the company's competitive capacity by improving product quality, show profit, utilize scale economies, effectively use the company's raw material assets and entail further processing (thereby building opportunities for a profitable future). SCA also decided not to expand its timber business, wood products sales and pulp operations. Taken together, all these statements indicated that SCA wanted to have a more 'concentrated, integrated and differentiated production' – a rather 'wobbling' expansion idea.

Finally, in 1955, market development and financial conditions made an investment in a new paper mill possible, although SCA lacked experience in that kind of production. However, that huge investment did not materialize as an expansion of the Matfors unit, where newsprint was already produced, mainly because of its inappropriate geographical location (expensive timber sourcing, high transportation costs and no harbour). Kramfors was not considered an alternative either, because its recent modernization made investments in a new kind of production unprofitable. CEO Enström was among those who promoted Ortviken as the best place for a newsprint investment; he even suggested that Matfors's production should be moved to that site (but that did not occur). Paradoxically, one of Ortviken's strengths was its bad shape; because the plant was run down and showed only a minor profit (its unbleached sulphite was not competitive), the alternative to a new investment there would have been to close it down entirely.[24]

So, beginning in the 1950s, SCA gradually altered its core business from pulp to paper, which implicitly meant a commitment to continue investing in that new field. Ortviken's first newsprint machine started production in 1958, and already in 1959 a second one followed. Since other forest-based companies were also building newsprint mills at the time, it was important to be among the first to be able to win a strong market position. Another important strategic decision taken then was to expand the bleaching at Östrand, so that all of its production could attain that quality. A sack plant was also discussed as an alternative production line, but it was concluded that it represented a less flexible path, particularly in light of the big newsprint investment that already had been decided.[25]

At about the same time, SCA had become concerned about its large production of unbleached sulphate pulp. Therefore, a special management team investigated whether it was possible to combine it with some kind of paper production or somehow increase the total bleaching capacity. Eventually, SCA decided to go both ways. The team considered various alternatives, and production of paper manufactured in smaller batches was rejected rather quickly since it did not fit with SCA's size and structure – the company was adapted to more bulky productions. SCA also hesitated making sack paper one of its core products because the distribution of raw materials was carried out increasingly in batches, and the investigating team anticipated incipient overcapacity. The possibility to produce fluting was rejected as well, as fluting could not do better than the bleached sulphate pulp.

For kraftliner, however, the future looked much brighter. Its market was increasing considerably (in Europe 15–20% each year), and producers were rather few (most of them were situated in the US). SCA had an advantage in its production of kraftliner, a much better product than testliner, which most of its competitors offered. In the end, SCA decided to invest in the kraftliner field and expand that production at some of its sites. Only Munksund and Östrand were eligible, and as the latter unit was producing an output to which management ascribed a bright future (bleached pulp), the former was chosen. So during 1959–61 Munksund got the liner production, which almost created a compulsion to integrate forward into corrugated.[26] Director Tore Browaldh[27] (board member 1960–80) saw the choice of the liner path at Munksund as a very important strategic decision.[28] At the same time, the unit at Obbola was expanded (unbleached long-fibre sulphate pulp) rather than shut down. The company had decided to keep it, since the board wanted to defend SCA's market share for pulp and saw a possibility that, in the future, Obbola might begin to produce liner.[29]

The market for liner (used in the production of corrugated) was rapidly growing due to changes in the distribution of staples and groceries to retailers. Once the decision to invest in liner was made, SCA began to discuss forward integration into transport packaging. So, in 1959, Head of Technology Hellerqvist and the head of the Munksund group made a journey to the US and observed that the corporations on that continent frequently included production of both liner and corrugated. However, unlike liner, corrugated was often produced in rather small units close to the customers (due to high distribution costs). Therefore, adding production of corrugated did not quite fit with SCA's strategy to be a large-scale producer of bulky products. Nevertheless, the need for knowledge about corrugated in order to deliver suitable liner qualities to its customers swayed SCA's decision to combine the two (one should note that it was liner – not corrugated – that was the 'high status product'[30]). The fact that 80 per cent of US corporations in the field were integrated probably also influenced that decision. So, the idea to integrate forward was soon presented to SCA's board, and the listed pros were safer (i.e. internal) selling of the liner, less exposure for cyclical variations and strong market growth (making healthy profit likely). There was basically one con – the obvious risk that other producers of corrugated would refrain from buying liner from SCA.[31]

13.2.2 Forward Integration and Internalization

Gradually, SCA's planning ambitions grew driven by the 'Working team for R&D' led by CFO Lindström. The team included Chief Technology Officer Hallerström (who became its leading 'philosopher'[32]), incoming CEO Mossberg, Head of Sales Kastrup, Head of Forestry Swan, Head of R&D Tydén and Team Secretary Brändström. The team's general task was to find ways for SCA to utilize its raw material base and industrial tradition in northern Sweden to win advantageous positions on selected markets in both

Europe and North America. With an assignment to focus on both industrial and corporate matters, it soon won a strong position in the company. For example, it evaluated the impact on SCA of the expected European free trade agreements and compared SCA's product costs with those of its international competitors.[33]

In 1960, Eje Mossberg succeeded Enström as CEO. That appointment came as a surprise to many actors. Director Tore Browaldh promoted Mossberg's candidacy and advocated that SCA needed that kind of person – one who (also) mastered political processes. Browaldh considered such a personality as a necessity, given that SCA's profitability was expected to be poor during most of the coming CEO period and that rationalizations and closures would thus be necessary. Mossberg was an appellate attorney, who had been both Minister in a Social Democratic government and Governor, so it was a daring step to appoint him as CEO in a large listed corporation.

Mossberg took full responsibility for the painful restructuring of SCA and consequently also most of the criticism. He claimed that, in order to survive, SCA needed 'full-scale' plants, high product quality and operative efficiency, and that made several closures ($\approx$ 20) unavoidable. Production quadrupled despite the shrinking number of pulp and paper machines. So, in practice, Mossberg delivered almost a 'set table'[34] to his successor. However, as Mossberg was a socially engaged and caring person, he led that necessary transformation with a heavy heart. The massive critique also hit him hard, but he never 'took shelter' behind the Chair or anybody else.[35]

The closures entailed large financial losses, but SCA's main bank Handelsbanken supported Mossberg's ambition to build a strong SCA. Browaldh (Chair of that bank) was simultaneously board member of both SCA and its 'rival' MoDo. That very unusual arrangement might be explained by his diplomatic skill and likeable personality and by the fact that Handelsbanken, which also was the main bank for MoDo, adopted a neutral/passive position. SCA's board (including Browaldh) also kept a low profile during Mossberg's time as CEO, so Browaldh's dual board membership never became a problem. Mossberg listened to the board's opinions on important issues, but (like the shareholders' AGM) the board was a rather weak agency.[36] Still, it had the formal power to decide SCA's future.

In the 1960s, it was no longer considered possible to expand SCA's pulp operations based on Swedish timber only. SCA had to go abroad, a decision that the company shared with many of its competitors. Thus, the bulk of the pulp investments was expected to be shifted from Western Europe to Eastern Europe and developing countries in Asia and the Americas. In its ambition to utilize the cheaper timber and more favourable growing conditions abroad eventually the idea to invest in British Columbia emerged. That same ambition also brought about discussions regarding activities in South America, as even a limited shareholding in a pulp producer on that continent could make it possible and profitable to import pulp to Europe. Later SCA took a step in that direction when its CEO of that time visited Brazilian Aracruz,[37] but despite the attractiveness of that site, SCA refrained from investing because of limited financial resources.[38]

For the other basic non-human input resource – electric power – certain re-arrangements were made. A new company (Korsselbränna) was founded and partially owned by BÅKAB (50%). SCA put much of its power resources in the new construct, while the other parties provided financial capital. A 50–50 construct was chosen to avoid further burdens on SCA's balance sheet. Later (1963) Industrivärden and Handelsbanken's

Pension Foundation together suggested that BÅKAB should be co-ordinated with its other power-producing unit Hammarforsen, as both companies operated in the same geographical region. SCA accepted that solution, although it represented a substantial financial commitment on SCA's part.[39]

In 1961, SCA's board approved Mossberg's strategic plan for the company. Basically, he suggested that the large investments that were needed had to focus on the existing plants to make them more effective. He also wanted them to add to SCA's competitive power by including further processing stages. However, the financial platform for those investments was poor so SCA needed to borrow substantial sums, which weakened its solidity (1959: 45%; 1972: 30%), worried shareholders and affected the share price negatively. However, Swedish financiers supported SCA, as they were well aware of the company's impressive timber and water-power resources. In the mid-1960s, because Handelsbanken was forced by the Swedish Bank Inspection to lower its exposure to the forest-based industry, it had to reduce its lending to SCA. However, other banks immediately entered the scene and solved that problem.[40]

Nordic forests grow slowly, which makes timber expensive and puts extra emphasis on its efficient use. The forests contain lots of spruce, which is a 'long-fibre tree' that possesses certain unique qualities for pulp and paper production. So, eventually it became more and more obvious that it was important for SCA to utilize that fibre advantage. Pushed by Hellerqvist's efforts, SCA therefore decided to aim for fewer and larger production units focusing on Munksund (kraftliner), Obbola (kraftliner), Ortviken (printing paper) and Östrand (pulp). Ultimately, that strategy would result in the closure of many units.[41]

The market prospects for the various kinds of pulp differed significantly. In the 1950s the dramatically declining competitiveness of both bleached and unbleached sulphite pulp led SCA to co-operate with Billerud to try to find a more efficient way to produce a quality suitable for liner. On the basis of initial success, a full-scale unit started test operations in 1963. The new kind of pulp was then used for liner production at a Danish plant, and the liner was tested at several corrugated units. By 1964, after some modifications, the process seemed to work well. So, CEO Mossberg suggested then that SCA change some of its production to that kind of pulp, and in 1965 the board decided that the Kramfors plant should be transformed to a fully integrated unit based on the new pulp process and liner production.[42]

Early in 1966, however, SCA received a message from a German customer, who claimed that the new liner was too brittle to use for corrugated 'in dry circumstances'. As a result, the board decided not to build a new integrated unit at Kramfors. Shutting down the rather small and old existing sulphite plant was for a long time unthinkable, as it was the core unit in a troubled region. SCA had declared several times that it intended to keep Kramfors as a production unit for forest-based products. Thus, there were discussions about adding a newsprint machine at that site (given that Ortviken's planned expansion was postponed). However, by 1968, it became obvious that such an investment in Kramfors would be unprofitable in its own right, and that the new newsprint machines recently set up in the Nordic countries and North America would make such a venture that much more risky. New environmental legislation that went into effect in 1969 made conditions even worse for Kramfors. In 1972, SCA finally decided to close Kramfors and instead build a third paper machine at Ortviken.[43]

CEO Mossberg saw entry on the European market for corrugated and packaging as a priority. It was essential that SCA controlled at least one of the outlets for its pulp, and corrugated was the natural first choice once sacks had been excluded. Already in the late 1950s, with encouragement from the board to try to find international partners in that field, former CEO Enström contacted, for example, Belgian actors with the goal of participating in an investment in Belgian Congo[44] (42%, sold in 1965). Mossberg considered building a packaging plant close to Stockholm, but abandoned the idea after negotiations with the Swedish competitors. Instead, SCA bought a corrugated producer situated in the countryside (Värnamo Wellpappfabrik, 1966).[45] At the time, 'all' Nordic forest-based companies expressed ambitions to integrate forward, so SCA's aspirations were far from unique. The purchase of Spanish Papelera Navarra (50%) in 1961 was the first significant step in SCA's internationalization process. It represented vertical integration, production of cardboard and the opening up of a potential liner market (for sacks). The acquisition of a large holding (40%) in Skeena River followed, establishing a presence for SCA on the US pulp market. Both purchases could be seen as outcomes of a tentative process that was running before the new strategy was finally set. So, most vertical integration paths (i.e. fine papers, graphic papers, hygiene papers and packaging papers) remained open.[46] However, neither of the two foreign investments was successful, so both holdings were rather soon sold.

SCA also expanded its corrugated business to Denmark with its 1963 acquisition of Columbusgruppen, which controlled one-third of that country's market. One year later, SCA, together with a pulp customer,[47] established Colon Emballage, and that new unit became the dominating actor on the Danish market for corrugated. In France, SCA took over one of its large liner customers, Papeteries Léon Clergeau (which owned two corrugated plants), after the big American competitor Weyerhaeuser had shown interest in it. SCA also took over Lutecia, a producer of corrugated located close to Paris, and installed cardboard machines and doubled production (1967). To enter the West German market, SCA began by strengthening its business relationship with Vereinigte Papierwerke Schickedanz (VP), a large producer of paper and cardboard. Thus, by the mid-1960s, SCA concluded that it had reached one of its goals and become an important actor on the European liner market. Only four companies had a larger market share: Reedpack (UK), Bowaters (UK), Container Corporation (US) and International Paper (US).[48]

In 1966, SCA acquired a holding (20%) in a sulphite pulp and printing paper[49] producer, Aschaffenburger Zellstoffwerke (AZ), Germany's third largest forest-based corporation (it actually used some of Östrand's pulp production). Bayerische Hypotheken- und Wechselbank and Landesanstalt für Aufbaufinanzierung (a state-run credit unit), two of the other owners, had sought a partner experienced in the forest-based business. Since SCA fit their 'specifications', it gained control together with Hypo-Bank of more than 50 per cent of AZ's votes. According to the consortium agreement, SCA should take the lead (i.e. manage AZ). Though AZ's machines were relatively small and rather outdated (except at Stockstadt), it had a differentiated product portfolio containing fine paper, wood-free printing paper, fluting, greaseproof paper, carbon paper, paper bags, carrier bags, napkins, and the like. SCA saw that product variety as an advantage – it provided rich opportunities for SCA's management to learn about later production stages and end customers in the pulp processing chain. Not long after SCA's acquisition, AZ merged with Waldhof, the second biggest forest-related business company in West Germany, which produced pulp, paper and paper products (corrugated, cardboard and tissue). Together the two companies formed Papierwerke Waldhof-Aschaffenburg (PWA). SCA kept its leading role also in the new constellation (and got 26% of the votes), and Bayerische Hypotheken- und Wechselbank continued to be its most important partner.[50]

To learn about tissue production and to attract additional users of its bleached pulp, SCA's American sales company bought a holding in Patrician Paper. That purchase also increased SCA's know-how in the food packaging business for possible future production of 'food board' at Östrand. Thus, SCA wanted to get more knowledge about one of the processing stages that follows pulp production to reduce some of the remaining uncertainty about which of the available paths it should choose.

In the 1960s, some of the leading executive actors in the Swedish forest-based industry began informally discussing possible restructuring opportunities. For example, Wallander (leading actor in the Handelsbanken/Industrivärden sphere) and Sundblad (CEO of Stora Kopparberg and a member of the Wallenberg sphere [cf. Ch. 11]) made some proposals about how to proceed and establish serious cross-sphere talks. They realized quickly that both the ownership situation as such (competing spheres) as well as poor personal relationships prevented what looked like rational structural changes. For example, two powerful leaders (Jacob Wallenberg Sr [Stora Kopparberg] and Carl Trygger [Iggesund]) would have to be convinced, and they did not trust each other at all.[51] However, in 1965, something finally happened when SCA and Stora Kopparberg made a 'castling', and Wifstavarf was transferred to SCA and Bergvik & Ala to Stora Kopparberg. SCA's interest in carrying out that swap was explained not solely by geographical conditions and expected synergies, but also – and perhaps foremost – by strategic gains through the elimination of a possible competitor in the upcoming rationalizations in the company's core region.[52]

In the mid-1960s pervasive changes occurred in the global forest-based industry. Until then most pulp, paper and sawn timber had been transported by smaller ships freighting from many harbours. As a consequence, a significant and growing part of the product price consisted of distribution costs. To reduce the cost CEO Mossberg decided that SCA should invest in a new transport strategy developed by internal actors. It was a brave managerial initiative and board decision (1965), as neither the ship owners nor the competitors were willing to participate and invest in new ships and terminals. Another radical change that took place during that period was that the Nordic forest-based companies abandoned timber floating and opted for timber transport by lorries and railways. More generally, technological developments changed many business conditions at the time.[53]

In 1968, SCA created a special unit for planning and co-ordination to make its growth process more solid. Wahlström, later Deputy CEO, became unit head. Since the operative managers did not applaud that solution, however, it was soon abandoned. Instead, SCA reorganized into divisions. SCA also initiated collaboration with its rival MoDo and Canadian Industries to develop a method of using oxygen in the pulp bleaching process. MoDo and Canadian Industries took responsibility for the process development, and MoDo built a pilot plant at Husum (sulphate). SCA's main contribution to the effort was the machines that were built internally at Sunds Verkstäder.[54]

At the same time, to make Sunds more independent of the investment cycles in the pulp business, SCA changed its strategy. Thus, Sunds began to manufacture machines for production of corrugated and to participate in the construction of entire plants. It even started to produce certain equipment for the plastics industry. Sunds also tried to acquire Defibrator – a company with a supplementary product repertoire. For financial reasons Sunds could not buy Defibrator right away, but received an option to buy it later. In 1970, when complications were encountered, SCA (Sunds) abandoned that agreement.[55]

SCA had in fact chosen its long-term international strategy at the end of the 1960s. The company had decided to integrate its output with European producers of corrugated. At the same time, SCA had decided to abandon the idea of investing abroad and utilizing the cheap foreign 'excess timber' that existed in certain regions (e.g. South America). As a consequence of the new strategy and revised business portfolio, SCA changed its location-based organization to a product-based one. Three divisions (i.e. quasi-profit centres) were established: one for pulp and printing paper (Matfors and Ortviken), one for pulp and packaging paper (Munksund, Obbola, Kramfors, Svartvik and Wifsta-Östrand[56]), and one for chemical products, foreign production stakes[57] and corrugated.[58]

13.2.3 Rydin Becomes New CEO

Early in the 1970s, SCA stood at the crossroads and had to make a crucial choice regarding its future involvement in the hygiene sector. The outcome of that decision had its roots in the R&D efforts made back in the mid-1960s. At that time, an engineer at SCA's research laboratory discovered that a water-soluble cellulose derivative together with paper could be used for producing sanitary napkins. In 1968, SCA granted Stille-Werner a licence to produce and sell such napkins on the Nordic market. Based on the success of that effort, SCA became interested in selling that product outside the region as well. When research results indicated that SCA ought to act on its own, it established Sancella in the UK and built a plant in Newcastle (1971). However, because it was not easy to sell a single product to the retailer chains – the big suppliers dominated the scene – the effort was basically unsuccessful.[59]

At that time MoDo's controlling shareholder Carlgren signalled that 'his company' was interested in buying SCA, and that it was prepared to pay well. However, it is unclear if SCA's leading shareholder Industrivärden and SCA's leading actors actually became informed about Carlgren's thoughts, and regardless of this, they did not see MoDo as a serious buyer (both for financial and competence reasons).[60] Instead, SCA considered acting itself on the buying side and analysed both Iggesund and MoDo. Iggesund's packaging business looked interesting, as did its geographical location. However, Iggesund did well, and its top management was unwilling to give up the company's autonomy. MoDo was simply unattainable because of Carlgren's (and other family members') ambitions for that company. Such a solution could only materialize in a severe crisis (then Handelsbanken would act and probably favour[61] SCA).[62]

The early 1970s also saw a shift at the CEO level. Mossberg retired in 1972 and was succeeded by Bo Rydin, an economist who had been on SCA's board since 1970. Rydin had made a great impression on Chair Browaldh and on SCA's main owner Industrivärden's CEO Nils Berggren, both of which had promoted his candidacy. Browaldh had met Rydin already in the early 1960s, when Rydin acted as CFO at Gullhögens Bruk. There he was seen as an up-and-coming CEO. Because Browaldh saw it as most important to keep Rydin inside the Handelsbanken/Industrivärden sphere, he listed him in his book of 'promising young managers'. Rydin was also favoured by some of SCA's top managers, who saw him as a business economist with the aim to improve profitability and please shareholders. Rydin's main competitor was Wahlström, who for a long time had been active in the company, particularly in its restructuring processes (rationalizations and closures), something that probably had hurt his internal popularity.[63] However, like Rydin, Wahlström also had strong supporters, but they lacked the formal positions to tip the coin. By far his strongest merit (aside from his leadership in the restructuring processes and leading role in the establishment of the new shipping system) was that he made the merger with Mölnlycke possible (cf. subsection 13.2.6).[64]

Rydin hesitated to take the assignment as SCA's new CEO, both because the company's situation was rather problematic (e.g. the forests were in bad shape ['thin sticks'], and many plants were run down[65]) and because he had other offers, too (e.g. as CEO of AGA).[66] In the end, it was the opportunity to manage a large Swedish forest-based company that became irresistible for Rydin – that industry was seen as 'Sweden's core business' – so he accepted SCA's proposal.[67] At the same time, Browaldh offered Wahlström the position as Deputy CEO. Eventually, however, realizing that his and Rydin's personalities were too different to allow successful co-operation over a long time period, Wahlström left SCA in 1976.[68] That decision was also triggered by his ambition to become CEO in a large company, and he had several offerings.

With the change of CEO, Brändström, who had been on the planning team under Enström and Mossberg, returned to SCA from a short period at Handelsbanken. Soon he – together with Chair Browaldh – became the person with whom Rydin discussed most issues.[69] Brändström was also the one that eventually succeeded Wahlström as Deputy CEO. Although Rydin initially considered Daun (Deputy CEO, Mölnlycke; cf. subsection 13.2.6), he was convinced about Brändström after having many favourable discussions with SCA directors.[70]

As his predecessor had executed most of the restructuring processes, Rydin had the opportunity to launch an expansion strategy. However, aside from the Mölnlycke acquisition discussed below, he pursued a cautious and conservative strategy.[71] Some managers even described Rydin as an extremely guarded and risk-averse person – as somebody who checked everybody and everything to the greatest extent possible.[72] So, the rather risky acquisition path was not often taken during his period as CEO. Instead, his rationale was tailor-made for a consolidation strategy. Rydin's particular strengths were his understanding of the crucial figures, his superb analyses and proven good judgement.[73] His emphasis on costs and profitability led him to reorganize SCA in a way that corresponded to such a focus. Divisional units stressing economic performance replaced the old cost-focused entities, where the specialist units had substantial influence.[74] All in all, he was seen as a brilliant administrator rather than as an energetic entrepreneur.[75] Some actors also stressed his pedagogical capacity, which made him capable of explaining ideas and decisions to many kinds of actors and audiences.[76]

Rydin's four main goals for SCA were: high self-sufficiency regarding timber, lower dependence on the USD, increased integration of the different businesses and closer relationships with (end) customers.[77] He also wanted to build greater autonomy for SCA vis-à-vis its main bank Handelsbanken, and that required improving most key financial figures. Moreover, as financial resources were limited, SCA sometimes had to use solutions involving divided ownership and control ('the poor man's solution') – it simply could not wait for a better balance sheet to materialize. Such a delay would put SCA on the sidelines when the restructuring process within the forest-based industry really took off. Another financial problem referred to the volatile exchange rate between SEK and USD ('it moved like a stray dog'[78]). The imagined catastrophic situation would combine high Swedish timber prices with a low USD exchange rate. That risk triggered efforts to move away from products that contained lots of timber and reinforced the need to move closer to the end customers. Rydin was particularly keen to learn whether SCA could compete with US producers – and if so, in what fields. Newsprint seemed to be the best alternative, so SCA decided that it should explore that path (the outcome would then influence the future of the Obbola and Ortviken plants). He also wanted to build an SCA that further processed its pulp (and timber), although the transition had to be done in a capital-saving way.[79] Basically, he advocated a strategy where SCA was in control of the whole value chain ranging from forests (timber) and power plants to 'non-bulky' end products.[80] Not long after his start as CEO, Rydin soon received the board's approval to pursue that strategy.

To improve its financial situation and free substantial capital, SCA sold its building material activities (units producing and selling windows, floors, woodwork, etc.) to ASSI and Ncb. Ncb – in particular – was keen to buy units from SCA, and that urge certainly facilitated SCA's restructuring process (cf. Ch. 6). Ncb bought most of the small old plants that SCA wanted to divest. ASSI's interest in some of SCA's units was also driven by a growth strategy (its newly appointed CEO had expressed that ambition).[81] In the case of both ASSI and Ncb, prices became favourable for SCA.

Still Rydin had to deal with the reality that many of the company's production plants were in rather bad shape. Thus, he used a good portion of his first months as CEO visiting production sites and speaking with the leading actors in the forest-based industry. In that way he built a genuine understanding of SCA's operations and its context. When summarizing the situation, he declared that SCA currently operated much like 'a raw material peddler' with a product portfolio that soon could be obsolete.[82] As it turned out then, Rydin did not arrive to a fully 'set table', even though his predecessors had taken care of many of the basic structural problems. He also knew that the company's poor financial situation made 'plant patching' the only possible alternative – larger new investments had to wait. To be able to carry out these rationalizations and closures without agonizing fights, Rydin contacted the Swedish Social Democratic government[83] and the unions and explained SCA's tough situation: SCA needed to carry out radical changes, and for financial (and other) reasons that process had to run 'smoothly' without lots of protests and delays.[84]

Rydin also looked into SCA's PWA engagement (11%). The fact that PWA accounted for 44 per cent of SCA's sales of bleached sulphate pulp and 15 per cent of its liner made it obvious that SCA and PWA had become co-ordinated companies. Thus, the PWA engagement had become of utmost importance for SCA's long-term development.[85] The PWA investment was made to take advantage of a golden opportunity to simultaneously integrate forward and internationalize. Since that investment had crowded out other possible alternatives, it was crucial that it become a success. Rydin therefore asked Wahlström to scrutinize PWA's plants (particularly its pulp producing ones) from both technical and economic perspectives. If his investigations indicated that there could be problems with PWA's profitability in the long run, SCA would try to keep its corrugated operations, but get out of the rest.

In early 1973 Rydin asked Wahlström to test the idea that Bayerische Hypotheken- und Wechselbank should acquire PWA's corrugated business, which would then free PWA to write down its poor plants. SCA and Bayerische Hypotheken- und Wechselbank would then simultaneously establish a new corrugated company in which SCA would put Colon, its Spanish and French companies and SCA Emballage (Sweden). SCA could also put in 25 per cent of Obbola to secure a majority in the new company. SCA would then gain control over a substantial kraftliner market without adding fresh capital (but Bayerische Hypotheken- und Wechselbank preferred a 50–50 ownership). However, in the long run SCA intended to get out of its PWA holding entirely and saw St Regis as a possible buyer.

PWA had considered selling its hygiene business to Mölnlycke (dominated by Custos, but with Industrivärden as an important shareholder). For SCA, it was crucial that the outcome favoured PWA (in which it was a large owner). However, Industrivärden was not interested in owning holdings of the offered type, so the sale did not take place. In addition, since Waldhof produced considerable quantities of corrugated, its owners decided in 1974 to separate that business from PWA and create a new company (Zewawell) in which SCA got 50 per cent of the shares.

SCA's continued co-operation with PWA soon turned into another joint project (at Wifstavarf). SCA was eager to process the fibres in optimal ways to acquire three basic qualities: printability (graphics), protection (packaging) and absorption (hygiene). Yet, Wifstavarf's unprofitable integrated production of pulp and kraft paper did not meet any of those requirements. Liquid packages and liner could not replace current production for technical reasons, but an investment in fine paper might work (together with Östrand's pulp). Because SCA had no experience in the fine paper business, it needed a partner. Fortunately, SCA could build on its well-established co-operation with PWA, as that company certainly knew fine paper. Eventually Wifstavarf was made a separate legal unit owned equally by PWA and SCA. It produced non-coated, bleached wood-free fine paper (rolls), but it quickly became obvious that the selling side (PWA Grafische Papiere) did not function as well as expected. So, SCA gradually took over PWA's ownership in Wifstavarf and became sole owner in 1989.[86]

In his managing, Rydin was a man who combined the use of broad strokes with the mastering of many details. He read many reports thoroughly and spent significant time in seeking to grasp even seemingly trivial details. His background as an MBA led him to listen extra cautiously to technical specialists. Basically, he offered freedom with responsibility and expected managers to take initiatives and make suggestions. His management model thus implied that the operative actors presented ideas, which Rydin carefully evaluated and in the end either approved or rejected. He was also anxious to establish trusting relationships among SCA's top managers, so he encouraged socializing activities (also ones that included spouses).[87] Those interactions were important to him, as he had decided not to use a GMT. Instead, he talked to the top managers one at a time, a model that made him a powerful CEO.

In reality, Swedish CEO's in general were often powerful[88] in those days in comparison with boards and shareholders. That was certainly valid for a company like SCA that lacked a private controlling owner. As a result, share prices and stock market activities were rather seldom prioritized (financial capitalism had not yet began to replace industrial capitalism[89]). Thus, SCA[90] was basically governed by its top executives, and most of them were then in one way or the other associated with the Handelsbanken/Industrivärden sphere. Still, the board process was professionally run, and most of the directors were deeply involved in the company's strategic decisions. Rydin was careful to have correct formal procedures and high-quality material for the board discussions. In fact, those actors that were to be responsible for carrying out the different proposals/decisions were asked to make the presentations and provide the necessary documents. Rydin also established a practice by which important and/or difficult decisions (almost) always had to be dealt with at least two meetings to enable 'second thoughts'. For most efforts and investments SCA was (still) dependent on its main bank Handelsbanken, but that was not a big issue, as its Chair Browaldh had made clear that the bank's support was strong for the path SCA had chosen (thus, a substantial part of the financial risk was taken by the bank).[91]

In 1972, SCA was offered the opportunity to acquire more than its current 50 per cent holding of Spanish Papelera Navarra, but Rydin was hesitant. SCA had not yet decided what path to follow, and Papelera Navarra's pulp and paper machines were regarded as too small. Still, he visited the company during the first part of 1973 and talked to one of the major owners, and a holding was eventually bought. SCA also initiated a special analysis of Papelera Navarra's operations to identify what investments might be required in the near future. One alternative was to increase the production of corrugated at that plant and let pulp production run down without any substantial new investments. However, it soon became obvious that the investment needs at Papelera Navarra were sizeable. If SCA could not limit its capital input there, selling its holding was almost unavoidable. Rydin therefore visited Papelera Navarra's owners and clarified that SCA had to refrain from participating in the new issue of shares needed for investments in Papelera Navarra's aged pulp and paper production. He also informed them that if Papelera Navarra could not be divided so that SCA could continue as co-owner in its corrugated business, then SCA would have to sell.

13.2.4 Obbola

Packaging had become a core business in SCA in the late 1950s, when a liner plant was built at Munksund. In order to secure demand for the liner and justify the investment, SCA entered the corrugated business. As the packaging business grew in Sweden, several of the producers[92] of raw material for corrugated founded the 'Swedish Development Group for Corrugated' (SUW) in 1968 to learn more about the customers and thus be able to better adapt to their requirements. R&D organizations also existed at the industry level (e.g. STFI and Packforsk), and together with SUW they became a world-leading constellation. Alf de Ruvo, future head of SCA's R&D, led the efforts, which eventually became crucial for SCA Packaging's development.[93]

Obbola was not expected to survive the 1970s as a producer of unbleached sulphate pulp, so some action had to be taken there. The forecast for liner was favourable, and rather few companies or regions had the right timber quality to compete. It was also too risky for SCA to rely on only one machine (Munksund). It was not inevitable, however, that the new liner machine should be built at Munksund – Obbola was also a strong possibility. Munksund's advantage was that a location nearby the existing machine would allow for integration gains, while Obbola's advantage was that a location there eliminated a painful closure (SCA could show social responsibility). Munksund's disadvantage was that the region's timber supply might not be sufficient for another liner machine (ASSI already had two units there). Furthermore, it used a less-well-situated harbour. Obbola had a potentially strong advantage over Munksund in terms of the timber situation: SCA expected that its two regional timber competitors would have to give up in the near future. Their absence would leave room for a new investment, and SCA was eager to prevent other competitors (e.g. ASSI) from entering 'its territory'. Still, the timber sourcing for Obbola could eventually become a problem, as a timber shortage could not be solved by an increased use of waste fibre.[94]

To reduce the timber sourcing risk, Rydin met with a delegation from the Swedish government led by Prime Minister Palme. Rydin stressed that an investment in a liner plant at Obbola would be dependent on substantial timber supply from the state-owned forest company Domänverket. He insisted that if a stable supply could not be arranged, SCA would have to leave Obbola entirely. Though the Swedish constitution prohibited the state-owned company from signing agreements that were valid for longer than five years, Domänverket's DG made clear in a document that his organization intended to continue its business relations with SCA (Obbola) far longer – a statement that made the investment possible (cf. Ch. 6).

Once the decision was made to proceed at the Obbola site, SCA also had to finance the investment, and for this it needed a partner. SCA sought a joint venture for three reasons: the size of the project, the need for subsequent investments (corrugated) and the lack of its own forests in the region. The ideal partner would be a foreign corporation that needed liner for its production of corrugated. Deputy CEO Wahlström therefore contacted Bowaters, Reedpack and a few French producers, but none of them was interested in investing 'upstream'. Instead, both St Regis and International Paper expressed interest.[95] SCA decided to begin discussions with St Regis, one of its relatively big customers.[96] Wahlström went to his good friend working there, and asked him whether St Regis might be interested in becoming part owner of Obbola. Wahlström's friend took the question to the leading shareholder at St Regis, whose friendship with Enström (the former legendary CEO at SCA) made it easier to make the case.[97] Therefore, it did not take long for CEO Rydin and St Regis Chair Kneeland to agree on the price for a St Regis holding (1973). St Regis's decision could also be explained by the fact that increased liner demand in the US had reduced its possibilities to continue exporting to Europe. Obbola's new liner investment made it possible for St Regis to supply its units in continental Europe from Sweden. Such a location had become interesting, as customs duties for liner had been lowered between the EFTA[98] and EEC.[99]

13.2.5 A Few Unsuccessful Attempts

At that time Rydin and his team discussed several strategic paths that did not materialize. In January 1973, Rydin met with the main owner of Graningeverken, Versteegh, who indicated interest in selling his company's forests, but keeping its power plants. Statsföretag (the Swedish state's holding company) had together with ASSI also shown interest in Graningeverken and placed a bid that also included its power resources (which state-owned Vattenfall would absorb). However, disagreements in the Versteegh family prevented such a solution. Eventually SCA lost interest in Graningeverken, both because that company's involvement in Great Lakes Carbon (US) proved to be a fiasco, and because it owned several small plants in Ådalen (Sweden) that had to be closed.[100]

SCA also discussed with Statsföretag's CEO Sköld whether something could be done (together) with ASSI. Sköld's suggestion that ASSI should buy Munksund never took off. Talks held with ASSI's CEO Bahrke regarding co-operation in the liner field also failed to yield any action. Esselte was contacted by SCA about the possibility of co-operating with SCA Emballage, so Rydin met Esselte's CEO Mannerfelt. Since Mannerfelt would not allow SCA to acquire more than 25 per cent, the idea was not pursued further. Several years later (1979) Rydin suspected that Esselte might be planning to sell its large corrugated business and feared that it might be acquired by a competitor (e.g. St Regis). So, Rydin made Esselte's new CEO Wallgren aware of SCA's interest in buying it.[101]

Rydin and Wahlström discussed various strategic options with Enso-Gutzeit in 1973–74. Enso-Gutzeit was experiencing problems with its newsprint operations, while SCA wanted to learn more about how to produce coated paper. The two leaders continued their talks, as they knew that their companies' businesses were basically complementary (Enso-Gutzeit produced mainly processed products, while SCA focused on standardized raw materials). Despite this, however, no substantial joint efforts materialized at the time.

On another front, a Dutch actor that planned to build a plant for coated paper in Holland contacted SCA in order to secure a safe supply of pulp. The Dutch investors offered SCA co-ownership of the plant. In the background, the Dutch government wanted to see the establishment of a modern production of printing paper in the country. At a lunch in his home, Rydin met the Dutch company Van Gelder's CEO Sundstrom, who presented the proposal. The outcome of the talks was not given, since SCA had alternative uses for its pulp. What tempted Rydin in this case was that SCA could learn more about the production and marketing of coated paper. In the end, however, because the price was high and SCA would have had to earmark quite a lot of its pulp production for the Dutch plant, nothing significant materialized out of the talks.[102]

13.2.6 The Acquisition of Mölnlycke

Already in late 1972, it was clear to CEO Rydin that something had to be done about SCA's operations in the hygiene business. One alternative was to sell; the other was to expand organically through investments in R&D and/or through acquisitions. It was simply not possible for SCA to continue running a business that only contained one product that from both a technical and a market perspective differed substantially from its other goods. The selling path was given priority but made contingent on the offered price.[103]

Back in 1970, three members of SCA's top management (Enander, Norberg and Nordenö) had participated in the most prestigious management education in Sweden, and there they carried out an assignment that addressed SCA's strategic situation. In their report they concluded that SCA had to get closer to its end customers, and one of the suggested paths for that was to acquire Mölnlycke – basically a textile company (a filature).[104]

Just before WWII a new CEO (Thulin) began a radical transformation of Mölnlycke. He encouraged the company to develop knowledge about the absorption capacities of various fibres, which materialized in the production of bandages, diapers and sanitary napkins.[105] Custos became sole owner of Mölnlycke in the middle of the 1940s, and Custos's shareholders were offered the option to buy 65 per cent of Mölnlycke's stock thus making the company eligible for listing on the SSE. Mölnlycke's top management understood early on that textile production would face difficulties if located in Sweden (too high salary level), so those units were sold. Instead, Mölnlycke invested in the production of hygiene products (disposables), but by 1960, still only 20 per cent of Mölnlycke's production was directly linked to the lucrative 'absorption business'. At that time, the big problem was that losses in the textile operations ate the profits made in the hygiene business, and around 1964 Mölnlycke was close to bankruptcy.[106] That situation made Mölnlycke dependent on its banks.

The leading actor in the tough but necessary transformation process was Dahlsten, who succeeded Thulin as CEO in 1965. He started his career at Mölnlycke back in the 1950s when the company first and foremost ran a classic textile business. Soon he became head of its hospital products, and eventually of all its hygiene operations. Through his travels in the US he had learned that such products could probably be distributed in ways other than what was currently considered best practice in Sweden. That in combination with Mölnlycke's competence in gauze fabric production created a business opportunity that Dahlsten seized upon. It became possible for him to act on his ideas, as the company recently had introduced a radically decentralized organization that provided him with substantial freedom of action.[107]

Initially, it was one of SCA's competitors – Billerud – that showed most interest in Mölnlycke's ideas and development. That interest could to a large extent be explained by its CEO Pihlgren's attitude. A sign of his engagement was that Dahlsten became a member of Billerud's board. His basic and radical idea was to sell hygiene products through supermarkets – not as before in pharmacies. Such an approach required a radical change in distribution and marketing. Its success in Sweden initiated a growth process in the whole Nordic region.

Mölnlycke had granted licences relating to hygiene products to several corporations, and entered part ownerships in the UK, Australia, Canada and Mexico. Still, Mölnlycke's top management felt a bit uncomfortable by 1970, because they had become uncertain about the company's capacity to carry out its expected fast and massive expansion on its own. Eventually Mölnlycke realized that it needed a partner and that its leaders therefore had to give up some of their freedom of action.[108] A merger or close co-operation with a big(ger) company would make growth through acquisitions possible, an important alternative since purely organic growth was regarded as being too slow in the current competitive situation.[109] Mölnlycke had entered the tissue market when they bought Nättraby Bruk (1961) and Dutch Papierfabrik Friesland (1969). Those acquisitions provided control of raw material for such production. Since Mölnlycke was both a rather small buyer and one that needed special qualities, such control freed it from a situation in which the few producers that supplied Mölnlycke could jointly organize a decrease in their market output to raise the price. Moreover, knowledge about tissue production was valuable in the R&D work for the company's whole hygiene business (diapers did not contain only pulp and weave – tissue was used, too). To be able to deliver both hygiene and tissue products also strengthened Mölnlycke's attractiveness for the retail chains.[110]

Dahlsten had noticed that SCA's CEO Mossberg had indicated interest in Mölnlycke. According to Dahlsten, Mölnlycke could not on its own raise the financial resources to make the necessary R&D and market investments. Mölnlycke was primarily supplied by Billerud's Aspa unit, although SCA also contributed with its pulp. One problem was that Billerud was unable (or unwilling?) to increase its deliveries (and its eucalyptus fibre was not particularly fitting for Mölnlycke's hygiene products). Another obstacle was that Billerud's new CEO Hindemark (1966) was not as interested in co-operating with Mölnlycke as his predecessor Pihlgren. A third problem was that Mölnlycke had a tough competitor in Stille-Werner, a company that sold tampons, a product that Dahlsten was eager to incorporate in Mölnlycke's portfolio. So, in 1972, SCA's new CEO Rydin and Dahlsten discussed the 'Stille-Werner path'. Somewhat later Rydin also talked to the target company's main owners (the Hedberg family) about the possibility of acquiring its hygiene operations, but Mrs Hedberg hesitated. Mölnlycke's Daun continued the talks with the owner family, but a year later (1974), it suddenly became clear that MoDo's leading actor Carlgren had bought Stille-Werner (cf. Ch. 8).[111]

Rydin and Carlgren met in 1975 to discuss the possibility of streamlining their respective consumer activities through product swaps. It thus became obvious that MoDo, too, were focused on tissue. During another meeting in 1976 (also attended by Dahlsten), they discussed the continental consumer market and the various ideas that foreign actors had communicated. Rydin, Dahlsten and Carlgren quickly concluded that the optimal solution for the European hygiene business would be that Mölnlycke's operations in France, Holland and Belgium were merged with PWA's corresponding operations, and that MoDo would become part of that process.[112]

SCA's pulp delivery to Mölnlycke was the main link between the two companies. Mölnlycke gradually increased its pulp sourcing from SCA, drawing Wahlström more heavily into the inter-company talks. He visited Mölnlycke several times together with Rydin to discuss SCA's pulp deliveries, particularly with Daun.[113] Mölnlycke's CEO Dahlsten asked his purchasing manager why he bought so much pulp from SCA (Dahlsten had had less pleasant experiences with SCA and feared a growing dependence on that supplier).[114] However, after he and Daun had met with Nordenö, SCA's Head of Pulp Operations, the current annoyances and misunderstandings were eliminated (1971). That meeting also involved discussion about SCA's Sancella unit. Nordenö was impressed by Mölnlycke's clear strategy and well-structured organization and suggested to Wahlström that SCA should get 'closer' to that company.[115]

In 1972, a member of SCA's top management (Löf) informed Rydin that the company had the opportunity to make a favourable licensing agreement in the Benelux region with the American corporation Pfizer, but SCA decided to wait until the talks with Mölnlycke had come to an end. However, co-operating with Pfizer could have offered an interesting path, particularly as Rydin claimed that SCA lacked the capacity to successfully enter a consumer's market on its own.[116]

The same year, Mölnlycke's Daun was invited to visit SCA's HQ at Sundsvall. The reluctance on the part of both the responsible managers to sell Sancella to Mölnlycke disappointed Daun. Wahlström got involved in the discussions and formulated the situation in a way that Daun appreciated. Wahlström's entrance became seminal, as it made a continuation of the discussions possible.[117]

At the same time, Rydin and Wahlström tried to find out if Mölnlycke might be interested in co-operating in the sanitary business. The discussions became rather difficult, as Mölnlycke was successful and its CEO Dahlsten rather self-reliant. Daun was more relaxed, and he and Wahlström got along well; eventually they became convinced that the two companies ought to co-operate more closely. Such a development would integrate SCA forward and bring the company closer to its end customers, while Mölnlycke would get capital for a rapid expansion and a secure sourcing of suitable pulp qualities.[118] Mölnlycke named its search for such a competent and capital-strong partner 'Project Rich Widow' – a label that basically indicated that the company wanted to find a well-capitalized firm that lacked a strong future. Because the production process was another crucial ingredient in a possible deal, technical specifications mattered. Over time, the competitors dropped away one by one. Billerud had excellent R&D activities but was not interested enough (able?) to deliver the required air-dried pulp. Uddeholm had the necessary technical capabilities, but poor financial resources. Thus, Obbola (SCA) was the only supplier that met both of Mölnlycke's criteria.[119]

Wahlström had introduced Daun to SCA's leading technicians in 1973, but nothing materialized from that meeting. Rydin continued to be active in his search for a new path for SCA, and became more and more convinced about Mölnlycke's high potential. Together with Wahlström he went to SCA's Sancella plant in Newcastle (UK), where they concluded that its machines were poor and the overall efficiency low. At the same time, discussions were underway regarding extended hygiene production at the Belgian site. Wahlström advocated the sale of the Newcastle unit and a halt to continued investments in Belgium. Rydin, by contrast, saw instead a reason to co-operate with Mölnlycke and asked Wahlström to take further steps in that direction. Consequently, Wahlström met with Dahlsten and Daun in Gothenburg and explained that if SCA and Mölnlycke did not increase their co-operation, SCA would have to eliminate the production of Mölnlycke's pulp, sell the Newcastle plant and leave the hygiene sector.[120] Mölnlycke was keen to secure its sourcing of suitable pulp, so it investigated every alternative – Swedish, Nordic and American – and concluded that SCA would indeed be its best partner. Although Dahlsten and Daun were fully aware that Mölnlycke needed lots of capital to continue its rapid expansion, they were not interested in selling to a big global actor. In their eyes, SCA provided suitable pulp, secure sourcing, technical skill and reliable actors (and it did not threaten their positions).[121]

Complicating matters, Unilever (cf. Sunlight) had 'courted' Custos's owners and board already in 1969 with the intention to buy Mölnlycke, and this time it offered an attractive price. Thus, Custos's owners faced the choice between 'cashing in' from an instant sale and waiting for even bigger (but uncertain) future profits. At the board meeting at which Unilever's offer was considered, CEO Dahlsten convinced the owners/board that they would be better off staying as shareholders. He had even borrowed money himself to buy Mölnlycke shares to demonstrate his firm belief in the company. He also stated that he would not stay as CEO if the company were sold. The board then changed its initial position and decided not to sell to Unilever.[122]

Eventually Sunlight (Unilever) also expressed the desire to acquire SCA's hygiene operations (and offered cash payment), but SCA regarded the sale of its Sancella unit to Mölnlycke as a better alternative.[123] Other companies showed interest in Mölnlycke in the early 1970s as well. For example, Esselte, through its CEO Carl Mannerfelt, wanted to start discussions, but Dahlsten hesitated – he saw no point in such a combination. Initiatives were taken in the other direction too. Mölnlycke's CEO Dahlsten was interested in Swedish Match's[124] large international network and strong brand and approached the company. However, since its Deputy CEO and spokesperson Sundberg showed no particular interest, nothing materialized.[125]

Wahlström made it clear that SCA would accept shares in Mölnlycke as payment for Sancella (Mölnlycke did not have the necessary financial resources for a cash payment[126]). Dahlsten responded positively to Wahlström's suggestion – he was interested in seeing a new substantial owner in Mölnlycke. Thus, in 1973 SCA received 6 per cent of Mölnlycke's shares in exchange for Sancella. That deal also brought about a seat at Mölnlycke's board for Rydin.[127] The insight Rydin gained about Mölnlycke from his board position stimulated SCA to buy more of Mölnlycke's stock (eventually making the holding exceed 10%). SCA kept the purchases secret to avoid raising suspicions that control fights were on their way. That was seen as particularly important, as Mölnlycke lacked a majority owner (although Custos dominated the scene).[128]

There were many talks in those days between SCA and Mölnlycke regarding pulp qualities. Mölnlycke was interested in integrating backwards and building a large new plant that would produce a modified thermo-mechanic pulp. For its part, SCA hoped that the growing co-operation between SCA and Mölnlycke would make Custos realize the merits of a stronger ownership link. Without that connection SCA hesitated to give Mölnlycke a more prominent role in its pulp production.[129]

In June 1974, Rydin discussed with Dahlsten whether SCA should increase its shareholding in Mölnlycke. As Custos was in practical control of the company, Dahlsten found it rather pointless for SCA to buy additional shares. However, Rydin thought that Industrivärden might be interested, and as Dahlsten liked that idea, Rydin went ahead and activated Industrivärden. He stressed that SCA was not interested in acquiring a majority position; it would be satisfied if it could buy Custos's holding. According to Dahlsten it was quite possible that such an opportunity would emerge over the coming years.[130] So, gradually SCA strengthened its position, and by 1975 the company had acquired about 12 per cent of the shares. However, that level began to worry Dahlsten, who was concerned about Mölnlycke's future autonomy. Dahlsten wished to find a formula that both preserved Mölnlycke's independence and secured its pulp sourcing. For its part, SCA began discussing instead whether it ought to double its investment (or even merge with Mölnlycke). SCA's increasing share also worried the Wallenberg sphere, which had a substantial holding in Custos (although it was not a core investment).[131]

The relationship between Rydin and Dahlsten never became particularly close – their personal chemistries did not match that well.[132] Still, together with Daun and Wahlström, they had several informal talks both during journeys and through hikes in the Swedish Alps. There, various constellations of the four leaders exchanged information about the two companies and built trusting relationships. Rydin talked primarily with Daun, who he found both pensive and well prepared.[133] One problem for SCA was that Dahlsten initially had ambitions to become CEO or Chair of a merged corporation – something that SCA could not accept.[134] However, many leading actors in the two companies found Dahlsten's high aspirations reasonable, as Mölnlycke was both a big (and growing) part of the new SCA, and very much a product of Dahlsten's ideas and efforts.[135] Mölnlycke's leaders had a more positive attitude towards a merger than did SCA's managers, many of whom disliked being associated with a low-status 'diapers company'.[136]

The bilateral talks continued under the leadership of Daun and Wahlström, who took them towards a 'happy ending'. Once the basic outlines of an agreement had been worked out, SCA's top management had to convince its controlling owner Industrivärden. Mölnlycke's leaders had to persuade their board, a task that had become easier, as the directors had concluded recently that the company needed a financially strong partner – top management had showed them what the big competitors looked like (and what they planned).[137] The second step then became convincing Mölnlycke's larger shareholders about the merits of a merger. Bergkvist, Custos's CEO and Mölnlycke's Chair, firmly supported the idea despite the fact that Custos was (at least weakly) connected to the Wallenberg sphere (and despite Marcus Wallenberg Sr's negative stance). The third step in the process was to win over Custos's owners as well, who were reluctant to put in more capital. Indeed, they required that SCA guaranteed the necessary financial resources for Mölnlycke's future expansion.[138]

Rydin ran the negotiations at the shareholder level, that is to say, he talked to Custos, while Wahlström mainly talked to Mölnlycke's executives. Custos wanted to see – and got SCA's approval for – a shareholder acceptance rate that exceeded 90 per cent. Custos also wanted tax exemption, and that request materialized, too. As a subsidiary in SCA, Mölnlycke demanded high-grade autonomy and a 'guarantee' of its special status through an agreement between the two companies. That status had to include a 'special' Mölnlycke board and 'secure' capital sourcing. Thus, Mölnlycke was guaranteed that it could grow without competing with the other SCA units over the new constellation's total capital resources. With all these stipulations, SCA ultimately – despite its initial declaration – became majority owner of Mölnlycke.[139]

Mölnlycke justified its decision to allow the acquisition first and foremost by its urgent need for secure sourcing of suitable pulp for its rapid expansion. In addition, being part of SCA could also create opportunities for joint R&D efforts, which in turn could produce interesting new (hygiene) products. For SCA's part, its problem with the expected shortage of forest resources was solved, as the new step represented forward integration instead of an increased use of timber. Moreover, SCA's exposure to cyclical variations in (pulp) demand declined, and it was believed that many of Mölnlycke's other textile activities would have advantages for SCA.

In the 'merger' document it was made clear that SCA would hand over its hygiene business to Mölnlycke, and in return it would get shares (not cash – SCA had become interested in remaining a dominating shareholder). Mölnlycke's autonomy was guaranteed through several 'mechanisms': the recruitment of its directors should take into account the special character of the company's operations, no changes would be made in its top management and decentralized organization, it could keep its own main bank connection (Handelsbanken's main competitor Skandinaviska Enskilda Banken, which was connected to the rival Wallenberg sphere) and a board seat was promised to Dahlsten.[140] When the acquisition was finalized in 1975, the new constellation had some 17000 employees and a turnover amounting to about SEK 4 billion (forest-based products 2 billion, Mölnlycke 1 billion and the rest 1 billion).

In an unsigned summarizing document produced at a meeting in Stockholm between Rydin, Wahlström, Dahlsten and Daun, Mölnlycke was also authorized to choose two of its directors (of which one directorship was intended for a representative from Skandinaviska Enskilda Banken). Mölnlycke also got a credit limit guaranteed by SCA, half of SCA's accumulated investment fund and profits from its forest-based operations (estimated to be around SEK 100 million each year). Its supply of pulp was also 'guaranteed', and SCA planned to build a TMP-plant to secure that sourcing. Moreover, if SCA succeeded in acquiring PWA's hygiene operations, it was agreed that it should be organized as part of Mölnlycke. SCA would also refrain from streamlining the rather diversified Mölnlycke.[141] Mölnlycke stressed that it was important that SCA's 'pulp-culture' was prevented from interfering with – hampering – the rapid expansion of the hygiene business. In reality, SCA was almost forced to accept all these terms in order to get Mölnlycke's approval.[142]

Thus, Mölnlycke's status had become very special in the new SCA – it was a favoured unit inside another larger unit. Practically, that arrangement meant that SCA's top management was prevented from directly intervening in Mölnlycke's operations. They had to go through Mölnlycke's board – an agreed-upon procedure that SCA's leading executives Rydin and Wahlström firmly defended. The Mölnlycke acquisition also radically changed SCA's financial capacity to invest in paper production, although its resources were still considerable thanks to the profitability of the pulp and paper investments made in the 1960s. This meant that Ortviken had to stand back again, and that crucial decisions had to be made about what to do with Wifstavarf-Östrand.

SCA's acquisition of Mölnlycke constituted a bold step, as it represented a very different business from the ones the company previously had run. Here CEO Rydin acted as a risk-taker in a way that clearly deviated from his basic action rationale. However, to make that step Rydin had found it of utmost importance to become very familiar with both the target company (products, processes, techniques, markets, culture[s], etc.) and its leaders; and he did so in a rather long process. It was also important to him that the acquired company delivered something that SCA urgently needed, and that desired feature was the opportunity to further process the pulp.[143]

Rydin's toughest challenge in connection to the acquisition was winning the approval of SCA's board. Only after a long lunch in Paris together with Browaldh did the Chair finally become convinced. It was not surprising that the talks took time, because it was a brave strategic move that put SCA on a new path. The board's hesitation had to do in part with Mölnlycke's total product portfolio – it resembled that of a conglomerate. The new businesses were unfamiliar to many directors, although they liked the linkage to SCA's pulp operations, and that the hygiene business represented forward integration.[144] The two companies' divergent cultures also made some directors concerned – SCA was a slow-growing, 'sluggish', process-intensive, forest-based business-to-business company, while Mölnlycke was a fast-moving, flexible and innovation-intense consumer-oriented company.

The purchase of Mölnlycke was brought up with SCA's larger shareholders. The idea was that SCA should acquire all shares in Mölnlycke by offering its shareholders an exchange of their Mölnlycke shares for newly issued SCA shares and convertible bonds. Mölnlycke's AGM became rather 'stormy', as particularly one of the bigger shareholders firmly opposed the whole merger idea.[145] However, at SCA's EGM and among most of Mölnlycke's shareholders, the idea was received with appreciation. Rather quickly more than 90 per cent of Mölnlycke's shares were exchanged,[146] and the remaining ones were eventually also acquired.

The composition of SCA's new board became problematic for a short period. Rydin thought that Dahlsten should be offered a position as deputy director, but Dahlsten expected an ordinary seat. Chair Browaldh's suggestion that the board be enlarged solved the problem. Dahlsten's appointment equipped SCA with something unusual in Swedish (or Nordic) corporate governance – a subsidiary's CEO as director. Rather soon, it also became clear to Dahlsten that he would become neither CEO nor Chair in the new constellation, and that disappointed him. Like most other leading actors, he understood that his and Rydin's different personalities and action rationales sooner or later would create governance complications. Dahlsten had initially agreed with Rydin that he would stay as Mölnlycke's CEO for two years, but when Thunholm (Chair of Skandinaviska Enskilda Banken and of Swedish Match) contacted Dahlsten and asked if he might be interested in becoming CEO of Swedish Match,[147] Dahlsten took him up on the offer.[148] However, he stayed as SCA director until 1989.

In the meantime, Rydin approached Daun and asked if he could foresee becoming CEO of Mölnlycke in the near future, and he answered 'yes'.[149] With Dahlsten's departure in 1976, Daun was named Mölnlycke's CEO and got a board seat at SCA. Mölnlycke's remarkable autonomy inside SCA continued during Daun's tenure as CEO. Indeed, an almost impermeable shelter existed around that subsidiary until Martin-Löf succeeded Rydin as CEO. Mölnlycke's urge for autonomy even made Daun hesitate to accept SCA's CFO as a member of Mölnlycke's board (1987). It was actually not until the 1990s that Mölnlycke became more integrated into SCA, particularly after Forsgren left as Mölnlycke's CEO in 1993, and after SCA's acquisition of PWA in 1995.[150]

Because Mölnlycke's leaders were particularly fond of 'fluff' operations, that kind of hygiene product dominated its repertoire. SCA's CEO Rydin, however, was keen to add more consumer tissue to Mölnlycke's repertoire, and discussed that with Daun.[151] Lilla Edet (tissue) became an acquisition candidate in 1976, when the Swedish Paper Workers' Union Chair Carlsson (later Minister of Industry) contacted Rydin and informed him that a competitor, Procter & Gamble, considered buying that company from Akzo. In the end (1977), however, Ncb won the race and bought Lilla Edet (cf. Ch. 6).[152] Since Mölnlycke remained interested in buying Lilla Edet, certain joint actions were discussed with Ncb that addressed the Swedish, Norwegian and French tissue markets. Rydin hesitated because Lilla Edet's products did not fit particularly well with SCA's new strategy (increased concentration within Sweden and not high-quality [sophisticated] products), and the volumes were too small to justify the necessary R&D efforts.

A few years later Lilla Edet once again emerged as an acquisition candidate. Ncb had run into difficulties and considered selling. Lilla Edet was still attractive to Mölnlycke, as it offered complementary products and based much of its production on waste fibres. Moreover, Mölnlycke sold to the industrial/institutional market, while Lilla Edet catered to retailers. Together the two companies would improve scale economies in both production and R&D. When MoDo, too, showed interest in Lilla Edet, Rydin contacted its leaders. The talks indicated a 50–50 solution, but Daun was concerned that such a construct would provide MoDo with too strong a sales capacity. MoDo considered merging Lilla Edet with its own unit MoDo Konsument, but suspected that the Swedish competition authority would not allow such a move. It was not until 1986 that SCA could finally buy Lilla Edet, having won a bidding race with the Wallenberg sphere's paper producer Papyrus.[153]

A co-structuring of PWA's and Mölnlycke's hygiene operations in Germany was also discussed in those days. One idea was to merge the activities in Germany and France, and put SCA and Mölnlycke as co-owners (50–50) in a new company (Mölnlycke would be expected to pay with shares). However, the integration attempt failed partly because of dissatisfaction among shareholders regarding the 1974 Zewawell agreement, partly because of the attitude expressed by members of Mölnlycke's top management.[154] Rydin also discussed strategic matters with the main shareholder in VP. Such talks with VP and PWA took place frequently during the late 1970s and early 1980s, both because SCA delivered lots of pulp to VP, and because SCA was part owner of PWA.

Together with Dahlsten, Rydin tried to buy French Aubry (tissue) and a diapers production where Cellulose de Pin held 98 per cent of the shares. In addition, SCA sought to buy a holding in a sales company, which would sell both Mölnlycke's and Aubry's products, and to buy units in the packaging business (Lafarge's operations in that field). In 1977, discussions were held regarding a deal between Mölnlycke and Béghin regarding the French market. Béghin had become concerned about Mölnlycke's talks about possible co-operation in (fifteen) other markets with Scott Paper, which wanted to extend its product repertoire. Ultimately SCA sold its French plants to Béghin for shares in that company and licence agreements.[155]

Mölnlycke was still a rather diversified subsidiary inside SCA at the end of the 1970s, with an output basically organized in two 'Groups', each containing several divisions: a 'Hygiene Group' containing consumer products and a 'Leisure Time Products Group' containing clothes, sewing cotton and marine products.[156]

At the end of the 1970s, SCA's five biggest shareholders were Industrivärden (20%), Custos (13%), Handelsbanken's Pension Foundation (4%), Skandia (3%) and Trygg-Hansa (3%). The 'only' significant changes in that structure that occurred during the last quarter of the 20th century were Custos's entry and exit (1975 and 2001 respectively). SCA's stable ownership situation was an invaluable strength during the tough years in the late 1980s – a period that was difficult for the whole Swedish forest-based industry. Many of its actors actually advocated devaluation, and the government was approached and pumped with arguments in favour of such a step. However, all companies did not agree – Stora Kopparberg, for example, expressed its opposition through its CEO Sundblad.[157] Soon (in 1979), however, Sweden left the European common margins arrangement, something that was in line with what Rydin advocated.[158]

13.3 SCA IMPROVES ITS COMPETITIVE POSITION

13.3.1 The Presence of Cartels

Cartels emerge when volumes grow slowly for standard products, when the number of producers is neither few nor many and where each company's investments are substantial (cf. capital-intensive production). In such settings, each new major investment triggers imbalances (market surpluses) that lower prices. Profitability is then to a large extent achieved through 'internal' regulation of market output. However, such regulation does not work particularly well if there are numerous actors on a market (often correlated with low capital needs and low barriers to entry). If the actors instead are few, cartels are not needed at all, because the fact that there are so few actors means that each is well informed about the others (however, a 'natural cartel' – an oligopoly – might emerge).[159]

Cartels had been common in the forest-based industry for most of the 20th century.

Until WWII that was an unproblematic way to conduct inter-firm co-operation, but from the 1950s onwards the merits of cartels was increasingly questioned and criticized (and eventually also made illegal). The 1970s period was no exception – the European forest-based corporations still discussed informal regulation of market output and prices. As usual, the Finnish companies led most of those 'organizing' efforts. These 'regulative' agreements could take forms like: (1) 'the Finnish companies have decided to stand still for two weeks on the condition that the Swedish companies do the same', (2) 'the Finnish companies suggest an urgent meeting of the "Copenhagen club"[160] to decide what price to use in Holland' or (3) 'the Finnish corporate Chair urged the Swedish competitor's CEO to enforce the suggested production restriction.' Local 'cartel-like' organization also existed at the time in Sweden, for example, Scannews and the Swedish Association of Pulp Producers.[161]

13.3.2 Drivers

SCA's actors expressed differing opinions about what driving forces were most important for pushing/pulling the company onwards. Norberg,[162] for example, maintained that it was the technicians that would lead the company into the future, that is to say, that corporate development was driven 'from below'. His view was widely shared inside and outside the organization. Norberg believed that technicians almost always could convince the executive actors about the merits of the suggested additional/marginal investments. Most current managers also found production and quality considerations decisive for SCA's development, and they justified their stance by referring to the standardized and 'bulky' character of the company's output (low degree of customizing).[163]

However, there were also other views. Director Francke, for example, claimed that it was the CEOs (i.e. Enström, Mossberg and Rydin) that (had) occupied SCA's driver's seat.[164] Still others added that the board and its Chair also contributed substantially to the company's development, but nobody mentioned that the (major) shareholders had any impact. Basically, SCA's strategic decision-making process followed the formal hierarchical set-up that was stated in the Swedish Companies Act. Yet, Rydin adapted those legal rules in certain ways. For example, he decided that group management should select board members for SCA's subsidiaries and bigger part-owned companies. That made it possible for those boards to take decisions on their own regarding major issues.[165]

13.3.3 Improving Current Operations

SCA was a large owner of forests and controlled substantial hydropower resources. The company decided to diverge from the mainstream trend and keep its natural assets in-house. Many of its competitors engaged in making their 'hidden values' visible, and sold many of them to 'improve' their balance sheets and free capital for expansion investments.[166] SCA, too, discussed sell back solutions with various kinds of investors, but none of these ever materialized. Basically, the company was afraid that those scarce resources could land in the hands of a competitor.[167] However, Rydin stressed that forests are only valuable for those corporations that have plants in the vicinity, since long-distance timber transports erode profitability. So, SCA did not buy larger quantities of (expensive) timber abroad, as it could hurt its possibilities to run low-cost large-scale production. Moreover, first and foremost SCA wanted to utilize its Swedish quality timber (spruce [long fibre]) and integrate forward (invest in further processing).[168] From time to time discussions also arose regarding whether SCA ought to buy additional hydropower plants, but SCA discarded that idea, as such resources were difficult to evaluate.[169] Regarding waste fibre, the new promising alternative to 'fresh' timber, SCA bided its time (and became a rather late adopter).[170]

The shortage of capital resources and uncertainty about the future USD rate led Rydin to seek a partner for SCA's forthcoming 'inescapable' investment at Östrand. During the first quarter of 1979, SCA began negotiating with the Swedish Ministry of Industry, whose officials suggested a three-party solution that involved the founding of a new company. SCA was supposed to put its Wifsta-Östrand constellation in that new construct, Ncb its Dynäs plant and the state a substantial amount of capital. The new company's sole mission would be to build and run a plant in Ådalen,[171] preferably a LWC one, and carry out the modernization of Östrand. Nobody was supposed to gain a majority position.

The consequences of closing down Östrand were difficult to estimate. In addition to the substantial social costs, there were also many business consequences that were hard to calculate. Rydin found it economically rational to have (at least) one large activity in that area (Wifsta-Östrand currently used around 30% of SCA's timber in the region). As new environmental requirements required a rather prompt investment decision, the board soon approved the new Östrand arrangement with Ncb and the state. SCA also decided to build a CTMP plant there to secure the long-term sourcing of pulp to Mölnlycke (that pulp became cheaper than the chemical one that currently was produced). However, one undesired consequence of the Östrand investment was that SCA had to postpone its planned machine at Ortviken.[172]

SCA had decided to try to become one of the biggest packaging companies in the world within a decade or two, and then, possibly, in high-tech carton. SCA would accomplish that by combining scale advantages in raw material production (particularly kraftliner) with market leadership (corrugated) on all local markets SCA decided to enter. Initially, SCA planned to expand in Sweden, then in the Nordic countries and finally in Europe.[173] Obviously, such growth could not be carried out in perfect geographical order – SCA would also have to take up opportunities as they presented themselves. One such opening arose in Ireland and the UK, where SCA lacked packaging businesses. In 1979, SCA bought a position[174] in those countries from the Jefferson Smurfit Group. The process leading to the deal actually started when Chair Michael Smurfit met SCA's Head of Pulp at an industry meeting in Montreux. As head of a family that wanted to both expand (enter the US market) and keep control, Smurfit was looking for partners for some of his company's businesses. He was the one who suggested the transaction, which also included a long-term kraftliner contract (15% of SCA's liner). The decisive negotiations were – as so often – carried out during long evenings.[175]

Thus, at the end of the 1970s, SCA's packaging operations contained two wholly owned companies, SCA Emballage (Sweden) and Papeteries Léon Clergeau (France), and several part-owned ones in Denmark, West Germany, the UK and Ireland.[176] At that time it also became obvious that the two operations – liner and packaging – that constituted the business were rather different. Scale economy, capital-intensive production, high production costs, productivity sensitivity, international customers, dependence on the USD and tough competition characterized liner operations. In contrast, local markets, customer orientation, small-scale production, low currency risk and high marketing costs characterized packaging. Because of these differences, a separate unit for packaging was formed in 1979, and Nordenö, SCA's Head of Pulp Operations, became its head. The new order implied that it now was packaging managers that bought liner, rather than liner managers using packaging as an outlet for their output.[177]

For SCA it was important to find out whether there were scale advantages (also) in packaging operations. In box making, scale economies were found primarily in purchasing power and in the sharing of experiences between local units. Thus, SCA Packaging utilized and expanded its extensive information and knowledge networks. SCA also looked for scale economies in the production of paper for packaging, and the shutdown of 12 paper machines within a decade contributed to the company's efficiency goal. Several mills were also adjusted for specific outputs to gain a similar effect. SCA even abandoned the idea that all kinds (grades) of paper for packaging should be produced in-house, which also (indirectly) produced economies of scale. Many discussions were held about differentiating and upgrading the packaging boxes through a focus on design, new printing qualities and increased customer service.[178]

Swedish forest and power resources were scarce all through the 1980s, and therefore attractive to acquire. In 1985, a battle arose over a mid-sized, forest-based Swedish company named Svanö. Rich forest resources made Svanö the key to getting a dominant position in northern Sweden. Still, SCA hesitated to participate in the upcoming race – Björkå was actually seen as a better alternative. Then the problem was that SCA did not like to see its rival MoDo as the new owner of Svanö. Eventually SCA won the competition, but it had to pay a rather high price.[179]

Two years later a similar opportunity emerged when SCA was offered a large portion of Graningeverken. The price, however, was regarded to be too high, so SCA turned down the offer. Only one year later, that opportunity reappeared, although this time the purchase was to be done together with MoDo and AGA in a consortium. AGA would then get the power resources, MoDo and SCA the forests and SCA part (25%) of the Utansjö mill. Just as the deal seemed done, two initially unknown ingredients spoiled the mix. First, the second biggest owner of Graningeverken, the Nordin family (24%), declared that it was not interested in selling, and its members refused to negotiate. Second, it was revealed that the Utansjö site should be closed down, so no share in that unit was at stake. Thus, the bid turned out to be hostile, although the biggest owner Skanska (29%) and third biggest owner MoDo (10%) supported such a transaction. In the end, this second attempt failed, too, but a third opportunity soon materialized. This time, SCA joined together with a consortium of institutional investors that tried to acquire parts of Graningeverken. Rather quickly it became clear that SCA could not afford to pay the asking price (SEK 2 billion), as it had begun a series of large acquisitions abroad (cf. Ch. 14). Nevertheless, SCA never considered it a serious problem that it had to refrain from a Graningeverken deal.

13.3.4 Looking for Core Businesses

Among the more odd growth ideas during the 1970s was SCA's plan to invest in Cameroon. Another long shot was the idea (proposed by Volvo, but never pursued) that

SCA would benefit from an acquisition of Volvo's leisure product unit. Another – more realistic – thought was that Bahco's[180] operations might fit well together with Sunds, SCA's manufacturing arm. In the mid-1970s, SCA actually bought a holding in Bahco and took a seat on its board. Not long after (1978) the idea emerged that SCA might buy the whole company and create an expansive manufacturing business (Bahco + Sunds). The alternative was to leave Bahco completely, and eventually SCA did just that.

Instead, the discussions of the late 1960s regarding a merger between Sunds and Defibrator were revived. The effort bore fruit in 1979, when SCA bought Defibrator's parent companies from a Swedish family and four of the companies' top managers. The main reason for the acquisition was that the market for Sunds's classic products was stagnating, thus making it necessary to expand the company's repertoire. A combined Defibrator and Sunds were expected to become a leading supplier of technical solutions to the world's newsprint and journal paper industry.[181] Despite these expectations, SCA ran into problems with Sunds's profitability during the 1980s. Still, SCA continued to invest there, and CEO Martin-Löf (later SCA's CEO) was given responsibility for its development before a possible sale. Therefore, Jylhävaraa[182] was purchased in 1983 from UPM, and an acquisition of Sprout Waldron[183] was considered. Discussions regarding a takeover of – or co-operation with – Impco[184] were also held (though it did not occur), and most of Hagfors Malsegment[185] was bought from Uddeholm (1987). In 1988, Rauma Repola[186] became part owner of Sunds, which reduced SCA's holding to 33 per cent. All through the 1980s SCA debated whether Sunds really belonged among SCA's core activities, or if it was to be seen as a financial investment.[187]

SCA also scrutinized Mölnlycke's business palette to identify the units that qualified as part of the enlarged SCA's core activities. Units that did not show clear synergies with hygiene operations – Mölnlycke Marin (1983), Mölnlycke Sytråd (1987) and Mölnlycke Mobility (1990) – were sold to free capital.[188] The company's total capital structure was actually the subject of many board discussions, not least how much of the profits ought to be kept for investments (and not used for dividends). In recent years a sharp dividing line had arisen on that subject between the directors that were appointed at the GMs and those that were elected by the unions.[189] That conflict might have been avoided had SCA not paid any substantial dividends in the 1960s and 1970s – a period when the many closures infected the relationship between the executive levels and the unions.[190]

13.3.5 Forward Integration

Together with a Swiss financial consortium, SCA discussed the establishment of a newsprint mill in Hessen (Germany) in 1975. The new plant's concessional financing made it tempting to go ahead (and healthy profit was expected). At the time it was important for SCA (or the Scannews cartel) to get the majority in the new company that was to be named 'Sontraprint Papierproduktions'. SCA's idea was to enter the project when the unit was ready for production, but the Swiss financiers preferred to see a 25 per cent contribution from SCA already at the construction stage. The Finnish actors feared that otherwise Scannews's cartel members might not invest at all (and probably not the Germans either).

Once again Wallander, who represented Handelsbanken on MoDo's board, asked whether SCA might be interested in discussing a merger with MoDo, but once again

Rydin said no. Wahlström thought that a purchase of MoDo would bring only greater dependence on the pulp market, which SCA had decided to leave. He also believed that the rivalry between the two companies would entail 'insurmountable' integration problems. MoDo did not like SCA, its 'hereditary enemy'. Wahlström also suspected that a merger would create such a large corporation that the politicians would not be able to stay away.[191] Nordenö, too, thought that the cultural differences between the two companies were huge, primarily because of the different ownership structures. MoDo was governed by a family dynasty with a strong leader, while SCA was run by professional managers in a setting that lacked a dominating private shareholder. Moreover, in MoDo the strategy was difficult to identify, as it only appeared 'ex post' through the actions of one person (Carlgren), while in SCA it was transparent, as it was formulated in accessible documents and actively promoted by several executives. The two companies' decision-making processes also differed. SCA was basically governed in accordance with legislation and proven experience, while MoDo instead ran a more diffuse executive process, where Carlgren (in his formal positions as major shareholder, Chair and CEO) sometimes acted without adhering to the company's juridical structure. However, MoDo also had obvious strengths, for example, its superior R&D unit, which over the years had produced many innovations.[192]

Åström (later CEO of SCA), too, agreed with most other actors that the companies' different historical track records had left strong marks. SCA had shut down many sites over the years, while MoDo instead had kept its plants and taken care of its employees. MoDo had also taken greater risks than SCA, a difference in rationale that currently both Carlgren (risk-seeking) and Rydin (risk averse) personified. The two companies' localization had also generated frictions between the companies, as it had created tough competition for the forest resources in southern Norrland. However, Åström also stressed that the two companies actually had exchanged several top managers (including him) over the years, so at least sometimes it had been possible for leading actors to adapt to the other company's values and traditions.[193]

At that time, the Wallenberg sphere initiated the announced new newsprint project at Hylte (1976). SCA wanted to stop the project, and the Scannews cartel was informed about its strong objections. Rydin even informed the German giant Feldmühle's head about his company's position. However, Feldmühle was prepared to convert some of its newsprint capacity to journal production, thereby 'making room' for Hylte. Still, Rydin was not calmed, but as Hylte's board was divided on the project, nothing happened (for a while).[194]

Another company that came across SCA's radar screen in the late 1970s was Munksjö.[195] At a dinner with Graningeverken's main owner Versteegh, Rydin talked a lot to Esselte's Chair Mannerfelt, his table companion, about Munksjö, and addressed particularly its corrugated cardboard operations. Esselte had been asked to have a look at that company but turned down the offer. Rydin and Mannerfelt agreed that Esselte should take up contact with Munksjö again and indicate interest in a deal that would also include SCA. In the end, however, SCA decided not to participate in a purchase of Munksjö both for market and financial reasons.[196] Instead, among possible Swedish acquisitions Nordenö, the head of SCA's corrugated business, prioritized acquisitions of Skarwell, Esselte Well and Kraftemballage.[197]

SCA's production of market pulp had decreased from 50 per cent to below 30 per cent in the late 1970s. In addition to that production, SCA contained four larger businesses: hygiene (Mölnlycke), newsprint (Ortviken), fine paper (Wifstavarf[198]) and corrugated. However, around 1978 the Swedish forest-based industry experienced severe problems, and some leading actors, particularly Rydin, began to bring up the idea of establishing something similar to the Swedish Steel construct, that is to say, a 'Swedish Pulp' company. That irritated the Conservative Minister of Finance Bohman, who disliked adding another engagement to the state's portfolio of base industries. At the same time Rydin and SCA were worried about discussions between Ncb and MoDo that seemed to involve some kind of joint venture that would include MoDo's Domsjö unit and result in a new paper mill. SCA was anxious to secure that – if the plant was built – it did not have access to state resources.

After extensive analyses, Rydin and the board again decided that SCA – except for Mölnlycke – foremost should invest in packaging. Rydin claimed that SCA needed at least two strong legs, and that packaging was to be preferred as the second one. Because newsprint was another business that SCA seriously considered continuing to run, the board put a lot of time and energy into discussing that path. A new newsprint machine at Ortviken would take up a major portion of SCA's investment resources and compete for capital with the prioritized hygiene operations (Mölnlycke). Rydin supported a modernization investment at Ortviken – he claimed that 'sooner or later it had to be done'.[199] Thus, a new newsprint machine that increased Ortviken's capacity by 50 per cent was approved, but it was not operational until 1985. SCA closed its production of chemical and groundwood pulp in 1984 but expanded simultaneously its production of TMP.[200] However, still Rydin worried about the future for newsprint (paperless offices and decreasing newspaper markets).[201] SCA's 'new' strategy not only described what operations should constitute its core businesses. It also restated that SCA foremost should expand outside Sweden, preferably within the EC to be 'on the safe side'. The geographical expansion was necessary to establish production close to the (end) customer, as that was crucial for both hygiene/tissue and carton/corrugated/liner.[202]

Deputy CEO Brändström wanted to see an SCA freed from most of its pulp operations. That could occur either by selling those business units to Ncb and Södra,[203] or by undertaking some kind of joint venture with one or both of these companies. That path was impossible for Rydin, who was determined to reduce SCA's dependence on raw material production. Ncb – through its head Hedlund – soon became the leading buyer of units that SCA wanted to get rid of. Rydin offered Hedlund several of SCA's smaller pulp producing units, with Ncb accepting most suggestions and prices. So, Hedlund's expansion ambitions actually 'solved' several of SCA's problems (cf. Ch. 6). Later in the early 1990s, AssiDomän's new and ambitious CEO Ahlgren acted in a similar way, and that, too, simplified things for SCA.[204]

Between the late 1970s and the early 1990s SCA became the most active Swedish buyer of European forest-based companies.[205] However, during the first part of that period, SCA saw few possibilities to make structural deals with Finnish and Norwegian actors. According to Wahlström, strong nationalism to a large extent explained that reluctance – these countries' leaders were simply unwilling to give away (some of the) control of their bigger corporate 'flagships'.[206]

In April 1981, SCA began planning for a time when St Regis might decide to give up its 50 per cent shareholding in Obbola. That time came in the second half of 1982, and

St Regis eventually left as part owner. Then SCA's first priority was to find a new partner, and Enso was mentioned.[207] At about this time, Weyerhaeuser offered to sell SCA all or some of its eight plants in Europe. However, with the exception of France, all offered units were situated in less interesting countries, so SCA purchased none of them.

Then, in late 1982, the Swedish government took a very important decision, which in many ways influenced SCA's operative profitability (higher) and capacity to make acquisitions (more costly). Sweden devaluated its currency by a remarkable 16 per cent. All in all, however, that move proved to be advantageous for SCA, as it recently had invested a lot both in Sweden and (particularly) abroad.[208]

13.3.6 The Iggesund Contest[209]

Like MoDo's Chair Carlgren, SCA and its leaders discussed Holmens Bruk in the early 1980s. Ratos CEO Söderberg, who represented one of Holmens Bruk's two main owners, claimed in his conversations with Rydin that, in the long run, Holmen would need a strong partner to be able to develop successfully. To Rydin, Söderberg's statement indicated that Ratos was considering selling its holding. Later Rydin met with Holmens Bruk's CEO Önnesjö at a sector meeting and informed him about SCA's plan to make Ortviken a plant for production of special papers, and that such a change would make co-operation with Holmens Bruk interesting. Rydin also thought that a quick decision regarding a further expansion at Braviken could prevent Stora Kopparberg from making certain large investments. Rydin mentioned that SCA might consider participating in a new issue of Holmens Bruk shares, if it was combined with some kind of industrial co-operation. However, Rydin was then careful to emphasize that a subscription of Holmens Bruk shares would not represent a first step in a long-term plan to take control of that company.[210]

The Holmens Bruk issue was still alive in September 1981, and it was discussed mainly with Wallander, who at that time (also) was Dagens Nyheter's Chair. It became obvious to Rydin that the Bonnier family preferred SCA shares if 'something happened' with Holmens Bruk. Rydin also discussed that path with SCA's Chair Browaldh, but like Rydin he was not particularly enthusiastic. Both were reluctant to invest further in newsprint – if they had to pick something in Holmens Bruk, they preferred its journal paper production. So, Rydin informed Wallander that SCA lacked sufficient interest to become a substantial shareholder in Holmens Bruk.[211]

However, already on 29 April 1981 it became important for SCA to decide how to treat the Swedish carton producer Iggesund. It was on that date that Stora Kopparberg and Billerud made a joint hostile bid for Iggesund, a move that certainly 'shook up' the competitive situation (for an extensive description of that process, cf. Ch. 9). MoDo had already begun to invest in Iggesund shares, and early in 1981 its holding had reached over 12 per cent. Rydin learned about the hostile bid on 30 April (he had been abroad), but he did not take it seriously, as it was so poorly constructed. Still, SCA's leading actors (including Browaldh and Wallander) immediately met, and several action alternatives were discussed. Browaldh thought that there still was some uncertainty about what path SCA ought to follow, aside from the Mölnlycke one.[212] Hellerqvist, too, favoured expansion in consumer products, and like Rydin he found a purchase of Iggesund's quality carton business less interesting ('lack of development opportunities', 'very different from

SCA's packaging operations' and 'too expensive'). For all these reasons, SCA decided not to participate in the Iggesund contest at all. However, if needed it could assist the Handelsbanken/Industrivärden sphere's backing of MoDo's attempt to get control of Iggesund.[213]

Wallander raised doubts about whether Carlgren (MoDo) actually would go ahead, especially when he learned that Iggesund had not developed as well as expected and became uncertain whether the support from the Handelsbanken sphere was wholehearted. However, Carlgren informed Rydin that he continued to buy Iggesund shares to keep up with Marcus Wallenberg Sr (i.e. Billerud and Stora Kopparberg). Carlgren also mentioned that he might get back to SCA and sell MoDo's hygiene operations to strengthen his financial capacity in the Iggesund race.[214] Daun found that potential offer most interesting, so Mölnlycke prepared for such a path.[215]

However, 1981 was not the first year that Iggesund was the topic of discussion at SCA. Already in 1977, Rydin understood that Marcus Wallenberg Sr was interested in acquiring that company, and at a dinner in September 1977 he mentioned that Wallenberg ambition to Iggesund's CEO Sundblad. Sundblad answered that he thought that Iggesund could defend itself against any hostile attack – management would fight them with 'all means'. At another dinner in early 1979, one of Handelsbanken's two CEOs, Ekman, re-opened the issue, and at that time two leading SCA actors indicated their company's potential interest in Iggesund. Ekman also mentioned that Marcus Wallenberg Sr might consider a takeover of that company. That information triggered Rydin to approach Iggesund's Chair Henrikson to 'protect SCA's interests'.[216]

One year later (June 1980), Rydin talked to Iggesund's CEO Lars G. Sundblad, as MoDo had begun to buy 'substantial amounts' of Iggesund shares. Like Sundblad, Rydin was of the opinion that Iggesund could survive on its own ('stand alone'). Indeed, both CEOs expressed uncertainty about Carlgren's true intentions. Sundblad did not rule out the possibility that it was an impulsive action rather than the start of a serious takeover process. However, it was important to understand that also a MoDo investment in Iggesund below 25 per cent[217] would be most risky, and indicated that Carlgren might have high ambitions. SCA's board once again discussed the issue, and as noted above, it remained disinterested in Iggesund.

The 'Iggesund serial' continued and attracted quite a few prominent actors. Rydin and Stora Kopparberg's CEO Erik Sundblad met and discussed the matter. Erik Sundblad mentioned that Stora Kopparberg had bought some shares to 'support' Iggesund. Carlgren's 'intrusion' irritated Lars G. Sundblad, but Erik Sundblad believed that his brother – if necessary – could defend Iggesund by mobilizing 'friends'. During a flight (March 1981), Carlgren told Rydin that MoDo and its associates might go up to a 25 per cent holding in Iggesund. Rydin answered that he was pleased that a Handelsbanken-friendly actor would get such a strong position in Iggesund. It meant that the sphere could act from a strong position if a takeover bid suddenly arose (e.g. from the Wallenberg family).[218]

At SCA's board meeting on 13 May 1981 shortly after the big announcement, Rydin brought up the question of whether SCA should react to Billerud and Stora Kopparberg's joint hostile bid on Iggesund. He presented two action alternatives – either enter a race with the bidders or try to buy a blocking 25 per cent holding. However, in both cases the expected returns for SCA looked poor. Iggesund's profitability was mediocre, and both its pulp and steel operations had problems. So, Rydin suggested that SCA bide its time, and the board agreed.[219] Eventually Carlgren and his MoDo allies won the fight with the Wallenberg sphere and became the main owner of Iggesund. However, MoDo could not reach the majority in Iggesund until it (as agreed) had acquired Billerud's and Stora Kopparberg's holdings (1983).[220] Still, a few years later (1985), United Brokers informed SCA that it had a large holding in MoDo for sale (the so-called 'Björkegren-holding'; cf. Ch. 9). However, SCA did not take up the offering both because its need to make financial investments in listed shares was low, and because the Carlgren–Kempe family was in control of MoDo anyway.[221]

13.3.7 Mölnlycke Expands

A decade after its decisive acquisition of Mölnlycke ('merger') – which occupied most of the executive actors' attention and capacity – the time had come for SCA to establish a strategy for the coming decade. In 1984 the board decided that the company should lower its ambitions for its classic forest-based businesses – the general focus should be on rationalization. It was also important that the packaging unit increased its profit level, and a planned machine at Obbola was expected to solve that problem. SCA also decided to keep Mölnlycke as an autonomous company and prioritize its geographical expansion, although its product portfolio was regarded as too 'profuse'. For Sunds and BÅKAB, however, disinvestment had become a serious alternative.[222]

Thus, SCA continued to prioritize Mölnlycke fully in accordance with the companies' initial agreement. Mölnlycke's CEO Daun led its internationalization process. The hygiene business was already strong in the Nordic countries, but there were quite a lot of difficulties associated with its expansion on the European continent (particularly in France and Germany). North America was seen as 'an impossible market' at that time, and Asia 'did not exist'. Mölnlycke was actually more successful in South and Central America and in Eastern Europe.[223] Daun's expansion ideas included the building of another plant in Sweden (it was too risky to rely on just one), investing in the UK (buy or build a plant) and organizing joint ventures in Mexico and Colombia. Those efforts were to be organized and carried out in the same way as its on-going activities in the UK, Australia, and Canada.[224] SCA used joint ventures to reduce country risks and to overcome the geographical distances to Sweden that made monitoring efforts difficult.[225]

SCA's preferential treatment of Mölnlycke was not uncontroversial internally. Enander, head of the Östrand plant (deliverer of pulp to Mölnlycke), expressed criticism and claimed that SCA gave advantages to Mölnlycke that overstated its profitability (e.g. incorrect internal pricing of the pulp). Enander also pointed out that SCA adjusted its fluff pulp to Mölnlycke's specifications and wanted to see those extra costs taken on by Mölnlycke (he even suggested that the 'tailored' pulp plant should be made part of Mölnlycke).[226]

In 1984, SCA noted that Swedish Match had bought shares in Grafoprint, a company controlled by the Bonnier family. Daun was worried that Swedish Match would get hold of Duni, Grafoprint's tissue-producing subsidiary. That looked to him like the start of a 'new Mölnlycke', a suspicion that might have emerged because Mölnlycke's former CEO Dahlsten had become Swedish Match's CEO. In that situation, Rydin advocated a direct purchase of Duni. The fact that SCA's Deputy CEO Brändström had been Chair of Grafoprint and knew the Bonnier family simplified the exploratory talks. Brändström tried to secure a promise from the Bonnier family that if they intended to sell Duni, they would first turn to Mölnlycke.

Two years later, Mölnlycke was offered the opportunity to buy Swedish Match's holding in Grafoprint. Mölnlycke's interest had escalated as its leaders had begun to worry that MoDo or Holmens Bruk might buy instead. However, to make a profitable investment in Duni, it would have been necessary to buy 100 per cent of Grafoprint, raising the price tag considerably. Rydin contacted Bonnier's CEO Måberg to come to some kind of arrangement, but the latter told Rydin that the Bonnier family's holding in Duni was 'strategic', so a sale was not on the agenda (not even to Holmens Bruk, where Bonnier was one of two main owners).[227]

Mölnlycke's relation to Swedish Match also appeared on the agenda when Kema Nobel[228] failed to take control of it. An exploration began into whether there were any synergies to be found between the two companies. However, Rydin found it difficult to 'see through' Swedish Match. One way to solve that problem was to gain a board position, but the Wallenberg sphere blocked that path. There was also the idea that SCA should acquire a holding in Swedish Match, but its CEO, among others, indicated that the main owner Peter Wallenberg never would sell.[229]

In 1985, Beijer[230] and Argentus[231] offered Mölnlycke a rather large holding in Cederroth.[232] Mölnlycke bought those shares and continued buying so that two years later the holding had grown to 33 per cent of the capital and 11 per cent of the votes. Mölnlycke wanted to buy a bigger share, but the majority owner was not interested in selling. SCA then considered making a (generous) hostile bid, but the idea was not pursued because the company's executive capacity was occupied by several other big issues (Peaudouce had recently been bought; Italcarta, Laakirchen, a Spanish corrugated unit and Reedpack were under discussion).[233] By the late 1980s, Cederroth had begun to worry about its continued listing at SSE. As it turns out, SCA had bought all the shares offered on the market, thereby reducing the number of shareholders in Cederroth to what SSE accepted as a minimum level.

When SCA in the early 1980s determined that it wanted to participate as a major owner in a European hygiene company, Scott Paper came into focus. Such a joint undertaking, which would involve merging Mölnlycke and Scott Paper's European operations, presupposed both that SCA would abandon its 100 per cent ownership in Mölnlycke, and that Scott Paper would leave the European market. Such a 'European company' would make SCA really big on the tissue market. However, it was not obvious that all top managers liked the idea. According to Rydin, Chair Browaldh was quite hesitant. Many of Mölnlycke's top managers also expressed scepticism – they were not inclined to take directions from new shareholders and executive bodies. Moreover, they regarded Mölnlycke's product portfolio as much better than the one Scott Paper offered. Another thing that spoke against a joint venture was that Mölnlycke intended to concentrate its tissue operations within the Nordic market, and Scott Paper had no presence there. Mölnlycke's decision to concentrate its hygiene activities on institutions also spoke against the new European construct, since Scott Paper was simply not needed for that effort. The American company was hesitant, too, mainly because it had bad experiences from the diapers market. Still, its CEO Lippincott in particular was eager to establish a strong link with Mölnlycke.[234]

Despite the many objections towards a jointly owned European hygiene company, Rydin met with Lippincott in 1986 and listened to his strategic ideas. They included expansion of the new unit with respect to both new products and markets. In addition to diapers, 'food service' (cf. Duni-Bilå) and absorption (cf. Mölnlycke and Johnson & Johnson) should be the focus. Rydin informed Lippincott that Europe (already) was Mölnlycke's home market, and that SCA's current cash flow made substantial investments possible in the hygiene businesses. He stressed that SCA would rather co-operate with Scott Paper outside Europe.[235] Roughly at that time, something dramatic occurred on the global market for diapers: Mölnlycke discovered that a Japanese firm had introduced an innovative diaper product (UniCharm) on its home market and managed to hit Procter & Gamble hard.

13.3.8 Defending the Shareholder Structure

In 1984, an unexpected actor showed interest in the forest-based industry: Philip Morris. Its strong cash flow led it to seek new investment fields (the company could no longer merely devote itself to reducing debts and redeeming shares), so the forest-based industry became one of its new target areas. Philip Morris set its sights on PWA and its tissue and fine paper. If SCA were to sell its holding – which it did not preclude – the sale would have to be combined with other structural changes (e.g. PWA would have to buy SCA's Wifstavarf investment, and SCA would have to get PWA's part of Zewawell). Philip Morris had analysed VP as well, but VP's controlling owner Schickedanz refused to sell. Although Philip Morris showed interest in both Feldmühle and Mölnlycke, none of those efforts led to concrete action at the time.

Also in the mid-1980s, SCA established a special company – Aeolus – to be used as a platform for share purchases. The original idea behind the creation of Aeolus was to prepare for the introduction of 'attractive' parts of SCA on the SSE. However, Aeolus soon acquired holdings in Custos (2%), Industrivärden (6%) and Pharmacia (4%), so instead SCA considered a listing of the new company.[236] The new company could also be used to defend SCA's ownership structure, making sure that the Handelsbanken/Industrivärden sphere could continue to decide SCA's future (however, Aeolus was never listed).

In 1986, SCA faced an 'attack' against its major owner Industrivärden. In that situation, SCA looked through its various options for securing the current power structure and included Aeolus as part of its defence strategy. For SCA, it was of utmost interest that Industrivärden was kept in 'safe hands'. Towards that end, a shareholder consortium was founded that 'secured' the Handelsbanken sphere's voting power in Industrivärden. The consortium agreement stated that all the contracting parties had to remain united and follow the majority in their voting. Therefore, when Ratos entered as a new and large shareholder in Industrivärden (13%, later 18%), its leading actors were informed about the consortium agreement and voting power (≈ 40%). Ratos did not object to such a construct, but its CEO Söderberg claimed that the consortium was obliged to report its holding to SSE. Rydin saw Ratos as a most appropriate shareholder in Industrivärden, although the Söderberg family often had been close to the rival Wallenberg sphere. Rydin informed Söderberg about the consortium's view regarding Industrivärden's basic investments (e.g. that certain ones were long term). He also stressed that it always had to be one main (or leading) owner in that investment company, and for the time being SCA played that role (≈ 15%).[237]

Industrivärden had a large amount of shares in SCA, so a cross-ownership arrangement existed between the two corporations. There also existed a 'rampart' upheld by four large Swedish companies that in addition to Industrivärden and SCA included Volvo and Skanska. The use of cross-ownerships and ramparts was actually criticized at the time, but SCA Chair Browaldh defended the system, as SCA currently was vulnerable and rather easy to acquire for an outside actor that, for example, was attracted by SCA's enormous forest resources.[238] As it was crucial for the Handelsbanken/Industrivärden sphere to keep its control of SCA, a revised consortium agreement was set up in 1987 that made Industrivärden almost impregnable.[239]

The arrangement between Industrivärden and SCA had consequences for how the latter company developed. For example, SCA could almost never pay for acquisitions with its own shares, as it 'had to' give precedence to its current owners when it issued new shares. Particularly in growth periods, that policy produced a risk that SCA might become short of equity capital, but the company's close link to the Handelsbanken sphere solved most of that problem. Economically well-motivated investments were usually financed.[240] SCA also used 'all' the existing legal opportunities to lower its tax payments to free up capital.

13.4 RYDIN BECOMES CHAIR AND MARTIN-LÖF CEO

In 1988, Browaldh left SCA's board and Rydin succeeded him as Chair. The directors appointed Rydin Chair because they wanted a person in that position that really knew the company's operations. Sverker Martin-Löf was then appointed CEO of SCA. Rydin, who was influential regarding whom to choose, had been impressed by Martin-Löf's achievements at Östrand (pulp) and Sunds Defibrator (machinery). A few years earlier, Rydin also considered Carlberg for that position, but Carlberg left and became new Nobel CEO in 1986.[241] As the directors wanted to learn more about Martin-Löf before they let him take full CEO responsibility, they encouraged Rydin to accept the position as Group CEO ('koncernchef') for a two-year period, during which Martin-Löf's actual role was more similar to that of a COO. Accordingly, Rydin acted as Chair of three important internal boards (Mölnlycke, SCA Packaging and BÅKAB). Not surprisingly Martin-Löf was not entirely satisfied with that arrangement, as it created some uncertainty in the organization.[242]

Several actors (e.g. SCA director Penser) claimed that Martin-Löf's internal position was strong, and that he was the obvious CEO choice, accepted by almost everybody. No other member of top management was regarded as a serious contender. Brändström, who was rather close to Rydin, was actually older than him, and Daun could not be appointed for 'political' reasons (since he was Head of Mölnlycke). Potential candidates working outside SCA were excluded for various reasons.[243] However, there were a few sceptics, too, that claimed that Martin-Löf's background was largely inappropriate, as he was not particularly knowledgeable in the crucial hygiene and consumer operations. Thus, his experience was not what SCA needed in 1988. Although the critics respected Martin-Löf for his achievements at Sunds and Östrand, they claimed that SCA now needed a market-oriented restructurer. The critics suggested instead that SCA should look outside the company, but there was weak support for that idea. SCA's managers, schooled in the classic forest-based businesses, preferred an internal solution.[244]

One outcome of Martin-Löf's appointment was that SCA's 'favouring of Mölnlycke' ended, and he was actually not convinced that Mölnlycke's relatively broad operations actually fitted into SCA's future business repertoire. However, he was well aware of Mönlycke's importance for SCA, as it represented around 60 per cent of the company's total turnover. So for the time being the three core businesses (Graphics, Packaging and Hygiene [Mölnlycke]) all received similar support.[245]

SCA's financial position had become much better since Rydin took command, and that suited the new CEO Martin-Löf's more risk-seeking personality. Martin-Löf's track record included the position as Head of Technology at SCA's rival MoDo, and that company's leading actor Carlgren had even hinted to Martin-Löf that he might become CEO there one day. However, that kind of 'promise' from Carlgren was not unusual, so most actors near him did not take those utterances particularly seriously.[246] As MoDo's Head of Technology, Martin-Löf was supposed to act as a 'counterforce' when the division heads presented their investment propositions to Carlgren (and the board). However, Martin-Löf faced many problems in that role with some of MoDo's more powerful top managers (e.g. Löf, Head of Pulp and Paper, and Sprängare, Head of Forestry). Over time, those tensions developed into 'emotional sediments' that had an impact on both companies' strategic discussions during the early 1990s – particularly when SCA became a large shareholder in MoDo.

Martin-Löf had moved from MoDo to SCA in 1977 after conversations with one of its top managers, Zetterberg, who told Martin-Löf that he intended to leave because he saw no chance of becoming CEO of SCA anytime soon (Rydin had recently been appointed). Despite that prognosis from Zetterberg, Martin-Löf decided to move to SCA and accepted a position that made him responsible for the pulp business and modernization of the Östrand plant. Indeed, his new position at SCA could have been regarded as less prominent than the one he left, but he also moved because he had found MoDo's culture too 'political' (i.e. full of intrigues, power struggles, and [unfulfilled] promises), and because of the tough internal competition regarding its next CEO appointment (cf. between Löf and Sprängare).[247] SCA had problems with its Östrand (pulp) unit at the time, particularly because it was economically disintegrated from the Wifsta unit (fine paper). Martin-Löf successfully addressed those problems, and gradually that strengthened his internal status.

Martin-Löf continued his predecessors' tradition of managing without a GMT. Instead, he organized a special group, composed of the business area heads and the Head of R&D (de Ruvo), which was instructed to work on the company's strategic development. Martin-Löf also decided to change SCA's decentralized organization structure. Because he believed the time was right for reaping advantages of scale and for building a more distinct corporate profile, he centralized certain policies and decisions. Martin-Löf was of the opinion that many of the core units in SCA had become too independent – almost self-governing and expanding more on their own merits rather than in a broader SCA context.

Martin-Löf's leadership style differed from that of Rydin in several ways. He was energetic, that is to say, a most active and 'pushy' actor, who closely followed the business areas. Thus, Martin-Löf quickly took command of SCA and started to accelerate its growth process. He participated personally in many of the crucial negotiations that followed from the expansion strategy. All in all, Martin-Löf was a businessman who stepped on the gas (while Chair Rydin used the brake).[248] He was also a straightforward leader, who could be frank and, when needed, express emotions.

One tradition that continued, however, was how the board worked – it continued to function foremost as an arena for 'syntonization' and control. Its respected directors prevented hasty proposals from even reaching that arena ('self-censorship'). The proposers (usually the core business heads) abandoned many of their ideas after discussions with Martin-Löf and/or Rydin. However, on the whole, and despite that board scrutiny, SCA continued to be a CEO-driven company.[249]

As Martin-Löf lacked formal education in Business Administration, he relied quite heavily on the company's CFO, Rietz.[250] Another important member of his top management was the Chief Legal Officer, Bertorp, who, for example, participated in most acquisition negotiations. The heads of R&D (de Ruvo), paper (Frölander) and pulp (Eriksson) were other top managers with whom he also interacted frequently (and some of them were part of his private circle).[251] Thus, from 1988 onwards SCA had a well-functioning top management where a 'family-like' atmosphere prevailed – the leaders liked each other and had fun together.[252] Yet, more formally speaking, Martin-Löf engaged in bilateral talks with his closest subordinates (thus, he had no GMT).[253]

NOTES

N.B.: When there is an 'i' inside a parenthesis below, that letter indicates that the note refers to an interview with the named person. All interviewees are listed in the Appendix. A complete listing of references is found at the end of the book.

1. Haslum (1993).
2. Utterström (1979).
3. Gaunitz (1979).
4. Haslum (1993).
5. Ibid.
6. A Swedish energy company.
7. Gaunitz (1979) and Haslum (1993).
8. Utterström (1979).
9. Utterström (1979) and Haslum (1993).
10. Utterström (1979).
11. Ibid.
12. Haslum (1993).
13. Wahlström (1999).
14. Haslum (1993).
15. Wahlström (1999).
16. Utterström (1979).
17. Utterström (1979) and Haslum (1993).
18. Gaunitz (1979).
19. Valeur (1997).
20. Rydberg (1990).
21. Haslum (1993).
22. Valeur (1997).
23. Gaunitz (1979) and Valeur (2000).
24. Valeur (1997).
25. Haslum (1993).

26. Gaunitz (1979) and Valeur (2003).
27. Ernfrid Browaldh's son.
28. Browaldh (2004i).
29. Gaunitz (1979) and Valeur (2003).
30. Nordenö (2005i).
31. Gaunitz (1979) and Haslum (1993).
32. Wahlström (2004i and 2006i).
33. Gaunitz (1979).
34. Mossberg even took some torturous decisions to save his successor Rydin from a bad start (the closures of Svartvik and Kramfors). Penser (2006i).
35. Wahlström (1999), Browaldh (2004i) and Wahlström (2004i and 2006i).
36. Wahlström (2006i).
37. Cf. Ch. 12.
38. Haslum (1993).
39. Ibid.
40. Ibid.
41. Ibid.
42. Gaunitz (1979) and Valeur (2003).
43. Ibid.
44. Caronnerie du Congo.
45. Gaunitz (1979) and Haslum (1993).
46. Nordenö (2005i).
47. De Forenede Papirfabrikker.
48. Gaunitz (1979).
49. Wood-free.
50. Wahlström (1999, p. 70), Gaunitz (1979) and Haslum (1993).
51. Wallander (1998, p. 17).
52. A memorandum to SCA's board from CEO Mossberg.
53. Norberg (2005i).
54. Haslum (1993).
55. Ibid.
56. Treated as one unit from 1966 (the Wifsta-Östrand industries).
57. Papelera Navarra, Papeteries Clergeau, Colon Emballage, AZ, Skeena River and Patrician.
58. Haslum (1993).
59. Haslum (1993) and Wahlström (1999, p. 66).
60. Browaldh (2004i) and Wahlström (2006i).
61. SCA was part of the Handelsbanken/Industrivärden sphere, MoDo was an autonomous corporation having Handelsbanken as its main bank.
62. Wahlström (2006i).
63. Wahlström (1999, p. 72), Wahlström (2006i), Dahlsten (2004i and 2005i) and Norberg (2005i).
64. Dahlsten (2004i and 2005i).
65. Yet Enström and Mossberg (together with Wahlström) had 'sorted out' the northern region, and made clear to which sites the prioritized production processes ought to be located.
66. Francke (2004i) and Rydin (2004i and 2005i).
67. Rydin (2004i and 2005i).
68. Wahlström (1999, p. 72).
69. Norberg (letter written in 2005).
70. Rydin's diary.
71. Francke (2004i).
72. Wahlström (2004i and 2006i).
73. Daun (2004i and 2006i).
74. Enander (2004i).
75. Penser (2005i).
76. Browaldh (2004i).
77. Rydin (2004i and 2005i).
78. Wahlström (2004i and 2006i).
79. Rydin (2004i and 2005i), Rydin's diary and Francke (2004i).
80. Martin-Löf (2004i and 2006i).
81. Rydin (2004i and 2005i).
82. When he visited Svartvik and Kramfors well aware of SCA's poor financial situation, he almost regretted that he had accepted the CEO position. Rydin (2004i and 2005i).

83. SCA had always cared about its relations with the politicians.
84. Nordenö (2005i).
85. Valeur (2003).
86. Nordenö (2005i).
87. Wahlström (2004i).
88. The strong CEO power was more based on custom than legislation.
89. Kallifatides et al. (2010).
90. In 1974, SCA decided to change its name from 'Svenska Cellulosa Aktiebolaget' to 'SCA' to protect that well-known acronym.
91. Lindholm and Wilke (2002).
92. ASSI, Billerud, Fiskeby and SCA.
93. Valeur (2003).
94. Ibid.
95. Over lunch in early 1973, Rydin also discussed with Hedlund a possible co-ownership of Obbola for Ncb. Since Ncb had very little to offer, the idea fizzled out. Still, Hedlund indicated that Ncb would be interested in buying Obbola (its sulphate plant), if SCA decided not to invest there (Rydin's diary).
96. Wahlström (1999).
97. Ibid.
98. Sweden was part of EFTA.
99. Valeur (2003).
100. Ibid.
101. Ibid.
102. Ibid.
103. Ibid.
104. Norberg (2005i) and Nordenö (2005i).
105. Valeur (2003).
106. Dahlsten (2004i).
107. Ibid.
108. Ibid.
109. Haslum (1993).
110. Daun (2004i and 2006i).
111. Rydin's diary.
112. Ibid.
113. Wahlström (2004i and 2006i).
114. Nordenö (2005i).
115. Ibid.
116. Rydin's diary.
117. Nordenö (2005i).
118. Wahlström (2004i and 2006i).
119. Dahlsten (2004i).
120. Ibid.
121. Daun (2004i and 2006i).
122. Dahlsten (2004i).
123. Valeur (2003).
124. At that time named Svenska Tändsticks AB.
125. Dahlsten (2004i).
126. Ibid.
127. Wahlström (2004i and 2006i).
128. Rydin (2004i and 2005i).
129. Wahlström (2004i and 2006i).
130. Rydin's diary.
131. Wahlström (2004i and 2006i).
132. Daun (2004i and 2006i).
133. Rydin (2004i and 2005i).
134. Ibid.
135. Daun (2004i and 2006i).
136. Wahlström (2004i and 2006i).
137. Dahlsten (2004i).
138. Daun (2004i and 2006i).
139. Wahlström (2004i and (2006i).
140. Ibid.

141. Daun (2004i and 2006i).
142. Rydin (2004i and 2005i).
143. Ibid.
144. Rydin's diary.
145. Lindholm and Wilke (2002).
146. The final terms stated that Mölnlycke's shareholders got either one SCA share for one Mölnlycke share or two SCA shares and one convertible bond (SEK 250) for three Mölnlycke shares.
147. Thunholm (2005, pp. 316–19).
148. Dahlsten (2004i).
149. Daun (2004i and 2006i).
150. Rietz (2004i).
151. Rydin (2004i and 2006i).
152. Rydin's diary.
153. Haslum (1993).
154. Wahlström (1999, p. 72).
155. Ibid.
156. Haslum (1979) and Haslum (1993).
157. The company's dominating shareholder Marcus Wallenberg Sr probably instructed him to do so.
158. Rydin's diary.
159. Rietz (2004i).
160. The group of forest-based corporations that upheld the cartel rules.
161. Wahlström (2004i and 2006i).
162. Head of SCA Graphic Paper.
163. Norberg (2005i).
164. Francke (2004i).
165. Rydin's diary.
166. Lindholm and Wilke (2002).
167. Rietz (2004i).
168. Rydin (2004i and 2005i).
169. Ibid.
170. Martin-Löf (2004i and 2006i).
171. A region in northern Sweden.
172. Valeur (1997).
173. Penser (2005i).
174. SCA got 49% in a Dutch holding company that became the mother company of those operations (named Smurfit-SCA).
175. Lindholm and Wilke (2002).
176. Haslum (1979).
177. Nordenö (2005i).
178. Williams, in Lindholm and Wilke (2002).
179. SCA board minutes (released by Martin-Löf).
180. A Swedish producer of professional hand tools.
181. Haslum (1993).
182. A Finnish manufacturing company.
183. An American industrial and chemistry company.
184. An American manufacturing company.
185. A Swedish company that produced grinding segments for pulp production.
186. A Finnish forest and metal company.
187. SCA board minutes (released by Martin-Löf).
188. Valeur (2003).
189. SCA board minutes (released by Martin-Löf).
190. Penser (2005i).
191. Wahlström (2004i and 2006i).
192. Nordenö (2005i).
193. Åström (2005i and 2006i).
194. Valeur (1997).
195. A diversified Swedish paper corporation (pulp, paper, hygiene and packaging).
196. Rydin's diary.
197. Nordenö (2005i).
198. Its production of kraft paper ended in 1982.
199. Rydin (2004i and 2005i).

200. Valeur (2003).
201. Rydin (2004i and 2005i).
202. As a step in the company's ambition to internationalize its operations, SCA listed its shares in both London and New York (Nasdaq) in 1983.
203. Södra was in crisis in 1982 and instead offered one of its pulp plants to SCA.
204. Rydin's diary.
205. Rydberg (1990).
206. Wahlström (2004i) and (2006i).
207. SCA board minutes (released by Martin-Löf).
208. Ibid.
209. For an extensive description of this process see Ch. 9, Ericson (1991) and Sjöstrand (1997).
210. Rydin (2004i and 2005i).
211. Ibid.
212. Browaldh (2004i).
213. Rydin's diary.
214. Carlgren (1994i).
215. Daun (2006i).
216. Rydin's diary.
217. Tax relief at that level.
218. Rydin's diary.
219. Valeur (2007) and SCA board minutes (released by Martin-Löf).
220. Sjöstrand (1997).
221. Rydin's diary.
222. SCA board minutes (released by Martin-Löf).
223. Rydin (2004i and 2005i).
224. SCA board minutes (released by Martin-Löf).
225. Daun (2004i and 2006i).
226. Enander (2004i).
227. Rydin's diary.
228. A Swedish chemical company.
229. Rydin's diary.
230. A medium-sized Swedish investment company.
231. Ibid.
232. A Swedish company with an extensive range of products in the healthcare sector.
233. SCA board minutes (released by Martin-Löf).
234. Rydin's diary.
235. Ibid.
236. SCA board minutes (released by Martin-Löf).
237. Ibid.
238. Browaldh (2004i).
239. SCA board minutes (released by Martin-Löf).
240. Rietz (2004i).
241. Rydin's diary.
242. Penser (2005i).
243. Ibid.
244. Dahlsten (2004i).
245. Haslum (1979).
246. Ibid.
247. Ibid.
248. Martin-Löf (2004i), Nordenö (2005i) and Penser (2005i).
249. Frölander (2005i).
250. Enander (2004i).
251. Nordenö (2005i).
252. Frölander (2005i).
253. Martin-Löf (2004i and 2006i).

14. SCA: a dramatic expansion period

14.1 A STRING OF ACQUISITIONS

14.1.1 Peaudouce

Mölnlycke's CEO Daun noticed that big international corporations showed increasing interest in Mölnlycke's products. They also looked at the Nordic countries as a potential new market, and Procter & Gamble, in particular, was seen as a threat. To address this threat, SCA had to decide whether it was possible for Mölnlycke to concentrate on the Nordic market, or whether it might have to expand its 'home domain' to all of Europe – or even go global. Daun was of the opinion that a sole presence in the Nordic countries would be impossible to defend, as the impact of diseconomies of scale in production and marketing would then hit hard. Mölnlycke's top management made a list of possible acquisitions in (primarily) Europe, and leading managers travelled around with that list in their heads and talked with high-level managers in the prioritized companies. If more 'serious' leads developed, Daun – and sometimes Rydin – would join SCA's staff in those meetings.[1] In packaging Nordenö's contribution mattered the most for many of the negotiations in that field – he knew almost everybody and everything in that business. However, for SCA as a whole, Martin-Löf (and before 1988 Rydin) – typically together with Bertorp (Chief Legal Officer) and Rietz (CFO) – led most acquisition processes. That team usually also carried out many of the crucial negotiations.[2]

SCA's dramatic expansion period started in early 1987 when 'Project Peaudouce' was introduced to SCA's board. The French Arnault family had decided to get out of the diapers business and concentrate on its operations in luxury consumables. Peaudouce had already been identified as an interesting target for SCA several years previously, as it was number one in diapers in France and ran a healthy business in Greece. Peaudouce was now put 'in play', and as it was active in geographical markets other than Mölnlycke's, it fitted SCA's strategy to expand beyond the Nordic region. Both Dahlsten (director, SCA) and Daun (CEO, Mölnlycke) favoured a purchase,[3] as there was an obvious risk that Peaudouce would be sold to another company that later could become a serious competitor to Mölnlycke in Europe.

Like most directors Penser regarded Daun's push for a purchase as well founded, and to some extent that opinion overcame both Rydin's cautiousness and SCA's traditional conservative governance principles. Rydin had trusted Daun's judgement ever since SCA bought Mölnlycke, and that ultimately tipped the coin in favour of a purchase.[4] Eventually it became clear that Peaudouce's plants were in rather poor shape, and that the acquisition price included a very 'expensive goodwill' on SCA's part. In addition, Peaudouce's product portfolio was almost too similar to that of Mölnlycke. It also became apparent that its products were not as good as Procter & Gamble's, but it was not seen as a problem at the time, as that company was not yet an aggressive actor in Europe.[5]

From the very beginning Rydin made clear that SCA must get majority ownership in Peaudouce (the seller finally accepted that). SCA was initially offered a 40 per cent holding plus an option to acquire an additional 20 per cent in order to avoid the scrutiny of the French authorities. A complication was that the seller Financière Agache, represented by Mr Arnault, did not accept shares as payment, but soon the parties agreed on a price just below SEK 2 billion. Rydin thought this was a good deal because of its strategic value, although it entailed many risks. However, when he received the 'Letter of intent' from Peaudouce, it was not phrased as expected. Furthermore, the seller seemed 'too eager' to close the deal. These two signs led Rydin to hesitate (his legal advisers had informed him that 'Arnault did not always act as a gentleman') and ask for certain guarantees (e.g. regarding Peaudouce's current profit level). Once SCA got those guarantees, the deal was closed in January 1988.

The acquisition of Peaudouce was a very important strategic step for SCA. That purchase made everybody aware that one main road forward for SCA was now set: hygiene. France became one of Mölnlycke's most important markets, and together Mölnlycke and Peaudouce were the largest companies in Europe in children's diapers, incontinence products and menstrual supplies (i.e. fluff products).[6] As late as during mid-1988, Peaudouce was regarded as a successful acquisition even though selling prices and some test-run troubles indicated that the economic result would be poor. However, Mölnlycke expected prices to rise once the potent newcomer Procter & Gamble had established a substantial market share (they had acted so on other markets).

Instead, Mölnlycke ran into serious problems rather quickly. Its Nordic management was not fully prepared to run a European consumer company, and they had underestimated how active Procter & Gamble would be. Moreover, Peaudouce's previous 'comfortable situation' in France, where its business was based mainly on well-developed domestic networks and close personal relationships, gradually eroded, particularly when its French owners were replaced by foreign (Swedish) ones. Peaudouce had simply never built high competence in fields like pricing and product strategies.

The new situation also worried Procter & Gamble. Suddenly, it faced a capable company (Mölnlycke) that might keep it in the second position for a long time. Added to that, the big US hygiene corporation Kimberly-Clark had entered the French market on a greenfield basis, and that further increased market pressure. There were also signs already in December 1988 that Peaudouce had lost market share, a development that continued during 1989.[7]

14.1.2 A Strategic Crossroads

In the late 1980s, SCA experienced a period of strategic uncertainty. Martin-Löf had not yet finally decided what path he preferred for SCA – it could either divest itself of Mölnlycke and focus on graphic papers and packaging, or concentrate on Mölnlycke and perhaps give up one of the other two businesses. As a third alternative, SCA could also go on investing in all three areas. If the 'Mölnlycke path' was chosen, then there was a need for streamlining, but that was difficult for SCA's new CEO, as Mölnlycke was (still) run by its internal board. For the time being, Martin-Löf decided that SCA should continue to support all its three core businesses, and do that without impairing its balance sheet. Thus, a break-up of SCA was not on Martin-Löf's agenda.[8]

The streamlining of Mölnlycke entailed both a reorganization of its units and disinvestments. Forsgren, who succeeded Daun as Mölnlycke's CEO in 1989, established seven business areas and several units that marketed and sold on behalf of those business areas. Before Forsgren took office, Mölnlycke had sold some of its more unrelated businesses (boats, sewing cotton, etc.).[9] So, the focus turned to fluff rather than tissue. In fluff, Mölnlycke concentrated on two 'legs', namely consumer products (like diapers) and incontinence care, with an emphasis on the AFH[10] segment (that soon became an expanding field).

When Mölnlycke was not able to reach first or second position on a consumer market, it concentrated its efforts on private ('retail') brands. At the moment its 'star' business was incontinence care, and Forsgren had granted that area a more autonomous standing within Mölnlycke. That freedom allowed for an expansion that involved both new products and new (geographical) markets. Outside Europe joint ventures were created, as Mölnlycke lacked experience from many of the 'conquered' markets.

In the late 1980s, the board decided that SCA should continue to treat Europe – rather than merely Scandinavia – as its home market. That also meant that most of the expansion should take place on the European continent and in the UK, rather than in Scandinavia. The geographical focus was to be on East and South Europe, and there Martin-Löf expected 'vertical' deals (to get closer to end customers). The Nordic countries should rather function as arenas for 'horizontal' activities (i.e. restructuring efforts). In Europe, Martin-Löf wanted to build SCA without part ownerships (i.e. no minority holdings, [50–50] joint ventures or majority positions) because he had found such constellations troublesome to run. As a result, in Europe SCA either expanded to full ownership or sold out. In South and Middle America and in Asia, however, he accepted part ownerships as a means to reduce both political and distance risks.

Martin-Löf's vision for SCA's packaging business was that it should maintain a sustainable balance between raw materials and further processing and keep its operations inside Europe (to export corrugated across the Atlantic was not economically possible). He also noted that, while SCA was strong on kraftliner, it still lacked substantial testliner production.[11] The Head of Packaging (Nordenö) was asked in 1987 to present a strategy for his business area. The resulting recommendation was that SCA only should acquire profitable corrugated companies, preferably those that produced testliner and fluting from waste paper. Nordenö and his team had identified all interesting target companies in Europe and organized their information gathering so that it was known in advance if and when those companies might be 'in play'. Ownership situations and changes were carefully checked – the managers within the packaging units were told to inform Nordenö 'if something was moving somewhere'. Thus, the focus was very much on the set-up and use of networks.[12]

SCA's goals were set high for graphic papers. However, the targets focused more on quality, productivity and integration with forestry operations than on volumes and market shares.[13] For graphic papers, what would become dramatic changes had just begun. The classic newsprint business was still profitable in the mid-1980s, but there were some signs that demand was declining. Moreover, waste fibre was increasingly used in that type of production, and its input share was in some cases approaching 100 per cent.

As a result, the expensive high-quality spruce fibre had to be used for something else. As TMP production used large amounts of electric energy, the cost for that input gradually became a problem, too. The conclusion was that SCA should move its production at Ortviken towards higher paper qualities (primarily coated ones). SCA intended to continue as a major supplier of standard newsprint in Europe but to re-locate that production to waste-fibre-based ones on the continent or in the UK (where that raw material 'grew best'). However, for the other graphic papers that allowed for better printing qualities, the situation looked much better – that market was actually growing (LWC and SC). Accordingly, SCA eventually started two LWC machines at Ortviken (1990 and 1995).[14]

The graphic business was treated as a 'cash cow' for the other two core businesses. It was well invested, but it gradually became obvious to everyone at SCA that it was not as highly prioritized as the other two businesses. Furthermore, to be competitive in most parts of the graphics industry, size had become very important. Because it would take quite a lot of capital to become 'big enough', Martin-Löf was reluctant to expand that business.[15] More generally, SCA was in a hurry – the number of potential acquisition candidates in the relevant parts of the forest-based industry was rapidly decreasing.[16]

Like his predecessor, Martin-Löf worked to strengthen SCA's reputation among potential sellers of (particularly) family-run forest-based companies. Selling families also often looked for other qualities in a deal than 'best price', and that suited SCA, as its financial resources were rather limited compared with those of the bigger competitors. In such situations, a buyer like SCA could make it more likely that the acquired company's values and traditions would be upheld. Now and then SCA also offered prominent executive positions to sellers.[17] In practice, the heads of the three business areas suggested most of the candidates (Daun [Mölnlycke; hygiene] and Nordenö [Packaging] were particularly active). Over the years, most top executives had built links to interesting firms (to their owners as well as executives) waiting for an opportunity to act. Martin-Löf was also very active – he was impatient and followed up on most signals that appeared on the market or popped up in informal small talk. However, as usual, most of the talks with the leaders of promising acquisition candidates never turned into actual deals.[18]

Martin-Löf's rather broad strategy for SCA (three 'legs') required quite a lot of capital, and that put the company's power plants in the spotlight as objects that could be financed more advantageously. Eventually 'partner financing' of those resources freed a good SEK 5 billion. In addition, divestments were simultaneously made that amounted to about SEK 3 billion (Sunds Defibrator, Zewawell and Smurfit Corrugated UK; all partly owned). There was also an issue of a convertible debt, and SCA began to consider a listing of its shares also outside Sweden.[19]

All through 1987 and 1988 SCA discussed the acquisition of the British forest-based company Reedpack (partially in parallel with the discussions with Peaudouce; cf. above), even though it was not certain that the company was 'in play'. In any case, such a purchase was soon seen as unrealistic. It was simply too large a 'bite' for SCA. It was also problematic because of the accompanying goodwill entry. Still, the low taxation in the UK made a purchase tempting, and with some financial creativity the actual price (SEK 4.5 billion) could be squeezed down to close to SEK 4 billion, an acceptable level. The idea arose to use KVBs[20] for the purchase with a limit at SEK 4.2 billion, but the Chair was pessimistic. He suspected that several other bidders would offer much more. SCA would also be short of managerial capacity, as it recently had acquired Peaudouce.

However, Rydin thought that Reedpack was far more interesting than Cellulose du Pin,[21] which in addition to corrugated contained a liner production SCA wanted to avoid. In addition to Reedpack, Rydin found Austrian Laakirchen (cf. subsection 14.1.3) and Italcarta (cf. subsection 14.1.4) particularly interesting. He also looked at BAT's[22] Wiggins Teape to see whether that unit was for sale and might fit. Champion was also analysed, but the price was a prohibitive obstacle. In most of these cases SCA acted indirectly through intermediaries so that its interest in purchasing would not push the price upwards and trigger activities from competitors.[23]

14.1.3 Laakirchen

In pursuit of a stable, long-term path in the graphics business, SCA looked for ways to enter the growing SC field and began the search for acquisition candidates on the continent. The focus was soon placed on Laakirchen, which produced and sold both SC paper and tissue.[24] Laakirchen's major owner (75%) Wilfred Heinzel wanted to 'cash in', so he contacted some of the actors he knew at SCA – a company he liked. SCA had earned a reputation as a responsible buyer/owner among many European industry families. One reason was that it was not uncommon for SCA to keep an acquired company's management. That was likely in this case, as well, since Wilfred Heinzel's son Alfred had managerial ambitions.[25]

So, Rydin, Martin-Löf, Enander (head of the Östrand plant), Frölander (Head of Paper) and de Ruvo (Head of R&D) all went to Vienna in June 1988 to meet with representatives from Laakirchen including Wilfred and Alfred Heinzel, who both seemed to favour SCA as a new major[26] owner of their company. The Swedish team checked the plants and machines and became seriously interested, although the company was not very profitable. Laakirchen's SC operations looked fine, but its tissue was in rather poor shape (SCA's management thought that Mölnlycke could overcome that problem). SCA was spared a bidding war, so it got a rather low price (SEK 2.6 billion).[27]

The acquisition of Laakirchen was done in 1988 during a period when SCA's leaders were a bit uncertain whether Mölnlycke with all its 'fiddly' businesses should be kept. At that time, the board and top management began to lean more towards packaging and printing papers as SCA's core businesses. The relatively prompt (1991) sale of Laakirchen's tissue operations to PWA also indicated that such ideas were gaining momentum.[28] The Laakirchen purchase was one of the first that took place under Martin-Löf as CEO, and it occurred at about the same time as the acquisition of Italcarta (cf. next subsection).[29] He allowed Laakirchen to continue its operations roughly as before, so its various units were not 'distributed' among corresponding ones in SCA. Thus, Mölnlycke did not get Laakirchen's tissue operations, but as they saw their own 'fluff' activities as more advanced, more amenable to proprietary product development and more profitable than tissue operations, they did not act. However, Martin-Löf maintained that SCA could not gain complete credibility as a major producer of hygiene paper products if the company did not also have comprehensive tissue operations.[30] Several managers suspected that a promise had been made to the seller that SCA would refrain from splitting up Laakirchen – otherwise it was hard for management to understand why Laakirchen's tissue was kept away from Mölnlycke. That suspicion grew when Laakirchen's SC operations were made part of a new SCA unit (SCA Graphic Paper, which also included SCA

Pulp, SCA Ortviken and Wifstavarf). Laakirchen's AFH products (for hospitals) were likewise moved to Mölnlycke's Health Care unit.

14.1.4 Italcarta and Bowaters

During the late 1980s corrugated showed healthy growth, but the situation for kraftliner was less favourable. Its position was challenged by testliner, which was quickly taking market share. The quality of testliner was previously lower than that of kraftliner, and therefore had been sold at cheaper prices. However, that quality gap was closing, which in turn meant that the pricing of kraftliner had to be reconsidered (particularly for the brown kind). Thus, SCA's lack of testliner became a problem.

Fortunately, Italcarta – an Italian company that primarily produced testliner and fluting (and some corrugated) – suddenly came into play. It was for sale for a classic reason – the major shareholder saw no successor among the younger family members. Martin-Löf and Nordenö pushed for a purchase, and Rydin made the crucial contacts with the selling family (Giomi, the founder of the company). Martin-Löf was interested both because it was a big company active on an important market (biggest producer of corrugated in Italy and with a substantial paper production), and because the offered selling price was acceptable.[31]

SCA was the owner family's favourite potential buyer. Like several owner families letting go of their heirlooms, the Giomi family sought a serious long-term owner that would not destroy (split up, etc.) their life's work. So, here again SCA was rewarded for its assiduous building of a reputation for sincerity and long-term orientation.[32] Families like Giomi often sell their heirlooms when industrial structures are changing, because their financial capability to run (or even participate in) such processes is limited. The most crucial factor at that point is timing – to get in contact with a selling family at the right moment (early, but not too early). Private owners and well-known families sometimes have an advantage there, as they often know each other and socialize. However, SCA had overcome that shortcoming and won a favourable reputation also among families/dynasties.[33]

Nordenö, too, had many solid contacts within Italcarta, although foremost at the executive levels, as he and part of SCA's sales organization already worked in Italy (selling kraftliner). SCA could also rely on Rydin and Martin-Löf, who knew Italcarta's Head of R&D. Indeed, SCA had already established relations with Italcarta, so they preferred – almost welcomed – SCA as buyer.[34] For some incomprehensible reason some characteristics of Swedish and Italian business cultures seemed compatible. Thus, as was the case with Laakirchen, SCA had no serious competitor in the takeover process, a situation that might to some extent explain the favourable price.

The head of the Giomi family was initially not healthy, but when his condition improved, he almost regretted the deal. In reality, the price SCA was offered was so favourable that the seller questioned the agreement and asked for additional payments. To make his case stronger, the family head even 'mobilized' the Italian bureaucracy – suddenly no permits were given and courts acted awkwardly. Thus, in a classic Italian way, the situation began to get messy for the foreigner. In the end, SCA raised the price in order to free itself from such obstacles.[35]

Despite the initial favourable atmosphere and 'cultural similarities', the concrete negotiations became difficult as (foremost) the state authorities allowed for quite different 'logics-in-use' and regulative practices than SCA was accustomed to in its Swedish context. For example, Italcarta's accounting system was rather 'indistinct', and, although the company was well run, that ambiguity created difficulties, especially regarding the purchase price. SCA's bad experiences during its recent acquisition of Peaudouce led it to decide to ensure stable operations by offering many former leaders key positions in the company.[36]

Italcarta's profit was actually better than its books indicated because the owners had made certain 'special arrangements'. It was also a company in which investments had been made well, and particularly its paper plant looked fine. Italcarta was in fact among Europe's most efficient paper producers. Still, Nordenö had begun to hesitate, but, since a 'Letter of Intent' existed, it was difficult for SCA to leave the process without both economic and reputational losses. The serious negotiations started in 1989, and they were stressful – also because another actor showed interest. However, by the middle of 1989 Italcarta and SCA had signed a preliminary agreement, and the negotiation process ended happily.[37]

For the Italcarta deal, SCA's board was not as involved in the decision-making process as several directors had expected and would have preferred. Italcarta was almost sneaked into SCA – and that in spite of the fact that the purchase effectively occurred twice (the seller managed to renegotiate both the price and some other terms).[38]

About one year after the purchase of Italcarta, SCA bought the British packaging company Bowaters's operations in Belgium and France. That was one step towards securing a market for SCA's kraftliner. SCA had been offered the chance to buy a large holding in Bowaters already in 1985 when it was 'under attack'. At that time Rydin hesitated but mentioned that some parts of Bowaters were of interest. This time the purchase was considered to be an obvious choice. The deal also brought Williams to SCA, a manager that would succeed Nordenö as Head of Packaging. SCA proceeded to buy additional packaging firms in both France and Holland, so the planned European expansion continued.

14.1.5 Feldmühle Nobel[39]

In 1989, both top management and the board of SCA began to discuss whether it was at all possible to get 'inside' Germany's Feldmühle Nobel. The opportunity to purchase a 5 per cent holding in that company had suddenly emerged (a family feud was going on). That offer was received at the same time as the discussions with Reedpack were underway (cf. subsection 14.1.6). Both alternatives interested Martin-Löf, who was eager to show results, and as it was not yet final which of the three businesses Graphics, Packaging and Hygiene should be given precedence, he continued to try to strengthen all of them.[40] However, as Feldmühle's top management disliked the family's selling intentions, it was not going to be an easy catch.

SCA's interest in buying the Feldmühle part of Feldmühle Nobel was solid – particularly as its own hygiene business (diapers) was in trouble. It was also a particularly attractive target because it was a leading actor in LWC – a growing segment in which SCA had ambitions. LWC was actually one of the few possibilities for SCA if it wished to stay in the graphics sector. The basic idea behind an acquisition of a modest 5 per cent holding was that it 'reserved a position at the table' for SCA, which could be important if additional holdings became available.

At the time, however, since SCA had many other negotiations in progress, the board hesitated. Furthermore, SCA expected resistance from the German authorities and the German unions. The expected price represented another potential obstacle. To get control of the company could amount to around SEK 10 billion, and that sum entailed both a 'country risk' and a squeezing out of other investments (particularly for Mölnlycke). Therefore, to improve its financial capacity, SCA investigated which units in Feldmühle Nobel might be sold off quickly if a takeover should become possible. A new issue of SCA shares to generate additional capital was out of the question because of the current low share price.[41]

Late in December 1989, VEBA (the owner of 50% of Feldmühle Nobel, the holding company that contained Feldmühle) turned down an American company's proposal. With this news, SCA's leaders thought that a bigger deal might be within reach, but it was still regarded as a risky path. SCA also learned that its Swedish competitor Stora was expected to arrive soon to enter into discussions with Feldmühle Nobel's owners about the possibility of a purchase. Martin-Löf told Rydin that the German negotiators seemed to prefer some kind of deal with Stora. Even so, SCA decided to try to acquire the 5 per cent holding that one of the Flick brothers had put on the market. Competition with corporate raiders was tough, but Flick picked SCA as the preferred buyer. So, SCA constructed an alternative that was supposed to be attractive for the Feldmühle part of Feldmühle Nobel. It addressed the graphics business, and included a possibility for SCA to get 51 per cent of Feldmühle.[42]

At about the same time, SCA also discussed an American acquisition. It seemed to be a more fitting company than the German one, but for financial and operative reasons MoDo, too, would have to be involved. So, SCA's leaders met with MoDo's leading actors to discuss the matter, but the American path ultimately did not materialize. While discussing the American option, Martin-Löf took the opportunity to check whether MoDo might be interested in participating in a purchase of Feldmühle (Nobel). However, he learned that MoDo (and Stora) simultaneously were analysing Charpel d'Arblais, so SCA continued on its own, and bought Flick's 5 per cent holding to establish a platform for the formation of a long-term solution for Graphics. That path required the purchase of a large producer of SC and/or LWC, and Feldmühle had now become a possible target.[43]

The discussions with Feldmühle Nobel indicated that it might be possible to separate out and buy its paper-producing unit Feldmühle. When the talks had gone so far that the pricing of the shares had become the core issue, Stora's CEO Berggren learned that something was going on around Feldmühle Nobel that he did not like at all. He immediately contacted Marcus Wallenberg Sr and got *carte blanche* to participate in an expected bidding contest (to get SCA out of Feldmühle Nobel).[44] SCA knew all the time that its purchase of 5 per cent went right to the heart of Stora, but SCA thought that Stora was more than fully occupied with the integration of its recently (1986–88) acquired companies Billerud, Papyrus and Swedish Match. However, that was not the case, so soon SCA came across Stora's leading actors. In April 1990 they 'met' Stora's team at the airport and at the hotel where the negotiations were being carried out. Eventually Feldmühle Nobel's shareholders found Stora's bid more attractive, so SCA lost the contest, but left with a minor profit by selling its holding.[45]

As Stora was eager to prevent SCA from getting any kind of holding in Feldmühle Nobel, it paid a substantial sum to win the race. However, basically Stora's 'victory' was made possible because its leaders were quicker, less risk averse and more flexible in their decision-making than SCA's corresponding actors.[46] There was also already a link between the leaders in Stora and Feldmühle, as they jointly ran both Norrsundet (pulp) and Hylte (paper). Thus, it was not only price that decided the outcome. SCA's CFO Rietz even suspected that Feldmühle Nobel might have used SCA to get a better price from Stora.[47]

The outcome of the Feldmühle Nobel struggle made the graphics business less attractive to SCA, which was more inclined to invest in its packaging business and take a 'big bite' and buy Reedpack. If SCA had bought Feldmühle, it would probably not have had the financial and managerial resources to buy Reedpack, too.[48] So, in 1989, SCA summarized its strategic position in its annual report. Its strengths were: solid balance sheet, EC presence, low dependence on cyclical variations, expected 'healthy' demand in its expanding hygiene business, environmentally friendly operations and products, and favourable supplier situation. However, there were also weaknesses and worries: increased competition from non-European corporations, temporary overcapacities on several paper markets, low speed in the Swedish adaption to EC regulations and costly Swedish energy regulations.[49]

Frölander, Head of Graphic Papers, saw the Swedish EC and EU discussions as first and foremost a rash of political rhetoric. As he saw it, Swedish membership would substantially affect neither the country's economic realities, nor SCA's opportunities to act successfully on the continent. Since all significant trade barriers were already eliminated, SCA would face a similar competitive situation regardless of Sweden's membership.[50] Martin-Löf regarded Sweden's connection to the EC/EU as primarily a 'psychological issue' that might help SCA to define Europe as its (new) home market. An entry into that continent also meant that SCA could learn about new production methods and more processed products – the Nordic pulp and paper production was (still) rather 'bulky'. Since (particularly) the Finnish competitors had a similar output repertoire as the Swedish firms, the Swedes tried to expand on the continent in the same way as their rivals. Thus, neither of them tried to solve the upcoming situation through intra-Nordic restructurings. That process took place a little later among those units that were left after the European race.[51]

14.1.6 Reedpack

Packaging was still treated as a core business in the 1980s. In those days SCA added Fiskeby's packaging unit Skarwell to its Swedish operations, a company that Nordenö had courted for a long time. SCA's executives also kept an eye on Reedpack, although most of them did not believe that it would come into play. Nordenö, however, had noticed that the owner company Reed sought to become a publishing group, and that change indicated to him that the owners might soon be interested in divesting the Reedpack unit. Following up on his hunch, Nordenö contacted Reed's CEO, who confirmed that the sale of Reedpack was on the agenda. SCA placed a tentative bid for that unit, but the sellers had already decided to go for a management-buy-out solution.

However, Nordenö did not give up – he kept the relationship with Reed and Reedpack alive – and eventually those efforts paid off. To SCA's surprise the new owners began to invest heavily in the acquired unit thereby eroding their financial capacity. So once again, SCA began to discuss a purchase of Reedpack. Once these talks turned into straightforward negotiations, Martin-Löf entered the acquisition process. The price for Reedpack had risen, but as the new owners had invested significantly, it was nevertheless acceptable. Nordenö considered the purchase of Reedpack to be crucial if the board really wanted to make SCA a leading company in the European packaging business. In addition, some parts of Reedpack could be sold and contribute to the financing of the acquisition, an element that helped calm the risk-averse Rydin.[52]

Still, since Rydin generally distrusted financial owners, he was not convinced that Reedpack's current ones had played with 'clean cards' and invested as much as they should have. As Rydin saw it, such owners often used the acquired firms' cash flows for mortgage repayments and interest payments instead of for investments. He was so reluctant that if some of the other board members had expressed doubts about the deal, it would probably have been stopped. Rydin was well aware that Reedpack was the first large strategic move made by Martin-Löf, who was eager to show results (particularly after the Feldmühle [Nobel] contest?). Therefore, it took Martin-Löf some effort to finally convince Rydin.[53] Nordenö noted that if SCA instead had succeeded in buying Feldmühle (Nobel), it would not have been able to buy Reedpack too, and then SCA would probably have become another kind of company.[54]

So, in 1990 SCA spent around SEK 10 billion buying Reedpack. It had a leading position in corrugated on the European market, and it also contained newsprint production, office material sales, cardboard operations and a plastics business. It also ran a waste paper business involving both collection and sorting. That 'big bite' increased SCA's turnover by about 50 per cent. Analysts regarded the price as a bit too high, but the estimates from those actors were seen as less interesting, as they (as usual) were made from a roodloft position and lacked solid knowledge about possible rationalizations and synergies.

This time the board was involved in the classic SCA way – the acquisition was thoroughly processed over the course of several meetings and was based on many studies and analyses. Reedpack's sellers were financial actors that had improved Reedpack's profitability with the intent to sell.[55] Director Penser described that kind of seller as a financially competent actor motivated by greed, as contrasted with a seller that (also) cared about the buyer's competence and intentions. SCA was seen as serious, so it had got a seat at the table.[56]

Reedpack suited SCA perfectly, but the price was high (boom times), particularly in light of the large Swedish currency devaluation that occurred rather shortly after the purchase.[57] Nevertheless, most important was that the acquisition substantially increased SCA's presence in Europe, as Reedpack was an actor in four major countries (Belgium, Holland, Ireland and the UK). It also needed large quantities of brown liner, which in itself generated a substantial integration effect. Yet, Reedpack also brought some disappointments. Several parts were not in good shape, and the planned sale of selected units became troublesome, as they were booked too high. Thus, the purchase initiated a spate of rationalizations, selling of units (at lower than expected prices), depreciations and issues of new shares. Still, the acquisition significantly increased SCA's indebtedness, so SCA was downgraded. SCA also had difficulties getting rid of some of the other units on its selling list (e.g. Spicers, Europe's biggest wholesaler [and leading producer] of office material[58]). However, paradoxically, an advantage of Reedpack's bad shape was that it offered vast improvement possibilities.[59]

With Reedpack, SCA also acquired Aylesford, a subsidiary that produced newsprint from waste fibre. In its efforts to improve the capital base, SCA sought a part owner for that unit. Though MoDo was consulted first, Mondi ultimately became the preferred partner. Mondi demanded a 50–50 solution – its ownership policy demanded (at least) that shareholding for all its engagements. SCA accepted that construct as it at least kept Aylesford outside SCA's gradually more strained balance sheet. Still, SCA had to put in around SEK 2 billion.[60]

Eventually SCA became Europe's leading producer and seller of packages for transport. This development gradually placed its liner production more in the background. Instead, it was the demand for packages that determined the performance of the liner business. The integration between liner and corrugated increased and by 1993 it had reached 50 per cent (1977: 25%). At the end of the 1980s Packaging contained about 60 plants in seven countries (Belgium, Holland, Ireland, France, Italy, Sweden and the UK), and it was organized into three business areas (Corrugated, Raw Material [for all kinds of corrugated[61]] and Waste Paper). All that remained were wholly owned companies – the others were divested. For example, in 1990, SCA sold its holdings in Smurfit Corrugated (Ireland and the UK), the remaining 25 per cent in Zewawell and, in 1991, the 50 per cent holding in Colon Emballage.[62]

Meanwhile, SCA's board continued discussing whether it would be possible in the future to run three different capital-intensive business areas (hygiene, graphics and packaging). SCA had in a short period of time made substantial acquisitions in all three of its core areas, but had even bigger ambitions for each of them. To develop its graphic operations SCA currently considered both a larger holding in KNP, and (again) some kind of co-operation with MoDo. For the further expansion of its hygiene operations SCA considered Germany and VP (tissue). To be able to fulfil these and other ideas and continue the expansion, SCA needed to improve its financial capacity.[63]

14.1.7 Divesting BÅKAB

SCA's overall strategy stated that products based on long-fibre timber should be given priority. Products containing a low proportion of fresh fibres were also preferred, as were outputs taking the company closer to its (end) customers. A key goal was to process the raw materials as far as possible.[64] This gradually changing product portfolio simultaneously lowered SCA's dependence on electric power. For example, the move from newsprint to further processed graphic papers had dramatically reduced the cost of electricity. However, the idea that power plants represented a backbone in SCA's operations was deeply rooted, so it took some time before any significant move was made in that field.[65] They were particularly pleased with the steady cash flow that SCA's hydroelectric power operations generated (cf. BÅKAB). When the Swedish deregulation discussions gained momentum in the mid-1980s, SCA began to realize that those cash flows were threatened. In light of this threat, the company conducted several studies about how a deregulated market for electric power would work in Sweden and the Nordic countries.[66]

The financial stress that followed SCA's dramatic expansion in 1987–90 put an even stronger focus on what would be the best use of its power plants. The company's key performance figures also became much weaker, and 1992 turned out to be a really bad year. Moreover, as SCA's expansion ambition was unbroken – both Rydin and Martin-Löf wanted SCA to expand further – even larger sums of capital were needed for the coming years.[67] Parallel to all that, the deregulation of the markets for electricity actually was implemented in the early 1990s, both in Sweden and in some other European countries, and that required a decision about what to do with BÅKAB.

Because the executive actors believed that SCA lacked the necessary resources to participate in the upcoming restructuring of the electric energy industry, they were inclined to sell the company's power resources. Otherwise, SCA would have to acquire numerous distribution companies to obtain sufficient scale for its operations. SCA actually started buying such firms, but learned at an early stage that the required amount of investments would be too high.[68] Inspired by most economists SCA also believed that the price of electricity would decline as a consequence of the expected tougher competition.[69]

However, SCA's forest resources – its other backbone – were not sold, as they differed from power plants in important ways. First, controlling forests close to production sites is always crucial, as the price of timber is directly linked to its transportation costs. Ownership of that resource is also necessary, since lack of 'forest control' would put a producer in a weak bargaining position. SCA also preferred to be highly self-sourced to avoid being forced to buy timber abroad. Second, forests are storable, as it is possible to postpone timber felling. Moreover, to moderate business cycles, a company could cut a few more of the distant trees during good times, and exploit the closer forests during bad times. By contrast, electric power is always available, and for a market price that the power plant owners do not decide. So, SCA could either keep its power plants and use them to subsidize its operations when the price for electricity is high, or sell them and use the capital for other purposes.[70]

In 1990, SCA freed capital (SEK 5 billion) by organizing partnerships for its power resources, but only two years later the board decided to reconsider that ownership strategy. Its conclusion was that SCA should divest that resource entirely. So, late in 1992, BÅKAB was sold to Sydkraft – a transaction that was reasonable from a financial standpoint but emotionally and psychologically troublesome. Rydin handled that decision carefully, and even brought it to the AGM (which was not necessary). He was actually also prepared to cancel the deal if the shareholders had demanded such a move (but they did not).[71] Sydkraft paid SEK 11.5 billion, which provided SCA with a capital gain amounting to SEK 6.7 billion (and almost SEK 10 billion was lifted from SCA's balance sheet). SCA claimed that the sale was the right decision both because it secured the asset value of BÅKAB for SCA and its shareholders, and because it provided BÅKAB and its employees with the best possible future on a dramatically changing market.[72]

However, there were also critics claiming in internal conversations that it would be a mistake to sell, but once they saw that Rydin had been convinced, they did not obstruct. Rydin's decision was fostered by his increasing worry about SCA's current debt situation – the company's balance sheet had become rather weak after all the purchases (adding up to SEK 20 billion). Not even Martin-Löf's position as CEO was safe in that situation – the falling price on the acquired MoDo shares (cf. Ch. 9) and the bad 1992 had put strong pressure on him.[73]

14.1.8 Unlocking Mölnlycke

In September 1989 Martin-Löf informed SCA's board that Mölnlycke did not stick to its financial commitments. That was a first clear indication that the relationship between the CEO and Mönlycke's new CEO Forsgren had become strained. Forsgren wanted Mölnlycke to continue its rapid expansion, although its profitability had fallen ('the diaper crisis', cf. Ch. 13). In that troublesome situation, Forsgren made the mistake of questioning the merits of Mölnlycke's current ownership structure. That initiative and some other initiatives and utterances upset Martin-Löf. That worried Chair Rydin, who suspected that it might be necessary to replace Forsgren, but the relation between Martin-Löf and Forsgren improved during 1991, so Rydin bided his time.[74] Forsgren wanted to keep the raw-material-dependent scale-economic operations (i.e. SCA) apart from the fast-paced consumer-driven operations (i.e. Mölnlycke).[75] However, eventually Martin-Löf and Rydin decided to abandon that separation and integrated Mölnlycke fully within SCA (the top-down 'revolution'). That change was facilitated by the diaper crisis, which also in 1994 ultimately 'produced' a new Mölnlycke CEO: Feltner.[76]

At the end of 1989, SCA's strategic strengths were summarized as follows: strong balance sheet, solid presence in EC countries, low sensitivity to cyclical variations (due to more than 50% consumer products and net buying of pulp), healthy demand (for the hygiene business), increased environmental awareness among customers (favourable for SCA) and better supplier structure in southern Europe. On the negative side, SCA stressed four factors: more competition from non-European corporations, periods of overcapacity in the paper businesses (due to new investments in machines around the world), remaining harmonization problems versus EC (trade issues) and unfavourable national energy policy (prices expected to rise).[77]

14.2 TRYING TO INCORPORATE MODO[78]

For a rather long time SCA had considered the possibility of co-operating with MoDo's Holmen unit. It was regarded as a serious alternative to Feldmühle and other similar acquisition opportunities. Director Hedelius believed that there might be changes in MoDo's shareholder structure in the future that could open up the situation, but Martin-Löf[79] saw substantial problems linking to MoDo, primarily because of historical clashes and diverging cultures. However, he had good relations with MoDo's major shareholder Carlgren, so at least one personal platform was in place.

In late November 1990 Rydin contacted Carlgren to express his view regarding structural alternatives for the two companies' printing paper businesses. Rydin suspected that Carlgren was in financial trouble, but as SCA was unwilling to acquire a large holding in MoDo, he wanted to bring the MoDo issue to SCA's board before anything happened that changed that company's ownership situation. Braun (CEO Marieberg) expected to be offered Carlgren's shares, and he was willing to consider a sale of both those and Marieberg's own holding. However, it was not on SCA's agenda to try to buy 'all' of MoDo – if it were, SCA would first have to free capital, and that would have to be done in Packaging, Mölnlycke (its chemical/technical business) and Laakirchen (its tissue operations). Moreover, such an acquisition would be contrary to SCA's strategy to grow outside of Sweden.[80]

On Friday 7 December Rydin and Martin-Löf discussed SCA's calculations regarding MoDo. The conclusion was that SCA could offer Carlgren and Marieberg around SEK 2 billion. One absolute condition for a deal was that SCA would reach more than 50 per cent of the votes. However, to get to that figure, it would be almost necessary to buy the Kempe foundations' MoDo holdings, and SCA saw that as difficult for anybody (for SCA as well as for its bidding competitor Lundberg). SCA also decided to leave the contest if Lundberg should out-trump SCA's current bid. However, SCA also saw the possibility that Lundberg in the current situation might be interested in co-operating in the upcoming restructurings.[81] At an extra board meeting on Sunday 9 December, SCA decided that it should not officially bid for MoDo until it had received acceptance of its proposal from MoDo shareholders representing at least 50 per cent of the votes, that is to say, acceptance from Carlgren, the Kempe foundations and Marieberg. The bid premium was planned to be 45 per cent, and some of it would be paid in cash.

How to approach Lundberg was also discussed at the meeting, and the conclusion was that SCA did not have to inform him before a public bid was made. SCA was fully aware that the intended bid would put both Carlgren and Marieberg in difficult positions, as rejecting it would hurt the other shareholders in MoDo.[82] The situation for the Kempe foundations was a bit special, as their statutes did not allow them to sell their holdings in MoDo for cash (but they were allowed to accept shares). Eventually Carlgren and Marieberg tried to get SCA to raise its bid above that of Lundberg, but SCA refused.[83] In that situation Marieberg decided to sell its MoDo holding to avoid ending up in a classic middle position, so its CEO contacted Lundberg, but he turned down the offering because he did not want to overextend his financial position – he had already offered a substantial sum for Carlgren's MoDo shares.[84] However, eventually SCA bought those shares, as Carlgren had informed Martin-Löf that SCA was the preferred buyer.

Rydin contacted Zetterberg[85] and informed him that he knew that Lundberg was bidding for Carlgren's holding. Zetterberg mentioned that Lundberg might be interested in a structural solution, but Rydin found that idea difficult to realize, as SCA was unwilling to give up its influence in MoDo (he expected that Lundberg wanted a holding of similar size). Then Rydin phoned each board member in SCA and learned that Gyllenhammar, Hedelius and Penser favoured a purchase at the suggested level, while Feinsilber, Öberg and (particularly) Francke were hesitant, basically because of the difficult shareholder combination (SCA–Lundberg–the Kempe foundations). However, an agreement with the Kempe foundations would convince Francke. They all understood that Lundberg's position was rather difficult, as all he could do was wait for improved results or sell to SCA.[86] It was at the end of the time limit, at 17.59, that Carlgren called Lundberg and told him that he had sold his MoDo holding to SCA for the same price that Lundberg had offered.[87] Rydin phoned Lundberg on 11 December and learned that Carlgren had contacted Lundberg the day before (that was unknown to SCA). In their conversation Lundberg claimed that Rydin ought to have contacted him before the deal to see if 'a better solution' could have been achieved. Rydin answered that SCA only had resources for a large but not controlling holding, and that SCA expected that its 'minor' move would still make it possible to co-operate in ways that would be beneficial for both companies. However, Lundberg was not as confident as Rydin about that.[88]

SCA had previously tried to establish an alliance with International Paper to make a bid for all of MoDo, where the latter company then would take care of the fine paper. Because International Paper found the country risk (!) too high, that path never materialized.[89] Instead, SCA bought both Carlgren's and Marieberg's MoDo holdings (taken together 32% of the votes and 16% of the capital[90]), although SCA had to act (almost too) fast and 'shoot from the hip'. The huge investment was a clear departure from SCA's strategy that it should concentrate its efforts on the European continent (in the EC). Nevertheless, it was seen as easier to invest in a Swedish company – the culture, thinking, institutions and language were well known, and it was therefore easier to exploit the synergies – at least in theory. However, Rydin thought that the basics of the deal were right, so he backed the idea and presented it to the board. A possible merger between SCA's and MoDo's forest-based businesses would be good for the Swedish industry's structure, and that was something that Rydin liked. He was proud of Sweden and wanted to do things that also were beneficial for the country.[91]

Martin-Löf justified the purchase with the company's strong interest in developing its printing paper business. He also mentioned synergy possibilities in fields like R&D, marketing, forestry and energy. He expected that SCA and MoDo together could make both structural re-arrangements and rationalizations for the benefit of both companies. He also stressed that SCA had not acquired (control of) MoDo – it had made a large investment in its shares. MoDo had two other big shareholders and many smaller ones, so MoDo was still an autonomous company that had to act for its own benefit.[92] Rietz, SCA's CFO, was of the same opinion as Martin-Löf regarding possible synergies, but was concerned about both companies' fine paper businesses.[93]

Frölander, Head of Paper, saw SCA's efforts to buy a large holding in MoDo as a way of better sorting out its short- and long-fibre activities. Such joint efforts would at the same time improve both companies' paper-based operations. He noted that the negotiations between the companies' leading actors were sluggish, although particularly SCA made serious efforts to find solutions – however, without success. Frölander's impression was that both Lundberg and MoDo CEO Löf were rather uninterested in co-operating with SCA.[94] Other actors saw structural possibilities between MoDo's combine Alizay and SCA's Wifsta-Östrand constellation, and between SCA's coated paper operations and MoDo's corresponding one at Silverdalen. Some actors also noted that an increased part of Husum's production could be processed further (coating). Generally, it was believed that the main obstacle to joint solutions was that MoDo's thought that SCA had not invested sufficiently in its units. However, there were also actors who thought that the poor personal chemistry[95] between the leaders of the two companies was the decisive barrier.

SCA director Penser, too, saw synergies between MoDo and SCA in their graphics business, and a promising complementary quality cardboard business in Iggesund. He was not aware of any intention on the part of SCA's board to split up MoDo, although he thought that the CEO might have such ideas.[96] Indeed, Chair Rydin did have such ideas, and was convinced that the split should first and foremost materialize in a SSE listing of the merging companies' printing paper operations. Rydin suspected, however, that MoDo's Carl Kempe Jr would dislike the idea, and that his firm opposition towards a split was the main reason why he eventually sided with Lundberg. Rydin also thought that SCA's less favourable reputation in northern Sweden might have contributed to

Kempe's stance.[97] Penser thought that Kempe's siding with Lundberg rather was based on a belief that such a coalition would give the family a better chance to continue being an important MoDo owner.[98]

Obviously the Kempe foundations and Carl Kempe Jr had the key position in the upcoming ownership struggle between SCA and Lundberg. SCA needed the foundations' shares to achieve more than 50 per cent of the votes in MoDo. At an early stage Rydin discussed the thought that Carl Kempe Jr should be appointed MoDo Chair with Wallander, Carlgren and Lundberg, but that idea received limited support. Later, in the efforts to sway Carl Kempe Jr's stance, SCA's leaders invited him to dinners where they discussed the shareholding situation.[99] Carl Kempe Jr was no industrialist, but a person who saw it as his responsibility to take care of the family heirloom (MoDo). SCA also had to deal with other SCA sceptics, namely Löf and Nordstrand. The relationship between the two CEOs was not the best either. Still, investigations were initiated to find out if it could be possible to find a way to co-ordinate some of the operations for the benefit of both companies – but those efforts failed.[100]

Lundberg preferred a renewal of MoDo's board, and suggested the Head of Sandvik (Eriksson) as the new Chair, and Zetterberg, Larsson and Welin from his own circle as directors. Former MoDo Chair Carlgren phoned Rydin declaring that Carl Kempe Jr lacked the necessary qualifications for the Chair position, and made at the same time clear that he himself was available.[101] SCA originally promised Carlgren a board seat, but then learned that he did not control the family's MoDo shares. In fact, Carlgren and Carl Kempe Jr were not on good terms, so the foundation's shares were out of Carlgren's reach.[102] Eventually Lundberg suggested Svedberg (Chair of Ericsson), and SCA accepted that solution.[103]

Rydin wanted a SCA that showed patience, while Martin-Löf wanted to see a more rapid MoDo process. Rydin believed that sooner or later MoDo would discover that the way to long-term profitability had to entail co-operation with SCA. Therefore, he wanted an SCA that made Lundberg both comfortable and confident. Lundberg disliked 50–50 solutions and was eager to have an agreement that did not restrict his opportunities to eventually sell his MoDo holding (i.e. he wanted to avoid being locked in a situation with only one buyer available [SCA]). So, Lundberg's stance limited SCA's options. Another factor that supported a cautious approach was that Rydin (and others) expected an impending change of MoDo's CEO, which would replace one of the more powerful opponents with somebody that might take a more neutral stance.

MoDo Chair Svedberg was concerned that SCA's CEO was present at MoDo's board meetings (also) in its strategic discussions. SCA Chair Rydin was also a board member, but as he represented the shareholder level, Svedberg saw no problem with that arrangement. Rydin defended the presence of SCA's CEO by claiming that the company had to have somebody that kept an eye on the return of its large investment, and he believed that Martin-Löf was the best person for that task. Thus, MoDo's directors had to rely on classic impartiality rules. The important thing was that MoDo's board work was carried out from a MoDo perspective, and Rydin was very careful to ensure that. One manifestation of that was when Rydin advocated in 1991 that MoDo purchase Alizay (SEK 4 billion), rather than the remaining shares in MD Papier. However, some actors instead saw his stance as a way of making sure that MoDo did not become too strong in printing paper – something that would affect the power situation between MoDo and SCA in the upcoming negotiations.

During the early part of 1991, talks between MoDo and SCA addressing printing paper still looked promising. By the middle of the year, it became clear that the co-ordination effects would be substantial, particularly if the investment side was included in the calculations. Rydin met Lundberg in July to discuss the idea from a shareholder perspective. However, Lundberg rejected a 50–50 solution, and was even prepared to refrain from some profit to maintain his discretion. Moreover, if he should sell his MoDo holding, he expected a substantial premium, and that level was far too high for SCA (and to bid for all of MoDo was financially impossible). Some months later, during Lundberg's fortieth birthday party, MoDo Chair Svedberg informed Rydin that Lundberg had begun to doubt whether co-operation with SCA could become a fruitful path. At the end of the year, SCA's further talks with Svedberg and Löf confirmed that Lundberg still was sceptical.[104]

Rydin met with Kymmene's leading actor Ehrnrooth in early 1992 to discuss a solution involving not only Kymmene and SCA, but (perhaps) also MoDo. The idea was to create and list a new printing paper company. Both CEOs (Pihl and Martin-Löf) were soon also involved in the talks, and together the quartet decided to investigate the idea further. In April the outlook looked promising (synergies were estimated to be around SEK 1 billion), but MoDo had not yet been included in the discussions. If the solution was to be built on MoDo as the base unit, the contribution of both Lundberg and the Kempe foundations had to be ensured (otherwise one of them might do). Rydin knew that the 'big' solution that involved all three companies meant that SCA would essentially need to 'leave' the forest-based industry, and he was concerned that it would be tough to justify that step with the shareholders. So, ultimately, he decided to continue to promote 'the MoDo path'.[105]

In March 1992, director Gyllenhammar (Chair of Volvo) talked with Rydin about some problems Volvo's CEO Zetterberg was having in that company. Gyllenhammar had talked to Lundberg (who appreciated Zetterberg) about naming him as new MoDo CEO. Rydin was positive, as he had been sceptical about Löf's capacity in that position for some time. However, Rydin thought that it would be best to await the outcome of the talks between SCA and Kymmene – to have a new CEO with all his expectations about the new position could be problematic in such an unstable situation. Still, Rydin decided to test the waters and asked Martin-Löf about his opinion regarding Zetterberg. To Rydin's surprise, both Martin-Löf and many other influential actors in the forest-based industry expressed negative views. Unfortunately, somebody leaked about the discussions, so that business media started to speculate that Zetterberg soon would replace Löf (but that did not occur).[106]

The talks between MoDo and SCA about possible ways to co-operate continued, but beginning in March 1992, SCA started to take a tougher stand, and later that spring the talks almost ceased. When Svedberg left as Chair in April 1992, instead, finding his successor took top priority. SCA hoped that the 'right' person might unlock the stalemate in MoDo. Carl Kempe Jr claimed that an internal solution would be best, but outsider names like Schotte (former CEO of Södra) and Lars G. Sundblad (former CEO of Iggesund) were also proposed. Rydin supported Schotte's candidacy but hesitated about Sundblad (age reasons), while MoDo's CEO Löf voiced the opposite ranking. Carl Kempe Jr also suggested Lundberg as Chair with Zetterberg as CEO, while Lundberg instead mentioned Palmstierna (Chair Nordbanken) and Zetterberg. Soon Lundberg added Önnesjö (former Chair and CEO of Holmens Bruk), a name that SCA eventually accepted. Önnesjö decided to shoulder that task if three conditions were met: no change in MoDo's top management (Löf was informed about that), a clear statement from all the three big shareholders that they backed the appointment and a confirmation from Rydin that he personally wanted to see Önnesjö as the new MoDo Chair.[107]

After the summer Rydin informed MoDo's Chair Önnesjö that SCA had reconsidered its holding in MoDo, and as it was no longer a strategic placement, SCA's CEO (Martin-Löf) would leave MoDo's board.[108] In autumn 1992 Ehrnrooth returned to the negotiations that Kymmene and SCA had conducted earlier the same year – talks that also concerned MoDo. Finland had recently devalued its currency, and that had put Kymmene (and most other Finnish companies) in a much better competitive situation, so he was not as keen to co-operate with SCA as he had been before (but still interested). Rydin did not want to meet with Lundberg about that issue, as that could be interpreted as going over the heads of MoDo's board and other shareholders. So, instead SCA again talked to Zetterberg, who expressed scepticism. Rydin then met with both Zetterberg and Ehrnrooth, who described many of the advantages that a joint effort was expected to bring about. Rydin made clear that SCA's forests could not be a part of an agreement, and he expressed worry that Lundberg would dislike Kymmene's high indebtedness. Rydin also soon learned that Ehrnrooth and Lundberg had talked to each other, and that the latter had made clear that a deal was impossible. Rydin could no longer act under those circumstances, since as MoDo Chair he had to play according to the rules, so that nobody could suspect that he favoured SCA.[109] Later during the catastrophic year of 1992, MoDo's share price fell, and SCA's board discussed selling its holding. However, Rydin insisted that SCA instead should show staying power and conviction that the investment would pay off in the future. Soon, Lundberg made a low-ball bid, but returned somewhat later to SCA with 'a decent one'. However, both offerings were made in a harsh context, as the relationship between Rydin and Lundberg had become rather frosty during the MoDo–SCA struggle.[110]

In early 1993 Carlgren visited Rydin and claimed that he had gathered a group of Swedes that wanted to buy SCA's MoDo shares and co-operate with the Kempe foundations in running MoDo in a long-term perspective. Carlgren was worried that MoDo was to be split up. He also claimed that his economic situation was not all that bad – his (25%) TV channel was profitable, so dividends were expected, and there were buyers for his Stille-Werner company.[111] However, Carlgren's ideas never materialized, and in August 1993 Rydin decided that all efforts to co-operate with MoDo should be ended, and that SCA instead should find an honourable way to exit. Before that, however, there had been talks about MoDo's Holmens Bruk unit (printing paper). SCA had decided not to bid for it, but could consider part ownership even of the whole MoDo, if the other parts of that company were sold out. Such a construct presumed an agreement that Holmen should specialize in newsprint, and that Aylesford then would be included. Eventually SCA also could be the dominating owner of that printing company through a purchase of Lundberg's holding.

Both International Paper and Burda had also indicated an interest in Holmens Bruk, but SCA regarded the prices they were willing to pay too low. SCA also discussed a SSE listing of Holmen, but the problem was then that the stripped MoDo would be rather unattractive.[112]

All through 1992 SCA had carefully observed how the Conservative government's idea to privatize the state-owned forest-based companies ASSI and Domän was developing (cf. Ch. 7). SCA was interested in entering into some kind of deal with ASSI, as substantial synergies could be expected. However, a solution required that some units were excluded from the agreement, and that was regarded to be a difficult task. SCA acted in several ways to negotiate with ASSI. It warned the government that a sale to foreign investors would make close-downs in the northernmost Sweden highly likely. SCA also offered a solution for the problem unit Karlsborg (a change of its production to fluff). Still, the indication from the Conservative government was that it preferred a foreign buyer. So, SCA turned to the Social Democratic opposition and tried to convince them about the merits of its offer (and prevent a sale to somebody else).

State secretary Ametier from the Ministry of Industry visited Rydin and informed him that the ministry was not particularly fond of the way ASSI's board ran the privatization process. That was encouraging, but nevertheless ASSI kept its books closed to SCA and treated SCA as a less preferred buyer. ASSI's management simply did not appreciate SCA's ideas, probably to some extent because it would involve tough rationalizations. However, in early 1993 the Swedish 'ombudsman for freedom of business' somewhat unexpectedly encouraged SCA to contact the actors in the ASSI privatization process and explain its plan to establish a new company together with the Swedish state. Such a new construct was expected to release substantial synergies. ASSI's remaining businesses would then be sold to SCA for further 'processing', with the exception of the liquid packaging operations. Either of Korsnäs and Stora were the planned harbours for that business.[113]

Later in the same year SCA discussed with Smurfit how ASSI's SSE listing could be stopped. The problem was that ASSI probably would be supported by a substantial allotment of forests from Domän – something that would make a merged and privatized AssiDomän highly competitive. A combined SCA–Smurfit solution was to be presented to the ministry, although it seemed clear that a merger between ASSI and Domän would occur anyway – the real uncertainty was how much of Domän's forests would be included in the new AssiDomän.[114]

14.3 DECIDING THE PATH FORWARD

14.3.1 A Unique Path

When summarizing developments over the 1970s and 1980s, Rydin concluded that SCA had taken a rather unique path. Unlike its Nordic competitors SCA had decided to leave large parts of its current business, and therefore had not been particularly active in the internal restructuring of the Nordic forest-based industry. Instead, SCA had bought Mölnlycke, and that represented a substantial step outside the core of the forest-based industry. Indeed, it was the first step in the new path that focused on further processing and products for end consumers with the expectation that those markets would expand and bring higher profitability. However, it was a rather risky path, as it meant that SCA challenged some of its big American competitors.[115]

Thus, SCA stressed forward integration (e.g. hygiene) and expansion in Europe, while most of its Nordic competitors stayed in their businesses and acted 'horizontally' (restructured and rationalized). Martin-Löf had another explanation for why SCA fell outside the internal Swedish processes in the 1980s: its lack of capital. It was simply not financially capable of participating until the end of the decade. However, at that time there would not be much left to do in the Nordic context, as the competitors had by then 'occupied' most of the possible business and market positions. So, either SCA had to become a significant European actor in selected fields, or it would face a future as a takeover candidate. Crucial for SCA's development was, paradoxically, its failure to acquire Feldmühle (Nobel). With that failed effort, the graphic business lost its status as a core business – instead SCA prioritized its hygiene and packaging operations.[116]

The 1970s and 1980s also led to rationalizations in SCA's production structure. Cost efficiency had become a requirement for all its operations, so plants were closed, staff reduced and new technologies introduced. Those two decades also saw the first substantial consolidation process in the European forest-based industry. The US companies had been far ahead in that respect, but Europe began to catch up, as many small and mid-sized family-controlled companies were bought (or failed), making room for economies of scale and professional management techniques.[117]

The year 1992 was a terrible one for the Swedish forest-based industry. However, that deep crisis also produced something good, namely much-needed rationalizations and restructurings. The Central Bank also 'assisted' the Swedish corporations that year by substantially devaluing the Swedish crown. Some actors claimed that those cost-reducing factors, taken together, added up to 40–50 per cent, making the Swedish forest-based industry's production costs among the lowest in the world.[118] However, leading SCA actors expressed different views about those effects on their own company. Some, for example, director Penser, claimed that SCA was not that affected at all, as it had been rather conservatively managed despite its risk-taking, while others, including Hedelius and Rydin, claimed that without the devaluation, the situation might have become really troublesome. The latter actors also stressed that Finland, which housed several severe competitors, had devaluated its Mark the year before.

Other external decisions that had a strong impact on SCA and its Swedish competitors were the new laws in the environmental field. In fact this legislation determined several plants' future (invest/close down). However, these laws also enhanced competitiveness on the international market – SCA, for example, became a certified supplier and a pioneer in using waste paper in its production.[119]

14.3.2 The Mölnlycke Crisis

Mölnlycke's diapers were unprofitable by 1991 (cf. below), but management continued to try to change that situation in several ways, including through the establishment of joint ventures in Eastern Europe and the sale of its Cederroth engagement to Alberto-Culver. SCA also entered into a 50–50 joint venture in the US with Scott Paper regarding incontinence products (Scott Health Care). In autumn 1992 ambitious discussions were conducted with Scott Europe. SCA's interest in Scott was based on its concern that Kimberly-Clark would be a tough competitor in a future fluff race, as it currently utilized a technical advantage in the diaper field.

CEO Forsgren pushed for (brand-based) expansion and global presence; a sole focus on Europe was in his eyes too risky (new technology could emerge anywhere, and the capacity to strike back required worldwide presence). Scott Europe represented one such expansion path, and that company had showed interest in a 50–50 merger with Mölnlycke. However, SCA's directors did not like such ownership solutions, and they were eager to ensure that SCA would get an easy way out. Its leaders therefore considered some kind of cross-ownership, but because Scott was not interested in discussing such constructs, those negotiations ended. However, the general talks with Scott continued, although the focus switched instead to two other product areas: AFH assortments and institutional products. Rather soon, however, Mölnlycke's managers got 'cold feet', as they found reason to question Scott Europe's profit reports.[120]

When VP (Germany) showed interest in selling its hygiene operations in exchange for shares (25%), SCA's leaders took up a discussion about whether the company should welcome partners at all in Mölnlycke. Once again, the question of whether SCA should run part-owned businesses in Europe was brought to the fore. Rydin believed that SCA would be forced to accept such solutions in hygiene (but still keep a majority holding) and graphics (accept a minority holding). Part ownerships also opened up for SSE listings (e.g. of Mölnlycke). Talks were conducted with VP in the first half of 1992, and they were so successful that SCA began to draw up a consortium agreement. However, the whole competitive situation became complicated when Procter & Gamble and Kimberly-Clark entered the scene. Sometimes it looked like VP and Kimberly-Clark were close to a deal, sometimes that Procter & Gamble was about to buy VP without its hygiene business, which instead then would be offered to Kimberly-Clark or SCA.

In the second half of 1992, when it became clear that VP had abandoned its negotiations with Kimberly-Clark, Rydin and Martin-Löf visited VP. But it was not to be easy: it suggested an ownership share in Mölnlycke (50%) and its indicative price for that holding was unsatisfactory (DM 1 billion). Still, Rydin thought that if SCA could get Scott into the race, the price might go up. Soon, however, SCA learned that VP considered instead leaving the hygiene business entirely, and that made the 'Scott path' even more interesting. The idea was to buy VP together with Scott, but in the end (late 1993) SCA bought VP on its own. For SCA, that meant that Kimberly-Clark was kept out of Europe (at least) temporarily.[121]

It was not sufficient for Mölnlycke to remain a big Nordic player with local/regional brands. One indication of that was that the company's overall profit was declining. Many competitors had invested heavily in the 1980s, so product prices fell when demand slowed down. SCA was also involved in a price war on diapers in France, and it even faced a threat to be replaced as second brand in many stores (by Kimberly-Clark). Eventually it became obvious that it would be difficult to beat Procter & Gamble globally in a 'brand fight', so SCA decided to focus on its private label business and become 'the retailer's best friend'.[122] SCA's production logic and market resources suited that business better. Moreover, the alternatives to SCA were rather few for the big retail chains, and barriers to entry rather high, so SCA could keep prices at a profitable level.[123]

Around 1990, the successful Mölnlycke 'machine' began to waver. Procter & Gamble had entered the European business arena as late as the mid-1980s, but very quickly established strong market presence for its diapers and sanitary pads. Many SCA actors were shocked when they finally understood with whom they were competing.[124] Procter & Gamble had low prices in Europe, actually around 25 per cent lower than its US ones.

It also took customers away from SCA on its Nordic home market. To find out the relative strength of Procter & Gamble, SCA asked a consultancy firm to compare the two companies' diapers operations. Its report showed that Mölnlycke's production and distribution costs exceeded those of Procter & Gamble by 22 per cent, and that the latter company's diapers had quality advantages.[125] Moreover, Mölnlycke's global market share for diapers was only 6 per cent, as compared with Procter & Gamble's 40 per cent.

Mölnlycke's board and management had not taken note of the threat from Procter & Gamble until it was 'too late'. Suddenly, Procter & Gamble introduced diapers based on a superior technique that, for example, allowed for flexible production, something that perfectly suited a consumer market based on brands (it allowed for 'continuous' product development). Procter & Gamble was also very strong in marketing (particularly advertising) and had the necessary economic muscle for promoting and selling branded products on a global scale.[126] Thus, Mölnlycke had simply underestimated Procter & Gamble – some of Mölnlycke's leaders had been hit by hubris and did not read the actions of its competitors correctly. They had fallen into 'the success trap' and become too self-confident.[127] In this crisis situation – the diaper crisis – Forsgren decided that the best strategy was to expand globally, and that stance, together with his assertion that it was Procter & Gamble's dumping of its products in Europe that triggered Mölnlycke's crisis, pushed SCA to replace him.[128] However, as late as September 1993, director Daun expressed his confidence in Forsgren, who also had a solid reputation in the industry. Actually, many outside actors criticized SCA's decision to push Forsgren out (that critique also hit Martin-Löf). A specialist on consumer businesses, Augustsson,[129] soon succeeded Feltner as CEO (and Alfred Heinzel from PWA soon replaced Augustsson).[130]

14.3.3 Looking for a Partner in Mölnlycke

In an attempt to get out of the diapers crisis, Mölnlycke promised SCA both significant cost reductions and new competitive products. Rydin then decided to trust Mölnlycke's technical department – that they actually could produce a product 'revolution'.[131] SCA also understood that a private label business supported a branded one by creating large volumes. So, SCA acted offensively,[132] and project 'Fenix' was launched – a big investment amounting to SEK 1 billion. At the same time, SCA learned that Procter & Gamble had problems on its home market (US), and that the company therefore considered increasing its European prices. With this in mind, SCA decided to continue to fight. There were also other reasons as both diapers and incontinence, where SCA still was globally strong, housed economically and technically connected products, which would enable both joint R&D efforts and production efficiency.[133]

Mölnlycke successfully restored its competitive power, but it took some time. Its efforts radically lowered production costs, and the new products proved to be as good as the ones sold by Procter & Gamble. SCA also got back to a 50–50 market situation in the Nordic countries, despite the fact that Kimberly-Clark, too, tried to enter that market.[134] Then SCA's most urgent task became to try to stop Kimberly-Clark's entrance on the European market for children's diapers. Basically, that could be accomplished in two ways. SCA could either sell them (parts of) Mölnlycke's operations in France and Holland, or start negotiations about co-ownerships (of course, the alternative to sell them all of Mölnlycke's diaper business also existed).[135]

In 1993, SCA issued new shares (SEK 1.4 billion) partly because of the problems in Mölnlycke, but also because of the current situation in MoDo. SCA generally disliked such moves, as the present controlling owners disliked having new (substantial) shareholders. However, SCA soon disinvested from MoDo, sold Spicer (SEK 1 billion) and handed over its vessels to a shipping company (Gorthon). From mid-1994 things began to look much better for Mölnlycke – everything except children's diapers was doing well. There were several reasons why Mölnlycke recovered. Rydin mentioned in particular that the investments in AFH, private brands and ladies sanitary products did not cost much (thus, no expensive brands were introduced).[136]

In mid-1994 Rydin and Mölnlycke's new internally recruited CEO Feltner discussed Mölnlycke's strategy. Feltner wanted to continue investing in diapers, as they were related to incontinence products. His plan was to rationalize its production by changing machinery, closing plants, and concentrating production to Falkenberg (Sweden) and Lille (France). Feltner also wanted to expand in Eastern Europe because that would prevent its companies from exporting private label products to Western Europe (including the Nordic market).[137]

In the latter half of 1994, SCA resumed its talks with Kimberly-Clark. Director Daun favoured some kind of co-operation, as he worried about both Feltner's and SCA's capacity to handle the tough competition with both that company and Procter & Gamble. A solution that involved Kimberly-Clark would have cost SCA about SEK 2 billion. However, Kimberly-Clark's European management hesitated – they found it too complicated and costly to end all agreements that both companies currently had with other parties. Thus, SCA instead continued its discussions with PWA. At the same time Martin-Löf talked to Johnson & Johnson, which had similar products, and also was of about the same size as Mölnlycke. The synergies were substantial, so the discussions continued until April 1995, when Johnson & Johnson backed out. Six months earlier a rumour told that Kimberly-Clark and Scott were considering a merger, and in mid-1995 those discussions materialized when Kimberly-Clark bought Scott.[138]

However, Kimberly-Clark had to sell two units when it merged with Scott Paper (called for by the European Commission). SCA and Kimberly-Clark then agreed to make a structural deal, where SCA got a plant at Lincelle (France) and Kimberly-Clark two tissue plants (one in France and one in the UK). When PWA was acquired in 1995 (cf. subsection 14.3.4 below), the balance in SCA's hygiene repertoire both with respect to its product portfolio and its geographical coverage changed radically. PWA's strong presence on the large European retail markets made it possible for SCA to begin to build up a profitable and leading private label diaper business throughout all of Europe.[139]

SCA Hygiene Products was established in 1996. In addition to SCA's own tissue operations in that sector, it also contained PWA's soft paper products. The idea was to expand that business in two ways: on the AFH markets and on the private label markets. SCA was world leader in the private label market segment, but also had strong brands on several local markets (Austria, Belgium, Denmark, Germany, Holland, Ireland, Norway, Sweden and the UK). SCA Hygiene Products also held SCA's fluff goods, which were sold both through retailers and to institutions. SCA marketed its hygiene products in some 25 non-European countries as well.

SCA continued its rapid expansion in (foremost) tissue. In 1998 SCA acquired all shares in Svetogorsk Tissue (Russia) from Tetra-Laval and increased its shareholding to

50 per cent in Productos Familia (Colombia), which in turn owned the tissue producer Tecnopapel (Ecuador). SCA also tried to buy 50 per cent of Melhoramentos Papeis (Brazil), and increased its presence in Asia through a purchase of Holland Pacific Paper (tissue; the Philippines).

14.3.4 Acquiring PWA

SCA's leaders concluded in 1995 that it was not possible to scale down the graphics business if it were to be able to continue to support the other businesses. However, they were concerned that such a decision made it almost compulsory to invest in a new LWC machine, which in turn could make it necessary to either sell the whole graphics unit or restructure it together with another company. Already in 1991 some other divestments were made (Spicers Board Mill, Colthrop Board Mill and Lower Darwin Mill), and Laakirchen's tissue was unexpectedly[140] sold to PWA. As SCA wanted to maintain a strong presence in all the major kinds of printing paper (LWC, SC and newsprint), it looked at KNP, and also considered expanding in Aylesford. Together with Mondi Paper, SCA finally decided to invest in a waste-paper-based machine at Aylesford (SEK 3 billion).

MoDo's bad financial situation made a new issue of shares necessary, and Lundberg suggested an amount around SEK 1.5 billion (cf. above and Ch. 9). He had secured support from the Kempe foundations (which intended to borrow capital to subscribe[141]). Lundberg's initiative forced SCA to seriously reconsider its position in MoDo. Selling the holding was discussed, and some directors favoured that path. To abstain from the new issue, however, would result in a certain loss, so SCA decided to subscribe (if SCA remained passive, the value of its holding would probably drop).[142]

Late in 1993, Lundberg made a bid for SCA's MoDo holding that Rydin thought was far too low, so he informed Lundberg that SCA was not interested at that price level. SCA also tried to convince Carl Kempe Jr to co-operate with SCA, but he refused, referring to the foundations' independence. Martin-Löf then suggested that SCA should try to interest Lundberg and Carl Kempe Jr in an exchange of their A-shares for B-shares (and get a premium). At that time, SCA was uncertain whether Lundberg could raise the necessary capital, but soon he actually raised his bid for SCA's holding in MoDo. The foundations had been given a put option[143] if Lundberg should get over 50 per cent, and SCA secured the same right for most of its own holding (SCA wanted to avoid a weak minority position).[144] Under these circumstances, SCA's leading actors finally agreed that it was the right time to give up the fight to acquire MoDo, and as a first step in that divestment process it switched its A-shares for B-shares. Four million A-shares furnished SCA with 5 million B-shares (including an option to sell 1 million of them for a fixed price).[145]

In mid-1994 SCA got indications that PWA might be up for sale, and that the price level would end up around DM 2 million. Most leading actors thought that PWA would be the ideal purchase for SCA. It was like a 'mini-SCA' that offered an excellent platform for further European expansion (particularly in France, Germany and the UK). PWA had not been doing well lately, explained to some extent by the strong German currency. Mondi, SCA's partner already in Aylesford, suggested a merger between Aylesford, Laakirchen and PWA, in which Mondi and SCA would own 50 per cent each. SCA was interested in acquiring PWA because of its product repertoire – it contained tissue, newsprint and packaging paper. Eventually PWA's main owner offered SCA 43 per cent of PWA in the first round, and an additional 10 per cent soon afterwards. Most of SCA's directors favoured that deal, but some thought that 53 per cent was too low. At a meeting the day before Christmas Eve, the board decided to see if it was possible to go for 100 per cent.[146] A complete purchase of PWA would manifest that the tissue business was a core activity for SCA (that path had recently been questioned).

In early 1995, SCA managed to buy as much as 75 per cent (+ one share) of PWA for DM 1.5 billion, and Germany became its biggest market. That shareholding figure was needed in Germany to be able to efficiently run a company. As that country lacked a system for compulsory redemption, SCA had to arrange both AGMs and a trading of the shares over many years to come.[147] Rydin saw the PWA purchase as both offensive and defensive. It not only suited SCA's current strategy well, it also blocked Stora from buying it and becoming too powerful. The seller was a federal state, and as its politicians were anxious to have a serious buyer, they had not arranged for an auction. Instead, its representatives introduced new (politically motivated) contract terms at almost every stage of the negotiating process. Still, Rydin and Martin-Löf managed to get a final agreement and price that was 'acceptable'.[148] Penser was one of the deal's rather few critics. He thought that the price was so high that it 'destroyed' some of SCA's key figures.[149]

Soon after the PWA purchase, SCA's board began to discuss whether its fine paper had a future, or whether that part of PWA perhaps ought to be sold.[150] Bertorp, SCA's Chief Legal Officer, actually thought that the very presence of fine paper in PWA had worked to SCA's advantage, as that business kept several other possible (serious) buyers away. Once the new Head of Fine Paper (Åström) had developed that business successfully,[151] it became possible to separate it from Graphic Papers. That split allowed SCA to be better prepared to participate in the expected structural changes in the fine paper industry. At that juncture, SCA Fine Paper included Stockstadt (Germany), Hallein (Austria) and Wifsta (Sweden), as well as several wholesaling units.

In late 1995, two Finnish competitors – Kymmene and UPM – merged. That move was expected to result in fewer new paper machines on the market. Not long after, UPM-Kymmene announced its alliance with the South Asian company April, thus establishing the first 'fine paper link' between Europe and Asia. In addition, Abitibi-Price (US) and Stone Consolidated (US) merged, which created the world's biggest newsprint company. In early 1996, SCA met with Weyerhaeuser's top managers, who wanted to see extensive co-operation between the two companies. It was not the first time these companies had discussed joint activities (it happened already in 1973 and 1992), and they had begun to co-operate in Asia (packaging).

SCA's Martin-Löf met with Stora's Chair Berggren in late 1995 in regard to issues that covered more than just fine paper co-operation. In addition, Berggren, Dahlbäck (the Chair of Investor [Stora's main owner]), Rydin and Reuterskiöld (CEO of Industrivärden [SCA's main owner]) met and discussed structures and synergies, but no concrete action came out of the talks. Rydin pointed to two major obstacles that stood in the way of building such a link: the companies' ownership structures – they belonged to two different spheres – and the presence of Custos (belonged to neither of them). So, both SCA and Stora also checked other alternatives. Rydin saw almost no substantial advantages from closer co-operation (or a merger) between SCA and Stora, although he realized that the new constellation would acquire a larger capital base, which would make it a powerful actor fully capable of taking global initiatives. In early 1998 SCA once again examined a potential arrangement with Stora, but found it too highly valued, particularly as it contained some poor plants. Moreover, SCA was currently focusing on its hygiene and packaging operations, and therefore decided to reduce its engagement in the traditional forest-based industry (including fine paper).[152]

14.3.5 Conflicts about SCA's Future

Swedish media and industrial leaders intensively debated cross-ownership constructions during 1995. Neoliberals and market fundamentalists, as well as many analysts and economic journalists, had then taken the lead in the public discussions, and the US corporate governance system was held up as the most effective one. 'Shareholder value' was the market liberals' slogan, and basically it should be created through the establishment of 'efficient' (i.e. frictionless) global capital markets. That would make it easier for all sorts of capital to move freely around the world to bid for (and buy) companies.[153] The pressure on the current ownership spheres to abandon constructs that could be accused of obstructing 'free' acquisition opportunities was therefore intense. So, eventually SCA – reluctantly – gave up the consortium agreement that 'protected' Industrivärden, and sold some of its Industrivärden shares stopping at a holding of 15 per cent of the votes. That holding was further reduced in 1997, when SCA through its Dutch subsidiary issued bonds. SCA's CEO also left Industrivärden's board.[154] However, the risk involved in ending the consortium agreement was seen as rather low, as the sphere foremost was based on strong personal ties (cf. the concept 'actor risk').[155]

SCA's board conducted a new comprehensive strategic analysis in 1996, but that effort did not alter the previous conclusions. SCA should still develop its capacity as a customer-oriented integrated paper and packaging company with Europe as its 'home market'. Starting from its unique knowledge of the fibre, SCA should meet customer requirements in three areas: liquid absorption (hygiene), mechanical solidity (packaging) and high-quality printing surface (graphic papers). The ambition should still be to add further customer value and become a market leader in most segments. SCA's critical mass (and financial capacity) had to be increased through establishing an expanding, competitive hygiene business, defending the strong packaging position in Europe (and expanding it in fast-growing markets), effectively utilizing the current machines in printing paper and fine paper, and by active participation in international consolidation processes (e.g. for fine paper). So, from 1997 it became quite clear that SCA prioritized hygiene and packaging – that these two businesses constituted its core businesses.

However, SCA's strategic discussions did not end there. The board intensively debated whether it would be a good idea to split up SCA. One of the directors, Gardell, had even tried to arouse some media pressure in support of his view, something that the other members of the board disliked. Gardell was of the opinion that SCA was too complicated for the stock market and its analysts, who could not cover (master) SCA's business repertoire. Moreover, SCA contained both cyclical and non-cyclical activities, and, according to Gardell, that made things more difficult for investors.[156] One consequence of Gardell's noise making was that the board adopted a policy regarding contacts with analysts, economic journalists, and so on.[157] The board was also concerned about Gardell's direct contacts with SCA's top management, and that he occupied quite a lot of their time asking for various analyses.[158] So, all in all, Gardell was a very active board member, something that became even more apparent when he began to advocate a strategic path that differed substantially from the one defended by the other board members.[159]

Basically, Gardell wanted to split up SCA, and then sell the forests and sell or list Hygiene, Graphics and Packaging. Gardell claimed that SCA was 'an underperformer' that gave the shareholders (e.g. Custos) too little value. SCA had invested heavily, but the return had been too low. Gardell also put down his thoughts in writing and sent that memo to the other directors. He had underpinned his ideas utilizing analyses produced by Custos's staff, so it was a serious attempt to change SCA's course. He also discussed his proposal both inside SCA and with actors from some of SCA's institutional shareholders, and met support 'everywhere'. Gardell saw SCA as too close to a conglomerate organization and pushed the idea that each business should be treated entirely on its own terms or be moved to better contexts. He claimed that all the basics differed for each of the core businesses: technology, customers and production. Gardell also thought that, since graphic paper had begun its decline on many of SCA's markets, that business should only be kept in 'good condition', that is to say, provide healthy cash flow for all new investments that instead should be made in the hygiene and packaging businesses. Furthermore, SCA's hygiene operations should be kept together because, although operations differed significantly, customers preferred one supplier for both tissue and incontinence products. A problem for Gardell was that SCA's board was a rather weak arena, and to some extent that fact might have influenced his predilection for 'unconventional' opinion-building methods. Gardell had the impression that most issues already were settled before the board ever became involved. The Chair and CEO both sat in the driver's seat (now and then together with the heads of core units). No director or shareholder was capable of seriously challenging the leading duo.[160]

Not all directors shared Gardell's view about the board's power, however. Enander, Francke and Penser, for example, agreed that the SCA's CEOs had played an important role, at least since WWII, and that Rydin was a much stronger Chair than his predecessors. Still, they claimed that the board had increasingly become a demanding 'sounding board' that produced a kind of 'self-censorship' in top management. Board work was actually very professional with excellent material and time to consider and discuss proposals. Rush was rare (with the exception of the acquisition of the MoDo holding). Decisions about large issues were always 'automatically postponed' to the next meeting, so that every director got an opportunity to collect more information and form a well-founded independent opinion. Moreover, the three large shareholders (Industrivärden, Handelsbanken and Custos) all acted exclusively through their board members.[161] The emerging criticism regarding the former CEO's promotion to Chair was refuted. Director Hedelius and several of the other directors claimed that such a solution actually is often to be preferred in situations where continuity is important, and when the Chair's and the CEO's personalities match. The advantage is that the Chair really knows the operations, the actors and the competitors in the industry, and that makes the board an agency that is capable of challenging and advising the CEO. However, it is then of utmost importance that the Chair refrains from acting operatively ('stepping on the CEO's toes').[162]

Rydin (and most other directors) was critical of Gardell's proposals, and argued that Gardell's calculations were unrealistic and that his suggestion destroyed synergies. Some directors even claimed that Gardell seemed to prioritize Custos's interests before those of SCA. However, Rydin admitted that Gardell's ideas could create shareholder value in the short run, but maintained that they would deliver lower value in a longer perspective. Like CFO Rietz,[163] Rydin stressed that each of the businesses was highly dependent on a large backing financial body if they intended to expand – none of them could manage that on its own.[164]

Director Gyll[165] stressed that Gardell's ideas lacked support at SCA's board. To make the forest reserves active (and for sale) would create problems, as all the businesses (Packaging, Graphics and [to some extent] Hygiene) needed a safe sourcing of forest resources and stable timber prices. He also emphasized that most of SCA's plants in northern Sweden were horizontally linked. The leading actors actually regarded SCA as a well-integrated and effective whole.[166] In that situation, Rydin took some time together with Gardell to explain SCA's current structure and operations, and to justify why the other board members advocated a strategy that differed from the one he had proposed.[167]

The controlling shareholders and the executive actors (with the exception of Gardell) expressed the same view: SCA could and should continue as an integrated unit. So, in December 1996 the board endorsed SCA's strategy, which eliminated most of the public uncertainty about the company's future path. Rydin was of the opinion that Custos had to support that strategy explicitly – otherwise it ought to sell its holding.[168]

To explain the chosen strategy to the remaining sceptical actors, Frölander was asked to compile an overview of the synergies that existed between SCA's businesses. His conclusion was that these synergies existed primarily in raw material sourcing, similar input goods, shared sales channels, overlapping R&D and joint logistics. Frölander also estimated these strengths in economic terms.[169] In order to build on these strengths, SCA then integrated its operations even further, for example, through product swaps between SCA Mölnlycke and PWA Hygiene, and by establishing a new unit for raw materials and logistics (1997). Moreover, in 1998 SCA merged SCA Hygiene Paper with SCA Mölnlycke.

When Custos failed to realize its split-up strategy for SCA, Gardell turned and expressed that he was happy with the current situation in SCA. By doing so, he also defended Custos's investment in that company, although he actually simultaneously tried to 'sell it' to a global competitor. When no one bid high enough, Custos decided to distribute its holding to its shareholders.

14.3.6 Taking SCA Packaging Global

SCA was world leader in packaging early in the 1990s, although its position in the US was weak. So, SCA decided to invest on that continent, too. An agreement with Weyerhaeuser (the third largest US packaging company) in 1992 was a first step. However, SCA also continued to invest in Europe, including in Turkey, Germany and Hungary. At the time, SCA's expansion activities were a bit tentative in character – it was a company that still was a bit uncertain about which business activities should be its future core ones.

SCA tried to buy Otor (packaging, France) in 1994, although it would have been a costly purchase. Several directors were concerned about the price, as they had hoped that SCA could expand its packaging operations in smaller steps. There was also concern that ASSI would intervene in the process and make a deal without really having considered all aspects. However, the really serious problem that emerged was that Otor's controlling owner had given Stora an advance purchase right (10–20%), and SCA's interest was dependent on the acquisition of that holding, too. That condition triggered a meeting between the leading actors in all three companies. Eventually Stora decided to block SCA's effort. Moreover, in April 1994 new, previously unannounced deals were revealed between Otor and other (to SCA unknown) actors. That revelation wiped out SCA's confidence in Otor and its main owner, so the negotiations stopped. The end of the talks was particularly embarrassing for SCA, as its leaders already had announced the acquisition (and even provided notice of a new issue of shares).[170]

Under those circumstances, the board began to question SCA's current expansion path for packaging. Several directors thought that the concentration on Europe was too strong.[171] Still, Martin-Löf met with European Cellulose du Pin's leading actor in March 1994 and expressed SCA's interest in certain parts of that company (coated fine paper and kraftliner were to be excluded). Later that year Cellulose du Pin returned and told SCA that the company was for sale. But SCA's leaders soon learned that Smurfit, too, was competing in the race, and that SCA's stood no chance of winning. Later that year SCA instead bought Champion's 25 per cent of Obbola and 60 per cent of Le Sac (UK).[172]

At that time, SCA Packaging was Europe's leading producer of corrugated (93 plants in 12 countries and 12% market share). It also produced substantial quantities of kraftliner and testliner. The customers on the corrugated market had become rather big, but due to transportation costs and customer stipulations, production had to be local, and therefore also of a small-scale kind. The preferred expansion method was to follow the big customers to their new markets (particularly then Asia and Eastern Europe). SCA Weyerhaeuser Packaging Asia (Shanghai) was established, as was SCA Packaging's first plant in China. SCA also bought 11 per cent[173] of Central Package Group (HQ in Singapore; production in China, Singapore, Malaysia, Thailand and Indonesia).

However, SCA also made quite a few company purchases in Europe during the last half of the 1990s and the first years of the 21st century.[174] SCA also bought several plants in Europe.[175] Almost all those companies had activities on several markets, thus providing SCA Packaging a very strong presence all over Europe. But SCA did not act alone in those days. Its competitors were equally active. In fact, several large mergers occurred: Jefferson Smurfit bought Stone, International Paper acquired Union Camp and KNP and financial investors took on BT's[176] corrugated business (Kappa).

At that time Martin-Löf began to question whether SCA's current economic reporting really constituted the best possible platform for making larger investment decisions (including acquisitions). So, in partnership with leading academics, SCA started a project to find models that worked better in such situations. Eventually SCA settled for a model based on cash value-added. In addition, SCA reorganized its top management. Åström, Head of Paper, was appointed Deputy CEO; de Ruvo, Head of R&D, retired; Rietz was made responsible for North America (and left as CFO); Bertorp, Chief Legal Officer, was appointed Head of Strategy and Market Communications; and Angwald was promoted to Head of SCA Hygiene.

SCA issued new shares[177] in 1999 (SEK 4.6 billion) to secure its capacity to expand further. Management analysed possible mergers – first and foremost with Stora, but also with Jefferson Smurfit, SAPPI, AssiDomän, Metsä-Serla and Norske Skog. In almost all analyses, Jefferson Smurfit came out as the best alternative. AssiDomän also seemed rather interesting, as it had supplementary operations, while Metsä-Serla looked less attractive because of its large graphics business. Soon SCA was also offered the chance to buy its favourite target the Smurfit Group from Michael Smurfit (2001), and the suggested price seemed reasonable. It was a unique opportunity to establish a leading position in packaging, but some uncertainty emerged both about Smurfit's product repertoire and indebtedness and regarding an upcoming integration process.[178] Overall, the Smurfit Group was in a difficult situation and wanted to leave certain of its businesses, but it was not obvious that the competition authorities would allow SCA to buy all of it. So, eventually, SCA refrained from buying any part of it.[179]

14.3.7 Acquire AssiDomän?

At the end of the 1990s, SCA's top management entered into serious discussions with AssiDomän about a structural deal. One idea was that SCA would buy AssiDomän (except some of its forests) using shares as payment (AssiDomän's owner, the Swedish state, was positive about that idea). However, directors Ramqvist, Gardell and Hedelius disliked it, as the state then would become a substantial owner of SCA (≈ 10%). They claimed that such a deal would lower the value of the new company and make other actors less interested in co-operating. Ramqvist also worried about AssiDomän's sack operations, Gardell about SCA's share price (valued too low) and Hedelius about the new constellation's large raw material operations. All of them also believed that SCA could survive even if somebody else bought AssiDomän. Still, however, all of them supported continued talks with AssiDomän, particularly as that company was worth much more than its current valuation indicated. Thus, there was room for a substantial bid premium.[180]

In January 1999 the Swedish state made SCA an offer regarding AssiDomän. Metsä-Serla also made SCA a proposal, and that construct looked even more promising (less risk and more value for SCA's shareholders). Soon Martin-Löf met the Swedish Minister of Industry, who liked SCA's concept for AssiDomän. Martin-Löf also met with AssiDomän's Chair Magnusson to find out whether it was possible to merge and list the two companies' packaging operations. As a potential buyer of AssiDomän's liquid packaging business (Frövifors), Korsnäs became part of the process, but decided to await further progress in the on-going talks between SCA and AssiDomän (cf. Ch. 7).[181]

Martin-Löf found it difficult to conduct discussions with AssiDomän's CEOs (initially Ahlgren and later Palme) because both of them seemed to advocate some kind of joint venture solution for the two companies' corrugated operations.[182] Soon SCA learned that another alternative existed: it could attempt to buy all of AssiDomän (except the forests). Such a 'big bite' represented a much more complex and demanding path, as the buyer had to orchestrate a solution that would involve many outside actors and tie up management capacity for a long time. In that situation SCA director Gardell offered Custos (where he was CEO) as a possible organizer and executor of the restructuring of AssiDomän. SCA's board took him up on the offer, as Martin-Löf, Gyll[183] and some of the other directors disliked the idea that SCA should handle the complicated split-up and selling process (neither did they like the price indication SCA got from the state's representatives).[184]

Eventually SCA learned from State Secretary Rekke that the state only wanted to keep the forests and sawmills in AssiDomän. Thus, the future for all its other businesses lay outside the company, and that included packaging, too. Eventually, however, both SCA and Custos ended up in the backwater, as AssiDomän's board decided that the company should itself undertake the split-up and sale. The board also decided to invite 'all capable actors' to make bids on (parts of) the company. Thus, SCA was never invited to engage in exclusive buying discussions about AssiDomän's packaging operations and, ultimately, (at least) one competitor (Kappa) offered a better price for that business than SCA did.

14.4 EXPANDING THE HYGIENE BUSINESS

When the board in 1997 discussed SCA's hygiene business, it was decided that three areas should be in focus: incontinence products, tissue for the AFH market and carefully chosen private label products (both tissue and fluff). The expanding incontinence business was a multi-channel affair (including the AFH one) that should be expanded globally. At the same time, SCA considered reducing its more slowly growing and less profitable menstrual products business. When Kimberly-Clark indicated an interest in acquiring SCA's diaper brands (i.e. its operations in the Nordic countries, Holland, Greece and Eastern Europe), that shift suddenly became feasible. At the time Kimberly-Clark wanted to include the Falkenberg plant and certain distribution contracts. However, as private label operations required large-scale production, SCA's board expressed reluctance to sell that plant. One director (Gardell) regarded the expected purchase sum as too low (SEK 1.5 billion), another favoured a sale (Ramqvist) and a third (Augustsson) was worried that Kimberly-Clark would enter the Nordic market anyway. Eventually SCA's board decided to discuss selling at the suggested price, but Kimberly-Clark changed its mind and declared that the price it initially had suggested had become too high.[185]

The integration of all SCA's hygiene business into one unit allowed for rationalizations and closures, but it also stimulated additional purchases and other forms of expansion. The current joint venture in Japan with UniCharm developed well and expanded into Taiwan and the Philippines. In 1997, Procter & Gamble informed SCA that it wanted to buy SCA's tissue operations. Procter & Gamble also made clear that if its proposition were rejected, it would invest around SEK 8 billion and build its own tissue plants in Europe. Thus, Procter & Gamble's offer was formulated in a rather threatening tone. SCA then pondered whether it should reply with a counter bid, propose a purchase of Procter & Gamble's incontinence operations, and in return for that business offer the American company selected tissue plants (e.g. Stembert) and brands. Instead, Procter & Gamble wanted to take over the Mannheim plant, a move that SCA could not agree to because it needed a big plant in Europe to stay competitive on the tissue market. In that somewhat tense situation, SCA also considered blocking Procter & Gamble's ambitions by buying a controlling holding in Metsä-Serla's tissue company.[186]

Growing companies continuously check and analyse emerging rumours and proposals, and SCA was no exception – it had prepared itself for almost 'everything'. To get early 'signals' from (or about) influential market actors, SCA had developed a dense information network all over Europe (and a broader one globally). Despite such information advantages, time pressure and unforeseen occurrences tended to turn many well-planned expansion processes into 'unstructured games'.[187] SCA's discussions with Fort James represented one such messy process that for some time did not even reach the board level.

The talks between the two companies finally became more structured in 1998, when Fort James declared that it wanted to buy SCA's hygiene business. The board immediately discussed the offer but turned it down.[188]

One year later, Fort James got back to SCA and proposed a kind of merger. Since SCA was interested in Fort James's European operations, Martin-Löf met with its leaders in Chicago. SCA's board even discussed a full merger, but some directors hesitated (Reuterskiöld: too difficult; Gyll: there's probably a reason why Fort James's share price had fallen), while others were more positive (Gardell:[189] attractive price, rather strong southern European position and a trimmed industrial structure).[190] Chair Rydin brought up the risk of taking such a huge step. He suspected that one outcome of a merger would be an Americanized company culture that might erode SCA's value base. As it would be impossible to work with shares with different voting rights, Rydin also believed that the Swedish actors soon would lose control of the merged company. Such a development was certainly not attractive for Industrivärden.[191]

In the meantime, SCA continued its expansion strategy by acquiring European companies: A.M. Paper Group (UK, tissue, SEK 2.5 billion), Panosa (Spain, tissue, SEK 0.2 billion) and Nisa (Portugal, tissue, 0.175 billion). SCA also started joint ventures in Chile and Jamaica, and expanded its operations in South Africa and Tunisia. Once again (2000) Fort James emerged as a topic, but Rydin was unwilling to discuss a merger. Various ideas involving Europe, the US and markets outside those two continents were discussed, but nothing materialized. Instead, SCA and Metsä-Serla agreed that SCA should buy an additional 65 per cent of Metsä-Serla's tissue unit (Metsä Tissue). Ultimately, however, the European Commission did not accept that purchase (cf. next section).[192]

One reason why SCA had failed to expand in the US market was its high pricing – the corporations (or even their parts) were too expensive for SCA. To change that situation, SCA would have been forced to issue substantial amounts of new shares, in a situation in which the SEK–USD exchange rate was unfavourable. SCA made no progress there until the US competition authorities conditioned Georgia Pacific's purchase of Fort James on the sale of a part of it. Fortunately, the sale suited SCA well – both content and price were attractive (cf. section 14.6).[193]

14.5 MODO AND SCA ESTABLISH MODO PAPER[194]

Slowly newsprint became a global business, while other kinds of printing paper continued to be regional products (thus, basically, each regional market housed unique producers). However, SCA's efforts to expand globally did not prevent it from announcing an investment in a newsprint machine within Europe at Aylesford and a SC machine at Laakirchen. Both machines were expected to be operational by 2000, making SCA even stronger in 'white papers'. Gardell expressed doubt as to whether those large investments in 'white papers' represented the best path for SCA.[195] He also stressed that SCA had to act carefully, as its competitors were investing, too. Like Palm Paper (UK), Norske Skog invested in a new newsprint machine, Haindl built a big LWC machine (Germany), Lang a machine for non-coated journal paper (Germany), and Perlen a LWC machine (Switzerland). Obviously, competition was tough – the 'good old cartel days' were gone.

At that time, most investment banks ran around and talked structural solutions with the leaders of the fine paper industry. SCA tried to find its own way in that messy situation, primarily looking for a partner for PWA's plants at Stockstadt and Hallein. Discussions were held with KNP, Enso, Stora and SAPPI,[196] although only the last two were regarded as capable of running a consolidated fine paper business. Gardell also added Metsä-Serla (to prevent Procter & Gamble from entering the Nordic market) and International Paper to that list of potential partners. Burgo and CVC also entered SCA's considerations. A problem for SCA was that most of these players did not want to include Wifstavarf in a future deal.[197] So, once again SCA chose the 'MoDo path', despite the two companies' long history of unsuccessful integration attempts. The rather obvious operative merits of such a solution was the primary motive for taking up that path again, but the fact that both companies were from the same country also contributed to the decision. The common cultural setting reduced value-based clashes.[198]

The discussions with MoDo's controlling shareholder Lundberg indicated that Deputy Chair Carl Kempe Jr, who represented the company's second largest shareholder, continued to regard fine paper as one of MoDo's core businesses. Kempe seemed to have a strong say,[199] so that unit was currently not for sale. It was not only Kempe's stance that obstructed a fine paper deal between SCA and MoDo. Actually, neither company wished to be on the buying side (although both wanted to sell). Gradually, therefore, the idea developed that they ought to merge their fine paper businesses and then list the new construct on the SSE (or sell it).[200] In the meantime, SCA also discussed some kind of co-operation with Norske Skog, but nothing materialized.

It was not easy to resume the talks with MoDo, as previous failures still gnawed at many actors. Moreover, communication between former CEO of MoDo Löf and SCA's CEO Martin-Löf had been quite strained, and the two chairs had a rather frosty relationship, too. Over time, however, the atmosphere had become better, especially once MoDo appointed a new CEO (Pettersson), who had a more neutral relationship with SCA's leading actors. It became therefore possible for SCA and MoDo to begin meeting again (spring 1999), although the initial gathering had to be carefully prepared to secure a factual discussion. The leading actors (Rydin, Martin-Löf, Åström ['investigator'], Lundberg and Pettersson) held several meetings determined to find a common solution, and eventually their efforts paid off. MoDo and SCA formed Modo Paper (owned 50–50), which included SCA's Wifstavarf but neither MoDo's Domsjö nor any forests. It became the third biggest fine paper company in Europe (only Stora Enso and UPM-Kymmene were bigger).

The parties discussed a listing of Modo Paper, but the idea was postponed because of the weak stock market, which would produce a too low valuation of the new unit. Thus, the selling alternative once again came to the fore, and that suited SCA, which needed more capital for its upcoming investments in hygiene and packaging. SCA's leaders therefore discussed whether the two companies should be obliged to keep their shareholdings in Modo Paper (and if so: how much and for how long). Lundberg stated that MoDo intended to keep some of it, and that the holding was a long-term investment.[201] In any event, neither MoDo nor SCA was given the right to sell shares in Modo Paper before 2003. SCA also soon learned that MoDo considered distributing (some of?) its Modo Paper shares to its shareholders.[202]

To the surprise of many, Metsä-Serla acquired Modo Paper in 2000 (cf. Ch. 10). With that capital, SCA tried to buy Metsä-Serla's tissue unit in turn, but the European

Commission stopped that transaction. The sale of Modo Paper contributed to streamlining SCA Graphic Paper, which soon became integrated with SCA's other units for forests and woodware into a new business area named Forest Products. SCA's graphics business then had available four strategic alternatives: 'business as usual', gradual regional expansion, participation in globalization or organic expansion. The choice of path was complicated, as the steps the other players in the industry took to survive also played an important role. In Europe, Holmen (formerly MoDo) bought Papelera Peninsular (newsprint, Spain), Stora Enso Consolidated Papers (printing paper, North America), UPM-Kymmene Repap (printing paper, North America), and Norske Skog Fletcher Challenge (pulp and paper, New Zealand). SCA itself was approached in 2001 by UPM-Kymmene, which wanted to assess whether a full merger between the two could be a possibility. However, Rydin (in his capacity as Chair of SCA's major owner Industrivärden) expressed scepticism – he could identify neither synergy nor shared business logic. A return to the fine paper segment was not a particularly attractive path either.[203]

14.6 BREAKTHROUGHS IN ASIA AND THE UNITED STATES

14.6.1 Exit Custos

In May 2000 Gardell asked Martin-Löf about his opinion regarding a possible buy-out of SCA from the SSE conducted by a UK/US fund. Martin-Löf saw that as an issue for SCA's shareholders and board. Industrivärden, SCA's biggest shareholder, was firmly against such a change, as SCA could end up as minority shareholder, with a majority composed of Custos and some external funds. At the same time, rumours emerged that SCA was to be split up into three parts, and that Martin-Löf advocated such a development. The latter was not true – still it brought to the fore the question of how SCA should act to better explain and communicate its strategy. It was also questioned whether Industrivärden would be able to defend SCA from a hostile takeover in the future. One way to avoid that threat was to substantially increase the capital base, for example, by merging SCA with another big company (e.g. with Smurfit that currently was in a similar situation).[204] That, however, did not happen.

Gardell continued to favour a sale of SCA (or some of its parts), so Custos and Goldman Sachs looked for actors that might be interested in putting forward bids. Industrivärden then considered swapping its B-shares for A-shares, but the Swedish insider regulation made that path dubious. Instead, Rydin informed Goldman Sachs that Industrivärden did not intend to participate in any 'financial' purchases of SCA. Eventually it became clear that the better alternative would be for Custos to leave as a shareholder. Several methods for that exit were discussed including, for example, the use of options, but in 2001 Custos decided to distribute its shares in SCA to its shareholders.[205]

14.6.2 Expansion in the United States

SCA tried to expand both its packaging and its hygiene businesses in the US. A few tentative attempts had been made already in 1998 (e.g. Chesapeake, tissue and packaging), but they had not materialized.[206] Bertorp actually thought that SCA's decision to stay out of

North America until the 1990s had been wise. SCA had decided to grow its packaging and hygiene operations in Europe and bring them in order so that they would be ready to try such challenging market entries.[207]

SCA's purchase of Johnson & Johnson's activities in North America was its breakthrough on that incontinence market, as was its agreement with Johnson & Johnson to sell some of its consumer products. That deal gave SCA access to the US (and Canadian) retail market. SCA also talked to Georgia Pacific, but the offering was a disappointment. However, in November 2000, a window of opportunity emerged when the Federal Trade Commission approved Georgia Pacific's acquisition of Fort James under the condition that Fort James sold certain units (which suited SCA's expansion strategy). The decision was written in such a way that few actors other than SCA were eligible. So, SCA could be rather tough in the upcoming negotiations. Eventually SCA paid SEK 8 billion for Georgia Pacific's North American AFH operations, making SCA number three in size on that market. That acquisition was an important step in SCA's globalization efforts, and it also created a platform for a more general expansion in North America.[208]

The acquisition of Encore Paper Company (providing AFH products and converted paper) was another of SCA's more important expansion steps in the hygiene business. That move made it possible to offer US customers both tissue and ready-made 'hygiene concepts'. By 2001, SCA had become number three in the world in the comprehensive hygiene business (13%), following Procter & Gamble and Kimberly-Clark, and it had come to be the biggest provider of quality products for the retailers' private brands (cf. Ahold, Carrefour, Aldi, Metro, etc.). Overall, SCA controlled several strong regional tissue and fluff brands, as well as quite a few global brands for incontinence and menstrual products. In terms of its US packaging business, SCA's expansion included a SEK 2.2 billion bid for Tuscarora, which produced packaging for fragile goods. SCA's leaders knew Tuscarora rather well, as they had co-operated for some time.[209] The Tuscarora deal represented another important step for SCA, as its packaging solutions (brown boxes with fittings) also included non-paper materials at the time. The purchase indicated that SCA had found it important to build up a 'balance' between box material and fittings material.[210]

In the early 2000s SCA also bought two other US companies engaged on the market for 'protective packages' – RPA (high-tech packages) and Insulated Shipping Containers (cold chain packages) – and part of Marko Foam Products (protective packages). All these US acquisitions prompted SCA to establish a new holding company: SCA North America.[211] SCA also continued its activities on the European packaging market. For example, together with Mondi, SCA discussed with AssiDomän a purchase of its Lövholmen plant. However, many (local) actors were sceptical, as SCA already owned a plant there. SCA also returned to the Smurfit case and conducted many analyses of its operations and potentials. At one point, it became clear that Smurfit's owner might consider giving up the company's US unit. That information changed the situation radically – suddenly SCA saw a viable deal and began to check Smurfit's US figures (undertook a limited due diligence). The analyses resulted in a surprise that made an acquisition less attractive. In reality, SCA was most interested in Smurfit's American packaging business, but its figures turned out to be rather poor (but for the other parts of Smurfit they looked much better). Because the target unit was also more indebted than expected, SCA cut its bid substantially. Rydin thought that the new lower offering might thwart a deal, but he was not particularly concerned, as he considered the acquisition to be risky.[212]

In the first years of the millennium SCA was running more than 220 sites in Europe, North America and Asia. It had become Europe's leading producer of corrugated and its raw materials, and world leader in the segment for tailor-made protective packages. SCA concentrated its packaging efforts on two kinds of products: special packages (for mobile phones, wine, liquor, perfume, etc.) and industry packages (car parts, bulk chemicals, etc.). In geographical terms, it continued its European growth (70% of its business took place on that continent), but put more and more effort towards expanding in North America and Asia. Williams, Head of Packaging, particularly pushed for investments in Asia, building on the idea that SCA should 'follow its customers' (as they usually prefer to know their 'packers').[213] Usually SCA tried to establish a foothold on such new markets – investments that were kept low to lessen country risks (and often made together with local partners).[214]

In Europe, attention was drawn to SCA's Aylesford unit when its co-owner Mondi unexpectedly announced that it did not wish to invest in a new machine there. However, Stora Enso was interested in entering that site because then it could postpone a planned investment in Germany. To ward off Stora Enso, SCA was inclined to buy Mondi's 50 per cent share in Aylesford, but hesitated because of the on-going (large) investments in North America.[215]

14.6.3 New CEO: Åström

In December 2001, SCA's nomination committee decided to suggest Martin-Löf as the new Chair to succeed Rydin, who had served in that position for 14 years (1988–2002).[216] But then SCA needed a new CEO, and several candidates competed for that attractive position. Ultimately, the board appointed Jan Åström, who was certainly no newcomer to the forest-based industry. He was actually born close to MoDo's Husum site, where his father had been a manager.[217] Thus, it was no surprise when Åström was recruited in the 1980s to MoDo. That family relationships and domiciles often influence careers is far from unusual, and Åström's career was no exception to that tradition.

Åström left MoDo when he was offered the position as Head of SCA Munksund. When SCA acquired PWA, its fine paper operations had to be put in order, and as Head of SCA Fine Paper, Åström took on the challenge. It was a most difficult task that also included the problematic Wifsta plant (operatively but not legally part of SCA Fine Paper). To get a better picture of the situation, Åström went to Germany and met with PWA's Group Head Heinzel. Rather quickly things improved for fine paper, and that strengthened Åström's authority and position both in SCA in general and – in particular – in its Austrian and German units.[218]

When Modo Paper was established, Åström was appointed its first CEO, and, together with the other leading actors, he planned for a listing of the new company. However, when Modo Paper was bought by Metsä-Serla, Åström was not interested in staying as CEO. Instead, he soon got an offer to become Deputy CEO at SCA and was made responsible for strategic development. In that capacity he participated in several acquisitions (e.g. in the US), which also came to function as preparation for even more demanding assignments.[219]

Rydin and Martin-Löf had actually discussed SCA's CEO succession several years before it took place. It had already been implicitly decided that Martin-Löf should replace Rydin as Chair, so the board had to find a CEO that was comfortable with that arrangement. Alfred Heinzel was then one of the leading internal candidates, but some of the directors were hesitant about appointing him.[220] Some talked about his age (roughly the same as that of the current CEO) as a problem, although they simultaneously praised his track record and great potential. In any event, Heinzel was reluctant to move from Austria to Sweden due to growing engagements in his home country, including both private business and his new role as the Austrian government's 'Head of Privatization'. So, the board asked Martin-Löf if he would agree to continue as CEO for some time, and as he liked the idea, he accepted. Martin-Löf did not leave as CEO until 2002, when he was appointed Chair, four years after the initial replacement discussions. The board then appointed Åström as the new CEO – a decision that had strong internal support, but was met with some raised eyebrows outside SCA (some actors regarded him too inexperienced for such a position and too much of a 'fine paper' man).

NOTES

N.B.: When there is an 'i' inside a parenthesis below, that letter indicates that the note refers to an interview with the named person. All interviewees are listed in the Appendix. A complete listing of references is found at the end of the book.

1. Daun (2004i and 2006i).
2. Rietz (2004i).
3. Daun quickly involved Rydin in the acquisition process (Daun, 2004i).
4. Penser (2005i).
5. Norberg (2005i).
6. Haslum (1993).
7. Martin-Löf (2004i and 2006i).
8. Ibid.
9. Haslum (1993).
10. Away from home.
11. Martin-Löf (2004i and 2006i).
12. Nordenö (2005i).
13. Bertorp, quoted in Lindholm and Wilke (2002).
14. Valeur (1997).
15. Frölander (2005i).
16. Francke (2004i).
17. Hedelius (2004i and 2006i).
18. Enander (2004i).
19. SCA board minutes (released by Martin-Löf).
20. Cf. Ch. 9.
21. SCA refrained from buying Cellulose du Pin in 1989 (Rydin's diary).
22. British American Tobacco.
23. Rydin's diary.
24. Croon (2005).
25. Rietz (2004i).
26. Heinzel wanted to keep 25%.
27. SCA bought 75% of Mill Holding, which in turn held 75% of Laakirchen.
28. Croon (2005).
29. Bertorp, quoted in Lindholm and Wilke (2002).
30. Ibid.
31. Martin-Löf (2004i and 2006i).

32. Rydin (2004i and 2005i).
33. Francke (2004i).
34. Martin-Löf (2004i and 2006i).
35. Ibid.
36. Croon (2005).
37. Nordenö (2005i).
38. Penser (2005i).
39. Cf. Ch. 12 for an extensive description of the process.
40. Nordenö (2005i).
41. Rydin's diary.
42. Ibid.
43. Frölander (2005i).
44. Haslum (1979).
45. Ibid.
46. Penser (2005i) and Rietz (2004i).
47. Rietz (2004i).
48. Martin-Löf (2004i and 2006i), Rydin (2004i and 2005i) and Bertorp, quoted in Lindholm and Wilke (2002).
49. SCA Annual Report 1989.
50. Frölander (2005i).
51. Martin-Löf (2004i and 2006i).
52. Nordenö (2005i).
53. Lindholm and Wilke (2002) and Rydin (2004i and 2005i).
54. Nordenö (2005i).
55. Lindholm and Wilke (2002).
56. Penser (2005i).
57. Martin-Löf (2004i and 2006i).
58. It was sold in 1993.
59. Rietz (2004i).
60. Frölander (2005i).
61. Testliner and kraftliner in Sweden (Munksund and Obbola), and testliner and fluting in Holland (Eerbeek), Italy (Porcari) and the UK (Aylesford).
62. Valeur (2003).
63. Rydin's diary.
64. Francke (2004i).
65. Haslum (1993).
66. Bertorp, quoted in Lindholm and Wilke (2002).
67. Francke (2004i), Penser (2005i) and Rietz (2004i).
68. Bertorp, quoted in Lindholm and Wilke (2002).
69. Rietz (2004i).
70. Hedelius (2004i and 2006i).
71. Martin-Löf, quoted in Lindholm and Wilke (2002).
72. Haslum (1993).
73. Rydin's diary.
74. Ibid.
75. Enander (2004i).
76. Rydin (2004i and 2005i) and Rydin's diary.
77. SCA Annual Report 1990.
78. For a complementary description of the MoDo contest see Ch. 9.
79. Martin-Löf in Lindholm and Wilke (2002).
80. Rydin's diary.
81. Ibid.
82. Ibid.
83. Ibid.
84. Croon (2005).
85. Member of Lundbergföretagen's board.
86. Francke (2004i).
87. Lundberg (2006i). He also recalls that SCA Chair Rydin phoned him at 19.30 and confirmed his deal with Carlgren, but that call is not recorded in Rydin's diary.
88. Rydin's diary.
89. Rietz (2004i).

90. Haslum (1993).
91. Martin-Löf in Lindholm and Wilke (2002).
92. Martin-Löf, quoted in Svensk papperstidning, No. 1, 1991.
93. Rietz (2004i).
94. Frölander (2005i).
95. Croon (2005).
96. Penser (2005i).
97. Rydin (2004i and 2005i).
98. Penser (2005i).
99. Rydin's diary.
100. Enander (2004i).
101. Carlgren (1994i).
102. Martin-Löf (2004i and 2006i).
103. Ibid.
104. Ibid.
105. Rydin's diary.
106. Ibid.
107. Ibid.
108. Croon (2005).
109. Ibid.
110. Rydin (2004i and 2005i).
111. Carlgren (1994i).
112. Rydin's diary.
113. Rydin (2004i and 2005i).
114. Ibid.
115. Lindholm and Wilke (2002).
116. Martin-Löf (2004i and 2006i).
117. Bertorp, quoted in Lindholm and Wilke (2002).
118. Lindholm and Wilke (2002).
119. Frölander (2005i).
120. Rydin's diary.
121. Ibid.
122. Martin-Löf (2004i and 2006i).
123. Hedelius (2004i and 2006i).
124. Angwald in Lindholm and Wilke (2002).
125. SCA board minutes (released by Martin-Löf) and Martin-Löf (2004i and 2006i).
126. Penser (2005i).
127. Ibid.
128. Rietz (2004i) and Rydin (2004i and 2005i).
129. E.g. former CEO of Marabou, the market leader on the Swedish market for chocolate and candy.
130. Rietz (2004i).
131. Ibid.
132. One board member disagreed and argued for another path for Mölnlycke.
133. Martin-Löf (2004i and 2006i).
134. Rietz (2004i).
135. Rydin's diary.
136. Rydin (2004i and 2005i).
137. Rydin's diary.
138. Ibid.
139. Angwald, quoted in Lindholm and Wilke (2002).
140. A part of hygiene. At the time Mölnlycke lacked the managerial capacity to take care of those operations.
141. Whether that was in accordance with the statutes or not was not obvious.
142. SCA board minutes (released by Martin-Löf).
143. A right but not an obligation to sell.
144. Rydin's diary.
145. SCA board minutes (released by Martin-Löf).
146. Ibid.
147. Rietz (2004i).
148. Lindholm and Wilke (2002).
149. Penser (2005i).
150. SCA board minutes (released by Martin-Löf).

151. Bertorp in Lindholm and Wilke (2002).
152. Ibid.
153. Kallifatides et al. (2010).
154. Board notes released by Martin-Löf, 2007.
155. Hedelius (2004i and 2006i).
156. Gardell (2005i).
157. SCA board minutes (released by Martin-Löf).
158. Martin-Löf (2004i and 2006i).
159. Gardell (2005i).
160. Gardell (2005i) and Penser (2005i).
161. Enander (2004i), Francke (2004i) and Penser (2005i).
162. Hedelius (2004i and 2006i).
163. Rietz (2004i).
164. Rydin's diary and Rydin (2006i).
165. Gyll replaced Penser.
166. Gyll (2005i).
167. Rydin's diary.
168. Ibid.
169. Hedelius (2004i and 2006i).
170. SCA board minutes (released by Martin-Löf).
171. Ibid.
172. Ibid.
173. Could be increased to 51%.
174. For example, in Austria Welpa; in the Czech Republic Obalex; in Denmark Danisco Pack; in Finland Metsä-Serla's corrugated unit Pakkausjaloste; in France Anjou Emballages, Caronnages Industriels Méchunois, and Nicollet; in Germany Nestler Wellpappe; in Holland Mendels Cartonnage; in Italy Alto Adige, Biopack, Cochis, and Lubelli; in Ireland Len-Pak; in Spain Lantero (25%); in Switzerland Widmer-Walty Group (49.9%); and in the UK Rexam.
175. For example, two in Poland (Pila and Kwidzin) and one each in Hungary (Nagykata), Italy (Emilia) and Turkey (Tarsus).
176. Bührmann-Tetterode.
177. Back in 1996 SCA had ratified precedence for the current owners to subscribe in proportion to its (A and B) shareholding.
178. SCA board minutes (released by Martin-Löf).
179. Hedelius (2004i and 2006i).
180. Gardell (2005i); and board notes released by Martin-Löf, 2007.
181. Rydin's diary.
182. Martin-Löf (2007i).
183. Gyll (2005i).
184. SCA board minutes (released by Martin-Löf).
185. Ibid.
186. Ibid.
187. Rydin (2004i and 2005i).
188. Gyll (2005i).
189. Gardell (2005i).
190. SCA board minutes (released by Martin-Löf).
191. Rydin's diary.
192. SCA board minutes (released by Martin-Löf).
193. Martin-Löf (2004i and 2006i).
194. Cf. also Ch. 10.
195. SCA board minutes (released by Martin-Löf).
196. A South African pulp and paper company with global operations.
197. SCA board minutes (released by Martin-Löf).
198. Åström (2005i and 2006i).
199. Some actors claimed that Carl Kempe Jr's strong position derived from an informal agreement with Lundberg from the time when Lundberg had struggled for control over MoDo.
200. Martin-Löf (2004i and 2006i).
201. Åström (2005i and 2006i).
202. SCA board minutes (released by Martin-Löf).
203. Rydin's diary.
204. Martin-Löf (2006i).

205. Gardell (2005i).
206. SCA board minutes (released by Martin-Löf).
207. Bertorp, quoted in Lindholm and Wilke (2002).
208. SCA board minutes (released by Martin-Löf).
209. SCA's purchases of companies were frequently based on such (longer) relationships with influential owners, directors or members of top management. However, it was usually the leaders of subsidiaries, divisions, and the like who took care of most of the small talk and kept the relationships 'warm' and alive. Thus, it was often the operative managers that met and tested ideas and picked up (and spread) rumours. There were also professional networks around companies like SCA, and usually they mattered a lot in the strategic processes.
210. Williams, quoted in Lindholm and Wilke (2002).
211. SCA board minutes (released by Martin-Löf).
212. Rydin's diary.
213. Williams, quoted in Lindholm and Wilke (2002).
214. Martin-Löf (2004i and 2006i).
215. Williams in Lindholm and Wilke (2002).
216. Rydin was simultaneously appointed Honorary Chair.
217. His father has even been a mentor to Martin-Löf.
218. Åström (2005i and 2006i).
219. Rydin's diary.
220. Ibid.

PART III

Analyses and conclusions

15. The impact of nature, occurrences, institutions and actor collectives on corporate paths

15.1 DIFFERENT DATA SOURCES

The analysis of the extensive empirical material is divided into two parts, this one that ends with WWII, and one that starts with the 1950s and runs into the first decade of the 21st century. The basic reason behind that division is that the opportunities to obtain primary data erode with time, since the actors that were active as (major) shareholders, board members or CEOs before the second half of the 20th century were not around when the extensive primary data was collected (2004–08). Thus, primary data is available only for the period starting with WWII and ending about 50 years later (cf. Appendix). That observation implies that for the many decades preceding that period, the analysis has to rely on secondary data, and therefore some of the major issues that this study addresses cannot be discussed in depth. Instead, those analyses have to wait until Chapter 16.[1]

In the long period ending with WWII the available secondary sources allow for descriptions of most of the basic forces that influence corporate paths. However, it has not been easy to determine whether available secondary data actually provides a convincing picture regarding which individuals (and actions) were important for the formation of corporate paths during that time period. The existing sources (books and articles) are relatively few, and it is thus likely that several influential actors might have been overlooked or forgotten (at least some of those that were active before the mid-19th century). As a result, it has been more difficult to evaluate the impact individual actorhood has had on corporate paths than to assess that of the other driving forces, which are easier to identify and describe even for periods long before the 20th century. As a result, the first part of the study – ranging from the 19th century (in some cases even longer ago; cf. Ch. 4) to WWII – will therefore focus on two of the boxes presented in Figure 15.1, namely forces (left side) and corporate paths (right side). From WWII onwards until the early 21st century, all three boxes will be discussed, as both secondary and – particularly – primary data could be used.

A reading of Chapters 4 ('Before World War I') and 5 ('The first half of the 20th century') makes it rather obvious that corporate paths are determined by intricate interactions of forces rather than by any individual force alone. Nevertheless, the following analyses (cf. sections 15.2–15.7) will focus on one force at a time. Those discussions will then be followed by a section that addresses corporate paths (15.8). In the final section of this chapter (15.9) a few tentative conclusions will be presented.

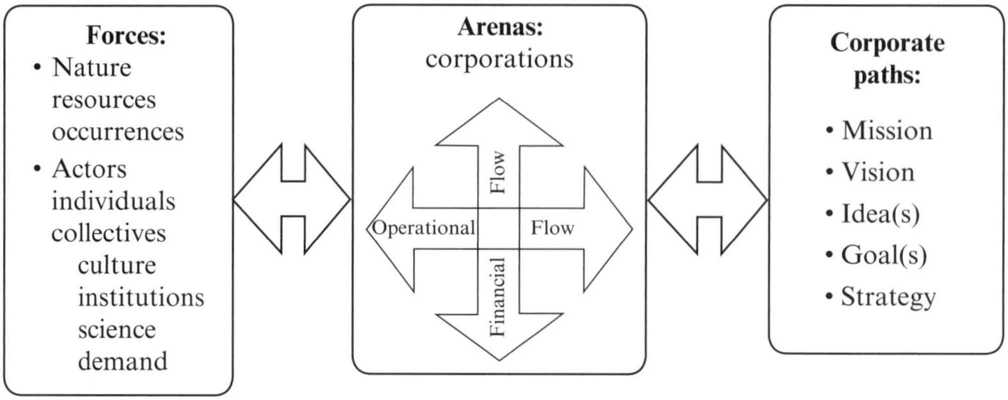

Figure 15.1 Corporate governance: its deciding forces, arenas and manifestations (identical to Figure 1.1)

15.2 NATURE-DRIVEN FORCES

In the original model (cf. Ch. 1), nature was described as a force causing occurrences, that is to say, phenomena that are difficult to deal with until they actually happen. In many cases their impact on corporate development is both sudden and strong. However, as is shown in the figure above, nature also plays another important role when corporate paths are determined, namely as a potential resource for human production and consumption. Still, something does not become a natural 'resource' until at least one actor decides to treat it that way. The most obvious resource for the forest-based industry is of course the timber (suitable forests), but initially (i.e. up until the second half of the 20th century) rivers and other water-based formations had almost similar status (power sources).

The more official recognition of the Swedish forests as a significant natural resource dates from the 16th century, when the state introduced regulations about how to utilize them.[2] Such forest-related legislation then became more and more detailed up until the middle of the 18th century. Still, in the 17th century the Swedish state owned most of the forests and waters. After that, however, when the state sought to encourage the colonization of northern Sweden, a large part of the forests were distributed to farmers. This transfer coincided with the rise of small-scale paper production located close to small rivers (which provided the power). At that time, the crucial raw material input consisted of linen lump.

In the early 19th century, in its effort to bring sawmill owners and raw material producers closer together, the state distributed additional forests to the farmers, making them landowners. The whole operation did not turn out as well as expected, so the state did not proceed further along that line. Instead, it kept the remaining forests and established a central supervisory unit responsible for all state-run forests (National Forestry Board). Initially, the primeval forests were used as raw material because of the opportunities provided by the rivers. When the restrictions regarding felling rights were abolished, a huge supply of high-quality forests became available. That new supply situation became a decisive factor for the Swedish firms' expansion and export of timber and sawn-wood products. Those businesses developed despite the fact that the firms were still small and used obsolete technologies. For example, until the middle of the 19th century, most of the timber was used in water power based sawmills. Because the sawmills were located inland, export remained rather modest.

Secure sourcing of linen lump was a necessity for the small paper mills that existed in the 18th century. Eventually, however, the supply could not match the growing demand for paper products. The state tried to improve the situation by organizing regional and national collections of linen lump, but soon it became obvious that those efforts did not deliver a sustainable solution. Instead, many experiments started looking for a new (cheap and abundant) natural resource that could be used as raw material in paper production. The comprehensive R&D efforts resulted in a revolution in the second half of the 19th century, when it became possible to use timber (wood fibres) as raw material.

More specific knowledge about what nature-initiated occurrences might have significantly influenced the development of the forest-based industry before the 20th century is rather limited. Although one can often trace how natural catastrophes have affected Swedish society as a whole (cf. crop failures [starvation], flooding, wildfires and climate/weather extremes), reliable accounts describing their effect on the forest-based industry are hard to find. Of course, many of those rather extreme nature-based forces now and then also struck forests and forest-based activities, but none of that seems to have significantly changed the ways the firms developed.

During the first half of the 20th century, the natural resources situation changed somewhat. For obvious reasons, pine and spruce still provided most of the basic raw material, although technological breakthroughs had made it possible to utilize certain leafy trees, too. At the same time, rivers lost in importance both as means of transportation (cf. railways and lorries) and as power sources (cf. steam and electricity). Those changes also affected the location of new production units (to the coast instead of inland), as they required water resources for the long distance transport of finished goods, that is to say, conditions that the Baltic Sea and the Atlantic Ocean usually provided (i.e. [ice-free] harbours).

The huge demand for forest-based products affected the supply of the industry's key natural resource, that is to say, timber. In the wake of several studies that indicated that cutting had been too extensive, a committee was formed in the early 1930s to find a solution. The committee concluded that a serious timber shortage would result if the industry began to produce at its full capacity. That statement influenced many corporate decisions over the next decades.

Thus, the Swedish forest-based corporations expected timber sourcing problems, and to avoid such a situation they could pursue one or several of six different paths: (1) 'business as usual' (expecting that the timber shortage would hit other forest-based companies), (2) expand sourcing by finding ways to utilize unused sorts of wood (e.g. birch, and small or low-quality timber), (3) get timber from sources outside Sweden (because eventually new innovations had made short-fibre trees competitive for certain products), (4) increase forest growth (by introducing new forestry methods), (5) develop more fibre-efficient production methods and (6) move along the value chain and integrate forward (i.e. make paper). All six of those paths were used to solve the expected raw material shortage, although each corporation applied its own strategic 'mixture'.

15.3 TECHNOLOGICAL BREAKTHROUGHS AND INNOVATIONS

Until the middle of the 19th century most of the forest-based goods that were produced in northern Sweden were sawn timber and wood products. Water-based power, river-based distribution and a large supply of suitable timber (mainly from primeval forests) were the crucial natural resources. Swedish paper mills were still working in old-fashioned, manual ways using linen lump as raw material and a poorly developed technology. However, steam-based sawmills located at the coast gradually began to replace the water-powered inland ones. That fundamental change of technology was a prerequisite for the emerging industrialization of the forest-based industry. Still, it took several decades before the new technology really began to make a difference and enabled substantial production increases for the forest-based firms. The new technology involved machinery, and eventually it made the whole business capital intensive, turning small firms into (relatively) large corporations.

The really significant expansion of the forest-based industry took place in the 1870s, when it became technologically possible to use wood fibre to produce pulp for paper production. That breakthrough made the Swedish forests an even more valuable raw material source (not only for Sweden, but also for many other parts of Europe, particularly the UK). Eventually the technology allowed for large-scale production of mechanical wood pulp, sulphite pulp and sulphate pulp (and somewhat later continuous, machine-based paper production). However, the entry of such chemical pulp on the marketplace was not the product of a few specific occurrences or of initiatives from solitary actors. Instead, the chemical pulp followed from many more or less co-ordinated contributions to a long sequence of scientific developments. The sulphate method appeared on the scene first, but the economic results of its first practical applications were rather poor, mainly due to substantial technical problems. Thus, for some time that method lost its credibility.

The situation for wood-based pulp production improved significantly when the sulphite method was put into practice. It could use cheap raw material (i.e. spruce), and the pulp's colour was easy to bleach. Still, the sulphite method also had its disadvantages. Because it required a considerable capital base (large-scale production was almost a 'must'), the financial risks were higher, and therefore the method was sensitive to demand fluctuations. Another problem was that it required spruce, while the sulphate method could use almost any kind of tree. The sulphate-based paper was also stronger than the sulphite-based one. Thus, the choice of method was not straightforward, although the initial failures with the sulphate technique contributed to the sulphite method's dominance during the last decades of the 19th century. In the early 20th century, however, plants using the sulphite method began to face increasing environmental costs, a burden previously placed only on the sulphate method. That cost drift spoke in favour of a 'comeback' for sulphate production.

The decades around WWI saw significant technical breakthroughs and innovations. Most parts of the value chain were affected: the cutting of the trees (chainsaws), the transportation of the timber to the plants (improved roads; trucks instead of horses and rivers), the production processes (e.g. radical mechanization and continuous cooking) and the transportation of the finished goods to the wholesalers/retailers/ultimate customers (railways and lorries). Almost all corporations benefitted from those improvements, but some took greater advantage of the developments than others by taking the lead in the transformations, a leadership that also included product development.

Spruce-based sulphite production continued to expand during the first decade of the 20th century, and several new plants were built. However, as sulphate production (also) could use weak pines and birch, and as a surplus of such trees existed in the northernmost part of Sweden, the state decided to encourage the location of such production units to that region (e.g. Obbola [Holmsund/SCA], Husum [MoDo/Holmen] and Kalix [Baltiska Trävaru/Sveaskog]). That state initiative changed the situation and became a platform for a coming revaluation of the relative merits of the sulphate production method.

Over time most of the larger corporations continued to re-position themselves along the value chain and focused their production on different paper qualities. Four corporations, Stora Kopparberg, Holmens Bruk, Matfors (SCA) and Skönvik (SCA), invested heavily in newsprint. Holmens Bruk expanded its textile operations as well, and thus developed two core businesses. MoDo was particularly active in R&D, and its leader at the time, Frans Kempe Sr, envisioned a MoDo that would bring radical innovations to the marketplace. WWI had already 'forced' the company to deliver many new products that differed from those of its classic core businesses: the new output repertoire actually resembled that of a modern chemical business (it included 'everything' ranging from dynamite to cosmetics).

Continuing the strategy of his predecessor Frans Kempe Sr, Carl Kempe Sr actively supported MoDo's R&D activities, for example, by establishing a laboratory building and recruiting highly competent people. Its leading actors made many 'minor' contributions to the company's production processes and its product repertoire, but the really important breakthrough that determined MoDo's path for many years was the invention of a technically and economically exploitable method for pulp bleaching. That new (chlorine oxide-based) process made it possible to use deciduous forests, particularly birch, something that dramatically expanded the supply of usable timber. That combination made MoDo the leading seller of a superior product for nearly a decade. Another important technological step the company took at the time was to start the production of wallboard, thereby making profitable use of 'waste' from sawmills (i.e. sawdust). Eventually other companies also became interested in setting up their own R&D units. The Swedish state followed suit and established a national forest research institute (in collaboration with the industry).

15.4 RAPIDLY RISING DEMAND

In the 18th century foreign capitalists still treated the Nordic countries as an underdeveloped region of Europe. What brought them to the Nordic market was primarily the combination of low-priced raw materials and cheap labour. Particularly Sweden became regarded as a reliable supplier of forest-based products. The first wave of foreign demand for raw timber and wood was driven by the emergence of industrial capitalism, the heavy investments in infrastructure (e.g. railways) in many parts of Europe and an emerging freedom of trade between some European countries. That gradually growing demand stimulated the establishment of numerous water-powered sawmills in Sweden in the 18th and 19th centuries.

It was not until the end of the 19th century that the forests became recognized as one of the most valuable assets of the Swedish territory (forest-based exports increased tenfold between the 1840s and 1890s), even though the mechanical wood processing industry had had a long history in the country before that. The main driver of the forest-based industry's extraordinary expansion was the growing demand from many parts of Europe (particularly the UK) for products for their buildings, infrastructures and carpentry industries. In addition, a rapidly growing demand for printing paper (for books and newspapers) could be met with new, machine-based production techniques.

Still, most paper production continued to be a domestic business, as most of the foreign demand was for pulp intended for processing in those countries' own mills. Several continental European and British companies had already captured a dominating position in that part of the value chain and had become dependent on Nordic pulp for their operations. Furthermore, because the pulp producers and the paper manufacturers had informally agreed to preserve the status quo, the Nordic corporations refrained for the time being from integrating forward to such an extent that they would need to export some of the paper they produced and compete with their own customers.

The first half of the 20th century represented a radical period of expansion for the Swedish forest-based industry, although several periods of serious setbacks changed the industry structure and ownership patterns. Newsprint demand grew rapidly (also from abroad), and particularly Stora Kopparberg and Holmens Bruk invested heavily in that market segment. Moreover, already during the century's first decade, some 15 pulp plants, mainly based on the sulphite method, were built, including Skutskär (Stora Kopparberg[3]), Loddby (Holmens Bruk), Domsjö (MoDo) and Svartvik (consortium of country squires/SCA). At the time Wallenberg established a sulphate production at Wifstavarf (Stora Kopparberg, later SCA), and Iggesund (later MoDo and Holmen) put up a combined sulphite–sulphate plant at Hjälmåsen.

A radical dip in demand for Swedish forest-based industry products occurred in 1920, triggered by a deep international recession. That crisis led to substantial changes regarding both corporate sizes and ownership. However, demand recovered already in the mid-1920s, with some of it now coming from the US (sulphate pulp for packaging paper). Thus, this time the rapid expansion almost exclusively involved investments in sulphate production (e.g. at Karlsborg [Swedish state/Sveaskog[4]], Munksund [Handelsbanken/SCA], Norrsundet [Kopparberg-Hofors/Stora Kopparberg] and Östrand [SCA]). Investments in the sulphate process continued from the 1930s on, making sulphate the dominant method for pulp production. Investments were also made in mechanical grinderies and in kraft paper production. Because almost all of these investments were carried out before any structural alterations or ownership changes had taken place, the boundaries between the different ownership spheres became (even) more rigid.

15.5 INSTITUTIONAL CHANGES

The Swedish state has regulated forest use since the 16th century, although the more organized efforts did not start until the 17th century. The state was particularly keen to ensure that the growing iron industry would benefit from good conditions by securing its sourcing of charcoal. For the forest-based businesses, the state's priority meant that the

Swedish export of timber and wood products was almost negligible before 1850. As noted above, the state distributed land to farmers in the 1820s, but the new owners did not take as good care of the forests as had been expected. As a result, the government's belief in the merits of private ownership and in the capacity of farmers was turned on its head. In order to take a firmer grip in that worrisome situation, the state centralized control by establishing a National Forestry Board (1859) that later, in conjunction with a merger, was renamed Domänstyrelsen (1883).[5]

By the mid-18th century, the emerging insight that it was possible to use timber for pulp and paper production not only changed the state's understanding of the forest industry, but also stimulated many firms to buy land from farmers in order to secure the sourcing of raw material (also) for forest-based production. It was actually not until that time that forests became regarded as a scarce (and crucial) natural resource, the locations and tree compositions of which had to be considered in the choice of output. All four global corporations addressed in this study – that is to say, what in the 21st century had developed into Holmen, SCA, Stora Enso and Sveaskog – participated in a first general buying race that culminated in the late 19th century. Previously, corporations had bought felling rights to secure timber sourcing, but this time real estate (forests) became the primary buying target. Unfortunately, those purchases were too seldom carried out in decent and honourable ways. Consequently, that deceitful practice brought about new legislation that prohibited limited companies and economic associations from buying real estate (in 1906 [applicable to the provinces] and in 1925 [applicable to the whole country]).

The rising ambition to decentralize and deregulate business activity in general that appeared in the 19th century materialized in several ways, particularly in fields that were associated with industrial investments. The abolishment of the legal restrictions regarding felling rights (1842) and opportunities to establish new sawmills (1863) were important elements in the liberalization process. However, the most important change that occurred at the time affected business in general: it was the establishment of the first Swedish Companies Act (1848), that is to say, a new law that regulated economic activity and (collective) risk-taking, which significantly simplified the sourcing of capital for organized ventures. That new law introduced a construct – the 'limited company' – that (among other things) made ownership transformations much easier, with such changes beginning to occur more often during the first decades of the 20th century. Industrial risk-taking was also made easier in those days when the regionally active commercial banks were founded. The opportunities to export forest-based products also improved, as, for example, both Swedish export duties and British import duties were lowered.

The decades following WWI also saw several significant institutional changes. Some of them came in the form of self-regulation – in many ways a reflection of war experiences that made many leading actors inclined to find co-operative (and national) solutions. The Swedish producers of kraftliner formed a joint organization in 1927 and initiated a Nordic network in 1932 (Scankraft). Both associations had the ambition to create a common pricing policy for their respective businesses. Similar informal organizations were formed a few years later in the wrapping paper sector and for newsprint (Scannews). The latter constellation grew in importance after WWII, when other countries such as Canada and the UK joined. Separate Swedish cartel-like associations were also founded during those years (i.e. Scanfin [fine paper], Scanpapp [packaging] and Scanpergamyn [printing paper]), and an older one was revived (Scansulfit [pulp]). At that time all (these) cartels were seen as legitimate institutions that contributed to wealth in society by improving export prices and preventing economic crises (by making extraordinary price fluctuations less probable). International co-operation also became increasingly popular, particularly after WWII and in the newsprint sector. For example, the International Committee on Newsprint was established with the goal of promoting the common interests of sellers and buyers of newsprint. The general idea was to guarantee certain sales volumes for each producer and stable price levels for the consumers.

In the early 1930s, several leaders of Swedish forest-based corporations felt that their companies' R&D efforts had to be strengthened (MoDo's earlier initiative became the archetype). Eventually they founded such a joint unit (1936). The state acted, too, and decided to take more responsibility for the financing of the industry's basic research. Together with many of the leading forest-based corporations, it also supported an institute for applied R&D efforts. Those two R&D organizations later merged and became part of the Swedish university system. Several of the corporations also formed a joint trading company that took care of pulp sales (1931). That organization, however, was founded primarily to obstruct the expansion of the newly established holding company SCA.

The government's regulatory efforts sought to promote the country's export of forest-based products. For example, a joint trade agreement on customs tariffs and quantity limits was concluded in 1925 between three Nordic countries and the UK. However, most other European countries still enforced high customs rates and low quotas, which almost stopped the Swedish forest-based industry's exports to countries such as France and Holland. Thus, the international market for forest-based goods continued to be full of obstructions up until WWII. For obvious reasons the demand for timber, sawn wood and other forest-based products rose dramatically after that destructive period, as many parts of Europe had to be rebuilt (houses, plants, infrastructure, etc.). In that situation the state feared inflation and introduced export regulations, a policy response that was repeated in connection with the Korean War.

However, after that period a more liberal economy began to emerge globally, so the Swedish (forest-based) companies accelerated their internationalization processes. Although protectionism was on the decline, some of the tough restrictions surrounding the Swedish capital market were maintained even into the 1970s and 1980s (e.g. the currency control), and specific monetary policy tools were added that included investment rules, liquidity quotas, loan regulations, interest regulations and issue controls.

15.6 ACTOR-GENERATED OCCURRENCES

Some occurrences – positive as well as negative – that hit the forest-based industry were caused by nature. For such events, actors are offered only two choices: try to foresee them and/or deal with their consequences. However, most occurrences have a quite different origin, namely (constellations of) individual actors. This volume is not the place for any thorough description and analysis of such events that hit the forest-based firms hard before the 20th century (cf. Ch. 4). However, one particularly striking man-made occurrence could be mentioned as a concrete example, as it specifically had consequences for one of the four corporations that are the focus of this study: the Russian galley fleet's burning down of Iggesund's plants and buildings in 1721.[6]

From the 20th century the richer empirical material makes it easier to identify significant man-made occurrences that have influenced the forest-based industry substantially, and particularly those that have affected the corporations highlighted in this volume. One such occurrence with its accompanying chains of events resulted in WWI, but the devastating consequences of that warfare actually did not significantly affect the Swedish forest-based industry, particularly not in a material sense as Sweden remained neutral throughout that war, so its corporations' plants remained intact. It was rather the rising inflation during those years that affected the Swedish forest-based industry, creating financial 'turbulence' and, as a consequence of that, radical structural changes. Thus, the period of relative owner stability that had prevailed in the century before WWI was replaced by a period in which the companies grew from small to medium-sized (although most of them remained family owned). Two of the ownership changes in particular entailed long-term consequences for the Swedish forest-based industry. One involved Handelsbanken (a bank later linked to MoDo/Holmen and SCA) when it acquired the relatively large pulp and paper producer Bergvik & Ala. The other targeted Stora Kopparberg, a corporation managed by the Wallenberg family together with Skandiabanken. At that time that Wallenberg-led constellation held only 3 per cent of the votes, but the family's position in the corporation was much stronger than that low figure indicated, as the Wallenbergs controlled Stora Kopparberg's top positions. Together, those two seemingly minor circumstances represented the beginning of a process that in the mid-20th century would establish the Wallenberg family as a prominent actor in the Swedish (and later global) forest-based industry.

Another severe man-made crisis hit the forest-based industry hard in 1920, when a deep international recession eliminated most of the demand for its products. The crisis lasted two years and produced significant problems for the industry. Many reputable families were hit hard and lost their positions as owners and leaders in Swedish business life. Several of the newer companies, in particular, failed (went bankrupt) because of excessive financial risk-taking (speculation). Many of the newly established corporations were fragile creations swiftly put together during the boom years (cf. financial consortia and issuing syndicates) and were poorly governed and highly indebted. So, after WWI several banks had to enter as shareholders by converting (unpaid) debt into equity, which in turn made them substantial owners of forest-based corporations. The Kempe family was one of the rather few ownership dynastics that not only survived the crisis, but actually came out strengthened, and that despite the fact that MoDo had invested heavily, but luckily mainly before WWI. Thus, the Kempe family's early efforts had built a financially robust business that survived the crisis. Another 'winner' was the Wallenberg family. Among the other corporations that benefitted from the crisis one finds Bergvik & Ala, Holmens Bruk, Kopparberg-Hofors, Papyrus, Stora Kopparberg and Wifstavarf.

The new ownership situation also brought about a deeper intertwining between certain banks and many of their already (partly) owned corporations. These tighter relationships contributed to the emergence of a more divided industrial structure in Sweden. Eventually two ownership spheres that would dominate 20th century economic life in Sweden emerged, one of them controlled by a dynasty (the Wallenberg family), and the other by the executives of a large bank (Handelsbanken) and the managers of its client corporations. Thus, the recession crisis triggered a radical change of the power distribution in Swedish industry, and for at least a century. Over a decade or two, trading houses (or families with that background) had lost their dominating position as owners of most of the (forest-based) companies; instead, financial and industrial capitalists had taken control.

Eventually several of the rather distinct boundaries that had existed between many forest-based companies during the 19th century disappeared or faded away when the 1920 recession led to the loss of company control for many families. That new situation created an opportunity for restructuring initiatives, but the leading actors refrained from making such efforts. The economic crisis had also severely reduced the number of capitalists capable of initiating such structural changes, and as the banks were prohibited from buying corporate shares (except in specific situations), they could not step in to fill the gap. Instead, the borders between each sphere's holdings became sharper, and that increased the Swedish industry's structural inertia. Thus, for several decades most of the rationalizations and integrations occurred within rather than between ownership spheres, and inside Sweden rather than inside the Nordic countries or on a European basis.

So, from the mid-1920s one could talk about a new era, that of industrial capitalism, which replaced the classic trade capitalism that had dominated the 19th century. Most current researchers use the 'industrial' label to define a period starting at the beginning of the 20th century and ending almost one hundred years later. However, it is also possible to claim that around WWI another kind of capitalism had emerged, although it only lasted for a short period: financial capitalism. That rationale set the tone for almost a decade, but the economic crisis of the early 1920s put an end to that era. However, it would return late in the 20th century, and then in a much more forceful and enduring manner.

15.7 ENTREPRENEURS AND CAPITALISTS

It was not only nature (through its unexpected occurrences and its [potential] resources), technological breakthroughs, rising customer demand, institutional forces and man-made occurrences that determined how the Swedish forest-based industry developed up until WWII. Obviously, many individual and collective actors also contributed actively to that process, though, as mentioned before, it is difficult to collect material that covers all of the more important actors that were involved before WWII. The available secondary data is merely sufficient for providing reliable descriptions of – at best – some of the more high-profile actors' efforts, that is to say, a handful of those individuals whose accomplishments have been regarded as so outstanding that their lives and efforts have generated biographies, chapters in corporate jubilee books and similar texts. Keeping that lack of information in mind, it could still be meaningful to describe the efforts of a handful of the supposedly prominent actors who had leading roles in the forerunners to the four corporations addressed in this study.

A rather clear-cut example of individual entrepreneurship in the 19th century is found in what was to become MoDo (later Holmen), when J.C. Kempe established a sawmill business at Mo in 1823. With time, J.C. Kempe became publicly known and remembered as an entrepreneurial businessman and energetic risk-taker – a combination that was regarded as a virtue by some (but certainly not all) of his descendants in MoDo. In spite of family disagreements, those attributes were usually referred to as requirements for any Kempe aspiring to run the growing corporation. Thus, J.C. Kempe left not only an economic legacy to his 11 heirs, but also guidelines regarding the future family heads' personalities and rationality mixes. Two of his heirs held board positions in MoDo, namely Frans Kempe Sr (CEO 1884–1917) and Seth Kempe. They were active financial as well as operative risk-takers and acquired several firms. That expansion process, however, made MoDo indebted to banks, and that dependency followed the company through most of the 20th century.

Olsson was another important actor in the late 19th century. Basically, he restructured forest-based firms in the northernmost parts of Sweden. His risk-taking was less adventurous than that of the Kempes since he was actively supported in his efforts by a prominent Swedish bank (Stockholms Enskilda Bank). Although Olsson's ambitious effort failed in the end, the bank expanded its activities in the forest-based businesses and formed a constellation that included, for example, the largest sulphite plant in Sweden. One of the acquired firms (Wifstavarf) recruited Marcus Wallenberg the Elder (cf. Ch. 11, Figure 11.1) as Chair and Knut Sundblad as CEO. That represented the start of a long engagement for those two families in the forest-based industry (Wallenbergs as owners and Sundblads as CEOs). Other renowned entrepreneurial actors in the 19th century included, for example, members of the Tamm (Iggesund), Dickson (Matfors, Svartvik, Baggböle and Holmsund) and Versteegh (Graningeverken) families. Alongside those actors were also many 'unnoticed' entrepreneurs that significantly contributed to the Swedish forest-based industry's development. Although most of their investments were small-scale ones, taken together their efforts were sizeable.

Capitalists – and somewhat later banks – supported many of the entrepreneurs in the forest-based industry. That support became essential, especially as handicraft (capital-saving) production was rapidly replaced by machine-based (capital-intensive) operations. So, a broad 'supply of capitalists' was necessary to finance growth. Most of these capitalists were involved in trade and came either from the regions where the industry was located or from Sweden's trade centres in Gothenburg and Stockholm; some were foreigners, coming mainly from the UK and continental Europe. Regardless of country of origin, most of the investors hailed from influential dynasties, so, basically, it was families that governed the rising Swedish forest-based industry in the 19th century.

MoDo's position as a leading forest-based company during the first half of the 20th century has been ascribed to a large extent to the efforts made by its second leader Frans Kempe Sr. Like his father he was a risk-seeking entrepreneur looking for both new business opportunities and new ways of developing MoDo's core activities. As mentioned, one of Frans Kempe Sr's most cherished ideas was to build the company's expansion on innovations that had scientific origins; that ambition led him to establish a unit for systematic R&D within MoDo. He also modernized MoDo's industrial structure by acquiring steam-based sawmills, and made sure that the necessary raw material was secured by buying forests (and forest-owning companies).

MoDo's experiences during WWI also influenced its growth path, as the wartime production of forest-based chemicals aroused the interest of Frans Kempe Sr's successor Carl Kempe Sr in investments in that emerging new industry. Carl Kempe Sr became MoDo's CEO in 1917, and, although he had the reputation as 'bon vivant', he was also described in classic J.C. Kempe terms as a courageous, visionary and risk-taking entrepreneur with a special talent for doing business. In 1920, Carl Kempe Sr also joined the board of the large Swedish bank Handelsbanken, which at that time tried to establish a potential competitor to MoDo, namely what would become SCA. By 1926, however, Carl Kempe Sr left Handelsbanken's board because he simply could not accept that the bank was working to build a new competitor, and thereby simultaneously making its incoming[7] CEO Hèrnod – someone Carl Kempe Sr disliked – an industrial bigwig. So, the tension between MoDo and SCA that now and then became visible throughout the 20th century could at least to some extent be traced back to the early Hèrnod–Kempe rivalry.

Kreuger was perhaps the most famous Swedish industrial actor in the 1920s and early 1930s. At that time, his almost unparalleled business efforts certainly generated lots of attention and admiration. Among many other things he was the architect of the biggest restructuring that had ever taken place in the Swedish forest-based industry. Together with two relatively large Swedish banks (one of which was Handelsbanken), he acquired and merged many minor forest-based companies with the ambition of creating a unit big enough to take the lead in an international cartel. Actually, it was a coincidental meeting of two prominent business actors (Kreuger and Handelsbanken's CEO Stén) on a ferry that initiated the formation of SCA in 1929, and Handelsbanken's swift sale of that new constellation to Kreuger & Toll. At about the same time, Kreuger also battled with Marcus Wallenberg the Elder, as Stora Kopparberg's shareholding situation was rather 'open'. Indeed, in 1929, Kreuger's and Wallenberg's holdings were almost equal. When the parties decided to meet to solve the deadlock, Marcus Wallenberg the Elder claimed that Stora Kopparberg (like Kopparberg-Hofors and Wifstavarf) were 'Wallenberg companies'. Kreuger disagreed, and the controversy between the two tycoons lasted until the Kreuger crash in 1932 – a time when Wallenberg controlled 12 per cent of the votes and Kreuger 9 per cent. In the end, Kreuger's unfortunate suicide simplified the Wallenberg family's effort to gain control of Stora Kopparberg.

As Handelsbanken was the Kreuger group's largest creditor, it assumed the role as SCA's governing body. Eventually the SCA shares were auctioned, and Handelsbanken became SCA's sole shareholder. However, the bank intended to get out of its ownership (Swedish banks had to do that), and in 1934 sold about 80 per cent of its SCA shares to another Swedish industry bigwig, Wenner-Gren (but on such terms that the bank maintained control). That sale, too, was primarily a product of initiatives from two individual actors that met by coincidence. SCA's CEO Hèrnod happened to run across Wenner-Gren, who had begun to consider phasing out his engagement in the global Electrolux group and settling down in Sweden. Wenner-Gren was interested in acquiring a new large undertaking that he could run from home, and SCA fitted that ambition.

MoDo's CEO Carl Kempe Sr was responsible for MoDo's introduction on the SSE (1936). When he noticed the structural changes that had taken place in the late 1920s/early 1930s (particularly the founding of SCA), he and other family members worked to secure family control over MoDo. The solution became to establish two foundations, J.C. Kempe's Memorial Foundation (1936) and Seth M. Kempe's Memorial Foundation (1941), whose sole purpose was to act as long-term shareholders in the company (initially they owned 15% of the stock). The foundations continued to buy shares, for example, from family members who sold when the share prices were high, and eventually they ended up as the dynasty's sole shareholders in MoDo. There was one important exception: the future leader of the Kempe dynasty Carlgren, whose private shareholding in MoDo became sizeable.

Among other influential capitalists that started their careers in the 1930s, two members of the Wallenberg dynasty stand out, namely the successors to Marcus Wallenberg the Elder: Marcus Wallenberg Sr and Jacob Wallenberg Sr. Marcus Wallenberg Sr became the leading actor in the Swedish business society up until the early 1980s; though Jacob Wallenberg Sr also attained a very strong position, he never became as influential as his brother. In time, they divided the governance tasks in their wide-ranging business sphere to avoid dual control and intra-family conflicts. However, one exception of that division of responsibility was Stora Kopparberg, which became a chief concern for both of them.

Both brothers had been trained in banking environments, but it was usually Jacob Wallenberg Sr that emphasized the financial perspective. He was risk averse (cf. low debt, high liquidity, low costs, low dividends, sizeable depreciations, large hidden reserves, etc.) and employed a long-term perspective. He was also a cautious person, who delegated most operative decisions to boards and CEOs. Marcus Wallenberg Sr, instead, favoured work in and around large industrial corporations, that is to say, he concentrated his efforts on issues that affected the corporations' operative flows. He was also a more risk-seeking actor, who, for example, promoted the early use of new technologies. Marcus Wallenberg Sr's leadership differed from that of his brother, as it was exceptionally centralized and connected to himself. He acted in both the financial and the operative flows and on all the crucial decision levels.

15.8 EMERGING CORPORATE PATHS

The four corporations that are the focus of this study, that is to say, what were to become Holmen, SCA, Stora Enso and Sveaskog, have all moved along the value chain, although in somewhat different ways. Stora, the oldest still active company in the world, started as Kopparberget in 1288, and was engaged in forestry, running mills and mining activities (ore mining was its core activity until the 20th century). The company was firmly located to the left in the value chain up to WWI, when a prestigious bank's activities in the late 19th century stimulated Stora Kopparberg to expand its forest-based businesses, a journey that would continue throughout the 20th century (and longer). During the years around the turn of the century, Stora Kopparberg actively bought forests and built sawmills, and among all its activities Wifstavarf stands out as the perhaps most important acquisition of them all. The company also reconditioned several of its plants and built both a sulphite plant (biggest in the country) and a sulphate plant (1907–14). Gradually, Stora Kopparberg began its movement to the right in the value chain.

Holmens Bruk became a paper producer already in 1633, but only for about a decade. Paper production was actually not re-introduced at Holmens Bruk until 1807. The same century, two additional paper mills were added and specialization began (newsprint). Holmens Bruk also became an early producer of pulp (1897). Iggesund started its activities in 1685 (a furnace close to a river). Until the late 19th century iron production was its core business, but it also engaged in forestry and sawmills. Iggesund integrated backward and invested in forests outside its home ground. Late in the 19th century, after complicated ownership transactions, Iggesund, led by the Tamm dynasty, concentrated its operations on the forest-based industry.

MoDo could be traced back to 1759, when a small water-based sawmill was built at

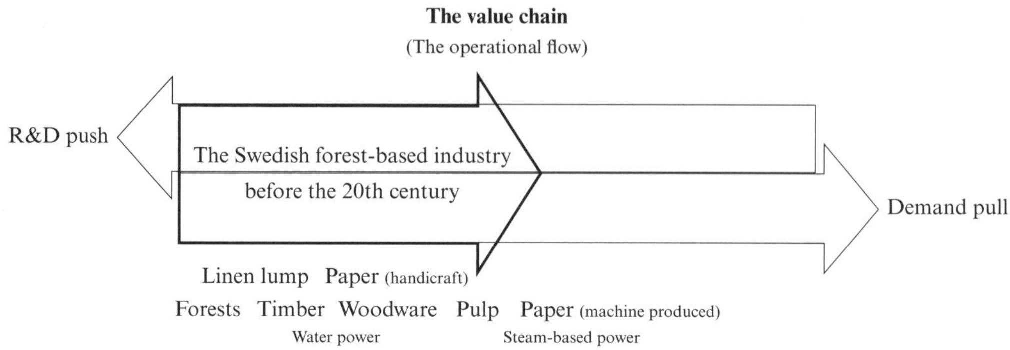

Figure 15.2 The Swedish forest-based industry's presence in the value chain in the late 19th century

Mo, though some have suggested other founding dates, for example, when its forerunner 'Firma J.C. Kempe' was established. However, MoDo's official 'birth year' was 1873, when J.C. Kempe's 11 heirs founded it as a limited company. At the time MoDo strengthened its position on the left side of the value chain by acquiring additional forests and several sawmills.

So, in the 19th century the Swedish firms and corporations had their common 'centre of gravity' to the left in the forest-based industry's value chain (cf. Figure 15.2), that is to say, in forestry, manual paper production, timber cutting, sawn wood and pulp production. Obviously, each individual firm was not involved in all these stages, but usually in at least two of them. That situation changed radically as early as the first half of the 20th century, when most of the (surviving/merged) corporations began their expansion by both utilizing advantages of scale and integrating forward in the value chain.

If one put together all corporate activities during the 19th century a fairly clear picture crystallizes, namely that most forest-based firms/corporations have developed in rather similar ways driven by nature-based resources (i.e. forests [fibres] and rivers [power]), technological breakthroughs, rising (foreign) demand, changing laws/regulations, entrepreneurs and capitalists. Almost all firms/corporations have gradually moved along a value chain composed of forestry, timber cutting, woodware production, manual (linen lump based) paper manufacturing, pulp production and industrial (timber-based) paper production. Although the choice of pulp production method varied somewhat among the forerunners to the four corporations highlighted in this study, most other features looked rather similar. One such striking similarity was that their forest-based activities were overshadowed for a long time by their own metal and mining operations.

After WWI, production not only increased substantially (despite some setbacks), but also became more and more differentiated over time. The growing demand for (brown) packaging paper (cf. kraftliner) stimulated the establishment of units for kraft paper production. As a result, several sulphate plants were built in the 1920s. A similar tendency could also be seen for newsprint, which stimulated the production of raw material for paler paper qualities.

During the 1930s and 1940s MoDo focused on modernization and organic expansion. CEO Carl Kempe Sr's idea was to secure competitiveness by keeping all plants up to date, and, where appropriate, upgrade production scale. At the same time, MoDo continued its intense R&D efforts in order to be able to introduce profitable innovations on the market. When soon after WWII MoDo was able to offer bleached sulphate qualities to the pulp market and thus provide customers both price and quality advantages, it placed itself in the driver's seat in the global pulp business for at least a decade. That innovation also instantly expanded MoDo's timber supply, as both birch and other deciduous trees could be used. The success with the bleached pulp led MoDo to stick to that particular stage in the forest-based industry's value chain for quite some time, and it became the platform for the company's future investments in the fine paper business. Even before that, however, MoDo differentiated its output in other ways. For example, in the early 1930s it became a pioneer in the building material field by establishing the biggest wallboard factory in Europe. But the idea to build a fine paper mill at the pulp-producing unit Husum was rejected by Carl Kempe Sr in 1937 – a decision that blocked that path for several decades. Instead, his interest in the chemical industry continued to grow, and in the 1930s production of, for example, sulphite spirit, glycol and chorine potash began.

Holmens Bruk, too, expanded considerably during the early 20th century. The modernization and expansion in Hallsta were certainly not the company's sole investments during those years. Holmens Bruk's cotton unit was also modernized and even merged with another firm. Moreover, a large textile company was acquired, power resources expanded and a grindery was built. Substantial forest areas in the middle of Sweden were also purchased. So, Holmens Bruk expanded both of its core businesses (textiles and newsprint). However, several prominent members of the company's controlling family disagreed about the merits of that growth strategy. In contrast with its CEO (Carl Wahren), the family doyen (Ernst Wahren) preferred fewer investments (lower risks) and more emphasis on the textile operations.

Iggesunds Bruk (Holmen) had woodware as its main product in the 19th century, but pulp became Iggesund's core business after WWI. Production of a paler sulphate pulp started in 1931, and semi-bleached sulphite pulp was marketed a few years later, which gave Iggesund a rather strong position. At the same time, many sulphate plants were built in the US, so CEO Gunnar Sundblad found it necessary for Iggesund to continue to invest substantially in bleached qualities. At the end of the 1930s, the company's situation looked promising, as its pulp sold well in the US, and prices on its woodware were increasing. Iggesund also expanded its sawmills and established factories for producing boxes, wooden houses and pieces of joinery work. However, WWII put an end to that growth, as almost all of Iggesund's production was intended for countries that participated in the war.

Stora Kopparberg gained momentum when its new major shareholder – the Wallenberg family – took control early in the 1920s. Company executives focused on modernization and expansion at the Kvarnsveden unit (its grindery, pulp plant and paper mill [newsprint]). The Skutskär plant had produced pulp since the 1890s, and the Wallenberg regime encouraged its management to improve the sulphite processes, for example, by trying to bleach sulphite pulp. Rather quickly Skutskär became capable of bleaching both sulphite pulp (around 1900) and eventually sulphate pulp (about two decades later). The Norrsundet site, another of Stora Kopparberg's[8] units, also began to bleach its sulphate pulp production beginning in 1925. While Korsnäs and MoDo patented their superior bleaching method in the 1940s, Stora Kopparberg purchased corresponding American patents, so that it too could introduce a competitive bleached product in the late 1940s.

When SCA was founded in 1929, the new holding company was composed of about a dozen mid-sized and small companies located in the northern half of Sweden. If their daughter companies are included, the number of firms under SCA's umbrella increased to about forty. That figure became even higher early in the 1930s, when additional firms were bought (one of those, Munksund, alone added many small firms to the emerging SCA constellation). However, SCA was established during a most difficult time period that included both the Great Depression (a crisis that hit 'everybody') and Kreuger's suicide (the latter, too, seriously affected SCA). In these circumstances, the immediate challenge for the new constellation was just to try to survive.

The SCA constellation was created not just to co-ordinate the incorporated firms' inefficient (i.e. unco-ordinated) export sales, but also to establish a capacity to utilize the large amounts of wood waste. None of its firms had the financial capacity to build a sulphate plant on its own, but the joint construct SCA could take on that task. Ultimately, it built the biggest sulphate unit in the world (Östrand). SCA also made investments in sulphate production in its other units (e.g. Munksund, Obbola and Wifstavarf), in sulphite production (e.g. viscose[9]) (cf. Svartvik) and in pulp bleaching (e.g. Essvik, Skönvik/Ortviken and Svartvik). When SCA's total production of the slow-selling unbleached sulphate pulp became too high, two other paths forward were investigated – to bleach it or to make paper out of it (i.e. kraft paper, sack paper or kraftliner). SCA's leaders began to discuss other ways to further process its pulp, and around the time of WWII the company considered starting cardboard production at Munksund (rejected), production of various kinds of paper and paper processing at Frånö (rejected) and board production at Wifstavarf (carried out in 1944).

15.9 A FEW CONCLUDING REMARKS

It is rather obvious from what is explained above (and described in more detail in Chapters 5 and 6) that natural resources, natural occurrences, culture and institutions, and collective and individual actorhood, all matter for how industries emerge. The forest-based industry's[10] dependency on the utilization of natural resources is not unique. Even the most modern businesses established in the early 21st century tend to rely on natural resources of some kind (e.g. oil, water and rare earth metals), and are usually also exposed to natural (e.g. tsunamis) as well as man-made (e.g. wars) catastrophes. Industries are also embedded in specific national or transnational cultures and are exposed to local as well as widespread institutions (some of which address specific industries) that regulate activities and assist in making the production and exchange of goods and services safe and effective. Actorhood linked to entrepreneurial, managerial, employee and capitalist roles is also basically a universal force, as the 'rationality repertoires' of human beings do not differ very much around the globe (cf. Ch. 1), although their concrete manifestations might vary depending on contexts and circumstances. Furthermore, actor constellations are formed in similar ways across societies, although their concrete configurations and manifestations might differ. Finally, it follows from this and other chapters that industrial and corporate development also requires technologies that make it possible for their users to stimulate or respond to people's demands.

However, the forces that shape corporate paths – natural resources, natural (or man-made) occurrences (initiatives), institutions, individual/collective actorhood, scientific and technological breakthroughs and customer demand – seldom, if ever, work in isolation. As already mentioned at the beginning of this chapter, it is first and foremost the interactions between them that create the actual drive. Such processes were described in detail in Chapters 4–14, and there it becomes obvious that usually (almost) all the identified forces are active when corporate paths are determined. It is actually difficult to claim that any one of them has been the sole decisive factor when the development of individual corporations is to be clarified.

Thus, one important conclusion from the chronological texts presented in Chapters 4 and 5, and from the force-by-force descriptions provided in sections 15.2–15.7 above, is that the original theoretical model presented already in Chapter 1 (cf. Figure 1.1) can be used to structure the forces driving corporate development. Apart from 'luck', the empirical material does not disclose any 'new' forces that the model has failed to consider. So, judging from the first part of the empirical material, it seems that most (all?) significant key forces that determine corporate paths have been identified, categorized and described. What is left to examine is how these forces work and interact in different settings, and, as mentioned both in Chapter 1 and initially in this chapter, what role and impact should be ascribed to actorhood, and in particular to two actor categories: the corporations' owners and executives. That question will be dealt with extensively in the following chapter of this volume.

NOTES

1. As this chapter directly builds on all the earlier ones, notes will not be repeated. Only new information qualifies for a note in this chapter.
2. Before the regulation efforts started any piece of land was 'owned' and handled by its settlers.
3. Each parenthesis denotes in which of the four focal corporations each of the plants or firms 'finally' ends up.
4. Ibid.
5. However, in 1905 the superintendence of the forests was moved back to the county level.
6. At that time Iggesund's activity was in the iron business.
7. Hèrnod was CEO of Holmsund (1922–26), Munksund (1926–29) and SCA (from 1929).
8. At that time it was part of Kopparfors (from 1978 part of Stora Kopparberg).
9. WWII led to a boost in demand for that kind of pulp. Viscose became raw material for a textile fibre (rayon), which several of the continental countries needed as substitute for cotton.
10. In this study the focal industry, that is to say, the forest-based industry, was chosen because it is a crucial export business for Scandinavian societies that has driven an extensive and impressive globalization process that eventually has involved activities on all continents.

16. The impact of individual actors on corporate paths

16.1 PLATFORM AND BASIC STRUCTURE

Two principal research questions were presented in Chapter 1, a more general one and a more specific one.[1] The more general question asks which are the main forces that determine the long-term development paths for large global corporations and how – and under what circumstances – do these forces operate? The specific question focuses on one of those forces – 'actorhood' – and in particular how the owners of the corporations act in those development processes.[2] Six dimensions of ownership are given priority in the analysis (cf. Ch. 2), namely its category (e.g. private or state), form (e.g. foundation or limited corporation), structure (e.g. concentrated or dispersed), status (e.g. sphere dependent or autonomous), organization (e.g. exerted inside or outside the board) and enactment rationales (e.g. risk-seeking or risk averse). The first, more general question was discussed in Chapter 15 and will be addressed in this chapter as well. However, the second, more specific question could not be examined in depth in the former chapter, as only secondary data is available for the time period covered, that is to say, before WWII (cf. the Appendix). In this chapter, the extensive primary data that underpinned the four 'master cases' described in Chapters 6 to 14, along with secondary data, provides the basis for a more extensive focus on the behaviour and rationales of (particularly) the owners.

This chapter is divided into five parts including this initial section (16.1) and thorough analyses of the four master cases (16.2–16.5). In the next chapter, the final one in this volume, some of the main theoretical and empirical results are reflected upon and summarized (Ch. 17). All four master cases contain descriptions, analyses and tentative conclusions that (also) involve all the minor cases (companies/'subcases') that in one way or another have contributed significantly to the development of the four large, global corporations that this study addresses. The analyses of the master cases (and their respective subcases) are based on the theoretical model presented in Chapter 1 (Figure 1.1) and use the concepts that were highlighted in Chapters 2 and 3.

The following section 'From Domänverket to Sveaskog' (i.e. the first master case) is divided into five subsections (16.2.1–16.2.5), each of which is based on one subcase (i.e. Domänverket, ASSI, Ncb, AssiDomän and Sveaskog) and focuses on each unit's development path, followed by a subsection (16.2.6) with some tentative conclusions. The following sections are then built up in the same way as section 16.2 and include the second master case 'From MoDo to Holmen' (16.3), the third master case 'From Stora Kopparberg and Stora to Stora Enso' (16.4) and, finally, the fourth master case 'The Emergence and Development of SCA' (16.5).

16.2 FROM DOMÄNVERKET TO SVEASKOG

16.2.1 Domänverket

Basically, the development trajectory of today's Sveaskog can be traced through analyses of five linked subcases, namely – in chronological order – Domänverket, ASSI, Ncb, AssiDomän and Sveaskog. The post-WWII processes towards what was to become Sveaskog started with activities in and around Domänverket, by far the oldest unit of the five involved companies. It actually lost many of its businesses during WWII, when the Swedish state moved the sawmills and the pulp production into a new state-run unit named ASSI ('Swedish Forest Industries'). That huge transformation reduced Domänverket's operations to forestry alone. Because Domänverket was state owned, and because forestry was seen as a public good that had to be protected, the owner (i.e. the state) implemented a reproduction strategy for that unit and stopped its attempts to integrate forward. Instead, it had to build its expansion on the benefits that usually followed from specialization and increased size.

Some 30 years after the owner had implemented its concentration strategy, Domänverket made a new attempt to integrate forward. This time, however, rather than merely focusing on its former businesses sawmills and pulp and moves to the right in the current value chain, the new effort entailed moves even to sometimes rather distant value chains.

Man-made occurrences were the main triggers behind Domänverket's second, rather radical deviation from its proven reproduction strategy. The company had become one of the targets of public criticism that had arisen suddenly regarding state-owned companies' performance. In that debate, some key opinion-makers claimed that Domänverket was far too ineffective, and that its situation could be improved only if it were allowed to add new businesses. The public pressure became so strong that the parliament soon took a decision that made it possible for Domänverket to run even unrelated activities (i.e. non-forestry operations), although those new businesses then had to be run as subsidiaries.

Somewhat later, the state enforced those institutional changes that were required to adapt Domänverket's legal construct to the new concessions parliament had granted. The changes allowed Domänverket to create a joint-stock subsidiary (Domänföretagen) that had as one of its assignments the governance of the company's non-forestry activities. Ultimately, the new constellation employed a rather radical differentiation strategy, with new products and new markets tested simultaneously. That meant that the owner had allowed Domänverket to adopt a path that significantly deviated from the trajectory decided when ASSI was formed.

Eventually Domänverket's new expansion strategy, organized in part in the Domänföretagen unit, proved to be unsuccessful. Not only had some of its forest-related businesses failed, but also the forward integration had taken unplanned and unprofitable turns when some of its units began to run wholly unrelated businesses. Soon Domänverket was instructed to divest those peripheral activities and again concentrate on its original business. Thus, in the early 1980s the company turned back to its roots and extracted itself from those activities that took place on the more distant value chains. While the owner initiated that change, the new DG became its architect when he simultaneously rationalized and reorganized the whole company. The DG even questioned Domänverket's form of association (state enterprise) and suggested that it should be converted into a (listed) limited corporation (with a majority holding for the state). However, the Minister of Industry rejected that idea, mainly because Domänverket's forests were seen as a national resource that should be kept far away from the market for corporate control. The owner also saw it as important that its timber deliveries to ASSI continued without disturbances.

Obviously, several forces contributed to Domänverket's development path, although some seem to have been more important than others. The fact that its business was based on a very special natural resource – forests – seems to have had implications for how the various actors and actor constellations behaved. As they saw it, forests were not only valuable for the forest-based industry – they also offered great benefits to the general public (i.e. recreation in a broad sense). Thus, to most actors it did not come as a surprise that the presence of public utilities impacted on Domänverket's path, and that such a rationale actually became decisive for how the company grew during the coming decades.

The politicians exerted their influence as a vicarious owner collective (i.e. through the parliament and/or the government) rather than as individuals with high-handed powers. Another important factor for the governance process was that it was the state that was Domänverket's controlling owner. Moreover, ownership form also mattered a lot, as one of the key strategic transformations actually required a new organizational construct (cf. the creation of Domänföretagen). Furthermore, the introduction of that construct forced the politicians to make further institutional changes (i.e. establish new regulations for Domänverket).

16.2.2 ASSI

As noted above, the Swedish state separated the sawmills and the sulphate plant from Domänverket during WWII and put all those operations into a semi-autonomous, limited company named ASSI, which initially was put under the control of the Swedish Forest Agency. Beginning in 1957, when ASSI got a new controlling actor (the Swedish Ministry of Trade), it was governed as a traditional business corporation. That shift did not represent a change of owner category, however, as it still was the state that had the ultimate power,[3] albeit from another platform that was more directly connected to the government level and its actors' ideals and ambitions.

Until the 1970s, ASSI's strategic development followed the forest-related industry's classic path, that is to say, it was characterized by attempts to move to the right in the value chain based on its unique business history and specific resource set-up. Accordingly, soon after its foundation ASSI began to look for possible uses of the by-products from its sawing business. That resource surplus combined with the executive actors' ambitions influenced the way it integrated forward (e.g. into board manufacturing).

The fact that ASSI lacked its own forest resources made its total operational risk substantial, particularly since its leading actors wanted to see an even bigger company that both used new technologies (i.e. utilized scale advantages) and integrated forward. However, because its main timber and pulpwood supplier Domänverket had the same controlling owner (the state), ASSI's operational risk was not as big as it seemed. ASSI's financial risk-taking was 'in principle' sizeable, too, as the company's high growth ambitions were concurrent with rather poor financial ratios. However, ultimately, the state's ownership substantially reduced that risk, too.

More generally, the (changing) ownership setting influenced ASSI's long-term development. It was important that the company was owned by the state and that its ownership was concentrated. Moreover, it was also crucial which actors decided and carried out the will of the owners and what distribution of power existed between the different corporate bodies (AGM, board and CEO). The impact of those ownership conditions became particularly evident when the government changed its corporate governance mode in the early 1970s. It introduced a holding company with the name Statsföretag ('State Enterprises') that would run most of the government's corporations, and ASSI became one of its larger subsidiaries. That change of ownership mode made ASSI subject to an entirely new governance structure that involved (at least) three superordinate levels, namely the parliament, the government and the board/CEO of Statsföretag.

The new holding company complicated the governance process even more, particularly for the incorporated companies, by introducing an additional decision level (Statsföretag's board/CEO) between the owner level and ASSI's two executive bodies. As a result, ASSI's development path became lined with somewhat unco-ordinated governance initiatives to which its executive levels had to respond. That ambiguity hampered the possibilities for ASSI's executives to shoulder full responsibility for the company's long-term development. In that setting Statsföretag's CEO (rather than its directors or owners) managed to take a leading role and became an actor who to a large extent determined ASSI's strategy. One example of his considerable personal power was when Statsföretag transferred certain peripheral businesses to ASSI against the will of that company's leaders. Over time, ASSI's board became a rather weak entity, often carrying out what already had been decided at the Statsföretag level (or sometimes by the government).

ASSI's kind of ownership influenced its development in many other ways. For example, the government persistently enforced a regional policy that encouraged investments that secured or increased employment in the northernmost parts of Sweden, the region where ASSI had most of its production facilities. That policy reduced the possibilities to expand abroad, thereby also narrowing ASSI's strategic options, particularly for its sack business and packaging units. The importance of state ownership also became clear when an investment was of such a size in relation to ASSI's balance sheet and risk-taking capacity that it required active support from both Statsföretag (operatively, particularly from its CEO) and the government (financially, particularly from its Minister of Industry). That became visible, for example, when ASSI's executives wanted to put a pioneering product (LPB) on the market, a most risky enterprise, as it involved both a new product and – initially – only one customer. ASSI tried to reduce the risk by joining forces with another corporation, but that path did not materialize partly because of the state's ownership as such (influential private actors disliked having that kind of partner). Eventually, however, the Ministry supported the new LPB path, so ASSI could take that risk even though it went far beyond what its balance sheet could match.

Over time ASSI made attempts to concentrate its activities, yet it continued to house a rather differentiated portfolio with production and sales units spread over large parts of Western Europe. Its businesses included sawmills, board production, building materials, pulp, kraft paper, kraftliner, LPB, sacks, plastic coated paper and packaging paper. In that situation ASSI's main ambition became to reduce that output variety and instead focus on liner production and its use for the further expansion of the packaging business (to become the biggest in that field in Europe). However, it was not at all clear how to proceed since ASSI's economic result was rather miserable in the late 1970s.

ASSI entered the 1980s in financially bad shape. Its losses continued and seemed to be so large that it might become necessary to set up a liquidation balance sheet. For obvious reasons a state could not allow such a situation, and the government injected fresh capital. The dilemma ASSI then faced was that a strategy solely based on operative considerations called for large investments in its core businesses to stay competitive, while a strategy solely based on financial considerations required consolidation.

So, for a change, ASSI focused on its financial flow. It asked the owner (the Ministry of Industry) for more economic support, and in 1982 the government decided to increase its capitalization. ASSI was also forced to strengthen its finances the classic way, that is to say, by reducing operative complexity (disinvesting). Some of those divestments were rather uncontroversial, since the units were sold to owners who continued operations. However, particularly one became controversial – the closing of the chipboard plants. The Minister of Industry did not permit such a move; however, when he was abroad, ASSI still took that radical step, thereby disregarding (!) the will of its controlling shareholder. That closure was probably only practicable because of the complicated ownership hierarchy (lengthy with weak ties).

ASSI's development also benefitted from external, man-made occurrences like the Swedish devaluation of its currency in 1982, and from initiatives launched by the informal global production networks that still existed in the liner industry. Those favourable circumstances made it possible for ASSI to continue to expand its packaging businesses, but that growth at the same time made it urgent to secure the timber supply from Domänverket over the long term. Still, the relationship between the two organizations continued to be strained during the early 1980s, and although ASSI pushed for a solution, Domänverket – particularly its internal actors – hesitated. The poor personal chemistry between the leading actor of ASSI's mother company Statsföretag and the Head of Domänverket hampered any steps towards a merger. To come to terms with those frictions, the owner of the two organizations orchestrated a move that at least formally brought them closer to each other – the owner, that is to say, the state, asked Domänverket to take 65 per cent of a new issue of ASSI shares (the state took the remaining 35%). That transaction made Domänverket a large shareholder in ASSI (25%). The owner also simultaneously made sure that Domänverket was converted into a limited company ('Domän') to make it legally capable to merge with ASSI. The transformation of Domänverket to Domän was actually more than merely a change in form of association, since some of Domänverket's forest resources were moved to a new public authority (Fastighetsverket), and some of its capital was transferred to the state. Yet Domän got most of Domänverket's forests (i.e. the 'commercially interesting' ones) and was simultaneously equipped with a strong balance sheet.

On the whole ASSI's development benefitted from the state's ownership. Its lack of own forests never became a serious problem, as ASSI and its main timber supplier had the same owner. The state's owncrship also made it possible for ASSI to make larger investments than its financial capacity actually allowed, since the state 'guaranteed' the required economic resources. So, it was operative experiences and institutional set-ups rather than certain individuals' ingenious rationales that determined ASSI's development during those years, although some executive actors also contributed substantially when concrete steps forward were taken. Another distinctive feature of ASSI's growth process was that its two flows – the operative and the financial ones – seldom met at a well-defined corporate hub. They were often handled separately and implemented by different, poorly co-ordinated agencies. Still, ASSI could go on expanding, as the owner ultimately could (had to?) support the operative efforts with the necessary financing.

ASSI's development could also be explained in terms of path dependence. As mentioned above, the company started as a spin-off of Domänverket, and was made responsible for most of that organization's further timber and pulpwood processing. A constellation of political actors took the decision to split the functions and furnished the new unit with both sawmills and a pulp plant. From that platform, ASSI followed the same base strategy as most other forest-based companies did in those days and alternated between forward integration and more or less temporary returns to earlier stages of the value chain. Thus, ASSI's operational strategy was a quite straightforward industrial one, although perhaps at times a bit more scattered than the ones pursued by most other forest-based corporations.

16.2.3 Ncb

In 1959 most of the Swedish farmers active in the northern half of Sweden joined to found a new company: Ncb. Nine forest-owners' associations, the National Association of Farmers (Riksförbundet Landsbygdens Folk) and Sweden's Farmers' Association (Sveriges Lantbruksförbund) became its initial owners. Their idea was that by establishing its own pulp production Ncb would level out the power inequalities that existed between buyers and sellers of timber and pulpwood, that is to say, between (cartels of) private corporations and forest farmers. Such forward integration was expected to give the forest farmers control of a larger segment of the value chain, which in turn would make it possible for them to reap more of the profits.

One legal institution – the economic association – significantly shaped how Ncb was founded, organized and governed. That construct – the co-operative structure – made it rather easy to mobilize the forest farmers, as it offered a suitable form for organizing large numbers of small, privately led units. The founding of Ncb was also stimulated by the presence of a similar construct that already had united and organized forest farmers in southern Sweden. However, tension soon arose between the 'southern' and 'northern' forest farmers, as well as among their respective leaders. Eventually Ncb imitated the southerners' construct, but without any active support from that constellation's actors.

Based on a rather straightforward business idea, Ncb's development path was the product of a classic entrepreneurial strategy and of the power distribution that had emerged among its key agencies and among its leading actors. The (initial) absence of power concentration that often characterizes co-operative associations usually makes the definition of the executive functions and the leadership standards particularly important. The formation of such definitions is usually the outcome of an iterative process through which the leaders and their followers define each other's roles. In the Ncb case, the numerous interactions between the forest farmers (re)produced an exceptionally powerful leader, who also accepted (some would say took) the formal position as company Chair (Hedlund). He became the one that both decided on and ran Ncb's expansion process. Yet, his actions did not differ significantly from those of most other entrepreneurs. Thus, Hedlund succeeded in governing the company towards a strategy similar to the one most competitors in the forest-based industry already practised: forward integration.

The importance of the individual person who fulfils the ownership function became particularly evident in the case of Ncb. Hedlund's personal ambitions and relationships certainly mattered when he managed the company. For example, his rivalry with the undisputed leader of the corresponding organization of southern forest farmers influenced his way of running Ncb, his rush to make it big and renowned and his eagerness that Ncb should take the lead in the upcoming structural rationalization of the northern forest-based companies. So, when Hedlund decided that Ncb must grow fast, making acquisitions became the only possible path forward (as building new plants would take too long).

In essence, Ncb's strategy was an entrepreneurial one, as it both addressed new products/markets that were already populated by experienced competitors (high operational risk) and rested on a small amount of equity provided mainly by a handful of small farmers' co-operatives (high financial risk). However, Ncb (and Hedlund) was lucky because the recent technological advancements and the ways forest firms were owned at the time (families dominated the scene) made the conditions for the purchase or sale of corporations favourable. Several of the targeted company owners were quite uncertain about their capacity to equip their firms with the big new machines that had become almost a necessity. So, Hedlund's vision for Ncb corresponded well with the underlying regional supply of forest-based firms. Another positive element in Ncb's purchasing process was that the company was sometimes favoured because of its ownership kind/category (regional forest farmers) and ownership form (a co-operative), both of which were seen as guarantees for further industrial activities in the region. Thus, in some cases the sellers' ideals and values undoubtedly influenced the outcomes.

When Hedlund tried to realize his grand vision for Ncb, competitors did not welcome the company's attempt to enter 'their' market. They organized an informal coalition to try to block Ncb's efforts to make acquisitions by agreeing not to sell. That coalition soon cracked, however, when one of its 'members' (Versteegh) broke the informal pact and sold a pulp plant to Ncb. Among other factors explaining that move, the close personal relationship between Hedlund and Versteegh that had evolved over time through their business relations was certainly important for the outcome. Moreover, since Versteegh long had been a bit of an outsider in the Swedish forest-based industry, his loyalties to the other actors were not particularly strong. When Hedlund and Versteegh had broken the ice, other owners also showed up ready to sell their firms to Ncb/Hedlund.

Ncb's initial expansion was of a classic kind marked by Hedlund's efforts to move it further right in the value chain. That expansion raised the company's operative risk, as the current supply of acquisition targets determined what kind of businesses Ncb could enter, that is to say, what parts of the value chain the company was allowed to occupy. As such, Ncb became a differentiated constellation that housed fine paper, fluting, tissue, sack paper, sacks, kraft paper and building materials (investments in both LWC paper and journal paper were seriously considered, too, but those ideas did not materialize). Some of Ncb's businesses also entered the other Nordic markets and even the European continent (e.g. tissue and sacks). Within a decade its expansion had produced considerable operational risk. The fact that some of its expansion activities were undertaken to meet some of the special interests of local/regional forest-owner groups added to that risk.

The differentiation of its operations and the high operational risk were not the only things that characterized Ncb's development during the 1960s and 1970s. Co-ordination between its operational and financial flows was also lacking. That problem partly emerged from Hedlund's predilection for acting through the operational flow rather than through the financial one. Like most forest farmers in Ncb, he felt more comfortable with operational matters. In combination with his undisputed power, that bias led to a situation where the two governance flows were never discussed on equal terms in proper decision-making bodies. Eventually that mismatch led to serious economic problems for Ncb. The growing financial strain could actually be traced back to Hedlund's early commitment to make Ncb expand almost 'at any cost'. He (and Ncb) was prepared to pay high prices for suitable firms, and sellers sensed this and took advantage of it.

Ncb's capacity to manage its severe financial strain was somewhat limited because of its ownership form (co-operative economic association), which made it difficult to get fresh capital from both the current owners and external sources. Furthermore, because the large banks often favoured corporations that belonged to their own spheres (i.e. Ncb's competitors), lending conditions were tight, too. Ncb also lacked the possibility of offsetting its losses by changing its bookings of property, as it did not own forests or power plants.

When the situation worsened, Hedlund initiated talks with the Swedish Minister of Industry at the time (a fellow member of the Centre Party) about Ncb's precarious situation. It became obvious that Ncb needed state support – a request that divided the current liberal-conservative government. The Minister of Industry (new from the Liberal Party) suggested that Ncb should sell its best units. To avoid an internal crisis, however, the government instead decided to support Ncb's current path (so it could keep its core units) and offered the company a large loan. At the same time, Hedlund, who undoubtedly was responsible for Ncb's failing expansion strategy, was replaced. The new CEO decided to try to ease Ncb's financial strain by entering joint ventures, but none of his more ambitious attempts materialized (i.e. those involving MoDo [fine paper], Stora Kopparberg [journal paper] and SCA [paper mill]).

Eventually discussions also began about how a reconstructed Ncb ought to be controlled (by the state and/or by the forest owners [through their associations]). When the dust finally had settled, the state had gained control (74% of the votes). This meant that Ncb faced the risk of losing its main strength – its privileged timber and pulpwood sourcing. Its business repertoire was soon radically reduced and in the end concentrated at two sites: Dynäs (pulp, kraft paper and sack paper) and Vallvik (pulp).

16.2.4 AssiDomän

During the early 1980s changing demand forced Domänverket's leading actors to reconsider the company's business structure. Its timber and pulpwood buyers had become fewer and much bigger, which made them more powerful. The institutional setting also changed, as a new neoliberal government changed both the owner's agenda and several regulating norms. The new owner representatives spoke of 'privatization' and established a special team to investigate how a merger between ASSI and Domän might be carried out (as a first step towards [partial] privatization). But changes in the timber demand and in the institutional setting were not the only forces that influenced those companies in the 1980s. For example, Sweden devalued its currency, a change that lowered the prices of Swedish corporations such that several competitors approached ASSI and declared their interest in buying certain of its businesses. However, as most buyers wanted to acquire precisely those units that ASSI wanted to keep, those proposals were turned down. Once again ASSI explored whether it might be possible to engage in joint efforts with some of its Swedish competitors, but nothing materialized.

Finally, ASSI and Domänverket (by that time renamed Domän) merged after having overcome some of the institutional, economic, organizational and personal hindrances described above. From the perspective of Domän, that forward integration was largely determined by those forces that contributed to the (re)production of the existing paths (i.e. cultural sediments and resource arrangements). By contrast, from the perspective of the other party, ASSI, the merger represented a backward integration to secure its possibilities to expand and utilize new technologies. Noteworthy is also that the merger was carried out soon after Domän had announced its intention to buy Ncb.

Domän's executive actors did not push for its integration with ASSI and Ncb; rather it was mainly the owners who promoted it to avoid a serious intra-government conflict (the Centre Party wanted to save Ncb). To do so, the state handed over its holding in Ncb to AssiDomän – a transaction that strengthened AssiDomän's kraft paper capacity and sacks businesses. The state remained a controlling shareholder in the new constellation and provided AssiDomän with a strong balance sheet that made it able to continue its major investment programme (and remain competitive). The leading actors of several of its Swedish competitors fiercely opposed the formation of the new company and criticized the liberal-conservative government for that decision because they expected that a state-run AssiDomän equipped with a large production capacity and 'endless' forest resources could become too strong a competitor, particularly in the packaging businesses. Ultimately, however, the state did not surrender to the strong pressures from parts of the Swedish business elite.

AssiDomän's board was reconstituted. Although it was populated with reputable 'professional directors', most of them[4] lacked deeper experience in the forest-based industry. As a consequence, the new, experienced and energetic CEO Ahlgren had won substantial freedom to build the new AssiDomän, and soon the growth process wore his personal signature. Yet his favoured strategy was a rather traditional one – it represented classic path-dependent forward integration (e.g. from sack paper to sacks), supplemented with substantial investments in the existing plants. Thus, the path he proposed was associated with rather low operative and financial risks, as it was based on well-known businesses and a strong balance sheet. However, the CEO also wanted an expansion of the company's young LPB business, which was operatively a much more risky path, as LPB was a new product that only involved a few (big) customers.

As mentioned above, the (state) owner had provided AssiDomän with a financial position that was almost too good. In light of that favourable situation, the company considered expanding into Eastern Europe by acquiring low-cost production units located close to its customers (i.e. near the Western European markets for sack paper, sacks and/or packaging). At the time such thinking was backed by strong institutional forces that offered advice, capital and re-regulation, as many politicians were eager to support the transformation of the former Soviet republics' planned economies to market-based ones. Consequently, a Czech company (Sepap) came into AssiDomän's focus and was soon bought from its American investors.

By far the most important consequence of AssiDomän's acquisition of Sepap was that it also involved an ownership link to another – much larger – corporation, namely Segheza, a gigantic Russian sack paper producer and sack manufacturer.

AssiDomän's executives saw Segheza's very existence as a major threat and feared that Segheza would start to sell large quantities of its sacks on the Western European market, or that another corporation would acquire it and do the same. Both alternatives were seen as potentially detrimental to AssiDomän, as the European market for paper-based sacks had already begun to shrink. Thus, acquiring Segheza was important not only for growth reasons; a strong defensive motive was involved as well. Moreover, a Segheza investment would offer AssiDomän the benefits of both scale-based integration and profitable forward integration, so from a strictly operative perspective, it was the perfect purchase. Still, the associated risks were substantial, both because of Segheza's large size and complicated shareholder situation and because of the political, cultural and legal risks that existed for investors at the time in Russia.

It did not take long for AssiDomän's combined investment in Czechoslovakia (Sepap) and Russia (Segheza) to turn into a catastrophe, with the Russian part of the deal soon proving to be the great mistake. In the end, AssiDomän withdrew from Segheza without any compensation for its huge investment. The shares that had been bought were impossible to sell, as it was unclear if they were bought in a correct way (according to the Russian authorities). However, the financially strong AssiDomän could take that massive loss and still be capable of investing in its other businesses (e.g. packaging and LPB). In the case of LPB, AssiDomän tried to reduce the high operative risk associated with having only one customer by becoming its sole deliverer. The sack strategy was also still going strong and led to new investments.

Several factors explain the great failure in Segheza. For one, the executive actors lacked experience in Russia; most of them simply did not understand that country's special business culture and institutional arrangements (cf. legislation, courts, custom, codes, etc.). Ultimately, it was the ownership issue that became the really serious problem. AssiDomän had bought Sepap from certain American investors ('Bahama capitalists') in a way that later created difficulties, not only because it was conditioned on a purchase of 50 per cent of Segheza, but also because the Russian authorities repudiated the American investors' original purchase of that stock. Consequently, the Russians declared AssiDomän's shareholding 'invalid'. Once also all the other calamities were taken into account, AssiDomän's board decided that the company should give up its Segheza investment.

16.2.5 The Emergence of Sveaskog

In the mid-1990s Sweden once again got a Social Democratic government, and that meant that neoliberal ideas and values that had dominated the scene during the first half of the decade disappeared from the discussions about how the Swedish state-owned corporate sector should be composed. Thinking about public utilities was again brought to the fore, particularly when the new Prime Minister stated that certain parts of a country's natural resources ought to be state owned, particularly those that required long time horizons or involved high risks or produced large civic benefits. Indeed, those criteria were met by much of AssiDomän. Still, for economic reasons,[5] the Prime Minister was reluctant to re-nationalize AssiDomän.[6] Together with a leading member of a political party that had many forest farmers as supporters/members, he instead suggested to the parliament a split of AssiDomän into two parts: one should get those forest resources that needed protection from commercial exploitation (initially that unit was named Vasaskog) and the other both the 'productive' forest resources and the processing plants (that unit kept the AssiDomän name). Though AssiDomän's CEO did not like that solution, he could not stop the divestment.

Even after the separation of most forest resources into Vasaskog, AssiDomän[7] controlled a lot of forests. Some actors therefore argued that Vasaskog ought to get more of AssiDomän's forests and that the state should re-nationalize AssiDomän. When the CEO opposed that strategy and hindered other moves that the owner supported, he was dismissed. Before his dismissal, however, he had proposed a new strategy for AssiDomän by which it would give up two of its (related) core businesses, namely sack paper and sacks. Those ideas reappeared once the new executive actors had been installed.

At that time prominent members of the Swedish government concluded that AssiDomän ought to be transformed to 'a new Domänverket', that is to say, get out of all its businesses except forestry and the sale of timber/pulpwood. The political directive given to the new Chair differed somewhat from that radical vision, as it encouraged AssiDomän's new executives to keep the packaging business, too. AssiDomän then encompassed units for pulp, kraft products, sacks, corrugated, cardboard, containerboard, forestry and barrier coating, making the task of selling any of these businesses both enormous and complex. Moreover, the units were also encumbered by state ownership, which usually tended to make international M&A processes more difficult.

The state allowed the new Chair to select all the board members but one – a 'direct representative' of the state. In essence, the Chair carried out AssiDomän's intricate divestment process almost exclusively with actors from his own circles. The board picked the new CEO, who was engaged to carry out its decisions. Basically, the stripping of AssiDomän ended as planned with two notable exceptions: the intended core business (packaging) was sold and the LPB operations remained in the company. It was actually the ruling government that made the about-face possible, since its leading actors were reluctant to keep the forest-based industries under the state's ownership. Ultimately, the outcomes of the selling process changed the government's instruction to AssiDomän's executives from one in which forestry and one core business were to be kept and developed, to one in which 'a new Domänverket' should contain only forestry. In the final stage of the process a struggle emerged between those who wanted to make what was to become Sveaskog privately owned, and those who wanted to keep it state owned. A conflict ensued regarding what ownership kind was to be preferred.

The idea emerged to transform AssiDomän into a wholly state-owned forest named Sveaskog 2.[8] Such a change was problematic, however, since the state initially was unwilling to buy (out) AssiDomän's forests and thus favour the existing shareholders. At about the same time, the management of Vasaskog – renamed Sveaskog 1[9] – expressed ambitions to buy additional forests. The situation became even more complicated when AssiDomän's executive actors made clear that they wished to transform 'their' company to a large, private forest-owning corporation. That idea worried its owners, that is to say, the government, whose Minister of Industry informed AssiDomän's Deputy Chair that the owner intended to intervene to implement earlier decisions taken by the parliament. The owner was in a hurry, as the leading executives at AssiDomän worked intensively to make it more costly for Sveaskog 1 (i.e. the state) to buy AssiDomän. So, Sveaskog 1 rapidly made a somewhat unexpected bid for AssiDomän's shares, and the outcome of that process finally established a state-governed, forest-owning corporation named Sveaskog 2. In 2001, it contained an LPB plant, sawmills and forests.

16.2.6 From Domänverket to Sveaskog: Some Tentative Conclusions

The analysis of this master case indicates that the impact of nature-based occurrences was negligible in Domänverket's transformation into Sveaskog. Instead, it was the presence of certain natural resources – especially forests and power plants[10] – that determined a good portion of the nuts and bolts of that development process. The need for secure sourcing of timber and pulpwood stimulated corporations to acquire and keep nearby suitable forest resources, and the outcome of those struggles often decisively affected what paths the companies could take.

Moreover, Domänverket's sizeable forest holdings also almost forced the company to integrate forward into sawn-wood and/or pulp production and to thereby reap the profits embedded in a further processing of its timber. For ASSI, the situation was reversed, as it lacked a holding of that crucial input. Its executive actors' ambition to eliminate that deficiency became a strong driving force for ASSI over several decades, and eventually those efforts were crowned with success when the long-awaited merger with Domän materialized. The impact of forest holdings on corporate development was also evident in the Ncb case. Ncb was a co-operatively organized constellation involving many (small) forest owners who wanted to make better (i.e. more profitable) use of their forest assets by investing in pulp production. Thus, natural resources rather than increasing demand guided that development.

The most striking example of how forest resources might determine a company's path was the process whereby AssiDomän was gradually stripped of its (other) core businesses. In that case, the forests were ascribed special status (even in comparison with other natural resources), as many – but not all – actors involved saw the forests as a public good. That view made it necessary for the state to secure ownership of a substantial share of the Swedish forests. Those belonging to AssiDomän became an obvious target. So, forest owning as such became a political hot potato, forcing AssiDomän to make a series of divestments (cf. Fastighetsverket, Vasaskog, Sveaskog 1 and Sveaskog 2). That value-based controversy regarding private versus state forest ownership certainly affected Domänverket's transformation to Sveaskog.

In the theoretical chapters it was argued that many of the external occurrences that hit corporations are man-made (i.e. initiated by [collectives of] individuals) and that the interpretations of those incidents often have a strong impact on how corporations develop. The man-made occurrences were clearly visible in the Domänverket case, in which a political debate suddenly arose that intensely criticized the inefficiency of state-owned companies. In light of that controversy, the government concluded that Domänverket should be given the opportunity to integrate forward, in turn triggering institutional changes. For Ncb the sudden emergence of a 'cartel' that opposed its expansion represented a similar kind of occurrence that had to be interpreted and handled. The same could be said for ASSI when the state unexpectedly subordinated it to a new holding company.

However, of all the units involved in the transformation of Domänverket to Sveaskog, AssiDomän was perhaps the corporation that was most exposed to external man-made incidents. The exposure started already during its Russian adventure, when (negative) surprises became almost an everyday occurrence. It continued when the neoliberal Swedish government decided to privatize a large part of AssiDomän and ended when the subsequent Social Democratic government both made sure that sizeable forest resources remained state owned and later allowed AssiDomän's executive actors to divest all company businesses except the forestry one (creating Sveaskog).

Path dependences – resulting from unique corporate cultures and idiosyncratic resource arrangements – substantially affected the courses followed by the companies involved in the transformation of Domänverket to Sveaskog. Both past and current activities in the value chain significantly determined the ways the forward integration was carried out. Sometimes, however, path dependences might be radically broken, and such dramatic changes are then usually linked to some kind of actorhood (individual or collective).

Two actor-driven forces that often alter corporate paths are those that involve technological breakthroughs (cf. innovation) and/or substantial changes in customer demand. As most of the five subcases evidenced, particularly new technologies that offered sizeable scale advantages made a significant impact on how the corporations developed. For Domänverket, for example, the changing demand situation at the end of the 1970s made its executives more inclined to accept a merger with ASSI. For its part, ASSI was influenced by the possibility of utilizing the potential scale advantages following from new technology by securing its raw material sourcing. Once AssiDomän was established, technological development combined with demand changes affected the merged company's strategic path (cf. e.g. the emergence of its innovative LPB operations and the declining demand for its paper sacks). For Ncb, finally, the evolving technology played a major role in making acquisitions easier, as it almost forced some family heads to sell their firms.

Institutions represent another force that certainly mattered in the transformation of Domänverket to Sveaskog, and that in several ways. Like other forces, institutions originate from various kinds of actor activity, so, basically, they affect corporate development processes in the form of outcomes of past actorhood, that is to say, through regulations previously established by various kinds of actors. All five subcases show that existing as well as changing legal constructs, rules, codes and customs have affected both the ways governance processes were conducted and their outcomes. However, those historically (re)produced institutions influenced many development processes in ways that were not always easily recognized even by the actors themselves (as many institutions are taken for granted). The shareholder-favouring Swedish Companies Act[11] represents one such powerful institution, whose ideas and values have been successfully (re)produced for more than a century without major controversies. The Act's ideological base has had a major impact on what forces have really mattered in the governance and development of the companies studied. First and foremost that legislation (and its associated rules, codes and customs) has influenced what kind of actor has taken the driver's seat: the (controlling) shareholder. So, in the Swedish/Nordic context actorhood in the sense of corporate governance becomes almost synonymous with the enactment of ownership, and that connection is very marked in the empirical material. While many other sources of actorhood also matter, the cases clearly indicate that it ultimately is the (controlling) owner that has the greatest impact on which corporate paths are pursued.

Thus, both the institution that regulates the basic elements of corporate governance efforts – the Companies Act – and the legally favoured actor category – the shareholder – had a strong impact on how Domänverket became Sveaskog. The founding of Ncb stands out as a clear-cut example of such a legal impact. The Companies Act affected Ncb's choice of ownership form – co-operative economic association – as well as the way it organized its governance processes. The chosen legal institution made it fairly easy for Ncb to attract many private actors (owners of forest farms) to form a large pulp business.

In the other subcases it was primarily institutional changes that were of importance for the corporate paths. For Domänverket the changes in its legal statutes were a decisive force, and for ASSI the introduction of Statsföretag altered the basic institutional set-up. For AssiDomän the almost 'revolutionary' change of government to one that was dominated by neoliberal ideals brought dramatic institutional changes, as did the subsequent Social Democratic government, which both re-established and changed several institutions in its efforts to secure that a substantial part of the Swedish forests would continue to be state owned.

However, the institutional revolution that took place in Eastern Europe when the Soviet Union collapsed represented perhaps the most striking example of them all. Initially, AssiDomän's expansion in that region was vigorously supported by many kinds of institutions (primarily Western European ones), but soon ambiguous and capricious institutions (exclusively Russian ones) instead thwarted its expansion and ultimately forced AssiDomän to abandon its investment in Segheza.

Turning to actorhood based on individual initiatives again puts the corporate owners in focus. In all subcases, the owners set the scene for how each of the corporations is governed and for how it develops. Many examples in this master case illustrate that it often is the owners' interpretations of occurrences, cultures, institutions, technologies, demand, performance, and so on, that influence corporate paths.

In the Domänverket case it was the controlling owner that encouraged the company to expand by integrating forward (and even to diversify some of its output), only to later instruct it to divest its more 'peripheral' activities and return to its core business. The same kind of owner subsequently asserted that the character of Domänverket's forestry business significantly differed from commercial businesses in general, and therefore quashed the idea to convert it to a limited company (and then some time later, when the merger with ASSI was underway, promoted the creation of the limited company Domän). It was also that owner that made sure that Domänverket delivered a substantial amount of its timber and pulpwood to ASSI, as both of them belonged to the same sphere (the state), and divided Domänverket into two units thereby creating ASSI in the first place. So, obviously ownership kind mattered for how Domänverket developed.

Ownership kind very much influenced ASSI's development as well. Having the state as owner made both the expansion of its current business and a forward integration possible, in spite of the fact that it lacked both own forest resources and the necessary financial capacity. The owner's instruction to Domänverket to supply ASSI with raw materials solved the first problem (the operative risk), and its economic capacity the second one (the financial risk). The state's strong impact on ASSI's operative development became particularly visible when it created a holding company that was put in charge of ASSI (and several other companies). The owner even used that parent company to force ASSI to accept certain peripheral or even unrelated businesses in its portfolio. Moreover, the owner hampered ASSI's development by enforcing certain values that actually reduced the company's expansion alternatives (cf. the regional policy). However, the state simultaneously ensured financing that in a rather unique way made big and risky investments possible (e.g. the LPB one) and provided fresh capital when ASSI's financial situation became strained.

The ownership setting also very much determined Ncb's long-term development. Its chosen form (co-operative economic association) left room for the emergence of a strong leader whose personality and rationale had a strong impact on Ncb's corporate path. Ncb's growth pattern also illustrated the importance of circles, coalitions and spheres for the building of the new constellation. Such relationships between Ncb's owners and members of the Swedish government explained why and how Ncb merged with Domän and became part of AssiDomän. While friendships paved the way for Domän(verket) and ASSI to merge their operations rather smoothly and create AssiDomän, the ownership setting – the fact that all three companies had the same controlling owner (the state) – made the merger agreement possible in the first place. Soon the new constellation's expansion path showed similarities with the one ASSI had previously followed in the sense that the owner (represented by the Social Democratic government at the time) 'guaranteed' its financial risk-taking, although in the case of AssiDomän that took place beforehand (it was equipped with a strong balance sheet already when it was founded).

A new owner representative (a liberal-conservative government) was also a decisive force when AssiDomän was partly privatized in the early 1990s. The state continued to act as owner when the Social Democratic government returned to power in the mid-1990s and decided to strip AssiDomän of most of its businesses, but make sure that it kept both its forests (as they were seen as a public good) and one of its core businesses (packaging). Although the executive process that transformed AssiDomän to Sveaskog did not fulfil the ambition to maintain the packaging business, the owner did not see that partial 'failure' as a problem (rather the opposite).

Thus, from the master case detailed in Chapters 6–7 and the preceding section, it becomes obvious that shareholding kind does matter for how corporations are governed and develop over time. Clearly, much of what happened in the transformation of Domänverket to Sveaskog was influenced by the fact that it was the state that held the controlling position. Still, several of the other aspects of ownership seem to have been at least as influential. In the case of Ncb, for example, it also mattered that there were many owners and that it had to organize both those shareholdings and the accompanying executive functions. So, evidently that (lack of) ownership concentration had consequences, too. Without such an open ownership structure, quite different governance processes would probably have been established from the start. Ownership form was also important for Domänverket's development path (from state enterprise to [part of a] listed company, and then back to state enterprise), as was the organization of the ownership (particularly for ASSI [for a short period part of a state-run holding company] and Ncb [built as a co-operative]). Finally, several of the subcases illustrated the importance of how the various ownership roles were performed (e.g. for Ncb Hedlund, and for AssiDomän Göran Persson).

Another tentative conclusion from the Domänverket to Sveaskog case is that it seems to be important for the companies if the actors in the operative and the financial flows actually are brought together within the prestigious arenas (i.e. at the AGM, board and/or CEO levels). Several of the subcases show that the corporations ran into trouble when one of those two flows was given lower priority (cf. Ncb) or if they were considered one at a time (cf. AssiDomän) or by different actors (cf. ASSI). Thus, in this master case successful long-term development would have required well-integrated corporate flows.

16.3 FROM MODO TO HOLMEN

16.3.1 MoDo before the 1980s

Like most other forest-based corporations, MoDo had anticipated a shortage of timber and pulpwood after WWII. A technological development that offered more efficient large-scale machines that required larger quantities of raw material lay behind those expectations, as did the rising demand for various kinds of pulp and paper. To try to secure its capacity to both continue to run a profitable pulp business and expand into other parts of the value chain (integrate forward), MoDo followed several paths. MoDo had several options for handling its timber situation without giving up the growth ambitions. Like other corporations, MoDo could possibly buy more forests, acquire forest-owning firms, improve its forestry activities, organize its timber buying (cf. cartels), launch afforestation projects abroad and invest in R&D to make more effective use of its timber and expand the usable kinds of trees. MoDo did most of that, although not everything at the same time. For example, together with 15 larger forest-buying companies in northern Sweden, MoDo participated in a timber-buying cartel to gain some control over volumes and prices (1947). In the 1960s MoDo systematically bought firms that held large forest resources, and looked abroad (South America) for opportunities to run forest plantations. MoDo also expanded its already impressive R&D unit to make it even more capable of dealing with fibre-related issues. As an example, the R&D unit contributed substantially to MoDo's expansion of its pulp operations by developing a superior method for the chlorine bleaching of pulp and by making pulp production based on birch possible.

Though MoDo had developed quite a differentiated – almost diversified – product range during the first half of the 20th century, it was still mainly a large, successful pulp producer that sold its output to other corporations that processed the pulp further by making various kinds of paper. Around 1950, MoDo took a rather small, yet important step to the right in the value chain when it integrated forward into fine paper through the acquisition of a paper mill. That acquisition was not really the result of strategic planning and thorough analyses, although the experience later had some influence on the company's development. Indeed, that unit was sold only a decade later, partly because MoDo needed the timber for its pulp production, and partly because MoDo was reluctant to compete in the fine paper market with its pulp customers.[12] Its wallboard company was also sold, so some capital was freed for the core businesses.

In the early 1950s, in an attempt to concentrate the company's rather straggly business repertoire, MoDo's CEO Erik Kempe launched a reproduction strategy with a strong focus on pulp production. Nevertheless, it was during his time as CEO that MoDo took its first step into the fine paper business and invested further both in power plants and in the chemical industry. Eventually the chemical business also earned 'core' status. The move into chemicals represented radical differentiation, but, as the business largely was based on forest-related raw material, it was not seen as a diversification step. When petroleum replaced forest substances as the basis for the chemical industry, MoDo was faced with a strategic dilemma. To become a successful player on the rapidly growing (and ever more petroleum-based) chemical market required huge amounts of capital, and as MoDo's ownership situation was locked (i.e. in the hands of a dynasty that wanted to stay in control), most of that capital had to be generated either by profitable pulp operations or by increased debt, and in both cases the needed sums were unrealistic. Rather quickly it became clear to MoDo's leading actor Carlgren that it was impossible for the company and its controlling owner to finance that expansion without selling most of its other businesses. It took some time before that insight was transformed to action, but in 1973, finally, MoDo's board and CEO reluctantly sold its chemical business to Statsföretag.

MoDo's strategic goal in the 1950s was the classic one, namely to integrate forward through the further processing of its main product (pulp) in order to reap some of the profits that usually could be accrued in the later stages of a value chain (and which simultaneously would reduce the operative risk). MoDo's dependence on 'bulky' standard pulp was seen as a problem since that market was exposed to huge price/volume fluctuations that created both operative and financial strain for the producers (the customers were not willing to assume any of those costs). MoDo had also learned that its marketing of special pulp qualities did not solve the problem.

With the expansion of its pulp production creating pressure to find new customers, MoDo decided to make a serious entry on the European continent and establish a sales company. The initial investments were made in France, since MoDo already had a successful pulp-selling agent there. MoDo mainly purchased minor regional/local units, because its customers were usually to be found in such settings. However, the French business did not gain momentum until later when MoDo became the sole owner of a French fine paper plant (PPSM) after an unsuccessful joint venture with a Swiss forest-based company. Eventually, the French unit became rather decisive for MoDo's long-term development (i.e. for its choice of fine paper as a core business).

Soon internationalization became the key goal for MoDo, both for its pulp sales and forward integration. MoDo even founded a special unit in 1961 to intensify its European efforts. In the end, the effort to find suitable firms failed, as none of the ones identified was interested in selling any of its businesses to MoDo. At the same time that unit sought new raw material sources, and South America came to be the preferred continent and Brazil the favoured country for that activity. Despite the promising results from several investigations, nothing materialized.

During the first decades after WWII most forest-based corporations tried to decide what paths they ought to follow, and MoDo was no exception. Its history and resources at the time spoke in favour of the continuation of its work in forestry, sawmills, pulp production and chemical production. Probably paper production of some kind could be considered, too. A fine paper path had already been tried, and somewhat later MoDo pondered 'brown papers', that is to say, liner and sacks, as well. Its owners, board and top management also analysed the possible production of kraft paper and bleached cardboard, and later (around 1970) Carlgren even took up a discussion in a close circle about trying to buy its rival company SCA, but eventually these new ideas were abandoned.

MoDo adopted a rather aggressive and diversified expansion strategy in the 1960s, when the company's controlling owner Carlgren entered the driver's seat. At that time MoDo was considering another new engagement, this time in the hygiene business, and that path was pursued in the form of acquisitions both within and outside Sweden. That effort was supposed to continue at full strength, since the initial investments were insufficient to ensure long-term competitiveness. However, the path followed was not straightforward, coincidences played a certain role, and some hygiene products were introduced in several countries without success. Moreover, those somewhat straggly hygiene operations were not organized under a common label until 1968, when MoDo Consumer Products was established.

MoDo began to question the earlier disinvestment of its fine paper plant (Hörnefors), and instead its leaders took up discussions about how to invest in that business, this time at Husum. As the 'Swiss failure' at least brought PPSM to MoDo, it had in all events provided the company an opportunity to learn more about fine paper production, which was helpful in the current strategic discussions. Soon the idea emerged that a pulp and paper 'combine' ought to be built at Husum. Such an investment would solve its timber-sourcing problem and at the same time lower MoDo's total operational risk.

When MoDo decided to follow a fine paper path, it invested heavily in a large, new paper machine at Husum. That forward integration triggered quite a lot of rethinking regarding the sales organization and eventually also the acquisition of a large Swedish wholesaler – a transaction that at the same time brought the production of high-quality coated paper and a packaging company. So, once again MoDo's product repertoire widened.

However, entrance on the fine paper market was not the only expansion path that was discussed at that time. A newsprint mill was also considered, with the idea of locating it either at Domsjö or Husum. Nevertheless, several MoDo actors saw those talks as first and foremost a way of influencing the competitors' strategic planning, and not as signs of a serious investment idea.

Two other forces influenced MoDo's choice of fine paper as the preferred way forward, namely path dependency (cf. its large output of pulp and its growing experience in fine paper operations) and competition. Indeed, the steps taken by the other large forest-based corporations in practice limited MoDo's alternative futures, as its competitors already had 'occupied' several of the possible paths, for example, liner and packaging (ASSI and SCA), quality cardboard (Iggesund) and newsprint (Holmens Bruk and Stora Kopparberg).

MoDo's large fine paper investment in the 1970s turned out to be a tremendous success, which encouraged the company to invest in two additional fine paper machines at Husum. The first of them started its production in 1976, but a decline in market demand and strong internal competition for the investment resources required the postponement of the second one until the 1980s. Those new investments also 'forced' MoDo to strengthen its position on the wholesale market, particularly in Europe (several such firms were bought in France, Germany, Holland, Italy and the UK). Thus, MoDo entered the 1980s as an international corporation.

At the same time, MoDo had also gradually become an indebted company, as its investments and acquisitions could be paid neither with profits (for they were not large enough), nor with company shares. The latter method was impracticable, as the ruling Kempe dynasty wanted to maintain control of MoDo. However, in that strained situation, Carlgren, by far MoDo's most powerful actor, began to build up his own 'parallel company' (Sanna Holding), whose main purpose was to support MoDo financially particularly when times were bad in the forest-based industry. Sanna Holding was composed of a diversified collection of non-forest businesses that taken together were expected to neutralize MoDo's operative risk.

MoDo continued to expand its hygiene business in the 1970s and acquired Stille-Werner, a company that produced and sold not only diapers and sanitary protection products, but also medical instruments. As so often, Carlgren and the Kempe dynasty hesitated to sell something that MoDo had acquired, so the increased differentiation was vigorously defended. MoDo's expansion in hygiene included its purchase of Klippan, which placed it in the same position in Sweden as the market leader Edet. Carlgren (MoDo) tried to buy Edet as well, but it instead ended up at Ncb. MoDo's expansion ambitions in the hygiene field were also hampered by an international hygiene cartel. Moreover, because of a lack of financial resources, MoDo was unable to assume the costs associated with full integration of all its acquired hygiene operations, a weakness that later would lead to radical strategic changes.

MoDo's leaders continued their efforts to secure the supply of timber, and participated in the establishment of two timber-buying cartels in Sweden (one northern and one southern). They also tried to solve the problem of sourcing MoDo's key units by eliminating capacity in some of the more peripheral businesses (board production, a few sawmills and a sulphite plant). In addition, the company continued its attempts to acquire forest-rich firms (preferably those with run-down plants). However, those activities were far from the most important ones that MoDo carried out in the 1970s. It had launched a record-breaking investment programme, and that, in combination with the losses made during the bad business years of 1977–78, put MoDo under intense financial pressure. Eventually the banks contacted Carlgren about the company's total debt status. As a result, planned investments were postponed, maintenance was reduced and some forests were sold. Nevertheless, Carlgren remained both optimistic and proud of how he had so far developed the family heirloom (i.e. MoDo), and he was committed to taking even more risks to make it possible to pass on an even bigger and more successful MoDo to his heirs/successors. Thus, at the end of the 1970s the crucial strategic question was not whether MoDo should continue its rapid growth, but rather in which directions and how such efforts should be financed.

16.3.2 Iggesund before 1981

Iggesund continued to focus on pulp, although its leaders' ambition to secure bleaching capacity rather resulted in a kind of partial diversification when EKA – an alkali and chlorine producing firm – was bought for that purpose. Basically, however, Iggesund followed a reproduction strategy, which meant that no new paths were taken up, even though discussions about possible futures were held (e.g. regarding kraft paper). Since Iggesund's 'free' capital was allocated in a low-risk securities portfolio instead of being invested, the company continued to keep its finances in good shape. Thus, up to the middle of the 20th century, Iggesund's strategy was basically 'linear', conservative and risk averse.

When Lars G. Sundblad replaced his father Gunnar as CEO in 1956, he saw a need for many minor investments to improve the efficiency of the existing pulp plants. He also recognized that Iggesund had to expand its machine sizes to be able to utilize the possibilities that the new, more efficient large-scale technologies offered. Iggesund's first step towards that end was to invest in the expansion of its sulphate-based pulp production, and some years later it closed down its sulphite unit (as it did not fit Iggesund's emerging core business). Like most actors in the forest-based industry in those days, and for similar reasons, Sundblad thought that it was necessary for Iggesund to integrate forward. As the company primarily produced bleached pulp, Sundblad advocated expansion into fine paper, tissue (hygiene) or (white) cardboard.

To determine the best path forward, Iggesund's board asked Sundblad to take a trip to the US with the goal of finding out how tissue and cardboard operations were run on that large innovative market and how demand for those two product groups had developed after WWII. Sundblad also sought advice from many of the most recognized specialists in the forest-based industry. In the end, the final strategic decision was based on thorough analyses and many and long discussions. Like most companies Iggesund's chosen path built both on its long track record (cf. its culture and competences) and its current resources. Eventually Sundblad became convinced that investments in bleached quality cardboard probably would generate the best future for Iggesund. After he informed the board about his conclusion, it approved his proposal early in the 1960s. That investment was so successful that a second cardboard machine was built only half a decade later, and eventually new qualities were added to the product offerings. The company's timber-sourcing problem also contributed to – but certainly did not determine – Iggesund's choice of the cardboard path. The expected timber shortage made forward integration into quality cardboard much more attractive than scale-based expansion in pulp. However, Iggesund still needed to acquire more forests, a need that explained at least to some extent its acquisitions of Boxholm and Ström-Ljusne.

By the mid-1970s, Iggesund lacked a controlling shareholder (constellation), something that was[13] rather unusual in Sweden. With its well-trimmed organization, healthy finances and promising new core business (quality cardboard), Iggesund became an attractive takeover target. To stave off such a move, Iggesund tried to grow in size and value by merging with another forest-based company (Billerud), whose operations fitted Iggesund well. Though the merger attempt failed, that was not the end of their attempts to co-operate.

16.3.3 Holmens Bruk before 1988

Holmens Bruk encompassed two core businesses after WWII, namely newsprint and textiles. In the 1950s newsprint boom, many companies entered that market. That rush prompted Holmens Bruk to expand into journal paper production, and soon the company had become the market leader in Sweden in that segment, too. The expansion of its printing paper operations made it necessary for Holmens Bruk to acquire even more timber resources, leading its executive actors to buy several forest-owning companies over the next two decades.

Holmens Bruk's top management was used to working rather independently of its owners since no major shareholder had been in control for some time. However, that ownership arrangement changed in the early 1950s when two new large shareholders (two reputable families) with aspirations to influence Holmens Bruk's development came on the scene. One of the new shareholders controlled a large media company[14] that consumed huge amounts of printing paper – particularly newsprint; its investment in Holmens Bruk was made primarily to control its sourcing costs. Indeed, some actors questioned the wisdom of having a big customer enter as one of two major owners, especially when the customer/owner also sought executive positions (board seats). In any event, the new entrant nailed Holmens Bruk even more firmly to its newsprint path.

In the late 1960s the question arose as to whether Holmens Bruk ought to keep two core businesses or pursue only one of them. The CEO (Önnesjö) advocated the latter path and led Holmens Bruk's decision to invest substantially in its printing paper business in order to expand its repertoire in that market segment. At the same time Holmens Bruk also resolved to divest its textile operations. The new strategy was soon implemented through the acquisition of a relatively large producer of coated journal paper (Wargöns Bruk). Moreover, physical realities forced Holmens Bruk to modify its geographical strategy and plan to build its new pulp plant in a different area (Bråviken[15]). However, to avoid a competitor establishing a large newsprint unit in the same region, Holmens Bruk agreed not to build its planned sulphate pulp plant.

In the early 1980s Holmens Bruk's interest in non-woven production grew, resulting in a fiberweb unit at Braviken. That investment represented a first step into the hygiene sector and the start of what was to become a new core business. In addition to the classic pulp and paper operations and the new hygiene business, Holmens Bruk produced chemicals with a special focus on lignin (a usable waste product from its other operations). The company's new CEO (Zetterberg) welcomed that relative diversity and used it as a platform for the company's forward integration.

With market interest in LWC paper increasing, the CEO proposed that Holmens Bruk should decrease its heavy dependence on the bulky non-coated qualities of newsprint by diversifying into chemical products and by pursuing fiberweb to a greater extent. To do so, acquisitions in the hygiene sector were put high on the company's agenda, and eventually 'the perfect candidate' (Fiskeby) was acquired (with its forests and sack business, but without its packaging operations). At the end of the 1980s Holmens Bruk again housed two core businesses: printing papers and hygiene. Soon the hygiene business was organized as a separate unit – Holmen Hygien. The reorganization intensified the company's efforts to find ways to grow, and in that search process MoDo Consumer Products came to the forefront.

16.3.4 The Third Bloc

Back at the beginning of the 1980s, MoDo had decided to concentrate its efforts even more intensely on its core businesses, that is to say, fine paper, through investments particularly at Husum, and hygiene, through acquisitions of Swedish firms. When Ncb collapsed at the end of the 1970s (cf. section 16.2), MoDo wanted to discuss joint fine paper investments with Ncb's controlling owner. Although plans were produced, none materialized in concrete investments. Instead, MoDo sought possible fine paper acquisitions abroad, but those efforts failed too, primarily due to MoDo's limited financial capacity. To improve that situation, MoDo began to divest and sold both its mechanical business and its med-tech firm (the latter to Carlgren's Sanna Holding).

In 1981 Carlgren resigned as MoDo's CEO and became its Chair, a change that underlined what already was well known, namely that his strategic ideas were what mattered. During his decade as CEO, he had experienced a growing problem: MoDo's long-term development was to a (too) large extent decided by 'countless' investment propositions put forward by the company's operative managers. None of the proposals was particularly large or important, but taken together they tied MoDo ever more firmly to its fine paper path. The root of the problem was that most directors did not have enough technical competence to make qualified evaluations of all the propositions, and, since the calculations always looked fine, the directors had no choice but to trust the assessments that the CEO and his staff had made. However, as Carlgren felt somewhat uncomfortable being on his own in that part of the operative flow, he recruited a Head of Technology, who acted as a 'gatekeeper' and examined all investment proposals in advance.

Like most of the other larger Swedish forest-based corporations, MoDo faced restrictions when it tried to expand its businesses, both because most acquisition targets already were locked up in different ownership spheres and because cross-national M&As at that time lay beyond what was considered possible. MoDo's weak financial position continued to limit its capacity to grow. Not surprisingly, the question arose now and then about how many core businesses the company actually could run. That discussion became particularly intense when MoDo considered an acquisition of a big producer of high-quality cardboard (Iggesund), at the same time as it expanded both its fine paper business and its hygiene operations.

When MoDo conducted its strategic discussions in the late 1970s, fine paper had obtained particularly high status both because of its success (cf. the Husum investments) and because most of the other pulp-processing paths were already 'occupied' by its competitors. Thus, the fine paper business was what remained for MoDo to 'colonize', and fortunately that segment fitted well with both its past achievements and its contemporary competences/resources. However, Carlgren had even bigger ambitions for MoDo – he was convinced that it could house and expand all its core areas, that is to say, fine paper (through organic growth), hygiene (through acquisitions) and quality cardboard (through the acquisition of Iggesund). Moreover, he believed that such growth could be carried out without loss of family control. So, basically, his ambition was to create an even more grandiose MoDo, which he later would hand over to impressed descendants.

Over time several M&As occurred in the Swedish forest-based industry – all with the ambition to utilize larger production scales and more customer-close sales organizations. However, most structural changes still took place inside the existing business spheres. For example, the Wallenberg dynasty used Stora Kopparberg as the hub in its M&A efforts (cf. section 16.4), and the Industrivärden sphere did the same, assigning SCA the leading role (cf. section 16.5). It was then not a surprise that Carlgren decided that MoDo should try to become the Swedish forest-based industry's third big constellation. This was not so easy given that MoDo's expansion opportunities were rapidly decreasing, as the other two spheres already had absorbed most of the candidates, one after the other. Yet, two attractive acquisition targets were still both 'free' from sphere connections and lacking a single controlling shareholder, namely Holmens Bruk (printing paper) and Iggesund (quality cardboard). Carlgren launched the idea that those companies together with MoDo ought to form a 'third bloc', and both the leading members of the Kempe dynasty and MoDo's board supported that vision. He firmly believed that such a new constellation would both bring scale advantages and result in reduced operative risks, as each of the involved companies' businesses involved radically different products/markets.

MoDo's poor financial situation did not allow a purchase of both Holmens Bruk (which had two controlling owners) and Iggesund (which lacked a controlling owner). Nevertheless, when holdings of Iggesund shares became available on the market, Carlgren/MoDo started to buy most of them, and rather soon MoDo had acquired about 12 per cent of the stock. To discourage other possible buyers from competing, Carlgren wanted to hold more than 10[16] per cent. Contrary to his expectations, his purchases instead aroused interest from the Wallenberg sphere, whose leading actor Marcus Wallenberg Sr wanted Billerud and Stora Kopparberg to act fast together and try to block Carlgren's attempt to take control of Iggesund. The Wallenberg sphere had discovered Iggesund's merits during Iggesund's failed effort about a year earlier to acquire (or merge with) Billerud. Wallenberg was also eager to keep Iggesund away from the competing Handelsbanken/Industrivärden sphere.

The Iggesund struggle was tough (cf. Ch. 9), but eventually MoDo gained control (1983: > 50%[17]), thereby adding one more 'leg' (quality cardboard) to its business repertoire. That acquisition actually improved MoDo's financial situation, as Iggesund soon disinvested both Boxholm (its steelworks) and EKA (chemicals). These sales, together with a new issue of shares, gathered about SEK 1.4 billion. To demonstrate to the capital market and its stakeholders that Iggesund still was to be treated as an autonomous company, Iggesund bought 10 per cent of MoDo (1985). Notably, Carlgren interpreted that transaction quite differently from most market actors – he saw it as a transaction that strengthened MoDo's control over Iggesund.

MoDo's fine paper expansion continued through the 1980s, an effort that was made possible by a remarkable improvement of its balance sheet. The Head of Finance introduced a financial model that exploited the interest rate differences between Sweden and (particularly) Germany. However, more had to be done to create a financial situation that could support a realization of Carlgren's Third Bloc vision. The selling of the power plants (with repurchase option) represented one important step towards solving that problem, but was still insufficient. MoDo was obliged to use expansion modes that involved other companies (but that was difficult to accomplish) and decided to keep its third fine paper investment at Husum outside the balance sheet to be able to show acceptable financial numbers.

Despite its limited financial capacity, MoDo continued to look for expansion opportunities. When the French company Alicel went bankrupt and substantial state subventions were promised to the new owner, Carlgren and the Head of MoDo France (Lejeune[18]) saw a possibility for MoDo to cheaply obtain a pulp production unit in France that could become a platform for further expansion in continental Europe. Although it was usually difficult for foreigners to acquire companies in France, the severe crisis at Alicel together with Lejeune's French citizenship simplified the transaction. A catch was that foreign ownership of companies in France was restricted to a maximum of 35 per cent of the stock, but Carlgren and Lejeune solved that problem by forming a French consortium

(Calanda) that bought 65 per cent of Alicel. While MoDo did not become the controlling owner, Carlgren made sure that MoDo through its PPSM unit got a large holding. Basically, that investment represented another step in MoDo's pulp and fine paper strategy and contributed to MoDo's ambition to expand on the continent.

The forest-sourcing situation and the need to expand the hygiene business created problems for MoDo. Further investments in Graningeverken (from 4% to 10%) partly 'solved' the first problem, but the second one remained unsolved, as MoDo could not raise the necessary capital. As a result, its attempts to buy Edet, Klippan and Fiskeby failed (competitors bought those firms). Still, however, the Swedish tissue producer Duni was acquired (from the Bonnier dynasty). The new investment in Alicel (pulp) also triggered ideas about integrating forward, preferably by adding a fine paper unit (Alipap). That move was fully in line with MoDo's current focus on fine paper. Like Lejeune, MoDo's CEO at the time (Löf) supported that investment, which – if carried out through PPSM – would double MoDo's total holding to 34 per cent (with an option to get 51%). At the same time MoDo strengthened its cardboard business by making Iggesund a subsidiary.

Though MoDo's financial situation did not improve, Carlgren was not deterred from trying to create the Third Bloc. After having acquired Iggesund, he began to look for ways to gain control over Holmens Bruk. Towards that end, Carlgren started to buy that company's shares using Iggesund as the buying unit (its capital came from the disinvestments of EKA and Boxholm). For some time, another actor (Lundberg) had a 7 per cent holding in Holmens Bruk, but he decided to exit that engagement when it became clear that neither the Bonnier[19] nor the Söderberg family intended to sell their holdings. Taking advantage of the situation, Carlgren (Iggesund) acquired Lundberg's and some other actors' holdings,[20] making it possible for Iggesund to announce that it had reached 15 per cent of the votes in Holmens Bruk (1986). That statement worried both Bonnier and Söderberg, so the Söderberg family bought 10 per cent of Iggesund to try to block the situation. However, instead it became more complicated, as a link had previously been established between the Bonnier family and Carlgren, when the latter had helped the former to get out of a problem company (Duni). That process initiated a lasting friendship relation between Carlgren and a leading member of the Bonnier family ('Joja' Bonnier). That new link worried the Söderberg family, who feared an imminent Bonnier–Carlgren alliance in Holmens Bruk.

In 1987 MoDo sold one of its core businesses, namely MoDo Konsument (i.e. its hygiene operations) to Holmens Bruk. Carlgren wanted payment in the form of Holmens Bruk shares to take another step towards the realization of the Third Bloc, but in the end he and MoDo had to accept cash. The same year the leader of the Söderberg dynasty (Sven Söderberg) came to the conclusion that it would be impossible for the family to stay in Holmens Bruk with its 30 per cent holding, if the combination of Carlgren (MoDo/Iggesund) and the Bonnier dynasty together controlled around 47 per cent. So, the Söderberg family decided to sell both its Holmens Bruk holding (30%) and its shares in Iggesund (10%) to Carlgren. Those transactions put the Bonnier dynasty in a difficult situation, as they provided Carlgren with close to a majority position in Holmens Bruk (47%). However, because Bonnier's holding in Holmens Bruk (30%) also attracted other actors, Carlgren felt forced to try to prevent those (potential) rivals from entering the bidding arena. Ultimately (in 1988) the rather extended acquisition process came to an end, when Bonnier/Marieberg, too, sold its Holmens Bruk shares to MoDo. That transaction confirmed that Carlgren's long-awaited Third Bloc had at last been formed.

The purchases of all of Holmens Bruk's and Iggesund's shares put new and severe pressure on MoDo's already strained finances. To relieve some of that pressure, MoDo had to take the biggest loan in its centuries-old history. That situation still did not worry Carlgren, who saw several ways for the family to maintain control. But the former shareholder in Holmens Bruk Lundberg detected an opportunity in the current ownership situation, as MoDo's limited financial capacity had produced a market full of MoDo convertibles. Lundberg started to buy such securities and offered a rather high price for Iggesund's shares in MoDo.[21] Lundberg also acquired some of those shares, and in due time his holding in MoDo reached 20 per cent (Carlgren 15%, the Kempe foundations 19% and Bonnier/Marieberg 11%).

MoDo was financially 'paralysed' after having both formed the Third Bloc and invested heavily in Alizay (Alipap). Carlgren had allowed MoDo to take high financial risks to maintain family control. As a result, the company was highly indebted, and the situation was rather similar for Carlgren himself (Sanna Holding included). Lundberg, who acted from a strong financial position, continued to buy MoDo shares. Those purchases began to worry Carlgren, who was also concerned about all the large investments that were required in the coming years to keep all the businesses in the new MoDo constellation competitive, particularly as he suspected that neither the dynasty nor the company itself would be able to raise the required sums. The only thing that might change that outcome was if MoDo began to earn unrealistically high profits. A partnership financing of Holmens Bruk's power plants was carried out to free some capital, but that solved only part of the financial problem.

In mid-1990, Sweden's two largest banks contacted Carlgren and declared that his personal financial status had become too fragile. That initiative was at least partly triggered by a domestic financial crisis in which almost all larger banks feared great losses and reconsidered quite a lot of their credits. Within a short time, Carlgren was forced to sell all his MoDo holdings, and after several turns, SCA won a tough race with Lundberg and bought Carlgren's shares (cf. Ch. 9 and Ch. 14). SCA also acquired the Bonnier/Marieberg holding in MoDo, thus making SCA its biggest owner (≈ 30% of the votes). That large holding did not put SCA in the driver's seat, however; it rather represented a strategic investment – a platform for co-operation between the two companies. As both MoDo and SCA ran extensive fine paper and newsprint operations, those two businesses came into focus. Several attempts were made to co-ordinate those (and other) areas, but the shareholder stalemate hampered all those efforts.

The start of the 1990s turned out to be a tough period for MoDo (especially [as usual] financially), so its CEO Löf proposed several sizeable divestments. At the same time, he advocated a large investment in Alizay through the acquisition of Calanda's holding in that combine (Alicel–Alipap), and eventually Löf won the board's support for such a purchase. Thus, MoDo continued to expand its fine paper operations, although on shaky financial ground. Particularly 1992 became such a miserable year for MoDo (and for many other Swedish forest-based corporations) that it actually came down to a fight for its future existence. MoDo needed new capital either from a new major shareholder or through a large issue of shares guaranteed by its current owners (i.e. by the Kempe foundations, Lundberg and SCA).

Once SCA changed its course and decided to treat its large investment in MoDo as non-strategic (as pure allocation of capital), SCA favoured the entry of a new big owner over a capital injection. Towards that end, SCA's leaders discussed the idea with a large US corporation. As nothing concrete had come out of those talks and the idea to split MoDo had been rejected, the shareholders embarked on the rights issue path. It was Lundberg that took the initiative in the crisis and suggested a sizeable figure that would make MoDo financially strong; reluctantly, SCA accepted. When SCA exchanged its high voting A-shares for Lundberg's low voting B-shares, Lundberg gained control of MoDo. The change of ownership triggered a radically new governance approach, as Lundberg did not focus exclusively on MoDo's operative flow; for him, it was equally important to master the financial flow. For MoDo, that meant the beginning of a radical shift of its financial strategy (from a high-risk to a low-risk one).

16.3.5 Holmen

In 1994 MoDo's incoming CEO (Pettersson) expressed a view similar to that of his predecessors – MoDo was comprised of too many core businesses for its size and financial capacity. Like the new controlling shareholder (Lundberg), he wanted to establish a decent capital structure and get all operations 'in order' before he presented the board any substantial expansion ideas. Therefore, several disinvestments were soon made (e.g. of a CTMP plant, Rentch, [the 25% holding in] Slave Lake Pulp, [somewhat later] Skärblacka and [the 25% holding in] MD Papier). One intended big investment – the remaining 75 per cent of shares in MD Papier – was stopped, even though it included an attractive LWC paper business that would have strengthened MoDo's newsprint position.

CEO Pettersson sought to clarify the relative strengths and weaknesses of each of MoDo's core businesses – operatively as well as financially – before he proposed which one(s) to keep and develop. He presumed that three 'legs' were at least one too many and that MoDo's international activities were too scattered. Moreover, the CEO noted that its successful history had given fine paper a unique status in the company, but it was not written in stone that a continuation of that special treatment would be beneficial for MoDo. Eventually he became rather convinced that even the opposite situation could emerge, that is to say, that fine paper might turn into a problem business. So, when both MoDo's new controlling owner and its leading executives thoroughly analysed possible futures for the company, they came to the somewhat unexpected conclusion that the quality cardboard business (i.e. Iggesund) was both the current and the expected star performer among the three 'contestants'. It was followed by the printing paper business (i.e. Holmens Bruk), while the fine paper business was placed only third (i.e. MoDo). For obvious reasons, the leading representatives of MoDo's former owner dynasty became worried when they learned about that new ranking.

Beginning in 1995 MoDo began to develop so well that it could both halve its indebtedness and make substantial investments in all its core businesses – more offensive ones in newsprint (Braviken and Hallsta) and cardboard (Iggesund), and more defensive ones in fine paper (Husum). In 1997 MoDo's board once again reviewed all its businesses as well as its strategy. Every stone was turned especially regarding the fine paper operations. Three crucial questions were posed: Should the French units PPSM and Alizay be sold? Should Husum be converted to a cardboard producer? Should the wholesaling business be maintained, and perhaps even developed? All in all, the answers to those questions strengthened the recent ranking of the core businesses: the fine paper business was the one that ought to be divested, but without hurry and in an orderly way. Unlike most of its competitors, MoDo decided to keep all its forests and power plants. MoDo actually tried to increase its forest resources, but at that time other bidders won the crucial contests.

In the second half of the 1990s MoDo began to consider how to separate out its fine paper operations while retaining the forests, the wholesale business and the Domsjö unit. The idea was to establish the fine paper business as a separate legal unit and distribute its shares to MoDo's shareholders. However, several weaknesses were linked to that solution, as no forests would be included, no synergies would emerge and no listing at SSE would be possible (too small a unit). To qualify for the SSE, the new unit needed a strong partner. SCA's fine paper business was the obvious candidate for that role, and to MoDo's surprise that company's leaders showed interest in discussing a joint fine paper unit. At that time MoDo's financial standing had become so strong that it could use that new position to take the time needed for making thorough analyses and the necessary contacts. In 1998 discussions were once again resumed between MoDo and SCA, and MoDo's Chair (Lundberg) and SCA's CEO (Martin-Löf) agreed that a partial merger (fine paper) might be a wise step. At the time nothing concrete materialized. MoDo also discussed similar solutions with other corporations (e.g. Enso-Gutzeit, Neusidler and Soporcell), but without any success.

MoDo was still determined to find a new harbour for its fine paper business, so the talks with SCA continued. In 1999 that path was given priority, and finally the two companies agreed to establish a new joint fine paper company named Modo Paper. MoDo would then change its name to Holmen. MoDo and SCA saw three alternative ways to handle the new company: list it on the SSE, sell it to a big forest-based company or distribute it to the shareholders. When MoDo ranked the three paths, it put the third one first, while SCA preferred a combination of the other two. Although initially the two companies agreed to try to introduce the Modo Paper shares on the SSE, that idea never materialized because investor interest was too low (partly because of the IT hype at the time). When the stock market crashed in 2000, SCA definitively abandoned the SSE introduction path, and then (due to the terms in the agreement) Holmen had to stop its planned distribution of Modo Paper shares to its shareholders. As a result, Holmen still housed several core businesses, but offensive investments were made only in printing paper and quality cardboard. To strengthen the cardboard business, Holmen considered an acquisition of an LPB producer (Frövifors from AssiDomän), but in the end it refrained from buying that unit. Holmen also tried to develop its newsprint operations and analysed two possible development paths: an expansion at Braviken or an investment in Spain (a country that lacked its own newsprint production). Eventually the latter alternative was chosen, and rather soon Papelera Peninsular was acquired.

Unexpectedly the CEO of Metsä-Serla indicated his company's interest in buying Modo Paper as part of its ambition to become the largest fine paper corporation in Europe. That sizeable transaction was concluded in 2000. The same year Domsjö was sold, in that case to a Swedish investor consortium. So, finally, the classic MoDo had become a 'Holmen without MoDo'. The new Holmen continued to invest substantially in printing papers and bought back previously sold hydroelectric power assets. That year Holmen decided to invest in a large newsprint machine in Spain.[22] In the beginning of the

21st century Holmen continued to develop its combined reproduction–industrial strategy, which involved ownership of both forests and power plants and the running of two core businesses (printing papers and quality cardboard).

16.3.6 From MoDo to Holmen: Some Tentative Conclusions

The analysis presented here and in the chapter on this master case indicates that nature-driven occurrences had near-negligible impact on the lengthy process by which MoDo, Iggesund and Holmens Bruk were transformed into Holmen. Instead, the presence of certain natural resources – especially forests and power plants – played an important role for that development. The demand for those forest resources increased continuously during the decades after WWII, partly because of the advantages of scale that the new technological solutions offered, partly because of the steadily rising demand for forest-based products. In many companies, that development created an uncertainty regarding future timber sourcing, which in turn stimulated thoughts about forward integration (e.g. from pulp to paper), as such a path was expected to both solve the problem of timber shortage and lower the risk for market crowding (pulp).

However, MoDo, Iggesund and Holmens Bruk did not merely try to reduce their timber and pulpwood use by various moves to the right in the value chain. They also increased their timber sourcing through assiduous forest purchases, utilization of buying cartels, looking abroad to find unexploited forest resources (e.g. in South America [MoDo]) and investing in R&D to make more effective use of the timber and/or expand the usable kinds of trees (e.g. birch [MoDo was a pioneer]). In addition, all three companies retained their forests and power plants even in those periods when many 'experts' recommended selling (a piece of advice that was followed by several competitors).

Although occurrences triggered by nature had negligible impact on how MoDo, Iggesund, Holmens Bruk and Holmen developed during the second half of the 20th century, several of the external man-made ones certainly mattered, for example, WWII, the Korean War in the early 1950s, the Swedish[23] and Finnish[24] devaluations of their currencies and the Swedish real estate crisis of 1990. The two wars had a rather positive impact; the import difficulties that WWII generated encouraged many forest-based corporations to enter new product areas, and the Korean War increased the international demand for forest-based products in a way that both boosted the expansion of the existing production plants and stimulated the establishment of new ones. By contrast, the Swedish real estate crisis struck the forest-based industry hard and particularly affected the situation for the Carlgren–Kempe dynasty, which had controlled MoDo since its founding in the 19th century. The most serious consequence of that crisis for the dynasty was that the two leading Swedish banks required Carlgren to sell all his MoDo shares within a short time frame. The forced sale of shares turned out to be transformative for MoDo, as it was impossible for the Kempe foundations to buy them.[25] Instead, it started a process that eventually provided MoDo with a new controlling shareholder (1993, Lundberg), who soon launched a radically different strategic course for the company. Until the 1990s, MoDo had basically adhered to a conservative entrepreneurial strategy that over time had generated a rather broad palette of businesses, but its new owner followed a completely different strategic rationale. From that period on, MoDo (later Holmen) rather pursued a combined reproduction–industrialist strategy.

Iggesund's development was partly determined by external man-made occurrences, particularly when the company abandoned its pulp-based, risk-averse reproduction strategy and instead adopted an entrepreneurial kind of strategy by integrating forward into quality cardboard. That move to the right in the value chain was partly triggered by market changes in the US, where innovations addressing the transportation and selling of various kinds of consumer goods had enticed manufacturers to invest in new packaging solutions. Like both MoDo and Iggesund, Holmens Bruk was exposed to the Swedish currency changes, which strengthened the company's competitive power on the European market. However, as its core business (printing paper) was monitored by a cartel, the impact of the Swedish devaluations on its performance did not become as massive as one might have expected.

MoDo's, Iggesund's and Holmens Bruk's development illustrates the explanatory power that is built into the idea of path dependence. MoDo, for example, gradually became fixed to a fine paper path, although the company also ran two additional core businesses from the 1980s, when it had acquired both Iggesund (quality cardboard) and Holmens Bruk (printing paper). Similarly, Iggesund and Holmens Bruk had been caught in their special paths for many decades before they became part of the enlarged MoDo constellation, and those ties did not weaken even in that new setting.

However, path dependence was certainly not the only phenomenon that explained the development of those corporations over time. Obviously, such an idea could explain neither why they added unrelated businesses, nor why they divested older ones. In the MoDo case, for example, path dependence does not explain why the Third Bloc emerged. It also fails to elucidate why Holmen in the late 1990s decided to disinvest its most classic and cherished core activity – its fine paper operations. On the other hand, for Iggesund's choice of quality cardboard in the late 1950s, path dependence has at least some explanatory power, although the company's pulp capacity at the time allowed the pursuit of other strategic choices as well. Holmens Bruk's strong position in printing papers in the late 20th century has a similar explanation, as its past accomplishments continuously built capacity and competitiveness in that core area. Yet, the Holmens Bruk case deviates from such 'linear' development processes, both when it divested its classic textile business and when it added its hygiene operations.

Path dependence could also assert itself through the impact of institutions, that is to say, via remnants of past human efforts that originate from initiatives taken either by single individuals or by different kinds of collectives. As such, institutions continuously (re)produce norms that influence contemporary human action. However, (constellations of) individuals also in never-ending processes dissolve, destroy, create and/or replace institutions. Such institutional changes have several different causes: nature-driven occurrences, discoveries and/or revaluations of natural resources, man-made occurrences and individual or collective actorhood. All of these factors have led to institutional changes of one kind or another at MoDo, Iggesund, Holmens Bruk and Holmen. For example, all four companies were exposed to new scientific knowledge, which prompted the Swedish authorities to introduce new environmental legislation that radically changed the opportunities available to produce certain kinds of products (e.g. sulphite pulp). These companies have also seen changes in many of those institutions that influence to a large extent their possibilities of expanding outside Sweden (e.g. the gradual dissolution of the regulating cartels in the 1970s). Still, during the second half of the 20th century, the EEC,

EC and EU, in turn, have probably been the most important foreign regulating institutions for the Swedish industry – and perhaps particularly for its largest export sector, the forest-based one. There, everything ranging from tariff rates to product specifications has been decided.

A particular difficulty in most analyses of the impact of institutional forces is that they are frequently taken for granted by the actors involved, and therefore these forces are often acted upon almost unconsciously. One such institution that often influences actors without arousing notice is the Swedish Companies Act (and its associated regulations, rules, standards and norms), which at the same time is probably also the most decisive factor shaping how Swedish corporations have been governed since the 19th century. Two ideals in particular have been used as the foundation for that legislation: the value of strong shareholder power and the indispensability of an unequivocal hierarchy. That special[26] Swedish institutional set-up as such partly clarifies why ownership (i.e. qualities associated with shareholding) has been so crucial for how MoDo, Iggesund, Holmens Bruk and Holmen have been governed, and, consequently, also for what paths they have followed. The four subcases also illustrate the importance of how the hierarchical relationships between owners and executives are conducted in the legally formed governance arenas.

Thus, ownership activity as such (or lack of it) stands out as an important force in the lengthy process by which MoDo, Iggesund and Holmens Bruk were transformed into Holmen. However, as mentioned initially in this chapter, owners do not merely govern corporations through their activities' frequency and intensity; ownership also impacts through dimensions such as its type, form, structure, status, organization and enactment.

MoDo stands out a little when it comes to owner activity as such, as it has been governed by a strong controlling owner. After WWII Carl Kempe Sr (until the 1960s), Carlgren (from the 1960s to 1990) and Lundberg (from 1993) have actively governed MoDo and thereby exerted substantial influence on its strategic path. In the few exceptional years in the early 1990s when no one was in charge (neither Carlgren/Kempe nor Lundberg nor SCA's leaders) that stalemate situation led to strategic passivity.

Iggesund lost its controlling shareholder constellation in the 1970s when the Trygger family and some other families substantially reduced their holdings and gave up their leading roles in the company, and then it did not take long before that company became the subject of a takeover struggle between the Wallenberg sphere (led by Marcus Wallenberg Sr) and MoDo (led by Carlgren). Ultimately, Iggesund was one of the two losers in that contest (the Wallenberg sphere was the other one), as it lacked an active controlling owner constellation that could support its autonomy and financially contribute to its further development. Its executives' devoted efforts to foster Iggesund's interests were not sufficient to compensate for that weakness, largely because the fight was carried out on a too high actor level (i.e. at the market for corporate control). The executive actors could not turn for support to the Swedish Companies Act, for it has put boards and CEOs in weak positions, particularly when it comes to takeover fights and ownership changes.

For Holmens Bruk, the ownership setting was quite straightforward from the early 1950s, when it got two major owners that together controlled the company. Those two owners, however, fulfilled that ownership function rather passively, thus handing the executive actors considerable freedom to run the company (even strategically). That moderate level of owner activity also followed from the fact that one of them was one of the company's key customers, and was therefore challengeable in certain decision situations.

A consideration of the ownership settings of all four cases indicates that high owner activity seems to correlate with a controlling shareholding (cf. MoDo, Iggesund and Holmen). If the latter is absent, executive forces will instead at least partly enter in its stead (cf. Iggesund and Holmens Bruk). However, such informal swapping is usually not possible for pure ownership issues, because in those situations only shareholdings as such can mobilize the necessary power (cf. Iggesund). Also worth noting is that a controlling shareholding is not always accompanied by active ownership (cf. Holmens Bruk).

Ownership kind, too, mattered in all four cases, in particular for MoDo from its founding until 1990. During that long time period ranging over two centuries, the controlling dynasty's overriding aim was to remain in that position. That stance both stimulated and hampered the company's expansion possibilities: stimulated because the company's leading actors felt an obligation to make it reputable, but hampered because it was difficult to pay for large acquisitions with the company's own shares (or merge in other ways that entailed the risk of losing a voting majority). Notably, that restriction was not present in all the family-run corporations analysed in this second master case. In one subcase the families actually preferred to sell their major holdings because of (expected) changes in the overall ownership structure (cf. Holmens Bruk), and in another subcase the head of the leading owner family eventually sold most of his holdings because he could not convince any of his children to assume responsibility as principal owner (cf. Iggesund).

Corporate paths are sometimes influenced by ownership form as well. That was a particularly decisive force for MoDo when it acquired Holmens Bruk and its controlling shareholder Carlgren refused to carry out that transaction in such a way that MoDo could control the new constellation with a relatively limited capital input. He could have made Holmens Bruk the buyer and used its shares with its highly differentiated voting rights[27] to gain control, thereby more likely avoiding the financial strain that later contributed to his loss of MoDo. A similar mistake was made somewhat later when Carlgren refrained from using the holding company form and instead merged both Iggesund and Holmens Bruk with MoDo. To accomplish that fusion with rather limited financial resources and yet maintain control, he let MoDo introduce a special form of convertibles that the shareholders in the acquired companies (and other market actors) could obtain. However, the industrialist Lundberg, who looked for (large) suitable investment objects and who previously had been a shareholder in Holmens Bruk (1984–85), found the offered form of convertibles attractive. So, to MoDo's, Carlgren's and his advisers' surprise, Lundberg bought many of them and began to exchange them for MoDo shares, thereby starting to build up a holding that ultimately would lead to his control of MoDo. So, for MoDo both its ownership kind (private dynasty) and the special form of the new securities (convertible profit-sharing debentures) had a decisive impact on its development over time.

As mentioned above, both the focal unit's status, that is to say, its degree of autonomy, and the way ownership governance is organized substantially influences which actors and agencies determine the corporate paths. In the Holmen case other considerations were seldom taken – the company was never subordinated to any superior constellation (sphere). However, when it comes to the organizational set-ups, this master case reveals a variety, although most of the practices can be explained in a rather straightforward way through references to legislation, regulations, codes, and so on. The most obvious deviation from the standard arrangements is found in the way Carlgren acted during his many years as MoDo leader. Basically, he worked in a similar way regardless of which organizational position(s) he held (i.e. as controlling owner, Chair, [acting] director or CEO). Both the owner family and MoDo's executives contributed to the emergence of that unique governance 'structure' by treating him – 'constructing' him – as the 'Great Leader', free to act almost irrespective of situation and circumstances. He was sometimes even allowed to cross the boundaries between his own holding company and MoDo. One of many striking examples of Carlgren's unique status was when he managed to organize one of MoDo's key activities – its large French operations – entirely outside the company's hierarchy, and consequently won acceptance for an arrangement that its head should report directly to him.

Furthermore, many times Carlgren acted on behalf of MoDo without feeling obliged to listen to – let alone take into account – the counterarguments that several autonomous, competent and respected directors and top managers raised. That meant that his strategic ideas and initiatives seldom were challenged or vetted. Given all this, for about three decades MoDo's strategy was largely a product of one man's thinking and acting, and that arrangement did not change until a new owner took control of the company (Lundberg). At times, Carlgren's reluctance to take guidance from the company's executive actors or other competent advisers created problems, particularly because of the huge discrepancy that often existed between his operative ambitions for MoDo and its financial capacity.[28] That 'Carlgren way' of running MoDo's internal processes had no counterpart whatsoever in the other three subcases. Iggesund, Holmens Bruk and Holmen were instead organized and managed in modes that much better corresponded with the legal prescriptions, and therefore the required agencies (AGM, board and CEO) were all equipped with appropriate powers and responsibilities.

Most of the key dimensions linked to MoDo's ownership were roughly the same for Carlgren and Lundberg, that is to say, its kind (private/family), form (listed limited corporation), structure (controlling shareholder) and status (autonomous unit). However, for two of the dimensions the differences were substantial: the organization of the governance processes and how they were enacted practically. Lundberg governed MoDo in a radically different way to that of Carlgren. For example, he put an end to the rather arbitrary informal governance methods that had dominated MoDo for several decades and instead ran the company in a more classic way using the formal procedures that the Swedish Companies Act prescribed. He also complied with most other governance regulations, behavioural codes and proven practices. Lundberg actively utilized MoDo's executive bodies to discuss both operative and strategic issues, and took the leading role in many of those talks (e.g. as Chair of the board). Thus, although Lundberg was a powerful and determined owner, the framing of MoDo's/Holmen's strategies was done in a rather broad actor constellation. In contrast with Carlgren, Lundberg also recognized the importance of active owner involvement in both governance flows (the financial and the operative) and stressed the need to integrate the two all along the executive hierarchy. He further claimed that MoDo's financial status should be regarded as a constraint to what the company could do operatively. To him, it was important that MoDo's production facilities were in order before any expansion ideas could be discussed seriously.

The opposite – the absence of a (constellation of) controlling shareholder(s) – often tends to generate quite different arrangements and uses of the prescribed governance bodies. As noted earlier, that ambiguous state affected MoDo for a few years in the early 1990s, when most of its shares were distributed among three actors/agencies: the Kempe foundations, Lundberg and SCA. In that stalemate situation, MoDo's independent directors and CEO had trouble acting at all.

For Iggesund, the decade without a controlling owner constellation (the 1980s) produced a rather powerless board that, for example, left to its top management, unions and employees the task of defending the company against hostile takeover attempts. In the end, that 'delegation' of responsibility did not solve the basic problem, as those internal actors, too, were at the mercy of the leading actors (owners) of the two 'attacking' companies (i.e. Carlgren [MoDo] and Marcus Wallenberg Sr [Billerud/Stora Kopparberg]). Still, Iggesund's managers made serious efforts to determine both the terms of the takeover (maintain Iggesund's autonomy) and its outcome (Iggesund preferred Carlgren/MoDo as its new major [not controlling] owner). It is also worth noting that, with few exceptions, its shareholders at the time of the takeover battle refrained from defending Iggesund's interests (none of them had a sufficiently large holding). In the Holmens Bruk subcase, however, there existed a controlling ownership constellation, but as it was built on rather fragile ground (a two-party agreement made by two acquaintances), the circumstances allowed the executive bodies substantial influence in the strategy-forming process. That situation was reversed in 1988, when Carlgren took control of Holmens Bruk and rather autocratically determined its path.

As was described previously in this section, several examples of inverted relationships among the core governing agencies could also be found in all the corporations studied, including among those with strong controlling owners. That anomaly could be illustrated, for example, by Carlgren's concern regarding the impact of MoDo's top management on its long-term path, as they continuously confronted board members with proposals for purportedly indispensable and highly profitable additional investments in the existing plants. As Carlgren and most other owners and directors were non-technicians, they felt incapable of evaluating the merits of all those proposals. So, to some extent, MoDo's path was determined in a way that neither he, as controlling owner and Chair, nor the directors fully could grasp (until afterwards).

As noted earlier, the impact of ownership also depends on how it is enacted, that is to say, which actor rationales are involved. The subcases of MoDo, Iggesund, Holmens Bruk and Holmen involve many instances and processes where actor-based forces not only are present but are actually even decisive for the paths taken. In the MoDo case, Carlgren is the most striking example of such sovereign actorhood, and from the very start his actorhood was based on membership in the right faction of the controlling dynasty (the one that was supposed to deliver the talented business leaders). Eventually Carlgren's track record also 'confirmed' to the family members that he was best suited to govern MoDo.

Carlgren's performance was built on a rather complex mix of rationales involving classic calculation as well as judgement based on values and emotions. The importance of the last two drivers was clearly visible in his continuous search for ways to make the family heirloom MoDo more 'grandiose'. At the time of his retirement, according to Carlgren, MoDo should flourish and be one of the few large surviving constellations in the Swedish forest-based industry. His (Third Bloc) vision actually became reality in the late 1980s, although that great achievement slipped out of his (and the Kempe dynasty's) control just a few years later. That family trauma was at least partly as a consequence of Carlgren's personal character, which included both a risk-seeking attitude and a considerable focus on non-calculative qualities (e.g. he acted as spiritualist, asking his late predecessor for advice). However, his risk-taking was first and foremost financial, while his operative acting was composed of a rather atypical combination of high risk-taking (cf. his entrepreneurship) and risk reduction (cf. his differentiation [and diversification] ambitions for MoDo).

Carlgren's approach as MoDo leader included an inclination to focus on operative matters (his 'comfort zone'), leaving the financial ones to other actors. His perspective was usually long term, which often translated into remarkable staying power. His rationale-in-use entailed the unusual combination of self-reliance and capacity to build persistent personal networks and friendship-like relationships. The way he expanded MoDo was to a large extent based on that duality, which was evident in how he, for example, ran MoDo's French business (cf. his relation to its head Lejeune), won the Iggesund contest (cf. his relationship with its CEO Sundblad) and acquired Holmens Bruk (cf. his friendship with one of its two major shareholders [Joja Bonnier]). That special blend of self-reliance and capacity to build relationships was also visible in the way he approached most of the owners of the other firms MoDo acquired (or tried to acquire).

Yet, his inclination to build MoDo's expansion on friendship-like relations had a downside, which affected MoDo's development negatively. Carlgren's genuine honesty and tendency to trust acquaintances and business partners sometimes created difficulties for the company. For example, when Alizay was to be fully incorporated into MoDo in the early 1990s, Alizay's head Lejeune did not act as friendly as Carlgren had expected. That naïveté together with his self-confidence also contributed to his conviction that his 'friends' in the banks would continue to assist him in 1990 when his financial situation had become disastrous. To his great surprise neither they nor his other 'friends' supported him in his efforts to keep the Carlgren–Kempe dynasty in control of MoDo. Together Carlgren's strong family identification, risk-seeking behaviour, self-sufficiency, honesty/naïveté, network-building capacity, stamina, optimism, operative bias and scout-like rationale permeated his governance of MoDo and the successful creation of the Third Bloc (but it also contributed to his personal bankruptcy).

His 'successor' as controlling owner in MoDo (Lundberg) applied a very different business rationale starting from a slightly different ownership base, as he represented nobody but himself. Lundberg encouraged MoDo/Holmen to follow a mixed reproduction–industrialist strategy, that is to say, he made sure that the company held the financial risk low and its operative risk low to moderate. Lundberg was a studious actor, who based much of his activity in MoDo on a calculative rationale, discussions with its board and judgements obtained from carefully selected advisers. His actions were usually based on a long-term perspective, and his staying power was extraordinary.

Lundberg had strong links to the Norrköping region (where he grew up), but it is unclear whether that affinity actually influenced his investment in Holmens Bruk shares in the mid-1980s and his transformation (and renaming) of MoDo to Holmen. In the process during which he conquered the shareholding majority in MoDo, he also showed considerable capacity to build professional alliances with key persons. Ultimately, the alliance that became decisive for MoDo's ownership situation and long-term development was the one he established in the early 1990s with the Chair of the third largest owner of MoDo, the Kempe foundations (Carl Kempe Jr). That relationship tipped the balance in favour of Lundberg in his fight with SCA over control of MoDo.

As the focus here is very much on those forces that have a substantial impact on how corporate paths develop, most of the influential actors were found among the major/controlling owners and corporate executives. Indeed, such strategic decisions and activities have to involve those (legal) bodies through which those sets of actors make most of their contributions. While that does not imply that all ideas and initiatives are generated at such high hierarchical levels, it means that they sooner or later have to be evaluated and decided on by actors in such leading positions. That function makes the major/controlling shareholders, the directors and the CEOs the crucial individual forces in the processes that determine corporate paths.

It is also evident from the described subcases that actors other than the corporations' major/dominating shareholders, directors and CEOs have affected how the corporations have developed. Some of them have acted as members of the companies' management teams, while others have acted from platforms outside the companies studied. Among MoDo's managers, individuals such as Altbäck (MoDo's general strategic development), Brändström (MoDo's financing), Erik Diedrichs (MoDo's fine paper business), Lejeune (MoDo's French business), and Peppler (MoDo's internationalization) significantly contributed to its long-term path. Among the external actors that had a strong impact on MoDo's development too, one could mention, for example, Martin-Löf (SCA, the creation of Modo Paper) and Rydin (SCA, its entry as major shareholder in MoDo). In the Iggesund case, while CEO Lars G. Sundblad stands out among the internal actors, one could also mention, for example, Haglund (who defended Iggesund's autonomy) and Svensson (who initiated Iggesund's acquisition of a major holding in Holmens Bruk).

Many external actors also substantially influenced Iggesund's course, for example, Carlgren (who was behind MoDo's acquisition of Iggesund), Marcus Wallenberg Sr (who prompted Billerud's/Stora Kopparberg's hostile bid for Iggesund) and Wallander (who supported Carlgren's acquisition effort, acting as MoDo director and Handelsbanken Chair). The strategic processes were run in a rather similar way in Holmens Bruk, that is to say, the large owners and the CEOs governed most of the activities. However, Önnesjö maintained his influence as Chair, and the previous Chair (Mannerfelt) played an important role, particularly for the process that ended with a rather dramatic change of ownership.

Finally, from all four (sub)cases it also becomes obvious that one important factor is absent in the theoretical model presented in the beginning of this chapter, namely luck. That attribute refers to interpretations that actors tend to make when their performances are favoured or disfavoured by unexpected 'autonomous' forces. All the companies studied, that is to say, MoDo, Iggesund, Holmens Bruk and Holmen, provide examples of such linking of favourable/unfavourable outcomes of human action to unforeseen situations and circumstanccs. For example, MoDo's controlling owner Carlgren's personal bankruptcy was partly the result of bad luck (most share prices fell dramatically because of an unexpected crisis in the Swedish real estate sector). However, MoDo's investment in its first fine paper mill at Husum instead turned out to be perfectly timed (luck) and generated both economic success and further similar investments. Lundberg's 'remake' of

MoDo/Holmen in the early/mid-1990s could also be used as an example of the impact of luck, as it coincided with an unexpected and rapid improvement of market demand in most sectors of the forest industry.

16.4 FROM STORA KOPPARBERG TO STORA ENSO

16.4.1 Sphere Disharmony

The third of the four master cases presented in this volume contains a description of how the large Swedish steel and forest-based company Stora Kopparberg eventually (in 1998) became the even bigger Swedish–Finnish corporation Stora Enso, one of the world's leading forest-based constellations. It particularly focuses on Stora Kopparberg's/Stora's development during the second half of the 20th century, but does not provide a similar in-depth study of how the Finnish constellation Enso-Gutzeit evolved over those years.

Stora Kopparberg entered the 1950s as a rather traditional and relatively large steel and forest-based company with Sweden as its operative base and Western Europe as its main market. For many corporations and actors, the years after WWII represented the start of a new development, and that was also true for Stora Kopparberg. Its R&D activities began to regain momentum, and the output from those efforts became important for its future path. Particularly its core business pulp[29] evolved in several ways: improved production methods were introduced, new (competitive) chlorine-bleached pulp qualities were launched and fluff production started (i.e. a first step to the right in the value chain was taken). During the same period Stora Kopparberg also integrated forward into sacks by acquiring Strömsnäs Bruk (a company that included forestry, pulp and newsprint operations as well).

As in other forest-based companies, the leading actors of Stora Kopparberg continued to express deep concern for the company's future sourcing of suitable timber. To come to grips with that expected shortage, Stora Kopparberg acquired several minor forest-owning companies throughout Sweden. In addition, the company also began to consider the possibility of making such investments also outside Sweden. As Stora Kopparberg already was active in North America through a subsidiary, it was 'natural' to expand that unit's assignment from selling pulp to include searching for new raw material sources. An appropriate opportunity soon emerged when it became possible to buy crown forests in Nova Scotia. Since that investment required support from the Canadian government, Stora's capacity to deal with cross-national politics turned out to be an important ingredient in the further establishment process.

However, the situation was a bit complicated for Stora Kopparberg in those days, as the efforts of its two leading owner representatives – the brothers Jacob Wallenberg Sr and Marcus Wallenberg Sr – were poorly co-ordinated. One reason for that lack of synchronization was that the governing Wallenberg sphere controlled several legally autonomous forest-based companies, not just Stora Kopparberg, and each of the two brothers ran his part of the holdings independent of the other. As a consequence of that divided governance, intra-sphere rationalizations never took off in the 1960s. As a result, Stora Kopparberg as well as Bergvik & Ala and Kopparfors continued to act on their own.

Stora Kopparberg's faltering decision-making process regarding the Nova Scotia project clearly demonstrated the Wallenberg sphere's internal co-ordination problems. The two brothers ended up on different sides – Marcus Wallenberg Sr supported the idea, while Jacob Wallenberg Sr hesitated. The latter claimed that an investment in a new pulp plant at Nova Scotia represented scale-based expansion in an existing field rather than forward integration, and that such a path would make Stora Kopparberg even more exposed to (pulp) market fluctuations. He also questioned whether there was enough demand for the produced pulp, and whether the Canadian timber qualities actually fitted the planned production. However, his main worry for the project concerned how it would be financed.

CEO Abenius, who supported the Nova Scotia investment, clarified most issues that were linked to its operative flow, but he admitted that the financing of the project was a major problem. Still, Marcus Wallenberg Sr claimed that at least four operative circumstances supported the planned investment. It would make Stora Kopparberg the first European forest-based company that could exploit the benefits of a cross-Atlantic effort, provide the company with a unique opportunity to buy a large forest area on the North American continent that contained suitable pulpwood, make it possible for Stora Kopparberg to utilize its superior large-scale technology and offer the company an excellent location for a new mill.

The Wallenberg brothers' differing opinions regarding the planned Nova Scotia investment even resulted in an emotionally flavoured clash, but they calmed down and agreed to provide the CEO with a right to buy the necessary property. That was a crucial step towards actually investing in a sulphite unit in Canada. However, the financing problem was still unsolved, and despite positive results from certain disinvestments, Stora Kopparberg had to seek partners for its Nova Scotia investment. Eventually Scott Paper decided to take a substantial minority position.

Thus, Stora Kopparberg's internationalization of its forest-related business went from merely being based on sales agents/companies to including production far abroad. Still, that new strategic path did not focus on forward integration like that of most of its Nordic competitors. Instead, it represented further concentration on a well-known segment of the value chain (the pulp one). Still, the Nova Scotia unit ran into many problems, including unexpected legal expenses, unfavourable currency rates, personnel problems, technical deficiencies and weak demand. As a result, that investment soon became an economic catastrophe that seriously – and for a long time – circumscribed its mother company's strategic activities. To tackle the miserable situation at Nova Scotia, Stora Kopparberg considered both forward integration into fluting (for corrugated cardboard) and a 'more-of-the-same' path, that is to say, an expansion of the existing pulp plant. During that process Stora Kopparberg replaced its CEO Abenius with Erik Sundblad, an important change, as the CEOs usually were the 'locomotives' in Stora Kopparberg.

Once at the helm, Sundblad launched a consolidation strategy that included both restructuring and shutdowns. The separation of the organization into two main groupings (steel and forest-based operations) was his most important achievement in terms of restructuring. When that division was accomplished, he showed interest in broadening the company's forest-based repertoire, but the financial situation at the time did not allow that (most of the available investment capital was already allocated to the Nova Scotia site). Nevertheless, Sundblad brought about one notable partnership that later would be rather decisive for Stora Kopparberg's choice of strategic path – he convinced the big

German forest-based corporation Feldmühle that it ought to invest substantially (25%) in the Hylte unit (newsprint). He also built an important link to a Finnish company that produced LWC, a printing paper quality that Stora Kopparberg was eager to incorporate into its organization.

After lots of investigations and lengthy discussions, Stora Kopparberg's board decided that the best path forward was to make further investments at its Nova Scotia unit, which included expansion of its pulp production as well as forward integration into newsprint (a segment Stora Kopparberg already mastered). However, those new investments did not solve the problems with the Canadian unit, and at least until the early 1970s, the CEO felt obliged to inform the Chair that the unit had developed less well than he had expected. The cash flow and the net result were (still) negative, but the operating profits had begun to improve.

Until the mid-1970s, the Wallenberg sphere was incapable of effectively co-ordinating its holdings of forest-based companies. The two brothers' view on that topic continued to differ – Marcus Wallenberg Sr favoured integration, while Jacob Wallenberg Sr wavered. Thus, for the time being, Marcus Wallenberg Sr – from his position as Papyrus Chair (since 1959) – had to limit his restructuring efforts to 'his' part of the sphere's forest-based companies (i.e. Kopparfors, Papyrus, Nymölla and Hylte). His initiative led to the establishment of a modern pulp mill at Nymölla (1960), which was expected to supply much of Papyrus's fine paper production. Nymölla was also built to lower Papyrus's dependence on timber from local farmers (particularly as they planned to build their own pulp plant). In addition, the new pulp mill would make it possible to meet the rising demand from continental Europe that followed from the lowering/removal of many trade barriers (cf. the establishment of EEC and EFTA). Thus, the Nymölla investment had both defensive and offensive motives, and it represented backward integration as well as scale-based expansion. However, it did not embody the most typical path tried by most competitors – forward integration. Despite all its potential qualities, Nymölla was unsuccessful, particularly because it used an untested, innovative technique that for several years simply did not work.

It was not until the late 1960s when Nymölla had become a stable part of the expanding Papyrus that the owner considered various paths for the rather worn-down Hylte site. Marcus Wallenberg Sr then decided that it should become the biggest newsprint unit in Europe, but such a sizeable forward integration was so financially risky that Jacob Wallenberg Sr opposed it, which made it impossible for the family's own holding companies Investor and Providentia to meet the financing requirements. However, since Marcus Wallenberg Sr soon found other sources, the investment was made (and became a success). At that time, Hylte was transformed from a classic division (i.e. a unit without its own balance sheet) to a subsidiary (although without its own forests and power plants) – a construct that made it easier for Feldmühle to enter as co-financer.

In the late 1970s Stora Kopparberg broke up its combination of steel and forest-based businesses, although, once again, the two brothers' opinions differed. Jacob Wallenberg Sr did not support the divestment of steel, but in a complicated process Marcus Wallenberg Sr finally forced through that change. The end result was a new steel company named Swedish Steel (SSAB) that the Swedish state founded and owned together with Stora Kopparberg and Grängesberg. Not long after (1981), Stora Kopparberg managed to withdraw from that consortium.

At that time Stora Kopparberg's leading actors also began to discuss various ways to expand the company's forest-based operations. They focused particularly on the possibilities of making further efforts in the printing paper field – that is to say, how to expand in wood-containing papers and journal papers – as well as on how the company could become a producer and seller of LWC. Thus, soon after its big steel disinvestment, Stora Kopparberg announced a new – forest-based – strategy, which implied that three core businesses should be operated and developed, namely pulp, fine paper and printing paper.

In the 1970s certain old regulations still determined many of the conditions for Stora Kopparberg's strategic development. The cartels were still going strong in the pulp and newsprint businesses, but were no longer legal. As such, intense discussions were held about how to relate to such illicit organizing. For corporations like Stora Kopparberg, which ran large, modern plants, cartels were actually a hindrance, as such arrangements favoured the smaller competitors with their often undersized and rather obsolete machines. However, the cartel arrangements lowered the investment risk for everyone, including major corporations like Stora Kopparberg. There also existed another most informal regulating 'institution', namely the Finnish consultancy firm Jakko Pöyry, which had captured a very strong global position in technical consulting, engineering and project management for the forest-based industry. Thus, when a particular investment was considered, it was often possible for an investing company to 'calibrate' that idea in light of the total running and planned capacities that existed around the world by checking with Jakko Pöyry. In that situation Stora Kopparberg had to choose between, on the one hand, pursuing its own path based on its quite unique resources and capacities and, on the other hand, accepting a path that to a large extent was determined by external actors, that is to say, by the cartels or by certain competitors' activities. Eventually Stora Kopparberg's owners decided that the company should go its own way and continuously work against all anti-competitive arrangements.

In 1981, Marcus Wallenberg Sr used two sphere-controlled corporations, Stora Kopparberg and Billerud, to try to capture control of Iggesund. Such a purchase was certainly not a first priority for Stora Kopparberg, but it suited Billerud rather well. Furthermore, a takeover would prevent both its rival sphere (Handelsbanken/Industrivärden) and either of two of its associated companies (MoDo and SCA) from acquiring Iggesund. Importantly, Iggesund's leading executives did not appreciate Stora Kopparberg's and Billerud's (hostile) bid – if they had to choose, they clearly preferred the competing bidder MoDo. In the end the Wallenberg sphere lost the Iggesund contest and sold its holdings to the winner MoDo. That defeat kept Stora Kopparberg off the quality cardboard path for some time. In any case, that lost opportunity was actually not a major problem, as the board had decided already a few years earlier to make wood-containing paper its third core activity (together with pulp and fine paper).

After the Iggesund failure CEO Erik Sundblad continued Stora Kopparberg's efforts to expand into new fields to reduce what he saw as a too high dependency on a few segments of the forest-based industry. He saw the hygiene business as the only expanding sector that still had room for new large efforts on the Nordic market (outside those countries, four US corporations dominated the scene). However, to get a substantial market share acquisitions had to be made urgently, and the remaining targets were few and decreasing in number. For the pulp business CEO Sundblad regarded purchases of minority holdings on the European continent as the best possible path forward. Building up a fine paper business in North America might be possible, but such a path, too, required acquisitions. At the time, Stora Kopparberg also showed interest in buying Esselte, which would both add another potential core business – special papers – and simplify future internationalization efforts. For the latter reason, Swedish Match was analysed as well (1980), but Marcus Wallenberg Sr rejected the idea of a deal.

In the early 1980s Stora Kopparberg still treated fine paper as one of its core businesses. CEO Erik Sundblad explored several growth possibilities in that field, but nothing concrete materialized. Generally, the early part of the 1980s was characterized by faltering attempts by the CEO to find the way forward for a corporation that had been stripped of one of its two core businesses (steel) and been forced to fully concentrate its activities on forest-related operations.

In the early 1980s radical changes occurred in the Wallenberg owner sphere, which controlled among others Stora Kopparberg, with extensive strategic consequences. Both Jacob Wallenberg Sr and Marcus Wallenberg Sr passed away, and for a while a situation of uncertainty prevailed regarding the sphere's leadership. The uncertainty emerged because Jacob Wallenberg Sr lacked children, and because Marcus Wallenberg Sr had lost his eldest son Marc, who was supposed to succeed him. His second son Peter stood next in line, but his father had not considered him as capable of governing the sphere. In order to fill that successor 'gap', Marcus Wallenberg Sr informally and secretly contacted a leading non-sphere actor – Gyllenhammar, the CEO of Volvo – and suggested to him that he take up one of the leading roles in the sphere. One of the consequences of those talks was that Volvo entered as a large shareholder in Stora Kopparberg, and its Chair Gyllenhammar became one of its more influential board members.

Peter Wallenberg certainly did not appreciate Volvo's shareholding and Gyllenhammar's presence in the two companies within his family's sphere, so soon a power struggle emerged between him (and his associates) and Gyllenhammar (and his supporters) concerning how those two corporations should be governed – and by whom. The conflict also produced a battle for the position as Chair of the sphere's bank (however, in the end neither of them was appointed). Some two years after the struggle between the two tycoons began, it was finally settled, and Gyllenhammar (and Volvo) left Stora Kopparberg and Atlas Copco. When that tough period was over in 1984, Peter Wallenberg (the controlling owner), Dahlbäck (CEO of Wallenberg's holding company Investor) and Berggren (new CEO of Stora Kopparberg) could return to their 'constitutional roles', that is to say, govern the sphere and its corporations, and, for example, decide on Stora Kopparberg's future path.

16.4.2 Uniting the Sphere

Once established, Stora Kopparberg's new leadership troika (Peter Wallenberg, Dahlbäck and Berggren) began to explore in what ways the corporation ought to develop. In the mid-1980s it was too small to act as the leading player and to depend on standardized bulk products. In general, the emerging strategy tended to stress market and customer perspectives at the expense of the production ones that had dominated during the cartel era. Thus, the first question the troika addressed was whether it would be possible for Stora Kopparberg to customize its pulp; the outcome of that analysis was not too encouraging. When attention moved to those areas where a customer perspective seemed to fit better, fine paper came into focus. CEO Berggren suggested a non-cash acquisition of Papyrus (i.e. a restructuring inside the Wallenberg sphere) implying that Nymölla would get certain of Papyrus's units and continue as a listed unit under the name of Papyrus(!). Peter Wallenberg was not yet convinced, so the idea was not pursued at that time. But CEO Berggren had other – and even bigger – plans for Stora Kopparberg. He wanted to see it acquire not only Papyrus but also Billerud and Swedish Match (in that order). Yet, many leading actors in Stora Kopparberg were sceptical of such audacious expansion ideas because they believed that the company above all needed to divest, as it was composed of too many small units that often were weakly related.

One thing that influenced Stora Kopparberg's development at that time was an unexpected proposal from a Swedish financier (Wall), who together with his partners was interested in selling their majority holding in Billerud – a company that Iggesund had tried to buy in 1980 (Billerud – together with Stora Kopparberg – had then tried to take over Iggesund in 1981). Wall made his sudden offer during an accidental meeting with Peter Wallenberg in 1984. Papyrus had actually tried to buy Billerud earlier the same year, but at that time Billerud's CEO showed no interest at all in such a transaction, despite its obvious attractiveness. The synergies between Billerud and Stora Kopparberg were not expected to be high, making it difficult to justify a purchase on 'rational' business grounds. However, the deal would provide a strong European presence, a recognized R&D unit, a solution for part of Stora Kopparberg's timber-sourcing problem (add eucalyptus), a both sizeable and more international pulp business and at least one promising new development path (cardboard). Nevertheless, Stora Kopparberg's purchase of Billerud was basically seen as an opportunistic move rather than the outcome of a well-thought-out strategic plan.

It became quickly clear that the Billerud deal was an economic success. It moved Stora Kopparberg slightly to the right in the value chain, although that change never was mentioned as a motive for the purchase. However, the acquisition of Billerud also made Stora Kopparberg's pulp-based operative repertoire even more sprawling with quite a few businesses: newsprint, magazine paper, coated fine paper, LPB, packaging paper, fluting and sack paper. That large variety indicated that the company very soon needed to determine its core businesses and lay down a long-term path.

The other large investments made at that time signalled that Stora Kopparberg still prioritized both newsprint and fine paper, but the acquisition of Billerud made it a bit more uncertain whether those two paths would be the only ones in the future. The purchase coincided with (triggered) the board's selection of a new name for the constellation: 'Stora'. Still, neither the change of name nor the large acquisitions/investments solved Stora's seemingly 'eternal' problems: lack of timber, high exposure to pulp and woodware and involvement in too many different businesses. In order to reduce the diversity problem, Stora eventually got out of sack paper, most industrial papers and some of its minor and/or unprofitable operations.

Once again Papyrus, the most preferred acquisition candidate, came into Stora's focus. About two years after Berggren first proposed such an initiative, Peter Wallenberg finally gave clearance for a merger. The move represented a significant step to the right on the value chain, as Papyrus (after having incorporated Nymölla and Ry) contained newsprint, fine paper and cardboard, the three businesses that Stora more and more began to treat as its core ones. The merger also brought forests and lowered the production of pulp for external sale.

Gradually, Stora's strategy began to unfold, and in 1987 CEO Berggren presented his plan for the company's development. The processed products were to be expanded radically and the strong fine paper position – as well as magazine paper and newsprint – were to be developed further. For packaging paper and cardboard the situation was more complicated, as some product lines – for example, fluting, white liner and LPB – showed healthy growth, while others – for example, sacks and boxboard – instead were on the decline. Outside the core activities, Stora still had problems with some of its timber sourcing, and its investment at Aracruz was too small to improve the situation (5%).

While Stora was occupied with the integration of its two large acquisitions Billerud (1984) and Papyrus (1986), it suddenly became necessary to seriously consider the third acquisition candidate that CEO Berggren had listed back in 1984: Swedish Match. That company was brought on the agenda much earlier than planned and not by those actors that necessarily applied a Stora perspective on things. Instead, it was the controlling owner – Peter Wallenberg – that had become worried about how one of the family's core holdings was governed. His unease concerned both the quality of Swedish Match's top management and the strategy the company was following. Initially, the Wallenberg group tried to solve Swedish Match's governance problem by appointing new board members and a new CEO. When those efforts failed to create change, the sphere decided to acquire the majority position and from that platform control its board. After several rounds the sphere's holding companies Investor and Providentia together reached more than 80 per cent[30] of the votes in Swedish Match (1988) and decided to sell their shares to Stora, which was thought to be a more suitable environment.

In essence, the acquisition of Swedish Match was carried out outside of Stora's board (except for the formal decision). That was not surprising, as its businesses did not fit Stora particularly well. Swedish Match included Tarkett (floor producer), Consumer Products (matches, etc.), Kitchen Products, Åkerlund & Rausing (packaging), Swedoor and Alby (chemicals). Obviously, the synergies with Stora were rather weak. Still, CEO Berggren argued for the purchase at Stora's board because it lowered the overall trade fluctuations, decreased the average need for capital and increased the capacity to compete globally. Moreover, Stora's woodware production fitted Swedish Match's Kitchen unit and Åkerlund & Rausing would become a major customer for Billerud. Yet the general impression among both external and internal actors was that the purchase of Swedish Match was made for the benefit of the Wallenberg sphere – not for Stora.

Thus, once again Stora's development path was difficult to decipher, as it housed many and various weakly related businesses. Most external actors therefore expected that Swedish Match would soon be split up and that most of its parts would be sold, leaving only a 'hub' unit that the sphere could utilize. To eliminate some of that uncertainty CEO Berggren tried to clarify Stora's strategy by confirming the rumours that indicated that several parts of Swedish Match were for sale (e.g. Consumer Products) and by explaining that Stora henceforth intended to be a 'two-legged' company containing a forest-based business (i.e. an industrial [large-scale], cyclical and capital-intensive one) and a building material business (i.e. an entrepreneurial, [almost] countercyclical one with low capital needs). Many parts of Swedish Match were indeed sold, and the 'rest-Match' that remained after those extensive disinvestments constituted a rather modest part of the 'new' Stora that still showed conglomerate features. Propitiously, the financial resources that Stora obtained from the sale of the former Swedish Match units significantly contributed to its rapid international expansion (cf. below).

16.4.3 Expanding Abroad

The deregulations and re-regulations in Western Europe in the 1980s radically changed the competitive situation for Stora, and consequently its strategy. The key issue was whether Sweden would apply for EC/EU membership, but the general view in the industry was that such a move would take place in the distant future. For forest-based corporations, it was a problem that Finland, where many of their competitors were based, was expected to apply earlier. Furthermore, the pressure on Stora to make large investments in Western Europe was not lowered when the European Commission presented 'a path towards a free European market' (1985). Given the new situation, Stora began to carry out its 'EU-ropeanization' by purchasing several Danish, French and Italian companies. It also listed potential acquisition objects inside the EC, for example, Burgo (Italy), Feldmühle (Germany; already partner in Hylte and Norrsundet), Haindl (Germany), KNP (Holland) and Wiggins Teape (UK). Stora contacted several of them, but got no positive responses. Most of them were seen as 'crown jewels' in their respective countries.

Stora also pursued a non-EC path and investigated the possibility of expanding its pulp business in South America and Asia, mainly because major parts of those two continents seemed to have a much better timber situation than did other continents. Stora already had a small holding in Brazil (5% of Aracruz) that could have been used as a platform for further expansion, but after a conflict with some of the other shareholders, the board instead decided to exit that investment. For its international short-fibre business Stora still relied very much on its Portuguese plant Celbi and hoped to expand there, although management continued to look for other global timber sources, particularly in Chile and Ireland. Stora actually already had a partner in Chile (Auraco) that owned a forest-based company (Pedro de Valdiva) that looked interesting, so eventually Stora bought 50 per cent of that unit.

Another source of raw material that gradually became more important was recycled paper, and Stora was eager to include that fibre source (particularly) in its production of printing papers. Several competitors on the continent already used that 'new' raw material, so the quickest way for Stora to learn how to produce (partly) waste paper based products was to acquire companies that already utilized such sourcing. To some extent that influenced Stora's search for acquisitions, though still prioritizing expansion of its presence in Europe (i.e. in the EC). Thus, new potential target companies were added to the list, with Kymmene (LWC, Finland), Chapelle-Darblay (France) and Soporcell (Portugal) thoroughly analysed, but nothing came of these efforts.

Stora carefully examined the bigger Swedish forest-based corporations for targets, but most of them did not fit with Stora's current 'European' strategy (AssiDomän [unsuitable products], MoDo [not for sale], Ncb [bad shape], SCA [too diversified] and Södra [backward integration]). Korsnäs, however, was approached because certain of its businesses corresponded well with those of Stora, and because it was important that the company did not land with a competitor. Initially, Stora acquired 15 per cent of Korsnäs from another Wallenberg company, but, since the leading actor of Korsnäs's owner family

(Jan Stenbeck) was not particularly fond of the Wallenberg dynasty, he kept his shares. To buy Finnish corporations was not even considered, as it was regarded to be too difficult to make acquisitions in that country. By the end of the 1980s, many alternative paths had been studied, which illustrated that Stora still was groping its way ahead.

All other acquisition ideas were mothballed when an opportunity suddenly emerged to buy the West German corporation Feldmühle Nobel which, inter alia, contained Stora's actual target unit Feldmühle (Europe's biggest forest-based company). The major owner of Feldmühle Nobel, the Flick family, had offered Stora a 30 per cent share in that holding company. Yet because of the complexity of the company's rather diversified business portfolio, time pressure and incomplete information led Stora to reject that proposal. Instead a unit named VEBA bought that Feldmühle Nobel holding and increased it to a majority one (51%). But, as the Flick family had a repurchase option for 38.5 per cent of the shares and still controlled another 30 per cent,[31] no radical changes of ownership had actually taken place. Thus, Stora's controlling owners were not surprised when, a year later, they were again offered another substantial holding in Feldmühle Nobel – 5 per cent with an option to buy an additional 20 per cent. When Stora's executives met with Feldmühle's top managers to discuss the offered shareholding, however, it became obvious that they opposed a deal because in their eyes it threatened the autonomy of their company. So, Stora stated that it respected that position as long as no one else tried to buy a substantial holding in Feldmühle Nobel. That meant that Stora was back to square one both regarding its EC strategy and with respect to its more general development plan.

It was no coincidence that Flick's offer was made to a family company like Stora. In the late 20th century most corporations around the world were run by that kind of owner, and Europe was certainly not an exception. Moreover, owners of family firms tended to prefer selling their 'heirlooms' to corporations with a similar kind of ownership, as that was supposed to 'guarantee' that their lifework would be taken care of both seriously and for a long time. It was actually also rather common that families that owned large corporations knew each other and even met regularly at various business gatherings, events or festivities. Flick approached Stora (Wallenberg) for both reasons, namely because it was a well-reputed family firm and because Marcus Wallenberg Sr and the Flick family had socialized since the 1950s. That long-standing relationship between the two families had already been converted into action about a decade earlier in Feldmühle's and Stora's joint operations at Hylte (newsprint) and Norrsundet (pulp).

Stora's leading actors saw Feldmühle as the perfect acquisition. It was the largest paper manufacturer in the EC, and its product mix fit Stora quite well (Feldmühle was particularly strong in LWC and journal papers, although it housed packaging paper, fine paper and tissue as well). As such, Feldmühle and Stora did not compete – instead, several complementarities existed, for example, regarding pulp (Stora net sold and Feldmühle net bought). Feldmühle also fulfilled Stora's desire to establish a long-term course by providing a large and stable platform for international expansion right in the heart of the EC (West Germany). However, there was a catch – a takeover would require permission from the West German authorities.

The period of strategic ambiguity that followed the pause in the Flick–Wallenberg discussions did not last long, as Stora's rival SCA suddenly bought a 5 per cent holding in Feldmühle Nobel, and Scott Paper (US), too, showed interest in investing in that company. Those new occurrences seriously threatened Stora's ambition to pursue its European/global printing paper strategy and complicated its joint operations with Feldmühle at Hylte and Norrsundet. CEO Berggren informed VEBA and Feldmühle Nobel that it opposed SCA's entrance as owner. Stora immediately won support from the executives in Feldmühle Nobel, and this time the issue was not whether the holding company would get a new large owner, but which one of the three contenders would win the race.

After several rounds Stora won the contest and bought Feldmühle Nobel, and that sizeable purchase determined much of Stora's business set-up, strategy and path for the coming years. It made Stora a weighty global actor in four business areas: pulp (large producer), printing papers (leading position), fine paper (large producer) and cardboard (doubled capacity). Although most operations looked fine, the big question was how to finance the purchase. Since large disinvestments were necessary, Stora sold several parts of Feldmühle Nobel (those unrelated to its forest-based business). Due to actions taken by the latter company's internal board ('Vorstand'), that divestment was restricted both regarding buyers (one was allowed: Metallgesellschaft) and form (had to be sold in one piece). Thus, the total revenues from those sales turned out to be much lower than Stora had expected.

After the Feldmühle Nobel acquisition, and when most non-forest-based businesses were divested (1991), Stora 'finally' became what it had been striving for in the late 1980s, namely a rather sizeable forest-based company based on large-scale operations in four core businesses: pulp, printing papers, fine paper and cardboard. At that point Stora began to review all its strengths and weaknesses across the chosen core businesses and found several weak points: an underdeveloped R&D operation, a lack of technical excellence and an insufficient marketing and sales organization. Particularly the last two points were crucial for a scale-based corporation like Stora. However, the most serious problem of them all – financing – was to a large extent 'solved' by an outside force, namely the Swedish government, which unexpectedly let the Swedish currency float. That move made Stora's domestic business much more competitive in the global market for most of the coming decade.

16.4.4 Consolidation Period

Stora's governance arrangement changed radically in 1992 when Peter Wallenberg had to step down as Chair for a few years because of failing health. CEO Berggren replaced him as Chair, and Helgesson was appointed CEO. However, Berggren continued to act as 'Group CEO'.[32] Though such a position did not exist in Swedish company law, many corporations used that arrangement to make room for both a formal CEO and an informal Group CEO. Its use in Stora made clear that Chair and Group CEO Berggren intended to carry on as an active strategist and that CEO Helgesson was primarily expected to devote his time to operative matters. CEO Helgesson was not entirely happy with that arrangement as he, too, aspired to be a major strategic actor in accordance with the classic Swedish governance tradition. So, from the very beginning the linkages between the controlling shareholders and the two executive levels faced an inherent conflict. That solution gradually undermined CEO Helgesson's internal authority, as his decisions and directives were not always seen as the final ones by several of Stora's leading managers. His decision to exclusively use corporate staff for his GMT further weakened his position vis-à-vis the leading operative managers.

Berggren was also appointed to be one of two deputy chairs in Investor, the investment company that controlled Stora. At that time Peter Wallenberg's eldest son Jacob Wallenberg Jr entered the scene and broadened 'the governing troika',[33] making clear that the family intended to stay in control. Stora's respected Deputy CEO Pettersson was included, too, creating what almost looked like a quintet. Essentially, Chair Berggren continued to govern Stora, although more and more from his Investor platform. That owner–executive arrangement certainly was not to CEO Helgesson's advantage when he launched a consolidation strategy to try to get Stora in order. Its implementation was not easy, as its content was controversial both inside Stora and at the Investor level.

Since many of Stora's products were difficult to differentiate both marketwise and technically, most of the profits had to come from cost-efficient production. Therefore, Helgesson stressed the need to establish effective operative flows, which in turn – because of all the recent acquisitions – required substantial rationalizations and restructurings. Other circumstances, too, contributed to that conclusion: the overcapacity in the forest-based industry, the effects of deregulation, the recession-like times, the dissolved cartels, the establishment of non-European competitors on the European market and the currency exchange rates that had turned unfavourable. However, perhaps the most decisive factor behind the CEO's effort to consolidate was the financial stress created by the large acquisitions starting with Billerud in 1984, which had squeezed Stora's finances almost to the limit. CEO Helgesson tried to improve Stora's financial standing further by deconsolidating Kopparkraft and by selling the holdings in Forestal Valdiva and Ireland. He also sought to depreciate certain assets, but the Chair did not allow it. Also sold were assets or units that lay outside the forest-based industry, as well as several of the ones linked to the core businesses. Several capacity reductions rounded out the strategy to resolve the financial problem.

Not only were finances strained, but Stora's operational stress had also increased during the second half of the 1980s, when quite a few new units and businesses had been acquired. Thus, both the scale advantages and the synergy effects from those extensive efforts needed to be captured. The effort turned out to be rather difficult, as the internal support for one of the two main elements of the CEO's consolidation strategy was rather weak. The first element – the rationalization programme – certainly paid off. Stora's productivity improved, as did the quality of its products, and its net debt was halved. However, the CEO's attempt to implement the second element – the restructuring programme – met resistance. His idea was to centralize Stora's decision-making by breaking up the rather autonomous 'sub-companies' and instead building a structure based on the businesses as such. Opposition emerged not only from the heads of certain of the operative units (cf. the acquired companies), but also from the Chair, who preferred a more decentralized approach. Despite the resistance, CEO Helgesson managed to enforce a new formal organization that was founded on his vision. Thus, Stora's different businesses – not the acquired companies as such – constituted the basic structure for his continued managing efforts.

To add to the challenges, CEO Helgesson inherited the Nova Scotia problem (large losses). The board considered two alternatives for that site: to concentrate on SC paper production or closure. The concentration alternative involved a sizeable investment, which in itself was not a problem, as it was consistent with Stora's current printing paper strategy. Obviously, there were both pros and cons involved in such an effort, but as one of Stora's goals was to act on the North American market, the cons would have to greatly outnumber the pros for Stora to abandon the goal.

At that time several institutional conditions changed that significantly influenced Stora's path ahead. For example, the signing of the GATT treaty eliminated most of the customs fees for the majority of paper products. This, together with the abolition of cartels, meant that Stora's (and all other large players') core businesses had to be globally competitive. So, once again Stora had to reconsider its long-term strategy and development path. It could either try to grow substantially and become a truly global actor, or continue as a regional (i.e. European) player. A global ambition required a completely different company size, so if Stora decided to take that path, it would have to find a large partner.

16.4.5 Trying to become a Global Player

Stora was ready to expand again after a few years of consolidation. The new ambition to compete on the global scene brought up the 'eternal issue' regarding how many core businesses the company could house and still be competitive. The answer to that key question was discussed in relation to what size Stora would need to reach to be able to reduce the extensive operative risks, as well as in relation to what financial resources Stora would need to support that growth. When most of the consolidation process was completed in the mid-1990s, the CEO organized a systematic listing and analysis of possible acquisition candidates. Haindl (printing papers) was the preferred target, but the price was regarded as too high. Stora also explored Papeterie de Condat (fine paper and packaging), but it was turned down for the same reason: the high price. A third analysed target was S.D. Warren (fine papers), but eventually its product mix was considered to be less attractive. Thus, initially Stora faced great difficulties in realizing its grand plan to become a global player.

Once again Stora reconsidered its strategy, and this time (1995) two of its core businesses were given priority: graphic papers (particularly journal paper) and quality cardboard. For journal papers Stora intended to stay as number three in the world and for cardboard to be among the top ten (with an edge in LPB). That meant that newsprint and fine paper were given lower priority. The first two areas were growing, and to a large extent were based on Nordic raw material (long fibres), while demand for the last two products was more uncertain, and the raw material sourcing less favourable. Stora's recent investments in LPB (Skoghall) and journal paper (Nova Scotia) fitted its revised strategy quite well. In order to expand its fine paper operations, Stora instead sought a partner and contacted MoDo, Norske Skog and SCA. Nothing came out of those discussions, mainly because of lack of mutual confidence between the leading actors. However, those negative outcomes were not particularly surprising, as 'everybody' wanted to get out of that business, preferably by creating new, jointly owned – but independent – fine paper companies.

For Stora, the timber sourcing continued to be a strategic problem that involved both its access to waste paper (recycled fibres) and how to arrange for a steady flow of short fibres. Chair Berggren was convinced that forest owning in itself was essential, and then both the tree species and their locations mattered. Towards that end, Stora bought cutting rights in Russia and started timber-buying units in Estonia to source its Swedish production units. For its global needs Stora established a task force that was expected to find out where it would be best to establish a pulp plant that would produce raw material for newsprint and magazine paper for further processing in Southeast Asia.

For some time Stora wavered between Asia and South America, but after careful investigations it chose South America (Brazil) over Asia (Indonesia), principally because corruption was too widespread in many parts of Asia (particularly in Indonesia). Furthermore, Stora preferred Brazil to Chile, because its reputation was spoiled in Chile as a consequence of its previous unexpected and unappreciated exit from that market. As so often, the choice of Brazil was coincidental – it could as well have been, for example, Argentina or Uruguay. However, Stora's Head of Forestry Hägglund happened to come across the Veracruz project, a Brazilian effort that seemed to fit well with what he and his task force were seeking, so Stora decided to go ahead there. Thus, once again, Stora was faced with a major project that required large-scale financing.

The Wallenberg family was enthusiastic about the business potential for Stora in China and India, which represented two 'gigantic' markets for future expansion that simultaneously could moderate the company's total operative risk. Stora also had an advantage over the other non-Asian corporations, as its controlling owner, the Wallenberg family, had built close relationships since WWII with important actors in those markets, particularly in China. Eventually Stora managed to buy the majority of the Souzho Paper Mill (fine paper). That acquisition demonstrated that Stora's new global strategy – the combined South American–Asian path – actually worked, and that the company finally had become a truly global corporation. The obvious merits of the new path towards South America and Asia slightly modified Stora's strategy, as it contributed to a relative downgrading of the North American market, which began to lose its special status. The Brazilian and Chinese investments also influenced Stora's strategy in another way: they contributed to a comeback for fine paper based on short fibres. Another reason for keeping – and expanding – the fine paper operations was that Stora's 'corporate body' otherwise would be too small. Thus, the exclusive focus on long fibres was abandoned.

In the meantime, Stora continued to implement its 'old' strategy and expanded its two other core businesses, that is to say, packaging (LPB and quality cardboard) and printing papers (journal and magazine papers). For the packaging business Enso-Gutzeit was the best merger candidate, but its ownership setting at the time made such an action close to impossible (it was owned by the Finnish state with a restriction regarding the minimum size of its holding). For printing papers Kymmene was the most obvious merger candidate, and as its controlling owners – the Ehrnrooth family – had a good relationship with Stora's key owners the Wallenberg family, the dialogue between the two companies' executive actors went smoothly. The major Swedish owner (Investor, represented by CEO Dahlbäck) and Stora's Chair Berggren supported the idea, but Stora's top managers (including CEO Helgesson) were hesitant because they felt that yet another merger could create excessive strain in a situation where the integration of the other recently acquired companies – particularly Feldmühle – continued to absorb significant energy and resources. Despite these concerns, an investigation was conducted as to what synergies could be expected from such a merger. To most actors' surprise a combined Kymmene–Stora would bring only minor operational improvements because both companies were already well managed and 'fully' rationalized. So, at least for some time, Stora's expansion of printing paper was put on hold.

Two years later Stora once again contacted Kymmene, which in the meantime had merged with UPM and formed UPM-Kymmene. Again, nothing concrete came out of those discussions for several reasons: the newly merged Finnish company was fully occupied with its internal integration processes, some of UPM-Kymmene's larger shareholders did not support its director Ehrnrooth (who was one of the initiators and biggest supporters of the merger idea) and most of the merger was expected to be stopped by the ECN (fine paper would probably have been the only business for which that authority would accept a merger, and both companies actually wanted to leave that market).

In its continued search to find a way to realize its 'two-core' strategy, Stora contacted Dutch KNP, which was a possible acquisition candidate because of its large fine paper operations. However, the contacts with KNP indicated that the company was not in the very best shape, and that conclusion – together with the fact that many of Stora's leading actors instead preferred expansions in printing papers and cardboard – decided the matter, despite CEO Helgesson's view that fine paper also in the future could be a core business. The disagreement regarding Stora's strategy aroused the long-smouldering conflict between the Chair (Berggren) and the CEO (Helgesson), making the current governance arrangement untenable. The solution was to replace Helgesson as CEO with Hägglund, the Head of Stora Forestry. Hägglund then took up the helm of a corporation that only just had begun its journey towards becoming a truly global corporation with a focus on printing papers and cardboard markets.

Eventually, however, even Chair Berggren's position in Stora was threatened, but not because of any disagreements about Stora's current and future strategy. Instead, Berggren became involved in a power struggle with ABB's CEO Barnevik regarding the Chair position in the Wallenberg sphere's investment company Investor. To the surprise of many, neither the Wallenberg family nor Dahlbäck (Investor's CEO), his partner for many years, supported him publicly after he had misinformed the general public about how Stora's former CEO Helgesson was separated from his position. The Wallenberg sphere's passivity was surprising considering the long years of dutiful service Berggren had contributed within that constellation. Barnevik – at that time regarded as an international executive superstar – won the fight with Berggren, with the result that Berggren had to leave all his sphere positions (including that as Stora Chair).

One consequence of the simultaneous changes in the two top executive positions was that the recently installed CEO announced a revised strategy for Stora. It envisioned both consolidation, that is to say, a goal to make the European plants more effective (and divest some units), and expansion, that is to say, an aim to develop the growing engagements in Brazil and China. Stora would also continue to seek ways to realize its overriding goal of becoming a large influential global player in selected segments of the forest-based industry. At the time, however, there were not that many really attractive partnership alternatives remaining, but as so often during the 20th century, SCA emerged as one of those rather few alternatives. Such a merger was expected to provide substantial synergies, particularly in Stora's core areas of printing papers and packaging. Despite the perceived advantages, the ownership setting was an insurmountable obstacle, as SCA (Handelsbanken/Industrivärden) and Stora (Wallenberg) belonged to different spheres that had been rivals for more than half a century. Stora also analysed several other European candidates, for example, Norske Skog (Norway), Burgo (Italy), Haindl (Germany) and Mayr-Melnhof (Austria), but – as so often in those days – nothing materialized.

16.4.6 Stora Enso

In 1996 when the Finnish state had begun to look for a partner for Enso-Gutzeit, an investment bank contacted Stora about that possibility. Although nothing happened that year, a seed was planted. The next year Berggren, still Stora's Chair at the time, took up the idea again and began to discuss it inside his own company. Enso-Gutzeit fitted Stora's globalization strategy well – the obstacle remained its ownership setting. Berggren contacted Enso-Gutzeit's CEO Härmälä anyway, and analyses were made to describe and quantify the possible benefits of a merger. Initially, both Enso-Gutzeit's major owner (the state, 80%) and its board opposed the idea, but Stora's interest grew for a joint Finnish–Swedish solution when it became clear that the Finnish state might consider removing its ownership restriction (a high minimum holding). The Wallenberg family's reputation as a responsible, long-term shareholder impressed those attending a hearing in the Finnish Parliament, so much so that the parliament agreed to unlock the ownership setting provided that Enso-Gutzeit's current CEO was appointed to the same position in the new constellation.

Initially, the newly dubbed Stora Enso got a rather 'Finnish' touch, since not only the CEO but also most of the top management came from Enso-Gutzeit. The reason for that was simply that Stora had lost talent when first CEO Helgesson and somewhat later Berggren had to leave and other Stora managers – among them several 'up-and-coming' men – resigned as a result. Particularly Berggren (but also Helgesson) had an almost unique 14-years-long experience as Stora's leader both as Chair (1992–98) and as CEO (1984–92) that could have been used in the new constellation (which actually was very much a result of his own efforts). Berggren's successor Dahlbäck, who became Chair of Stora Enso in 1998, had much less operative experience. He was first and foremost a financial strategist, who had worked close to Berggren for many years.

Hägglund officially began as CEO for Stora in March 1998, but that appointment only lasted a very short period. He had been informed about his forthcoming promotion to CEO in autumn 1997, that is to say, before the decision was made public in December. However, when he was told informally that he was to be promoted, he was not informed about the on-going discussions with Enso-Gutzeit regarding a possible merger (neither was Deputy CEO Petersson). It was Berggren that conducted the talks with Enso-Gutzeit's CEO Härmälä, although Berggren's sudden dismissal forced his 'partner' Dahlbäck (CEO of Investor) to take over and finish the negotiations. When the merger between Stora and Enso was carried out in autumn 1998, it was decided – actually stipulated by the Finnish owner – that Enso-Gutzeit's CEO should become the new constellation's CEO. Hägglund then agreed to become Stora Enso's Deputy CEO, a decision that contributed to the smooth running of the merger process. Thus, Stora merged with Enso-Gutzeit late in 1998, once the EU had approved the merger. Thus, at last, Stora had become the large global player it had strived to be for almost a decade. At that time the new constellation Stora Enso actually qualified as the largest forest-based company in the world.

16.4.7 From Stora Kopparberg to Stora Enso: Some Tentative Conclusions

Based on an analysis of Stora's strategic paths, it can be said that nature-driven occurrences had little influence on the process by which Stora Kopparberg became Stora Enso over time. Externally generated man-made occurrences, however, played a rather important role for Stora Kopparberg, particularly those that were generated by its competitors. Two control fights stand out as by far the most dramatic occurrences that influenced Stora (Kopparberg). The first of the two was actually produced by Stora Kopparberg itself, when it made a sudden hostile takeover bid for Iggesund. That bid was in turn triggered by the actions of the leading actor of a rival company (MoDo), who rather unexpectedly had begun to buy Iggesund shares. The second of those two cases hit Stora when SCA all of a sudden made attempts to take a position in Feldmühle Nobel. Both these man-made occurrences had decisive consequences for Stora's long-term development. In the former case the quality cardboard path was shut (at least for some time), and in the latter case Stora was 'forced' to buy a company in a situation that it did not fully control, which led to a rather high price and difficulties with the financing. The purchase of Feldmühle Nobel also determined Stora's path for quite a long time by making other large acquisitions financially impossible.

Another force that played an important role in Stora Kopparberg's development was its access to certain natural resources – especially forests (i.e. timber), but also power plants. Its search for new forest resources continued – almost accelerated – after WWII, partly because of the advantages of scale that new technological solutions offered, and partly because of the steadily rising European demand for forest-based products. So, during most of the 20th century Stora Kopparberg was looking for new forest resources, and gradually it widened its search area such that it finally covered almost all continents.

The first really big foreign investment in forest resources was made in Canada (Nova Scotia) in the 1950s with the intention of establishing pulp production. In addition to purchases inside Sweden, Stora also sought the possibility of getting timber from its neighbours, ultimately establishing opportunities in, for example, Russia (cutting rights) and Estonia (timber-buying units). It even made an (unsuccessful) attempt to invest in Ireland. However, the most important effort to solve the sourcing problem was made in South America, as those forests offered cheap timber that was competitive even when transportation costs to other continents were added. Stora Kopparberg's ambition to expand its pulp business on that continent was visionary, although it had to give up its earliest investment in Brazil (Aracruz, 5%).

Eventually Stora Kopparberg returned to the South American continent and invested in Chile together with a highly reputable domestic partner (Auraco) that owned a forest-based company (Pedro de Valdiva). However, the financial strain that followed from the purchase of Feldmühle Nobel forced Stora Kopparberg to leave that partnership, an awkward exit that spoiled its possibility of returning to that market. The fact that Stora Kopparberg somewhat later established a special task force with the assignment to look around the globe to find the best location for (forestry and) pulp production demonstrated how important it was for the company to secure its raw material sourcing. Again South America was preferred (that time to Indonesia), but because Chile was no longer an option, Argentina, Brazil and Uruguay came into focus. In the end, Stora Kopparberg decided to invest in a gigantic project in Brazil (Veracruz), which solved a substantial part of the timber and pulp-sourcing problem for the coming decades. As so often happens, that choice of path evolved from a combination of an articulated plan (the task force was well prepared and knew what it was looking for) and coincidence (the sudden 'appearance' of the Veracruz project).

Perhaps the most significant occurrence during the second half of the 20th century was that it became possible to use waste paper in production instead of – or as a complement to – pulpwood/timber. In the beginning, waste paper was used mainly in brown papers, but gradually the technique improved so that it could be used at least as an ingredient in most kinds of papers including, for example, some qualities of fine paper. That meant that 'forests' also began to 'grow' in the cities and not just in the woods, a development that certainly influenced Stora's production arrangements in many ways (location, technology, product mix, etc.). That gradual change of input material (from fresh to waste fibres) affected Stora in two ways: It had to adapt several of its production units to that new sourcing situation, and it had to put more focus on products where fresh (long-fibre) timber still was competitive.

So, both the availability of natural resources (including waste paper) and the repercussions from external man-made occurrences clearly influenced Stora Kopparberg's strategic development. However, collective actorhood manifested as regulating institutions also greatly affected how that path evolved. One such institution that had a significant impact on Stora's way ahead was the Canadian government. Stora's investment in Nova Scotia would not have occurred without certain guarantees and permissions from the state. That huge effort – with all its problems – effectively blocked the possibility of seriously exploring alternative paths. Another institution that had an effect on Stora Kopparberg's strategy was the cartel. Several such informal (sometimes illegal) organizing arrangements around the world regulated prices and volumes on most of the submarkets for forest-based products, and that 'invisible' organizing substantially reduced classic market competition. Those non-state 'regulations' (re)produced rather stable product and sales conditions over time, which reduced the need for strategic initiatives and reorientations. To get rid of that locked situation, Stora decided to contact the European authorities, so that they could put a stop to those anti-competitive networks.

Regulations established by the ECSC,[34] EC and EFTA – and later the EU – influenced Stora's development path as well. In the 1980s Sweden was neither a member of the EC nor acting to become a member of its upcoming 'successor' the EU, but even more important, most leading industrial actors did not expect such a membership for several decades. This meant that Stora, which had significant exports within Europe, believed that it had to establish a position within the EC (later EU) to avoid a competitive handicap. The situation became more acute in the early 1990s when Finland, home of several of Stora's toughest competitors, announced that it was ready to apply for membership.[35] In response, Stora decided to increase its growth ambitions in terms of both speed and scale, and tried to establish a (production) platform inside the EC. The first concrete outcome of that goal was the purchase of De Forenede Papirfabrikker (Denmark) in 1987, but by far the most important step was taken in 1990 when Stora acquired Feldmühle Nobel (Germany), a purchase that became most decisive for Stora's future development. That acquisition was also in itself to a large extent affected – restricted – by certain German institutions, which in the end caused Stora considerable financial strain.

Stora made other purchases inside the EC as well, for example, in France (Moyer Perrin and Espalux [10%]), Italy (Veneta Cucine [80%]) and Germany (Bischof & Klein [40%]).

An example of another institution (i.e. regulating agreement or agency) that mattered was the GATT treaty, which, for example, eliminated most of the customs fees for paper products, and thus made it possible for substantial production volumes to move between continents. For Stora that development mainly affected shipments of SC paper (Europe–US), pulp (South America–Asia) and fine paper (Europe–Asia). Like most other Swedish forest-based corporations Stora also benefitted from the Swedish government's devaluations of the country's currency and the deregulations of the financial markets starting in the 1980s. However, Stora was hindered from certain paths by the European authorities (ECN), for example, when the idea arose to merge Stora and UPM-Kymmene. The only path that ECN was expected to approve was precisely the one Stora wanted to abandon. Notably, the very existence of that monitoring institution produced quite a lot of self-adjusting or even self-censorship; that is to say, certain attractive alternatives were not even investigated.

However, the most influential force behind Stora Kopparberg's transformation into Stora Enso seems to be various kinds of actorhood, and particularly those activities that are linked to different aspects of ownership (its kind, form, structure, status, organization and enactment). When it comes to ownership kind, that factor certainly mattered for Stora's development, particularly when it considered potential acquisition candidates in its ambition to become a large global player. It was in that analysis that Stora actually excluded Enso-Gutzeit from its candidate listing because it was state owned, and ownership by external actors was restricted. It was not until the CEO of Enso-Gutzeit communicated that it might be possible to overcome that limit for shareholding that Stora considered a merger. Nevertheless, in most other acquisitions described in this master case, it was less the kind, form or structure of ownership that mattered, but more so – and often to a large extent – its organization and enactment.

In most of the process that took Stora Kopparberg to Stora Enso, ownership organization was a key factor. From the time when Peter Wallenberg became family head in 1982 until Stora Enso was founded in 1998, Stora (Kopparberg) was governed by its controlling family through its investment company Investor, in collaboration with one or two of Stora's leading executives. Before that, from WWII to the early 1980s, Jacob Wallenberg Sr and Marcus Wallenberg Sr governed the 'sphere companies' and had actually divided them between themselves. Notably, Stora Kopparberg was unique in that respect, as it was the only sphere company in which both brothers were active simultaneously. Jacob Wallenberg Sr became a board member in Stora Kopparberg in 1941 and its Chair in 1950, and left that position in 1976. Marcus Wallenberg Sr became a board member in Stora Kopparberg in 1944, assumed its Chair in 1976, and left that position in 1980. Basically, that period of 'dual command' was marked by constant friction between the two leaders of the Wallenberg sphere, which made it almost impossible for the family to restructure and rationalize the sphere's total engagement in the forest-based sector. Marcus Wallenberg Sr made some attempts to reorganize the part he controlled, but eventually he decided to force his will through in several of the holdings that were jointly led, as well as in some of the companies that 'belonged to' his brother. Over time he became the Great Leader of the family, although with increasing age not always unchallenged.

Thus, the organization of the ownership of Stora (Kopparberg) was sphere based, and the problems associated with that situation had a substantial impact on its long-term development. The most important strategic decision before the early 1980s was when Stora divested its steel business, in accordance with Marcus Wallenberg Sr's wishes but without support from Jacob Wallenberg Sr (that divestment became a success). Another very important decision for Stora that Marcus Wallenberg Sr pushed through against the will of his brother was the large investment in Nova Scotia (that investment became unsuccessful). There were also several other issues where the positions of the two brothers differed. That owner dissonance created ambiguities and frictions in Stora that seriously influenced its governance processes, that is to say, the ways the operational and financial flows ought to be handled. The sphere perspective continued to be strong when Peter Wallenberg acted as peak co-ordinator, but when he was in command it was no longer a question of dual command, but of what interest was given priority: that of the sphere or that of the individual corporation. For Stora, that difference was particularly striking when Swedish Match was acquired. That purchase was carried out because the Wallenberg sphere had recognized a problem within that key holding – not because Stora's executive actors saw Swedish Match as a fitting acquisition.

A troika composed of Investor's Chair and CEO together with the Chair of Stora governed Stora from the time Peter Wallenberg took full control of the company in 1984 (he became director in 1974, Deputy Chair in 1980 and Chair in 1985). When it came to the really important strategic issues, these three leaders usually acted outside the board. The Swedish Match case illustrated that kind of process, as it was run from the sphere (Investor) and only involved Stora's board when the formal decision was to be taken. The same governance mode was in effect when Stora acquired Billerud and Papyrus, although in that case the initiative came primarily from Stora's CEO Berggren.

However, it was Peter Wallenberg who had the final say, both regarding whether a certain purchase ought to be undertaken and – if so – when it should be carried out. Furthermore, he was usually the recipient of the more significant M&A proposals, for example, when Billerud's controlling owner at an accidental encounter asked if he (the Wallenberg sphere) was interested in making a deal. Billerud did not fit Stora particularly well, yet that purchase was made. It was also Peter Wallenberg who gave the final clearance for Stora's purchase of Papyrus, an acquisition that suited Stora's operations much better.

Thus, it is rather obvious that the way ownership is organized matters for corporate development. In the Stora case, that organizing impacted in two different ways. Before the early 1980s, the unclear internal organization of the sphere's ownership exposed Stora's executives to ambiguous and erratic governance processes that created obstacles which prevented them from taking strategic initiatives. Beginning in the early 1980s, the same difficulties remained for the executive actors, although this time not generated by divided governance. The executives were still largely excluded from the strategy-making process, but for a different reason.

As mentioned above, the enactment of ownership usually has a strong impact on corporate paths, and this master case contains several striking examples of how that force works. Marcus Wallenberg Sr was probably the most influential actor in Swedish business life in the second half of the 20th century, and his impact on Stora's development was extensive. He had the final say in many decisions that directly or indirectly formed Stora's strategy and development path, for example, regarding the investment in Nova Scotia, the establishment of Nymölla, the conversion of Hylte, the divestment of the steel business, the hostile bid for Iggesund, the end to a hygiene business effort, the stopping of an early merger with Swedish Match and the ownership deal with Volvo.

Marcus Wallenberg Sr continuously monitored the CEOs and even discussed issues with managers further down the corporate hierarchies. He felt free to contact anybody anytime anywhere about anything. Thus, he acted as if he were a member of all the legally prescribed corporate agencies (AGM, board and CEO) and acted outside those agencies through innumerable informal contacts (cf. Carlgren's standing in MoDo, subsection 16.3.6). He participated in countless concrete business discussions and gained experience that allowed him to master even many of the details in the crucial strategic and operative matters.

Jacob Wallenberg Sr was also active in Stora, but as his influence gradually declined, he never had the same impact on how the company evolved. He tried to hinder several of the strategic decisions that his brother favoured, but in most cases he lost the struggle. Jacob Wallenberg Sr always acted in accordance with the principles manifested in the Swedish Companies Act, that is to say, the legal platform designed for the owner(s). Consequently, he also focused on the financial flows and let the executive actors take care of operations.

If one should briefly summarize the governance rationales of the two brothers, it would be fair to state that Jacob Wallenberg Sr preferred to act in the financial flow, while Marcus Wallenberg Sr rather stressed the operational one. That difference is clearly visible all through the master case, in which Jacob Wallenberg Sr regularly pointed to the financial risks and problems that were present in the different investment projects at the same time as Marcus Wallenberg Sr tended to focus on operative novelties and tried to provide ways to circumvent the financial difficulties.

Peter Wallenberg, too, was a significant actor, but unlike his father, he did not act fully on his own. He relied more on the highly qualified people he had attracted to the sphere's key governance bodies (the investment companies Investor and Providentia). For the governance of Stora, he had created a troika that took all the crucial decisions, for example, those that involved acquisitions (e.g. Billerud, Papyrus, Swedish Match and Feldmühle Nobel), as well as those that had to do with how Stora should expand outside Sweden (acquire a platform inside the EC/EU, work on the North American market, establish a business in China, etc.).

If one looks for owners outside Stora that have affected its long-term path a few stand out, for example, Carlgren (who won the Iggesund contest), the Flick family (who presented the opportunity to acquire Feldmühle Nobel), Wall (who offered Peter Wallenberg controlling shares in Billerud) and Stenbeck (who refused to sell Korsnäs to someone he did not trust [the Wallenberg family]). If one goes beyond the owner category, several other actors become visible that have also contributed substantially to Stora's development, for example, Swedish Match's top executives (Nicolin and Thunholm), Dahlbäck (who assisted Peter Wallenberg in most of his efforts in Stora), Barnevik (who dismissed Berggren as Stora Chair) and Härmälä (who opened up Enso-Gutzeit for a merger with Stora). Looking within Stora, Berggren stands out because he was involved in most of what occurred in and around Stora for some 15 years, that is to say, between 1984 (when Stora Kopparberg became Stora) and 1998 (when Stora became Stora Enso). Others too played important roles, for example, Erik Sundblad (cf. the dividing of the company into one steel and one forest-based unit and Stora's initial partnership with Feldmühle [at Hylte]), Pettersson (who had Peter Wallenberg's ear) and Helgesson (who transformed a rather sprawling Stora constellation into a more integrated one).

16.5 THE EMERGENCE AND DEVELOPMENT OF SCA

16.5.1 Pursuing Scale Advantages

The fourth and final of the four master cases presented in this volume contains a description of how about a dozen independent firms were integrated into one common constellation soon named SCA, and how that construct after WWII developed into a large global corporation that operated both in the hygiene business and in certain parts of the more 'traditional' forest-based industry.

All through the 1950s SCA worked to become a truly integrated company, and certain reforms in that direction started in the early 1950s. CEO Engström acted to limit the founding firms' freedom and managed to establish a rather cohesive SCA. Since it was also important to improve the new constellation's financial situation, the Swedish devaluation in 1949 was welcome, as were the boom years that followed WWII. With increasingly stronger finances, SCA was soon able to cut its formal ownership link to Handelsbanken and to begin considering various ways to integrate forward to reduce its strong dependence on the pulp market. The new expansion opportunity could then be utilized in two ways: through purchases of firms and plants supported by strong finances and/or through organic growth supported by scaled-up plants and upgraded R&D resources. Both development paths made it necessary for SCA to match its strategy to the changing circumstances that had emerged for its production processes (new technology offered scale advantages) as well as its sales and marketing activities (closer customer relations required local/regional sales companies). To take advantage of those changes required large amounts of investment capital, and that, in turn, necessitated enhanced financial planning and new organizational solutions.

The Swedish production of 'market pulp' was still significant in the 1950s, and SCA was among the larger suppliers of that commodity. However, it was newsprint that was Sweden's largest export product at the time, and SCA was a major producer of that commodity, too, although not as big as Holmens Bruk or Stora Kopparberg. For SCA it soon became a problem that half of its pulp export went to North America, as the favourable conditions for export to that continent were weakening. In the 1950s SCA had to seek out possible new investments (products and markets), a search that was inspired both by the current success of the co-located pulp and paper combines (they seemed to be more effective than separate mills) and by the expected timber shortage that thwarted a large expansion of pulp production. Generally, SCA based its new expansion path on the utilization of (technological) scale advantages, product differentiation, effective raw material use and further processing of the pulp. To avoid negative reactions from pulp customers, SCA decided to concentrate its move to the right in the value chain (it should only involve few commodities and a handful of [carefully selected] geographical markets).

However, a growing SCA had to solve the same basic strategic problem faced by most other large forest-based corporations in those days, namely to determine on what kind of paper it should concentrate its expansion. Initially, SCA chose newsprint, primarily because that commodity was already produced, but also for several other reasons: the producers were rather few and mostly Nordic, the current cartel worked well, the newsprint market was growing and the risk of political regulations was low. To pursue the newsprint path, SCA did not expand its Matfors site, but instead began sizeable newsprint production at Ortviken in the late 1950s. SCA was in a hurry, both because substantial first-mover advantages had to be captured, and because several competitors simultaneously invested in similar production.

SCA's analyses of possible futures indicated that kraft paper could become another profitable business – perhaps even a better way to integrate forward than its current newsprint operations (and probably better than efforts in journal paper, fluting, sack paper and fine paper). The basic idea to exploit an advantage linked to the use of Nordic spruce (its high-quality long fibres) spoke strongly in favour of investing in kraftliner production, particularly as that market was growing rapidly (basically because the market for paper-based packages for consumables exploded). Also favouring the liner path was SCA's ability to offer a superior product, as its kraftliner was a much better paper quality for the production of packages than that offered by most of its competitors (testliner). However, unlike newsprint, kraftliner was not an 'end product' for the customer, as it constituted only one of its two main components. To produce packages (cardboard, wrappings, boxes, etc.) corrugated had to be added, and that ingredient was produced in a very different way from kraftliner. Kraftliner was a bulk product that suited SCA's ambition to act as large-scale producer of selected forest-based products, while corrugated instead was a 'voluminous' product that was produced in rather small-scale units located close to customers. Despite that basic difference in production and distribution modes, many large corporations decided to include both liner and corrugated in their operations. SCA recognized that it had to do the same in order to defend and develop its liner position on the expanding packaging market.

The vision to build SCA's future on large-scale production of selected bulk products did not fit particularly well with its current structure, as it was composed of many minor production units that sometimes also manufactured rather obsolete products. Its CEO Mossberg (appointed 1960) therefore formulated a restructuring and rationalization strategy for SCA that involved quite a few closures in regions where the forest-based units were the dominating (or only) industries, and where consequently entire communities would be negatively affected. A focus on fewer and larger production units implied that SCA ought to concentrate its main investments at three sites: Munksund (kraftliner), Obbola (printing paper) and Östrand (pulp). Moreover, new environmental legislation in Sweden influenced the radical restructuring process, as the cost of complying with the legislation made certain units unprofitable. All in all, the transformation of SCA into a cohesive and effective corporation was a tough process particularly for the employees and the local communities. It also entailed large financial losses that for some time thwarted the company's attempt to integrate forward. However, as the sphere's bank (Handelsbanken) fully supported SCA's integration and expansion strategy, the company at least had access to the capital necessary for the restructuring.

Like most other Nordic forest-based corporations SCA worried about its future timber sourcing. To be able to expand its operations, it seemed at the time as if it had to go abroad either to find new timber for its (expanding) domestic units or to establish new timber-based plants. SCA decided to follow the first path, investing in forests in British Columbia. It also considered investing at the Brazilian Aracruz site, but strained finances made it less tempting to make that investment as well. Moreover, unlike many of its competitors SCA eventually decided to abandon the idea of investing in timber resources abroad. Instead, the company decided to concentrate its efforts on establishing new outlets in Europe for its pulp and liner production.

Despite certain financial strain the CEO saw it as absolutely necessary for SCA's long-term survival that it integrated forward and gained more control of one of the two main outlets for its pulp and liner, namely the European market for packaging products (earlier strategic discussions had excluded the sacks market). The fastest and most effective way to accomplish this was to buy quite a few of the rather small European producers of corrugated. That buying ambition soon gathered momentum, and SCA acquired (parts of) Danish, French and Spanish firms. As SCA finances were rather weak at that time, it used part ownerships as well as other kinds of collaborative arrangements for its European expansion. Since some of the investments that were made outside Europe seemed rather 'capricious' (e.g. the ones in Belgian Congo and at Skeena River [US]), a rather general impression evolved among outsiders that SCA lacked a clear vision about what part (or range) of the value chain it wanted to 'colonize'. Thus, most growth options were still open: pulp, fine paper, graphic papers (e.g. newsprint, journal paper, SC and LWC), hygiene papers (e.g. fluff and tissue), packaging papers (e.g. liner and corrugated) and special papers. Though two of them were already being pursued, that is to say, newsprint and packaging, SCA continued to look for new and better alternatives.

SCA took an important strategic step in the mid-1960s when it acquired 20 per cent of a large German forest-based company, Aschaffenburger Zellstoffwerke (AZ), which at the time consumed some of SCA's pulp production. The other owners (banks) of AZ needed a competent actor in the forest-based industry as a partner, and they chose SCA. Since AZ had a rather differentiated product portfolio that included fine paper, printing paper, fluting and various special papers, the acquisition as such did not clarify SCA's expansion direction. Not long afterwards AZ merged with another big German forest-based company, Waldhof, which produced corrugated, cardboard and tissue, and established Papierwerke Waldhof-Aschaffenburg (PWA). Waldhof's contribution to AZ added further to SCA's already impressive involvement in various kinds of forest-based products, and as a large owner and leading executive actor, SCA's management gained a unique opportunity to learn about how to produce and market almost all kinds of forest-based products. That broadening of SCA's repertoire continued when it invested in the US company Patrician Paper (a buyer of SCA's pulp), which made it possible to learn more about both tissue production and the North American market.

16.5.2 Looking for Core Businesses

In the early 1970s SCA again stood at the crossroads and had to take crucial decisions regarding its future development. It had decided to integrate forward into newsprint and packaging, but it also housed a small but promising hygiene business (sanitary napkins) that was licensed to another company for the Nordic market. SCA had built a plant in the UK to sell that product in certain other parts of Europe, but as it was difficult to offer just one product to retailer chains, SCA's leaders had to decide how to move ahead. Thus,

SCA had to either sell that unit and leave the hygiene sector or use some of its managerial and financial resources to develop that business (e.g. add new products and markets).

When Rydin was appointed CEO in 1972, he acquired the same strong position as his predecessors, very much due to SCA's ownership setting. Since SCA lacked an individual actor (or family) as major/controlling owner, the leading professional executives in the Handelsbanken/Industrivärden sphere governed the company, and by tradition they had granted the CEO substantial freedom of action. Still, however, the board mattered, and Rydin was careful to follow formal prescriptions and established practices. The board's material and discussions were thus of high quality, and all truly important decisions had to be dealt with at (at least) two separate meetings to make it possible for the directors to informally discuss the crucial issues and – if necessary – ask for (or collect) more information.

Rydin soon discovered that several of the production plants were in rather bad shape. As he was made aware of SCA's poor finances already from the start, he realized that he initially had to rely on 'plant patching' rather than grand new investments to improve the situation. Rydin even contacted the current Social Democratic government and the unions to make sure they understood that SCA's situation was acute, and that radical measures had to be taken to get the corporation back on track. However, unlike his predecessors Rydin rather quickly got the opportunity to launch at least a partial expansion strategy. That did not mean that SCA's finances were in good shape, but at least the company was not in a crisis situation, and it was not forced to use all of its limited economic resources on restructurings.

Slowly but surely the financial risk was moving back from the banks to SCA, and eventually that gave Rydin greater freedom of action. In any case, his basic approach actually suited a conservative consolidation strategy better, as he was a careful, risk-averse and pensive actor. He combined the capacity to use broad strokes – formulate visions and strategies – with a mastering of many details. He was both a listener and a pedagogue, and simultaneously both forceful and cautious. Thus, like most actors, Rydin's rationale was complex, although it had its marked characteristics. It was therefore rather unexpected that it was during his stay as CEO that SCA took its boldest and most crucial strategic decision since its establishment in the 1930s, namely its decision to acquire the textile and hygiene company Mölnlycke.

Rydin could not delay action until SCA's finances had become strong because then the company would end up on the sidelines during the decisive 1970s, when most larger forest-based corporations grew out of their home markets and together formed a new globalized industry structure that set many of the competitive conditions for the last quarter of the 20th century. Thus, during that decade, most companies participated in the 'forward integration race' and had to decide what paths they should follow to survive and prosper. SCA was no exception, and like many of its competitors it tried to secure solid presence all along the value chain, which covered everything from forestry to (some kind of) production. Rydin's vision implied both a move away from 'timber-intensive' products and a concentration on a few product segments. Newsprint was then considered to be the best alternative, but gradually packaging reached a similar status. To acquire capacity to implement his vision, Rydin needed to free capital, so SCA sold its building material activities and some plants to ASSI and Ncb. SCA was lucky because Ncb in particular was at that time eager to expand its operations.

It was not long before Rydin looked into SCA's most crucial international engagement, namely its large investment in PWA. Because the size[36] of that undertaking had crowded out some other possible expansion investments, it had to pay off quickly. SCA was particularly interested in PWA's corrugated operations, leading Rydin and his team to suggest certain organizational re-arrangements to avoid deeper engagement in PWA's other businesses. A short time later, corrugated was detached from PWA and put in a separate company (Zewawell), in which SCA got a 50 per cent shareholding. SCA also used PWA's know-how to improve Wifstavarf's performance, as that plant's production of pulp and kraft paper was not functioning particularly well. After some investigations, it was concluded that Wifstavarf would be better off making fine paper (using Östrand's pulp). Though fine paper was not a business that SCA prioritized, SCA decided to continue its efforts in that field since PWA mastered such operations.[37]

SCA had already begun its journey towards making packaging one of its core activities when it built Munksund back in the 1950s and started to produce and sell kraftliner. As being dependent on one machine only was seen as operatively too risky, and as the market forecasts for liner looked promising, SCA decided to add one more machine. Eventually it was decided to locate that new one to Obbola (not to Munksund) because the discussions with the Swedish government had led to a guarantee from Domänverket[38] that it would deliver the necessary quantities of timber, and because the planned investment eliminated the need for what would have been a painful and costly site closure. Still, SCA needed a partner, as the project in itself was large and entailed substantial follow-up investments. Obviously, the best partner would be a corporation that used Obbola's liner, and eventually one of SCA's customers, the US company St Regis, turned up as a serious candidate. As SCA's Deputy CEO was friends with one of its leading executive actors, the negotiations soon reached the ownership level. St Regis's major shareholder in turn had a good relationship with one of SCA's earlier CEOs, so eventually a satisfactory agreement was reached.

Despite its increased presence in the packaging industry (basically as supplier of kraftliner), SCA continued the search for a more stable way forward. Its leaders discussed various possible acquisitions/collaborations with, among others, the owners/managers of Graningeverken (forest resources), ASSI (packaging), Esselte (packaging), Enso-Gutzeit (coated paper) and Van Gelder (printing paper), but none of those attempts materialized. SCA's leaders also discussed what to do with the company's relatively small (one product) – but promising – hygiene operations. Most alternatives were considered: sell off, expand organically (through increased R&D efforts) or expand through acquisitions. Something had to be done, and ultimately the sale alternative was given priority.

Already during Mossberg's period as CEO SCA had indicated a certain interest in Mölnlycke, a producer of textile-related products that also had extensive knowledge of timber-based fibres' absorption capacities (cf. bandages, diapers and sanitary napkins). Mölnlycke needed a partner that was capable of financing its (expected) fast and massive expansion. At the time making acquisitions was Mölnlycke's preferred path, as organic growth was considered to be too slow to be effective in the on-going race on the expanding hygiene market. Furthermore, the company needed to secure the sourcing of special qualities of pulp, so it would be an advantage if a future partner could deliver that raw material.

The main link between SCA and Mölnlycke in the late 1960s was SCA's pulp deliveries.

That led to many contacts between the two companies' executive actors, and Mölnlycke's strategy and organization impressed SCA's leaders. At a certain point Rydin and Wahlström (Deputy CEO) tried to find out if Mölnlycke was interested in increasing its co-operation with SCA. Such a step could solve one of SCA's remaining really difficult strategic issues, namely whether it should try to make hygiene a core activity or leave that sector. Rydin slowly became convinced that hygiene could be the 'missing' core business that SCA had sought, and that it would be best to pursue it in collaboration with Mölnlycke, which he believed to be a corporation with great potential. So, again SCA stood at a crossroads – it should either exit the hygiene field (i.e. stop producing special pulp for Mölnlycke, sell its UK plant, etc.) or make a serious effort in that business (i.e. co-operate further with Mölnlycke).

Other corporations, too, showed interest in buying Mölnlycke, for example, the big US company Sunlight. However, because Mölnlycke's leading executives were not keen on becoming a small unit in a large US corporation, they convinced its board that the company would develop much more successfully on its own, a stance that opened the door to a deal with SCA. Sunlight also wanted to buy SCA's hygiene businesses, but SCA preferred to sell it to Mölnlycke and accepted its shares as payment (Mölnlycke did not have the necessary cash, and SCA wanted to become part-owner of that company). Rydin won a seat on Mölnlycke's board, which made it possible for him to learn more about its businesses and its capacity to contribute to a strong future (also) for SCA.

Mölnlycke's executive actors were running the company very much according to their own visions and rationales, and they were eager to preserve an ownership setting that lacked an intervening controlling shareholder. At the time the company had one major shareholder that gave its top management plenty of freedom (Custos). Rydin assured Mölnlycke's leaders that SCA did not aspire to get a dominating ownership position in 'their' company, but that SCA would be interested in acquiring a holding of about the same size as the one Custos had. Gradually, SCA increased its ownership, and by 1975 it had doubled. Over time the leading actors of the two companies developed trusting relationships, and discussions about a possible merger between the two companies began. With such an arrangement, SCA would finally get its longed-for additional core business, and Mölnlycke the necessary supply of both capital (for expansion) and special pulp (for product quality). One potential stumbling block involved how to distribute the various executive positions in the newly merged constellation, but eventually that classic obstacle was solved.

As the initiative to 'merge' was taken at the two companies' top management level, it remained for them to convince the shareholders and directors that such a merger would be the best solution for both companies. They were indeed successful. One important outcome of the negotiations was a special solution for Mölnlycke (as part of the enlarged SCA). Although Mölnlycke formally became a subsidiary, a special regulating document guaranteed it an exceptionally strong internal position (i.e. a high degree of autonomy). For example, Mölnlycke retained substantial influence over the composition of its board (and appointed some of its outside directors), secured capital sourcing (i.e. no internal competition regarding investment resources) and ensured that SCA's top management would not be allowed to govern its operations (through channels other than Mölnlycke's board).

Rydin was convinced that a successful hygiene business had to include both fluff-based products (where Mölnlycke was strong) and consumer tissue. When SCA tried to strengthen its position in the latter field, Lilla Edet came into focus as the result of the tip Rydin received from a member of the Swedish government that Procter & Gamble considered buying that company from Akzo. Somewhat unexpectedly Ncb won the contest, but that outcome was not a setback for SCA/Mölnlycke, as Lilla Edet's products and market channels did not fit that well with its new hygiene strategy. When Ncb then ran into difficulties (1978), SCA/Mölnlycke again examined the possible merits of acquiring Lilla Edet, but did not act. Over the next few years both MoDo and Nokia discussed purchasing the company, but in the end SCA/Mölnlycke was the one that incorporated Lilla Edet into its organization (1986).

SCA considered solutions for its hygiene business that involved both PWA and Vereinigte Papierwerke (VP), but nothing materialized. Furthermore, SCA tried to buy a plant from Cellulose du Pin (diapers), entered Sany (50%, a French sales company) and discussed co-operation with French Béghin (tissue). However, all those efforts made to build a competitive and relatively concentrated hygiene business could not hide that Mölnlycke still was a rather diversified subsidiary. In addition to its hygiene operations, the company encompassed units for marine products, clothes, sewing cotton, and so on, so a 'full' merger process would be complicated. Most of those unrelated units had to be sold, but that did not happen until the 1980s.

SCA's acquisition of Mölnlycke was a major strategic step that incorporated a business that was very different from the ones it previously ran. It represented high operative risk-taking and a huge step to the right in the value chain, getting as close to end customers as possible. It also brought both geographical market extension (new countries) and product differentiation (consumer goods) to such a level that it almost represented a diversification. However, that move was taken in a situation in which SCA was well informed through the numerous bilateral talks that had been conducted between the two corporations' top managers as well as through the information Rydin got as a member of Mölnlycke's board. As a result, some of the operative risks were handled in advance, and the acquisition as such did not significantly increase SCA's financial risk, although it had some impact on how the other core businesses developed. Thus, from the mid-1970s hygiene began to look more and more like a third core business supplementing the packaging and printing paper ones. Though SCA ran fine paper operations and pulp production as well, neither had core business status.

Unlike most of its competitors SCA decided to maintain its position to the left in the value chain (i.e. keep its forests and power plants). Since effectively utilizing the Nordic quality timber (the long fibre) was another important ingredient in SCA's strategy in the late 1970s, it was essential to find a profitable way to further process that unique resource. An unintended consequence of that priority was that SCA became a rather late user of waste fibres.

Nevertheless, not all investment activities were driven by such forward-looking considerations. At the time SCA had to decide urgently what to do with certain of the existing plants. In this regard, the pulp plant at Östrand came into focus. Because of a capital shortage SCA discussed a possible three-party solution with the Swedish Ministry of Industry that would include SCA's Wifstavarf–Östrand combine, Ncb's Dynäs plant and state capital. SCA's board approved that arrangement but added CTMP production to improve Mölnlycke's long-term pulp sourcing. The board made clear that such a large investment made it necessary to postpone the planned printing paper machine at Ortviken.

SCA's newsprint business developed in the 1970s as well. Although the Östrand investment had temporarily crowded out Ortviken's expansion, SCA continued to discuss other newsprint activities, albeit, usually along with potential partners. One such possibility that emerged in 1975 was a newsprint mill that would be established in Hessen (Germany) together with a Swiss consortium, but for various reasons that idea never took off. When the Wallenberg sphere's new ambitious newsprint project at Stora Kopparberg's Hylte site was revealed (intended to be the biggest mill of that kind in Europe), SCA tried to stop that venture by informing both the head of the German forest-based company Feldmühle and the international newsprint cartel about its strong objections. But since Feldmühle was changing some of its newsprint production to journal paper, it did not oppose the new Hylte investment (and Feldmühle was also already linked to the Wallenberg sphere through co-operation with Stora Kopparberg). By then Rydin had begun to worry about the future of newsprint in SCA. His concern was further strengthened by the emerging discussions about 'paperless offices' and possibly decreasing newspaper markets. Yet he was convinced that Ortviken had to be modernized and expanded, and eventually that step was taken (the renovated plant was actually not taken into production until the mid-1980s).

The 1970s also saw further developments in SCA's third core business, packaging. SCA's goal was to become one of the largest packaging corporations in the world before the turn of the millennium and dominate the 'high-tech segment'. That vision was based partly on SCA's superior raw material sourcing (i.e. kraftliner) and partly on its strong position on all the markets for corrugated it had entered. The initial expansion was to take place in Europe with a special emphasis on Sweden and the other Nordic countries. As so often happened, however, fast-moving opportunities determined much of that growth process. As an example, the Jefferson Smurfit Group offered SCA a position in the UK and Ireland, which added to SCA's existing packaging operations in Denmark, France, Sweden and West Germany. During the rapid growth process it became more and more evident that the two bases for the packaging business – liner and corrugated – differed significantly in important respects (i.e. production scale, capital needs, customer structure, exchange rate dependence and competitive setting). In light of this realization, SCA decided to organize a separate packaging unit that did not include its liner operations (1979). From then on, packaging sat in the driver's seat, not liner.

During the severe crisis that hit many forest-based companies in the late 1970s, Rydin raised the question – perhaps inspired by the recent formation of Swedish Steel – whether a 'Swedish Pulp' company ought to be established. That idea, which stemmed from SCA's standing wish to get out of (most of) its production of market pulp, irritated the conservative Minister of Finance, who did not want to see yet another base industry as part of the state's business sphere. At about the same time the Chair of Handelsbanken brought up the 'classic' idea that MoDo and SCA ought to merge, but he received almost no support, as SCA's leaders regarded such a path incompatible with the company's current strategy. They claimed that such a constellation would contain more market pulp and more fine paper, two businesses that SCA had given lower priority to since the mid-1970s.

In the early 1980s SCA explored the possibility of doing something in the printing paper business together with Holmens Bruk, which had two major shareholders that together controlled the company. An opportunity emerged when one of the dominating owners, the Söderberg family, indicated that Holmens Bruk needed a strong partner to survive the on-going expansion race in the forest-based industry, where plant and machine sizes became more and more decisive for competitiveness. The other main owner, the Bonnier family, seemed to be interested in getting SCA shares 'if something would happen' with Holmens Bruk. Rydin interpreted the current shareholding setting in that company as rather favourable for SCA. However, he was mainly interested in co-operating with Holmens Bruk if it invested further in journal paper production – its newsprint operations were less attractive to SCA.

Over time SCA's interest in Holmens Bruk decreased, but during that period another large Swedish forest-based corporation came into play, namely the 'ownerless' packaging company Iggesund (high-quality cardboard). That development was triggered by a hostile bid from two of SCA's competitors – Stora Kopparberg and Billerud – and their joint initiative made it necessary for SCA to react. The fact that the two bidding companies belonged to the Wallenberg sphere made SCA's response particularly important, although its own ownership sphere Handelsbanken/Industrivärden already was involved in the contest through a close associate (SCA's rival MoDo).

Initially, Rydin and SCA did not take the hostile bid that seriously because it was rather amateurishly constructed, but as SCA's long-term strategy in the packaging field still was not fully determined, its executives carefully discussed various possible ways to participate in the contest. They concluded that Iggesund's packaging operations differed significantly from SCA's own activities in the field and that they lacked 'development opportunities'. Given this and the fact that the Handelsbanken/Industrivärden sphere and its associate MoDo did not need SCA's support, SCA decided to do nothing. That stance was made easier to maintain since MoDo soon got the upper hand in the control fight. MoDo hinted that SCA might get the opportunity to acquire its hygiene business, and to Mölnlycke's leaders that seemed like a very promising idea.

16.5.3 Expansion on Three Fronts

Into the early 1980s SCA continued to prioritize Mölnlycke in accordance with the original agreement from 1975. Mölnlycke's European expansion was also high on the agenda, as was coming to terms with its still far too 'bushy' product repertoire. Its hygiene operations were strong on the Nordic market, but its expansion in the other northern parts of Europe was problematic. The company was strong in South and Eastern Europe and on distant markets such as Australia and parts of South and Central America. In South and Central America in particular, joint ventures were preferred, and Mölnlycke stayed with that formula when it expanded to 'similar' new markets in the region (e.g. Mexico and Colombia). Mölnlycke also tried to further develop its hygiene operations through acquisitions/partnerships with quite a few national and international actors, for example, the Bonnier family (Duni, tissue), the Wallenberg family (Swedish Match), Beijer/Argentus (Cederroths, healthcare), Scott Paper (the European hygiene market) and Philip Morris (SCA's holding in PWA). Yet, it was not until the second half of the 1980s, when SCA had got a new CEO (Martin-Löf) and Rydin had been promoted to Chair, that SCA's international expansion really took off – and that growth took place not only in the hygiene business – it occurred on several fronts.

Martin-Löf decided to give SCA's three core businesses roughly equal status before he (possibly) suggested any changes. 'Equal status' then meant that the privileged treatment of Mölnlycke (hygiene) was to be abandoned (not entirely executed until 1995). The new CEO also increased SCA's risk level, a move that was possible because finances had improved radically since Rydin took office. Indeed, the time had come to catch up with the competitors and make expansion investments to survive the current race, and to become one of the remaining players in the increasingly globalized forest-based industry. Martin-Löf's more risk-seeking approach fitted such a situation, particularly as the risk-averse Chair functioned as a counterforce. The new CEO was an energetic, 'pushy' and straightforward businessman, who acted in SCA's operative flow, particularly in the acquisition processes, where he performed as a clever and cunning negotiator. However, he did not run the company on his own – he also used his top management team that almost operated like an ideal type circle (cf. Ch. 1).

Mölnlycke's success again attracted interest from several of the big international competitors and increased their inclination to do something on the Nordic market. That development accentuated the need for Mölnlycke to decide which geographical territory should constitute its home market. Its CEO was convinced that it was impossible to act solely in a Nordic context, as scale advantages in both production and marketing would make such a position indefensible. In preparation for moving beyond the Nordic region, Mölnlycke's leaders listed potential acquisition candidates in Europe and visited and talked to several of those companies' executive actors.

SCA's dramatic expansion period started in 1987, when the French family Arnault decided to disinvest their holdings in the hygiene sector and put Peaudouce 'in play'. Peaudouce was already on Mölnlycke's listing of potential acquisition candidates, as it was number one in the diapers business in France and active in some other geographical markets where Mölnlycke was weak. Initially, SCA's Chair Rydin hesitated, but in the end he trusted Mölnlycke's CEO Daun, who favoured a purchase. So, in 1988 SCA bought Peaudouce after intense negotiations regarding the size of the offered holding and the price. That acquisition became decisive for SCA's further development, as it made clear to everybody that the hygiene path, although it had lost its special status, still kept its position as one of the company's core businesses. Together Mölnlycke and Peaudouce became the largest European constellation for fluff products (i.e. diapers, incontinence products and menstrual supplies). However, because Mölnlycke's management was not ready to run such a big non-domestic business, and because much of Peaudouce's strength rather lay in personal relationships (i.e. in French business networks and circles) than product qualities and marketing skill, the situation soon became problematic.

In the late 1980s SCA entered a period where uncertainty about its future path grew both inside and outside the company. The CEO had not yet made clear which of the three core businesses he preferred to run in the future – all of them, that is to say, graphic papers,[39] packaging and hygiene, were still given equal attention. What complicated the strategic situation and made it unclear were some rather unexpected setbacks in the hygiene field (i.e. Mölnlycke's profits were down, Peaudouce was not as successful in France as expected and competition grew). Therefore, Mölnlycke streamlined its hygiene business by focusing on fluff rather than tissue (i.e. on consumer products and incontinence care) and prioritized expansion on the AFH market. Moreover, when its brand did not reach the position as number one or number two in a market, Mölnlycke changed focus and tried to become the leading supplier of 'private brands'. Outside Europe, however, it continued to utilize joint ventures to reduce country risks and the problems associated with governance at a distance. All those efforts indicated that Mölnlycke finally had formulated a robust strategy for its hygiene business – a vision that could last for at least a decade.

For the two other core businesses – graphic papers and packaging – SCA chose Europe as its home ground, although its strategy for the Nordic countries differed somewhat from the one implemented in the UK and on the continent. In the Nordic countries SCA pursued scale-based integration, that is to say, restructurings in already covered segments of the value chain, while in the rest of Europe SCA practised forward integration. A common strategy for the whole of Europe was to situate all activities in fully controlled corporations, requiring the company to sell off minority holdings and exit joint ventures.

SCA had set high goals for its graphic papers, although quality, productivity and integration with forestry operations rather than volumes and market shares were put in the forefront. Basically, that well-invested business functioned like a 'cash cow' that made sizeable expansion investments possible in hygiene and packaging. For newsprint, which faced a declining market, it was crucial to keep down production costs and increase the use of waste paper, while for LWC and SC the market looked better. Therefore, SCA eventually decided to invest in two new LWC machines. For packaging it was crucial to maintain a balance between raw materials and further processing. SCA was relatively weak on testliner, fluting and the use of waste paper, so acquisitions of packaging/corrugated units that helped to reduce those shortcomings were preferred.

Implementing SCA's comprehensive operational strategy required matching finances. Towards that end, SCA freed substantial amounts of capital through partner financing of its power plants and the sale of business units (Sunds Defibrator, Zewawell and Smurfit Corrugated UK), which made its high expansion ambitions much more realistic. Thus, by the late 1980s it was (financially) possible for SCA to consider acquisitions beyond Peaudouce, for example, Cellulose du Pin (France, liner), Champion (US, coated paper), Laakirchen (Austria, graphic papers and tissue), Italcarta (Italy, packaging), Reedpack (UK, packaging) and Wiggins Teape (UK, special papers). As SCA particularly looked for ways to enter the growing SC paper market, Laakirchen became its first target. It was 'in play' at the time, since its owner family wanted to 'cash in'. Its family head (Alfred Heinzel) decided to forgo a bidding race; instead he contacted potential buyers that the family liked, and SCA qualified as one of those. After several site visits and extensive negotiations it became possible for SCA to buy Laakirchen at a decent price. That acquisition not only completed SCA's printing paper 'palette', but also strengthened graphic papers within the company, thereby reducing the internal doubts about its future status as a core business. That purchase occurred roughly at the same time as the board discussed whether the troubled Mölnlycke unit perhaps should be sold. The uncertainty about the long-term position of the hygiene business increased when it was rumoured that Laakirchen's tissue operations might be sold to PWA.

In the late 1980s and early 1990s, SCA's vigorous expansion was not limited to Laakirchen (graphic papers) and Peaudouce (hygiene). Finally, its top management's well-established contacts with Italcarta (packaging) paid off. That Italian company fitted SCA's strategy almost perfectly, as it used both testliner and waste paper in its products. However, it took some time before the deal was finally closed, as the Italian owner (a family head) mobilized his country's 'efficient' bureaucracy (i.e. authorities and courts began to obstruct the takeover). Soon after that purchase SCA added several other packaging firms, for example, two subsidiaries of the British packaging corporation Bowaters (i.e. those in Belgium and France), one company in Holland and one in France. So, by the time Italcarta and the others were bought, SCA had invested heavily in all three of its core businesses, still leaving open the question of whether that trio was to be reduced or not (because of overwhelming capital needs).

Somewhat out of the blue something occurred that indirectly influenced SCA's choice of path, namely the opportunity to acquire 5 per cent of the German Feldmühle Nobel, a holding company that included a big forest-based company with a similar name: Feldmühle. Two qualities made that company particularly attractive to SCA, namely its leading position in the European graphic paper business (which included attractive LWC operations) and its generally strong position on the continent (which corresponded with SCA's ambition to make Europe its home market). Feldmühle was thus an attractive target, especially since it was one of the few options left if SCA wanted to remain in the graphic paper business and become a significant global player. The negotiation process became rather complicated, as SCA at that time also was considering a purchase of Reedpack (packaging), and already one of those two corporations was regarded as almost 'too big a bite'. SCA's leaders were well aware that an acquisition of either Feldmühle (Nobel) or Reedpack (or both) would determine much of SCA's path for more than a decade.

SCA expected problems with the German authorities and unions if it were to invest substantially in Feldmühle Nobel; as such there existed a kind of 'country risk'. In addition, such a big purchase could also squeeze out the necessary expansion investments in Mölnlycke (hygiene). Therefore, the intention was to sell off most of Feldmühle Nobel except Feldmühle to free capital for other urgent investments. SCA knew that Feldmühle co-operated with Stora at Hylte and Norrsundet and noted that Stora's leading actors had been meeting with Feldmühle Nobel's owners to consider buying a 25 per cent holding in Feldmühle (and then put Hylte and Norrsundet in the same unit). Still, however, SCA continued to try to get the 5 per cent in Feldmühle Nobel that was put 'in play' by two brothers in the owner family. SCA's ambition was to construct a 'package deal' that would be so interesting for Feldmühle that it later would be possible to get a majority shareholding. Thus, for the time being the important thing for SCA was to single out Feldmühle from Feldmühle Nobel and thereby establish a long-term solution for its graphic papers business.

At that time SCA considered an American acquisition, but as that solution also involved its Swedish rival MoDo it was difficult to come to an agreement. SCA used those discussions to find out whether MoDo (instead) might be interested in participating in a Feldmühle Nobel purchase, but as its leaders were analysing another alternative, nothing materialized. Instead, SCA continued the tough battle with Stora and Scott Paper over control of Feldmühle Nobel – which eventually Stora won. In practice, that defeat triggered a downgrading of the graphic paper business within SCA (although explorations still were conducted with both MoDo and KNP about possible future joint efforts in that field).

On the other hand, SCA's negotiations with Reedpack were successful, and a sizeable sum was spent on that acquisition. In that purchasing process, the sellers were financial actors, an owner category that Chair Rydin did not fully trust. In the end SCA's CEO (and others) convinced Rydin and the purchase went through. Reedpack not only brought SCA a leading position on the European corrugated market; it also ran a large waste paper business and organized both newsprint and cardboard operations. The Reedpack acquisition featured a mental and visionary dimension as well, as it 'confirmed' that packaging continued to be a core business.

Reedpack suited SCA's geographical strategy well, as it had a strong presence in four major European countries (Belgium, Holland, Ireland and the UK). Moreover, Reedpack consumed large amounts of brown liner, one of SCA's major products. Through the Reedpack purchase, SCA obtained the Aylesford unit, a daughter company that produced newsprint from waste fibres. Because bulky newsprint did not have the highest priority, SCA sought a partner for the Aylesford unit and found Mondi, which showed interest in participating. Eventually a 50–50 solution was implemented. Together with all other (smaller) purchases during that time, the acquisition of Reedpack made SCA the leading producer of transport packages in Europe. Despite this overall success, some problems emerged; not all of the plants were in good shape (i.e. rationalizations were needed) and certain of the units that SCA planned to sell were booked high (i.e. large depreciations were required).

SCA's rapid and massive expansion (cf. particularly Laakirchen, Peaudouce, Italcarta and Reedpack) highlighted the need to establish an adequate financial flow to back up all the new (and upcoming) investments. To free capital, the company even considered selling its forests and power plants. In fact, the power plants came into focus as the Swedish energy industry was undergoing a restructuring process that required significant capital. Once SCA concluded that it did not have the necessary financial muscle to successfully participate in that transformation, it instead decided to divest all its power resources (i.e. BÅKAB), and in 1992 they were sold to Sydkraft for a considerable sum. At the same time it was concluded that forests (timber) represented 'a different kind' of natural resource, so it was kept in-house.

16.5.4 More of the Same

Although the packaging unit's internal position had been strengthened after the purchase of Reedpack, the graphic papers business was still going strong. While SCA sought a long-term solution for that activity as well, its efforts were more defensive in character and included finding ways to divest some segments (e.g. fine paper and [perhaps] bulky newsprint) and strengthen others (e.g. LWC paper and SC paper). As so often in the past MoDo came into SCA's focus. Though a purchase of that company did not correspond with SCA's geographical strategy since it would entail further investment in Sweden, a combination of the two companies would allow for various structural solutions (cf. particularly for newsprint and fine paper).

As described in the MoDo master case, when MoDo's controlling owner (Carlgren) lost control, SCA moved to acquire a large holding in that company in a tough race with another bidder (Lundberg, the head of a young family dynasty). Ultimately, SCA was offered the opportunity to buy Carlgren's MoDo shares (and some other holdings in that company) and thus became a major owner ($\approx$ 30% of the votes) like Lundberg and the Kempe foundations. At the time SCA did not have the financial muscle needed to bid for all (or a majority) of MoDo, but it had tried to build an alliance with International Paper to be able to do just that. The idea was that International Paper would handle fine paper and SCA the other businesses (i.e. printing papers and cardboard). In the end, however, International Paper found the 'country risk' too high.

The Kempe foundations' Chair Carl Kempe Jr played a key role in MoDo, as both Lundberg and SCA needed his support to gain the upper hand in MoDo. Both contenders courted Carl Kempe Jr, but he finally sided with Lundberg, probably because he regarded Lundberg's ownership (kind) more advantageous for the Kempe family's future role in MoDo. He might also have suspected that SCA was interested in splitting the family heirloom (i.e. MoDo's classic businesses) and selling it piece by piece, which would wipe out the bulk of his ancestors' achievements. Despite this setback, SCA's leading actors began discussions about possible re-arrangements, since SCA's intention had in any case been to engage in operative collaborations between the two companies. In the end, nothing materialized because of the deadlocked ownership setting (three major owners) and because of the poor personal chemistry that prevailed among several of the leading actors.

In the early 1990s, while the MoDo issue still was pending, SCA thought that its printing business might benefit from the participation of the large Finnish forest-based company Kymmene. Discussions with the leader of that corporation then began with the idea that the two companies should combine their fine paper operations and list them as a new separate company. However, since such a re-arrangement would make the remaining part of SCA look quite different from the classic forest company it had been since its founding, that move was controversial in the eyes of many shareholders and employees. For that reason, SCA's leaders hesitated to take that step and concentrated their efforts instead on the 'MoDo path'. Somewhat later, after Kymmene declared its withdrawal from the talks, the MoDo path remained as the only one available.[40]

SCA decided to abandon its active role in MoDo in 1992, stating that its large investment in that company would henceforth be treated as a non-strategic capital allocation. At some point, MoDo's former head Carlgren looked up Rydin and claimed that he had established a group of Swedes who wanted to buy SCA's MoDo shares and together with the two Kempe foundations take control to avoid a splitting of MoDo. Even so, that (possible[41]) offer did not change SCA's determination to cut all links with MoDo at the time. There had also been talks about a split of MoDo, by which SCA would get Holmens Bruk (newsprint and journal paper) and Lundberg both MoDo 'classic' (fine paper) and Iggesund (quality cardboard). Other companies had shown interest in Holmens Bruk (e.g. Burda and International Paper), but SCA found all the offered prices too low. SCA even considered the possibility of re-listing Holmens Bruk on the SSE but concluded that the 'residual MoDo' would be unattractive for both itself and other investors.

SCA's path during the 1970s and 1980s differed significantly from that of most of its competitors, as the company maintained a low profile in the restructuring that took place on its home market. Instead, by buying Mölnlycke, SCA had taken a step into a new value chain that was rather weakly linked to the classic forest-based industry. It was not entirely unproblematic to follow that alternative path, and that became obvious in the early 1990s when Mölnlycke entered a severe crisis that even brought up the question of whether it should continue as part of SCA. It was particularly the diapers business that had run into difficulties.

To become a large, profitable hygiene player in Europe in the 1990s, SCA would have to handle the competition with Procter & Gamble, a major US company that had entered the continent about a decade earlier with its diapers and sanitary pads. In addition, SCA would have to deal with the growing price competition on the French market, which threatened its position as that market's 'second brand'. Soon, SCA understood that competing with Procter & Gamble meant challenging a giant corporation that held low prices in Europe to capture market share and expand on Mölnlycke's home market. In reality, Procter & Gamble offered a better product that was more efficiently manufactured. That company's strength and determination surprised not only SCA's executives but also Mölnlycke's top management. The Mölnlycke team had seriously underestimated Procter & Gamble and for some time had explained away its achievements as a temporary phenomenon. At that time SCA realized that it never would be able to beat Procter & Gamble in a 'brand fight', as the latter company's superior size[42] allowed for higher efficiency in most parts of the operative flow (from R&D to marketing). Instead Mölnlycke decided to become the retailers' best friend and focus more on the private label market. Its leaders also promised SCA that in a short time it would radically improve its cost efficiency and market new competitive products. SCA's executive actors accepted those pledges, and Mölnlycke could carry out the necessary (huge) investments. Thus, SCA stayed on the market for diapers and incontinence products. Eventually Mölnlycke's management kept its promises and restored the company's competitive power, so from the mid-1990s most of its businesses looked fine again.

Mölnlycke's expansion continued throughout those tough years, for example, through the establishment of new joint ventures in Eastern Europe (e.g. Poland and Czechoslovakia), sale of the engagement in Cederroths and co-operation with Scott Paper in the US (incontinence products). It was also discussed whether SCA ought to welcome partners into Mölnlycke (VP showed interest in selling its hygiene operations for shares) and prepare it for a listing. Like SCA, Kimberly-Clark and Procter & Gamble were active on the market for corporate control, complicating SCA's strategic efforts. For example, at times it appeared as if Kimberly-Clark and VP were close to an agreement, and at other times it seemed as if Procter & Gamble would buy VP (without its hygiene business which Kimberly-Clark or SCA would be offered); at times it looked like VP would buy 50 per cent of Mölnlycke, and at other times VP seemed to want to leave the hygiene sector altogether. In the end (1993), however, SCA bought VP.

SCA continued to debate Mölnlycke's future strategic path, and those talks involved, for example, Kimberly-Clark, PWA and Johnson & Johnson. In the meantime, Kimberly-Clark bought Scott Paper, and the European authorities required that the new constellation sold two units, one of which SCA acquired.

However, SCA's acquisition of PWA in 1995 was a much more important step because it had a lot to do with SCA's strategy for its graphic papers business, particularly with the conclusion that it was impossible to scale down those operations and still be competitive. As SCA at that time wanted to stay in the graphic papers business and maintain presence in all its major segments, it both took a renewed look at KNP and considered investing in a new LWC machine (together with a partner). Together with Mondi Paper, SCA decided to make an expansion investment at Aylesford (waste paper based newsprint). However, the PWA purchase overshadowed all those other efforts, both because of its size and because of the stable platform it provided for SCA's further European expansion.

Thus, PWA was almost the perfect acquisition for SCA. The company corresponded well with SCA's strategy and kept one of SCA's main competitors – Stora – from growing too big and powerful. The PWA transaction was successfully carried out without an auction, although the German system complicated the negotiation process and (re)produced certain unconventional terms. Soon after that purchase SCA again began to question the merits of running a fine paper business and whether that part of PWA perhaps ought to be sold. Eventually the fine paper business was put in order and separated from the other graphic paper operations to create 'SCA Fine Paper' – an arrangement that made future structural deals easier.

16.5.5 Internal Conflicts about SCA's Future

In the 1990s the impact of Anglo-American corporate governance ideals increased dramatically in Sweden and many other countries as a consequence of the deregulation of the financial markets (including the one for corporate control). As so often, Sweden was one of the nations that was most keen to adapt to US and (particularly) UK practices, but the EU, too, began to promote similar market liberalism, and discussed, for example, the merits of a governance system that put stronger emphasis on 'shareholder value'. Most European countries and many countries in Asia and the Americas had regulations that in some way hampered extreme market liberalism (and that was actually to some extent valid also for the UK and the US). For the Nordic countries that already had regulations that gave the shareholder the upper hand, the invading Anglo-American ideology and practice tipped the balance further in that same direction (strong shareholder power).

In those days[43] many special national regulations, codes and customs counteracted the 'free' market for corporate control (foundations, golden shares, shares with different voting rights, stakeholder rights, etc.). Among many of the issues the Swedish corporate governance debate critically addressed were the cross-ownerships between companies. So, eventually SCA was 'forced' to give up its participation in the consortium that protected its main owner Industrivärden (and indirectly therefore SCA) from hostile takeover attempts. SCA's executives were also compelled to leave Industrivärden's board. However, neither of the outcomes had a significant impact on the governance processes, as the Handelsbanken/Industrivärden sphere also was based on strong personal ties, and they were not broken just because the cross-ownerships had to be abandoned.

In the late 1990s SCA's strategy was still based on its three 'classic' core businesses – packaging, hygiene and printing papers[44] – although signs had appeared within the company that the last was losing ground. More and more the printing paper business was discussed in terms of how efficiently its machines were utilized, rather than in what ways it could be expanded. Europe was still regarded as SCA's home market, although the ambition for the hygiene business in particular was for it to become an important actor on the global scene. Market leadership was sought everywhere possible, and it was important to participate in certain of the on-going international consolidation processes, particularly in those involving fine paper. At the same time, the idea of splitting SCA began to gain momentum, as particularly Gardell, a board member who represented a minor holding, tried to put pressure on SCA's controlling shareholder to support such a path. Gardell claimed that SCA was a too complicated construct for the stock market to handle (i.e. the analysts were unable to understand and value its wide range of businesses), and that its mix of cyclical and non-cyclical products made it difficult for (potential) investors to act. Gardell wanted to split SCA using its three core businesses as base units that could be either sold or listed. Thus, each of them should either be moved to a more fitting constellation or made capable of standing alone. However, he had trouble gaining support for his idea, and the fact that the board was a rather weak agency did not improve his chances of acceptance. Such crucial strategic discussions were usually held 'somewhere else' outside SCA's board, that is to say, in informal discussions conducted in various arenas in the Handelsbanken/Industrivärden sphere.

In the end, the board decided not to follow Gardell's suggestion that SCA ought to be divided, and that stance was decisive for how SCA continued to develop in the early 21st century. The main argument for a coherent SCA was that each of the core businesses needed the combined (financial) strength of all three to be able to successfully expand its business in the on-going global races. In addition, strong operative links existed between the different businesses that comprised SCA, because each core business needed secure sourcing of forest-based resources at competitive prices, and because most of the plants in northern Sweden were both well integrated and horizontally linked.

16.5.6 Further Expansion Efforts

SCA had become a world-leading packaging company with one striking weakness – a very thin market position in the US.[45] To remedy this, its leaders decided to try to expand the company's businesses in that country. Since that would take some time, the efforts to expand in Europe continued and utilized some of the available financial resources. New investments were made in Germany, Hungary and Turkey. In addition, SCA tried to take a 'big bite' by buying the French packaging company Otor, but because of a competitor's (Stora's) efforts to block the attempt and discoveries of undisclosed deals between Otor and other firms, SCA decided to withdraw. SCA also showed interest in (parts of) French Cellulose du Pin, but as Smurfit competed for that purchase, SCA saw no chance of winning and abandoned that path as well.

All those difficulties in expanding in the packaging businesses led the board to question whether Western Europe should be the main focus of SCA's efforts. Those doubts did not disappear even after Champion's 25 per cent in Obbola and 60 per cent of the UK company Le Sac were acquired. The board increasingly stressed that management should implement SCA's 'new' packaging strategy and expand that business to the new markets that were rapidly emerging in Eastern Europe and Asia (and continue to seek a better position in North America). That strategy soon bore fruit in Asia in the form of a joint venture (in China with US Weyerhaeuser), a part ownership (16% of Central Packaging Group with operations in China, Malaysia, Indonesia, Singapore and Thailand) and a large plant (in China).

Nonetheless, most of the purchases of companies still took place in Europe (foremost in Western Europe, i.e. in Austria, Belgium, Denmark, Finland, France, Germany, Holland, Italy, Ireland, Spain, Switzerland and the UK). As a large part of the acquired firms also had operations in countries other than their homelands, SCA's packaging business soon covered most parts of Europe. SCA also bought individual plants all over the continent, for example, in Hungary, Poland, Italy and Turkey. However, it is important to note that SCA did not act alone on the market for corporate control – its competitors were at least as active, and several sizeable mergers occurred (e.g. Jefferson Smurfit bought Stone, International Paper acquired both Union Camp and KNP, and 'financial investors' took on Kappa, BT's corrugated business).

Due to the intense competition in the global packaging industry around the turn of the millennium, SCA decided to issue new shares to secure sufficient financial muscle to be able to act forcefully and expand its activities. Its expansion discussions then foremost addressed various possible mergers and other kinds of far-reaching joint efforts, particularly with AssiDomän, Jefferson Smurfit, Metsä-Serla, Norske Skog, SAPPI and Stora. After some time it became clear that Jefferson Smurfit would be the best merger alternative (or partner). The problem with that combination, however, was that SCA was convinced that the European regulating authorities never would accept it, as the new constellation would be too dominating. Given that obstacle, SCA decided to abandon that path. Acquiring AssiDomän, however, looked to be a good idea, and as it was expected that the authorities might accept such a step, the two companies began to discuss some kind of joint effort.

One possibility was that SCA would buy AssiDomän and pay with its own shares. That would provide the Swedish state with a 10 per cent holding, a solution the state found perfectly acceptable. However, several of SCA's board members did not like that idea. They thought that state ownership might make private actors less interested in investing in the new constellation, and that they actually might be reluctant to co-operate in other ways, too. Thus, a state minority position was expected to lower the value of the current (controlling) shareholders' holdings. As regards the operations, SCA disliked getting both a large sacks business and a sizeable raw material production. Still, since AssiDomän was valued at a rather low level, there was certainly room to make a favourable deal. Indeed, the possibility of dividing the target company and keeping the most fitting parts tempted SCA.

As the government was eager for the state to exit most of its timber processing activities in the forest-based sector, it made SCA an offer in 1999. SCA was mainly interested in finding out whether it would be possible to merge and list the two companies' packaging businesses, while AssiDomän's CEOs leaned more towards some kind of joint venture. SCA then considered the alternative to buy all of AssiDomän except the forests (which the state would never sell), which would represent a much more complicated operation for which the buyer would have to orchestrate a highly demanding mix of restructuring and selling. SCA director Gardell proposed that Custos, where he was the CEO, should shoulder the responsibility and organize and execute AssiDomän's divestment process, but the owner (represented by the government) instead asked AssiDomän's board to do that work themselves (and reap the profit from that effort). As it turned out, AssiDomän invited bids for most of its businesses, eventually also for its packaging business. For that business, Kappa offered the highest price, and to some actors' surprise the Swedish state had no problem accepting non-Swedish owners (and private equity). So, in the end and despite all efforts, SCA got no part of AssiDomän.

Back in 1997 SCA had decided that its hygiene business should focus on incontinence products (as a multi-channel affair), tissue (for the AFH market) and selected private label products (tissue and fluff). Thus, the incontinence business should continue its global expansion, but how to deal with the diapers in Europe became an open question. One idea was that Mölnlycke should sell the brands to Kimberly-Clark, but a catch was that the buyer also wanted to include Mölnlycke's Falkenberg plant and certain selected contracts in a deal. That was not acceptable for Mölnlycke because it needed that unit's effective large-scale production to run its private label businesses.

The same year another US corporation – Procter & Gamble – also approached SCA/Mölnlycke with the intention of acquiring the tissue part of its hygiene business. Procter & Gamble in fact indicated ('threatened') that it would build its own tissue plants in Europe if SCA/Mölnlycke did not agree to sell. SCA/Mölnlycke considered responding with an offer to sell certain tissue plants (e.g. Stembert) to Procter & Gamble in exchange for the opportunity to buy the American company's incontinence business. However, as was the case with Kimberly-Clark, Procter & Gamble was most interested in acquiring the unit that SCA never would sell (the Falkenberg plant). Taking the fight with Procter & Gamble in Europe further, SCA bought a major holding in Metsä-Serla's tissue unit, thereby blocking some of Procter & Gamble's targets and ambitions. Because of the very tough competitive situation in Europe in the hygiene sector, SCA had to devote sizeable resources to investigations of many more or less realistic strategic alternatives. Basically, since SCA had to be prepared for 'everything', it refined its network to be able to get early and reliable information about its competitors' aims and plans.

Another US corporation, Fort James, informed some of SCA's executive actors in 1998 that it wanted to buy SCA's hygiene business, but that offer was immediately turned down. Merely a year later Fort James returned to SCA and suggested some form of merger. Because it was interested in Fort James's European operations, SCA decided to meet with that company's leaders and discuss the matter. SCA's board members expressed quite different opinions about the merits of a grand merger between the two companies. Those in favour particularly stressed two advantages: the valuation (pricing) of the US company and its well-run European operations. Those opposing a deal instead put emphasis on the high operative risk (following from huge cultural differences and an expected dominance of US-flavoured governance and management practices) and the high risk that SCA would lose control (because shares with different voting rights would probably not be accepted). In the end, the proposed merger did not take place.

While continuing its efforts to develop its hygiene business in the US, SCA expanded its tissue operations in Europe by buying firms in the UK, Portugal and Spain, and it also grew in other parts of the world (i.e. outside Europe and the US), for example, through new joint ventures in the Americas (Chile and Jamaica) and expansion in South Africa and Tunisia. SCA's growth problems in the US continued for some time, as the prices for the companies that acted on that market were high. Acquisitions usually required issues of new shares, but SCA regarded the current SEK–USD exchange rate as too unfavourable for that kind of financing. Suddenly a breakthrough occurred, as the US authorities conditioned Georgia Pacific's purchase of Fort James on the sale of a part of it, and fortunately that part fitted SCA's needs (both content and price). Thus, at last SCA's US expansion took off, and there was more to come.

16.5.7 Establishing MoDo Paper

There still remained the problem of what SCA should do with its large graphic paper operations, particularly after that business lost priority in relation to hygiene and packaging. Concern about the future of the more and more globalized newsprint business had not prevented SCA's board from approving sizeable investments in Aylesford (newsprint) and Laakirchen (SC paper), making the company even stronger in 'white papers'. Some directors actually expressed doubts about whether such investments were really the best strategy for SCA, particularly as several competitors also invested heavily in that field (Norske Skog [newsprint], Haindl [LWC], Lang [journal paper] and Perlen [LWC]). That intense competition and the high increases in capacities led the investment banks to begin discussing structural solutions with most leaders in the 'white paper' industry. SCA tried to navigate in that messy situation and sought a partner for some of its PWA plants. Discussions were held with Enso, KNP, SAPPI and Stora, even if only the last two were seen as fully capable of running a consolidated fine paper business. Soon a few more candidates were added to that listing: Metsä-Serla, International Paper, Burgo and CVC. A major obstacle for SCA was that none of those corporations wanted to include the Wifstavarf unit as part of a deal.

That meant that MoDo once again became the main candidate for a partnership. The operative fit between the two companies' graphic papers was adequate, but everyone seemed to expect co-operation problems because of the long history of unsuccessful attempts to integrate (parts of) the two companies and the difficult personal relationships among some of the leaders. Still, both companies were Swedish, so that cultural similarity ought to make at least some parts of a merger process a bit easier. A stumbling block on MoDo's part was that its second biggest shareholder, the Kempe foundations through its Chair Carl Kempe Jr, regarded fine paper as the core of its (former?) family heirloom, so MoDo was not ready to give it up easily. However, for SCA (and MoDo) it was probably an even bigger obstacle that neither of the two corporations wanted to be on the buying side. Both parties realized that the only possible path forward was to merge their fine paper businesses and remain as joint owners (at least for some years). After much toing and froing, the negotiations bore fruit in 1999 creating Europe's third largest fine paper unit (Modo Paper), equally owned by MoDo (soon renamed Holmen) and SCA. That agreement had been preceded by talks about listing Modo Paper (rejected because of a lack of interest from the investors) and about distributing its shares to the owners of the two founding companies. Questions had also been raised about how long Holmen and SCA should be obliged to keep their holdings in Modo Paper. The deadlock was suddenly broken up less than a year later, when Metsä-Serla stated that it wanted to acquire Modo Paper and was willing to pay what the sellers saw as a favourable price. So, in the year 2000, after having tried many alternative paths, SCA succeeded in getting out of the fine paper business (with substantial profit).

The remaining graphic businesses were organized closer to SCA's units for basic resources (forestry, pulp, etc.), and then three crucial strategic choices had to be made: expansion or no expansion, organic growth or growth through acquisitions and global or regional presence. However, those three choices were indirectly affected to a large extent by the actions of the other corporations with big graphic papers operations. Basically, two paths were available for the competing corporations: either leave the graphic papers business (or parts of it) or expand and become one of the few actors remaining in the early 21st century. The most striking acquisitions that SCA's competitors made at the time were the ones in New Zealand (Norske Skog bought Fletcher Challenge [pulp and paper]), Spain (Holmen bought Papelera Peninsular) and the US (Stora Enso bought Consolidated Paper [printing papers] and UPM-Kymmene bought Repap [printing papers]). SCA was itself approached by UPM-Kymmene (2001), whose leading actors wanted to find out whether it would be possible to merge. As SCA did not want to return to fine paper, and as the other operative synergies seemed to be weak, its executives rejected the idea.

At the beginning of the 21st century, a rumour went around that certain financial actors might bid for a large part of SCA. Custos and Goldman Sachs were actually looking for US funds that might be interested in making such an offer. However, SCA's biggest shareholder Industrivärden strongly opposed such a development, which would put Custos and some external funds rather than SCA in the driver's seat (and set SCA [at least temporarily] in a minority position). Those talks put to a test Industrivärden's capacity to defend SCA from hostile takeover attempts (it withstood the test). At that time Industrivärden even considered swapping its B-shares for A-shares to strengthen its voting power within SCA (according to Swedish regulations that would have been a dubious step, and, consequently, it was not taken).

SCA's continued expansion efforts in the US included both a purchase of Johnson & Johnson's incontinence business in North America and an acquisition of a part of the new Georgia Pacific–Fort James constellation (cf. above). In addition, SCA entered into a deal with Johnson & Johnson under which it would sell some of SCA's consumer products on the US market. A third larger purchase was Encore Paper Company, which provided SCA with both converted paper and AFH products. By then SCA had become number three in the world in the comprehensive hygiene business (only Procter & Gamble and Kimberly-Clark were bigger). SCA had also become the largest provider of quality products for retailers' private brands and controlled several strong regional tissue- and fluff-based brands, as well as certain global brands for incontinence and menstrual products.

The packaging business was not left behind. In the US, SCA acquired Tuscarora (packages for fragile goods), RPA (protective [high-tech] packages), Insulated Shipping (cold chain packages) and (part of) Marko Foam Products. That expansion led SCA to establish a North American holding company for all its activities on that continent. So, a few years after the start of the new millennium, SCA had not only become Europe's leading producer of corrugated and its raw materials, but also world leader for tailor-made protective packaging. Broadly speaking its packaging operations focused on special packages and industry packages that were sold on three continents (Asia, Europe [70%] and North America).

16.5.8 SCA's Development – Some Tentative Conclusions

Close examination of SCA's strategic path reveals that the impact of nature-driven occurrences was minimal. However, nature-based resources played a much more important role and substantially impacted how SCA developed over time. The expected shortage of timber made SCA question both its heavy concentration on pulp production and its dependence on Swedish timber. Like most of its competitors SCA decided to look for (cheap) timber outside Sweden as well as find ways to integrate forward (invest in processing of the pulp rather than new pulp production). As a large exporter of pulp, SCA had to be very careful about how it carried out that move to the right in the value chain (i.e. it should not compete with its own customers).

SCA found suitable timber resources in British Columbia (Canada) and invested there. Though the company considered a similar effort in South America (Aracruz, Brazil), it did not have the financial resources to invest. That financial strain actually forced SCA to choose between, on the one hand, further efforts along that global raw material path, and, on the other hand, 'securing' the market for its pulp and liner production. Eventually the latter alternative – investments in (European) corrugated/packaging firms – was chosen. To a large extent, it was the abundance of high-quality long-fibres (cf. spruce) on the home front that led SCA to choose kraftliner as one of its core businesses, which in turn constituted the basis for its expansion into packaging, and later contributed to making it a global player in that field. For quite some time, it was also considered crucial to control another key nature-based resource that was abundant in Sweden – (hydro)electric power. However, in a critical period (the early 1990s) when most large forest-based corporations around the world competed to 'occupy' the most attractive parts of the forest-based industry's value chains, SCA decided that the sizeable capital that was tied up in the company's power plants could be better used as a financial platform for its expansion investments (the financial situation had to be restored after the purchases of Laakirchen, Peaudouce, Italcarta and Reedpack). Thus, unlike several of its competitors, SCA sold off its power plants.

When it comes to forces that basically are actor initiated, SCA – like most of its competitors – responded both to the rapid technological development (driven by scientists, innovators and mechanical engineers) and to the fast-growing demand. Thus, it was the advantages of the ever-increasing scale of machines together with changing pulp demand that in the 1950s forced SCA's executives to integrate the company's many small units into one coherent whole. These same factors also stimulated SCA to upgrade its R&D operations and identify possible ways to integrate forward.

Only a decade later SCA had to decide whether it should follow a path based on several minor specialized pulp and/or paper plants or concentrate its production within fewer and bigger bulk-producing units. SCA's CEO in the 1960s (Mossberg) favoured the 'bulky' option and executed the necessary – but for (particularly) the employees extremely stressful – rationalizations. That effort created the platform SCA needed to be able to compete for a position on the most attractive value chains in the forest-based industry, and perhaps even dominate some of those over the coming decades. So, although Mossberg did not solve all of SCA's scale and efficiency problems during his 12 years as CEO, he certainly took care of most of them and laid the groundwork for his successor to expand the company. The restructuring Mossberg oversaw was necessary because otherwise SCA would have been left behind its competitors in the decisive races that took off in the 1980s.

The industry's technological progress affected not only the operating scales and, consequently, SCA's growth, but also what products it could offer and their attractiveness on the market. That effect was particularly visible in the hygiene business, where SCA was successful in developing and producing pulp qualities that matched the specific requirements that its large, hygiene-materials-producing customer Mölnlycke lined up. That technological capability contributed significantly to Mölnlycke's choice of SCA as a partner and represented the first step towards the successful and sizeable business that SCA/Mölnlycke built during the last quarter of the 20th century. Later, however, Mölnlycke's own 'rusty' technological capacity produced a crisis when it was clear that its diapers were inferior to those of the big competitors (and inefficiently produced).

Market changes were massive as well and certainly had an impact on SCA's development. In the aftermath of WWII the demand for SCA's pulp from its biggest customer market (North America) began to weaken radically (50%). That decline stimulated the company's leaders to develop and implement a strategy that both reduced its dependence on pulp and processed that raw material further. Obviously, there was a third alternative, namely to find new pulp customers for the qualities that US customers no longer bought, but in a short- and mid-term perspective that path was found to be unrealistic. When the timber-sourcing problem was considered along with the pulp-surplus one, the preferred solution was to integrate forward in some way, and newsprint was the obvious candidate, as it already was produced in-house (cf. path dependence). However, the difficult question was whether SCA ought to also expand its pulp processing in some other direction – and if so, to what kind of product.

Actual and expected changes in demand had a strong impact on SCA's development all through the second half of the 20th century. Newsprint was a clear example of that. Initially (i.e. after WWII), demand for that product grew rapidly, so SCA responded to that opportunity by expanding and differentiating its output to the growing segments (SC and LWC). However, the increasing demand also attracted other corporations to that business, so the newsprint cartel became an important 'regulator' of volumes and prices. That 'informal organization' was even used to block large expansion investments (SCA tried to use that trick when Stora Kopparberg announced its Hylte investment). But doubts about the future of graphic papers began to slowly emerge (especially for bulky newsprint and fine paper) as new information technology was expected to decrease demand for printing papers, and instead allow for radically new ways of distributing information (i.e. through the Internet). On top of that, the newsprint cartel was declared illegal and eventually dissolved, so no 'help' could be expected from that source.

Yet, SCA's graphic papers as a whole were still profitable in the 1980s. They essentially functioned as 'cash cows' contributing to the company's expansion efforts in its other business areas. As late as in the 1990s, SCA invested in two new LWC machines, verifying that the expected decline in demand had not yet hit all kinds of printing papers. Because SCA's top executives still believed that it was possible to build a prosperous future in that business, they tried to expand it by making large acquisitions in Europe that would add to SCA's capacity in the more attractive SC and LWC segments. Some of those attempts failed (Feldmühle and MoDo), while others instead were more successful (Laakirchen and PWA).

However, the expansion of the market for graphic papers that had lasted all through the first decades after WWII stalled in the early 1990s, and the situation gradually began to turn in a downward direction, particularly for fine paper. SCA was rather quickly convinced that the overcapacity in that segment was there to stay and that structural changes were required. In order to prepare for that development, SCA Fine Paper was established. Not long afterwards, SCA joined with MoDo to establish a joint fine paper unit named Modo Paper. In the end, that new company was soon sold to Metsä-Serla, which had taken up the task of leading the European restructuring of the fine paper industry.

First and foremost it was the demand from the rapidly growing packaging industry that made the liner path so attractive that SCA never hesitated to keep it as one of its core businesses. The focus on liner could actually be traced back to the 1950s when SCA built its first plant for that product. Thus, liner's continuing status as a core activity could be seen as an outflow of 'path dependence', that is to say, as a product of the know-how SCA built up over time in that field. The decision was also facilitated by a raw material advantage, as SCA's kraftliner, which was based on the long fibres offered by the Nordic spruce, was superior to the competitors' testliner, which instead utilized various short-fibre trees. Thus, SCA possessed all the necessary process and market knowledge when the market turned in kraftliner's favour. Nevertheless, the situation for SCA's kraftliner remained somewhat complicated, as the production of packages required a second main ingredient, namely corrugated.

Thus, to become a significant and profitable actor in the packaging industry, SCA had to become a big producer of corrugated, too. That requirement very much shaped the way in which SCA expanded its packaging operations from the 1990s and onwards (i.e. through purchases of many smaller firms, as well as through 'big bites' like the acquisitions of Reedpack, Tuscarora and RPA[46]). Similar circumstances also affected SCA's choice of hygiene as one of its core businesses. At the beginning (i.e. before the acquisition of Mölnlycke), SCA housed only one hygiene product (which actually was licensed out). Because the actual and potential customers (retailers) did not appreciate such a meagre offering, SCA had to either leave that business or expand its product repertoire. The situation was not very different after the purchase of Mölnlycke, when SCA/Mölnlycke learned that the same customers expected to get both fluff- and tissue-based products from its suppliers. That pressure prompted SCA/Mölnlycke to increase its capacity to offer different types of tissue-based products. Thus, customer preferences had a strong impact on what path SCA decided to follow for its hygiene business.

Another force that originates in collective human efforts emanates from various kinds of institutions, that is to say, from formally and/or informally enforced systems of norms that have survived over periods of time. One such decisive institutional force that strongly influenced SCA's path after WWII was the set of new environmental laws that were enacted and made several of its older units unprofitable. That legislation certainly speeded up SCA's restructuring, that is to say, the process by which the collection of smaller companies was transformed to one integrated unit, although it was triggered primarily by the advantages linked to the new large-scale technologies. The cartels also represented a form of institution that (re)produced certain norms that SCA and most of the other member companies followed.

Some of the regulating institutions interfered with SCA more intensely when it was making acquisitions abroad or sought partnerships. The purchase of Italcarta represents one such example where national institutions activated culture-specific laws and regulations that almost brought the process to a halt. Such institutions mattered as well in Germany in the Feldmühle Nobel contest, for example, those that regulated possible shareholding levels and the form of stakeholder influence. Another decisive institutional force was manifested when the Swedish Minister for Finance obstructed SCA's attempt to establish a 'Swedish Pulp', which was supposed to reduce the industry's (including SCA's) problem with overcapacity. The national and regional institutions influenced not only how acquisition processes were conducted in general, but also how specific ones ended, for example, when the authorities conditioned approval of the Georgia Pacific–Fort James merger on a specific divestment (for which SCA became the 'perfect' harbour).

Important institutionalized norms were also activated in the intense debates that took place in Sweden as Anglo-American corporate governance ideals took hold in many (Western) countries in the 1990s. Some of the critique of the Nordic system addressed the presence of cross-ownerships, a way of organizing shareholdings used by some Swedish companies, among them SCA and its major owner Industrivärden. The critique was troublesome for SCA because Industrivärden's capacity to defend the company against hostile takeovers was suddenly at stake. Thus, two institutional systems – the Anglo-American and the Nordic – clashed, and the former had the upper hand at the time.

Actor impact works not only through those collectively established institutions that have survived the challenges of time, but also through current individual actions. This study has focused on those categories of actors that formally are the most responsible for how corporations develop over time, that is to say, shareholders and executives. For SCA, particularly the latter category mattered a great deal, since after WWII the company never experienced a situation in which one individual (or family/dynasty, etc.) had a controlling shareholding. Instead, the top executives at Handelsbanken (SCA's main bank) and Industrivärden (SCA's controlling owner) carried out the ownership function and populated the board. In essence, it is their rationales that have influenced how SCA developed after WWII.

Initially, the executives' contributions involved primarily the joining of quite a few relatively autonomous units to build a classic integrated corporation. SCA's CEOs Engström and Mossberg carried out most of that task, and later the latter also implemented profound rationalizations and restructurings. Even the most significant change of SCA's path since its founding in the early 1930s – the acquisition of Mölnlycke – was driven by executive actors. It was SCA's CEO Rydin and its Deputy CEO Wahlström that drove the process, and they were supported in turn by Mölnlycke's CEO Dahlsten and Deputy CEO Daun. Yet even after those four executives had made up their minds, they (at least two of them) still had to convince the boards and shareholders of the companies involved. For SCA's leaders who lacked a strong counterpart, that is to say, a sizeable shareholder outside the Handelsbanken/Industrivärden sphere, that was not a problem. In contrast, for Mölnlycke's top management who faced both a classic 'independent' group of shareholders and a classic 'independent' board, it took some effort to convince the disparate owners' board representatives. Obviously, the strong track record of Mölnlycke's CEO (and his team) contributed to the board's decision to approve the merger with SCA, despite the fact that another actor offered Mölnlycke's shareholders a most tempting price for their shares.

Within SCA it was quite clear to everybody that the company's strategic development since WWII was driven by the CEOs, and that the directors – foremost – functioned as critical examiners of the ideas and proposals top management put forward. The power of the CEO position made the rationales of those who over the years held that post almost critical for how the company developed. Rydin, for example, was perceived as a careful, risk-averse and pensive actor, so his rationale probably fitted best with a conservative consolidation strategy. His successor Martin-Löf was instead known as a straightforward, risk-seeking and energetic personality, and thus his approach corresponded most closely with a radical expansion strategy. Together, however, they created a rather balanced executive rationale that had a significant impact on SCA's long-term development (cf. e.g. the acquisitions of Peaudoce, Italcarta, PWA, Reedpack and Tuscarora).

The importance of the executives' approaches was also illustrated in the SCA case by the strong effect various personal friendships had on the company's choices of paths. For example, for the process that preceded SCA's pivotal acquisition of Mölnlycke, it was decisive for the outcome that some of the leading actors had built confidence in each other (e.g. Rydin–Daun and Wahlström–Dahlsten). Similar trusting relationships existed among several key actors in SCA and St Regis, which facilitated St Regis's decision to invest in SCA's liner production at Obbola. Differing actor rationales and the relationships among the actors (strained as well as close) had a strong impact on the MoDo contest (cf. the behaviour of Carlgren, Carl Kempe Jr, Lundberg, Löf, Martin-Löf and Rydin). The same held true when SCA sold some of its units to ASSI and Ncb. In the case of Ncb in particular, its CEO had a powerful position that he combined with high expansion ambitions, so that in the end his aggressive approach contributed to SCA's rather smooth exit from some less attractive plants. Other examples of the impact of individual actorhood could easily be found in the Iggesund contest (e.g. Carlgren, Marcus Wallenberg Sr and Lars G. Sundblad), the acquisition of Peaudouce (e.g. Arnault's network), Laakirchen (e.g. the Heinzel family), Feldmühle Nobel (e.g. the Flick brothers), AssiDomän (e.g. Gardell and Magnusson) and in the suggested splitting of SCA (e.g. Gardell, Martin-Löf and Rydin).

As regards the two main 'arenas' for corporate governance efforts – the operational and the financial flows – SCA worked hard to calibrate them, that is to say, make sure that they were in balance. Accomplishing that had been rather tough for SCA ever since WWII, despite the continuous and strong support the company got from its main bank and its business sphere. 'Full' bank backing was actually almost a necessity for SCA until the 1950s, when its improved finances made it possible to cut the formal link to the bank. From the time of that 'break', the financial risk gradually moved from the banks back to SCA itself, giving the new CEO certain freedom of action. At the time SCA also began to consider different ways to integrate forward to become less dependent on the volatile pulp market. Even so, the company's finances were not particularly strong. As a result, it had to, for example, give up its operative ambition to build a strong raw material position abroad, as it was regarded as more important for SCA to expand its market for pulp and liner.

In the early 1970s when Rydin took office as CEO he learned that several production plants housed machines that had to be radically rebuilt, replaced or even sold, but as SCA's finances were rather weak, he instead used various forms of 'plant patching'. Unlike his predecessors, though, Rydin eventually got the financial opportunity to expand SCA's operations. One major question at the time was whether the improved finances allowed for an expansion of the embryonic hygiene operations (in addition to the 'givens' in the classic forest-based businesses). That matter was soon resolved when the opportunity emerged to buy Mölnlycke, which urgently needed a company like SCA with strong financial muscle in order to implement its grand expansion plan. Although the Mölnlycke acquisition was a rather 'big bite', it did not seriously hurt SCA's overall financial situation, but it did, at least temporarily, affect how much the company could invest in the other businesses.

SCA could not postpone its expansion investments until the finances were in good shape, because then the company risked either becoming an acquisition target or being squeezed out of its current businesses. So, healthy finances were required in the 1980s, as most of the larger forest-based corporations had grown out of their home markets and a new globalized industry structure was forming that would set the competitive conditions for many years to come. To carry out all its planned acquisitions (cf. Laakirchen, Peaudouce, PWA, Reedpack, etc.) and investments (cf. MoDo), SCA needed to free capital and sold several businesses and – even more important – its power resources.

Early in the 21st century, the global race finally took SCA to the US market (e.g. [part of] Johnson & Johnson, Encore Paper, Tuscarora, RPA and Insulated Shipping), a move that was appreciated by many shareholders, analysts and economic journalists. At that time, however, critical voices were also heard that called for a splitting of the company, claiming that the benefits of keeping all its (core) businesses and their support operations together were too low. The most important counterargument that SCA's executives put forward was a financial one: they asserted that each of the businesses needed the combined (financial) body of them all to be able to successfully expand in the on-going global race (thus, the actual size of the balance sheet mattered). So, once again it became obvious how important it was for SCA to continuously calibrate its two basic governance flows – the operative and the financial one – and that it was a task that both the board and top management had consistently given highest priority.

NOTES

1. As this chapter directly builds on all the earlier ones, notes will not be repeated. Only new information qualifies for a note in this chapter.
2. In this study ownership is usually (but not always) equivalent to 'shareholding'.
3. Actually it was the Swedish citizens that had that status.
4. An obvious exception was the former CEO.
5. The forests had a very low book value.
6. The state owned 51% of AssiDomän at the time.
7. The state's shareholding in AssiDomän amounted then to 40%.
8. The number is used to distinguish it from Vasaskog that later was renamed Sveaskog (1).
9. The number is used to distinguish it from Sveaskog 2.
10. Based on water, wind, sunshine or uranium.
11. Swedish (and Nordic) legislation assigns shareholders an exceptionally strong position in corporations (the like of which is difficult to be found elsewhere).
12. MoDo also got a favourable price for the Hörnefors unit.
13. It is still unusual in the 21st century.
14. Dagens Nyheter/Marieberg (the Bonnier family).
15. Holmens Bruk decided to use the spelling 'Br*a*viken', as the letter 'å' seldom is used outside the Nordic countries.
16. ≥10% is in Sweden associated with strong minority rights.
17. Technically MoDo reduced its holding to below 50% because of a promise to Iggesund from Carlgren.
18. Carlgren had made Lejeune head of MoDo's French operations. Lejeune was even allowed to run his own forest-based operations, and he was not made part of MoDo's formal organizational hierarchy – instead, he reported directly to Carlgren, and eventually he even got a board seat in MoDo. So, Carlgren trusted him completely.
19. Bonnier's ownership was also carried out through another company that the family controlled, namely Marieberg.
20. E.g. Kooperativa Förbundet's holding.
21. Iggesund had to sell them when MoDo took full control of Iggesund.
22. Because of market problems that investment was postponed to 2006.
23. Particularly the ones in 1977, 1981, 1982 and 1992.
24. In the 1970s and 1990s.
25. Its statutes prohibited debts of the needed magnitude.
26. Legislation is similar in the other Nordic countries.

27. 1:1000.
28. Later that lack of capacity to link the operative and the financial flows significantly contributed to his personal bankruptcy, and also to MoDo's poor finances during the first years in the 1990s.
29. The company was also rather big on the newsprint market.
30. Soon the sphere reached more than 90%.
31. The general public owned the remaining 20%.
32. In Swedish: 'koncernchef'.
33. Stora's CEO Berggren, Investor's Chair Peter Wallenberg and Investor's CEO Dahlbäck together ran Stora.
34. The European Coal and Steel Community.
35. Finland applied in 1992.
36. PWA actually accounted for almost half of SCA's bleached pulp and about 15% of its liner, so obviously how to handle PWA was crucial for SCA's future development.
37. Wifstavarf became a separate legal unit equally owned by SCA and PWA.
38. A state-owned forestry company.
39. In which newsprint is a part.
40. Finland devalued its currency in those days, which immediately made Kymmene more competitive (and probably less eager to engage in joint efforts).
41. However, the actors disagree if there ever was such an offering.
42. For example, Procter & Gamble was globally seven times as big as SCA in diapers.
43. Many of them still exist in the early 21st century.
44. Printing papers here refer to graphic papers except fine papers.
45. SCA made an agreement with the third biggest US packaging company Weyerhaeuser in 1992, but that was only a minor step towards becoming a respected player on that continent.
46. A US speciality packaging company.

17. A few more general conclusions

In this final chapter a few more general conclusions are offered as tentative answers to the two comprehensive research questions initially formulated (Ch. 1), addressing both what main forces largely determine corporate development paths and – in that rather wide context – the particular impact of actorhood and ownership. However, these terse conclusions – and several others – have also been described in a more detailed way in the two preceding chapters (Ch. 15, 'The impact of nature, occurrences, institutions and actor collectives on corporate paths' and Ch. 16, 'The impact of individual actors on corporate paths').

This chapter is divided into four parts, each one addressing one of the more important findings that were generated through the extensive empirical study (cf. Chapters 4–14) and in the previous analyses (Ch. 15 and Ch. 16). Thus, tentative conclusions are presented regarding how intricate interplays between the driving forces seem to determine both governance efforts and development processes (section 17.1), what kind of forces usually make it possible for corporations to adopt radically new paths (17.2), why calibration of operative and financial flows enable corporate development over time (17.3), and why the overall ownership settings are crucial for the ways corporations move forward (17.4).

17.1 CORPORATE PATHS EMERGE FROM INTRICATE INTERPLAYS OF DECIDING FORCES

The four master cases described in Chapters 6–14 illustrate that corporate governance and the associated development processes are changeable, complex and difficult to predict, and that they tend to be shaped by intricate interplays among those driving forces that were listed and described in Chapter 1, that is to say, natural occurrences, nature-based resources, scientific/technological breakthroughs, demand pull, cultural and institutional pressures, and the activities of individual or collective actors. The master cases also indicate that it is not solely economic 'realities' that determine the governance activities and the formation of corporate paths, but also (changing) social, cultural and political circumstances.

If one tries to determine how the corporations studied have developed through the 19th century, a fairly clear picture crystallizes, namely that almost all of them have progressed in a similar way. They have gradually moved along the same value chain that was composed of (from left to right) forestry, timber cutting, woodware production, manual linen lump based paper manufacturing, pulp production and various kinds of industrial timber-based paper production (e.g. fine paper and newsprint). A similar picture emerges if one puts together all their activities during the 20th century (and also includes the first years of the 21st century) – almost all of them have continued their journey to the right in the value chain.

In the 20th and 21st centuries, however, each of the companies has also embarked slowly but surely on a rather different path forward, and some of them have even tried to enter more distant value chains. In some cases those relatively unrelated additions proved to be temporary (cf. e.g. MoDo's investments in the chemical industry), but in a few other cases that radical change became 'permanent' and moved the focus of some of the companies towards quite different kinds of businesses (cf. e.g. SCA's step into the hygiene sector). However, one has to keep in mind that, although most of the companies integrated forward in some way, they did not abandon all the stages to the left in the value chain – in many cases they continued those activities, although to a lesser extent, and mainly as input into the further processing stages (e.g. in the production of printing papers, liner, cardboard, fine paper and sacks).

In their efforts to get 'closer to the customer' most companies tried to enter paths that reduced head-on competition, particularly as, by the late 20th century, it had become impossible to lean on cartels[1] to solve that problem. Instead, they participated in the races to be (one of) the first to enter, dominate and/or 'occupy' a certain market segment – an achievement that put strong pressure on the competitors to find other paths. So, product specialization certainly emerged, although most corporations still continued to house more than one core business, and for several of them such a relatively broad repertoire was kept and still pursued in the early 21st century.

However, ultimately it was the link between the operational and the financial flows that determined the companies' product ranges and expansion possibilities, particularly as the increasing economies of scale put strong pressure on the corporations' technological and financial capacities. For example, in the 1990s Holmen decided to reduce the number of its core businesses to two (printing papers and fine cardboard), and SCA began to focus more and more on its hygiene and packaging businesses. For similar reasons Stora decided to concentrate its investments on newsprint and packaging, and AssiDomän planned[2] to divest all its businesses except two (packaging and forestry).

It is important to stress that it was not merely the ambition to avoid head-on competition that determined the corporate paths; in fact, the companies competed hard in some fields despite their efforts to avoid such situations. Rather, each corporation's unique accumulated experiences and resource settings mattered, too (cf. path dependence). That was obvious in most of the corporations studied, but perhaps particularly visible in MoDo (fine paper), SCA (brown papers), Stora (newsprint) and Sveaskog (forestry).

Thus, although the forces that structured corporate paths basically were the same for all corporations investigated, it is clearly visible in the empirical material that the intrinsic and complex interplay of these driving forces allowed for many different actor interpretations and behaviour that contributed to rather different futures. Thus, corporate paths were also to a large extent dependent both on a corporation's own track record (i.e. what businesses it had learned to master) and on what positions the other corporations in the industry had taken (or tried to take).

17.2 BREAKING PATH DEPENDENCE

Though 'typical' development paths and the forces that had had a decisive influence on those processes can be detected, it is also evident from the descriptions of the master cases and in the previous analyses (cf. Ch. 15 and Ch. 16) that corporate paths now and then – although not very often – are broken and replaced by quite different ones. Those breaks are obviously of particular importance for how corporations develop over time, and the question then becomes what forces precipitate such radical changes.

Looking at the focal corporations one at a time, one common denominator emerges – the revised/new path is usually triggered by a combination of some kind of transformational 'event' and one or several leading actors' shared interpretation of (the significance of) that new circumstance. However, one exception to that rather frequent combination of determining forces is to be found in most of Domänverket's, ASSI's and AssiDomän's gradual transformation into Sveaskog, where internal actor initiatives – often unprovoked by environmental forces – have determined many of the basic transformations. For example, when AssiDomän became Sveaskog through various temporary constructs, the Swedish Prime Minister was very active in defining the expected outcome of the transformation process and made sure that his[3] vision was effectively pursued by putting the Minister of Industry in charge of the process. In that case an actor rationale (an ideology) really mattered: what made the Prime Minister take action was his strong conviction that the state (its citizens) should own a substantial portion of a nation's forest resources. However, there were also other leading actors who expressed and promoted quite different values. So, it was a fight between political ideals rather than sudden external pressures that spurred that dramatic transformation process for about a decade.

A look at the second master case, which concerned MoDo, Iggesund, Holmens Bruk and Holmen, indicates that the more typical combination of, on the one hand, external forces and, on the other hand, actor interpretations and initiatives was prevalent when their respective corporate paths were formed. For Iggesund, the successful addition of a new core business (quality cardboard) is an example of just that. There, the CEO discovered that a whole new business was emerging in the US (cardboard boxes for consumers), and he firmly believed that a similar big change would hit Europe soon. So, at Iggesund's board meetings he suggested that the company should embark on the quality cardboard path (there were alternatives) and tried to ensure that the company's pulp investments in the years to come would suit the needs associated with that new product segment. That was a risky step that took Iggesund into a new direction (forward integration instead of scale-based integration), but rather soon its quality cardboard became a success and consequently a new core business that almost relegated the company's cherished pulp production to a 'support function'.

For MoDo the two world wars functioned as a powerful external force, as they created national shortages of many important commodities that the company found it possible to manufacture. Those new production experiences soon aroused the company's interest in building up a new core business: chemical products based on raw materials from the forest industry. Thus, in the first half of the 20th century, MoDo's leading actors (i.e. the heads of the controlling owner dynasty) believed that MoDo could and should build part of its growth and profitability on that market. However, that idea rather soon faced a radically new resource situation, when chemical products based on petroleum began to win out over most efforts based on forest-based raw materials. Moreover, the new oil-based technology required investments of such a magnitude that it became totally impossible for MoDo to raise the necessary capital for that business (too). As a result, the company (reluctantly) had to give up its efforts to become one of the leading players in chemical products.

In the third case, Stora (Kopparberg), similar combinations of external pressures and circumstances, on the one hand, and actorhood, on the other hand, were present on several occasions. The most radical change of path occurred when Stora Kopparberg decided to abandon its steel operations in the 1970s (about half of the company was sold). That huge divestment was primarily triggered by worries about the future development of the European steel market, as many governments seemed to be prepared to give their countries' steel corporations sizeable subsidies to ensure that they survived the increasingly tough competition (growing overcapacity). Those actors that shared that understanding of the situation – particularly the leading actor of the dynasty that had controlled Stora Kopparberg for a long time and the company's CEO – acted to convince most of the other larger shareholders and the company's executive actors about the merits of a steel divestment, and in the end they were successful.

For SCA, finally, the acquisition of Mölnlycke represented the addition of a radically new business, and that bold effort far excelled over all the other large acquisitions that took place about a decade later. The latter additions were not particularly surprising, as they did not alter the company's chosen strategy and path. Those purchases rather strengthened SCA's existing core businesses (graphic papers and packaging) and increased SCA's general competitiveness on the European market.

Mölnlycke's success in the hygiene sector represented an external 'circumstance' that eventually caught the attention of some of SCA's leading actors. Yet it was far from obvious that they would find that company particularly interesting, as it also contained sizeable textile operations that did not complement SCA's classic forest-based activities particularly well. In the late 1960s there were two links between the companies – SCA ran its own minor hygiene business and delivered special pulp to Mölnlycke. What really decided the matter in the end were the four executive actors' interpretations of the situation and the actions they took. After many and long talks the CEOs and Deputy CEOs of the two companies became convinced that it would be a good idea to merge the two companies (SCA bought Mölnlycke), and eventually they also convinced the companies' boards and major shareholders that this audacious joint effort represented the best way ahead for both corporations.

17.3 CORPORATE GOVERNANCE – CALIBRATING OPERATIONAL AND FINANCIAL FLOWS

From most of the (master) cases it is evident that all sizeable efforts in the operational flows have to be calibrated with the prevailing financial situations. Such calibrations were indeed carried out in most of the corporations studied. For example, when large acquisitions were made that created financial strain, immediate actions were usually taken to strengthen the balance sheets (often parts of the [acquired] companies were sold). Those flow calibrations were particularly intense when SCA and Stora made their large acquisitions in the 1970s and 1980s, respectively. The financial pressure that resulted was handled in both companies mainly through divestments of parts of the acquired companies. Holmen is another example of a corporation that in the 1990s, when a new owner had taken control, stressed the necessity to continuously calibrate the two flows.

However, among the corporations studied there are also several examples of how a failure/inability to calibrate the two flows led to severe consequences. In the case of MoDo, for example, the incapacity of the head of the dynasty to successfully manage that relationship, particularly in the 1980s, along with the passivity of his closest associates, led both to a radical change in how the company was controlled and to his personal bankruptcy. In many respects the situation was similar in ASSI in the 1970s and 1980s, but in that case poor economic results rather than excessive risk-taking made ASSI's financial capacity insufficient to match top management's investment ambitions. However, unlike MoDo, ASSI had a controlling shareholder (the state) with almost 'unlimited' financial resources and a willingness to use them. Thus, it is not always merely the company's financial status that matters, but also the financial capacity and operative ambitions of its controlling shareholder(s).

Though the discussion thus far has addressed the situation in which a corporation's finances do not match its operative needs, the situation could sometimes also be the reverse, that is to say, that the financial resources far exceed what the executives' investment ideas and proposals require. In that case a quite different scenario emerges, namely that the corporation's management might make a better contribution to its shareholders (and other stakeholders) by instead distributing some of the 'surplus' capital to them (for better utilization elsewhere). Despite the fact that most of the studied corporations had powerful owners, who in certain cases could be expected to favour such a procedure, it was seldom used (although in some cases it was discussed; cf. the discussions that took place when Modo Paper was established [Ch. 10]).

Thus, from these few examples and the analyses and empirical material presented in this book, it seems unproblematic to submit the conclusion that it is important for any governance effort that the two basic corporate flows are calibrated continuously – if not, there is a risk that a corporation will either run into serious difficulties or deliver a (unnecessary) low return on its capital.

17.4 CORPORATE GOVERNANCE – THE IMPORTANCE OF THE OVERALL OWNERSHIP SETTING

Perhaps the most striking impression gained from the extensive empirical material presented in Chapters 6–14 and from the analyses provided in Chapters 15 and 16 has not been fully captured in the summarizing conclusions presented above. As mentioned earlier, what seems to permeate most of the corporations examined is how the changing, intricate interplays between the driving forces determine both governance efforts and development processes. Thus, corporate governance set-ups more closely resemble the output of unique, customized tailoring efforts than mass-produced items from the garment industry. It is also rather easy to see in the different master cases that single-force explanations seldom – if ever – capture how governance processes and corporate paths evolve over time. Yet, one of the driving forces stands out above the others throughout the whole empirical material: owner actorhood. That force is present and important in almost all the corporate governance set-ups found in this study. However, as for deciding forces more generally, owner actorhood does not work in isolation – it is always connected in one way or the other to one or several of the other dimensions that make up the overall ownership setting. Owner actorhood also sets the conditions for the other leading actors, that is to say, influences the executives' goals and action spaces.

Thus, all four master cases contain extensive material that indicates that to a large extent it is each corporation's unique ownership setting that determines how (i.e. by which actor or collective) natural and man-made occurrences will be interpreted. That conclusion is valid also when the value of current and potential natural resources is estimated and when a corporation has to relate to various kinds of institutionalized norms. Thus, the ownership setting and the accompanying owner and/or executive performance in continuous interplay with (some of) the other main forces will define the governance procedures and map out the corporate paths. Though the empirical material contains numerous examples of such interactions, it is only possible to present a few of the more striking ones in this final chapter.

When the consequences of (various) ownership settings are described and analysed, the shareholding structure emerges as the number one 'explanation'. In effect, it is the degree of ownership concentration rather than any of the other ownership dimensions that largely sets the scene, although in most cases the other dimensions (i.e. ownership category, form and status, as well as how ownership is organized and enacted) also matter. Even so, the concentrated shareholding structure that is prevalent in the first master case, from Domänverket to Sveaskog, offers a surprise. Though one would expect strong shareholder power, the executives (particularly the CEOs) essentially run the changing constellation most of the time. The explanation for that arrangement might be found in one of the other ingredients in the ownership setting: the owner category. For a long time, the state used a sort of 'leaning back' governing logic, meaning that its company boards tended to include only a few directors that were picked directly from the ministries (cf. e.g. AssiDomän). Furthermore, professional executives recruited outside the state sector carried out most of the corporations' operational activities. However, in the rather few cases when the owner (the state) decided to act, it did so in a most forceful and decisive way in order to radically change the path for the organization involved. For Domänverket that intervention resulted in disengagement of its 'ASSI part', for ASSI and Domän it 're-established' a joint AssiDomän (but without some of Domänverket's initial forest resources), and for AssiDomän it resulted in the substantial divestments that generated Sveaskog.

'Ownership category' mattered in other ways, too, when Domänverket was transformed into Sveaskog. Political pressure and/or actor ideology were the main driving forces for the state when it made use of its dominating ownership position. What certainly mattered when Domänverket was transformed into Sveaskog through a long and complicated process was that a substantial part of the assets involved was forests, and that resource had long enjoyed an exceptional 'standing' and value in the eyes of most of the ultimate owners (the Swedish citizens).[4] The consequences of that perspective were particularly visible in the 1980s and 1990s, when first the Liberal–Conservative and later the Social Democratic government tried to transform AssiDomän on ideological grounds. The former government wished to see a privately owned AssiDomän and had a narrower notion of what forests the state ought to keep, while the latter government wanted to keep more of the 'productive' forest resources under state control. One could also easily see the impact of actor category in the 1980s, when the state as owner of ASSI placed almost all of its expansion investments in Sweden (particularly in its northernmost regions). It was also politics when the Liberal–Conservative government decided that AssiDomän should acquire (i.e. save) Ncb.

The legal form also mattered when Domänverket was transformed into Sveaskog. That was particularly visible when the idea to merge ASSI and Domän(verket) arose, as such a step required a change of the latter unit's legal status. The importance of form was evident when Ncb was founded as well. In that case the ultimate owners were (forest) farmers, whose large number in itself played an important role and made it possible for one single executive actor to take full control and to do so without having to 'balance' counterforces. Thus, the democratic co-operative ownership form led, paradoxically, to a situation in which almost all power was concentrated in one single person (initially in his capacity as Chair, but after two years as a most active CEO). That powerful actor's rationale also became decisive for how circumstances were interpreted and for how Ncb was governed and developed.

In the second master case (MoDo/Holmen) the importance of the overall shareholder setting becomes apparent, too. Particularly the shareholder structure set the scene, as it did for all the other corporations. For MoDo and Holmen a controlling shareholder was in place almost all the time, while Iggesund had a dispersed ownership for at least a decade. By contrast, Holmens Bruk had a rather special shareholding setting with two equally strong co-operating owners that together controlled the company for several decades.

The way the controlling dynasty had organized its governance of MoDo since the 19th century had a weakness that did not affect the company until the last decade of the 20th century. The problem was that it allowed its head to act freely in a way that made it difficult for any kind of counterforce to evolve.[5] Thus, the flaw was not that the family heads held power positions, but rather that no mechanisms existed that could compensate for their excessive risk-taking and challenge questionable action rationales. So, in MoDo it was a combination of ownership structure (concentrated), organization (informal and unstable) and enactment (an unchallenged actor rationale) that determined what happened in the early 1990s.

In several respects, Holmen's overall shareholding setting was similar to that of MoDo. Its shareholding was private (based on an emerging family dynasty), and it was run as a limited company. Like in the MoDo case, Holmen's ownership was both concentrated (the company had a controlling owner) and independent (it was not part of a sphere). However, in the Holmen case two ingredients in the ownership setting differed significantly from that of MoDo, namely the way the execution of ownership was organized (it followed the legal rules and was both stable and intelligible) and how it was enacted (through low risk-taking and active involvement in both corporate flows).

Iggesund's governance and long-term development were also highly impacted by shareholding arrangements. When its constellation of controlling shareholders vanished in the 1970s, it became an acquisition target for several other corporations, and despite its attempts to defend its autonomy, it eventually became a part of MoDo. Iggesund's intense attempt to maintain its independence again showed the importance of the ownership structure for corporate development. Soon it was MoDo's major shareholder that decided how Iggesund should be governed and what paths it should take. Thus, the ownership structure set the stage, and Iggesund became part of a sphere, which meant that its resources were used to further a constellation in which MoDo – not Iggesund – was the core unit. Later, the same thing happened to Holmens Bruk when MoDo, through its leading actor, managed to split the controlling shareholding duo and acquire both their holdings.

The overall ownership setting in Stora (Kopparberg) also impacted strongly on the company's long-term development. Like for several of the companies described above, a controlling shareholder continuously led Stora (Kopparberg), and it was the same family dynasty that was in control during the whole of the 20th century. In that time, that dynasty had purposefully built up a sizeable business sphere in which Stora was a cherished unit. However, it was not always the constituent companies that were in focus, but sometimes also the preservation (or advancement) of the dynasty's position and the development of the whole sphere.

Stora's governance was organized in a way that made its executive bodies rather weak, leaving room for the actors from the governing dynasty and its investment companies and foundations to take many of the crucial decisions. That was particularly visible in the 1980s both when the head of the dynasty at the time decided that Stora (and Billerud) should make a hostile bid for Iggesund, and when it some years later acquired Swedish Match. In the first instance the intention was primarily to prevent the rival sphere from usurping the flagship of the Swedish quality cardboard industry, and in the second instance the idea was to defend a large investment.

The way Stora's governance processes were organized was similar to MoDo's in one critical sense: it was quite extraordinary. In the Stora case a team of three to four actors with different affiliations led the governance efforts (its core included the dynasty head, the CEO of the dynasty's leading holding company and the Chair of Stora). So, unlike in the MoDo case, Stora was not run as a 'one-man show' – instead the various (possible) corporate paths were thoroughly discussed by a prestigious team before some of them were put into practice.

SCA's shareholding setting was unique among the four master cases. Although SCA, too, had a controlling shareholder constellation, those who acted as SCA's owners had themselves no (or negligible) holdings. Instead, 'the owners' were largely executive actors recruited by and from a business sphere (the executives of a large bank and an investment company held its peak positions).

Despite the overlapping relationships between shareholders and executives, SCAs governance principles were most traditional, so all formal requirements – legal as well as other regulations – were carefully fulfilled. However, the enactment of the ownership function became somewhat different to that in most of the other cases, as the executives that held those roles tended to apply rather operatively oriented rationales. Therefore, they lacked some of the overall perspective on the allocation process that was described in Chapter 2. The unusual situation where certain managers rather than separate (private) owners conducted the ownership function also made the impact from the executive levels particularly strong, both for the organization of the governance processes and for how the strategic paths developed. While there were some benefits to that rather unusual sphere construct, it simultaneously limited SCA's expansion possibilities, as its executive actors were anxious to stay in control of both the sphere and its companies, and therefore hesitated to issue substantial amounts of new shares, as that risked bringing in new, potentially influential shareholders. Owner category also seems to have mattered for SCA, particularly when discussions were held about some kind of co-operation with (parts of) the state-owned competitor AssiDomän. For example, the aversion of SCA's board to the idea of the state as a significant shareholder in the company closed off a possible way forward.

Taken together the arguments and examples provided above suggest that checking just one or two of the dimensions characterizing the overall ownership setting is insufficient when the aim is to understand not only how corporate governance processes are formed but also what development paths will emerge. Still, however, the shareholding structure stands out as perhaps the most important dimension of all those that make up the ownership setting, seldom on its own, but instead usually as part of various kinds of complicated and idiosyncratic interplays with the other dimensions.

Generally speaking, corporate governance processes and their accompanying development paths are determined by different kinds of forces (cf. Figure 1.1) – both nature-based ones (occurrences and resources) and actor-based ones (individuals and collectives [culture, institutions, demand and scientific progress/innovations]). The actions taken by individuals have a special status among the determining forces, as they not only generate impact in themselves, but also involve interpretations of the possible effects of all the other forces. Thus, for example, the consequences of natural occurrences are merely interpreted, while institutions are both (re)produced and evaluated. Ultimately, actors also determine which interpretations will be put into practice and how that should be done.

NOTES

1. They had become illegal.
2. However, that was not the final outcome.
3. He was not alone, cf. Ch. 7.
4. Individuals' legal right of access to (almost all) forests.
5. One of the non-dynasty CEOs actually tried to challenge a family head but without success.

Appendix: a methodological note[1]

A.1 A BASIC ASSUMPTION

The legitimacy of this and other extensive case studies ultimately rests on the assumption that a relatively limited number of in-depth investigations can be used to evidence socio-economic phenomena of a more general importance.[2] Such legitimacy also rests on the unique quality of the case study format to convey an understanding of such universal phenomena through their instantiations in particular cases and the opportunity those might present to develop or revise connections between established as well as emerging – or even novel – explanatory concepts, often then formulated as empirically based theories.[3] Chapters 4–14 in this volume contain that kind of empirical foundation.

This methodological note is brief for two reasons: this project has no ambition to make a significant methodological contribution, and the choice of methods and techniques is basically rather traditional, given the case study format. Like for most extensive case studies, the credibility of the empirical material presented rests on both how the material was produced (see below) and how it has been presented (the cases' clarity, internal consistency, accuracy, and so on).

In accordance with most research in socio-economics, this study did not start from some kind of 'tabula rasa'. When the research effort presented in this volume started there was already a running research programme at the Centre for Corporate Governance Studies at the Stockholm School of Economics addressing the governance and control issues associated with the emergence of global financial capitalism. Since 1977 that centre has been led by the author, and for some 40 years housed a long series[4] of longitudinal, multi-method studies of governance practices in large Nordic corporations, thus providing an extensive and trusting network of distinguished and influential (major) shareholders and corporate executives. That the author served on the boards of several large listed as well as unlisted corporations and acted as a senior adviser to many of the 'captains of the Nordic industry' also contributed to that unique network, which made comprehensive empirical access possible (in particular regarding the more delicate and contentious themes).

A.2 A HISTORICAL PERSPECTIVE

This book starts from the idea that history matters also in the world of corporations. This study has therefore been set up as a longitudinal one that takes the origins of the four focal corporations as its starting point. Each of those corporations (the 'master cases') is then followed closely until the turn of the millennium, covering also relevant environmental circumstances and forces (cf. Figure 1.1 in Ch. 1). The focus has first and foremost been on the corporation's owners and executives, as from the very beginning of the project it was expected that those two categories of actors were of particular importance for the formation of corporate paths.

Thus, the empirical study presented in Chapters 4–14 builds to a considerable extent on two rather different data sources, namely rich historical material (documents) and extensive new material (interviews) that contain direct reporting from those actors that have been most involved in shaping the focal corporations' strategic development during (parts of) the last 50 years. The results are partly presented as (case) descriptions, partly as analyses of the empirical material (based on the theories presented in Part I). The more general conclusions are mostly of a tentative character, and the main ambition is that they will contribute substantially to the refinement and further development of the conceptual apparatus relating to corporate governance (with emphasis on the contributions and impact of owners and executives).

The empirical material presented in Chapters 4–14 represents only a small part of the total material collected. As such, all the descriptions ultimately (have to) build on selections and interpretations made by the author (cf. below for more details). Those interpretations may in some cases differ from quite a few of those offered by individual interviewees, but that is inescapable as many of those interviewed also show considerable variation among themselves regarding many of the topics. To identify all those differences in the text is simply not possible, as writing such a book would take too much time and other resources – and such a book would also be far too voluminous for most (potential) readers.

A.3 FOCUS: CORPORATE GOVERNANCE AND CORPORATE PATHS

As it is obviously impossible to incorporate all the business decisions that sooner or later influence corporate paths, the focus in this volume will be on those actors and arenas where such strategic issues at some stage in the process have to land (at least for formal reasons). That means that owners and executives are given a privileged role in this empirical study, as are the decision-making bodies (the AGMs, the boards and the CEOs). It also means that 'only' those forces that substantially influence corporate paths are taken into account. The basic content of those paths, that is to say, the outcomes of the critical decisions and the actions taken, will also be addressed.

A.4 A GLOBAL PERSPECTIVE

This study of corporate governance and corporate development paths includes many companies from all over the world, although the focus clearly is on four Swedish corporations as defined by their configurations at the turn of the millennium. That focus is very much a consequence of the fact that most of the research addressing corporate governance and related topics has been (and still is?) carried out and published by UK and US researchers, and therefore is usually mainly based on empirical material from those countries (their home grounds). Although those studies contribute significant new knowledge (particularly of a theoretical kind), they are often of a more limited value for many European actors (practitioners as well as regulators), since most of the corporations in continental and northern Europe work in a radically different kind of environment (cf. its business culture, ownership situation and institutional set-up). Moreover, many US and European studies (particularly the non-Nordic) tend to base their investigations primarily on secondary sources and quantitative data – primary sources and qualitative data are (too) often absent. Sometimes that makes the theorizing efforts and practical conclusions rather superficial and too vaguely linked to actual governance practices. Probably the most important difference between, on the one hand, the continental European and Nordic corporations, and, on the other hand, the UK and US corporations relates to how they are owned and controlled. In Europe, since corporate ownership is much more concentrated (and the executive bodies rather weak), usually one finds a controlling shareholder (constellation) in most of its larger corporations. In the UK and the US the situation is rather the complete opposite – there, corporate shareholding is often dispersed and, consequently, the executive bodies relatively strong. All those differences underline that it is important that the theory building relating to corporate governance becomes truly international in character from now on, and that it be derived from a broader empirical platform.

A.5 CASE SELECTION

A.5.1 Four Master Cases and Several Subcases

As mentioned in Chapter 1, this volume addresses two fundamental questions that (too) seldom have been raised in the socio-economic sciences: (1) what are the main forces that determine the long-term (development) paths for large global corporations and (2) how and under what circumstances do those forces operate? These two more general research questions are accompanied by several much more specific ones addressing various aspects of shareholding, namely to what extent does a corporation's kind, legal form, structure, status, organizing and enactment influence corporate paths? To answer those two difficult questions it was considered best to carry out longitudinal, in-depth studies of more than one corporation, and in this study four corporations ('master cases') as they appeared around the turn of the millennium were selected.

Each of the four chosen corporations comprises dozens of other companies that have been acquired, merged or in some other way restructured. Thus the total number of firms included in the master cases amounts to several hundred, although 'only' about a dozen of them have played such important roles for the formation of the four focal corporations that they have the status of 'subcases'. While quite a few other companies 'among the hundreds' have also influenced the four focal corporations' development, they have not done it to such an extent that they qualify as subcases on their own.

A.5.2 One Industry and Four Corporations

To gain an in-depth understanding of the long-term development processes that have taken place in each of the four focused on corporations, the master cases were all selected from the same industry – the forest-based one. The master cases therefore involve most of the significant actors and other kind of forces in and around that industry that continuously – in one way or another – have determined its development. With such an approach it becomes possible to get (at least[5]) as many as four different corporate perspectives on a certain occurrence or activity – one from each of the four corporations (and in each corporation there might be several different views, too). Basically, the collecting of such rich empirical material has been motivated by the ambition to provide credible and reliable case descriptions, which – in turn – is expected to improve the premises for the accompanying efforts to develop theory.

The industry that perhaps has mattered most for Sweden's economic development over the last centuries – and at the same time expanded into a global one – is the forest-based industry. Therefore, it was chosen as the focus of the study. Once that decision was taken it was rather obvious which corporations should be selected. The ambition was to study the ones that were really significant for that industry's development also in an international perspective. The international aspect was particularly important, as Sweden for a long time has been – and still is – a small, open economy that is heavily dependent for its wealth on the performance of its exporting corporations. So, the study focuses on the four forest-based corporations that stood out in Sweden around the turn of the millennium both with respect to size and track record, that is to say, (in alphabetical order) Holmen, SCA, Stora and Sveaskog. The Holmen master case then also includes three extensive subcases, namely MoDo, Iggesund and Holmens Bruk. For SCA, particularly Mölnlycke qualified as a subcase, while Stora comprised three subcases – Billerud, Papyrus and Swedish Match – and Sveaskog four subcases – Domänverket, Domän, ASSI and AssiDomän.

A.6 DATA SOURCES

A.6.1 An Overview

The intense and extensive empirical work involving the leading actors in the four focal corporations was carried out from 2004 to 2007 with follow-ups from 2008 to 2010. A (preliminary) framework describing significant occurrences, actors involved, the timing of activities and crucial decisions served as a platform for these talks. This background information was obtained through the thorough reading of numerous documents of all kinds ranging from publicly available material, describing the corporation's governance activities and development processes, to confidential material, such as board minutes and private letters. Taken together those public and confidential materials formed a kind of framework that was used in the long interviews, although each question was 'open ended'[6] to make sure that as few as possible of the really important issues that might not have been captured through the document analysis slipped through. That approach was valid both for how single interviews unfolded, and when the same person was contacted more than once. It also influenced the questioning as the number of interviews accumulated and revealed new information.

The gathering of information began by temporarily assuming that the written texts of the more formal or published kind basically were correct representations of what had occurred. It was also assumed for the time being that what the informants were describing, particularly when it came to 'facts' such as dates, persons and themes for discussions, were, on the whole, reliable data. However, it was particularly important to be open minded from the beginning (and remain so) when it came to their explanations of motives and rationales (of themselves and of others). To a large extent, that principle has proven fruitful in establishing a detailed and basically incontrovertible timeline of events (the 'time–place–actor–action skeleton'). To a great extent, it has also been possible to get confirmation from at least two reasonably independent sources on every single item included in the text for each master case (such that a wide range of claims made by [single] informants have not found their way into the descriptions[7]).

The entire material is ultimately presented as (basically) chronological case descriptions, providing rather detailed information on four of the five necessary dimensions of any completed narrative: actors, their actions, their tools for action and the context for their action.[8] The fifth dimension, the intention and meaning of the actors' efforts is – as always – hidden for any outsider. It is ultimately up to the reader to decipher such intentions by reflecting on the different possible meanings that might be derived from a reading of the complete case stories.

A.6.2 The Interviews

Each interview started with more general questions about the corporation in focus and its overall governance practices and development paths. Then gradually more and more of the framework material and the information from previous interviews were brought into the discussion. As the interviews proceeded, information from various kinds of writings (documents, articles, statistics, etc.) also found its way into the talks. This 'funnel-like' technique for collecting information from interviewees was chosen to enhance data quality, to enable new information to arise (i.e. information not expected by the interviewer) and to allow for a crosscheck of information from a particular interviewee or between different interviewees. Thus, all these bits and pieces of information were used to enrich and reconfigure the continuously developing overarching case descriptions. Lots of details were then followed up methodically. Despite that, some of the numbers and spellings of names might be incorrect, but hopefully not the more important ones (and not too many).

The interviews varied in length, with some lasting up to five hours. A number of respondents have been interviewed more than once (in one case four times). During those additional rounds of interviews several individuals made elaborate comments, substantial additions and important corrections, and even provided well-founded criticism. This feedback from the informants also created opportunities for further interviewing. In those follow-up talks it was then possible to pose (even) more specific questions to fill gaps, check disagreements between informants and resolve discrepancies between certain texts and individuals' oral statements.

During the interviews notes were taken by hand. None of the interviews were recorded, enforcing the promised confidentiality and 'off-the-record' setting. The basic foundation for the case stories is then more than 100 such talks with 83 different actors (cf. below) that have had direct and profound insights on the processes covered. The interview material was transcribed in as much detail as possible within a few days. All those interviewed were given the opportunity to read the interpretations of their statements and make any necessary adjustments. Finally, they also confirmed the correctness of the interviewer's final notations with their signatures.[9]

A.6.3 Written Material

Many other sources of information also underpin the four master cases in addition to the many and long interviews described above. Access to voluminous corporate archives opened up another indispensable source (beyond the interviews) that made it possible to depict the corporate governance processes and corporate development paths in depth. Other written texts covering the whole period include both documents produced by the companies themselves (e.g. board minutes, company history and anniversary volumes, as well as individuals' memos, letters, CDs, and [auto]biographies and presentation slides), and documents published by leading business journals and daily newspapers in Sweden and abroad. Furthermore, several analysts' reports, diaries, private notations and correspondence have also been available. However, since written sources can never be entirely comprehensive, it is to be expected that some of the explanations provided in this volume are incomplete and/or skewed. Still, when all this is taken together and reflected on, the readers will hopefully acknowledge the quality of the material and have confidence in the (tentative) conclusions offered.

A.6.4 The Interviewed Actors

The following actor categories were prioritized for interviews: (major/controlling) shareholders, chairs, directors, CEOs and members of the (G)MTs. Their names were identified in the pre-interview work (readings). The selection of interviewees was to a certain extent also sequential; that is to say, some actors grew in importance as the interviewing proceeded and were thus chosen, too. The candidate population was also defined by time – they must have been active between 1970 and the turn of the millennium.

Holmen: Arne Altbäck (telephone), Matts Carlgren***, Ingemar Croon, Lars Dahlgren, Harry Diedrichs, Bo Fahlin, Johan Flodström*, Magnus Hall, Frans Kempe Jr, Carl Kempe Jr, Hans Larsson, Bernt Löf**, Fredrik Lundberg*, Göran Lundin, Carl M:son Mannerfelt (telephone), Arne Mårtensson, Lars Nabseth, John Nordlund, Anders Nordstrand, Wilhelm Peppler, Bengt Pettersson, Clas Reuterskiöld, Sven Söderberg, Björn Sprängare, Lars G. Sundblad*, Björn Svedberg, Lennart Svensson, August Trolle-Löwén, Jan Wallander, Per Welin and Christer Zetterberg* (31 interviewees).

SCA: Jan Åström, Michael Bertorp, Tore Browaldh*, Gunnar Dahlsten*, Tore Daun*, Jan-Sture Enander, Robert Francke, Ulf Frölander, Christer Gardell, Sören Gyll, Tom Hedelius, Sverker Martin-Löf*, Bernt Norberg, Börje Nordenö, Erik Penser, Clas Reuterskiöld, Åke Rietz, Bo Rydin* (including his diary) and Björn Wahlström* (19 interviewees).

Stora: Bo Berggren*, Claes Dahlbäck*, Nils Grafström, Ingemar Haegerstrand, Lennart Hagelin, Björn Hägglund, Lars-Åke Helgesson, Per Knuts, Karl-Axel Linderoth, Håkan

Mogren, Jacob Palmstierna*, Ingvar Petersson, Tom Wachtmeister, Marcus Wallenberg Jr, Jacob Wallenberg Jr and Peter Wallenberg* (16 interviewees).

Sveaskog: Lennart Ahlgren, Roger Asserståhl, Sigvard Bahrke*, Hans Carlsson, Bo Dockered, Bengt Hamrefors, Bo S. Hedström, Olle Lund, Bernt Magnusson*, Gunnar Olofsson, Gunnar Palme, Göran Persson, Karl-Henrik Pettersson, C.W. Ros, Björn Rosengren, Anders Sundström and Per Tegnér (17 interviewees).

A total of 83 interviewees and more than 100 interviews.
* = More than one interview ** = Three or more interviews. *** Several interviews in the early 1990s after which the author was appointed 'Matts Carlgren Professor of Management' at the Stockholm School of Economics. Those talks later became the platform for the study reported in this volume, although the other interviews for this project were not carried out until the first decade of the 21st century.

NOTES

1. This methodological note is influenced by the one the author previously has published together with two co-authors (cf. Kallifatides et al. [2010]).
2. Ragin and Becker (1992).
3. Helenius (1990) and Flyvberg (2006).
4. More than 100 separate studies that, for example, have produced about 50 dissertations (PhDs).
5. Subcases not counted.
6. Noaks and Wincup (2004).
7. However, despite that ambition sometimes only one source is listed in the empirical chapters' endnotes. Usually that is a consequence of specific requests from one or more of the actors interviewed to remain anonymous. In any event, more than one source has underpinned those statements.
8. Burke (1945).
9. However, that material was presented in Swedish only, so minor changes of the wording might have occurred as a result of the translation into the English language.

References

Abrahamson, E. and Fombrun, C.J. (1994), Macrocultures: determinants and consequences, *Academy of Management Review*, Vol. 19, No. 4, pp. 728–55.

Aguilera, R.V., Filatotchev, I., Gospel, H. and Jackson, G. (2008), An organizational approach to comparative corporate governance, *Organization Science*, Vol. 19, No. 3, pp. 475–92.

Alchian, A. (1950), Uncertainty, evolution and economic theory, *Journal of Political Economy*, Vol. 58, No. 3, pp. 211–21.

Alchian, A. (1979), Some implications of recognition of property right transaction costs, in Brunner, K. (ed.), *Economics and Social Institutions*, Boston, MA: Martinus Nijhoff Publishing, pp. 233–54.

Allen, F. and Zhao, M. (2007), The corporate governance model of Japan: shareholders are not rulers, Paper presented on 13 May 2007, University of Pennsylvania and Bentley College.

Allison, G.T. (1971), *Essence of Decision: Explaining the Cuban Missile Crisis*, Boston: Little Brown.

Althin, T. (1945), *Papyrus 1895–1945. På traditionsrik grund*, Göteborg: Esselte.

Amey, L. (1964), Diversified manufacturing businesses, *Journal of the Royal Statistical Society, Series A*, Vol. 127, pp. 157–74.

Andersson, T. (1993), *Strukturförändringar och utvecklingsstrategier inom svensk skogsindustri – tre exempel: MoDo, SCA och Stora*, Uppsala: SIMS/SLU.

Andrén, M. (1995), Idén om den ekonomiska människan, *Häften för kritiska studier*, Vol. 28, No. 3, pp. 36–45.

Ansoff, H.I. (1965), *Corporate Strategy*, New York: McGraw-Hill.

Ansoff, H.I. (1991), Critique of Henry Mintzberg's 'The design school: reconsidering the basic premises of strategic management', *Strategic Management Journal*, Vol. 12, No. 6, pp. 449–61.

Aoki, M. (2001), *Toward a Comparative Institutional Analysis*, Cambridge, MA: MIT Press.

Archer, M.S. (1995), *Realist Social Theory: The Morphogenetic Approach*, Cambridge: Cambridge University Press.

Arun, T.G. and Turner, J. (2009), *Corporate Governance and Development: Reform, Financial Systems and Legal Frameworks*, Cheltenham, UK and Northampton, MA, USA: Edward Elgar Publishing.

Åsling, N. (1996), *Skäl att minnas*, Stockholm: Ekerlids.

Åsling, N. (1999), *Hedlund, Gunnar, Politikern och industrimannen*, Stockholm: Ekerlids.

AssiDomän (1994a), *Erbjudande från svenska staten: Inbjudan till förvärv av aktier i AssiDomän*, Stockholm: AssiDomän.

AssiDomän (1994b), *Erbjudande till aktieägarna i Ncb*, Stockholm: AssiDomän.

Austin, J.L. (1955/1980), *How to Do Things with Words*, Oxford: Oxford University Press.
Bailey, A. and Johnson, G. (1992), How strategies develop in organizations, in Faulkner, D.O. and Johnson, G. (eds), *The Challenge of Strategic Management*, London: Kogan, pp. 147–78.
Barney, J.B. (1995), Looking inside for competitive advantage, *Academy of Management Executive*, Vol. 9, No. 4, pp. 49–61.
Baum, J.A.C., Calabrese, T. and Silverman, B.S. (2000), Don't go it alone: alliance network composition and start-ups, performance in Canadian biotechnology, *Strategic Management Journal*, Vol. 21, No. 3, pp. 267–81.
Becht, M., Bolton, P. and Röell, A. (2002), Corporate governance and control, European Governance Institute, Finance Working Paper No. 2/2002.
Bengtsson, E. (2005), *Shareholder Activism of Swedish Institutional Investors*, Stockholm: Stockholm University School of Business.
Berggren, B., Ahlqvist, B. and Ask, B.L. (1985), *Samtal om Stora*, Stockholm: Stora.
Berry, C.H. (1971), Corporate growth and diversification, *Journal of Law and Economics*, Vol. XIV, pp. 371–83.
Berry, C.H. (1974), Corporate diversification and market structure, *Bell Journal of Economics and Management Science*, Vol. 5, No. 1, pp. 196–204.
Berry, C.H. (1975), *Corporate Growth and Diversification*, Princeton, NJ: Princeton University Press.
Besanko, D., Dranove, D., Shanley, M. and Schaefer, S. (2003), *Economics of Strategy*, New York: Wiley.
Bhaskar, R. (1989), *The Possibility of Naturalism: A Philosophic Critique of the Contemporary Human Sciences*, Brighton, UK: Harvester.
Blumer, H. (1969), *Symbolic Interactionism: Perspective and Method*, Englewood Cliffs, NJ: Prentice Hall.
Blyth, M. (2002), *Great Transformations: Economic Ideas and Institutional Change in the Twentieth Century*, Cambridge: Cambridge University Press.
Borgström, H. and Haag, M. (1988), *Gyllenhammar*, Uddevalla: Bonniers.
Brantingson, C. (1994), *Stora och Peter Wallenberg*, Stockholm: Caslon Press.
Bratton, W. (2001), Berle and Means reconsidered at the century's turn, *Journal of Corporation Law*, Vol. 26, No. 3, pp. 737–70.
Brenner, R. (2002), *The Boom and the Bubble: The US in the World Economy*, London and New York: Verso.
Brodin, B., Lundkvist, L., Sjöstrand, S-E. and Östman L. (2000), *Koncernchefen och ägarna*, Stockholm: EFI and IFL.
Brown, C., Guillet de Monthoux, P. and McCullough, A. (1976), *The Access-Casebook: Social Scientists Account for How to Get Data for Field Research*, Stockholm: KTH.
Burke, K. (1945), *A Grammar of Motives*, New York: Prentice Hall.
Campbell, J.L. (2004), *Institutional Change and Globalization*, Princeton, NJ: Princeton University Press.
Caves, R.E., Porter, M.E., Spence, M. and Scott, J.T. (1980), *Competition in the Open Economy: A Model Applied to Canada*, Cambridge, MA: Harvard University Press.
Chaffee, E.E. (1985), Three models of strategy, *Academy of Management Review*, Vol. 10, No. 1, pp. 89–98.

Chandler, A. (1977), *The Visible Hand: The Managerial Revolution in American Business*, Cambridge, MA: Belknap.
Chatterjee, S. and Wernerfelt, B. (1991), The link between resources and type of diversification: theory and evidence, *Strategic Management Journal*, Vol. 12, No. 1, pp. 33–48.
Cicon, J.E., Ferris, S.P., Kammel, A.J. and Noronha, G. (2012), European corporate governance: a thematic analysis of national codes of governance, *European Financial Management*, Vol. 18, No. 4, pp. 620–48.
Collin, S-O. (1990), *Aktiebolagets kontroll*, Lund: Lund University Press.
Cool, K., Costa, L.A. and Dierickx, I. (2002), Constructing competitive advantage, in Pettigrew, A., Thomas, H. and Whittington, R. (eds), *Handbook of Strategy and Management*, London: Sage, pp. 55–71.
Croon, I. (2005), *Utveckling – förnyelse – omvälvning*, Stockholm: Spearhead Production.
Cyert, R.M. and March, J.G. (1963), *A Behavioural Theory of the Firm*, Englewood Cliffs, NJ: Prentice Hall.
Czarniawska, B. (1998), *A Narrative Approach in Organization Studies*, Thousand Oaks, CA: Sage.
Damasio, A. (1994), *Descartes' Error: Emotion, Reason, and the Human Brain*, New York: Avon Books.
Davis, G.F., Diekmann, K.A. and Tinsley, C.H. (1994), The decline and fall of the conglomerate firm in the 1980s: the deinstitutionalization of an organizational form, *American Sociological Review*, Vol. 59, pp. 547–70.
Demsetz, H. (1991), The theory of the firm revisited, in Williamson, O. and Winter, S. (eds), *The Nature of the Firm: Origins, Evolution and Development*, Oxford: Oxford University Press, pp. 159–78.
Dodd, R. (2005), Derivatives markets: sources of vulnerability in US financial markets, in Epstein, G. (ed.), *Financialization and the World Economy*, Cheltenham, UK and Northampton, MA, USA: Edward Elgar Publishing, pp. 149–80.
Downey, K. and Slocum, J. (1975), Uncertainty: measures, research and sources of variations, *Academy of Management Journal*, Vol. 18, No. 3, pp. 562–78.
Duhaime, I.M. and Stimpert, J.L. (1991), One more time: a look at the factors influencing firm performance, University of Illinois, Working Paper.
Durkheim, E. (1984/1893), *The Division of Labour in Society*, New York: Free Press.
Eisenhart, K.M. and Zbaracki, M.J. (1992), Strategic decision-making, *Strategic Management Journal*, Vol. 13, pp. 17–37.
Emling, E. (2000), *Svenskt familjeföretagande*, Stockholm: Stockholm School of Economics Research Institute.
Ericson, M. (1991), *Iggesundsaffären*, Stockholm: Stockholm School of Economics Research Institute.
Fama, E. (1980), Agency problems and the theory of the firm, *Journal of Political Economy*, Vol. 88, No. 2, pp. 288–307.
Faulkner, D.O. and Campbell, A. (2003), *The Oxford Handbook of Strategy, Vol. I: A Strategy Overview and Competitive Strategy*, Oxford: Oxford University Press.
Fisher, W. (1989), *Human Communication as Narration: Toward a Philosophy of Reason, Value and Action*, Columbia, SC: University of South Carolina Press.
Fligstein, N. (2001), *The Architecture of Markets: An Economic Sociology of Twenty-First Century Capitalist Societies*, Princeton, NJ: Princeton University Press.

Flyvbjerg, B. (2006), Five misunderstandings about case-study research, *Qualitative Inquiry*, Vol. 12, No. 2, pp. 219–45.
Freeman, R.E. and Reed, D.L. (1983), Stockholders and shareholders: a new perspective on corporate governance, *California Management Review*, Vol. 25, pp. 88–101.
Gao, B. (1998), Efficiency, culture and politics: the transformation of Japanese management in 1946–66, in Callon, M. (ed.), *The Laws of the Markets*, Oxford: Blackwell, pp. 86–115.
García-Castro, R., Aguilera, R.V. and Ariño, M.A. (2013), Bundles of firm corporate governance practices: a fuzzy set analysis, *Corporate Governance: An International Review*, Vol. 21, No. 4, pp. 390–407.
Gårdlund, T. (1951), *Mo och Domsjö intill 1940*, Uppsala: Almqvist & Wiksell.
Gårdlund, T. (1986), *MoDo 1940–1985*, Stockholm: MoDos informationsavdelning.
Gasslander, O. (1956/1959), *Bank och industriellt genombrott. Stockholms Enskilda Bank kring sekelskiftet 1900 (parts I and II)*, Stockholm: Esselte.
Gaunitz, S. (1979), Struktur, strategi och resurser. Några drag i strukturomvandlingen och den långsiktiga företagspolitiken inom SCA, in Utterström, G. (ed.), *SCA 50 år*, Sundsvall: SCA, pp. 143–218.
Geertz, C. (1973), *The Interpretation of Cultures*, New York: Basic Books.
Gilson, R. and Gordon, J. (2013), The agency costs of agency capitalism, *Columbia Law Review*, Vol. 113, pp. 863–927.
Glete, J. (1987), *Ägande och industriell omvandling*, Stockholm: SNS.
Glete, J. (1994), *Nätverk i näringslivet*, Stockholm: SNS.
Gort, M. (1962), *Diversification and Integration in American Industry*, Princeton, NJ: Princeton University Press.
Grandori, A. (2004), *Corporate Governance and Firm Organization*, Oxford: Oxford University Press.
Grant, R. (2002), Corporate strategy: managing scope and strategy content, in Pettigrew, A., Thomas, H. and Whittington, R. (eds), *Handbook of Strategy and Management*, London: Sage, pp. 72–97.
Gustafsson, C. (1994), *Om produktion av allvar*, Stockholm: Nerenius and Santérus.
Gustafsson, K-F. (2002), *Papper och massa i Småland, Skogsindustriernas Historiska utskotts skriftserie*, Köping: Christian Persson.
Guve, B. (2003), *Att bestämma sig utan grund*, Stockholm: Arvinius.
Gyllenhammar, P.G. (1991), *Även med känsla*, Stockholm: Bonnierfakta.
Hägg, I. (ed.) (1987), *Att äga stora företag. Några ägares erfarenheter*, Stockholm: SNS.
Hall, P.A. and Soskice, D. (2001), *Varieties of Capitalism: The Institutional Foundations of Comparative Advantage*, Oxford and New York: Oxford University Press.
Hamlyn, D.W. (1987), Kognitionen och behovet av känsla, *Ajatus*, Vol. 44, pp. 3–17.
Hannan, M.T. and Freeman, J. (1988), *Organizational Ecology*, Cambridge, MA: Harvard University Press.
Hansmann, H. and Kraakman, R. (2011), Reflections on the end of history for corporate law, Yale Law and Economics, Research Paper No. 449.
Haslum, B. (1979), SCA 1979, in Utterström, G. (ed.), *SCA 50 år*, Sundsvall: SCA, pp. 457–98.
Haslum, B. (1993), *Från Galtströms järnbruk till SCA. Återblickar i ett storföretags historia 1673–1993*, Köping: Christer Persson Tryckeri.

Hastorf, A. and Isen, A.M. (eds) (1982), *Cognitive Social Psychology*, New York: Elsevier.
Hawley, J.P. and Williams, A.T. (2000), *The Rise of Fiduciary Capitalism*, Philadelphia, PA: University of Pennsylvania Press.
Helenius, R. (1990), *Förstå och bättre veta*, Stockholm: Carlsson.
Helmfrid, B. (1954), *Holmenöden under fyra sekler. Studier i Holmens bruks historia*, Norrköping: Norrköpings Tidningar.
Henrekson, M. and Jakobsson, U. (2001), The transformation of ownership policy and structure in Sweden: convergence towards the Anglo-Saxon model? Stockholm, IUI Working Paper.
Henrekson, M. and Jakobsson, U. (2011), Globaliseringen och eroderingen av den svenska modellen för bolagsstyrning, IFN, Stockholm, IFN Policy Paper nr 48.
Henrekson, M. and Jakobsson, U. (2012), The Swedish corporate control model: convergence, persistence or decline? *Corporate Governance: An International Review*, Vol. 20, No. 2, pp. 212–27.
Hirschman, A.O. (1970), *Exit, Voice and Loyalty*, Cambridge, MA: Harvard University Press.
Hitt, M.A., Gimeno, J. and Hoskisson, R.E. (1998), Current and future research methods in strategic management, *Organizational Research Methods*, Vol. 1, No. 1, pp. 6–44.
Hodgson, G.M. (2007), Institutions and individuals: interaction and evolution, *Organization Studies*, Vol. 28, No. 1, pp. 95–116.
Hofsten, E. von (1984), *Historien om Domänverket*, Stockholm: Domänverket.
Höök, S. and Kihlström, L. (1983), *Billerud 1883–1983*, Karlstad: Billerud.
Hoskisson, R.E., Hitt, M.A., Wan, W.P. and Yiu, D. (1999), Theory and research in strategic management: swings of a pendulum, *Journal of Management*, Vol. 25, No. 3, pp. 417–56.
Huff, A.S. (1982), Industry influences on strategy reformulation, *Strategic Management Journal*, Vol. 3, pp. 119–31.
Iggesund (1985), *Iggesunds Bruks Historia 1965–1985 (Part I and II)*, Örebro: Ljungföretagen i Örebro.
Investor (1991), *Investor 1916–1991*, Lidköping: Investor och KREAB.
Izzard, C. (1977), *Human Emotions*, New York: Plenum Press.
Jackall, R. (1988), *Moral Mazes: The World of Corporate Managers*, Oxford: Oxford University Press.
Jacquemin, A.P. and Berry, C.H. (1979), Entropy measure of diversification and corporate growth, *Journal of Industrial Economics*, Vol. 27, pp. 359–69.
Jensen, M. and Meckling, W. (1976), Theory of the firm: managerial behaviour, agency costs, and ownership structure, *Journal of Financial Economics*, Vol. 3, pp. 305–60.
Johansson, S. and Nial, H. (2007), *Svensk associationsrätt i huvuddrag*, Stockholm: Norstedts juridik.
Johnson, E.J. and Tversky, A. (1983), Affect, generalization and the perception of risk, *Journal of Personality and Social Psychology*, Vol. 45, pp. 20–31.
Johnson, G. (1987), *Strategic Change and the Management Process*, Oxford: Blackwell.
Kahneman, D. (2003), A perspective on judgment and choice, *American Psychologist*, Vol. 58, pp. 697–720.
Kahneman, D. and Lovallo, D. (1993), Timid choices and bold forecasts: a cognitive perspective on risk taking, *Management Science*, Vol. 39, No. 1, pp. 17–31.

Kahneman, D. and Tversky, A. (1972), Subjective probability, *Cognitive Psychology*, Vol. 3, pp. 430–54.
Kahneman, D. and Tversky, A. (1973), On the psychology of prediction, *Psychological Review*, Vol. 80, pp. 237–51.
Kahneman, D. and Tversky, A. (1979), Prospect theory: an analysis of decision under risk, *Econometrica*, Vol. 47, pp. 263–91.
Kahneman, D. and Tversky, A. (1982), The psychology of preferences, *Scientific American*, Vol. 246, No. 1, January, pp. 160–73.
Kahneman, D. and Tversky, A. (1993), Timid choices and bold forecasts: a cognitive perspective on risk taking, *Management Science*, Vol. 39, pp. 17–31.
Kallifatides, M., Nachemsson-Ekwall, S. and Sjöstrand, S-E. (2010), *Corporate Governance in Modern Financial Capitalism: Old Mutual's Hostile Takeover of Skandia*, Cheltenham, UK and Northampton, MA, USA: Edward Elgar Publishing.
Kallifatides, M. and Sjöstrand, S-E. (2011), Kapitalmarknadens omvandling och skapande av värde, in Benson, I., Lind, J., Sjögren, E. and Wijkström, F. (eds), *Morgondagens industri. Att sätta spelregler och flytta gränser*, Lund: Studentlitteratur, pp. 23–38.
Karlsson Stider, A. (2000), *Familjen och firman*, Stockholm: Stockholm School of Economics Research Institute.
Kempe, M. (2006), *Försvinnande spår. Boken om Lotty Bruzelius*, Stockholm: Kempestiftelserna.
Kets de Vries, M. and Miller, D. (1984), Neurotic style and organisational pathology, *Strategic Management Journal*, Vol. 5, pp. 35–55.
Kogut, B. (2000), The network as knowledge: generative rules and the emergence of structure, *Strategic Management Journal*, Vol. 21, No. 3, pp. 405–21.
Krugman, P. (2008), *The Return of Depression Economics and the Crisis of 2008*, New York: W.W. Norton.
Lindblom, C.E. (1959), The science of muddling through, *Public Administration Review*, Vol. 19, pp. 79–88.
Lindgren, H. (1994), *Aktivt ägande. Investor under växlande konjunkutrer*, Stockholm: Norstedts.
Lindgren, H. (2007), *Jacob Wallenberg 1892–1980*, Kristianstad: Atlantis.
Lindholm, S. and Wilke, B. (2002), *Industrialisten Bo Rydin*, Örebro: SCA.
Lyberg, B. (1984), *Vandring i gamla kvarter – från Lustigknopp till Ekliden*, Stockholm: Louise Lyberg.
Lyles, M.A. and Schwenk, C.R. (1992), Top management strategy and organisational knowledge structures, *Social Forces*, Vol. 64, pp. 442–72.
McCahery, J., Moerland, P., Raaijmakers, T. and Renneboog, L. (eds) (2002), *Corporate Governance Regimes: Convergence and Diversity*, Oxford: Oxford University Press.
MacIntyre, A. (1981/1984), *After Virtue*, Notre Dame: University of Notre Dame Press.
McNeil, I.R. (1981), Economic analysis of contractual relations, *Northwestern University Law Review*, Vol. 75, pp. 1018–63.
Mallin, C.A. (2004), *Corporate Governance*, Oxford: Oxford University Press.
Mallin, C.A. (ed.) (2006a), *Handbook on International Corporate Governance*, Cheltenham, UK and Northampton, MA, USA: Edward Elgar Publishing.

Mallin, C.A. (ed.) (2006b), *International Corporate Governance: A Case Study Approach*, Cheltenham, UK and Northampton, MA, USA: Edward Elgar Publishing.
Mantzavinos, C. (2001), *Individuals, Institutions, and Markets*, New York: Cambridge University Press.
March, J. (1976), The technology of foolishness, in March, J. and Olsen, J. (eds), *Ambiguity and Choice in Organizations*, Bergen: Universitetsförlaget, pp. 253–65.
Markham, J.W. (1973), *Conglomerate Enterprise and Public Policy*, Boston, MA: Harvard Business School.
Markides, C. (2002), Corporate strategy: the role of the centre, in Pettigrew, A., Thomas, H. and Whittington, R. (eds), *Handbook of Strategy and Management*, London: Sage, pp. 98–112.
Masten, S. (1988), A legal basis for the firm, *Journal of Law and Economics*, Vol. 4, No. 1, pp. 181–98.
Melander, A. and Nordqvist, M. (eds) (2008), *Att förstå strategi*, Lund: Studentlitteratur.
Mintzberg, H. (1990), Strategy formation: schools of thought, in Fredrickson, J.W. (ed.), *Perspectives on Strategic Management*, New York: Harper & Row, pp. 105–235.
Mintzberg, H. (1994), *The Rise and Fall of Strategic Planning*, New York: Free Press.
Mintzberg, H. and Waters, J.A. (1985), On strategies, deliberate and emergent, *Strategic Management Journal*, Vol. 6, pp. 257–72.
Monks, R.A.G. and Minow, N. (2004), *Corporate Governance*, 3rd edition, Malden, MA: Blackwell.
Montgomery, C.A. (1982), The measurement of firm diversification: some new empirical evidence, *Academy of Management Journal*, Vol. 25, pp. 299–307.
Mueller, D.C. (2009), The corporation: an economic enigma, in Bjuggren, P-O. and Mueller, D.C. (eds), *The Modern Firm, Corporate Governance and Investment*, Cheltenham, UK and Northampton, MA, USA: Edward Elgar Publishing, pp. 43–60.
Nelson, R. and Winter, S. (1998), *An Evolutionary Theory of Economic Change*, Cambridge, MA: Belknap Press.
Noaks, L. and Wincup, E. (2004), *Understanding Qualitative Methods*, London: Sage.
North, D.C. (1990), *Institutions, Institutional Change, and Economic Performance*, New York: Cambridge University Press.
Ochs, E. (1997), Narrative, in van Dijk, T. (ed.), *Discourse as Structure and Process*, London: Sage, pp. 185–207.
Ohmae, K. (1995), *The End of the Nation State: The Rise of Regional Economies*, New York: Free Press.
Olsson, U. (1986), *Bank, familj och företagande. Stockholms enskilda Bank 1946–1971*, Almqvist och Wiksell International, Stockholm.
Olsson, U. (2000), *Att förvalta sitt pund*, Stockholm: Ekerlids.
Osborne, S. (2009), *The New Public Governance*, London: Routledge.
Östman, L. (1993), De vertikala och horisontella styrprocessernas betydelse för den ekonomiska effektiviteten, in Samuelsson, L. and Östman, L. (eds), *Redovisningens roller*, Stockholm: EFI, pp. 220–36.
Östman, L. (2006), *Lysande ögonblick och finansiella kriser*, Stockholm: EFI.
Östman, L. (2009), *Towards a General Theory of Financial Control for Organisations*, Stockholm: EFI.

Palepu, K. (1985), Diversification strategy, profit performance and the entropy measure, *Strategic Management Journal*, Vol. 6, pp. 239–55.
Parenteau, R.W. (2005), The late 1990s' US bubble: financialization in the extreme, in Epstein, G. (ed.), *Financialization and the World Economy*, Cheltenham, UK and Northampton, MA, USA: Edward Elgar Publishing, pp. 111–48.
Paues, N. (1998), *Stora Celbi – En svensks pionjär på eukalyptuspappersmassa*, Falun: Stora, pp. 102–3.
Pelikan, P. (1989), Evolution, economic competence, and the market for corporate control, *Journal of Economic Behavior and Organization*, Vol. 12, No. 3, pp. 279–303.
Penrose, E.T. (1959), *Theory of the Growth of the Firm*, New York: Wiley.
Peppler, W. (2006), *Speglingar* (private distribution, not publicly available).
Peteraf, M.A. (1993), The cornerstones of competitive advantage: a resource-based view, *Strategic Management Journal*, Vol. 14, No. 3, pp. 179–91.
Pettigrew, A. (1973), *The Politics of Organizational Decision-Making*, London: Tavistock.
Pettigrew, A. (1985/2011), *The Awakening Giant*, London: Routledge.
Pitts, R.A. and Hopkins, H.D. (1982), Firm diversity: conceptualization and measurement, *Academy of Management Review*, Vol. 7, No. 4, pp. 620–29.
Porac, J. and Thomas, H. (2002), Managing cognition and strategy: issues, trends and future directions, in Pettigrew, A., Thomas, H. and Whittington, R. (eds), *Handbook of Strategy and Management*, London: Sage, pp. 165–81.
Porter, M.E. (1980), *Competitive Strategy: Techniques for Analysing Industries and Firms*, New York: Free Press.
Porter, M.E. (1985), *Competitive Advantage: Creating and Sustaining Superior Performance*, New York: Free Press.
Porter, M.E. (1986), *Competition in Global Industries*, Boston, MA: Harvard Business School Press.
Porter, M.E. (1996), What is strategy? *Harvard Business Review*, November–December, pp. 61–8.
Pöyry, J. and Ryti, N. (1979), *Trender inom den Skandinaviska skogsindustrin*, Sundsvall: SCA.
Prahalad, C.K. and Bettis, R.A. (1986), The dominant logic: a new linkage between diversity and performance, *Strategic Management Journal*, Vol. 7, pp. 485–501.
Prahalad, C.K. and Hamel, G. (1990), The core competence of the corporation, *Harvard Business Review*, Vol. 68, No. 3, pp. 79–91.
Quinn, J.B. (1980), *Strategies for Change: Logical Incrementalism*, Homewood, IL: Richard D. Irwin.
Ragin, C. and Becker, H. (eds) (1992), *What is a Case?: Exploring the Foundations of Social Inquiry*, Cambridge: Cambridge University Press.
Rajagopalan, N., Rasheed, A.M.A. and Datta, D.K. (1993), Strategic decision processes: an integrative framework and future directions, in Lorange, P., Chakravarthy, B., Roos, J. and Van de Ven, A. (eds), *Implementing Strategic Processes: Change, Learning and Co-operation*, Oxford: Blackwell, pp. 274–312.
Ravenscraft, D. and Scherer, F.M. (1987), *Mergers, Sell-Offs and Economic Efficiency*, Berkeley, CA: The Brookings Institution.
Rhoades, S.A. (1973), The effect of diversification on industry profit performance in

241 manufacturing industries in 1963, *Review of Economics and Statistics*, Vol. LV, pp. 146–55.
Roe, M.J. (2003), *Political Determinants of Corporate Governance*, Oxford: Oxford University Press.
Rumelt, R.P. (1974), *Strategy, Structure, and Economic Performance*, Cambridge, MA: Harvard Business School Press.
Rumelt, R.P. (1987), Theory, strategy and entrepreneurship, in Teece, D. (ed.), *The Competitive Challenge*, Cambridge, MA: Ballinger, pp. 137–58.
Rydberg, S. (1990), *Papper i perspektiv. Svensk skogsindustri under 100 år*, Stockholm: Gidlund.
Sassen, S. (2001), *The Global City*, Princeton, NJ: Princeton University Press.
Savalainen, T. and Zacco-Broberg, L. (1985), *Iggesund 300 år*, Örebro: Ljungföretagen.
SCA (1979), *SCA 50 år. Studier kring ett storföretag och dess föregångare*, Sundsvall: SCA.
Schmalensee, R. (1985), Do markets differ much? *American Economic Review*, Vol. 75, pp. 341–51.
Schwenk, C.R. (1988), *The Essence of Strategic Decision Making*, Lexington, MA: D.C. Heath and Co.
Sevenius, R. (2007), *Bolagsstyrning*, Lund: Studentlitteratur.
Shleifer, A. and Vishny, R. (1997), A survey of corporate governance, *Journal of Finance*, Vol. 52, No. 2, pp. 737–83.
Shrivastava, P. and Grant, J. (1985), Empirically derived models of strategic decision-making processes, *Strategic Management Journal*, Vol. 6, No. 2, pp. 97–113.
Simon, H.A. (1957), *Models of Man*, New York: Wiley.
Sjödin, U. (2006), *Insiders' Outside/Outsiders' Inside: Rethinking the Insider Regulation*, Stockholm: Stockholm University.
Sjögren, H. (2005), *Den uthålliga kapitalismen*, Stockholm: SNS.
Sjöstrand, S-E. (1985), *Samhällsorganisation*, Lund: Doxa.
Sjöstrand, S-E. (ed.) (1993), *Institutional Change: Theory and Empirical Findings*, New York: M.E. Sharpe.
Sjöstrand, S-E. (1995), Towards a theory of institutional change, in Groenewegen, J., Pitelis, C. and Sjöstrand, S-E. (eds), *On Economic Institutions: Theory and Applications*, Aldershot, UK and Brookfield, VT, USA: Edward Elgar Publishing, pp. 19–44.
Sjöstrand, S-E. (1997), *The Two Faces of Management*, London: Thomson.
Sjöstrand, S-E. (2000), The organization of non-profit activities, *Voluntas*, Vol. 11, No. 3, pp. 199–216.
Sjöstrand, S-E. (2005), Om vertikala och horisontella organiseringsprocesser, in Lind, J. and Schuster, W. (eds), *Redovisningens teori, praktik och pedagogik*, Stockholm: EFI, pp. 255–72.
Sjöstrand, S-E. and Hammarkvist, O. (2014), *Om ägarstyrning i statligt ägda företag*, Stockholm: Stockholm School of Economics Institute for Research (SIR).
Sjöstrand, S-E., Sandberg, J. and Tyrstrup, M. (2001), *Invisible Management*, London: Thomson.
Sjunnesson, H. and Wahlberg, T. (2003), *Papper och massa i Östergötland – Från handpappersbruk till processindustri, Skogsindustriernas historiska utskotts skriftserie*, Köping: Christian Persson.

Spender, J.C. (1989), *Industry Recipes: An Inquiry into the Nature and Sources of Managerial Judgement*, Cambridge, MA: Basil Blackwell.

Stearns, L. and Allen, K. (1996), Economic behaviour in institutional environments: the corporate merger wave of the 1980s, *American Sociological Review*, Vol. 61, pp. 699–718.

Steen-Johnsen, K., Eynaud, P. and Wijkström, F. (2011), On civil society governance: an emergent research field, *Voluntas*, Vol. 22, No. 4, pp. 555–65.

Stora (1994), *Peter Wallenberg 1974–92*, Stockholm: Caslon Press.

Stymne, B. (1970), *Values and Processes*, Stockholm: EFI.

Swedberg, R., Himmelstrand, U. and Brulin, G. (1987), The paradigm of economic sociology, *Theory and Society*, Vol. 16, No. 2, pp. 169–213.

Swedish Securities Council (1988), *Fråga om det förelåg samband mellan tidigare aktieförvärv och ett senare offentligt erbjudande om aktieförvärv (Holmen, Iggesund, Marieberg, MoDo, Ratos)*, 1988:4, March 3.

Teece, D.J. (1986), Profiting from technological innovation: implications for integration, collaboration, licensing and public policy, *Research Policy*, Vol. 15, No. 6, pp. 285–305.

Teubner, G. (2001), Legal irritants: unifying law ends up in new divergences, in Hall, P. and Soskice, D. (eds), *Varieties of Capitalism: The Institutional Foundations of Comparative Advantage*, Oxford: Oxford University Press, pp. 417–41.

Thunholm, L-E. (2005), *Flydda Tider*, Rimbo: Fischer & Co.

Trotzig, K.G. (1963), *Den kanadensiska massa- och pappersindustrin. Marknadsläge och virkesförsörjning*, Stockholm: Svenska Skogsvårdsföreningen.

Tsoukas, H. and Knudsen, C. (2002), The conduct of strategy research, in Pettigrew, A., Thomas, H. and Whittington, R. (eds), *Handbook of Strategy and Management*, London: Sage, pp. 411–35.

Tversky, A. and Kahneman, D. (1974), Judgment under uncertainty: heuristics and biases, *Science*, Vol. 185, No. 4157, pp. 1124–31.

Tversky, A. and Kahneman, D. (1981), The framing of decisions and the psychology of choice, *Science*, Vol. 211, No. 4481, pp. 453–8.

Unger, G. (1967), *Carl Kempe: den siste patriarken*, Stockholm: Bonniers.

Utterström, G. (ed.) (1979), *SCA 1929–54*, Sundsvall: SCA.

Valeur, C. (1997), *Papper och Pappersmassa i Medelpad och Jämtland, Skogsindustriernas historiska utskotts skriftserie*, Köping: Christian Persson.

Valeur, C. (2000), *Papper och Pappersmassa i Ångermanland, Skogsindustriernas historiska utskotts skriftserie*, Köping: Christian Persson.

Valeur, C. (2003), *Papper och massa i Västerbotten och Norrbotten, Skogsindustriernas Historiska utskotts skriftserie*, Köping: Christian Persson.

Valeur, C. (2007), *Papper och Pappersmassa i Hälsingland och Gästrikland, Skogsindustriernas historiska utskotts skriftserie*, Köping: Christian Persson.

Venkatraman, M. and Subramaniam, M. (2002), Theorizing the future of strategy, in Pettigrew, A., Thomas, H. and Whittington, R. (eds), *Handbook of Strategy and Management*, London: Sage, pp. 461–74.

Volberda, H.W. and Elfring, T. (2001), *Rethinking Strategy*, London: Sage.

Wahlström, B. (1999), *En laber bris*, Falun: Ekerlid.

Wallander, J. (1998), *Forskaren som bankdirektör*, Stockholm: SNS.

Weber, M. (1978/1920), *Gesammelte Aufsätze zur Religionssoziologie*, Band 1, Tübingen: Mohr.
Weick, K.E. (1979), *The Social Psychology of Organizing*, London: Addison-Wesley.
Weick, K.E. (1990), Cartographic myths in organizations, in Huff, A. and Jenkins, M. (eds), *Mapping Strategic Thought*, London: Wiley, pp. 1–10.
Weick, K.E. (1995), *Sense-Making in Organizations*, Thousand Oaks, CA: Sage.
Wernerfelt, B. (1984), A resource-based view of the firm, *Strategic Management Journal*, Vol. 5, No. 2, pp. 171–80.
Wernerfelt, B. and Montgomery, C.A. (1988), Tobin's q and the importance of focus in firm performance, *American Economic Review*, Vol. 78, pp. 246–50.
Westerlund, G. and Sjöstrand, S-E. (1979), *Organizational Myths*, New York: Harper & Row.
Whittington, R. (1992), Putting Giddens into action: social systems and managerial agency, *Journal of Management Studies*, Vol. 29, No. 6, pp. 693–712.
Whittington, R. (1993/2002), *What Is Strategy and Does It Matter?* London: Routledge.
Whittington, R. and Mayer, M. (2001), *The European Corporation: Strategy, Structure and Social Science*, Oxford: Oxford University Press.
Williamson, O.E. (1975), *Markets and Hierarchies: Analysis and Antitrust Implications*, New York: Collier Macmillan.
Williamson, O.E. (1985), *The Economic Institutions of Capitalism*, New York: Free Press.
Williamson, O.E. (1991), Strategizing, economizing and economic organization, *Strategic Management Journal*, Vol. 12, No. 2, pp. 75–94.
Williamson, O.E. (2000), The new institutional economics: taking stock, looking ahead, *Journal of Economic Literature*, Vol. 38, pp. 595–613.
Windolf, P. (2005), Was ist Finanzmarkt-Kapitalismus? In Windolf, P. (ed.), *Finanzmarkt-kapitalismus. Analysen zum Wandel von Produktionsregimen*, Kölner Zeitschrift für Soziologie und Sozialpsychologie, Vol. 1, pp. 20–57.
Zhapira, Z. (1995), *Risk Taking: A Managerial Perspective*, New York: Russell Sage Foundation.
Zucker, L. (1986), Production of trust, in Staw, B. and Cummings, L. (eds), *Research in Organizational Behaviour*, Vol. 8, Greenwich: JAI Press, pp. 53–111.

Name index

Subject index